Ancient Native Americans

Ancient Native Americans

Edited by

Jesse D. Jennings

The University of Utah

W. H. Freeman and Company
San Francisco

Cover illustration for the paperback edition provided by Donald V.
Hague, Director of the Utah Museum of Natural History.

Library of Congress Cataloging in Publication Data

Main entry under title:

Ancient native Americans.

    Includes bibliographies and index.
    1. Indians—Antiquities. 2. America—Antiquities.
I. Jennings, Jesse David, 1909–
E61.A57   970   78-7989
ISBN 0-7167-0075-1
ISBN 0-7167-0074-3 pbk.

Printed in the United States of America

  2   3   4   5   6   7   8   9

Contents

Preface

This book is about the human history of the New World prior to the European invasion nearly 500 years ago, an event that marked the beginnings of modern knowledge of the aboriginal Americans—or, more commonly, the American Indians. The unwritten history of the two continents will here be called prehistory, which can be understood as the synthesis of data recovered through archeological excavations and information generated by a score of disciplines other than anthropology (palynology, meteorology, botany, geology, zoology, paleontology, chemistry, physics, medicine, conchology, and mineralogy, among others), with frequent contributions by other specialties in anthropology, such as ethnohistory, linguistics, physical anthropology, and social anthropology. To put it more simply, then, the book deals with New World archeology. The aim is to provide a coherent, if brief, outline of the culture history of each culture area in North, Central, and South America. Together the chapters provide a survey of the evolution of the American Indian civilizations from the Arctic Circle to land's end in Patagonia over a span of 15,000 to 30,000 or even 40,000 years.

The book is designed to be used as a text or text supplement in appropriate classes at either the graduate or the undergraduate level. It is also intended to appeal to serious lay readers who wish to know the prehistory but have no interest in reading technical jargon or tedious detail not required for appreciation of the complex flow of events. To facilitate reading, footnotes are omitted and intertext citations kept to a minimum. Each chapter, however, includes its own selected bibliography for the benefit of those who wish to pursue the study of one or more of the areas.

Authors were selected for their mastery of the subject matter and their ability to substitute English for professional jargon. They were invited to produce a simply written, straightforward, even orthodox account of the culture history of each major culture area in North, Central, and South America as those areas are understood today, and, where significant controversy exists, to comment briefly on the discrepancies in the interpretations and to express an opinion on the matter.

One of the readers of this manuscript pointed out that the papers that follow lack a consistent theoretical position and that perhaps as editor I should have imposed one. My unwillingness to do what the reviewer suggests rests on three points. First, I don't have a personal or consistent theoretical bias because my views change as new theories are advanced that seem to be viable and useful to the archeologist. Second, many of the authors have quite explicit theoretical biases of their own, which, I believe, they should be allowed to express and utilize without any interference from the editor. Third, and most cogent, is my assumption that anyone likely to use the book in instruction has, or certainly should have, a theoretical bias of his own. No matter what I or the other authors say, he will and should present the material in the light of his theoretical stance; I take this to be not only the instructor's prerogative but his responsibility as well.

The same reviewer remarked that not all the authors accepted my invitation to deal explicitly with controversial matters. The purpose of my invitation was merely to encourage the exercise of that option. Some readers may regret that topics specifically mentioned by the critic, such as the projectile point debate, the transition to agriculture, and the role of diffusion in accounting for culture change, were not more specifically dealt with by the appropriate authors. As editor, I have no strong feelings in the matter and do not feel that the volume is greatly weakened by the absence of these topics.

It should be noted that a very light editorial hand has been exercised (as will be evident from the fact that I did not alter the other authors' BC-AD dates to match my BP system). This I set as a condition when the authors were invited to participate, for several reasons. First, each individual must express his or her own views because they provide the guidance for the selection and presentation of the information. Second, an author's style reveals something of his or her personality; thus, a variety of styles adds another dimension to the context of the book. Finally, heavy editing might mask the fact that there are honest and strong differences in fundamental views between some authors. The readers *must* know this to be the case and realize that without controversy no area of study or knowledge progresses. In argument there lies stimulus; American archeology is being studied by literally hundreds of competent scholars whose guiding premises and readings of the evidence lead to differing and stoutly defended views. In this way, American archeology is a highly viable field where new data and finer interpretations keep the specialist scrambling to stay abreast in his own specialty.

The preceding sentence explains in large part why this book is needed.

Trusted conclusions of yesteryear are constantly being challenged and reformulated as new findings and new methods for examining data modify early interpretations.

The authors take a variety of approaches, which, to some degree, documents the disparity of viewpoints anticipated above. In the first chapter, I attempt only to set the stage and to arrange a welter of diverse material into a coherent statement about the development of the North American continental environment in the crucial centuries following the retreat of the ice. In passing, I try to lay to rest the ghosts of an "impassable ice barrier" and of the endlessly debated "ice-free corridor." The cultural synthesis that takes up the bulk of the pages tends to focus on recent finds, as these document an expanded chronological span for the early Americans.

Two of the authors, Dumond and Griffin, deal with scattered finds that are inadequately integrated as yet. In their opening sections, both choose an encyclopedic style, making sure that there is mention of sites and local cultures that must be noted even though their full significance remains obscure and offering tentative chronological-cultural placement of these dangling data. In their closing portions, each handles the more recent, better-studied materials in a more synthetic manner.

Wedel, a pioneer human ecologist, emphasizes the environmental stresses of the Plains from earliest times; he links the cultural changes with climatic fluctuations that have been characteristic of the Plains for millennia.

Lynch shares with Wedel a strong ecological stance. Moreover, he shows conservative restraint in his evaluation of the more exuberant claims for the antiquity of certain finds, rejecting all those where any portion of the evidence, or the authenticity of the artifacts, is doubtful.

Harp also organizes his chapter around subsistence and environment, linking the artifact inventory to these factors. The result is that the artifacts become more than mere objects; they become the tools for achieving a flexible adaptation to varying conditions. Harp tends always to connect the archeological record with the behavior of historically observed tribes.

Muller's treatment of the Southeast is not the usual one. He attempts to escape the restrictively heavy hand of accumulated scholarship by ignoring the typologies and local sequence names that are confusingly numerous in the literature. His aim is to provide a regional sequence of events, without becoming mired in the details.

Culbert similarly disregards the time-honored practice of dividing the Lowland Maya from the cultures of highland Mexico. He chooses instead to consider Mesoamerica as a single culture area, with mutually interdependent subareas. This holistic study results in less confusion and more coherence than traditional studies often do.

Moseley too abandons the orthodox treatments of the past. His basic assumption is that the Inca civilization of historic record was the final version of an ancient social, political, and environmental management pattern that evolved in the Andean area and persisted until the sixteenth-century conquest by Europeans. Use of that model allows him to point out the continuity of the Andean traditions without obscuring the well-known variations from river valley to valley.

Meggers and Evans are faced with many data, only recently generated, which must be placed in some kind of regional perspective. To establish an understanding of complex distributional, chronological, and cultural material, they have created a series of maps that add greatly to the substantive content of their chapter. Environmental factors are prominent in their discussion also.

Aikens has followed a more traditional course in utilizing the extant classifications and typologies without attempting a premature sweeping synthesis. He is conscious of environmental circumstances but adopts a less pervasive ecological position than some of the other authors have. Wherever possible, Aikens, like Harp, makes an effort to link the archeological findings to the ethnographic record; the result is a fully fleshed explanation of prehistoric lifeways.

Jett's chapter on transoceanic contacts is a dispassionate inventory of the claims or speculations about Old World cultural impact on the Americas. Two major waves of influence have been postulated: one 4000 years ago or earlier; the second about the time of Christ. Jett avoids fanatic defense of either cluster of claims, but his own reading of the evidence clearly leads him to support the idea that early Old World contacts influenced New World cultural development.

Lipe's chapter is cautious, even diplomatic. He treats each subregion separately and takes care to cite opposing interpretations. He describes the state of knowledge about the Southwest in an essentially orthodox format.

The epilogue is a series of subjective ruminations about archeology and some of its humanistic implications.

Such, then, is the nature of this book; there remains only the pleasure of acknowledging some of the many individuals who contributed to its completion. Marjorie Mitchell of McGraw-Hill and Marjory H. Mooney of Prentice-Hall graciously granted permission for the use of illustrations, and the following individuals and institutions gave permission for use of photographs: the National Geographic Society; the Smithsonian Institution; Dr. René Millon; Stephen Williams, Director, Peabody Museum; and William Coe, of the University of Pennsylvania Museum. John Staples, Executive Editor of W. H. Freeman and Company, through both encouragement and forbearance, made the preparation of this manuscript more pleasurable. Rulon Nielson, Senior Preparator of the Utah Museum of Natural History, prepared all the original illustrations, and Donald V. Hague, Director of the Museum, provided an original painting as the cover illustration and the frontispiece for Chapter 1. Finally, the highly competent Talma L. Day assisted with all author correspondence and did the typing and retyping necessitated by the editorial effort.

Jesse D. Jennings

About the Authors

Dr. C. Melvin Aikens is Associate Professor of Anthropology at the University of Oregon. His publications reflect his interest in the archeology of the Southwest, the Great Basin, and the Pacific Northwest and particularly in those relationships of the prehistoric populations that crosscut the arbitrary geographical boundaries that we have assigned to their world. Dr. Aikens, who received his Ph.D. from the University of Chicago in 1966, has served as Field Director of the University of Utah Statewide Archeological Survey, as Assistant Professor of Anthropology at the University of Nevada, and as an NSF Science Faculty Fellow in Japanese Archeology at Kyoto University.

Dr. T. Patrick Culbert is Professor of Anthropology at the University of Arizona. A specialist in the Mayan civilization, especially in its evolution and ultimate collapse, Dr. Culbert has done extensive fieldwork at Tikal and Poptun, Guatemala, and is the author of *City and State in the Maya Lowlands* and *The Origins of Civilization in the Maya Lowlands* (with R. E. W. Adams). Since receiving his Ph.D. at the University of Chicago in 1962, he has taught at the University of Mississippi and Southern Illinois University and served as Visiting Professor at the Universidad de San Carlos in Guatemala. Dr. Culbert has been active in several programs of the Society for American Archaeology and currently serves as cochairman of the Committee on Archaeological Employment.

Dr. Don E. Dumond is Professor of Anthropology at the University of Oregon and received his Ph.D. in 1962 from the same institution. Beginning archeological research in southwestern Alaska in 1960, he completed his tenth field season in that region in 1975. His publications include more than a score of titles devoted to Alaskan and Arctic prehistory, some of which are cited in Chapter Two. More broadly, he has written on various aspects of ecology, demography, social organization, archeological method, and the prehistory and ethnohistory of Mexico. During 1976 and 1977 he held a fellowship from the National Endowment for the Humanities to pursue documentary research on the Maya of nineteenth-century Yucatan.

Dr. Clifford Evans is Curator of Archeology and **Dr. Betty J. Meggers** is Research Associate at the National Museum of Natural History, the Smithsonian Institution. They have done fieldwork in much of South America, the Lesser Antilles, and the Caroline Islands, and are codirectors of the Smithsonian's research and training program for Latin American Archeologists. Additionally, Dr. Evans has been closely involved with the exhibits program of the National Museum. In 1966, Drs. Meggers and Evans were awarded the Order of Merit by the government of Ecuador and the Gold Medal of the International Congress of Americanists.

Dr. James B. Griffin is Professor Emeritus of Anthropology at the University of Michigan, Curator Emeritus of the University of Michigan Museum of Anthropology, where he served as Director for many years, and a member of the National Academy of Sciences. Educated at the Universities of Chicago and Michigan, Dr. Griffin received his Ph.D. in 1936 and since that time has been involved in both fieldwork and teaching in such diverse places as Siberia, Central Mexico, and Copenhagen. Although his archeological interests are cosmopolitan, Dr. Griffin's speciality is the eastern United States, and he is the author of such classic works as *The Fort Ancient Aspect* and *Archeology of the Eastern United States.*

Dr. Elmer Harp, Jr., is Professor of Anthropology at Dartmouth College and was for many years chairman of the Anthropology Department. Educated at Harvard, where he received his Ph.D. in 1953, Dr. Harp is a veteran of fourteen expeditions to the Arctic and sub-Arctic regions, including work as a consultant for the archeological surveillance of the trans-Alaska oil pipeline. Dr. Harp is the author of numerous papers and monographs concerning Arctic and sub-Arctic archeology and is especially interested in the uses of photography in archeological research.

Dr. Jesse D. Jennings is Distinguished Professor of Anthropology at the University of Utah and a member of the National Academy of Sciences. He was formerly chairman of his department and Director of the Utah Museum of Natural History, and is a past president of the Society for American Archeology. He received his Ph.D. from the University of Chicago in 1943 and was for many years associated with the National Park Service. Although originally interested in cultural or social anthropology, Dr. Jennings soon succumbed to the fascination of cultural history, change, and stability as seen through the archeological record. Although he has done research in the Great Basin, the Southwest, and Polynesia, Dr. Jennings disclaims any area of specialization. His real interest is in the kind of synthesis exemplified by this volume.

Dr. Stephen C. Jett is Associate Professor of Geography and acting department chairman at the University of California, Davis. His interests include cultural and historical geography, the Indians of the American Southwest, and, as reflected in this volume, pre-Columbian transoceanic contacts. Dr. Jett received his Ph.D. from John Hopkins University in 1964 and has also taught at Ohio State University. He is the author of numerous publications on geographical, anthropological, and conservationist topics, including *Navajo Wildlands,* which won awards from the American Institute of Graphic Arts and the Western Book Publishers Association.

Dr. William D. Lipe is Associate Professor Anthropology at Washington State University. He received his Ph.D. from Yale University in 1966 and has taught at the University of Oklahoma and the State University of New York at Binghamton. In addition, he has served as Research Archaeologist and Assistant to the Director at the Museum of Northern Arizona. His fieldwork has centered around the Colorado Plateau, especially southeastern Utah, and his rescarch focus has been prehistoric settlement patterns and resource use. He is also actively concerned with cultural resource management and public interpretation of archeology and has published several seminal articles on those topics.

Dr. Thomas F. Lynch is Professor of Anthropology at Cornell University, where he was formerly chairman of the Department of Anthropology and Director of the Intercollege Program in Archaeology. Dr. Lynch received his Ph.D. from the University of Chicago in 1967. His research interests and publications have involved early man in South America, the origins of agriculture, the European Paleolithic, and the history of archeology. Dr. Lynch currently serves as Research Area Editor for Andean South America for *American Antiquity.*

Dr. Michael E. Moseley is Associate Curator of Middle and South American Archeology at the Field Museum of Natural History. Although Dr. Moseley's fieldwork has included North America and Europe, his speciality is South America, specifically, Columbia and Peru. Since receiving his Ph.D. from Harvard in 1968, Dr. Moseley has been involved in research focusing on questions of plant domestication, early agriculture, maritime adaptations, irrigation agriculture, settlement patterns, and urbanism.

Dr. Jon D. Muller is Associate Professor of Anthropology at Southern Illinois University at Carbondale. Although he was originally interested in the northern and central Great Plains, Dr. Muller's dissertation work with Southern Cult art styles began his specialization in the archeology of the Southeast, particularly the settlement and organization of the Kincaid environs along the lower Ohio River. Dr. Muller received his Ph.D. in 1967 from Harvard University, where he was a Woodrow Wilson and Dissertation Fellow. In addition to his research and teaching activities, Dr. Muller serves on the Board of Directors of the Illinois Archaeological Survey.

Dr. Waldo R. Wedel is Senior Archeologist of the United States National Museum of Natural History, the Smithsonian Institution, with which he has been associated since 1936. He received his doctorate from the University of California, Berkeley. The archeology and aboriginal human ecology of the Great Plains and the relationships of Plains peoples at all periods with those of neighboring areas comprise his main field of interest. For his pioneer studies in human ecology of the Plains Indians, he received the 1947 award of the Washington Academy of Sciences in the biological sciences. He is a member of the National Academy of Sciences and the author of *Prehistoric Man on the Great Plains* and other works.

Ancient Native Americans

CHAPTER ONE

Origins

Jesse D. Jennings

Dr. Jennings tells the remarkable story of the slow, inexorable movement of man into the virgin territory of the two American continents. In a chapter that raises as many questions as it answers, we are introduced to many of the themes that will appear throughout the later chapters—climate, environment, dating, subsistence, technology. Those first men—the Paleo-Indians—began a fascinating chapter in man's history; it is appropriate that we should begin this book with them.

At once the most important and the least dramatic event in American history was the passage of the first man from Asia into the New World 30,000 or more years ago. No one knows just when it happened, or exactly where. Nor can one speak with certainty about the physical appearance, weaponry, or clothing of the long-forgotten first American. We do not know what motives led the emigrant eastward. Nor can the conditions he encountered be readily described except through inference. It is the consideration of such questions, and of others arising out of the search for convincing first answers, that shapes this opening chapter.

There is no reasonable doubt as to the ultimate origin of the human population that finally covered the hemisphere. There is consensus among scholars that the first American was of Asian stock. Research in biology, language, and archeology demonstrates this; no space need be wasted here in presenting the varied evidence pointing to the one conclusion. It is the timing of the entry that has not yet been determined.

Thanks largely to the findings of geologists, we can determine rather closely when it *could* have happened and, what is equally important, when it would not have been possible. During that last 40,000 years, conditions existed more than once that would have allowed passage on foot overland where the shallow waters of the Bering and Chukchi seas now separate Asia from North America. A time span so long, of course, goes back deeply into the last major episode of the Pleistocene, or Ice Age. It is widely realized that Ice Age events were never static; they were not merely periods of ice as opposed to periods of no ice. On the contrary, the ice masses, as with modern glaciers or vast ice caps, were dynamic entities. The Greenland ice cap, the interior ice of Iceland, and the enormous Antarctic ice fields today effectively display the dynamic actions—ice currents or rivers, lateral outflow, interior stresses—of the ancient masses. But the short-range studies made possible by modern technology are merely reporting the behavior and internal physical attributes of the ice itself. Concern here is with the effects that the behavior of an ice mass covering over half of North America had upon that continent and the rest of the world.

Turning to the timing of man's arrival, one must note that the Pleistocene, as a major geological epoch, endured for two million years or more. At least four times the high latitudes and high elevations of the world were alternately clear and covered with ice. The formation of glaciers and ice caps was evidently rather closely synchronized or simultaneous around the world, including South America, as were the warmer ice-free periods. As the ice deposits increased in depth or thickness, the ice flowed outward from a center so that the edges advanced and the ice area increased. Similarly, the ice margins retreated as warming conditions allowed the ice to melt. The advance-retreat rhythm was in response to meteorological-environmental factors not fully understood, but the effects on world environment are known. A major effect of ice fields around the world, and especially an ice cap covering all of Canada to a depth of perhaps 3 kilometers, was the locking up of tens upon tens of thousands of *cubic* kilometers of water, which lowered the level of the oceans by many meters. Lowering of sea level by as much as 100 meters would create very different continental outlines, with many now shallowly submerged areas left high above the ocean shores. The Japanese islands, for example, would be connected to the Asian mainland as the shallow waters of the Yellow and China seas retreated. At the same time, most of the islands of the East Indies (Sumatra, Java, Borneo, and so on) would be connected to Southeast Asia as the floors of the Jerva Sea and the Gulf of Siam were freed from sea waters.

Of more importance here, however, is the emergence of the floor of today's very shallow Bering and Chukchi seas to form a land bridge over 2000 kilometers in width, at its maximum. This vast area, known as Beringia, provided a wide path into what is now called interior Alaska, which was *not* ice covered, even when the Late Pleistocene ice was at maximum extent. The Beringian avenue was available to east Asians, including occupants of the Japanese islands, and to interior northeast Asian Siberian peoples.

Pleistocene geological history in the Northern Hemisphere is thus a history of ice formation and movement and of the climatic, geomorphological, and environmental changes attendant upon the behavior of the ice. The four major ice ages or glacial advances are thought to have lasted for short periods, to be measured probably in thousands of years, whereas the ice-free periods were very lengthy, to be measured in tens or hundreds of thousands of years. Of the sequence of ice ages, only the last, or Wisconsin glacial advance, is of interest here.

Thanks to radiocarbon dating, it is possible to fit the events of the Wisconsin stage into a reliable and reasonably tight chronological framework; because the entire period with its several advance-retreat cycles is short, the last half is well within the range of optimum radiocarbon dating. Although Figure 1.1, derived from Butzer (1971), shows the Wisconsin stage as lasting 60,000 years, some glaciologists would say that the first substage began after 40,000 BP. Figure 1.2, uses the short chronology, but it will be noted that, for the last 30,000 years, the two figures show the same events (retreats and advances) at about the same times; the chronology of the last half of both figures is particularly well documented by interlocking dates. The second chart stems from the work of the Arctic geologists (Hopkins 1967, particularly), work that helps establish the timing of man's entry into the New World. As both Figures 1.2 and 1.5 show, there were one major and two minor ice advances between 25,000 and 10,000 years ago. The Bering bridge was open for all but about 2,000 years of that time. It is even possible that the short retreats climaxing at 14,000 and 10,000 years ago were of lesser magnitude than the sea level graph shows, and that the land bridge never entirely disappeared until after 9,000 or 10,000 BP.

Thus, the time when man could walk from northeast Asia into Alaska is set; it was, in fact, almost any time during the Late Pleistocene. Admittedly, the timing is not precise, and an even *earlier* date for the entry is not precluded, though the next older emergence of the bridge (an event that occurred dozens of times during the Pleistocene) cannot be bracketed in time with certainty. However, the locations where good evidence of early man occurs are all dated later than 25,000 BP (Old Crow Flats is an exception—see below), so that knowledge about when the arrival *could* have happened and data on when it actually *did* occur are not in contradiction.

But arrival in Alaska does not mean that for travelers the whole New World always lay just ahead. When Beringia was broadest, because of low sea level, it follows that the ice was thickest and most widely distributed. At times the only portion of the New World open to Old World immigrants would have been the unglaciated portions of interior Alaska, called the Alaskan Refuge or Refugium. The path to the east was sometimes blocked at or near what is now the valley of Porcupine River, a west-flowing tributary of the Yukon, in the Yukon Territory. The ice barrier was probably not there during the slow buildup of the ice at the beginning of an advance, so a path southward out of the Refuge was open for long periods while the Canadian glaciers radiated slowly outward from two centers. One sheet was the Cordilleran, advancing eastward from the mountains; the other was the Laurentide, which spread in all directions from a center where Hudson Bay is now. When the ice

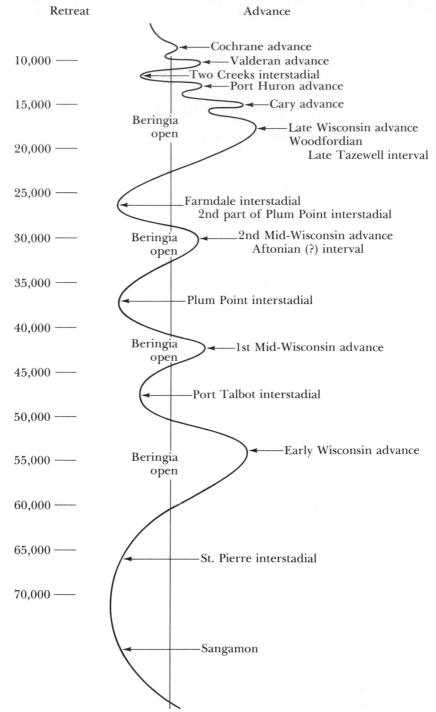

Retreat   Advance

Cochrane advance
10,000 —   Valderan advance
Two Creeks interstadial
Port Huron advance
15,000 —   Cary advance
Beringia open
Late Wisconsin advance
Woodfordian
20,000 —   Late Tazewell interval

25,000 —
Farmdale interstadial
2nd part of Plum Point interstadial
30,000 — Beringia open
2nd Mid-Wisconsin advance
Aftonian (?) interval

35,000 —
Plum Point interstadial

40,000 —
Beringia open
1st Mid-Wisconsin advance

45,000 —
Port Talbot interstadial

50,000 —

55,000 — Beringia open
Early Wisconsin advance

60,000 —

65,000 —
St. Pierre interstadial

70,000 —

Sangamon

FIGURE 1.1
Ice advance-and-retreat rhythm during the Wisconsin stage of the Pleistocene, in years BP.

Years ago	Hopkins chronology	Hough chronology	Haynes chronology
8,000	7.	Cochrane	
	6. Valders	Valders	Valders
10,500	5. Mankato	Two Creeks interval, Port Huron (Mankato)	Two Creeks interval
	4. Cary	Cary	Woodford
20,000	3. Tazewell	Bloomington (late Tazewell)	
	2. Iowan	Shelbyville-Iowan (early Tazewell)	
25,000	1. Farmdale	Farmdale	Farmdale

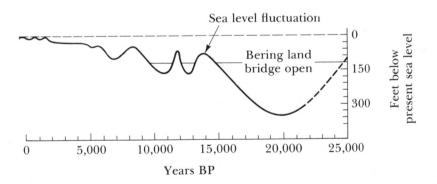

FIGURE 1.2
Three comparative chronologies and the exposure of Beringia during oscillations of the ice mass. (From *Prehistory of North America,* 2d ed., by Jesse D. Jennings. Copyright © 1968, 1974 by McGraw-Hill, Inc. Used with permission of McGraw-Hill Book Company.)

accumulation was at its maximum and the glaciers met, all of Canada seems to have been under ice up to 3000 meters thick. There was extensive downwarping of the area as it was depressed under the enormous weight of over 42 million cubic kilometers of ice in the Laurentide sheet alone. Then, of course, there would have been no open, ice-free route to what is now United States. Before 18,000 BP there would undoubtedly have been an ice-free route between the ice masses of the two centers, but at the height of the Woodfordian advance, from 18,000 to 14,000 BP, the way could well have been blocked. Beyond doubt, the open corridor existed again after 12,000 BP (see Figure 1.3).

It is necessary to emphasize that man *could* also have passed from Asia into the Refuge during at least three earlier times when major Wisconsin advances would have opened the bridge (see Figure 1.1). The late Wisconsin dating of the event is accepted here because it comfortably antedates all the evidence so far recorded for Early Man, or the Paleo-Indian.

Next it is necessary to review the probable environment that the newly arrived migrants faced. Located in the Arctic zone and surrounded by ice, the bridge and the Refuge would have been an entirely familiar environment for any northeast Asiatic. Both vegetation and fauna were the same. Butzer (1971) shows tundra ranging from the Yenesei River into Alaska, with some trees in the mountains rimming the Refuge and with woodlands in its central basin. The tundra is characterized by grasses, lichens, mosses, and sedges. Creeping shrubs—dwarf willow and birch—are also characteristic along streams and on sheltered slopes. The tundra is bright with flowers during the short summer but otherwise is bleak and gray. Yet except for the grass-covered plains, pampas, and savannas, the tundra has the greatest carrying capacity of any environment, supporting a biomass of fauna of over 800 kilograms per square kilometer. On the land bridge and in both Arctic Asia and America, the abundant game during the Pleistocene included the present species of those areas— reindeer and musk ox—as well as the now extinct long-horned bison and woolly mammoth. Presumably the quest for such customary game explains the spread of the human population into North America. With no obstacle toward the south until perhaps 18,000 BP, but with vast ice sheets present and advancing, there would have been an easy route south with familiar vegetation and available megafauna, especially elephant and bison, down into continental United States.

Now that the gross environment has been identified as Arctic at the point of entry, the next question is what the paleoenvironment was to the south of the ice during the Late Pleistocene. That environment was quite different from today's, and, equally, it was different from the Arctic scene, except at the time of the glaciers when there was still tundra and an adjacent taiga (boreal conifer forest) just south of the ice (see Figure 1.4). Vegetation is, of course, the clue to animal species. As Figure 1.4 shows, today's succession of continental biologic zones prevailed 10,000 years ago; they were, however,

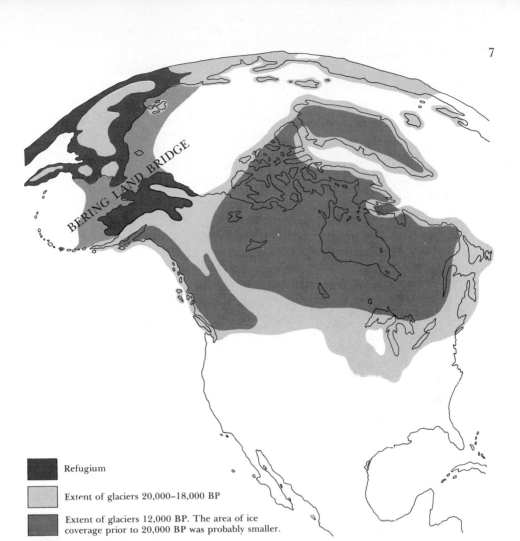

Refugium

Extent of glaciers 20,000–18,000 BP

Extent of glaciers 12,000 BP. The area of ice coverage prior to 20,000 BP was probably smaller.

Maximum extent of Bering land bridge 20,000–18,000 BP

FIGURE 1.3
Beringia, the Alaskan Refuge (Refugium), and the distribution of glacial ice.

much compressed. In the critical millennia between 20,000 and 10,000 years ago when the ice was achieving a maximum, the environment was not as it is now. The plains, for example, much smaller than today, were not a sea of grass but an equally rich savanna, a grassland studded with clumps of trees. Between the tundra at the edge of the ice and the steppe or plains vegetation in the southwest lay a zone of coniferous forest or taiga, which can support a very limited number of animals; such animals as there were would not have been herd animals.

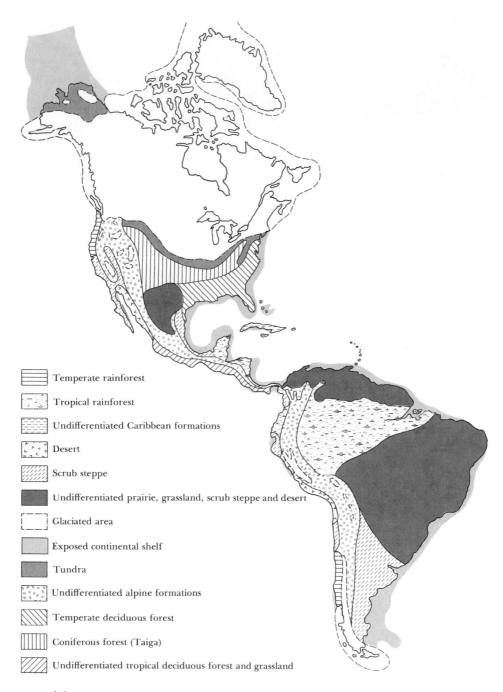

Temperate rainforest

Tropical rainforest

Undifferentiated Caribbean formations

Desert

Scrub steppe

Undifferentiated prairie, grassland, scrub steppe and desert

Glaciated area

Exposed continental shelf

Tundra

Undifferentiated alpine formations

Temperate deciduous forest

Coniferous forest (Taiga)

Undifferentiated tropical deciduous forest and grassland

FIGURE 1.4
Glacial (*left*) and modern (*right*) environments. (From *Prehistory of North America*, 2d ed., by Jesse D. Jennings. Copyright © 1968, 1974 by McGraw-Hill, Inc. Used with permission of McGraw-Hill Book Company.)

0   1000
Miles

Moreover, the entire southern third of the continent was well watered. Springs, streams, and lakes were abundant. An example is the high Llano Estacado of west Texas. There quite convincing but controversial studies show that the flora was more than 50 percent conifers (spruce and pine) during the Tahoka pluvial, which was a period of markedly cooler and moister climate from about 23,000 to 16,000 BP. Fossil lakes (recognizable today as dry playas) and stream courses (now dry) testify to a very well watered land. In central and east Texas, what is now grassland is described as having been an open woodland deciduous forest with an understory of grasses, herbs, and shrubs until about 16,000 BP. At the same time, between the pine-spruce forests of the Llano Estacado and mixed woodlands of east Texas, there lay a broad belt of juniper and piñon parkland. Thereafter, many arboreal species disappeared, so that woodlands became parklands. By 6000 BP, the treeless plains of today had come into being over most of Texas.

To the north, across the entire glacial front, the tundra zone fringing the glacier toe gave over to a band of boreal coniferous forest, in which spruce was dominant. The spruce forest persisted from 20,000 BP until about 11,000 or 10,000 BP; relict forest groves of pine and spruce are still to be found over the plains in the lee of scarps and in broken country. The shift to grasslands occurred swiftly as the ice, followed by the band of taiga, began its northward retreat. The change from the limited grassland zone of maximum glacial time shown in Figure 1.4 to the vast prairie of today was a relatively recent occurrence as well as a rapid one.

The world the newcomers faced was therefore still somewhat familiar, and they could exploit the resources with their imported technology so long as they were confined to the tundra or taiga. But the primary megafauna—elephant and bison—would not have inhabited the classic taiga; herbivores require grasses and sedges. In view of the distribution of early man sites and of the requirements of the now extinct beasts, one must conclude that between 15,000 and 10,000 BP the taiga in the present northern plains area must not have been classic taiga but much more open, with grassy, parkline vegetation among scattered clumps of conifers. The presence of the spruce forests is amply documented by a spate of pollen studies from Texas to Wyoming (see Wright 1970). What is uncertain is whether or not the boreal forest fringing the ice was the typical one where fauna is scant. It may be that the forest was an open woodland offering an easy transition from the tundra to the grasslands, where long-horned bison and elephants (southern species rather than those found in the Arctic) were available, as they were in the Middle West and Southeast.

In concluding the consideration of the paleoenvironment, I must emphasize that this description of broad continental conditions is supported by scores or hundreds of detailed studies (in palynology, plant macrofossils, and so on) of small areas or even single locations and can be accepted as correctly presenting the gross facts about climate and food resources. Thus, the environment was Arctic in Beringia and Alaska as well as along all the upper tier of states in the United States until about 12,000 BP. The situation would favor or even enforce a hunting economy; gathering of vegetable foods was undoubtedly minimal until after 9000 or 8000 BP.

After 12,000 BP, environmental changes were rapid and could perhaps even be called extreme. The changes in climate were those expectably correlated with withdrawal and final disappearance of the continental ice (except for local mountain glaciers and the Greenland ice sheet). There was a warming trend, and there was a reduction of overall available moisture. The reduction in moisture can be linked to a shifting of the west-to-east cyclonic belt-jet stream to the north, and to the resultant gradual warming. Vegetation followed the ice edge as ground and air temperatures rose; precipitation, in general, decreased.

One of the most interesting single papers on the paleoclimates of the Holocene is by Bryson, Baerreis, and Wendland (1970). Using data from radiocarbon-dated organic matter associated with geological events, paleosoils, palynology, and modern weather records, they present a dramatic graphic summary of the northward retreat of the ice and the summer-winter frontal zones of storm paths and of the concomitant shift of vegetational zones (Figure 1.5).

Moreover, the three men discovered that there was a sequence of times when the radiocarbon dates linked with significant environmental change showed a series of quick transitions to quasi-steady regional-continental climates. The point is that there was not a gradual or complacent linear progression of climatic change for the Holocene period. Rather, the climatic and biotic changes were swift and abrupt, or steplike. The concepts of steps and quasi-steady states are very useful for archeologists in their attempts to explain cultural adaptive changes that seem to occur suddenly. We may be sure, for example, that the expansion of the small grassland area of 12,000 BP to more or less its present range within about 1,000 years (see Figure 1.3) accounts for the wide distribution of the long-horned bison.

The climatic episodes listed in Figure 1.2 bespeak fluctuating climates with effective moisture differences. The general trend, however, from the end of the Wisconsin stage until today has been toward less effective moisture for the plains and western North America (see Jennings 1977). Many intensive microclimatic studies of small research areas (e.g., O'Connell 1975) tend to confirm the broader studies (e.g., Bryson, Baerris, and Wendland 1970). It becomes increasingly clear that the well-known work of Antevs (e.g., 1948), which identified three Holocene episodes (Anathermal, Altithermal, and Medithermal) or climatic states involving shifting moisture-temperature conditions, is not only too coarse and too widely applied, but is also in conflict with currently available evidence. Antevs's model is now recognized as being without great value in any fine-grained adaptive study.

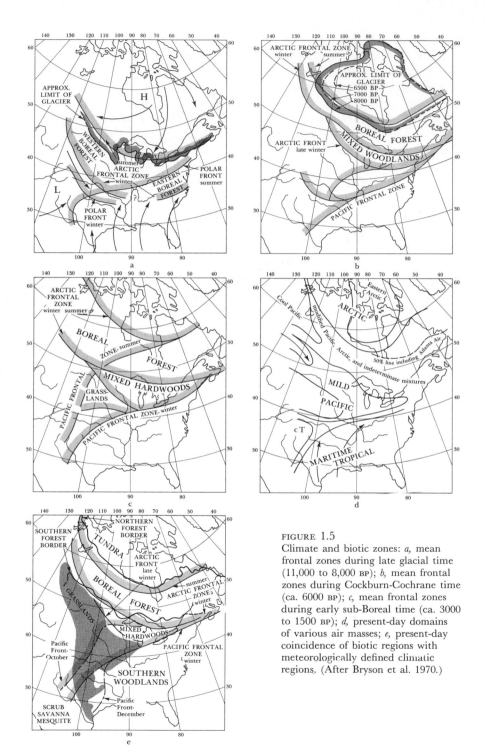

FIGURE 1.5
Climate and biotic zones: *a*, mean
frontal zones during late glacial time
(11,000 to 8,000 BP); *b*, mean frontal
zones during Cockburn-Cochrane time
(ca. 6000 BP); *c*, mean frontal zones
during early sub-Boreal time (ca. 3000
to 1500 BP); *d*, present-day domains
of various air masses; *e*, present-day
coincidence of biotic regions with
meteorologically defined climatic
regions. (After Bryson et al. 1970.)

All the evidence indicates that the Paleo-Indians were hunters of big animals, some now extinct, such as the caribou, mammoth, musk ox, and long-horned bison. In the limited southern plains or savannas of 12,000 to 10,000 years ago, there were, along with the mammoth, camelids, horses, tapirs, dire wolves, and other now extinct animals such as the peccary and a giant armadillo. In the Great Basin there were giant ground sloths, but firm evidence that they were preyed upon by man is lacking. All the others cited above were hunted, however, where they occurred.

Mention of the megafauna always raises the question of extinction. Why is there none left? The query, though reasonable, remains unanswered, but it has been much thought and speculated upon. One favorite and common-sense explanation is that the changing climates and rapid changes in vegetation mentioned earlier changed regional ecology so greatly that the habitat no longer favored several species. Reduction or disappearance of the late Wisconsin water resources would have rapidly reduced the amount of coarse grasses and reeds available for the elephant bands. For such species, an adaptation to a plains or desert ecobase is impossible; evidently the population dwindled and disappeared about 11,200 years ago. The big-horned bison held on longer, but they too were gone by about 9500 to 9000 years past.

Perhaps the most popular theory offered in explanation is that man, the world's most efficient predator, hunted the big beasts into extinction. The most determined and persuasive exponent of the theory that the Paleo-Indian was the agent of extinction is Martin (e.g., 1973). In an ingenious model, credibly presented but not likely to sustain proof, he suggests that hunting bands emerged onto the northern plains from the low-lying corridor between the retreating ice sheets and destroyed the elephants in only 1000 years as the human population increased and expanded. Figure 1.6 shows the Martin model, which combines predation overkill with the expansion of the population invading the New World south of the ice. It is at the "front" that the population was densest; there the kill would be greater than the animals could replace by propagation. Martin makes anew the unarguable point that the continent was rich in game, game unaccustomed to the lethal new enemy, and that slaughter would have been easy. "Easy living" would no doubt have accelerated the population growth. At best Martin's model can only be applied to elephants because only they are found in the earliest documented association with good evidence of human presence. As will be noted later, however, man was south of the ice well *before* 11,200 years ago, a circumstance that Martin does not deal with. His model is applicable only to the bands entering the northern Plains after 12,000 BP. One asks why the first human invaders did not achieve the extinction at the time of the earlier invasion. While I cannot challenge the model, I do suggest that with or without man climatic shifts would soon have led to extinction.

Although the reasons for extinction are of extreme interest, they are peripheral to the object of this chapter; it is the fact of extinction that is

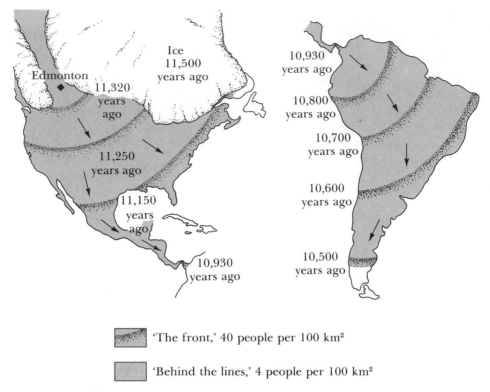

'The front,' 40 people per 100 km²

'Behind the lines,' 4 people per 100 km²

FIGURE 1.6
The Martin model of the extinction of the mammoth. Extinction occurred locally as the "front" progressed. (After Martin 1973.)

relevant in the archeologist's concern with adaptation to environment. The evidence is that elephant extinction was rapid, with long-horned bison (*B. antiquus*) disappearing next. All the other species cited in the preceding paragraphs seem to have disappeared at about the same time or a little later than the *Bison antiquus*. Thus, after about 8000 BP the megafauna consisted of a somewhat smaller bison (*B. occidentalis*) and modern species—pronghorn antelope, elk, deer, mountain sheep, and goats—animals that throve in both the vast reaches of the Plains and in the expanding woodlands, necessitating modified or new procurement techniques. The smaller modern bison (*B. bison*) appeared much later (see Figure 1.7).

The preceding paragraphs, of course, are concerned entirely with the Plains and the eastern woodlands. However, a series of entirely different events characterizes the third of the continent west of the Rocky Mountains. The largest physiographic-climatic-environmental province in the West is the Great Basin. There the evidence of an early moister regime is indisputable

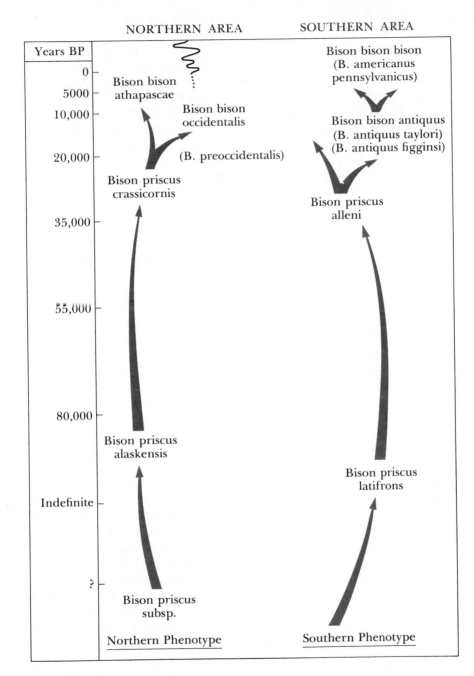

FIGURE 1.7
Evolution of the American bison. (After Wilson in Frison 1974.)

and widespread. Prior to 12,000 BP the entire West was characterized by large lakes and many swampy areas. The evidence for the water resources is best defined in the Great Basin because it lacks external drainage. The overall vegetable resources, however, were the same 12,000 or 14,000 years BP as they are today. The same can be said for the biotic environment, which can be generalized as a dry steppe environment; the dominant vegetation was sagebrush (*Artemisia*) with juniper-piñon communities on the many north-south-trending mountain ranges—a topographic feature lacking in the rest of the continent. Above the juniper-piñon forests were stands of spruce, fir, and pine. The entire region, however, was much richer in subsistence resources for man because of the vast lakes and attendant aquatic vegetation, animal life, and water fowl. By 12,000 BP the megafauna used by man was evidently the modern species known today. Although mammoth, horse, and camel fossils are found, no association with man is claimed. Thus we have, over most of the West and exemplified in the Great Basin, the anomaly of a semidesert studded with rich and concentrated subsistence resources not characteristic of the entire Plains area to the east. As will be apparent in later chapters, this desert environment had important implications for the cultural history of the area where man's adaptation to a series of specialized econiches was quite different. The evidence is, however, that the Great Basin was occupied well-nigh simultaneously with the rest of the continent.

Assuming that the time of entry, the climatic control of passage from Beringia to what is now the United States, and a sequence of changing environments at the conclusion of the Pleistocene are documented here adequately—if not in great detail—one must consider other matters. The physical attributes and appearance of the first Americans, for example, are of considerable importance. Again, probabilities rather than certainties must be invoked. Although today's descendants of the founding population—the American Indians—are recognized as a distinctive and unique population, the Indian is believed to have achieved his distinctiveness on the American continent. While the Asiatic affiliation of the American Indians is recognized, no one would describe them today as an Asiatic group. Several authorities point out, for example, that the first immigrants would have been an exceedingly hardy and viable small group or series of small groups that had survived the rigorous screening of the Arctic environment. Thus, there would have been a very small gene pool, and the distinctive American Indian attributes would have developed through normal genetic processes operating in isolation and without significant genetic increments after about 10,000 BP. As summarized in Jennings (1974b: 56), the American Indian can be described as

being of stocky rather than gracile build, regardless of overall stature which may be either short or tall. The stockiness applies to both sexes. The extent of skin pigmentation is less than seen in the Old World but the ability to tan is exceptionally high. The eyes are dark. The hair is coarse and straight, and body hair is scant in both sexes. Females often have the Mongoloid fold. Incisor teeth are distinct in the frequency of the shovel-shape. Blood types A^2, B, D^u, and r are lacking. The sickle cell anomaly is not found in Indian blood. The Indian male is rarely bald and rarely becomes grey in old age.

Moreover, the Indian has extreme susceptibility to common Eurasiatic diseases, such as the common cold, measles, and tuberculosis. The complete lack of immunity to these diseases is regarded as further evidence of the long period of isolation from the Old World.

There is scant evidence, so far as human skeletons are concerned, as to the appearance of the ancestors of the American Indian, but persuasive arguments as to their probable appearance have been provided by several authors. Based on his studies of modern Asian populations, Birdsell proposes that the first Americans can be described as generalized primitive Caucasoids, pushed further and further into the Arctic by the increasing population pressures in Eurasia. It is true that occupancy of the Arctic zone can be demonstrated as having occurred during and only during the middle and late Wisconsin periods. This early *Homo sapiens* Birdsell (1951) calls Amurian. The enclaved Ainu of Japan would be "living fossil" representatives of this strain. The latest fossil *Homo sapiens* at the famous Pekin site would be Amurian in type, as would the first Americans. Birdsell also suggests that the Mongoloid strain was beginning to evolve and that the Amurian group entering the New World might have had an infusion of the new Mongoloid genes. His entirely theoretical proposal is fully congruent with the conclusions reached by Neumann, whose interest in the original population was expressed in a more empirical manner. Neumann (1952) studied skeletal collections from early American sites on the assumption that he would be dealing with an essentially homogeneous population if he confined his study to skeletons recovered from a single site representing a short period of occupancy. He concluded that there were eight sequential population types over the last 10,000 years. The first two are of significance here. The oldest he calls Otamid, the next oldest Iswanid. He, too, sees similarities between the Otamid and the latest skeletal material from Pekin. The Otamid skull is long, of moderate height, with heavy supraorbital ridges that have a slight swelling or bun-shaped occipital morphology. He describes the body build as slender and gracile, the stature as short. Stewart (1973) in another study also allied the early Americans with the late *Homo sapiens* specimens from the Pekin locality.

In a restudy of Neumann's data, Long (1966) does not entirely agree with the Otamid strain but asserts that the Iswanid is a valid physical type and exists as a "basic and widespread group [from] archaic to historical times." In his study he goes on to emphasize his idea that the American Indian physical type resulted from genetic microevolutionary factors. He favors a small original population from which the American Indian developed rather than a series of continuous increments. It should be pointed out, of course, that none of the authors are concerned with the documented entry after

6000 BP of the Aleutian, Eskimo, and Deneid populations. Lacking better data, it is therefore taken here as given that the founding New World population was, in fact, Asiatic *Homo sapiens* of Caucasoid-Mongoloid mixture and that the American Indian evolved in the New World in response to a variety of environments and evolutionary processes.

Despite the assertions in the preceding paragraphs, there are but few ancient skeletal sources of information. The first of the early human remains that seems credible is Midland man. This find, reported by Wendorf et al. (1955), comes from a blowout near Midland, Texas. Although the specimen was discovered on the surface of a deep and extensive blowout in a cluster of dunes near Midland, the geological circumstances, carefully researched by the study team, make the find credible. The specimen is 10,000 or more years old and fits the Otamid description convincingly. The skull is that of a young female, described as having a slight and gracile body; the skull itself is long, highly vaulted, and even possesses the specified occipital bun. Many other finds have been described and claims for extreme age made about them, but in all cases there is doubt as to the exact provenience or geological or cultural association. These would include the Tepexpan find near Mexico City, the Santa Barbara skull from California, and the Minnesota woman, as well as several others. There is also a tantalizing hint (Lahren and Bonnichsen 1974) that a human burial in association with Clovis Fluted points has been discovered in Montana, but no description of the bones has appeared.

Even more vexing than the problem of physiology is the question of the tool kit and overall technology possessed by early man in America. It is obvious that his technology was suitable for an Arctic environment and the taking of big game. Very likely, tailored skin clothing was standard. Presumably his stone tool kit would have been Asiatic in all respects, but no definitive statements about the nature of the stone tools with which other utensils and tools were fabricated can yet be made. Krieger (1964) has long contended that there was a well-developed technology, which he characterizes as the preprojectile stage. Certainly this is compatible with the Asiatic evidence, particularly from Siberia and northeast Asia at the Pekin site, for example. Unfortunately, none of the complexes Krieger defines (see Figure 1.8) occur in well-controlled circumstances. Most of the complexes are surface finds and cannot be assigned either a geological or chronological age. Echoing Krieger is the more empirical study by Müller-Beck (1966). With an entirely European background and research experience, he presents a distributional pattern of European and Asiatic stone artifact complexes that supports Krieger. The hypotheses put forward by these two men were largely ignored by American prehistorians, yet both hypotheses are being substantiated by recent sites, as will be apparent in the description of the Meadowcroft assemblage.

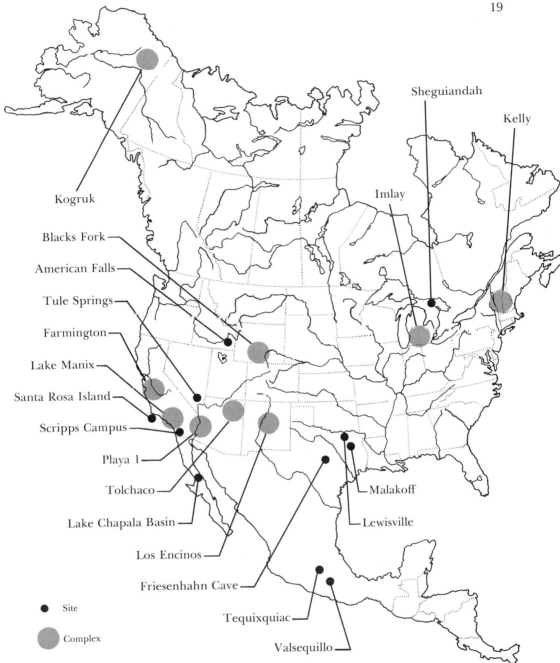

FIGURE 1.8
Chopper-scraper sites and complexes in North America. (From *Prehistory of North America*, 2d ed., by Jesse D. Jennings. Copyright © 1968, 1974 by McGraw-Hill, Inc. Used with permission of McGraw-Hill Book Company.)

Although Müller-Beck's argument is lengthy and complex, with many nuances, it can be readily summarized as having typological and distributional bases. He can recognize in the northwest Siberian artifact assemblages, of late or middle Wisconsin times, a complex with antecedents in the Aurignacian, even Mousterian, of central Europe. Müller-Beck calls the complex Aurignacoid. The chronological and distributional data he summarizes show that the relationship is possible. The timing is correct, and, moreover, some of the Aurignacoid components of the complex are those occurring in North America at the earliest sites. His proposed distribution and timing are summarized in Figure 1.9. The tool complex includes prismatic flakes, retouched flakes, bifaces, burins, and microblades, as well as bone projectile points. He further points out that the implements from Hokkaido dating around 16,000 BP are also Aurignacoid in affiliation. Müller-Beck was influenced by Krieger (1964), who insisted that the many chopper-scraper and crude biface objects at scores of North American locations argued a preprojectile point stage. Krieger's argument was not chronological but typological, being concerned with stages rather than age. Bryan (1969) also recognizes the possibility of Mousterian antecedents for the earliest American tool kit.

Following Müller-Beck and Bryan, one might hypothesize that the tool kit of the first American population blends the Aurignacoid of circumpolar Eurasia with the east Asian chopper-scraper complex. The finely chipped bifaces of North America that we shall examine later can, on present evidence, only be regarded as an American development. Some authors, notably Griffin and Wormington, feel that some of the Siberian artifacts, particularly some crudely chipped slender points from Malta, could be prototypes for the lanceolate blades associated with the Paleo-Indian cultures at 12,000 years BP and later.

The evidences of the earliest men can most economically be presented according to the simple scheme proposed by Haynes (1969). He has offered a three-period scheme that he keys to the chronology outlined in the opening paragraphs of this article. The early period would fall before 30,000 years BP; the middle terminates at 12,000 BP; and the late extends from 12,000 to 7,000 or 8,000 BP. Although there are no archeological sites that can be safely ascribed to the early period, Haynes, along with many students, presumes that acceptable evidence of human occupancy earlier than 30,000 BP will one day develop. For the middle period, there are but few convincing locations, and these will be dealt with shortly. About the late period there is no doubt, since there is abundant evidence of human activity on the continent at that time.

Now that the times, the place, the environmental circumstances, the probable tool kit, and the physical appearance of the founder population have been set, there remains only to describe some of the key locations where evidence of early man has been encountered.

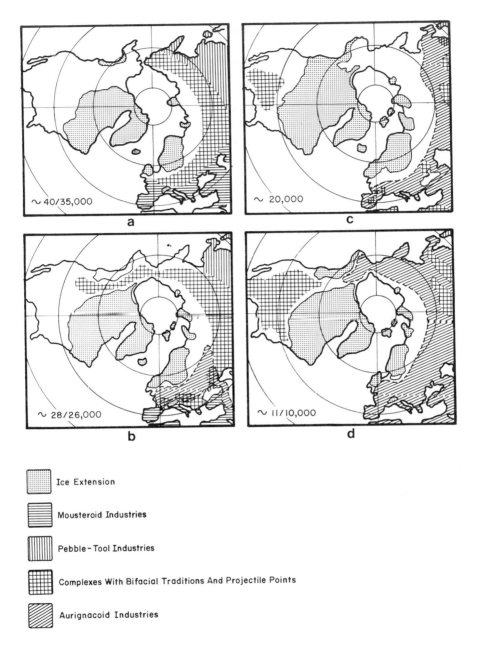

FIGURE 1.9
Distribution of Moustero-Aurignacoid cultures during late Wisconsin times: *a*, at the end of the Middle Upper Pleistocene; *b*, at transition between Middle and Late Neopleistocene; *c*, at maximum ice extension in Late Neopleistocene; *d*, at the end of the Late Upper Pleistocene, in years BP. (After Müller-Beck 1966.)

Haynes's early period can, as indicated, be dismissed for now. Only one location, the Calico Hills near Yerma, California, has been advanced as belonging to this little-known time. Here Simpson and Leakey discovered a location where much flaked chert was recovered. A very small percentage of the flakes were identified subjectively by them as of human workmanship. One can agree that the selected flakes, if found in a site with recognizable unquestioned chipped flint artifacts, would pass as debris. However, all the professional archeologists and geologists who viewed the specimens and the location of discovery at an invitational site visit in 1970 are highly skeptical that the site gives evidence of man. The most compelling reasons are (1) there are no acceptable archeological phenomena (charcoal, hearths, or recognizable artifacts) and (2) the geological formation containing the specimens is probably of pre-Wisconsin age. Haynes (1973) has dealt with the problem finally by rejecting the evidence unequivocally, as do I.

For the middle period at least four North American locations fit the criteria of archeological control, proper radiocarbon age, *and,* in some cases, the Aurignacoid affinities of the few artifacts: Old Crow site in Alaska; the Fort Rock caves, Fort Rock Valley, Oregon; Wilson Butte Cave, Idaho; and Meadowcroft Shelter, Pennsylvania. As will be discussed in Chapter 10, there are numerous South American locations that fall late in the middle period or at its terminal boundary. There are also questionable claims for several locations in Mexico, but for one reason or another each of them has been challenged as unproved.

The earliest of the North American locations is Old Crow Flats, located on the Porcupine River at the extreme eastern edge of the Alaskan Refuge area. Irving and Harington (1973) have issued a preliminary report. The site is a rich Pleistocene fossil bed at a locality labeled 14N. The bones in the bed appear to have been redeposited on a stream-side bar. Transport, however, was short; the bones are not battered or water worn. They are now covered by many feet of alluvial sediment. From the bone bed a well-made caribou bone flesher and two mammoth bones showing deliberate crushing or flaking when green were recovered. The flesher (see Figure 1.10) is remarkably modern in appearance, and there is no doubt that it is a tool created by human hands. Its age is 27,000 ± 3,000 BP. The age is from an apatite radiocarbon date derived from the tool itself. The mammoth bones are of the same age. Although no stonework was present, one has no hesitancy in accepting this find as authentic.

Equally authentic, but more informative about tools, is Meadowcroft Shelter near Avella in eastern Pennsylvania (Adovasio 1975). The deposits in the shelter are alluvial in origin, since the site is located on the banks of Cross Creek, a tributary of the Ohio River. Although occupancy was continuous, the concern here is only with stratum IIa. One date ascribed to the layer comes from charcoal from the lowest firepit in the stratum. The other is from a carbonized fragment of simple plaited basketry made from what

FIGURE 1.10
Fleshing tool from Old Crow Flat.

appears to be birch bark. The dates are 19,650 ± 2400 and 19,150 ± 800 BP. There is a lower stratum (I) from which only charcoal has been recovered. The dates from that stratum run from 37,000 to 21,500 BP. No cultural material such as chipped flint has yet been recovered from stratum I. From stratum IIa, however, there were three prismatic flakes, one chipped biface, and one "Mungai" knife, which can be described as a retouched, flat prismatic flake. These artifacts are shown in Figure 1.11. The objects, except for the prismatic flaked knife, do not resemble other Paleo-Indian finds except the collections from Fort Rock Cave and the Wilson Butte sites. It should be pointed out, however, that the prismatic blades and the "Mungai" knife are similar—if not identical—to finds both at Blackwater Draw and at the Lindenmeier location. It is proper to point out that the Meadowcroft evidence lends credence to some of the sites Krieger identified as falling in his pre-projectile stage, even though those sites are surface finds. The Meadowcroft site was evidently excavated with extreme care and is the most convincing of the middle period sites reported to date. It can be taken as establishing beyond reasonable debate the existence of a human population south of the ice toward the close of this period.

For the late period the evidence of human population is, of course, over-whelming. The problem is to select which of the locations should be de-scribed to exemplify the cultures of that period.

Most authors divide the late period into a more or less logical group of subseries or periods. These periods are the Llano, Folsom, and Plano. Al-though the three will be used here, it should be mentioned that retention of a brief Folsom period is based more on sentiment than on logic, because on cultural grounds the Folsom and Plano lifeways are but variations on a single theme whereas the first or Llano stands to some degree distinctive. In general the Llano culture and its remains are associated with a brief period of time when the mammoth was the preferred prey of the Paleo-Indian. From the rudimentary evidence, which is consistent from location to loca-tion, there is an association of the remains of one or more mammoths with a tool kit, always characterized by the Clovis Fluted point (Figures 1.12 and 1.13), prismatic flake knives, edge chipped flat flaked knives, smooth bone or ivory cylinders of unknown use, and very little else. At one site, Murray

FIGURE 1.11
Representative artifacts from the lowest cultural stratum at Meadowcroft Shelter: *a–c*, prismatic blades; *d–f*, flaking detritus; *g*, Mungai "knife"; *h*, biface. (After Adovasio 1975.)

Springs, a unique ivory "wrench" was found that has counterparts in objects from the Ukraine.

Hester (1975) has interpreted evidence from a number of Llano Estacado sites as providing a plausible description of the Llano lifeway. He points out, for example, that the major kill site locations are at the edge of ponds or stream channels with the campsite somewhere nearby, usually on a slight eminence or elevation. He thinks the animals were killed by stalking since there is almost always only a single individual. The tool types all point toward big-game hunting as the basic economy. In addition to the mammoth,

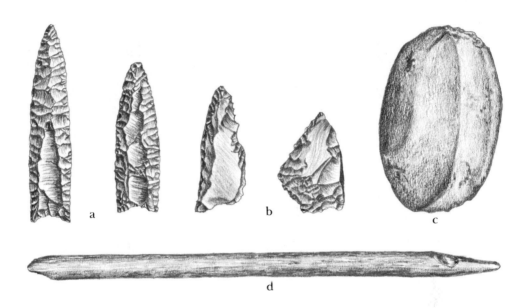

FIGURE 1.12
Artifacts from Blackwater Draw, locality 1: *a*, fluted points; *b*, scrapers; *c*, hammerstone; *d*, worked bone. (From *Prehistory of North America,* 2d ed., by Jesse D. Jennings. Copyright © 1968, 1974 by McGraw-Hill, Inc., Used with permission of McGraw-Hill Book Company.)

FIGURE 1.13
Clovis blades from Blackwater Draw, locality 1. (From *Prehistory of North America,* 2d ed., by Jesse D. Jennings. Copyright © 1968, 1974 by McGraw-Hill, Inc. Used with permission of McGraw-Hill Book Company.)

there are other animals represented, including camelids, the horse, the dire wolf, a giant armadillo, the four-horned antelope, and the sloth. Once taken, the kill was butchered on the spot, the butchery resulting in dismemberment and the scattering of the bones over a small area. Hester contends that life was a roving one—probably cyclical—with the people returning to the same sites year after year. He bases this assumption, quite reasonably, on the source of the raw materials used in making stone tools. The favorite Llano stone at Blackwater Draw was Alibates chert, with a more refractory material called Edwards chert a poor second choice. These famous two quarries were used by successive cultures from Llano times onward into historic times. Hester speculates that the normal socioeconomic unit was very small. His estimate is that the normal band would be only from 10 to 20 individuals. Even so, he reckons that in the Llano Estacado there are 10 pure Llano sites out of a total of some 80 Paleo-Indian locations known in an area 160 by 240 kilometers in extent. The total of 80 Paleo-Indian sites in the 38,400 square kilometers works out to one site in every 518 square kilometers. But for the pure Llano groups, there would be but one band for every 4,000 square kilometers. Although we must recognize that these figures are unreliable, being mere estimates based on the number of sites known when he wrote, they do support the concept of a sparse, mobile population.

There are many known Clovis sites, such as Blackwater Draw, New Mexico; Naco, Lehner, Murray Springs, and Escapule in Arizona; Dent, Nebraska; Domebo in Oklahoma; and Union Pacific in Montana, as well as some known but not yet excavated sites. None is more famous than Blackwater Draw (Hester 1972), which will be described here briefly. At the time it was used by the Llano hunters, Blackwater Draw was a large lake fed by strong springs. Around the edges were extensive swamp zones supporting large stands of aquatic grasses and other plants. Here it appears that the Clovis campsites were located close to the western shore rather than on the normal hillock or ridge. The many kills reported are of single individuals, some of which appear to have been mired in the boggy soil of the lake shore. This famous site remained in continuous use for several thousand years; there are Folsom and Plano campsites along the west shore.

The stratigraphy of the long-dry lake sediments at the BW1 location, the Llano-Clovis-type site, is sharp and clear, with the basal layer containing Llano materials, with Folsom above the Llano, and with the several Plano cultures occurring last or topmost in the stratigraphic column. Since the middle 1930s, this location has provided a yardstick and reference point for the basic Plains chronological sequence of cultures, a sequence that has been repeated time after time at other sites excavated later. Incredible as it seems, this site, worked by nine major expeditions, was never adequately reported by any investigator until Hester published a synthesis of the finds of these many expeditions in an effort to present a coherent picture of the data recovered, the artifacts removed, and the circumstances that made it such a desirable hunting spot.

Such neglect does not characterize all the important Llano locations, however. At the Lehner, for example, Haury and his associates conducted a careful excavation and published their observations on the details of this important find. Here the remains of nine mammoths were uncovered along with specimens of horse, bison, and tapir. The tools included not only the Clovis Fluted projectile point but also prismatic knives, uniface chipped scrapers, and flat flake knives. There was also evidence of fire. Pollen studies conducted later indicated that the environment at the time of the kills was very like today's so far as vegetation was concerned but that there was probably somewhat more moisture than there is today. The time span for the Llano period is very short. The radiocarbon date of nearly all the kills is between 12,000 and 11,200 BP. This short time span influenced the design of Martin's model that we discussed earlier.

Folsom, excavated in the late 1920s, is the most famous of all Paleo-Indian sites because it represented a scientific breakthrough. The location was the *first* fully authenticated find of bones of extinct bison in association with tools of human workmanship.

Although the Paleo-Indian-type sites lie in the western Plains area, more fluted points have been found in the Middle West and Southeast than in the Plains. The eastern specimens have usually been surface finds, often turned up by the plow, and their ages have not been determinable. There is also considerable variation in the form, making any typological equating of eastern and western projectile point types debatable. Moreover, no association of eastern finds with now extinct fauna has been documented, although mastodon, long-horned bison, and other megafauna were abundant. The upshot was that for many years the claims for equal age for the eastern and western Paleo-Indian occupancy were casually dismissed by most students.

The matter has now been settled. There were without doubt both eastern and western Paleo-Indian complexes closely related and almost coeval. It is possible to speak thus positively because of the finds at the Flint Run district in Virginia, the Shawnee-Minisink site in Delaware, the Debert site in Nova Scotia, and Bull Brook, Massachusetts (Figure 1.14). The Shoop site in Pennsylvania, the Dinwoodie area in Virginia, and other locations where provenience and chronology are not well controlled are, no doubt, of the same age. The evidence that offers certainty comes from four places where extensive search provided large numbers of artifacts, datable charcoal from fireplaces, and concentrations of artifacts and flint scrap. The concentrations marked the location of family camps or even houses in villages or settlements of several households. The first to be discovered was Bull Brook, dated at about 9,000 BP; Debert is somewhat earlier at 10,600 BP. At neither did the bones or other evidence of the preferred prey survive. At both, however, a

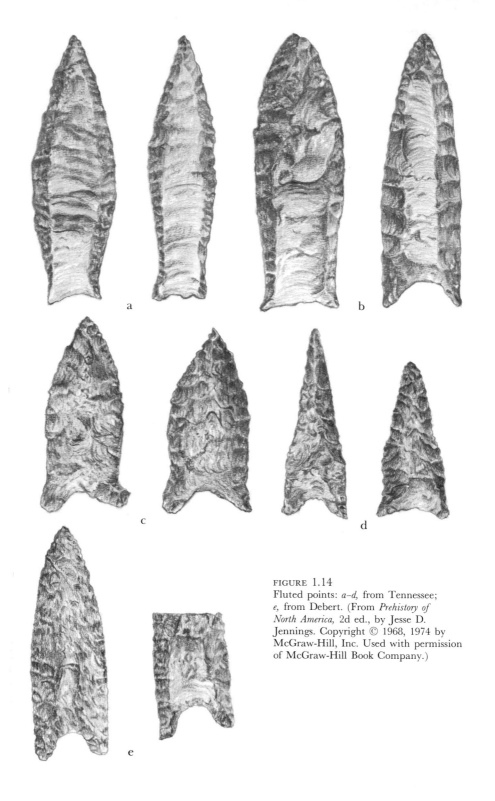

FIGURE 1.14
Fluted points: *a–d,* from Tennessee;
e, from Debert. (From *Prehistory of
North America,* 2d ed., by Jesse D.
Jennings. Copyright © 1968, 1974 by
McGraw-Hill, Inc. Used with permission
of McGraw-Hill Book Company.)

varied tool kit of retouched prismatic blades, fluted points of Clovis-like form, burins or engraving-cutting tools, steep-bitted scrapers or woodworking tools, and retouched flakes of irregular shape for butchery are found. The tool kit indicates a broad spectrum of activities, including on-site manufacture of other tools using flint tools. Both sites were buried, but lack clear-cut stratification.

But to date the most extensive and careful study of the eastern Paleo-Indian has been done by Gardner (1974) and his associates and by McNett et al. (1975). In a long-range program, Gardner, with a multidiscipline team, is conducting study of a complex of sites at Flint Run, in Virginia. The site is about 50 miles west of Washington, D.C., on the South Fork of the Shenandoah River. At Flint Run, there is an extensive, stratified village or base camp, the Thunderbird site; a long-exploited jasper quarry; and flint-processing camps, one of which is the Fifty site.

Thunderbird has been the scene of the most extensive excavation so far. It is located on a long ridge a few hundred meters west of and paralleling the river channel. There are hunting camps and processing camps on fans extending out onto the floodplain. Debris occurs at "hot spots" (as at Debert and Bull Brook) on the terrace where structures or shelters of vertical posts are associated with use surfaces and fired areas. These are the earliest (10,900 BP) possible house structures in the Americas. They are not, however, *firmly* associated with the Clovis level of occupancy and may relate to the next or Archaic level; the evidence has been blurred by recent farming activity. From the lowest levels at Thunderbird, a near-classic Clovis point and several other, more variant pieces were recovered. Above the Clovis finds are later Paleo-Indian and Archaic levels. Other "hot spots," apart from the structures, appear to be almost exclusively the result of final flint-knapping work; the evidence is in the presence of core fragments, myriads of flakes created by pressure or hammer (baton?) blows, and broken, not whole, tools. The quarry sites, like other such locations, yield largely cores, primary (percussion) flakes, and unfinished pieces labeled preforms. This is to say that production of half-finished tools went on at these quarries, which are usually found near outcrops of the chert or jasper.

Based on his work at Flint Run, Gardner (1975) suggests that there are three phases in the Paleo-Indian period. They are the Clovis (12,000–11,000 BP), mid-Paleo (11,000–10,500 BP), and Dalton-Hardaway (10,500–10,000 BP). Gardner further argues the Clovis phase in the East is essentially contemporary with the western Llano. Additional work will probably support his view, although earlier authors postulated an easterly lag, as has Martin.

The Flint Run investigators have gone rather carefully into the paleoclimate of the region. Using a widespread series of pollen studies, they reconstruct the floral chronology of the Flint Run district in a familiar sequence. At 10,000 BP, the mountain zone is characterized as having been tundra, and the foothills as spruce-pine dominated. There were extensive upland-plateau grasslands, with the floodplain showing deciduous species and many extensive bogs. The bogs, except in one or two instances, have long since been sealed off by deep Recent sediments. Fauna, at 11,000 years BP, was the already familiar, now extinct assemblage associated with tundra and boreal vegetation—mastodon, mammoth, caribou, two species of musk ox, moose, and bison. By 9300 BP the animals were modern species. Note that the timing does not exactly coincide with the vegetational data for the Plains, where grass must have been dominant by 10,500 to 11,500 BP.

At the Shawnee-Minisink site in Delaware, McNett has already recovered a near-classic Clovis point and many other tools in what seems to be a rich Clovis site that was barely sampled in 1975. This project is also a long-range study, so a large corpus of fully controlled new data will be generated in ensuing years. Dragoo (1976) offers his findings at Wells Creek in Tennessee as evidence of a strong and early Paleo-Indian use of the area. The site is described as an extensive stone-chipping deposit, where alleged Clovis points in all stages of manufacture have been recovered. The other tools found include pieces that may be preforms or blanks to have been taken elsewhere for finishing, prismatic flake knives, many scrapers, cleavers, spokeshaves, picks, and raclettes. Such tools correspond to specimens from Folsom; they fall as well into Müller-Beck's Aurignacoid-Mousteroid complex.

There are other locations where early Paleo-Indian debris is abundant all over the East, Southeast, and Middle West. The great surge of interest in this period during the 1970s has resulted in the mounting of programs such as the Thunderbird and Minisink efforts, which will beyond doubt establish the presence a heavy Llano-Clovis complex everywhere south of the 11,000 BP ice edge. (In fact, it is believed that Debert was occupied when the glacial ice was fewer than 96 kilometers away, with caribou and other tundra species being the prey.) Whether complete contemporaneity of the eastern and western complexes is soon demonstrated or is delayed a few years, it remains true that there are hundreds more fluted points reported in the East than in the West. The reluctance to fully accept the several fluted point types found east of the Plains as being of equal age with the Plains points is due to faulty control and lack of association. Most all of the eastern finds have been from the surface; radiocarbon dates have been lacking until recently; and no extinct megafauna have been proved to have been standard prey. That the last-mentioned lack is a hindrance to acceptance may be credited to scholarly myopia or sheer inertia; it is not derived from any real knowledge of the extinction dates for the eastern species of elephant, musk ox, or bison. Chapter 6 will offer slightly differing views on the eastern Clovis horizon; Chapter 4 will describe what little Clovis material there is available from the coastal West.

Returning to a review of the western sites where the data are abundant and in good control, mention must first be made of the epoch-making Folsom discovery in 1926–1927. As indicated earlier, Folsom was merely the be-

FIGURE 1.15
Folsom Fluted points from Lindenmeier.
(From *Prehistory of North America*, 2d ed.,
by Jesse D. Jennings. Copyright ©
1968, 1974 by McGraw-Hill, Inc. Used
with permission of McGraw-Hill Book
Company.)

ginning of a new cultural system, marked by the utilization of the trap or
fall technique of harvesting game. But to call the Folsom-Plano a "new"
cultural system is not entirely correct. The settlement patterns, the basic tool
kit, the areas and pattern of exploitation, and most other basic subsystems in
the culture persisted for several millennia. At Folsom, 23 *Bison antiquus* were
evidently trapped, killed, and butchered. During the butchery 19 fluted
points of a previously unknown type were lost, to be found in full association
with the bones of the kill. The points were unique in their delicacy and distinctive form (Figure 1.15). The site demonstrated the existence of a Paleo-
Indian population during Late Pleistocene times and opened up Paleo-Indian
study, which is still being actively pursued today.

But at Lindenmeier, which was probably a base camp, a broader understanding of the Folsom culture is to be gained. Lindenmeier, located near
Fort Collins, Colorado, suffered the same neglect as Blackwater Draw—that is,
inadequate reporting—from its excavation in the 1930s until after 1970. An
all-important difference is that Lindenmeier was excavated by the late
F. H. H. Roberts, who kept meticulous notes and records. He simply never
produced other than seasonal preliminary reports. Thanks to Wilmsen (1973),
some of the significance of the find becomes apparent.

Located on the marshy banks of a Late Pleistocene lake, long since covered
by sediment from the low hills surrounding the high valley, the site was
quite extensive. As at Thunderbird, there were many "hot spots" where
debitage, broken tools, fire-darkened hearths, and food scrap were abundant.
The location had also been used by Llano peoples, but the heaviest use was
by a Folsom group. An occasional mammoth and many bison were killed and
butchered there. The tool kit, aside from the delicate fluted points, includes
the crescent-bladed spokeshave used in shaping or smoothing spear or dart
shafts or other slender cylindrical objects, fine-pointed graving or cutting
tools, scrapers for a variety of tasks, prismatic flake knives, and drills.

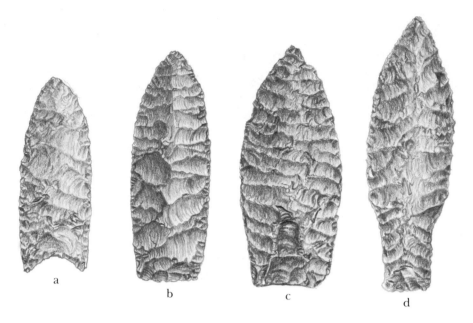

FIGURE 1.16
Plano points: *a*, Plainview; *b*, Milnesand; *c*, Browns Valley; *d*, Hell Gap. (From *Prehistory of North America*, 2d ed., by Jesse D. Jennings. Copyright © 1968, 1974 by McGraw-Hill, Inc. Used with permission of McGraw-Hill Book Company.)

It should be noted that at Lindenmeier, Plainview, Midland, Hell Gap, and other stratified sites on the Plains, there occur what have been called Plainview points. On the basis of form, this point has been described as an "*Un*fluted" Folsom. This term means merely that the point is very similar to the Folsom except that the long fluted flakes whose scars give the Folsom point its thin, biconcave cross-sectional outline were never removed (Figure 1.16). There is continuing debate over the relationship of the classical Folsom and Plainview points. Which is older? Are they contemporary? Neither stratigraphy nor radiocarbon nor typology provides a firm answer. My own opinion is that the Plainview is contemporary with Folsom but persisted to set a model for the many lanceolate unfluted types that follow in rather quick succession over all the Plains, although not in the East. From the Olsen-Chubbuck site, to be described below, Wheat (1972) found and described a Firstview point, which further confuses the issue; the Firstview and Plainview appear to be the same. The evidence at Bonfire Shelter (Dibble and Lorrain 1968) tends to support the brief popularity of the Plainview point as marking a transition from Folsom toward the varied unfluted, elongated, later projectile types. At Bonfire, deep in the southern Texas plains, three separate bison stampede kills were uncovered. With the lowest, dated at 10,200 BP, was a Folsom point. Immediately above, the slightly later second kill yielded only Plainview points. On the other hand, Irwin (1971) places the Plainview type ahead of Folsom on the strength of the Hell Gap site finds. The truth is that the stratigraphy (which is equivalent to time) for all these sites was probably correctly observed and reported. The differing stratigraphic positions may reflect a broad distribution over many hundreds of horizontal miles, with the Plainview point having developed in the northern Plains and later been adopted in south Texas as the type gained in popularity. Before the matter can be decided, more and better evidence will be required.

Hell Gap is one more location that assumes importance by having great chronological depth. The cultures represented there cover a 3,200-year time span—from 11,200 BP to 8,000 BP—about the full range of the Paleo-Indian occupancy of the Plains. Lying in eastern Wyoming, the finds consist of several contiguous locations that could be collapsed or combined to form a stratigraphic column-sequence on the strength of radiocarbon dates, geological formations, and internal evidence within the sequent strata. Figure 1.17 is modified from one that Irwin based upon the Hell Gap findings. Note that he uses the term *Itama* to indicate the culture sequence after Llano. His Itama thus includes Folsom; grouping the Folsom with the later Plano emphasizes their similarities to each other as contrasted with Llano. Actually the objects and other evidence found at Hell Gap were scanty; the importance of the site rests with the time depth and culture sequence presented in Figure 1.17.

At this juncture a pair of carefully excavated kill sites should be described in order to exemplify the wealth of information these sites contain. The first to be mentioned is the Olsen-Chubbuck kill in east central Colorado, not far from Kit Carson, near the Kansas line (Wheat 1972). It is Folsom-Plainview in age at 10,200 BP. The kill occurred where a long, narrow gully (3 meters wide by 2 meters deep) lay across the path of a bison herd (*occidentalis*) stampeding down a steep hillside. Approximately 190 animals of both sexes and all ages were injured or killed in the trap. Immediately butchery began, in the course of which (and during the kill itself) more than 60 tools—Firstview (Plainview) and San Jon points, cobbles for breaking bones, and flint flake knives and scrapers—were lost or discarded. By working slowly, with great care, Wheat exposed many heaps of bone and discovered that the butchery process followed a consistent pattern. It was doubtless efficient and rapid. The bone piles showed that after skinning, and removal of the savory hump meat, the forelegs and shoulder girdle were removed, stripped of meat, and discarded. Next, the hind legs and pelvic girdle were cut free, the meat removed, and the bones discarded on the foreleg bones. Usually in the scrap heap the hind legs lay above the pelvic bones. Next atop the heap were chains of vertebrae, with skulls attached. Animals wedged into the narrow bottom of the arroyo rarely showed any evidence of butchery, their bones being still articulated upon discovery. In addition to providing the details about butchering techniques, the site allowed for an analysis of the age components

Chronological chart of the Llano / Paleo-Indian cultural sequence

Phase	Subphase / Complex	Years BP	North					South
					Relative Geographic Position			
Horner phase	Lusk complex	8,000	Mangus / mummy cave		Hell Gap	Jimmey Allen / Lime Creek	Angostura / Greene site	Blackwater Draw
Horner phase	Frederick complex; Cody subphase	8,500	MacHaffie / Renner	Horner	Hell Gap; Scottsbluff / Finley	Lime Creek	Lindenmeier / Claypool	Olsen-Chubbuck / Jurgens / Lamb Springs
Horner phase	Alberta subphase	9,000	Fletcher / Bayrock		Hell Gap		Lindenmeier	San Jon / Blackwater Draw
Sister's Hill phase	Hell Gap subphase	9,500		Sister's Hill	Hell Gap			
Sister's Hill phase	Agate Basin subphase	10,000		Agate Basin	Hell Gap; Angostura	Gordon Creek	Frazier	Blackwater Draw / Milnesand
Lindenmeier phase	Midland subphase	10,500			Hell Gap	Gordon Creek		Blackwater Draw / Scharbauer / Bonfire
Lindenmeier phase	Folsom subphase	10,750		MacHaffie / Agate Basin	Hell Gap		Johnson / Lindenmeier / Folsom	Blackwater Draw / Lipscomb / Lubbock / Sandia / Bonfire
Plainview phase	Plainview subphase	11,000			Hell Gap		Domebo	Plainview / Bonfire
	Black Water phase	11,200		Simon	U.P.		Dent / Miami	Blackwater Draw / Naco / Lehner
		12,000						Murray Springs

llama culture

of the herd—calf, yearling, and so on. The chipped flint showed that a wide range of raw materials had been collected and utilized (including some Texas Alibates flint pieces), reinforcing the ideas widely held about the cyclical wandering of the Folsom-Plano bands.

In Wyoming, Frison has discovered and excavated a number of bison kill sites since 1965. One, the Casper site near Casper (Frison 1974), is of interest because it is not a fall but an instance of the trap or cul-de-sac technique. The site, dated 8000 BP, was an extensive bone bed between the horns of a fossil parabolic dune. The heavy animals could not ascend the shifting sand of the steep dune face. As they milled, their escape cut off by the hunters, they were slaughtered one by one by the lancers. This location also provided information on the herd composition; but the data suggest that selective killing was practiced, there being more carcasses in the 0.6-to-2.6-year range than a random herd would normally have. The associated points are almost exclusively of the Hell Gap type.

Frison et al. (1976) report a kill of yet a third type. Here in a fossil arroyo, very deep and ending headward with a steep walled jump up or knickpoint forming an unscalable barrier, are remains of a kill of about 100 bison. The technique involved pushing several small herds upstream until the animals were wedged helplessly against each other in the narrow gully. The date of this kill at the Hawken location (in extreme northeast Wyoming, near Sun Dance) is 6500 BP. Aside from the detailed paleogeomorphological reconstructions made by the authors, the site is the type site for a new Plano knife point, here called the Hawken Side Notched. The form is very similar to a quite distinctive style found farther west in the northern Great Basin, called Northern Side Notched. They are also similar to, but distinct from, an Idaho series of side-notched points called Bitterroot.

In view of their large number and the uniformly sketchy reporting, the Plano sites other than Hell Gap, Hawken, Plainview, Casper, and Bonfire, will not be described here. However, there are several named locations that give their names to distinctive and chronologically separate projectile knife types, and these must be listed. Some of these are Eden, Claypool, Scottsbluff, Milnesand, San Jon, Agate Basin, and Angostura. Some of these are kill sites; others may have been oft-used campsites.

During the Plano period, the now extinct *Bison occidentalis* gave over to the historic *Bison bison*. In Chapter 5 Wedel effectively deals with the apparent extreme fluctuation of bison herd size, the localization of herds in favorable areas, and the cultural results this fluctuation in numbers produced in the Plains area.

FIGURE 1.17 *(Opposite)*
Chronological arrangement of Plains big-game-hunter components. (From *Prehistory of North America,* 2d ed., by Jesse D. Jennings. Copyright © 1968, 1974 by McGraw-Hill, Inc. Used with permission of McGraw-Hill Book Company.)

Several Central American finds—Tepexpan, Valesquillo, Tlacopaya, and Hueyatlaco—have been ascribed an antiquity of greater than 10,000 years. On internal stratigraphic evidence and anachronistic archeological associations, these sites are not widely accepted. At Iztapan, however, mammoth bones aged about 11,000 BP with flint tools in good association were discovered. This is regarded as an authentic find. In Guatemala, Gruhn and Bryan (1975) have reported a site, dated at 11,200 BP, where the artifacts are not entirely consistent with other Paleo-Indian locations. The site lies very high, in a mountain meadow at 3200 meters, a few kilometers west and north of Guatemala City. Although bifacially chipped blades and two apparent Clovis Fluted point bases were recovered, many of the flint specimens are burins and gravers. The remains are scanty; no bones from food animals survived. The site, interpreted as a short-lived hunting camp, is entirely credible, albeit unusual.

The intent of this chapter has been to provide a succint survey of the beginnings of man's history in the New World. Hence, attention has been largely confined to North America. The sometimes scant evidence (and the areas of ignorance) that surround the saga of the first Americans has been emphasized. What the evidence says, as I read it, is that man crossed from Asia to the Americas by way of the Beringian land bridge, then a vast plain characterized by arctic vegetation and megafauna. The first dated evidence of man comes at 27,000 ± BP. After his arrival, there was an intensification of the ice buildup over Canada, which may have prevented southward movement of people for a time, but by 19,000 ± BP, small hunting bands were already below the southern edge of the ice in what is now the United States. They were using a Eurasiatic tool kit, typologically reminiscent of the Aurignacian level of technology.

Around 11,500 BP there was another influx at or near Edmonton, Canada, of a later and possibly a numerically larger population, which concentrated its subsistence activities upon now extinct megafauna. The physical environment was not arctic but was an open woodland that rapidly yielded to the endless grasslands that now characterize the Plains. These Paleo-Indian hunters can be divided on cultural grounds into the earlier Llano and the subsequent Folsom-Plano. The lifeways of the two groups were similar in their apparent concentration on big game that is now extinct, their cyclical wandering from one resource to another, and their frequent returns to favorable hunting locations. Villages, or at least base camps, as well as kill sites have been identified in both the Plains and the eastern United States; the eastern locations are numerous, with more being reported each year. The occupancies were no doubt contemporary, a fact that bespeaks a very rapid expansion of the hunters over the ice-free portion of the hemisphere.

The Llano peoples' preferred game was the mammoth, usually young, single individuals, and they normally hunted in ambushes or in boggy or marsh locations where the animal would presumably be hampered in movement. The environment was transitional from a well-watered Pleistocene one, characterized by open parkland—savanna and many wet locations where coarse grasses were abundant—to the drier grasslands of the Plains.

The Folsom-Plano groups concentrated on the long-horn bison (*antiquus* and *occidentalis*) that dominated the drier grasslands upon the extinction of the mammoth. Although the ambush killing of singles may have continued, the bison hunters developed the mass-kill technique. The procedure required a task force larger than the family, as it involved the driving of a small herd of bison over a cliff or into a box canyon or arroyo or other kind of blind trap, such as a crescentic sand dune. This mass-kill technique required control over a sizable group of hunters, while the Llano single-kill technique did not. The settlement patterns appear to have varied, with the Llano tending to camp near water sources (sometimes on knolls) and the Folsom-Plano camps tending to be slightly removed downwind but on elevations where the watering holes and the animal range could be constantly observed.

Although the preceding pages offer a sample of the literature and give the beginning reader a glimpse of how the Indian conquest of the New World began, this chapter can properly be regarded as but an introduction to the reams of data available on the ever fresh and increasingly deep (chronologically) story of the Paleo-Indian.

Again, one predicts that further research will continue to push the evidence of man on both continents deeper back into time, perhaps into the mid-Wisconsin (40,000 BP) range. The chapter, which has dealt almost exclusively with North America, with a very brief excursion into Central America, has exercised a certain selectivity for two reasons. First, research on Paleo-Indian matters in North America has been unceasing since the late 1920s and would exceed by a hundredfold the amount of study of the same time period by Latin American students, perhaps because of their greater concern for the vast, ruined cities of a later period. The second reason is that the early action is in North America, where it all began, leaving the later, more southerly manifestations to draw their essential credibility from the better-documented data to the north. Alas, as indicated, some of the few Central American sites are not accepted as fully authenticated examples from the alleged time span.

This chapter is an introduction in another sense. It provides an introduction to the chapters that follow in that it describes significant climatic changes between 20,000 and 10,000 years ago. The changes in climate, fauna, and flora since 10,000 BP are also implied. The adaptation the Native Americans made to the areal expansion of life zones and resources and to the continuous population increase constitute the cultural history unfolded in the following chapters. It is widely believed, even if not constantly reiterated, that the climatic changes following the retreat of the ice set up certain subsistence stresses that led to the marked shifts in adaptation to different resources that characterize the ubiquitous Archaic cultures of the two continents. Thus,

FIGURE 1.18
North American culture areas.
(From *Prehistory of North America*,
2d ed., by Jesse D. Jennings.
Copyright © 1968, 1974 by
McGraw-Hill, Inc. Used with
permission of McGraw-Hill Book
Company.)

some would argue that all subsequent American cultures after the Paleo-Indian are directly attributable to the new set of environments.

Anthropologists and geographers have long recognized the inescapable fact that the world environments, over broad regions, are so different that a variety of lifestyles or patterns would of necessity evolve to "fit" the broad environmental-resource attributes of the several regions. Examples would be the Desert West as opposed to the Plains, where the bison lingered after the Paleo-Indian. Sharply different from either is the Southeast. There, the deciduous hardwood forests and the dense canebrakes in the myriad swampy stream valleys supply even today a rich and varied fauna and flora, where the living is "easy" for the hunter and collector.

The remaining chapters of the book are organized around the culture areas of the hemisphere and the unique resources of each. Figure 1.18 shows the major areas and their different but interlocking culture sequences. To some degree, the exchange of culture traits and patterns between them is also noted. But the culture area treatment employed is emphatically *not* to imply that the regional events transpired in isolation. More correctly, the culture area idea should be recognized as the convenient, even traditional way in which archeologists have held the diverse and varied data down to a manageable mass. Even so, the bulk of the data to be compressed into the regional sections increases annually, and meaningful summaries become more difficult to prepare because of the difficulty of making decisions about the greater or lesser importance of a corpus of new data.

References Cited and Recommended Sources

Adovasio, James M. 1975 Excavations at Meadowcroft Rockshelter, 1973–1974: a progress report. *Pennsylvania Archaeologist* 45:3:1–30.

Antevs, Ernst 1948 Climatic changes and prewhite man. *In* The Great Basin with emphasis on glacial and post glacial times. University of Utah Bulletin 38:20:168–191.

Bedwell, Stephen F. 1973 Fort Rock Basin Prehistory and Environment. Eugene: University of Oregon Press.

Birdsell, Joseph B. 1951 The problem of the early peopling of the Americas as viewed from Asia. Papers on the physical anthropology of the American Indian, Delivered at 4th Viking Fund Summer Seminar in Physical Anthropology. New York: The Viking Fund, Inc.

Bryan, Alan L. 1969 Early man in America and the Late Pleistocene chronology of western Canada and Alaska. Current Anthropology 10:4:339–367.

Bryson, Reid A., David A. Baerreis, and Wayne M. Wendland 1970 The character of late glacial and post-glacial climatic changes. *In* Pleistocene and Recent Environments of the Central Great Plains, ed. Wakefield Dort, Jr., and J. Knox Jones, Jr., pp. 53–74. Department of Geology, University of Kansas, Special Publication No. 3.

Butzer, Karl W. 1971 Environment and Archeology: An Introduction to Pleistocene Geography. 2d ed. Chicago: Aldine Publishing Company.

Dibble, David S., and Dessamae Lorrain 1968 Bonfire Shelter: a stratified bison kill site, Val Verde County, Texas. Texas Memorial Museum. Miscellaneous Papers, No. 1.

Dragoo, Don W. 1976 Some aspects of eastern North American prehistory: a review, 1975. American Antiquity 41:1:3–27.

Frison, George C. 1974 The Casper Site: A Hell Gap Bison Kill on the High Plains. New York: Academic Press, Inc.

Frison, George C., Michael Wilson, and Diane J. Wilson 1976 Fossil bison and artifacts from an early altithermal period arroyo trap in Wyoming. American Antiquity 41:1:28–57.

Gardner, William M. 1974 The Flint Run Paleo-Indian complex: a preliminary report, 1971–73 seasons. Archeology Laboratory, Department of Anthropology, Occasional Publication, No. 1. The Catholic University of America.

————. 1975 Paleo-Indian to Early Archaic: continuity and change in eastern North America during the Late Pleistocene and Early Holocene. Proceedings of the IXth International Congress of Prehistoric and Protohistoric Scientists, Nice, France.

Gruhn, Ruth, and Alan L. Bryan n.d. Los Tapiales: A Paleo-Indian campsite in the Guatemalan Highlands. Unpublished manuscript.

Haury, Emil W., Ernest Antevs, and John F. Lance 1953 Artifacts with mammoth remains, Naco, Arizona: I, II, III. American Antiquity 19:1:1–24.

Haury, Emil W., Edwin B. Sayles, and William W. Wasley 1959 The Lehner Mammoth site, southeastern Arizona. American Antiquity 25:1:2–30.

Haynes, C. Vance, Jr. 1969 The earliest Americans. Science, 166:3906:709–715. 1973 The Calico site: artifacts or geofacts? Science 181:4097:305–310.

Haynes, C. Vance, Jr., and E. Thomas Hemmings 1968 Mammoth-bone shaft wrench from Murray Springs, Arizona. Science 159:3811:186–187.

Hester, James J. 1972 Blackwater Locality No. 1: A Stratified, Early Man Site in Eastern New Mexico. Ranchos de Taos, New Mexico: Fort Burgwin Research Center, Inc.

————. 1975 Paleoarchaeology of the Llano Estacado. *In* Late Pleistocene Environments of the Southern High Plains, ed. Fred Wendorf and James J. Hester, pp. 247–256. Ranchos de Taos, New Mexico: Fort Burgwin Research Center, Inc.

Hopkins, David M. 1967 The Cenozoic history of Beringia—a synthesis. *In* The Bering Land Bridge, ed. David M. Hopkins, pp. 451–484. Stanford: Stanford University Press.

Irving, William N., and C. R. Harington 1973 Upper Pleistocene radiocarbon-dated artifacts from the northern Yukon. Science 179:4071:335–340.

Irwin, Henry T. 1971 Developments in early man studies in western North America, 1960–1970. Arctic Anthropology VIII:2.

Irwin-Williams, Cynthia 1967 Associations of early man with horse, camel, and mastodon at Hueyatlaco, Valsequillo (Puebla, Mexico). *In* Pleistocene Extinctions: The Search for a Cause, ed. P. S. Martin and H. E. Wright, Jr., pp. 337–347. New Haven: Yale University Press.

————. 1968 Archaeological evidence on early man in Mexico. *In* Early Man in Western North America, ed. Cynthia Irwin-Williams. Eastern New Mexico University Contributions in Anthropology 1:4:39–41.

Jennings, Jesse D. 1974a Across an Arctic bridge. *In* The World of the American Indian, ed. Jules B. Billard, pp. 29–70. Washington, D.C.: The National Geographic Society.

————. 1974b Prehistory of North America. 2d ed. New York: McGraw-Hill Book Company.

————. n.d. Prehistory of Utah and the eastern Great Basin. University of Utah Anthropological Papers No. 97. In press.

Krieger, Alex D. 1964 Early man in the New World. *In* Prehistoric Man in the New World, ed. J. Jennings and E. Norbeck, pp. 23–81. Chicago: University of Chicago Press.

Lahren, Larry, and Robson Bonnichsen 1974 Bone foreshafts from A Clovis burial in southwestern Montana. Science 186:147–150.

LaMarche, Valmore C., Jr. 1974 Paleoclimatic inferences from long tree-ring records. Science 183:4129:1043–1048.

Laughlin, W. S. 1967 Human migration and permanent occupation in the Bering Sea area. *In* The Bering Land Bridge, ed. David M. Hopkins, pp. 409–450. Stanford: Stanford University Press.

Long, Joseph K. 1966 A test of multiple-discriminant analysis as a means of determining evolutionary changes and intergroup relationships in physical anthropology. American Anthropologist 68:2:1:444–464.

Martin, Paul S. 1973 The discovery of America. Science 179:969–974.

McNett, Charles W., Jr., Sydne B. Marshall, and Ellis E. McDowell 1975 Second season of the upper Delaware Valley early man project. A report for the National Geographic Society and National Science Foundation. Washington, D.C.: Department of Anthropology, The American University.

Müller-Beck, Hansjürgen 1966 Paleohunters in America: origins and diffusion. Science 152: 3726:1191–1210.

————. 1967 On migrations of hunters across the Bering land bridge in the Upper Pleistocene. *In* The Bering Land Bridge, ed. David M. Hopkins, pp. 373–408. Stanford: Stanford University Press.

Neumann, Georg K. 1952 Archeology and race in the American Indian. *In* Archeology of Eastern United States, ed. James B. Griffin, pp. 13–34. Chicago: University of Chicago Press.

O'Connell, James F. 1975 The prehistory of Surprise Valley. Ballena Press Anthropological Papers, No. 4, ed. Lowell John Bean.

Reeves, Brian 1973 The concept of an Altithermal cultural hiatus in northern Plains prehistory. American Anthropologist 75:5:1221–1253.

Shafter, Harry J. 1975 Early Lithic assemblages in eastern Texas. Paper presented at the Paleo-Indian Lifeways Symposium, Lubbock, Texas.

Stewart, T. D. 1973 The People of America. New York: Charles Scribner's Sons.

Wells, Philip V. 1970 Vegetational history of the Great Plains: a post-glacial record of coniferous woodland in southeastern Wyoming. *In* Pleistocene and Recent Environments of the Central Great Plains, ed. Wakefield Dort, Jr., and J. Knox Jones, Jr., pp. 185–202. Department of Geology, University of Kansas, Special Publication No. 3.

Wendorf, Fred, Alex D. Krieger, and Claude E. Albritton 1955 The Midland Discovery: A Report on the Pleistocene Human Remains from Midland, Texas. Austin: University of Texas Press.

Wheat, Joe Ben 1972 The Olsen-Chubbuck site: a Paleo-Indian bison kill. American Antiquity 37:1:2. Memoirs of the society for American Archaeology No. 26.

Wilmsen, Edwin N. 1973 Lindenmeier: A Pleistocene Hunting Society. New York: Harper and Row.

Wright, H. E., Jr. 1970 Vegetational history of the central plains. *In* Pleistocene and Recent Environments of the Central Great Plains, ed. Wakefield Dort, Jr., and J. Knox Jones, Jr., pp. 157–172. Department of Geology, University of Kansas, Special Publication No. 3.

The upper Naknek drainage on the Alaska Peninsula, looking southeast. Mile-and-a-half-long Brooks River drains Brooks Lake (*right*) into Naknek Lake (*left*), part of a complex of lakes and rivers that was formed by Late Pleistocene glaciers and that now provides spawning grounds for five species of salmon. The spruce forest visible south of Brooks River has become established only in the past 500 years. In the far distance is the Aleutian Range, beyond which is the Pacific coast. The mountains in the left background are blocked from view by a haze of volcanic ash from the eruption of Mount Trident, an active volcano near the Valley of Ten Thousand Smokes in Katmai National Monument.

CHAPTER TWO

Alaska and the Northwest Coast

Don E. Dumond

In this chapter and the one that follows, the remarkable adaptive qualities of man become immediately clear. Despite the seemingly bleak and barren nature of much of the Alaskan, Arctic, and sub-Arctic environments, man not only lived there but throve and developed a series of rich and diverse cultures. Dr. Dumond discusses not only the inhabitants of the frozen reaches of the far north but also the Indians of the Northwest Coast of North America—the great wealth of their material culture and their extremely successful adaptation to a region of bountiful resources.

GEOGRAPHY

Today, Alaska is a great plate that juts from North America into the northern seas (Figure 2.1). Millennia ago, however, it was a part of the Asian mainland from which it became separated at Bering Strait as waters rose to form the Chukchi Sea on the north and the Bering Sea on the south. Its importance to American prehistory is precisely the result of its unique geographic situation.

Running east and west across the northern portion of the modern state, and separating the relatively flat Arctic slope from the rest of Alaska, is the largely treeless and ice-free Brooks Range, in which a few glacier-scarred peaks rise to elevations above 3000 meters. In the south, a roughly matching but more angular ridge is the Alaska Range, which includes Mt. McKinley and a few other very high peaks, but in which most crests are no higher than 3000 meters. On its western end the spottedly glacier-laden Alaska Range merges with the Aleutian Range, an active mountain chain in which more than 80 identified volcanoes march southwestward along the Alaska Peninsula until, drowned by the waters of the Pacific, they become the 1700-kilometer string of Aleutian Islands.

FIGURE 2.1
Map of Alaska and the Northwest Coast.

Between the Brooks and Alaska ranges, the center of the Alaskan mainland is a trough of flat lowlands and low, broken uplands through which are channeled two major rivers—the Yukon, with its headwaters in western Canada, and the shorter Kuskokwim, which rises in the interior uplands of Alaska. With their mouths on the Bering Sea, both of these river systems receive massive runs of salmon, which, moving far into the interior, provide a rich seasonal resource. This resource is shared by the Northwest Coast to the south but is not matched in the northward-flowing streams that drain the great area of neighboring Canada at a similar latitude, nor in the smaller streams of Alaska's own Arctic slope.

Precipitation throughout all of Alaska except that portion lying directly upon the Pacific Ocean proper (the Aleutian Islands, Kodiak Island, the Alaska and Kenai peninsulas) is relatively light. But with the slow rate of evaporation of the cool climate, and with permafrost often inhibiting drainage, ground moisture is seldom lacking and flatlands are swampy.

In the Yukon Territory to the southeast, the Rocky Mountains, the Coast Mountains, and the St. Elias Range virtually coalesce to form a rugged backbone for the region. Farther south in British Columbia, the Rockies and the Coast Mountains separate, embracing the Columbia-Fraser Plateau. The Coast Mountains in turn divide to become the relatively low-lying Coast Range of Washington and Oregon and the much more formidable Cascades to the east. This great barrier of the Coast Mountains and Cascade Range is breached by only a few major rivers—such as the Stikine, Skeena, and Fraser in British Columbia, and the Columbia to the south—which are sufficient, however, to provide entry for the masses of ocean-matured salmon that migrate far into the interior to spawn.

Westward, on the lengthy and heavily fjorded Pacific coastal strip extending from Prince William Sound in Alaska through southern Oregon, rainfall, although subject to local variation, is generally heavy, exceeding 250 centimeters in numerous locations and reaching twice that in some zones. As mentioned in Chapter 1, vegetation in this region consists of dense forests of spruce, cedar, or Douglas Fir.

GLACIAL HISTORY

Central Alaska experienced a lesser amount of Pleistocene glaciation than did much of North America, including the Northwest Coast. During the height of the last glacial epoch, continuous ice in Alaska was confined to the east-west-trending mountain ridges of the south and the north.

East of the Alaskan border in the Yukon Territory, the mountain glacier systems of north and south Alaska curved toward one another and nearly joined along the northern extension of the Rocky Mountains, so that during the height of the Wisconsin epoch the Alaskan interior formed a relatively ice-free bowl, rimmed on north, east, and south by almost continuous glaciers. Out of this bowl a narrow ice-free corridor led eastward, passed between the Cordilleran glacier system of the west and the edge of the massive continental ice sheet centered around what is now Hudson Bay, and opened southward through Canada into what is now the United States.

According to one view, this hallway was open during all but the most pronounced glacial episodes of the Pleistocene and provided, during the Wisconsin epoch, a relatively continuous access from Alaska to the heart of the continent. According to a second view, however, this corridor was closed virtually throughout the entire Wisconsin when the major North American ice sheets met one another and coalesced, leaving a suitable pathway to the south only before about 23,000 BC and after a time that may have been as late as 6,500 BC. Each of these views carries its own specific implication for the early prehistory both of Alaska and of North America.

NATIVE PEOPLES

At the time of earliest European contact, the coast of Alaska north of the Alaska Peninsula was the home of people adapted to life along a winter-frozen coast, speakers of two distinct Eskimoan languages, one of which was also spoken by Pacific coastal people of the region around Kodiak Island and Prince William Sound. West of about 159° west longitude, on the tip of the Alaska Peninsula and throughout the Aleutian Islands, were to be found the Aleuts, existing by open-water hunting and fishing, and speaking one or more languages classified with Eskimoan in an Eskaleutian stock. The Alaskan interior was peopled by broadly adapted hunters and fishermen of the coniferous forest, Indians speaking several distinct languages, all of which are included in the Athapaskan family—the western extreme of a great linguistic block that extended eastward as far as Hudson Bay.

The northern Northwest Coast was the home of the Eyak, Tlingit, and Haida, whose languages are usually included with Athapaskan in the Na-Dene linguistic phylum. Farther south lived the Penutian-speaking Tsimshian of British Columbia, the Wakashan speakers—Bella Bella, Kwakiutl, Nootka, and others—and the coastal segment of the great Salish family, all of whom partook of classic Northwest Coast culture, with its maritime or littoral subsistence and its emphasis on property and social rank. South of the Athapaskans of the Fraser Plateau, to the east, lived river-fishing Interior Salish of standard Columbia Plateau culture type.

Other Penutian speakers, who occupied the lower Columbia River and the central and southern Oregon coast, were more peripherally involved in the Northwest Coast pattern and provided a transition to the cultures of northern California.

THE ARCHEOLOGY OF
ARCTIC ALASKA AND THE YUKON

By about 4000 BC, there is unmistakable evidence for some differentiation between the tool assemblages of the Alaskan interior and those of some areas of the coast, and this may be thought to relate to a comparable degree of ethnic differentiation among people who used them. In the pages that follow, therefore, the archeology will be set out in two divisions, the first relating to the time before about 4000 BC, the second to all later times.

Before 4000 BC

The earliest evidence to date of man's activities was discovered about 50 kilometers east of the modern border between Alaska and the Yukon Territory, a region that pertained to the unglaciated heart of Alaska when it formed an extension of Asia during the Wisconsin. As indicated elsewhere in this volume (Chapter 1), eroding sediments at the edge of the Old Crow River have produced a collection of fossil animal bone and some modified bones concluded to be artifacts, which yielded radiocarbon dates between about 24,000 and 27,000 BC. Although this redeposited material cannot be related in any systematic way to later cultural deposits from Alaska, it at least now appears to attest to the presence of man at that early date, before the peak of the late Wisconsin glaciation.

No equally early dates have been obtained from any products of human activity in Alaska proper. The earliest, from the Trail Creek caves of Seward Peninsula, are bison bones, thought to have been broken by humans in order to remove the marrow, which have been dated at about 13,000 BC (Larsen 1968b). With one exception, all other presumably early tool complexes in Alaska consist of stone rather than bone implements; bone trash is consistently rare or nonexistent.

THE PALEOARCTIC TRADITION (9000–6000 BC) □ The unequivocally early stone complexes already show considerable diversity, manifest particularly in the presence or absence of bifaces in general, of fluted points in particular, and of certain apparently specialized implements such as types of burins. What the collections have strikingly in common is that they are dominated by products of a blade technology and that they consistently tend to include at least some blade cores in which the wedge-shaped form of the core is created before blades are removed. Although notable differences in scale are present, it is most common for these cores to be small, having provided small blades, termed microblades. Examples of wedge-shaped cores from which the blades removed commonly do not exceed 5 centimeters in

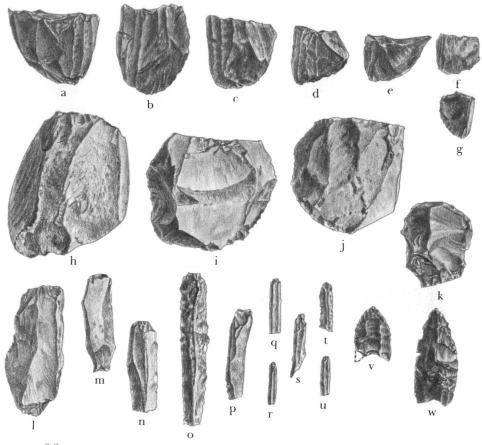

FIGURE 2.2

Artifacts of the Paleoarctic tradition: *a–g*, wedge-shaped cores; *h*, blade core; *i, j*, core bifaces; *k*, end scraper; *l–u*, blades; *v, w*, fluted and incipiently fluted points. *a, p, q*, Anangula blade site, Anangula Island; *v, w*, Batza Tena; all others, Alaska Peninsula.

length have sometimes been referred to as "campus-type" microcores, after the site on the University of Alaska campus where they were first discovered (Figure 2.2).

In addition, some collections include larger blades struck from a variety of types of cores, as well as more or less discoidal and bifacially worked flake cores, some of which reflect what might be called a Levallois technique of shaping the flake before detachment from the core. Certain collections also include specialized stone projectile points, while a few others lack bifacially chipped stone entirely. For present purposes, all of these are designated the Paleoarctic tradition (see Figure 2.3 for a chart of Alaska's cultural tradition).

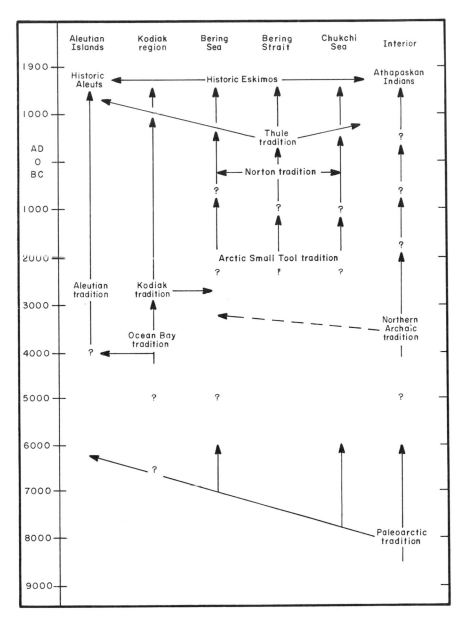

FIGURE 2.3
Major cultural traditions in Alaska.

Sites involved are located either in areas that were untouched by the latest major local glacial episodes or in zones that were deglaciated early, so that the sites may have been in fairly close proximity to remnant glacial ice. Dry Creek, in central Alaska, has yielded bone remains of horse and bison, reflecting the Late Pleistocene faunal assemblage. Paleoarctic collections have been dated by radiocarbon as early as 9000 BC and at least as late as 6000 BC.

The first-discovered and best attested Alaskan assemblages are those termed the Akmak and Kobuk complexes from the site of Onion Portage, on the Kobuk River more than 160 kilometers above its mouth, in northeastern Alaska. The Akmak complex includes wedge-shaped microcores, microblades, burins, ellipsoidal bifaces, large core bifaces reminiscent of Levallois cores, and large polyhedral cores and the blades removed from them; the complex is believed to date to about 8000 BC. The more recent Kobuk complex consists almost entirely of microcores and microblades and may well represent less than the full inventory of the artifacts used by the people involved (Anderson 1970).

Similar collections are found along the north slope of the Brooks Range and in the Noatak River drainage. On Seward Peninsula, the lowest artifact-bearing levels of the Trail Creek caves have yielded blades probably derived from wedge-shaped microcores, and levels believed to date around 7000 BC have produced slender bone points with grooves in the sides in which such microblades may have been set (Larsen 1968b). Farther south, a narrow game crossing between two lakes in the Ugashik River drainage on the Bering Sea slope of the Alaska Peninsula has yielded an assemblage strongly reminiscent of that of Akmak, and cores of the wedge-shaped type have been reported elsewhere in the immediate vicinity (Dumond 1977:37, 40; Dumond, et al. 1976).

In central Alaska, in addition to the Dry Creek site mentioned earlier, certain collections of what has been designated the Denali complex, with essentially the same content as those just described, have recently been shown to date from about 8000 BC (Hadleigh West 1975). Although the original Denali complex assemblage was the first of this kind to be formally defined (Hadleigh West 1967), its acceptance as a valid early entity has been hampered by the presence in some subsequently described "Denali" assemblages of artifacts that are unquestionably later in time, even as late as the Christian era. Nevertheless, accumulating evidence makes it clear that earlier elements of the Denali complex are an integral part of the Paleoarctic tradition.

Other assemblages of early date, which include the same basic blade and core artifacts, are somewhat more varied in their total inventory (Dumond 1977:41–43). At Healy Lake, in the Yukon-Tanana Uplands, the lowest levels of a shallow stratified site yielded a complex designated Chindadn, which includes some very thin, teardrop and triangular-shaped points slightly more than 5 centimeters in length, as well as microblades and burins; these levels are dated about 9000 BC. A few apparently valid collections contain both blades and stone projectile points with fluted bases. One surficial site on the Utukok River produced fragments of two such points, as well as blades, blade cores, and other tools. A mammoth tusk nearby was radiocarbon dated to about 15,000 BC; other mammal bone in the site dated about 400 BC (Humphrey 1970), leaving the date of the cultural material in doubt. At least two sites in the Sagavanirktok River region of the Brooks Range have also yielded such points, plus blades and microblades. One, the Putu site, provided a radiocarbon date of about 6500 BC on organic material in soil surrounding the artifacts (Alexander 1973). Similar points, again reported to be probably associated with microblades, have been recovered at undated flaking stations in the upper Koyokuk River valley, and they are known elsewhere, particularly in northern Alaska, from surface finds (Clark 1972). Although the dating of these fluted points in Alaska is not firm, the present evidence suggests strongly that they do pertain to the Paleoarctic tradition.

Another variant is represented by two important sites that are separated in space and time but nevertheless exhibit some striking correspondences to one another. One is the Anangula blade site, on Anangula Island just off the coast of Umnak Island in the eastern Aleutians, which has yielded an extensive blade and core industry, scrapers, scraping implements made by a transverse burin blow, and fragments of stone vessels. Despite the presence of some wedge-shaped cores, most blade cores were made without any serious attempt at shaping other than the flattening of a striking platform, and were often rotated in use so that multiple sets of blade scars may run in various directions. There is no clear distinction between blades and microblades, for sizes intergrade freely; there are no bifaces in the collection at all. The site dates to about 6000 BC (Aigner 1970).

The latest geological research in the Anangula area indicates that the sea level had risen to about its present height by the time the site was occupied, suggesting that the use of boats must have been known to the people (Black 1975). This circumstance seems to provide a convincing argument for an early coastal economic adaptation by a people of what is here called the Paleoarctic tradition, even though there is as yet no evidence of an artifact assemblage specific to sea-edge pursuits.

The second site of this variant, designated the Gallagher Flint station, is located on the Sagavanirktok River near the Putu site, north of the Brooks Range. The collection, an Anangula-like core and blade assemblage without bifaces, and lacking the burinized scraping implements of Anangula, is dated by radiocarbon about 8600 BC (Dixon 1975).

RELATIONSHIPS OF THE PALEOARCTIC TRADITION ☐ In north-central Canada, no remains of human occupations are known until substantially later than the period just under discussion—a fact in keeping with the glacial history of the region. Although attempts have been made to compare Paleoarctic tradition collections containing fluted points to early collections from what is now the continental United States (e.g., Alexander 1973; Humphrey 1970), the presence in the Arctic sites of the extensive and highly characteristic microblade industry seems itself sufficient to set these assemblages apart from those proceeding—for instance, from the Clovis levels of the southerly North American sites. Other evidence places the Alaskan collections considerably too late for them to reflect any development ancestral to the material culture of the Clovis hunters. Such collections may, however, indicate the beginning of communication, upon the final retreat of the glaciers, with people already present in the south.

In northeastern Asia, the past few years have revealed the existence of a prehistory with obvious relevance to that of the American Arctic. Oval, bifacially chipped projectile heads and knives, disc-shaped cores, wedge-shaped blade cores, blades, microblades, scrapers, and a variety of burins are characteristic of collections in the Aldan region possibly as early as 20,000 BC; these persisted to about 8,000 BC, by which time similar assemblages had appeared in Kamchatka and on the Chukchi Peninsula, as well as in Alaska. It thus seems clear that the Alaskan representatives of the Paleoarctic tradition hark back to the time when Alaska was a peninsula of Asia, thrusting against the continental ice of the New World.

OTHER PUTATIVELY EARLY ASSEMBLAGES □ The patinated chips, choppers, and fragmentary point of the supposedly early Palisades I complex, which were separated on grounds of typology and weathering from the side-notched projectile points of the Palisades II complex with which they were discovered on the hill behind Cape Krusenstern (Giddings 1967), have never been satisfactorily isolated elsewhere. They are now considered to be a normal part of a single Palisades complex, which has been securely dated to later times.

The British Mountain complex, described first from the stratigraphically untrustworthy Engigstciak site on the Firth River in northwestern Canada, consists of retouched flakes, relatively heavy bifaces, and some unifacial and often patinated points (MacNeish 1964:329, 362). The complex has been compared to certain crude but undated collections from northern Alaska, particularly the Kogruk complex of Anaktuvuk Pass (Campbell 1961a) and material from elsewhere in the Brooks Range (e.g., Solecki et al. 1973). An apparently valid British Mountain assemblage from a buried site not far from Firth River now appears to have been dated by radiocarbon to a time after 3500 BC (Gordon 1970).

After 4000 BC: The Interior

THE NORTHERN ARCHAIC TRADITION (4000–2400 BC) □ Well-dated deposits from the site at Onion Portage have produced material that can be divided into a series of sequential stages within what has been termed the Northern Archaic tradition (Anderson 1968). The earliest stages, beginning around 4000 BC by several radiocarbon determinations, include somewhat asymmetrical side-notched points with deep, wide notches and bases that are commonly rather convex; large unifacially chipped knives; and chipped end scrapers. As time goes on, some of the projectile points become shorter, the scraping implements change somewhat, and notched cobbles, apparently designed to be hafted as axes, appear. Still later, the bases of the side-notched points tend to evolve into stems produced by corner notching; notched water-worn cobbles appear, supposedly used as sinkers; and some slate objects with crudely polished or striated faces are found. All of these are aspects of what is designated the Palisades complex. By about 2600 BC lanceolate points are found with the stemmed points, and the stage is set for what is called the Portage complex of about 2500 BC, when all projectile points are of generalized leaf or lanceolate form, but with some other artifacts continuing without modification (Figure 2.4).

Other sites of the Palisades complex are known in northwest Alaska, including that of the original discovery on the coastal bluffs behind Cape Krusenstern, which is thought to represent the incursion of people from the interior (Giddings 1967).

The related Tuktu complex was reported first from an unstratified site at Anaktuvuk Pass, where it was dated by a single radiocarbon determination somewhere between 5000 and 4000 BC. It includes side-notched points and end scrapers very similar to those of the Palisades complex, as well as notched cobbles and some grinding of implements. Unlike Palisades, this complex contains numerous microblades, which were struck or pressed from cores having a nearly flat face, described as more "tabular" than the small wedge-shaped cores of the Paleoarctic tradition (Campbell 1961b). A component of this complex, not directly dated by radiocarbon, is reported from Healy Lake. A similar assemblage, in which side-notched and stemmed points are accompanied by small blades removed from rather simple cores made from trimmed pebbles, is also present in the upper Ugashik River drainage on the Alaska Peninsula; it has been termed the Ugashik Knoll phase and dated to about 3000 BC (Dumond et al. 1976). Thus it seems clear that some assemblages that may be assigned to the Northern Archaic tradition also include microblades.

A number of other collections characterized by side- or corner-notched points have been reported, the great majority of them from the Alaskan interior, and most of them without clear evidence of microblades; unfortunately, most of them are also little described in the literature and inadequately dated. Nevertheless, it seems that assemblages including both side-notched points and microblades are more common to the east. In southwest Yukon Territory certain collections characterized by this association have been assigned to three sequential phases designated Little Arm, Gladstone, and Taye Lake (MacNeish 1964). Although the dating of the phases is questionable in some respects, the association of notched, stemmed,

FIGURE 2.4
Artifacts of the Northern Archaic tradition; Palisades site, Cape Krusenstern. (From *Prehistory of North America*, 2d ed., by Jesse D. Jennings. Copyright © 1968, 1974 by McGraw-Hill, Inc. Used with permission of McGraw-Hill Book Company.)

and lanceolate points with microblades produced both from wedge-shaped cores and from somewhat more tabular cores seems clear in sites dating at least as early as 1500 BC and probably as early as 3000 BC; it also appears as though the production of all microblades ceased by the end of the Taye Lake phase. Stemmed and notched points also occur with microblades farther east, in the southwestern portion of the Northwest Territories, where on the basis of overall similarity of the sequences the dating may be presumed to be similar to that in Yukon Territory.

Sites of this last sort raise again the subject of the Denali complex. Where originally defined, the complex was asserted by its discoverer to be a very early manifestation dating from many millennia before the Christian era

(Hadleigh West 1967); unfortunately the dating evidence was then ambiguous. Not long afterward, based largely on material from Healy Lake and
Dixthada in interior Alaska and from Aishihik Lake in southwest Yukon
Territory, the Denali complex was redefined by other investigators so as to
include wedge-shaped microcores very similar to those of the Paleoarctic.
tradition, as well as side-notched and stemmed projectile points such as are
common in the Northern Archaic tradition. The complex was then said to
date from about 2500 BC to perhaps as late as AD 1000 (e.g., Cook and
McKennon 1970b).

Recent evidence (e.g., Hadleigh West 1975) indicates that both of these
definitions were of valid assemblages, the embarrassing result being two
Denali complexes, one of them of about 8000 BC and pertaining to the
Paleoarctic tradition, the other dating from after 3000 BC and assignable to
the Northern Archaic tradition. Despite the extremely late date suggested for
the end of the second "Denali complex," however, other evidence makes it
doubtful that microblades persisted anywhere in Alaska or the Yukon Territory substantially after the beginning of the Christian era.

LATER ASSEMBLAGES (AFTER 2400 BC) ⊔ A collection designated the
Kayuk complex was recovered from an extensive site at Anaktuvuk Pass.
Although notions of the date of the complex have varied (Campbell 1959;
1962), similarities with lanceolate projectile points of the Angostura type
from the northern Plains have been stressed by the excavator, who estimated
the dating between 5000 and 3000 BC.

More recently, a short-term occupation at Onion Portage was found to
include some well-made lanceolate projectile points of obsidian, in what
was designated the Itkillik complex. Suggested tentatively to pertain to
ancestral Athapaskan Indians, the materials have been compared to those
of the Kayuk complex and to some implements from the Noatak drainage
(Anderson 1972). The dating of the Itkillik complex at about AD 500 appears
to be secure; indeed, this and the probable dating of the extensive cache of
lanceolate points on a beach ridge at Cape Krusenstern to the centuries following 1000 BC (the time of the Choris aspect of local culture, to be mentioned in a later section) constitute the only relatively unquestionable dates
available in the literature for the appearance of well-chipped lanceolate
points within Alaska.

The still more recent Kavik complex was defined first on the basis of a
small collection from Anaktuvuk Pass (Campbell 1962; 1968). It is characterized by small contracting-stem projectile points, to which excavations
at the site of Dixthada added crude scraping implements sometimes called
"tci-thos," barbed and unbarbed bone and antler points, bone awls, and
awls and stemmed points hammered from native copper. This inventory
seems to have been in part duplicated in sites of the northeastern Brooks
Range and at the site of Klo-Kut near Old Crow in northwestern Canada,

in levels dating after AD 1400, and is strongly reminiscent of that of the phases termed Aishihik and Bennet Lake in southwest Yukon (MacNeish 1964; Morlan 1971). In view of its distribution and late date, the Kavik complex and its relatives are attributed to late prehistoric Athapaskans, the direct ancestors of the native people who were encountered by the first European visitors to the northeastern Alaskan interior. The combined evidence from Healy Lake and Dixthada is said to indicate a development of the Kavik complex from the earlier, redefined "Denali complex" of the millennia shortly before the Christian era, and hence ultimately from local manifestations of the Paleoarctic tradition (Cook 1969; Cook and McKennon 1970a).

By no means were all these late interior Alaskan cultural manifestations exact duplicates of the original Kavik complex, however. A late prehistoric site near Gulkana in the Copper River drainage in western Alaska, presumed to date from AD 1500 to 1700, yielded abundant artifacts of native copper—projectile points, knives, and others—as well as of bone and antler, and stone scrapers and wedges, but no stone projectile points. The copper implements have been compared to those from Dixthada, and some of the simple stone work to Klo-Kut (Workman 1976), although at the latter site Kavik points are also present whereas the copper industry is replaced by work in bone.

Farther west in Alaska along the lower Yukon River are sites that vary even more strikingly. Although almost certainly inhabited by late prehistoric Indians, these yield many implements generally thought typical of Eskimo sites—objects such as bone toggling-head harpoons, polished slate transverse knives or ulus, bow drills used with a mouthpiece to hold the upper end of the drill, and pottery (de Laguna 1947). This archeological impression of the acculturation of the recent lower river Indians is confirmed by the obvious Eskimo influence in the material culture of some of the ethnographically known Athapaskan groups of the region (e.g., Osgood 1940).

Thus, whatever the degree of ancient homogeneity of ancestral peoples in the Alaskan interior, the more recent Athapaskan-speaking Indians have displayed a certain regional variety in material culture.

CLIMATE AND CULTURE OF THE INTERIOR □ The time after about 4000 BC saw the warming trend of the Hypsithermal interval, which stimulated the complete forestation of the Alaskan interior and a northward shift of the northern edge of the Canadian boreal forest, with attendant changes in the distribution of major animals. Presumably these events formed the backdrop for the increasing appearance of the side-notched projectile points and other implements of the Northern Archaic tradition in Alaska, as well as some lanceolate point forms of Paleo-Indian derivation in north-central Canada. Although some bison appear in faunal collections of this period, the most important single food animal in the area under discussion was apparently the caribou.

As mentioned earlier, and in keeping with the glacial history, the plentiful microblades and blades of the earliest Alaskan assemblages did not appear east of the Yukon and lower Mackenzie Rivers except in collections representing a relatively brief intrusion of coastal people of the Arctic Small Tool tradition (to be mentioned later) shortly before 1000 BC; otherwise, interior Alaskan developments were in many respects paralleled by those of the northern Canadian interior. Yet there is a suggestive difference in the sequence of the appearance of well-developed lanceolate points on the one hand and of side-notched points on the other. In Alaska the notched-point assemblages appear by at least 4000 BC, whereas the approximately contemporary complexes in Canada appear to have been dominated by lanceolate forms. Side notching in interior Alaska apparently gave way to more lanceolate forms through time, while the reverse occurred in Canada. There, and particularly around Great Slave Lake and along the upper Thelon River, side notching tended to replace lanceolate forms after the beginning of the Christian era. Despite this difference, however, prototypes for both the lanceolate points of Canada and the side-notched forms of Alaska appear to be found in the more southerly regions of North America: in the Plains, various lanceolate point forms are known in early postglacial times; somewhat more to the west, on the Columbia Plateau and in the Great Basin, side-notched points are common by 5000 BC and before.

Thus the evidence seems to say that a large part of the content of the Northern Archaic tradition with its dominant notched points was ultimately derived from the more southern portions of continental America sometime after about 4000 or 5000 BC, despite the fact that the presence of microblade technology in some Northern Archaic sites may bespeak a measure of descent also from the Paleoarctic tradition.

After 4000 BC: The Coast

THE PACIFIC REGION □ Although there may have been the beginnings of a satisfactory coastal adaptation by 6000 BC, with the Anangula Blade complex, artifactual and faunal evidence for the coastal lifeway is unmistakable only after 4000 BC.

THE OCEAN BAY TRADITION (4000–3000 BC) □ In the Kodiak Island group, the earliest complexes, known as Ocean Bay I from Sitkalidak and Afognak Islands, are closely related to the Takli Alder phase from Takli Island just off the Pacific coast of the Alaska Peninsula. On the basis of multiple radiocarbon determinations all of these are dated between 4000 and 3000 BC (Clark 1966; 1974; Dumond 1971) and may be designated the Ocean Bay tradition (Dumond 1977: 56–59). The collections include large numbers of leaf-shaped, percussion-flaked knives or heavy projectile heads; percussion-flaked knives or projectile blades with rather weakly developed, tapering

FIGURE 2.5
Artifacts of the Ocean Bay tradition, Takli Alder phase: *a–n*, projectile points and knives; *o, q, p*, discoidal core; *r*, adze blade with polished bit; *s, t*, bone harpoon dart heads.

stems; and a variety of scrapers. One site yielded some better-made projectile blades with relatively long stems, triangular in cross-section, as well as a few gougelike adze blades with polished bits. A single stone vessel that was apparently used as a lamp to burn sea mammal oil has been found. Barbed bone harpoon dart heads, designed to hold within the animal by barbs alone, rather than by "toggling" or twisting sideways in the wound, were in use (Figure 2.5). Although little organic material is preserved in most collections, such waste as has been recovered is dominated by bones of sea mammals; but the location of at least one of the sites suggests that river fishing may also have been important. At least one site has yielded microblades from its basal levels.

In the Aleutian Islands, a large projectile blade of chipped stone from levels dated about 1750 BC from a site on an islet off the coast of Akun Island in the eastern Aleutians, has been compared to materials of the Ocean Bay tradition (Turner and Turner 1974). Analogous comparisons can be drawn concerning the elongated chipped projectile blades from a site on Sandy Beach Bay on Umnak Island, which may date from as early as 3000 BC (Aigner et al. 1976). Still more strikingly, Ocean Bay-like implements were reported in 1974 near the older blade site on Anangula Island and were dated at about 4000 BC (Laughlin 1975).

Materials of the Ocean Bay tradition comprise a horizon of the Pacific Eskimo region of the fourth millennium BC and may well have begun in an earlier blade-making tradition. Although some researchers have rejected the notion, the presence of the Ocean Bay tradition within the Aleutian Islands appears probable.

THE KODIAK TRADITION (3000 BC–AD 1000) □ By 2500 BC, the Ocean Bay II complex from Sitkalidak and Afognak islands, the earliest elements of the Takli Birch phase from the Peninsula coast, and the Old Islanders complex of Chirikof Island had appeared. Presumably descendants of the preceding complexes, these people were now polishing long thrusting implements of slate, while still relying to varying degrees upon chipped stone implements such as those in use by their ancestors. There is no evidence of any significant change in subsistence. Bone artifacts included harpoon dart heads, wedges, awls, and parts of what are apparently fish spears or leisters (Figure 2.6). In bone waste, individual sea mammals outnumber land mammals by about eight to one. These earliest manifestations, dated from about 3000 to 1500 BC, are referred to here as the *Takli stage* of the Kodiak tradition.

The next two complexes from Kodiak Island, designated Old Kiavak and Three Saints (Clark 1966), are apparently related closely to those known from Kachemak Bay (de Laguna 1934) and from the lower levels of the Uyak site on Kodiak Island (Heizer 1956); together they span the time from about 1500 BC to AD 1000. To them may be added the later part of the Takli Birch phase, dating from 1500 to 1000 BC, and a still later assemblage of the Pacific coast of the Alaska Peninsula, called the Takli Cottonwood phase and dating in the first half of the first millennium AD; all of these constitute the *Kachemak stage* of the Kodiak tradition.

The assemblages of the Kachemak stage include a great variety of implements of polished slate that were chipped to shape before grinding. The transverse knife or ulu appears; oil lamps of stone are plentiful, and a number of them are decorated with reliefs carved within the bowl; there are labrets of stone or bone; and a wide variety of bone implements are included, most notably harpoon dart heads. The primary orientation remained toward sea mammal hunting, with a strong subsidiary emphasis on fishing. Sites on the Pacific coast of the Peninsula contain large quantities of Pacific codfish and

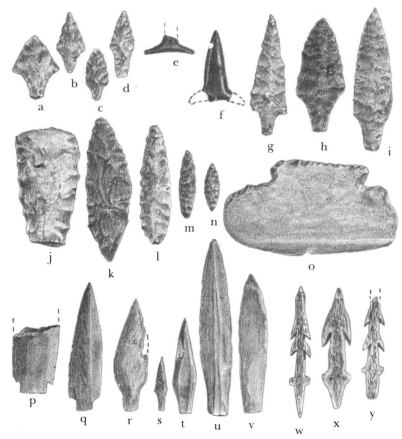

FIGURE 2.6
Artifacts of the Kodiak tradition, Takli Birch Phase: *a–d, g–i, k–n,* chipped projectile points and knives; *e, f,* labrets; *j,* adze blade with polished bit; *o,* polished slate ulu; *p–v,* polished slate projectile blades; *w–y,* bone harpoon dart heads.

halibut remains, as well as those of salmon, attesting to techniques for taking salt water fish in substantial quantities.

Thus, the Kodiak tradition, which was based to a significant extent on the earlier Ocean Bay tradition, saw the increased use of polished slate implements among coastal dwellers who, through time, manifested more and more diversity between subregions. By the height of the tradition, in the first millennium AD, people on the Pacific coast of the Alaska Peninsula were beginning to experience pressure from their neighbors of the Bering Sea slope, and would shortly capitulate to the expansion of Thule culture.

THE ALEUTIAN TRADITION (AFTER 3000 BC) □ In the zone west of that occupied by the Kodiak tradition—that is, west of about 158° west longitude—local specializations in tool form developed within a basic tradition of stone implements manufactured by chipping, rather than grinding. However, harpoon dart heads of bone extremely similar to those of the Kodiak area were also a part of the assemblage here. Although there is at present no known early and homogeneous archeological horizon throughout the region that represents its initial peopling by ancestors of recent Aleuts, both the much earlier blade collection from Anangula Island, described here as a part of the Paleoarctic tradition, and the Ocean Bay tradition have been suggested by various investigators to be related to that development. In any event, it is clear that people ancestral to modern Aleuts were occupying the Fox Island group at least as early as 3000 BC, the Rat Island group at least as early as 1000 BC, and the Near Island group at least as early as 600 BC. There is no evidence of any kind to suggest that the Aleutian Islands were populated from the west—that is, directly from Asia.

The most sustained research has been devoted to sites on Umnak Island in the western Fox Islands, particularly at Chaluka (Aigner 1966; Denniston 1966; Lippold 1966). There, polished stone artifacts were virtually nonexistent before relatively recent times, except that pecked and polished stone lamps occur throughout the occupation (Figure 2.7). Periods designated Early Chaluka and Middle Chaluka last from about 2000 to 1000 BC. The chipped stone industry is predominantly unifacial, but with fairly plentiful small, bifacially chipped projectile points. Houses found were built of large rounded stones and whale bones, in part paved with flat, angular stones, and were possibly 4 to 5 meters across. Upper Chaluka, beginning sometime in the first millennium AD, manifests a predominantly bifacial chipped stone industry with thick knives, stemmed knives with asymmetrical blades, stone chisels, and plentiful large, flat, two-notched pebble "sinkers." Only late in the period—certainly after AD 1000 and possibly after AD 1500—did polished slate appear among the implements.

Throughout all periods the bone industry included a large number of harpoon dart heads, both bilaterally and unilaterally barbed. Although styles of these vary throughout the various periods, the basic form is constant. Subsistence orientation was always toward the sea, with large numbers of fish, hair and fur seals, sea lions, sea otters, and some whales being taken.

As indicated earlier, occupation at Sandy Beach Bay, on the same island, apparently began somewhat earlier, around 3000 BC (Aigner et al. 1976). Houses were elliptical, about 3 by 5 meters in size, and were apparently entered from the roof. The stone industry, except for numerous elongated bifacial points, resembled that of Early Chaluka.

On Amchitka in the Rat Islands to the west, both stone and bone artifacts in a sequence beginning about 1000 BC are in a general way similar to those from the Chaluka midden, with the exception that there is no shift indicated from a predominantly unifacial industry to a bifacial one, but rather the reverse. Faunal trash included sea mammal, bird, fish, and invertebrates. Fish were ocean varieties, predominantly of the area close inshore (Desautels et al. 1970). A house from about AD 1500 was subrectangular, about 5 by

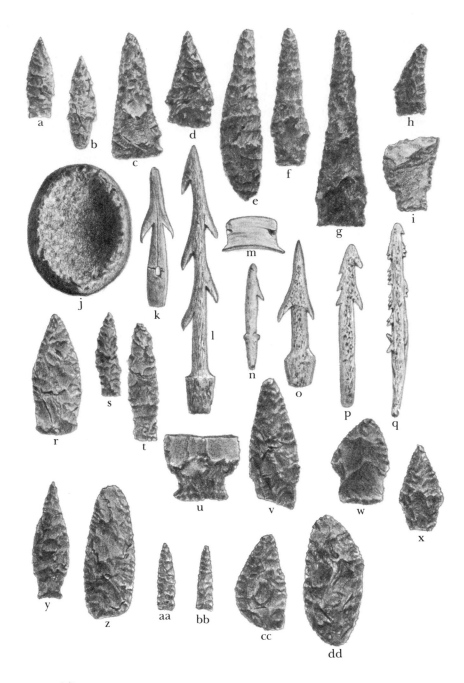

FIGURE 2.7

Artifacts of the Aleutian tradition: *a–i, r–dd,* stone projectile points and knives; *j,* stone lamp; *k, l, n–q,* bone dart heads; *m,* ivory labret. *a–q,* Umnak Island; *r–dd,* Chignik region, Alaska Peninsula.

6 meters in size, apparently entered from a hole in the roof. Associated tools included polished ulus—an occurrence that was thought to represent the earliest appearance of polished slate on the island (Cook et al. 1972).

Still farther west, collections from the Near Islands are stylistically the most variant of all those in the Aleutian chain of islands. Chipped stone artifacts include a very high proportion of elliptical to leaf-shaped bifaces, as well as long and relatively slender points, reminiscent of some of those from Sandy Beach Bay. The polished slate ulu appeared very late, perhaps little earlier than the arrival of the Russians in the eighteenth century (McCartney 1971; Spaulding 1962).

To turn eastward of Umnak Island, on the lower portion of the Alaska Peninsula—territory within the area of the Aleutian tradition—the Hot Springs site at Port Moller (Workman 1966; Okada and Okada 1974) has provided a collection dating after 1000 BC, in which stone artifacts are again dominated by chipped implements, including knives and projectile blades similar to those from the eastern Aleutian Islands. Two houses measuring about 4 to 5 meters across were elliptical in plan, were excavated into the ground surface, and were without a visible entry.

Eastward from Port Moller, similar stone material is known from the vicinity of Chignik. Westward, at Izembek Lagoon, excavations uncovered a semisubterranean house constructed with a framework of whale mandibles, while artifacts included both chipped stone implements reminiscent of those from Port Moller and polished slate and pottery such as are known around the Bering Sea at AD 1000 and later; radiocarbon determinations suggest a date of about AD 1000 (McCartney 1974). Still to the west, excavations on Akun Island in the eastern Foxes revealed a similar mixture of chipped stone and polished slate at about the end of the first millennium AD (Turner and Turner 1974).

In summary, there appears to have been continuous and undisturbed development in Aleutian territory, during which local cultures diverged only gradually from one another. Late in the sequences, a period of more rapid change came, with the introduction of polished slate ulus and other implement styles in what seems to have been a wave of influence from the Bering Sea or Kodiak Island to the east, a wave that ultimately washed lightly over the entire chain of islands.

The Bering Sea Region and Northward

THE ARCTIC SMALL TOOL TRADITION (2000–1000 BC) □ This tradition was first discovered at Cape Denbigh on Norton Bay, where it was called the Denbigh Flint complex (Giddings 1951; 1964). Manifestations of this far-flung tradition are now known to occur from the Bering Sea side of the Alaska Peninsula in the southwest, northward along a strip of land adjacent to the Alaskan coast, throughout the Brooks Range, and, beyond Alaska, along the coastal zone of northern Canada and the Arctic Archipelago to Greenland. The origin of the Arctic Small Tool tradition is unclear, but elements of the technology suggest it to have been derived ultimately from the Paleoarctic tradition.

In the various collections, variety in stone tools is commonly restricted to small endblades and sideblades, often bipointed; burins struck on small bifaces; microblades; some variety of carefully made scrapers; occasional larger knifelike bifaces; small adze blades with polished bits; and burinlike implements in which the struck burin facet is replaced by a polished face (Figure 2.8). Alaskan collections do not include oil lamps, and the finds include no organic artifacts, for reasons of poor preservation, but in the eastern Arctic some small toggling and nontoggling harpoon heads of organic material are attributed to this period, and stone lamps appear occasionally.

Alaskan sites are generally the remains of temporary camps, which appear both along the coast proper and farther inland in the adjacent tundra zone, where they are frequently along the courses of streams. Constructed houses, apparently intended for winter occupation, are known so far from only four locations, all of them between 55 and 250 kilometers from the coast: Onion Portage on the Kobuk River, Howard Pass between the Noatak and Colville drainages in the Brooks Range, and the upper portion of both the Ugashik and Naknek River drainages on the Alaska Peninsula (Dumond 1969a). In this last area the houses were square, about 4 meters on a side, excavated into the contemporary surface at times as much as half a meter, warmed by a central fire, and entered by an entryway that sloped downward into one side of the house in tunnel fashion.

By the time of the Arctic Small Tool tradition, Alaska and the Arctic were experiencing the last portions of the relatively warm Hypsithermal interval, with the temperature gradually cooling. Subsistence was apparently balanced between hunting and fishing, emphasis being upon caribou and salmon or other anadromous fish where fish were available.

Interestingly, there is nowhere direct evidence that sealing through the winter ice (a technique that has often been thought to be indispensable for permanent residence on the Arctic coast by hunting peoples) was practiced by carriers of the Arctic Small Tool tradition, or that boats were in use, or that there was any consistent use of dogs. That is, there is no real evidence for the existence at this early time of the key attributes of later Arctic Eskimo culture.

In Alaska, after the occupation of Small Tool tradition people, there is virtually everywhere a break in the sequence as it is now understood, a break that ends with the earliest manifestations of the succeeding Norton tradition. But most of the accepted dating suggests that this interval is not exactly contemporaneous through Alaska: in the north, the latest Arctic Small Tool occupations may date to about 1500 BC, with the earliest Norton

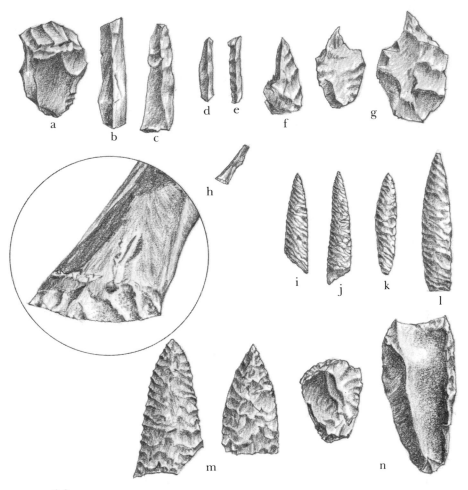

FIGURE 2.8
Artifacts of the Arctic Small Tool tradition, Denbigh Flint complex: *a*, microblade core; *b–d*, microblades; *e*, burin spall; *f*, *g*, burins; *h*, burin spall and much enlarged view of retouched cutting edge; *i*, *j*, sideblades; *k*, *l*, projectile endblades; *m*, large projectile (possibly harpoon) blades; *n*, scrapers. (From *Prehistory of North America*, 2d ed., by Jesse D. Jennings. Copyright © 1968, 1974 by McGraw-Hill, Inc. Used with permission of McGraw-Hill Book Company.)

tradition remains appearing at roughly 1000 BC; south of the Bering Strait the comparable interval seems to be from about 1000 to 500 BC. Additional data, of course, may tend to smooth out the apparent discrepancy.

Nevertheless, the seeming presence of such a break is sufficiently consistent to hint that the major subsistence base of the people disappeared rather suddenly. The late second millennium BC saw lowering of the average temperature, followed by a slightly warmer interval, and then another cold period. One of these periods of colder temperature has been suggested by at least one researcher to have inspired the strengthened adaptation to specifically coastal resources that is characteristic of later peoples (Dikov 1965); in any event, the climatic factor may have served to drastically restrict the patterns of caribou migration, which would be expected to affect the subsistence of the Arctic Small Tool people. This same period witnessed the unbroken transition from pre-Dorset to Dorset in eastern Canada and Greenland (see Chapter 3), with the Dorset people being somewhat more restricted to the coastline than their pre-Dorset, Small Tool tradition ancestors.

AN INTERVAL OF TRANSITION □ The time following the disappearance of the Arctic Small Tool tradition in Alaska was one of some cultural heterogeneity. Although most of it can be subsumed under what is here designated the Norton tradition, an exception is the enigmatic Old Whaling culture, known from only a single location on one beach ridge at Cape Krusenstern (Giddings 1961; 1967).

Old Whaling tools include chipped stone lance heads, knives, and blades that are presumed to be for whaling harpoons. Five deep semisubterranean houses are thought to have been for winter use, five shallow houses for summer. Bone litter was chiefly whalebone. The tools are not exactly comparable to those known from anywhere else, and although the assemblage appears to represent the earliest known example of a truly seaward economic orientation in Eskimo territory, there is no evidence that these people, whoever they were, had any impact upon cultural development in that portion of Alaska. They appear to have been strangers, strayed from somewhere in the north Pacific, who resided only a short time—perhaps a single year—and departed. Radiocarbon evidence, if taken at face value, suggests the date to have been around 1700 BC; this is hard to reconcile with the rest of the Krusenstern sequence, in which 1000 BC seems more suitable.

THE NORTON TRADITION (1000 BC–AD 1000) □ This tradition includes all collections of what have been called Norton culture, as well as those slightly earlier ones from the Chukchi Sea termed Choris culture, and the later ones of the same area assigned to Ipiutak culture. The Norton tradition is substantially equivalent to what some investigators have designated Paleo-Eskimo (Larsen and Rainey 1948).

The earliest known, or *Choris* form, of the Norton tradition is represented in few sites and by limited published descriptions (Giddings 1957; 1961; 1967). The original collections, dating from a few centuries after 1000 BC, were from large elliptical houses (about 12 meters long) that had been slightly excavated into the contemporary surface of the Choris Peninsula at Kotzebue Sound. Pottery, the earliest in Alaska, is fiber tempered and decorated over the outside with linear stamping. To compare this with the earlier Arctic Small Tool tradition, the use of microblades has been abandoned, the use of burins has changed, projectile points are larger, fully chipped adze blades have been introduced, and both the oil lamp and crudely ground slate tools are in use. At the original site, bone waste was chiefly that of caribou, despite the coastal location.

At Cape Krusenstern, finds are from small scattered campsites on certain beach ridges, on one of which was encountered a large cache of lanceolate points startlingly similar in many respects to some unfluted lanceolate forms of Paleo-Indian assemblages of the North American Plains (Giddings 1963). Similar points were found in levels of the Trail Creek caves that may date to the time of the Choris aspect of the Norton tradition (Larsen 1968b), although there were no other Choris items present. Elsewhere, as at Onion Portage, the occupation of the corresponding period displays some variation from the finds on the Choris Peninsula. One site immediately south of Point Barrow has yielded a complex with the characteristic Choris ceramics and with stone implements strongly reminiscent of those of the Arctic Small Tool tradition, and may be dated to the late second millennium BC. An analogous assemblage may also have been recovered in the vicinity of the Firth River in northwestern Canada (MacNeish 1956), but stratigraphic displacements by frost action in that site are so extreme that associations are suspect (Mackay et al. 1961). There are no clearly similar assemblages from the Bering Sea coast, where, instead, sites of the ordinary Norton aspect of the Norton tradition appear by around 500 BC.

Despite the impression of provincialism that is conveyed by the lack of homogeneity of tool assemblages during this time, important innovations indicate some widespread contacts. The pottery was clearly Asian in inspiration (Griffin 1970); clear precedents for the use both of ground slate and of oil lamps appear strongest in the Pacific coastal zone in the Kodiak region to the south; and the diagonally chipped lanceolate points seem to reflect a heritage from the American interior as well as from the Arctic Small Tool tradition.

The properly *Norton* aspect of the Norton tradition includes what has been called Norton culture in the Bering Strait vicinity (at Cape Denbigh, Cape Prince of Wales, Cape Krusenstern, Cape Nome, Unalakleet); phases of the Brooks River period of the Naknek drainage and the Ugashik Lakes phase of the Ugashik drainage on the Alaska Peninsula; early material from around Platinum; material of the Duchikmute phase of Nunivak Island; the so-called Near Ipiutak at Point Hope; recently discovered material from near Point Barrow; and some assemblages from the Firth River in extreme northwest Canada (Ackerman 1964; Bandi 1969; Bockstoce 1973; Dumond 1971; Dumond et al. 1976; Giddings 1964; 1967; Larsen and Rainey 1948; Lutz 1973; Nowak 1970; Stanford 1969). (See Figure 2.9.) The earliest manifestations appeared by about 500 BC, and the entire zone from the Alaska Peninsula to the Firth River in Canada was involved by the beginning of

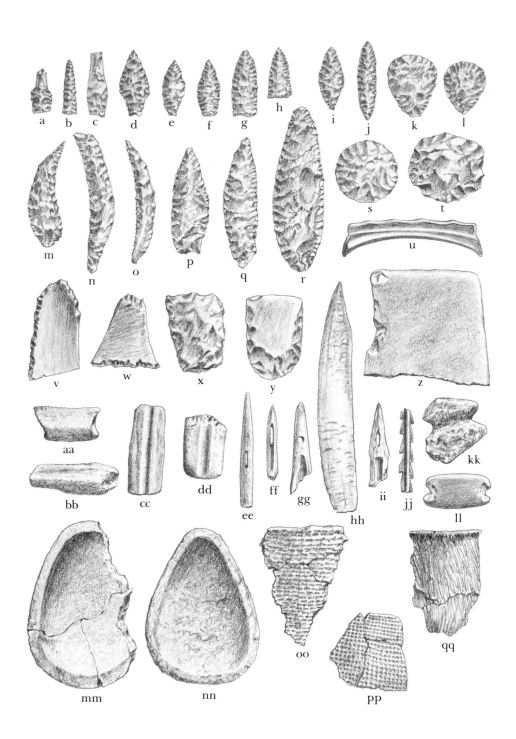

a b c d e f g h i j k l

m n o p q r s t

u v w x y z

aa bb cc dd ee ff gg hh ii jj kk ll

mm nn oo pp qq

the Christian era. Although there are some clear variations from site to site, the collections are rather homogeneous. The dominant pottery is now check stamped, although linear-stamped ware identical in all respects to that of Choris collections occasionally appears in some locations. Whereas the fine chipping techniques of the Arctic Small Tool tradition are noticeable in some of the smaller projectile point forms, the tendency to abandon the use of fine cherts in favor of basalts and other coarse volcanic rocks gives a cruder look to most of the projectile points; nevertheless, in some southern Norton culture sites occasional lanceolate projectile blades are beautifully made and strikingly Choris-like. Crudely polished slate implements and the oil lamp are present, although the former are rare in many sites. In all but the southern Bering Sea region houses appear to have been confined to the coast. The permanent houses that are known are usually square and excavated as much as half a meter into the contemporary surface, with relatively short, sloping entries—hardly distinguishable from houses of the Arctic Small Tool tradition known from the Alaska Peninsula. The *kazigi,* or Eskimo combination ceremonial house and men's house, was probably present (Lutz 1973). Preservation of organic artifacts in some sites makes it certain that the toggling harpoon was in use. At Point Hope, the deposits of Near Ipiutak include a large toggling harpoon head, presumably intended for whaling.

From the Bering Strait south, the Norton occupation was heavy, widespread, and durable. Attempts to divide collections into sequential phases have been made with materials from sites on Nunivak Island, Unalakleet, Chagvan Bay, and the Alaska Peninsula. In the Naknek drainage they have been divided into three sequential phases, the first of which is most like Norton cultural assemblages farther north while the second and third manifest local evolution of chipped artifact forms, a steady increase in the use of polished slate at the expense of chipped stone, and variations in pottery style. These changes in the assemblage appear to coincide with increased adaptation to the use of open-water resources along the coasts, increasing sedentation, and increasing population, and they culminate in a renewed interest in interior salmon streams with the harvest of resources that were once the mainstays of their ancestors of the Arctic Small Tool tradition (Dumond 1971; 1972). Although this process probably occurred generally, it appears to be especially noteworthy south of the Bering Strait.

FIGURE 2.9 *(Opposite)*
Artifacts of the Norton stage of the Norton tradition: *a–c,* drill bits; *d–h,* projectile points; *i, j,* side-blades; *k, l,* bifacial knives; *m–o,* scrapers; *p–r,* lance points or knives; *s, t,* discoidal knives; *u,* labret; *v, w,* polished slate fragments; *x, y,* adze blades; *z,* whetstone; *aa, bb,* faceted whetstones; *cc, dd,* sandstone abraders; *ee,* antler harpoon foreshaft; *ff,* antler arrowhead fragment; *gg,* antler harpoon head; *hh,* ivory harpoon head or possibly harpoon icepick; *ii,* antler harpoon head; *jj,* leister prong fragment; *kk, ll,* stone net sinkers; *mm, nn,* stone lamps; *oo, pp,* check stamped potsherds; *qq,* linear stamped potsherd. (From *Prehistory of North America,* 2d ed., by Jesse D. Jennings. Copyright © 1968, 1974 by McGraw-Hill, Inc. Used with permission of McGraw-Hill Book Company.)

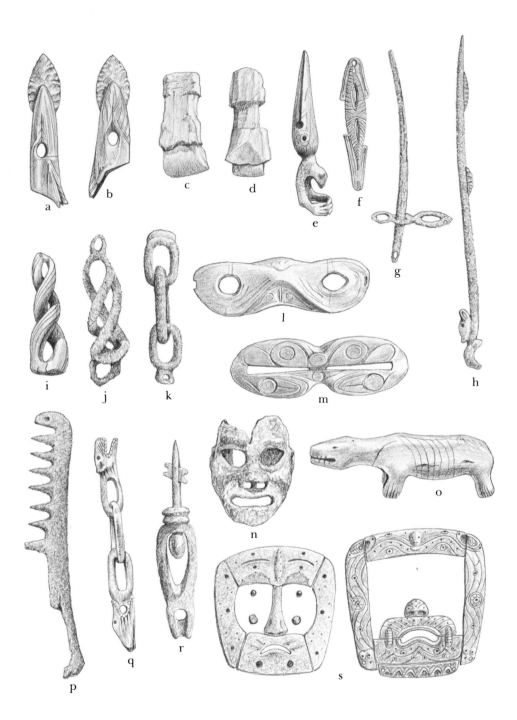

Coastal subsistence appears to explain the distribution of sites of Norton culture—plentiful along the coast from the Alaska Peninsula to Point Hope, absent from the Brooks Range, present at Point Barrow and at the Firth River. In the south, this subsistence pattern was apparently responsible for a progressive spread of Norton influences across the Alaska Peninsula to the north Pacific, beginning shortly after the initiation of the Christian era, and, by AD 800, all but overwhelming the local Pacific tradition on the coast of the Alaska Peninsula (Dumond 1969a; 1971).

The steady evolution of the specifically Norton form of the Norton tradition is confined to the south. Despite their early presence in such places as Cape Krusenstern, Point Hope, and Point Barrow, not long after the beginning of the Christian era the bearers of Norton culture were superseded by other people, perhaps their own descendants, of what has been called *Ipiutak* culture—a way of life that was to last as late as ca. AD 800. Characteristic assemblages lack some of the important Norton diagnostics, namely, pottery, ground slate, and oil lamps. Yet projectile blades, the side-hafted, asymmetrical knives called sideblades, and other implements are so obviously Norton that if one were to excavate an ordinary Norton camp in which the sometimes rare pottery was absent because no pot had been broken, and in which no tool of the even rarer ground slate had been lost, one would simply classify the site as Ipiutak (Figure 2.10).

Especially striking are the lavish burial goods from the cemetery at Point Hope (Larsen and Rainey 1948). In addition, permanent habitations—square, excavated into the contemporary surface, with a rudimentary entrance passage—are known from the same site, where they number in the hundreds and are scattered along several beach ridges; they are known also from Cape Krusenstern (Giddings 1967) and from Deering on the northern part of the Seward Peninsula. Temporary campsites are also apparently present along the Chukchi Sea coast in the same vicinity. Interior sites have been reported, but are not plentiful. Although it was suggested some years ago that the Ipiutak people were primarily hunters of the caribou herds of the interior, the distribution of sites that has gradually been revealed is more in keeping with a subsistence pattern like that of their immediate predecessors of the Norton aspect of the tradition, except that indications of whaling are even less clear.

FIGURE 2.10 *(Opposite)*
Artifacts of the Ipiutak variant of the Norton tradition: *a, b,* harpoon heads; *c, d,* bone adze heads with slate blades; *e,* ivory openwork carving; *f,* ivory ornament; *g, h,* ivory lance heads or daggers; *i,* ivory swivel; *j,* ivory openwork carving; *k,* ornamental linked ivory object; *l, m,* ivory snow goggles; *n,* human effigy of antler; *o,* ivory polar bear effigy; *p,* unidentified ivory implement; *q,* ornamental linked object; *r,* swivel; *s,* masklike ivory carvings usually found associated with burials. (From *Prehistory of North America*, 2d ed., by Jesse D. Jennings. Copyright © 1968, 1974 by McGraw-Hill, Inc. Used with permission of McGraw-Hill Book Company.)

THE THULE TRADITION (AD 100–1800) ☐ This tradition includes all prehistoric Eskimo remains from St. Lawrence Island and the nearby coast of Siberia, which date from after about AD 100, as well as remains from the northern Alaskan coast after about AD 500, and from the southern coasts after about AD 1000. In Canada and Greenland it includes all remains after about AD 1000. The Alaskan examples are characterized by a consistent heavy use of polished slate and by dependence upon coastal resources, with coast dwellers notably skilled in open-water hunting. It is what has been called Neo-Eskimo or the Northern Maritime tradition (e.g., Larsen and Rainey 1948; Collins 1964).

The earliest known manifestations of the Thule tradition are those termed *Okvik* and *Old Bering Sea* from the Siberian coast and from St. Lawrence and other islands around Bering Strait. Although it appears likely that they had their origin in the Norton tradition (Dumond 1965; Larsen 1968a), this has not yet been conclusively demonstrated. They are characterized by extensive use of polished slate; by pottery, some of which is impressed on the exterior with relatively broad corrugations (broader than the linear impressions of Choris and Norton pottery); and by an extensive organic artifact inventory including numerous toggling harpoons in different sizes designed specifically for seals, walrus, and whales. Their art, which was produced in the period from about AD 100 to 500, forms one of the high points of all Eskimo decorative work, and includes numerous elaborate ivory objects—carved human figures, ivory chains, and so on—as well as harpoon heads spectacularly covered with patterns of parallel lines, dots, and encircled bosses (Figure 2.11). Houses were about 3 meters square, with a flagstone floor excavated into the contemporary surface, and were entered by a relatively long (about 6 meters) entrance tunnel, the floor of which dipped lower than that of the house, in order to trap cold air and reduce drafts while still providing ventilation.

The collections upon which the major descriptions have been based were excavated from St. Lawrence Island (Collins 1937; Geist and Rainey 1936) and from the site of Okvik on one of the small Punuk Islands immediately to the east (Rainey 1941). Although the artifact collections display no clearly consistent difference from site to site, the art styles permit discrimination between two major stylistic groups, thus the designations Old Bering Sea and Okvik. There are two different views of the meaning of these stylistic differences. The first, and probably the most common, is that the Okvik style is the older, and some proponents of this view have suggested an origin for Okvik several millennia before the beginning of the Christian era. The second view, which is favored here, is that the two were substantially contemporaneous (e.g., Ackerman 1962); this is supported by radiocarbon evidence, the more recent determinations suggesting strongly that none of these remains predates the Christian era. In this view, both Okvik and Old Bering Sea developed during the time that Ipiutak culture was to be found on the Alaskan coast north of Bering Strait and the late phases of the Norton stage of the Norton tradition were to be found in Alaska to the south.

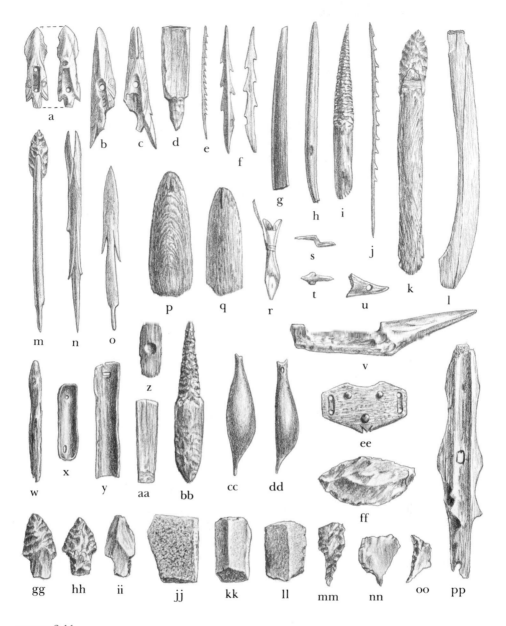

FIGURE 2.11

Artifacts of the early Thule tradition from St. Lawrence Island: *a–c,* ivory harpoon heads; *d,* ivory harpoon socket piece; *e,* ivory fish spear point; *f,* ivory sideprongs for bird darts; *g,* ivory harpoon foreshaft fragment; *h,* ivory harpoon foreshaft; *i,* ivory ice pick; *j,* ivory fish spear point; *k,* hafted knife; *l,* wooden adze handle; *m–o,* arrowheads; *p, q,* wooden wound plugs; *r,* walrus-tusk knife sharpener; *s, t,* ivory pegs for end of throwing board; *u,* ivory finger rest for harpoon shaft; *v,* ivory meathook; *w,* wooden drill shaft, *x, y,* ivory fat scrapers; *z,* ivory drill mouthpiece; *aa,* ivory wedge; *bb,* ivory ice pick; *cc, dd,* ivory fishline sinkers; *ee,* bone ice creeper; *ff,* ulu blade; *gg–ii,* knife blades; *jj–ll,* whetstones; *mm,* hand drill; *nn, oo,* gravers; *pp,* throwing-board fragment. (From *Prehistory of North America,* 2d ed., by Jesse D. Jennings. Copyright © 1968, 1974 by McGraw-Hill, Inc. Used with permission of McGraw-Hill Book Company.)

a b c d e f g h i j k l m n o p q r s t u v w x y z aa bb cc dd ee

In the second half of the first millennium AD, Okvik-Old Bering Sea was succeeded by another local development that has been termed *Punuk*, which was characterized by an art style that has much in common with its predecessors, particularly Okvik. The evolution of the Punuk style, which also involved the use of lines, dots, and circles on ivory implements, apparently was accompanied by no significant shift in subsistence or other workaday matters; items such as polished stone implements and pottery scarcely changed from earlier forms, although the pottery was by now plain and tempered with heavy gravel. After AD 1200, implements became still more plain and pottery shapes changed somewhat, resulting in the material culture of the late prehistoric Eskimos of St. Lawrence Island (Figure 2.12).

By AD 500, when the Punuk style was becoming recognizable on St. Lawrence Island, a related but different manifestation known as *Birnirk* (named for a site in the vicinity of Point Barrow) was spreading along the northern Alaskan coast from Bering Strait to Point Barrow, replacing Ipiutak, and was apparently appearing in some places on the corresponding Asian coast, where its implements mingled with those of Punuk style. The most thoroughly published analysis of specific stylistic and artifactual elements (Ford 1959) concluded that the major source of Birnirk material culture lay in Old Bering Sea–Okvik. The lifeways suggested by the collections are closely similar, but the mainland environment of Birnirk is indicated in some obvious ways, as in an increased use of antler over ivory for harpoon heads and other implements. Birnirk houses are square, entered by a sunken and relatively long tunnel, and sometimes have a raised area in the house floor—a platform for sleeping—along one side. Like the Punuk collections, Birnirk assemblages represent people oriented toward the coast; in areas favorable for whaling, the necessary harpoon heads were found, as well as numerous remains of buckets and other items made of baleen, and whalebone was used in house construction. The thick, gravel-tempered pottery, almost identical in paste to that of Punuk, was impressed on the outside with circular designs—targets or spirals—apparently applied with a paddle, and often overstamped heavily. Birnirk proper disappeared before AD 1000, but from it developed the lifeways of all the later prehistoric coastal people of northern Alaska. The final result was embodied in the northern Eskimos encountered by Europeans—people skilled in winter ice hunting, some of them settled in large villages at favorable whaling locations, and organized economically and ceremonially into whaling crews, each of which centered around a

FIGURE 2.12 (*Opposite*)

Artifacts of the Thule tradition from St. Lawrence Island: *a*, ivory vessel; *b*, *c*, wooden snow goggles; *d*, toy wooden kayak; *e*, drum handle and rim fragment; *f*, antler spoon; *g*, antler ladle; *h*, ivory browband; *i*, ivory comb; *j*, bark doll; *k*, bone drill point; *l*, *m*, ivory awls; *n*, baleen ice scoop; *o*, bone ladle; *p*, wooden pottery paddle; *q*, *r*, hafted slate knives; *s*, baleen vessel; *t*, wooden pail handle; *u*, wooden bow drill; *v*, *w*, slate ulus with wooden handles; *x*, pottery lamp; *y*, toy wooden bow; *z*, *aa*, ivory sled shoes; *bb*, toy wooden sled runner; *cc*, *dd*, ivory sled runners; *ee*, bone snow shovel. (From *Prehistory of North America*, 2d ed., by Jesse D. Jennings. Copyright © 1968, 1974 by McGraw-Hill, Inc. Used with permission of McGraw-Hill Book Company.)

whaleboat-owning, kazigi-dominating entrepreneur known as the *umialiq* (cf. Oswalt 1967).

The most southern house ruins of probable Birnirk affiliation have been reported around Cape Nome, on the southern coast of the Seward Peninsula, where they are dated to about AD 600 (Bockstoce 1973). South of this, the introduction of Thule tradition lifeways lagged a little. On the Bering Sea coast of the Alaskan mainland the earliest known representative of the Thule tradition is the collection termed Nukleet, from Norton Bay. There, thick, gravel-tempered pottery with concentric circle decorations appeared near the end of the first millennium AD—about AD 800, probably—with a tool assemblage predominantly of polished stone. Rectangular houses possessed the deeply sunken entrance tunnel or cold trap. Similar assemblages appear southward along the coast until they occur on the Bering Sea side of the Alaska Peninsula at about AD 1000. Only relatively minor evolutionary changes took place between that time and the arrival of the Russians shortly after AD 1800. By the later part of the Thule tradition, there existed throughout the Alaskan coast all of the major items of the ethnographically known Eskimo culture with its fully equipped kayaks, umiaks, dog sleds, sunken houses with deep entrances, and its almost staggering series of specialized tools and weapons. Of these last, artifacts of bone, antler, and ivory included parts for specialized arrows, darts, and spears for birds and fish; toggling harpoon heads and nontoggling harpoon dart heads for various sea mammals; dart heads for land mammals, often split to take polished slate endblades. Artifacts of stone included numerous varieties of polished projectile heads of slate, as well as some chipped ones of harder stone; varieties of double-edged knives; and, of course, the familiar transverse-bladed ulu.

THULE EXPANSION ☐ After about AD 1000, and without any depopulation of the coast, there was a general expansion of people upstream along the major rivers, where permanent settlements were established; this involved a steady diversification in the use of inland resources, as land hunting and especially river fishing came to be more and more important. The new lifeway of these people who penetrated the forested upper reaches of the rivers has been called the Arctic Woodland culture (Giddings 1952). Other groups moved onto the treeless north slope of the Brooks Range, where they concentrated particularly upon caribou hunting. Despite the weakening of their dependence on ocean resources, all of these new inland people retained a dependence upon the use of certain coastal products—especially sea mammal oil—which were obtained either by trade or by seasonal hunting trips to the coast.

This expansion into the interior was still going on at the time the Europeans arrived, and an obvious suggestion is that it was a response to a steadily increasing population. In some cases the territory entered by these Eskimos appears to have been substantially vacant; in many others, however, they must have displaced thinly settled Indian groups.

The most notable expansionist occurrence was the Thule migration across northern Canada to Greenland that apparently took place around AD 1000 or immediately thereafter (see Chapter 3). In the south of Alaska, however, an analogous movement occurred. As was indicated earlier, people of the Norton tradition had begun to drift across the Alaska Peninsula to the Pacific coast before AD 1000, presumably as a reflection of increased interest in hunting sea mammals in open water. This movement increased dramatically with the appearance of the Thule tradition. But, unlike the northeast where Thule people replaced or absorbed their Dorset cousins of substantially different material culture, the importation of Thule tradition stone implements to the Pacific coast resulted in a renewed emphasis on techniques and implement forms long known in that region; the developing Thule tradition culture of the north, in its increased use of polished implements devoted especially to sea hunting, had moved ever closer in material culture to the earlier peoples of Kodiak Island. There remained artifactual differences between north and extreme south—for example, the much more frequent use of the toggling harpoon head in the north in place of the harpoon dart head favored in the south—but the overall impression is one of convergence. The most exotic importation to the Pacific at this time was thick, gravel-tempered pottery that appeared on southern Kodiak Island around AD 1000 and yet was never used in quantity in the northern portion of the same island, even though it appeared elsewhere on the Pacific coast, in settlements of the Alaska Peninsula and along Cook Inlet, for instance (Clark 1966; de Laguna 1934; Dumond 1971; Dumond and Mace 1968).

Summary: Prehistory of the Alaskan Coast

By about 4000 BC a subsistence adaptation to the unfrozen Pacific coastline of the Alaska Peninsula and the Kodiak Island group had been made by people who after 3000 BC took up techniques of slate grinding, and from then on exhibited a remarkably stable technological tradition. A similar subsistence adaptation was clearly present in the Aleutian Islands by 3000 or 2500 BC (if not several millennia earlier) with a similarly stable technological tradition in which slate polishing did not figure.

Farther north on the Alaskan mainland, by about 2200 BC the Arctic Small Tool tradition represented a generalized hunting people adapted to life on the tundra strip inside the coast, based on river fishing, land mammal hunting, and the seasonal quest for sea mammals. These people spread across all of arctic North America to Greenland; in the east, their descendants of a millennium and a half later would be the bearers of Dorset culture. Although their precise origin is uncertain, the absence of any apparent immediate predecessors within Alaska suggests that they represent a new influx of people from Asia, probably as an Asian outgrowth of the Siberian-American Paleoarctic tradition.

By the last centuries before the Christian era, the presumed descendants of the Arctic Small Tool people in Alaska, those of Norton tradition, occupied the coast from the Alaska Peninsula northward. Equipped with new techniques derived in part from Asia, more sedentary, more completely adjusted to life on the seacoast, they spread as far east along the Arctic coast as it was possible for them to do and still maintain their customary life. At Bering Strait these same people initiated a cultural florescence based upon the heavy use of sea mammals, which resulted in the pattern of living represented in the Thule tradition. Succeeding centuries saw increasing specialization in the use of sea products by some of these people, as well as subsidiary developments by others toward specialized dependence on resources such as salmon and caribou.

Around AD 1000, possibly as a result of warmer weather that brought a change in the path of sea mammal migration, north Alaskan coastal hunters moved eastward across northern Canada to Greenland. Meanwhile, the interest in open-water hunting brought on a similar southward expansion to the coast of the Pacific, which is rich in sea mammals; pottery and other peculiarly Thule traits and probably some people of Thule tradition appeared on Kodiak Island. At the same time the techniques of slate polishing spread southwestward down the Alaska Peninsula and into the Aleutian Islands, there to be passed throughout the long island chain by the time of the arrival of the Russians or shortly after.

Thus, at the time of the arrival of Europeans (between about AD 1750 and 1850, depending upon the location) the coast of Alaska except for the southeastern panhandle was in Aleut or Eskimo hands, and Eskimos had also pressed some distance into the interior in certain areas. There, along the major rivers, they were in direct contact with settled Athapaskan neighbors, many of whom were becoming acculturated to Eskimo ways. In the Brooks Range, however, despite the fact that Eskimo immigrants of the late Thule period had taken with them aspects of social organization derived from the relatively sedentary whaling villages, their migratory pattern of life had more in common with that customarily found among the caribou-hunting interior Athapaskan Indians, with whom they were apparently in intermittent contact.

THE ARCHEOLOGY OF THE NORTHWEST COAST

As was the case in the block of Alaskan territory to the north, the earliest cultural remains from southeastern Alaska, British Columbia, Washington, and Oregon do not manifest any clear-cut differentiation between assemblages of the coast and those of the interior (Figure 2.13). Again like Alaska, such distinctions developed in the course of time, leading on the one hand to inland hunters and river fishermen—many of whom were Athapaskans similar

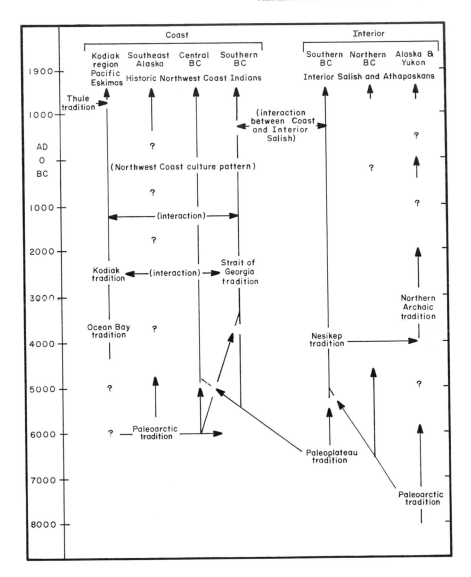

FIGURE 2.13
Major cultural traditions in the northern portion of the Pacific Northwest and adjacent regions.

in culture and language to those of Alaska, others of whom were of the ethnographically known Plateau culture type—and leading on the other hand to the well-known pattern of Northwest Coast culture, famous for its dense population, ceremonialism, and its emphasis on property, on rank, and on personal pride.

Before 5000 BC

Although lacking distinctions between coast and interior, the Northwest in the millennia before 5000 BC was nevertheless host to two distinct traditions, one of them derived from the north, the other apparently from the south.

THE PALEOARCTIC TRADITION (7000–5000 BC) □ In the vicinity of Juneau in southeastern Alaska, a coastal occupation with evident arctic affiliation is known certainly by 6000 BC, and may have been initiated 2000 years earlier, although details pertaining to these earlier millennia are scant (Ackerman 1973). This manifestation has been referred to by one scholar as the Early Boreal tradition (Borden 1969; 1975), but the term *Paleoarctic* has priority of publication (Anderson 1968).

Occupation of the coastal site at Ground Hog Bay by 6000 BC was characterized by a tool assemblage that included microcores and microblades, larger cores, choppers, scrapers, and at least some bifacially flaked implements, known now only from fragments. The cores have been compared to early wedge-shaped microcores from Alaska and the Yukon. This industry may have lasted as late as about 1000 BC, although such persistence is uncertain. Thus far, further local successors are unknown until the very late historic period, when the typical Northwest Coast pattern was present.

From east of the Coast Mountains in the upper Stikine River drainage in northern British Columbia, and only about 240 kilometers east of Juneau, is reported what has been termed the Ice Mountain Microblade phase, to which are assigned collections from three sites that yielded small wedge-shaped obsidian cores and microblades. Dating is limited to obsidian hydration measurements which, if interpreted by means of a hydration rate proposed from material from Onion Portage in northern Alaska, provide a mode between 3000 and 2000 BC, with a significant number of specimens dating as early as 5000 BC, and with a few possibly even earlier (Smith 1971: 201, Fig. 2). These components, apparently consisting solely of products of the blade-core microindustry, were thought to overlie a few relatively crude bifaces and retouched flakes presumed by the excavator to be earlier, but which have the appearance of other items typical of assemblages of the Paleoarctic tradition. The Ice Mountain Microblade components are followed after a substantial hiatus by triangular, side-notched arrow points attributable to historically known Athapaskans, the descendants of whom still reside in the area (Smith 1970; 1971).

Considerably farther south, at Namu on the central coast of British Columbia, another industry apparently of the Paleoarctic type has been found, in which microblades occur with a few relatively crude bifacial points or knives. These artifacts were deposited by people who occupied the region before 6000 BC, perhaps as early as 7000 BC, and who accumulated bones not only of deer, bear, river otter, beaver, and dog, but also of seal, porpoise, and sea otter. The habits of the last two, in particular, suggest that boats must have been used in the chase.

After about 5000 BC, additional microblade industries, presumably derived from the Paleoarctic tradition, appear farther south both on the coast and in the interior. These industries will be taken up in a later section.

THE PALEOPLATEAU TRADITION (8000–3000 BC) ☐ Toward the southern edge of the area covered by Pleistocene glacial ice, the assemblages for which greatest age has been claimed were obtained from the several terraces of the Fraser River in the vicinity of modern Yale, and make up a collection known as the Pasika complex. These pebble tools and scrapers have been said to date from the Late Pleistocene and to represent the ancestors of makers of later artifacts represented in the vicinity, but their validity as an early cultural assemblage has been called into question on various grounds (Borden 1968; 1969; see Borden 1975:55–60 for additional references). Because it is not yet possible to relate these tools and scrapers systematically to later remains in the area, they will not be further dealt with here.

These remains aside, the earliest evidence of what will here be called the Paleoplateau tradition is from locations in the Columbia-Fraser Plateau and from the canyon of the Fraser River in south-central British Columbia. It is most completely reported from the middle Columbia River region, where it includes the material from the Early Period at the Road Cut site at Five Mile Rapids near The Dalles, Oregon (Cressman 1960) and the sequential Windust and Cascade phases of the lower Snake River (Leonhardy and Rice 1970; Rice 1972; see also Figure 4.11, this volume). More fragmentary indications of the existence of the same adaptation proceed from the zone west of the Cascade Range and its northern extension, the Coast Mountains of British Columbia.

Between about 8000 and 6000 BC, the collections from the Columbia River region include projectile points with shoulders, relatively short blades, straight or contracting stems, and straight or slightly concave bases; occasional lanceolate or leaf-shaped points; lanceolate and ovoid knives; some burins, cobble choppers, and discoidal cores; some fairly large blades struck from polyhedral cores; and some projectile heads produced from discoidal cores through the use of a Levallois-like technique. Mullers or grinders also were apparently in use, although not common. Portions of the assemblage—the discoidal cores, the blades and blade cores—are reminiscent of portions of the Akmak and related complexes of the Paleoarctic tradition, but these southern collections lack all trace of microblades and include a characteristic congeries of projectile points that is unrepresented in the Arctic. The traces of early bison hunters at Lind Coulee (Daugherty 1956) apparently pertain to this culture type, but the bone refuse also includes deer, pronghorn, elk, rabbit, and beaver, and shell refuse consists of river mussel.

After about 6000 BC, the bipointed or leaf-shaped Cascade point became typical in an assemblage otherwise little changed, having perhaps more scrapers and milling stones, and many cobbles heavily ground along the edge. Game remains now include those represented earlier, plus salmon and steelhead bones, which probably indicates the use of a new resource. Around 5000 BC this assemblage was joined by a series of large side-notched projectile points.

For a time following 7000 BC, the basic Paleoplateau assemblage is reflected in the lowest deposits at site DjRi3 in the canyon of the Fraser River—a short distance west of the Fraser Plateau—in what are termed the Milliken and Mazama phases (Borden 1968; 1975); the presence of wild cherry pits indicates a late summer occupation that would have coincided with the Fraser River salmon runs. To the east, the Interior Plateau of the upper Fraser, the Thompson, and the upper Columbia River systems was sufficiently deglaciated by 7000 BC to support abundant plant and animal life, and around 6000 BC what has been termed the Lochnore complex of tools (Sanger 1969) appears there, apparently borne by a northward movement of people of the Paleoplateau tradition. In addition, some lanceolate points of the same date may also reflect the influence of Plano people from the Plains to the east, who were apparently moving northward in central Canada at the same time.

Similar Paleoplateau-like complexes are reported from the Cholcotin Plateau in British Columbia (Mitchell 1970), and have been thought to be present in both southern and northern Yukon Territory (MacNeish 1964: 344); their presence in the latter area, however, is not clearly documented.

Whatever the case for possible far northern affinities, it seems evident that the Paleoplateau tradition assemblages are related to those of the contemporary northern Great Basin, and perhaps to others, still farther south, of what has been termed a San Dieguito-like horizon (see Chapter 4).

The degree to which the Paleoplateau tradition is present on the coast itself is not yet clear. In the early deposits at the Road Cut site near The Dalles—on the western edge of the Plateau—seal bones appear, indicating some acquaintance with sea mammals, if only those taken while they pursued migrating salmon upriver. Paleoplateau tradition artifacts are clearly present in the lower levels of Cascadia Cave, on the western slope of the Cascade Range in Oregon (Newman 1966). More fragmentary collections from western Washington that probably pertain to the same tradition are those that have been referred to a hypothetical Coastal Land Hunting tradition (Bryan 1963). Some investigators (e.g., Butler 1965) have suggested that the Paleoplateau tradition was ancestral to later developments of the lower Columbia River, which culminated in the culture of the Penutian-speaking Chinook Indians; such evidence as is available from the region is reconcilable with this view, although not sufficient to demonstrate its accuracy.

On or nearly on the coast proper, most artifacts that might represent the Paleoplateau tradition are small and scattered finds from sites in Washington and British Columbia (Mitchell 1971:60, Table X). An apparent exception is the earliest component from the Glenrose Cannery site on the South Arm of the Fraser River about 22 kilometers above its mouth. Dating somewhere around 5000 BC, and perhaps earlier, the assemblage, with its leaf-shaped points, is reminiscent of the Mazama phase of the Fraser Canyon and of the Cascade phase of the Columbia Plateau (Borden 1975); it includes bone waste of elk, deer, beaver, mink, dog, and seal.

Additional suggestions that the Paleoplateau tradition played an important part in the development of Northwest Coast culture as it is known from ethnographic times proceed from as far north as the Prince Rupert area, in the country of the recent Penutian-speaking Tsimshian. This evidence will be discussed later.

After 5000 BC

Events of the next several millennia both in the interior and on the coast involved the interplay of two early traditions.

THE INTERIOR □ On the plateau, around the confluence of the Thompson and Fraser rivers, the assemblages of the Paleoplateau tradition were followed by those in which microblades and cores figure prominently. Indeed, microblades appear as early as 5000 BC. The blade technology climaxed around 3000 to 4000 BC, when microblades constitute about 50 percent of the collections that are assigned to what is locally termed the Nesikep tradition. Unlike many of the assemblages referred to heretofore, however, blades of this tradition were produced chiefly from cores in which weathered cortex surfaces formed the striking platforms. Products of this long-lived local industry were associated with a progression of corner- and side-notched projectile points, which appear early enough—5000 BC, at least—to have furnished a prototype for notched projectile points of the Northern Archaic tradition in the Yukon and Alaska (cf. Dumond 1969b).

The making of microblades was gradually abandoned by people of the Nesikep tradition around AD 500, and the period following is characterized by small, side-notched, triangular projectile points similar in form to those produced by late prehistoric residents of the Ice Mountain area farther north. This same late period also saw the use of polished nephrite adzes, of tubular copper beads, and the presence of steatite carvings and objects of ocean shell. The course of development of the Nesikep tradition from its blade-producing stages to the time of European contact is interpreted as representing a single people who evolved into the interior Salish of recent times (Sanger 1969; 1970).

The production of microblades continued in central British Columbia— although dated evidence is at present confined to the first millennium BC

(Sanger 1968:98)—and it extends as far south as the Plateau area of central Washington. There microblades are especially plentiful in a component of the Ryegrass Coulee site dating certainly to 2000 BC, and possibly as early as 3500 BC, where they are associated with leaf-shaped and side-notched points reminiscent of the latest stages of the Paleoplateau tradition. Other finds of microblades in central Washington are undated but are presumably somewhat later than those at Ryegrass Coulee (Sanger 1968).

As one investigator has emphasized (Sanger 1968), the Northwest assemblages in which blade technology appears are so varied that it must be concluded that the arctic influence is almost solely limited to the production of microblades. In view of the dating and distribution, however, it is difficult to avoid the conclusion that the microblades in the northwest interior were derived from the Arctic during postglacial times. Furthermore, the communication that made this possible must have been responsible for the movement of notched points northward. Indeed, the association of side-notched points and microblades in the Nesikep tradition of the fourth millennium BC suggests that communication with the north was already well established, probably along the corridor between the Coast and Rocky mountains.

THE COAST □ On the Queen Charlotte Islands, the earliest known occupation is by a group of microblade producers of around 5000 BC, who used cores of split pebbles and who made no bifacial stone implements (Borden 1975:20–25; Fladmark 1970; 1971a; 1971b). After about 3000 BC, the flake technology had changed to one described as a bipolar percussion industry, although the rest of the unifacial stone assemblage—retouched and used flakes, gravers, scrapers—was not substantially altered. Shortly afterward, however, the islands began to partake of the standard Northwest Coast development, with the accumulation of large shell midden deposits, and the appearance of implements of bone and polished slate such as are known also from the contemporary British Columbia coast around Prince Rupert. The roots of a recognizable Northwest Coast cultural pattern may begin to be distinguished in the latter area even as early as 2500 BC (MacDonald 1969).

At Prince Rupert, in a lowest horizon dated from about 2500 to 500 BC, chipped stone implements include heavy leaf-shaped points; chipped points with square bases; large leaf-shaped, knifelike bifaces; scrapers and cutting implements of boulder chips and pebbles; and numerous edge-ground cobbles. The Paleoplateau-like material from Prince Rupert does not represent people adapted only to life inland. This is made clear by the series of bone harpoons, barbed and with line guards to hold the line, or with gouged line holes.

Thereafter, evolution at Prince Rupert is toward the well-known Northwest Coast pattern. By the beginning of the Christian era stone labrets occur in burials; stone clubs and other implements of pecked stone appear, together with slender polished slate points. Later, stone implements become rare, with projectiles predominantly of bone, including both harpoons with line holes and composite toggling harpoons. Transverse, ululike knives are of shell, and there is much evidence of woodworking (MacDonald 1969).

That the earlier stone artifacts at Prince Rupert owed something of their character to the Paleoplateau tradition is partly supported by the presence of Paleoplateau-like leaf-shaped projectile points, crude bifaces, scrapers, and other implements of chipped stone in an assemblage known as the Cathedral phase, which occurs at several sites now under high tides in Kwatna Inlet, somewhat east of Namu (Borden 1975:34). This assemblage is dated, somewhat uncertainly, to 4000 to 3000 BC, and it apparently relates to the appearance of leaf-shaped points around 3500 BC at Namu, where such points joined the earlier microblades. At Namu, after 2500 BC shell middens began to accumulate, and bone projectile points, harpoon dart heads, awls, and wedges began to occur, while microblades disappeared. Bone waste includes significant proportions of sea mammals, some of which were probably taken by boat. Although one may presume that from this time onward development followed the typical Northwest Coast pattern, no implements of polished or pecked stone were represented anywhere in the relatively small Namu sample.

THE STRAIT OF GEORGIA TRADITION (AFTER 3000 BC) ☐ Still farther southward, a seaward shift in subsistence emphasis is suggested by data from the Eayem phase of the Fraser Canyon, dated from 3000 or 3500 BC to 1500 BC. During that time chipped, stemmed points were joined by chipped and partially ground slate points and knives (Borden 1968; 1975). Nearer the mouth of the Fraser, Eayem-like assemblages have been recovered from other sites, such as Maurer, Glenrose Cannery, and St. Mungo's Cannery, the latter only about 20 kilometers from the present seashore (Borden 1975; Calvert 1970). An apparently related assemblage is that from the Helen Point site on Mayne Island in the western Strait of Georgia, dating from 2500 BC and possibly earlier (Borden 1975:93; Carlson 1970). This last, as well as the collection from the Maurer site, departs from the inventory of the others in that it contains microblades.

It has been proposed that the Eayem phase and all those similar and contemporary components of other sites just referred to should be classed together as a regional cultural manifestation to be termed the Charles phase (Borden 1975:97), which could be presumed to be characteristic of the entire Strait of Georgia and southern coastal mainland of British Columbia at that time. It was this regional culture that was to form the base for the development of a tradition leading directly to the culture of the ethnographically known Coast Salish people. In keeping with the terminology used here, then, this manifestation will be termed the Charles stage of the Strait of Georgia tradition. The local Strait of Georgia tradition, in turn, may be taken as representative of the development of Northwest Coast culture throughout the great northwest area, although data are much less complete for other parts of it.

Furthermore, the Mayne Island assemblage has been compared to the Takli Birch phase of the Pacific side of the Alaska Peninsula (mentioned in a previous section), and together the Mayne collection and Takli Birch phase have been suggested to represent a common north Pacific cultural horizon of the third millennium BC (Carlson 1970). It seems reasonable to extend such a comparison to all collections of the Charles stage.

The next manifestation of the Strait of Georgia tradition is what has been referred to as the Locarno Beach culture type (Mitchell 1971) but which will here be termed the Locarno Beach stage of the tradition. Distinctive features include chipped basalt points, often with contracting stems, nearly identical to those of the preceding stage; microblades and cores that tend to flare outward at the edge opposite the striking platform; chipped slate knives; polished slate points and partially or wholly ground slate knives; small polished celts or adzes; labrets; earspools; and bone and antler implements that include bilaterally barbed points, wedges, foreshafts, and toggling harpoons of either one piece or composite form (Figure 2.14). Subsistence was based upon both land and sea products. Sites were predominantly located beside what was at the time of occupation salt water, both in the Strait Islands and the Fraser Delta region. The Locarno Beach stage is dated at least as early as 2000 BC and lasts to about 200 BC.

In the Fraser Canyon after about 1000 BC, a reflection of the developing Strait of Georgia tradition is seen in the Baldwin phase, in which appear microblades, polished projectile blades, labrets, earspools, and some small sculptures in stone (Borden 1968). Indeed, the conclusion that the Charles-Locarno Beach-Baldwin manifestation as a whole represents a part of a long coastal sphere of communication stretching from southern British Columbia as far north as the Kodiak zone of southwestern Alaska seems inescapable although information is still unavailable for most of the great length of intervening coastline.

From shortly before the Christian era until probably late in the first millennium AD, the Strait of Georgia archeological materials may be assigned to a Marpole stage of the Strait of Georgia tradition. Distinctive artifacts continue to include microblades and chipped stone points in a variety of forms, but now they include an increased variety of large polished slate points, and the transverse polished slate knife or ulu, apparently used particularly in the processing of fish. Barbed, nontoggling harpoon dart heads, tied by a line secured against projecting guards, were used for hunting sea mammals. Subsistence included obviously heavy use of the fish runs of the Fraser River, as well as other fish, birds, shellfish, sea mammals, and land animals.

Settlements were by now large; habitations were probably the long, cedar-plank houses known among historic Coast Salish. The presence of numerous

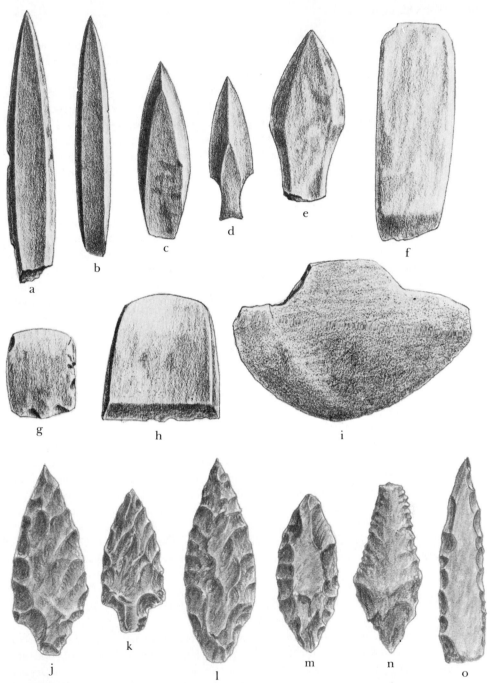

FIGURE 2.14
Artifacts of the Gulf of Georgia tradition, from the Fraser delta region: *a–e,* ground slate points; *f–h,* polished adze blades; *i,* ground slate ulu; *j–n,* chipped stone points; *o,* chipped and ground point. *a–d, g, j–o,* Locarno Beach Stage; *e, f, h, i,* Marpole Stage; *a–i,* after Borden 1962; *j–o,* after Mitchell 1971.

woodworking tools suggests the use of the dugout boat. Differences between burials—in the value and amount of grave goods and in the presence or absence of skull deformation—probably reflect status distinctions. Dentalium shells, disk beads, copper, and large, carefully chipped stone points or knives are thought to represent wealth items and to imply the presence of institutions for the manipulation of property analogous to the historic potlatch. Sculpture in antler and stone clearly presages historic Northwest Coast culture, and at the same time has been said to indicate close connections with the somewhat earlier people of the rich Baldwin phase of the Fraser Canyon. In short, the historical patterns of Northwest Coast culture were clearly present by the beginning of the Christian era.

By AD 1000, in the late prehistoric stage of the tradition, the ethnographic patterns reported for the Coast Salish at contact were even more clearly blocked out in the Fraser Delta, the Strait of Georgia, and the San Juan Islands. Distinctive artifacts include thin triangular points of polished stone, with thinned bases for insertion into a harpoon head of antler or bone; polished adzes; and various composite fish hooks and toggling harpoon parts. Although changes are evident in the form of the most favored harpoons and certain other artifacts, the heritage of the Marpole stage is unmistakable. A slight variant is present in the Fraser Canyon, where during the Esilao phase the long plank houses of the coast were replaced by circular pithouses, covered with poles, bark, and sod; this must have been an up-river Salish culture somewhat influenced by Salish relatives still farther to the interior, such as the late prehistoric people of the Nesikep area, mentioned earlier (Borden 1968; Mitchell 1971).

As one moves still farther southward along the coast, archeological materials are consistently late, and pertain to developed Northwest Coast culture. Many of the known sites are protohistoric and historic, such as the spectacular site at Ozette, Washington. Near the mouth of the Columbia River some recent unpublished excavations indicate the appearance of the Northwest Coast lifeway by the beginning of the Christian era. On the coast of Oregon south of about 43° north latitude, the Northwest Coast pattern seems to yield to the cultures of the subregion of northern California.

SUMMARY: THE NORTHWEST COAST

Hunter-collectors of the Paleoplateau tradition apparently moved northward with the recession of the Cordilleran glaciers between 9000 and 7000 BC, spreading into the coastal zone and at least as far north as central British Columbia. There they encountered and mingled with carriers of northern ideas, made manifest chiefly in the production and use of microblades in a technology derived from the Paleoarctic tradition. These northern ideas were then transported southward, arriving in the Fraser Plateau as early as

5000 BC. In their turn, southern ideas—such as those responsible for the fabrication of side-notched projectile points—were transmitted northward. This vast regional interchange was integral to the peculiar character of the developing coast and interior traditions of British Columbia and of the Northern Archaic tradition in Alaska.

Whether the earliest exchange of ideas resulted primarily from movements or contacts through the interior valleys of British Columbia between the Coast Mountains and the Rockies or from communication along the coast is not yet altogether clear; each view has been argued by prehistorians (e.g., Borden 1969; 1975; Fladmark 1971a). Both routes came to be important.

In any event, before 2000 BC northern and southern ideas were also merged in a coastal lifeway in the Strait of Georgia region, a lifeway so strongly reminiscent of that of the Kodiak area of southwestern Alaska of the same period that it suggests communication, once established with the north, continued along the coastline. This lifeway was ancestral to later cultures such as the maritime-oriented Pacific Eskimo and the Northwest Coast Indians. These last, based in the more southerly region, with its somewhat greater marine and intertidal resources and in particular its mountainous hinterland so rich in fish and game, surpassed their Alaskan cousins to produce the spectacular culture of abundance that is famous in the ethnographic literature.

It is not clear from the archeological evidence whether the transmission of ideas both northward and southward between the Northwest and Alaska resulted from relatively massive movements of people from the north, or simply from communication, once occupation of formerly glaciated zones was open to a slowly expanding southern population. If the former, then one might tentatively suggest that the ancestors of nearly all peoples of true Northwest Coast culture entered the New World as part of a post-Wisconsin migration. This would include the forebears of recent peoples speaking Salishan, Wakashan, and Na-Dene (with whom all the Athapaskans would of necessity be included), but not of the Penutian-speaking Tsimshian, whose linguistic relatives all lie to the south in a distribution more suggestive of derivation from people of the Paleoplateau tradition, and who must represent a part of the population already present in America before the latest glacial advances of the Pleistocene.

On the other hand, if the intermingling of northern and southern influences was the result almost solely of diffusion, it is possible as an extreme case to argue that only the Eskimo-Aleuts—reputedly the most Asian of all American natives in physique and language—were derived from the Old World by migration in post-Wisconsin times. In such a case, all others of the Northwest (and all other American Indians) must have been present in the New World since well before the time of the Paleoarctic and Paleoplateau traditions as they have been described here.

Unfortunately, although both constructions require the presence of people in southerly portions of North America before the recession of the major glaciers of the Late Pleistocene, neither Alaska nor the Northwest provides any clear and unambiguous trace of these supposed earlier immigrants to the Western Hemisphere.

References Cited and Recommended Sources

Ackerman, Robert E. 1962 Culture contact in the Bering Sea: Birnirk-Punuk period. *In* Prehistoric Cultural Relations Between the Arctic and Temperate Zones of North America, ed. J. M. Campbell, pp. 27–34. Arctic Institute of North America, Technical Paper, No. 11.

————. 1964 Prehistory in the Kuskokwim-Bristol Bay region, southwestern Alaska. Washington State University Laboratory of Anthropology Report of Investigations, No. 26.

————. 1973 Post Pleistocene cultural adaptations on the northern Northwest Coast. *In* International Conference on the Prehistory and Paleoecology of Western Arctic and Sub-Arctic, ed. S. Raymond and P. Schledermann, pp. 1–20. Calgary: University of Calgary Archaeological Association.

Aigner, Jean S., Bruce Fullem, Douglas Veltre, and Mary Veltre 1976 Preliminary reports on remains from Sandy Beach Bay, a 4300–5600 BP Aleut Village. Arctic Anthropology 13:2:89–90.

————. 1970 The unifacial, core and blade site on Anangula Island, Aleutians. Arctic Anthropology 7:2:59–88.

Aigner, Jean S., Bruce Fullem, Douglas Veltre, and Mary Veltre 1976 Preliminary reports on remains from Sandy Beach Bay, a 4300–5600 BP Aleut Village. Arctic Anthropology 13:2:83–90.

Alexander, Herbert L. 1973 The association of Aurignacoid elements with fluted point complexes in North America. *In* International Conference on the Prehistory and Paleoecology of Western Arctic and Sub-Arctic, ed. S. Raymond and P. Schledermann, pp. 21–32. Calgary: University of Calgary Archaeological Association.

Anderson, Douglas D. 1968 A Stone Age campsite at the gateway to America. Scientific American 218:6:24–33.

————. 1970 Akmak. Acta Arctica XVI. Copenhagen: Arctic Institute.

————. 1972 An archaeological survey of Noatak Drainage, Alaska. Arctic Anthropology 9:1:66–117.

Bandi, Hans-Georg 1969 Eskimo Prehistory. Translated by A. Keep. College: University of Alaska Press.

Black, Robert F. 1975 Late-Quaternary geomorphic processes: effects on the ancient Aleuts of Umnak Island in the Aleutians. Arctic 28:3:160–169.

Bockstoce, John 1973 A prehistoric population change in the Bering Strait region. Polar Record 16:793–803.

Borden, Charles E. 1962 West Coast crossties with Alaska. *In* Prehistoric Cultural Relations Between the Arctic and Temperate Zones of North America. ed. J. M. Campbell, pp. 9–19. Arctic Institute of North America, Technical Paper, No. 11.

————. 1968 Prehistory of the lower mainland. *In* Lower Fraser Valley: Evolution of a Cultural Landscape, ed. A. H. Siemens, pp. 9–26. Vancouver: B.C. Geographical Series, 9.

————. 1969 Early population movements from Asia into western North America. Syesis 2:1–2:1–13.

————. 1975 Origins and development of early Northwest Coast culture to about 3000 BC. National Museum of Man, Mercury Series, Archaeological Survey of Canada Paper, No. 45.

Bryan, Alan Lyle 1963 An archaeological survey of northern Puget Sound. Occasional Papers of the Idaho State University Museum, 11.

Butler, B. Robert 1961 The Old Cordilleran culture in the Pacific Northwest. Occasional Papers of the Idaho State College Museum, 5.

———. 1965 Perspectives on the prehistory of the lower Columbia River. Tebiwa 8:1:1–16.

Calvert, Gay 1970 The St. Mungo Cannery site: a preliminary report. B.C. Studies 6–7:54–76.

Campbell, John M. 1959 The Kayuk complex of Arctic Alaska. American Antiquity 25:94–105.

———. 1961a the Kogruk complex of Anaktuvuk Pass, Alaska. Anthropologica, n.s. 3:1:3–20.

———. 1961b The Tuktu complex of Anaktuvuk Pass. Anthropological Papers of the University of Alaska 9:2:61–80.

———. 1962 Cultural succession at Anaktuvuk Pass, Arctic Alaska. In Prehistoric Cultural Relations Between the Arctic and Temperate Zones of North America, ed. J. M. Campbell, pp. 39–54. Arctic Institute of North America, Technical Paper, No. 11.

———. 1968 The Kavik site of Anaktuvuk Pass, central Brooks Range, Alaska. Anthropological Papers of the University of Alaska 14:1:33–42.

Carlson, Roy L. 1970 Excavations at Helen Point on Mayne Island. B.C. Studies 6–7:113–135.

Clark, Donald W. 1966 Perspectives in the prehistory of Kodiak Island, Alaska. American Antiquity 31:3:356–371.

———. 1972 Archaeology of the Batza Tena obsidian source, west-central Alaska. Anthropological Papers of the University of Alaska 15:2:1–21.

———. 1974 The earliest prehistoric cultures of Kodiak Island, Alaska: 1971 fieldwork, preliminary report. Arctic Anthropology 11:1:41–46.

Collins, Henry B., Jr. 1937 Archaeology of St. Lawrence Island, Alaska. Smithsonian Miscellaneous Collections 96:(1).

———. 1964 The Arctic and Subarctic. In Prehistoric Man in the New World, ed. J. D. Jennings and E. Norbeck, pp. 85–114. Chicago: University of Chicago Press.

Cook, John P. 1969 Early prehistory of Healy Lake, Alaska. Ph.D. thesis, University of Wisconsin. Madison: University Microfilms 69–22, 365.

Cook, John P., E. J. Dixon, and C. E. Holmes 1972 Archaeological report, Site 49 RAT 32, Amchitka Island, Alaska. Las Vegas: Holmes and Narver, Inc.

Cook, John P., and Robert A. McKennan 1970a The Athapaskan tradition: a view from Healy Lake in the Yukon-Tanana Upland. Paper read at the annual meeting of the Northeastern Anthropological Association, Ottawa, 1970.

———. 1970b The village site at Healy Lake, Alaska: an interim report. Paper read at the annual meeting of the Society for American Archaeology, Mexico, D.F., 1970.

Cressman, L. S. 1960 Cultural sequences at The Dalles, Oregon. Transactions of the American Philosophical Society, n.s. 50:(10).

Daugherty, Richard D. 1956 Archaeology of the Lind Coulee site, Washington. Proceedings of the American Philosophical Society 100:3:223–278.

de Laguna, Frederica 1934 The Archaeology of Cook Inlet, Alaska. Philadelphia: University of Pennsylvania Press.

———. 1947 The prehistory of northern North America as seen from the Yukon. Memoirs of the Society for American Archaeology, No. 3.

Denniston, Glenda B. 1966 Cultural change at Chaluka, Umnak Island: stone artifacts and features. Arctic Anthropology 3:2:84–124.

Desautels, R. J., A. J. McCurdy, J. D. Flynn, and R. R. Ellis 1970 Archaeological Report, Amchitka Island, Alaska 1969–1970. Costa Mesa, Calif.: Archaeological Research, Inc.

Dikov, N. N. 1965 The Stone Age of Kamchatka and the Chukchi Peninsula in the light of new archaeological data. Arctic Anthropology 3:1:10–25.

Dixon, E. James, Jr. 1975 The Gallagher Flint Station, an early man site on the north slope, Arctic Alaska, and its role in relation to the Bering land bridge. Arctic Anthropology 12:1:68–75.

Dumond, D. E. 1965 On Eskaleutian linguistics, archaeology, and prehistory. American Anthropologist 67:5:1231–1257.

———. 1969a Prehistoric cultural contacts in southwestern Alaska. Science 166:1108–1115.

———. 1969b Toward a prehistory of the Na-Dene. American Anthropologist 71:5:857–863.

———. 1971 A summary of archaeology in the Katmai region, southwestern Alaska. University of Oregon Anthropological Papers, No. 2.

———. 1972 Prehistoric population growth and subsistence change in Eskimo Alaska. *In* Population Growth: Anthropological Implications, ed. Brian Spooner, pp. 311–328. Cambridge: MIT Press.

———. 1977 The Eskimos and Aleuts. London: Thames and Hudson.

Dumond, D. E., and Robert L. A. Mace 1968 An archaeological survey along Knik Arm. Anthropological Papers of the University of Alaska 14:1:1–21.

Dumond, D. E., Winfield Henn, and Robert Stuckenrath 1976 Archaeology and prehistory on the Alaska Peninsula. Anthropological Papers of the University of Alaska 18:1:17–29.

Fladmark, K. R. 1970 A preliminary report on lithic assemblages from the Queen Charlotte Islands, British Columbia. *In* Early Man and Environments in Northwest North America, ed. R. C. Smith and J. W. Smith, pp. 117–136. Calgary: University of Calgary Archaeological Association.

———. 1971a Early microblade industries of the Queen Charlotte Islands, British Columbia. Paper read at the annual meeting of the Canadian Archaeological Association, Calgary.

———. 1971b Radiocarbon dates from the Queen Charlotte Islands. The Midden 3:5:11–12.

Ford, James A. 1959 Eskimo prehistory in the vicinity of Point Barrow, Alaska. Anthropological Papers of the American Museum of Natural History 47:1:1–272.

Geist, Otto W., and Froelich G. Rainey 1936 Archaeological excavations at Kukulik, St. Lawrence Island, Alaska. Miscellaneous Publications of the University of Alaska, No. 2.

Giddings, J. L. 1951 The Denbigh Flint complex. American Antiquity 16:3:193–203.

———. 1952 The Arctic Woodland culture of the Kobuk River. Philadelphia: University of Pennsylvania, Museum Monographs.

———. 1957 Round houses in the western Arctic. American Antiquity 23:2:121–135.

———. 1961 Cultural continuities of Eskimos. American Antiquity 27:2:155–173.

———. 1962 Side-notched points near Bering Strait. *In* Prehistoric Cultural Relations Between the Arctic and Temperate Zones of North America, ed. J. M. Campbell, pp. 35–38. Arctic Institute of North America, Technical Paper, No. 11.

———. 1963 Some arctic spear points and their counterparts. Anthropological Papers of the University of Alaska 10:2:1–12.

———. 1964 The Archaeology of Cape Denbigh. Providence: Brown University Press.

———. 1967 Ancient Men of the Arctic. New York: Alfred A. Knopf.

Gordon, B. C. 1970 Recent archaeological investigations on the Arctic Yukon coast: including a description of the British Mountain complex at Trout Lake. *In* Early Man and Environments in Northwest North America, ed. R. A. Smith and J. W. Smith, pp. 67–86. Calgary: University of Calgary Archaeological Association.

Griffin, James B. 1970 Northeast Asian and northwestern American ceramics. Proceedings, VIIIth International Congress of Anthropological and Ethnological Sciences, Tokyo and Kyoto, 1968 3:327–330.

Hadleigh West, Frederick 1967 The Donnelly Ridge site and the definition of an early core and blade complex in central Alaska. American Antiquity 32:3:360–382.

———. 1975 Dating the Denali complex. Arctic Anthropology 12:1:76–81.

Heizer, Robert F. 1956 Archaeology of the Uyak site, Kōdiak Island, Alaska. University of California Anthropological Records 17:1.

Humphrey, Robert L., Jr. 1970 The prehistory of the Arctic slope of Alaska: Pleistocene cultural relations between Eurasia and North America. Ph.D. thesis, University of New Mexico, 1970. Albuquerque: University Microfilms 71–9277.

Larsen, Helge 1968a New Ipiutak and Uwelen-Okvik. Folk 10:81–90.

———. 1968b Trail Creek. Acta Arctica XV. Copenhagen: Arctic Institute.

Larsen, Helge, and Froelich G. Rainey 1948 Ipiutak and the Arctic Whale Hunting culture. Anthropological Papers of the American Museum of Natural History 42.

Laughlin, William S. 1975 Aleuts: ecosystem, Holocene history, and Siberian origin. Science 189:507–515.

Leonhardy, Frank C., and David G. Rice 1970 A proposed culture typology for the lower Snake River region, southeastern Washington. Northwest Anthropological Research Notes 4:1:1–29.

Lippold, Lois K. 1966 Chaluka: the economic base. Arctic Anthropology 3:2:125–131.

Lutz, Bruce J. 1973 An archaeological *karigi* at the site of UngaLaqLiq, western Alaska. Arctic Anthropology 10:1:111–118.

McCartney, A. P. 1971 A proposed western Aleutian phase in the Near Islands, Alaska. Arctic Anthropology 8:2:92–142.

MacDonald, George F. 1969 Preliminary culture sequence from the Coast Tsimshian area, British Columbia. Northwest Anthropological Research Notes 3:2:240–254.

MacKay, J. R., W. H. Mathews, and R. S. MacNeish 1961 Geology of the Engigstciak archaeological site, Yukon Territory. Arctic 14:1:25–52.

MacNeish, Richard S. 1956 The Engigstciak site on the Yukon Arctic coast. Anthropological Papers of the University of Alaska 4:2:91–112.

———. 1964 Investigations in southwest Yukon: archaeological excavation, comparisons and speculations. Papers of the Robert S. Peabody Foundation for Archaeology 6:2:201–471.

———. 1974 Prehistoric cultural integration along the Alaska Peninsula. Anthropological Papers of the University of Alaska 16:1:59–84.

Mitchell, Donald H. 1970 Excavations on the Chilcotin Plateau: three sites, three phases. Northwest Anthropological Research Notes 4:1:99–116.

———. 1971 Archaeology of the Gulf of Georgia area, a natural region and its culture types. Syesis 4, supplement 1.

Morlan, Richard E. 1971 Late prehistory of the middle Porcupine drainage, northern Yukon Territories. Ph.D. thesis, University of Wisconsin. Madison: University Microfilms 71-25491.

Newman, Thomas M. 1966 Cascadia Cave. Occasional Papers of the Idaho State University Museum 18.

Nowak, Michael 1970 A preliminary report on the archaeology of Nunivak Island, Alaska. Anthropological Papers of the University of Alaska 15:1:18–32.

Okada, Hiroaki, and Atsuko Okada 1974 Preliminary report on the 1972 excavations at Port Moller, Alaska. Arctic Anthropology 11 (supplement):112–144.

Osgood, Cornelius 1940 Ingalik material culture. Yale University Publications in Anthropology, No. 22.

Oswalt, Wendell H. 1967 Alaskan Eskimos. San Francisco: Chandler Publishing Company.

Rainey, Froelich G. 1941 Eskimo prehistory: the Okvik site on the Punuk Islands. Anthropological Papers of the American Museum of Natural History 37:4:443–569.

Rice, David G. 1972 The Windust phase in lower Snake River region prehistory. Washington State University Laboratory of Anthropology Report of Investigations, 50.

Sanger, David 1968 Prepared core and blade traditions in the Pacific Northwest. Arctic Anthropology 5:1:92–120.

———. 1969 Cultural traditions in the interior of British Columbia. Syesis 2:1–2:189–200.

———. 1970 The archaeology of the Lochnore-Nesikep locality, British Columbia. Syesis 3, supplement 1.

Smith Jason W. 1970 Preliminary report of archaeological investigation in northern British Columbia. In Early Man and Environments in Northwest North America, ed. R. A. Smith and J. S. Smith, pp. 87–104. Calgary: University of Calgary Archaeological Association.

———. 1971 The Ice Mountain microblade and core industry, Cassiar district, northern British Columbia, Canada. Arctic and Alpine Research 3:3:199–213.

Solecki, Ralph S., Bert Salwen, and Jerome Jacobson 1973 Archaeological reconnaissances north of the Brooks Range in northeastern Alaska. Department of Archaeology, the University of Calgary, Occasional Papers, 1.

Spaulding, A. C. 1962 Archaeological investigation on Agattu, Aleutian Islands. Anthropological Papers of the Museum of Anthropology, University of Michigan, No. 18.

Stanford, Dennis J. 1969 Recent excavations near Point Barrow, Alaska. Paper read at the annual meeting of the Society for American Archaeology, Milwaukee.

Turner, Christy G., II, and Jacqueline A. Turner 1974 Progress report on evolutionary anthropological study of Akun Strait district, eastern Aleutians, Alaska. Anthropological Papers of the University of Alaska 16:1:27–57.

Workman, William B. 1966 Prehistory at Port Moller, Alaska Peninsula, in light of fieldwork in 1960. Arctic Anthropology 3:2:132–153.

———. 1976 A late prehistoric Ahtena site near Gulkana, Alaska. Paper read at the annual meeting of the Alaska Anthropological Association, Anchorage.

The treeline at Nastapoka River, east coast of Hudson Bay. The small spruce tree in the foreground is about 100 years old. It is surrounded by a thicket of dwarf birch.

CHAPTER THREE

Pioneer Cultures of the Sub-Arctic and the Arctic

Elmer Harp, Jr.

Dr. Harp details the history of archeology in what must surely be one of the least hospitable areas on earth for carrying out fieldwork. Through his description we see the slow process through which knowledge about the prehistoric inhabitants of this little-known frozen world has come to light. The diversity and richness of their culture is reflected in the variety of their tool assemblages and the often aesthetically appealing quality of their workmanship.

THE REGIONAL ENVIRONMENTS

The northeastern quadrant of North America, here divided into the sub-Arctic and Arctic, consists of three major geographic provinces: the large eastern portion of the Canadian mainland that surrounds Hudson Bay; the Canadian Arctic Archipelago; and Greenland, the largest island in the world (Figure 3.1). The continental part of this vast region is transected from northwest to southeast by the treeline, which marks the northern limit of forest growth and serves as the nominal boundary between the sub-Arctic and Arctic environmental zones.

The first of these geographic provinces is essentially a shallow basin, with Hudson Bay in the center. Several large rivers drain into this depression, including the Thelon-Dubawnt system, the Kazan, Churchill, Nelson, and Albany from the west and south, and the Great Whale and Eastmain rivers from the east. The terrain west of Hudson Bay is a plain with low to moderate relief, extensively covered by marine deposits and glacial till; the Quebec-Ungava country to the east is a rocky, glaciated plateau with an average elevation of about 300 meters. As a whole, this province coincides approxi-

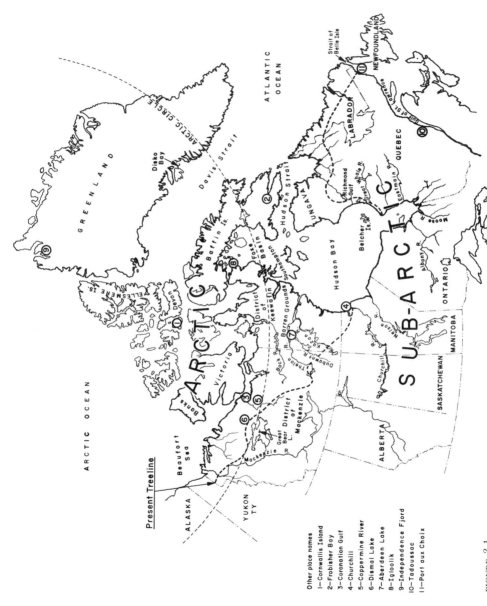

FIGURE 3.1
The Arctic and the sub-Arctic.

mately with the Canadian Shield, which is basically composed of ancient pre-Cambrian rocks, among the oldest on earth. In many areas the Shield has been stripped bare of all soil cover by past glaciation, leaving the rock surfaces striated or scoured to a high polish.

The Canadian Archipelago, with a combined land mass of about 1,300,000 square kilometers, is completely arctic in character, and one-tenth of it is covered with permanent ice and alpine glaciers. Along the eastern margin rises a mountain chain with elevations up to 3000 meters, and the coastlines are deeply dissected by fjords. Otherwise, the physiography of the islands is extremely varied, including plains, plateaus, rolling terrain, and rift valleys; the interior consists largely of rock-strewn barrens.

Greenland is notable as the northernmost land in the world, reaching to within 700 kilometers of the North Pole. Its massive inland ice cap, which covers about 1,800,000 square kilometers, extends down in some places to meet the sea, but elsewhere there are coastal fringes of ice-free land. The topography of this border country is predominantly mountainous and pierced by deep fjords, and it does not provide lavish life support for large animal populations.

Before the coming of the Europeans, each of these geographic provinces was successfully occupied by aboriginal peoples. These native hunters were precisely adapted to specific environments, and their culture areas correlated closely with the two major ecological zones that make up the region as a whole. This unity of cultural adaptation and environment was particularly the case in the Arctic, which was occupied solely by the Eskimos, or Inuit [Editor's note: The term *Inuit* is used here as a preferred substitute for *Eskimo.*] The sub-Arctic adaptation was more varied, and this region was occupied by several different Indian tribes and bands belonging to the Athapaskan and Algonquian linguistic families. The adaptations were also affected, of course, by the special character of the biomes that were inhabited.

The Arctic

The Arctic is commonly defined as the circumpolar zone that lies north of the treeline, a border that coincides roughly with the 10°C (50°F) isotherm for the month of July. Substantial forests cannot develop where the average temperature of the warmest month of the year is below 10°C. Note also that the treeline has no immediate geographic relationship with the Arctic Circle, the imaginary line that circumscribes the earth at about 66°67′ north latitude. That is a purely astronomical convention, which relates to seasonal changes and the alternation of night and day. However, despite the lack of linear correspondence between the treeline and the Arctic Circle, the polar pattern of diurnal variation, in association with the shifting seasons, exerts profound influence on all plant and animal life in the Arctic, as well as on the psychological states of the human beings who dwell there.

The Arctic is generally characterized by long, dark, severely cold winters and brief summers. In Keewatin District, for example, west of Hudson Bay, midwinter temperatures average below $-32°C$ ($-25°F$) for two months at a time, and during the frequent northwest storms such temperatures may be depressed by a wind-chill factor to $-73°C$ ($-100°F$). Winter snowfall averages from 1 to 2 meters in Keewatin, while in eastern Ungava-Labrador it may amount to over 3 meters. Summer is cool and short, with no more than 50 frost-free days in the southern Arctic, but it is a time of intense growth and flowering. There are several hundred species of mosses, lichens, and other ground-hugging flora, and they mature rapidly in the long hours of sunlight. Toward the south, dwarf willows, alders, and birch may flourish in protected microenvironments, but all species gradually fade out toward the north, until in the high latitudes of the Archipelago one comes finally to virtually lifeless landscapes of dry, rocky barrens.

The relatively few species of land animals in the Arctic include lemmings, ground squirrels, weasels, wolverines, foxes, the arctic wolf and arctic hare, polar bears, and occasional barren-ground grizzly bears, but the most important food animal is the barren-ground caribou. Several major herds of this species, totaling now less than a million head, roam the barrens west of Hudson Bay, and smaller aggregations are scattered in the Archipelago, the Quebec-Labrador peninsula, and Greenland. Another large land mammal, the musk ox, exists in small residual herds in the barren grounds of central Keewatin, the northern islands of the Archipelago, and Greenland.

Bird life is abundant throughout the Arctic, especially numerous species of shore birds and migratory waterfowl that breed and nest there in the summer. Insect life includes bees, spiders, and several species of flies, and in early summer hordes of mosquitoes parasitize man and beast alike. The surrounding marine waters afford rich food resources of sea mammals, although some species have suffered from excessive commercial hunting in the last century. The most common seals, including the Bearded, Jar, and Ringed varieties, are fundamental to the Inuit subsistence economy, and small herds of walrus still exist in some areas. Arctic char, salmon, and lake trout are the principal food fishes.

One peculiar feature of the Arctic, the widespread occurrence of permafrost, is noteworthy. Because the summers are chilly and brief, Arctic surface soils thaw only to shallow depths, and much of the land is therefore underlain by permanently frozen subsoil. This eliminates the possibility of seepage, and low-lying places consequently develop into waterlogged bogs or ponds that evaporate very slowly in the cool air. Hence, some areas become complex mazes of lakes and meandering waterways, and overland travel through them is extremely difficult.

The Sub-Arctic

The so-called treeline, which separates the Arctic from the sub-Arctic, is not, in fact, a line but rather a broad transitional zone that includes both the tundra and the boreal forest. Approaching it from the north, one first encounters outlying isolated clumps of stunted conifers in sheltered valleys; these increase in size and density toward the south, until at last the closed boreal forest appears. This forest is almost impenetrable for man, who must travel through it along the natural drainage systems. The boreal coniferous forest is frequently called the *taiga,* a term originally adopted by Russians from the Tungus reindeer herders of eastern Siberia; like the Arctic tundra, it has a circumpolar distribution across both hemispheres. Black and white spruce dominate the northern portions of the taiga, while hemlock, tamarack, and pine occur toward the south; along its southern edges the taiga is gradually supplanted by deciduous hardwood forests, or it disappears at the border of the high plains.

The winter climate of the taiga is as severe as that of the tundra, but summers are warmer and longer, having up to 100 frost-free days. Annual precipitation generally exceeds that of the Arctic, and winter snowfall tends to be deep and softly packed within the wind-sheltered depths of the forest.

Animal species are more numerous in the taiga than in the tundra. Woodland caribou are plentiful in the lichen meadows of the transitional zone, while moose is the chief game animal in the deeper forest. Migratory waterfowl constitute another important food resource. Various species of small fur-bearing animals, such as marten, lynx, beaver, fox, and mink, assumed primary economic significance with the advent of the Europeans.

In concluding this brief survey of regional environments, I must emphasize that the culture areas of the present and recent past do not coincide precisely in a geographic sense with those of prehistoric time. Although Arctic and sub-Arctic biomes have existed throughout mankind's presence in the New World, cyclical changes of climate in the post-Pleistocene era caused northward or southward shifts in the boundaries of these zones. Such alterations in the distribution of flora and fauna, in turn, stimulated a corresponding ebb or flow of peoples and cultures, all of which will be explained more fully in later sections of this chapter.

ARCHEOLOGICAL RESEARCH IN THE EASTERN NORTHLANDS

The earliest archeological activity in the eastern Arctic was completely unscientific and amounted to little more than surface collecting or random digging, usually as a subsidiary game on exploratory or whaling expeditions.

Finally, from 1921 to 1924, Knud Rasmussen, the noted Danish explorer, staged his famous Fifth Thule Expedition, which included ethnologist Kaj Birket-Smith and archeologist Therkel Mathiassen. Their fieldwork marked the beginning of scientific archeology in this quadrant of North America. Mathiassen explored widely on Baffin Island and around northern Hudson Bay, discovering an early whale-hunting stage of Inuit culture, which he named Thule. He concluded that the Thule culture had originated in Alaska and was ancestral to the modern Inuit of the central and eastern Arctic. Then, in 1925, a second major archeological landmark was established when Diamond Jenness described another hitherto unknown Arctic culture. This has since come to be known as the Dorset Eskimo culture, but it was not immediately accepted as such by all authorities. Nevertheless, Jenness made the interesting suggestion that Dorset was older than Thule and proposed that a still earlier pre-Dorset phase might yet be found in the eastern Arctic. Within the next several years Jenness and his colleague, W. J. Wintemberg, discovered other sites in Newfoundland that contained unmistakable Dorset materials, and most professional doubts about the authenticity of the Dorset culture evaporated.

In the 1930s, the status of Thule culture in Greenland was thoroughly investigated by Mathiassen, Helge Larsen, and Erik Holtved, who found no evidence of earlier occupations. However, W. D. Strong discovered traces of Dorset culture in northeastern Labrador, and other Dorset sites were excavated in northern Labrador by Douglas Leechman and at Igloolik, Foxe Basin, by Graham Rowley. It was now perfectly evident that Dorset culture was distinct from Thule, although its origins and degree of affiliation with the Inuit continuum remained obscure.

The years following World War II witnessed a dramatic extension of the Dorset spectrum—culturally, geographically, and chronologically. Eigil Knuth discovered the pre-Dorset Independence I occupation in northeastern Greenland, and excavations by Helge Larsen and Jorgen Meldgaard in Disko Bay, southwestern Greenland, delineated a longer sequence of Sarqaq (pre-Dorset), Dorset, and Thule. In the Canadian Arctic, Henry Collins obtained stratified separation of Dorset and Thule levels at Resolute, Cornwallis Island, and Frobisher, Baffin Island, while his T-1 site on Southampton Island yielded a new, early phase of Dorset culture dating from the seventh century BC. Other projects in this period included my investigations in Dorset and Archaic Indian sites in western Newfoundland and southern Labrador and Jorgen Meldgaard's research on seriated pre-Dorset, Dorset, and Thule occupations in the Igloolik area. Meldgaard proposed an Alaskan origin for the pre-Dorset phase and suggested that the later Dorset culture had derived from, or otherwise had been strongly influenced by, boreal-forest adaptations to the south.

That view was not accepted by most Canadian and American scholars, who professed to see a linear continuum of Inuit cultures in the central and eastern Arctic, stemming primarily from ancestral impulses out of Alaska. This latter interpretation received support in the mid-1950s when Louis Giddings explored along the treeline west of Hudson Bay and found an assemblage of microblade materials that resembled his Denbigh Flint complex core and blade culture in western Alaska. I found similar evidence at Dismal and Kamut Lakes, south of Coronation Gulf, and suggested that this was a link between the Dorset continuum and Alaskan forebears. In the 1960s, I also excavated the large Dorset site at Port aux Choix, in northwestern Newfoundland, and confirmed its essential Arctic relationships. The *coup de grâce* for the concept of southern origins for Dorset culture was ultimately delivered when Moreau Maxwell described a 3000-year span of pre-Dorset to Dorset evolution in southern Baffin Island, while William Taylor traced similar events in northern Ungava and Hudson Strait.

Within the past few years, the geographic borders of the Dorset realm have been opened still farther to the west and south. Taylor found more pre-Dorset and Dorset sites on Banks and Victoria islands, Ronald Nash excavated in sites of both stages in the vicinity of Churchill on the west coast of Hudson Bay, and Patrick Plumet examined a pre-Dorset occupation at Great Whale River in southeastern Hudson Bay. In that same area, I discovered a complex of surprisingly late Dorset sites in the entrance to Richmond Gulf, the most recent of which dated ca. AD 1400, and from 1974 to 1975 I surveyed further in the Belcher Islands, finding a long range of Dorset occupations dating approximately from 1000 BC to AD 1000.

Thus, after slightly more than half a century of scientific archeological research in the central and eastern Arctic, it appears that the outlines of Inuit prehistory in that region have been established. In contrast to that level of achievement, the sub-Arctic has received relatively little attention from archeologists, and that mostly in the post-World War II period. This inequity has generally been due to the differing patterns of European exploration in the two zones and, more particularly, to the delayed expansion of modern commercial enterprise and settlement into the forested interior.

In sub-Arctic Quebec-Labrador the earliest aboriginal occupations are related to the Archaic tradition, a term that denotes a major stage of Indian prehistory in which various semisedentary bands subsisted by means of hunting, fishing, and some gathering of wild foods. The first significant archeological find there was made in 1915, when Frank Speck reported a large Archaic concentration at Tadoussac on the north shore of the St. Lawrence River; this important site was later investigated more fully by W. J. Wintemberg and Gordon Lowther. From 1927 to 1928, W. D. Strong found Archaic materials in northeastern Labrador, and Edward Rogers, who explored the interior of south-central Quebec from 1947 to 1950, recorded a large number of sites that ranged from the Archaic into the protohistoric period. Somewhat later, I obtained a date of ca. 4300 BC for the earliest Archaic horizon in southern Labrador. Finally, William Fitzhugh, Robert McGhee, and James

Tuck have since added to our understanding of the northeastern Archaic by defining a subtradition called the Maritime Archaic, which emphasized a seasonal specialization for sea mammal hunting along the Atlantic littoral.

The archeology of the taiga and barren lands west of Hudson Bay has been tapped only during the last 25 years. During the 1950s Richard MacNeish traveled the Mackenzie River country, finding sporadic evidence of an early Paleo-Indian occupation that dated prior to ca. 5000 BC. My own survey, farther east along the middle Thelon River in 1958, indicated that the first people to exploit the barren lands were Indian hunters with lanceolate projectile points of a southern Plano type. Robert McGhee found similar, but considerably later, indications of Plano influence at Bloody Falls on the Coppermine River.

In the southwest Yukon Territory, MacNeish later identified a post-Plano stage of culture, which he named the Northwest Microblade tradition, and William Noble's surveys around Great Slave Lake and in the central Mackenzie District have begun to trace the evolution of these early forest-hunting groups into the historic Athapaskan-speaking tribes of that area.

James Wright, after years of fieldwork in Manitoba and Keewatin District, has hypothesized the existence of a specific Shield Archaic subtradition whose bearers may have been the first Algonquian speakers; most recently, Bryan Gordon excavated stratified sites on the upper Thelon River and proposed that discrete bands of early tundra hunters were ecologically associated with particular herds of caribou in regular migration territories.

Such, in brief retrospect, is the history of archeological research in northeastern North America. It has been clearly determined that man's exploitation of the austere sub-Arctic and Arctic environments has undergone a long and complex evolution. Given the still-fragmented nature of our knowledge, we can perceive some ancient cultural phases more vividly than others, and it is only fair to add that the transition from prehistory into modern times is the least well known of all. We see that throughout the 6000 or 7000 years of cultural development in this region some increments of change must be attributed to migrations and the influx of new people, but equally significant were the constant internal adaptations to the constraints imposed on the indigenes by fluctuating postglacial climate. It remains for us now to examine these ancient cultural responses in greater detail.

PREHISTORIC CULTURE SEQUENCES IN THE SUB-ARCTIC

Northeastern North America consists of the newest land surfaces to be found anywhere on the continent, for that region was last to emerge from the glaciation of the Wisconsin period. That part of the continent had been blanketed by the vast Laurentide sheet, which originated from a set of highland growth centers in Greenland, Ellesmere Island, Baffin Island, Labrador, and Quebec. From the evidence of terminal moraines we know that the sheet once extended as far as western Alberta and south of the Great Lakes-St. Lawrence River system. When deglaciation began, around 12,000 BC, there was a radial shrinkage of this ice cap back toward its centers of origin, albeit the process was not uniform either geographically or chronologically. The area southeast of Great Bear Lake was freed of ice by about 8000 BC, and central Keewatin District by 5000 BC. To the south, the Great Lakes had emerged by 9000 BC and the James Bay area by 5500 BC. South-central Quebec was in the clear by 5000 BC, and the ultimate disappearance of the ice cap in mainland Canada occurred about 3800 BC in the mountains of northeastern Labrador. Around 3000 BC the Laurentide sheet had dwindled to its present-day remnants on Baffin, Devon, and Ellesmere islands and in Greenland.

Thus, the spread of early man into this region became, in effect, a series of centripetal movements, mostly along the radii of deglaciation. As newly liberated landscapes surfaced in the periglacial zone around the periphery of the ice cap, the tundra flora migrated rapidly into the consequent biological vacuum, and various faunal species were then drawn forward by their shifting ecosystems. Man's response came last, and in some areas it was delayed for several centuries by residual postglacial features that physically barred his movements, such as ice-dammed lakes or marine submergence in the Hudson Bay lowlands. In this period of climatic amelioration we can discern two major thrusts of human influence into the northern frontier lands: the earliest came from the country to the west of Hudson Bay, and soon afterward the second developed east of the Great Lakes and diffused along the St. Lawrence corridor into the Quebec-Labrador peninsula (Figure 3.2).

The first active hunting cultures in present-day sub-Arctic latitudes west of Hudson Bay have been identified with the Paleo-Indian stage (see Chapter 1), but as the forest environment encroached toward the north, forming an ever-thickening barrier between the temperate grasslands and the periglacial tundra, new cultural orientations became necessary. The northern Archaic stage emerged in this period of flux, and it was a primary response to forest conditions. In general, this Archaic culture was founded on the ancient big-game-hunting patterns of the preceding Paleo-Indian stage, but as the centuries passed, a variety of regional modifications developed. Caribou hunting remained the chief economic activity in the northern fringes of the forest, but to the south and west other large species, such as elk, moose, and deer, became mainstays. In addition, there was a new emphasis on riverine adaptation and fishing in some areas, on shellfish gathering, and on wild-plant collecting. Far to the east, on the Atlantic littoral, Archaic people developed an important seasonal exploitation of sea mammals.

Furthermore, the Archaic stage was a time of slowly expanding human population. The regional density of hunting camps and larger settlements

104

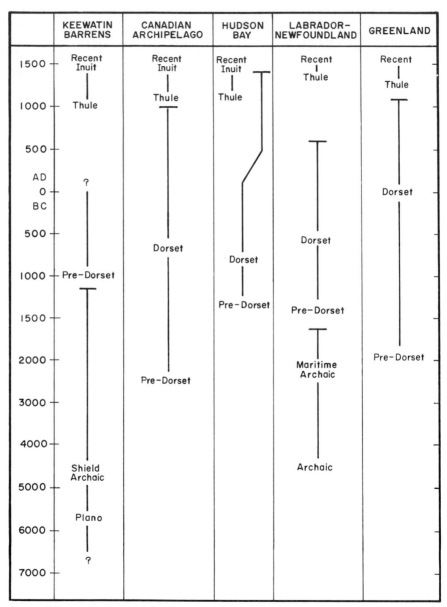

FIGURE 3.2
Prehistoric occupations in the eastern sub-Arctic and the Arctic.

increased, deeper midden deposits in some Archaic sites attest to prolonged or recurrent occupations, and even the clusters of dwelling units within specific sites are frequently more numerous. All such observations suggest a reduction of migratory habits and an enhancement of sedentary ways. So, as technological capabilities improved and exploitation of local food resources was intensified, the hunting-gathering life of the Archaic gradually evolved toward greater economic and social stability, and probably also toward firmer territorial relationships.

West of Hudson Bay, the archeological evidence shows that caribou were the most important game animals throughout the entire Archaic stage and into the historic era. The most significant part of this country was the transitional belt that stretched along the northern edges of the boreal forest; as an ecotone, this zone of mixed environments combined certain advantageous features of both the tundra and the taiga, including plentiful game, supplies of wood for fuel and artifacts, a degree of shelter within the limited forest, and ease of movement through semiopen country. Thus, it afforded a safe operating base for the forest-oriented hunters, from which they could sally forth in summertime, following the migrating caribou herds northward onto the barrens, and into which they could retreat as winter approached.

In this seasonal manner, Archaic hunters became the earliest occupants of the Barren Grounds during the first postglacial warm phase, prior to 1500 BC, when the forest reached approximately 240 kilometers north of the present treeline. Their caribou-hunting sites in central Keewatin were situated along the rivers and lakes that lay athwart the migration paths of the herds, and their northernmost penetration seems to have been along the Thelon River. There, at various narrows or other fording points, the caribou were most vulnerable to interception and ambush as they funneled along habitual paths into the water crossings; correspondingly, the camps, lookouts, and workshop sites of the Archaic hunters were located in these critical places.

One of the most extensive Archaic caribou-hunting sites on the Thelon lay at the west end of Aberdeen Lake, and investigations have shown that the site was occupied on a seasonal basis beginning ca. 5000 BC. The final Archaic occupation there left a semisubterranean house that has been dated ca. 1000 BC, a period when the weather was cooler and more unstable than it is today. As this site was most productive in late summer, when the caribou were returning southward toward the forest edges, the substantial lodge, in contrast to a simple summer tent ring, is probably a reflection of the deteriorating weather conditions. In any case, the Archaic hunters abandoned the site after that occupation, never to return.

The cold trend that began around 1500 BC caused the treeline to shift back southward, and we may assume that as of about 1000 BC the forest was so far distant from the Aberdeen site that journeying between the two had become impractical and even dangerous in the face of approaching winter. Thus, as the Archaic people were unable to cope with winter conditions in the Barren

Grounds, they had no choice but to retreat southward in order to stay within reach of their customary habitat. The vacuum left by their withdrawal was short-lived, however, because the same cold period stimulated an expansion of pre-Dorset Inuit hunters into the interior barrens. Thenceforward, as the climate oscillated in quickening cycles of several centuries' duration, the northern limits of Archaic summer occupation shifted conformably. In the early years of the Christian era the immediate ancestors of the historic Chipewyan came again to the Thelon country on their summer forays.

Recent studies of the Canadian caribou have shown that four separate herds are distributed from west to east across the Barren Grounds, and each of these herds forages in a discrete geographic area. Furthermore, ethnographic analysis of Chipewyan hunting practices has demonstrated that a direct relationship exists between specific Indian bands and one or another of these herds. Thus, the migratory lifeways of sub-Arctic hunters in the historic period have been governed essentially by the north-south seasonal movements of a single herd, in accordance with an ecological man-animal attachment that has obvious survival value, at least for mankind. This same relationship has also been convincingly proved for the pre-Dorset Inuit who infiltrated the Barren Grounds after 1500 BC, and, although proof is lacking, it is plausible to suggest that the Archaic Indian hunters might have operated according to a like economic pattern.

In any event, the caribou was the staff of life in this central region, and we see further testimony of its importance in the artifact assemblages found in Archaic sites. The fundamental kit of stone tools is much the same throughout the entire area, and, aside from frequency shifts in certain types of artifacts, its general character altered only slightly during the long Archaic stage. All of the surviving tool and weapon types were flaked from local varieties of quartzite, and they include the following dominant forms: several kinds of large, lanceolate spear or lance points; crude burins and gravers; leaf-shaped side blades for knives; discoidal biface knives; asymmetric and semilunar biface knives; triangular end scrapers; turtleback core scrapers; flat spall scrapers; denticulate or saw scrapers; wedge-shaped cores and coarse prismatic blades; rectangular adze blades; wedges; pebble hammerstones; and numerous amorphous scrap flakes showing edge wear (Figure 3.3). Artifacts made of organic materials, such as bone, antler, or wood, are seldom recovered, except in late period sites.

It is impossible to identify specific functions for all of these implements, but they clearly represent a considerable spectrum of job specialization. Here are all the basic tools for hunting and killing, skinning and butchering, cutting and splitting bone, scraping and softening hides, and cutting, scraping, or adzing wood, antler, and bone for the fabrication of other artifacts. Given the minimal inventories of perishable materials, it is difficult to make further inferences about cultural content or pattern. We must assume, however, that the Archaic hunters possessed, at the very least, sufficient skills and experience

FIGURE 3.3
Type specimens from the Shield Archaic, chipped from coarse-grained quartzite and found at several interior Barren Grounds sites northwest of Hudson Bay: *a, b,* Keewatin lanceolate points; *c, d,* burinated points; *e,* biface knife; *f,* skin scraper; *g, h,* snub-nosed end scrapers.

for successful winter survival in the boreal forest, particularly with respect to the manufacture of adequate clothing and shelter.

As for cultural evolution in the Archaic of this region, there are several artifact types that serve as dependable, if rather slight, indicators of both continuity and change. The fundamental relationship between Paleo-Indian and Archaic is best established through the medium of the Keewatin lanceolate point with ground basal edges, a type that derived from the Agate Basin style of the north-central plains and developed, in turn, by slow stages into several variants with contracting stems. Other such trait linkages are the denticulate or saw scrapers, wedges made from fragments of other kinds of bifacial tools, and the use of broken projectile points for the manufacture of burins. Otherwise, throughout the Archaic stage west of Hudson Bay there was an increase in the frequency of projectile points and scrapers, a gradual shift from large lanceolate points to smaller side-notched types, and a general decrease in the occurrence of large biface tools.

James Wright has suggested that this basic forest culture should be called the Shield Archaic, for its distribution around Hudson Bay conforms closely to the spread of the Canadian Shield itself; he has further postulated that the people of the Shield Archaic spoke an Algonquian language and thus were directly ancestral to the central and eastern Algonquian tribes of the historic period. There is considerable merit to both these hypotheses, inasmuch as they account for the strong cultural continuities that existed in the sub-Arctic forest zone from the origin of the taiga economy into historic time. Also, this terminology permits us to differentiate other localized specializations that developed elsewhere in the boreal forest, some of them resulting from external diffusion and others arising from internal change and adaptation.

We have seen, for example, that western caribou hunters with Paleo-Indian affiliations were probably the first occupants of the Canadian Shield region west of Hudson Bay. The archeological evidence from interior Quebec is still too scarce to trace these same influences there, but the few facts that we do have indicate the presence of the ancient taiga complex. However, in this region another significant impulse is detectable, one that derived from the northeastern woodlands south of the St. Lawrence (see Chapter 6) and gave rise to the early cultures of the Quebec-Labrador peninsula. In this area there was a distinctive sub-tradition that has been aptly named the Boreal Archaic.

So far, all evidence relating to the northeastern Boreal Archaic comes from a few sites around the coastal periphery of Quebec-Labrador. Typical of these are one small kill site on the east coast of Hudson Bay a few miles north of Great Whale River, seven workshop sites on raised marine beach lines at Tadoussac on the St. Lawrence River, a number of small locales scattered through the forest in south-central Quebec north of Lake St. John, a series of workshops and settlements in southern Labrador at the Strait of Belle Isle, an Archaic burial ground at Port aux Choix on the northwest coast of Newfoundland, the Old Stone culture along the central coast of Labrador, and a few other recent discoveries in central and northern Labrador. Of all these sites, only one, at Northwest Corners, Labrador, can be identified with any certainty as an interior caribou hunters' camp; all the others were oriented to inland waterways and lakes or toward the sea.

This distribution may not adequately reflect the overall importance of the caribou in Boreal Archaic economy, but it does indicate that there may have been a standard settlement pattern of seasonal migration, with periodic nodes of concentration at certain productive fishing camps. As I shall explain presently, the faunal resources of the sea played a key role in Archaic culture along the littoral of the St. Lawrence and the Atlantic, but the inland aspect of life probably depended heavily on fish and the small fur-bearing animal species, such as hare, muskrat, beaver, wolf, otter, and so on, that inhabit the taiga. The only large game available in the interior plateau country was the caribou, for moose and deer are known to have been quite recent arrivals in the area.

The highest of the sites at Tadoussac, and therefore presumably the oldest of the series, was found on an ancient raised beach that is believed to correlate with the postglacial Champlain Sea stage, dating to about 4000 BC. This site yielded a collection with a high frequency of crudely shaped, percussion-flaked core tools, similar to assemblages from several sites in the interior around Lakes Mistassini and Albanel. It has been conjectured that these finds may represent a pre-Archaic level of culture, perhaps related to a theoretical stage that has been noted elsewhere in North America and tentatively called the Unspecialized Lithic, or pre-Projectile Point stage. The general concept of such a stage is not accepted by all authorities, and it certainly has not been satisfactorily confirmed in the Quebec-Labrador area. On the other hand, it is fully possible that the anomalous inventories from these sites may be a simple reflection of their nature as workshops, where preliminary manu-facturing was done at a crucial lookout point, while hunters waited for the appearance of game, or else in the immediate vicinity of a quarry area. Otherwise, it can be stated positively that the oldest dates presently known for the Boreal Archaic in southern Labrador also reach back to around 4000 BC.

There are no analogs of Paleo-Indian projectile points in Boreal Archaic assemblages, but there are lanceolate forms, ranging from small to large, usually with tapered stems or corner-notched bases; other point variants are leaf-shaped, triangular, or lozenge forms. In settlement areas with a cus-tomarily broad spectrum of artifact types, the points are usually mixed with a great variety of chipped stone biface tools, including large leaf-shaped blades or knives, semilunar knives, percussion-flaked choppers and adzes, side and end scrapers, occasional gravers, and hammerstones and anvils (Figure 3.4).

In the middle and late phases of the Boreal Archaic most of these imple-ments were retained, but there was a marked shift in the frequencies of projectile point styles, notably a reduction of the stemmed, lanceolate type in the face of increasing dependence on side-notched points and finally on triangular points. Also, the manufacturing technique of pecking, grinding,

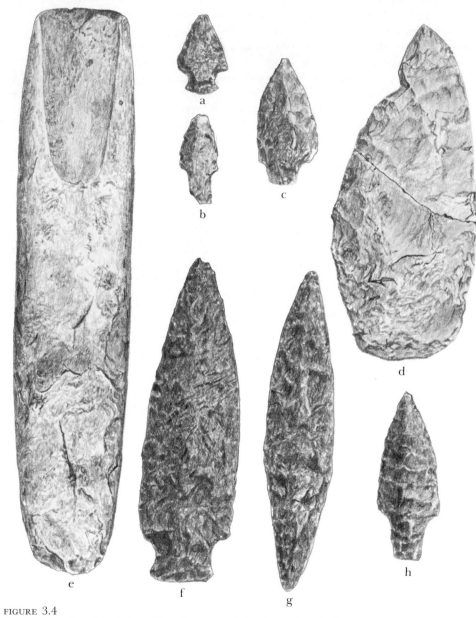

FIGURE 3.4
Northeastern Boreal Archaic artifacts from coastal sites in southern Labrador: *a–c,* small projectile points; *d,* biface knife; *e,* gouge; *f–h,* large projectile points.

and polishing came into fashion as the Boreal Archaic matured. Silicified slate was the favored material for grinding and polishing, and the predominant types made in this manner included long, bayonetlike projectile points with ovoid or faceted cross-sections and what are presumed to be heavy woodworking tools, such as chisels, adzes, and gouges.

Aside from this use of slate, several local varieties of colored quartzite, cherts, and chalcedony were chosen for manufacturing flaked tools. One preferred kind of translucent gray quartzite, which has been found in numerous northeastern Archaic sites, has been traced to a unique quarry near Ramah Bay in northern Labrador. This occurrence, in conjunction with an array of chipped and ground and polished tool types that are commonly found together in the same sites, serves to emphasize the highly uniform character of Boreal Archaic culture from Maine to Labrador. In fact, the combinations of traits are often so precisely alike in many sites throughout the area that one may plausibly regard this as an integrated diffusion sphere.

For years, the concentration of Archaic sites along the shores of the St. Lawrence and in the Strait of Belle Isle area has engendered speculation concerning the economic orientation of these particular locales. Their basic culture, of course, was Archaic, and their elaborate adaptation to the sub-Arctic forest fully justifies the term *Boreal Archaic*. However, these littoral sites confront deep waters that are exceedingly rich in marine species, especially seals and small whales, and it has been noted that similar ground slate bayonet points were successfully used for prehistoric whale hunting in southern Alaska. Therefore, it was suggested, this coastal expression of the Archaic might well have had a seasonal maritime specialization. Unfortunately, the evidence for such an inference was limited to stone artifacts, and the proposition could never be proved because these littoral sites were all stationed on acidic sands from which all organic deposits had long since disappeared.

Then, in the late 1960s, a large Archaic cemetery was accidentally uncovered in the village of Port aux Choix on the northwestern coast of Newfoundland, and extensive investigations there produced a rich and unprecedented inventory of coastal Archaic culture as it existed for a period of about 1000 years, between the late third and the late second millennia BC. The preparation of the more than 100 individual burials and the inclusion of red ochre and elaborate grave furnishings testified to a corpus of beliefs regarding the world of the supernatural and life in the hereafter; in addition, the grave goods afforded a comprehensive view of primary food-getting activities, showing strong emphasis on sea mammal hunting. The complement of stone artifacts included all the ground and polished slate tools and weapons mentioned above, but flaked stone tools were surprisingly few, possibly because they related to mundane, less significant work. But, most interesting of all, there was a well-developed harpoon complex consisting of barbed bone points, open-socketed toggling harpoon heads of bone, and

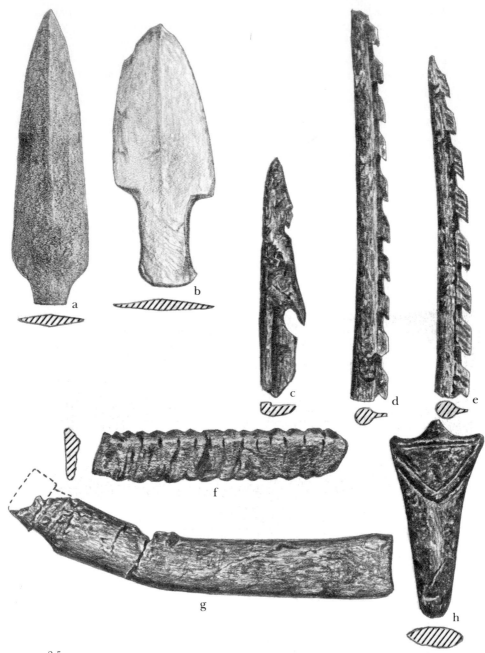

FIGURE 3.5
Northeastern Maritime Archaic artifacts, recovered from burial sites in western Newfoundland:
a, b, beveled slate projectile points; *c,* bone harpoon point with open socket; *d, e,* barbed bone fish spear fragments; *f,* serrated stone scraper or saw; *g,* bone knife handle with scarfed tip; *h,* soapstone (steatite) amulet.

whalebone foreshafts (Figure 3.5). Associated with these were daggers of walrus ivory, antler, and caribou leg bone, as well as eyed needles of bone, caribou scapula skin scrapers, bone beaming tools, and decorated bone combs. Alkaline soils accounted for the preservation of these materials, although wood artifacts did not survive. Finally, the cultural inventory included many shell beads, undoubtedly for the decoration of clothing, and numerous parts of animals and birds, such as seal claws, bird beaks, and so on, together with two conventionalized stone sculptures of killer whales. The latter strongly suggest the practice of wearing amulets and a belief in sympathetic, imitative magic.

Given its level of intricate specialization for marine hunting, this aspect of Archaic culture has been named the Maritime Archaic, a term that seems appropriate for all of the closely related bands that coevally inhabited the Atlantic shores from Labrador to Maine. Naturally, the emphasis on marine hunting was purely seasonal, and at other times of the year the Maritime Archaic people continued to exploit the land resources that were of fundamental importance everywhere in the sub-Arctic zone. Although there is no direct archeological evidence, we must infer that these people possessed considerable skill in boat building and seamanship, if only for inshore hunting. The woodland cultures of later periods are known to have had dugout and bark-covered canoes, and in the Boreal and Maritime Archaic we recognize the presence of specific tools, such as ground slate chisels, adzes, and gouges, that were potentially useful for the construction of similar craft.

According to the Port aux Choix cemetery dates, the Maritime Archaic flourished during the first postglacial warm period, and thereafter its influence may have waned as competitive pre-Dorset Inuit moved south along the Labrador coast. Later, in the early centuries of the Christian era, Dorset Inuit culture appears to have dominated these shores, and the last Indian practitioners of sea mammal hunting may have been the Beothucks of Newfoundland, before their ultimate obliteration by European settlers.

In the final analysis, we do not know precisely what became of Archaic culture in the sub-Arctic zone, although it seems eminently logical to assume that it evolved into the various Indian cultures that occupied the region at the time of European discovery. There is sufficient documentary evidence to show that such groups as the Beothucks of Newfoundland, the Montagnais-Naskapi of Quebec-Labrador, the Cree and Ojibwa of the Hudson Bay lowlands, the Chipewyan west of Hudson Bay, and other Athapaskan-speaking tribes living farther northwest all practiced a basic taiga economy, many elements of which are traceable back into archeological horizons.

Except for the Beothucks, all of these people have survived to the present day, although they lost most of their ancient heritage in exchange for metal knives, guns, blankets, beads, and rum. The dictates of the fur trade imposed on them the strange concepts of territoriality and property, an unbalanced stress on trapping and overkill, and artificial migration cycles keyed to isolated trading posts, while their universe of spirits was superseded by a Christian god. To these last representatives of the primeval boreal forest way of life, the Europeans brought decimating disease, social inferiority, and cataclysm.

THE INUIT: PIONEERS OF THE EASTERN ARCTIC

Even as the occupation of the eastern sub-Arctic by early Indian hunters was initially governed by deglaciation, the phenomena of the Laurentide retreat and subsequent postglacial climatic changes affected the spread of the Inuit across the Arctic. However, man's adaptation to this circumpolar biome represents a special peak in the long epic of human evolution, for, barring only Antarctica, it was the last terrestrial niche to be conquered. From present archeological evidence, we know that man had reached into the eastern Arctic by approximately 2500 BC.

Before recapitulating this story, we must consider two related matters. The first concerns the name of the arctic people conventionally referred to as Eskimos. Although it has been otherwise explained, this term is probably a French rendition (*Esquimaux*) of an Algonquian word that means "eaters of raw flesh." Eastern boreal forest Indians named the arctic hunters in this manner, and the pejorative overtones suggest that early contacts between the two peoples at various places along the treeline were not always congenial. Now, in our time, there is a trend toward use of the alternate term *Inuit* because this is the Eskimos' own word for themselves, it means simply "the people."

The second matter relates to the Inuit as an ethnic group: How are they identified and differentiated from other peoples and cultures, and, more specifically, how do they differ from the Indians of North America? These questions deserve detailed and complex answers, but here I can offer only a brief characterization of the Inuit and their culture, as known from the period of European contact. At that time they exhibited a remarkable degree of linguistic, cultural, and racial uniformity throughout their entire geographic range, from Alaska to Greenland, despite many regional adaptations to local differences in the environment. Further back in prehistoric time, such adaptational differences were even more pronounced.

Linguistically, the Inuit constitute a unique speech family that has no discernible relationship to any New World Indian language; some scholars believe that it may be akin to the Uralic stock of Eurasia. The Inuit language had an ancestral unity with Aleut, from which it diverged about 6000 years ago, and thereafter it evolved into two distinctive subfamily units: the *Yupik* of southwestern Alaska and *Inupik,* which includes all dialects between western

Alaska and Greenland. The dialects are mutually comprehensible within each of the subfamilies.

From a cultural point of view, the Inuit were the only people who achieved a successful year-round adaptation to the Arctic by means of hunting and fishing, without the benefit of any domesticated food resources. The primary food quest was the hunting of sea mammals, including seal, walrus, and whale, although some groups practiced a dual subsistence economy with seasonal dependence on caribou. The ultimate secret of their success is explained by their specialized weapons for hunting sea mammals, particularly the toggle-headed harpoon, and their elaborate methods for locating, stalking, and retrieving this game, whether in open water, at the ice edge, or through breathing holes in the sea ice in the depth of winter. Aside from the harpoon, they had other more common weapons, such as lances, knives, fish and bird spears, and the bow and arrow. In the characteristically barren arctic environment they capitalized on scarce raw materials with great ingenuity, using all animal parts in the fabrication of their material effects, including skin, gut, bones, claws, horn, ivory, sinew, and baleen. Their cutting implements were generally chipped from stone. Containers were made of skin or, in the case of cooking pots and lamps, of soapstone. The primary fuel was seal blubber, or sometimes caribou fat. The Inuit traveled and hunted at sea in skin-covered boats such as the kayak or the umiak and had sledges for winter use, pulled at first by human beings and later by dogs. Naturally, they also had efficient protection against winter cold, including tailored, double-layered skin garments, and a variety of house types adapted to particular seasons and available raw materials, of which the most ingenious was the snow house of the central regions.

Finally, the Inuit also stand somewhat apart from the New World Indian peoples in terms of biological anthropology. They represent a specialized branch of the Mongoloid stock of east Asia, and, together with the Chukchi, Koryak, Yukaghir, and Itelmen of northeastern Siberia, are sometimes referred to as Arctic Mongoloids. Aside from its general resemblance to other Mongoloid peoples, this variant group exhibits certain physiological and structural characteristics that apparently are advantageous for survival in arctic environments. For example, the flat facial morphology, with the depressed nasal profile and accompanying narrow inner aperture, is effective in reducing the loss of body heat. It has also been suggested that slight differences in metabolic rate and the vascular system may function toward the same end. Moreover, the average physical proportions of these people also enhance heat retention and maintenance of the body's core temperature; their typical body build is compact and arms and legs are relatively short in respect to trunk length. This means that there is less skin surface per unit of body mass and consequently a relative decrease in the amount of internal heat lost by radiation. Not all authorities accept this interpretation of the biological evidence, but if these are adaptive traits, then the Inuit and other Arctic Mongoloids are genetically better equipped than others to withstand some of the stresses of natural selection in polar environments.

The earliest known occupation of the central and eastern Arctic, beginning early in the third millennium BC, is called pre-Dorset. This is recognized as the ancestral stock of the Inuit in that region because it forms an unbroken continuity with the succeeding Dorset Eskimo culture. Unfortunately, no linguistic or skeletal evidence is available from this pioneering stage, but its derivation from known Alaskan forebears has been archeologically established. It was part of the wave of the Arctic Small Tool tradition that spread eastward along the North Slope of Alaska into Canada, and that tradition, in turn, originated in the Denbigh Flint complex in the Bering Strait area. The direct relationship between the Denbigh complex and pre-Dorset is unmistakable, as the basic tool kit of each contains carefully prepared cores and microblades, burins, retouched burin spalls, incipient side-notched knives, and several other types of artifacts.

The eastward spread of the pre-Dorset hunters occurred toward the end of the first warm period that wasted the Laurentide ice sheet to its present extent by about 3000 BC, and the evidence indicates that they were firmly established around northern Hudson Bay by 2000 BC. Their movement out of the west appears to have developed rapidly, within a span of several centuries, and it passed through the islands of the Canadian Archipelago into northern Greenland. So far, the oldest known sites, dating to ca. 2400 BC, are on the south coast of Baffin Island, and the pre-Dorset Independence I complex of northeastern Greenland has been dated close to 2000 BC.

The initial postglacial warm period lasted until 1500 BC, by which time the treeline west of Hudson Bay had advanced more than 240 kilometers north of its present position and pre-Dorset had begun to expand southward. During a cold-weather trend in the next four centuries this movement continued; the pre-Dorset hunters shifted back westward into Victoria and Banks islands, southward onto the Canadian mainland, into the Barren Grounds of central Keewatin, and down along the east and west coasts of Hudson Bay. The pre-Dorset Sarqaq occupation also appeared in southern Greenland at this time.

Pre-Dorset settlement patterns are not yet fully known, but their sites were coastal and based on seal and walrus hunting, with occasional emphasis in some areas on musk ox and caribou. Seasonal orientation is indicated by differing house types, including presumed summer tent locations in residual boulder rings and ovoid winter houses with central slab-rock hearth areas. As these latter dwellings lack well-defined perimeters, it has been inferred that the winter houses may have been constructed of snow blocks. In food-rich areas, a few deeper midden deposits suggest recurrent occupation of these preferred sites over long periods of time.

Tool assemblages were made of chipped stone, seal and walrus bone, and ivory. Major types used in hunting include toggle harpoon heads with open sockets, single line holes, and slotted ends for the insertion of triangular stone points (Figure 3.6). The throwing board was apparently unknown, although the possibility of a hooked spear thrower of antler has been reported from northern Foxe Basin. Spears and lances were used against caribou and musk ox, and their open-socketed antler heads frequently had inset side blades of chipped stone. The presence of a short, recurved, composite bow is proved by finds of bow segments and braces. Arrows had foreshafts of wood or bone with blunt tips for birds and small game; for larger game the arrows were fitted with triangular or tapering-stemmed chert points. In the Igloolik area, dogs were present throughout the pre-Dorset occupations and may have been used as hunting aids.

The most important manufacturing tools were burins, used for engraving and sectioning bone and ivory; burin spalls, many of them minutely re- touched, for engraving, sinew cutting, and other delicate jobs; numerous small end scrapers of chert, probably for shaping wood, antler, or ivory, and larger, more roughly flaked stone scrapers for hide dressing; a considerable variety of stemmed and side-notched knife blades for hafting in wood or bone handles; fine-grained, granitic abrading stones; adzes of silicified slate for woodworking or shaping soapstone pots and lamps; numerous random flakes of stone, sometimes retouched, for odd jobs of many kinds; and the ever- present microblades, which were useful for many cutting functions. Gen- erally, these implements were chipped from local varieties of chert, but quartz crystals were also a favored material for microblades. Ground and polished slate knives were used infrequently for butchering.

We cannot in all instances define specific functions for these tools, but it is clear that many of them were carefully specialized for particular tasks. Hence, the major game animals of land and sea were successfully hunted in all seasons, and suitable tools were at hand for butchering, food preparation, and the manipulation of all raw materials, such as hides, bone, ivory, antler, wood, and stone. Needles of bone and ivory attest to the making of tailored clothing, and small, ovoid soapstone lamps, as well as natural rock spalls, served as vessels for the life-sustaining fire of burning seal blubber. In some of the later pre-Dorset winter houses the central hearth boxes made of vertical stone slabs were probably lined with green skins to serve as cooking pots, the contents being raised to boiling temperature by the addition of heated stones.

There is still much to be learned about these pre-Dorset pioneers of the central and eastern Arctic, but we know that they met the progressive chal- lenges of the environment and endured for some 1500 years. Ultimately, in the period from 1100 to 950 BC, their culture evolved toward the patterns that we identify as Dorset, and thenceforward the archeological record be- comes more comprehensive. The emergence of the Dorset phase occurred in

118

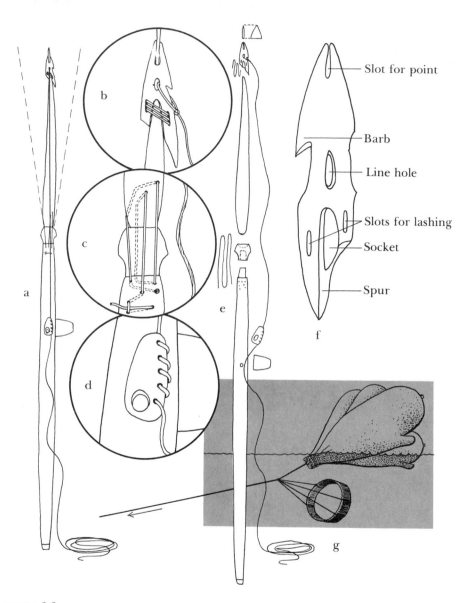

Slot for point

Barb

Line hole

Slots for lashing

Socket

Spur

FIGURE 3.6
Harpoon assembly: *a*, assembled harpoon (dotted lines indicate flexibility of foreshaft); *b*, harpoon head; *c*, flexible joint showing shaft, shaft head, and foreshaft lashed together; *d*, line retainer secured to shaft by knob; *e*, component parts of harpoon; *f*, idealized harpoon head; *g*, sealskin floats and drag attached to end of line. (From *Prehistory of North America*, 2d ed., by Jesse D. Jennings. Copyright © 1968, 1974 by McGraw-Hill, Inc. Used with permission of McGraw-Hill Book Company.)

another warm-weather trend, as the Inuit were spreading back once more into the high Arctic. It was a time of heightened culture change, especially in the core area around northern Foxe Basin and southern Baffin Island, where the genesis of Dorset culture is placed. Although stylistic variation was rapid in the Igloolik area, the overall transition out of pre-Dorset was a notably smooth process, marked by continuity rather than drastic upheaval. By about 700 BC Dorset had achieved its own distinctive character, and in the succeeding centuries it left an imprint of remarkable cultural homogeneity across the eastern Arctic. In addition, we know from skeletal evidence found in Ungava and Newfoundland that the Dorset people were physically related to the specialized Arctic Mongoloids, and thus were true representatives of the Inuit.

In general, Dorset subsistence and domestic activity patterns were much the same as in the pre-Dorset phase, yet even in the face of their obvious adaptive success we note several curious anomalies in their cultural mechanisms. For example, Dorset harpoon gear was lightweight and small, and it lacked the throwing board, but it was nevertheless used effectively against the larger species of seal, walrus, and possibly some of the smaller whales, such as beluga. Their sea mammal hunting techniques seem to have been focused more on winter and spring efforts, judging from the presence of ice creepers made of bone or ivory, small hand-drawn sledges with whalebone-shod runners, and the snow knife, which was presumably used for building snow houses (Figure 3.7). Also, there is no evidence of float and drag equipment for kayak hunting, and no indication of the *maupok* method of hunting seals at their breathing holes through the ice. Hence, the Dorset hunters must have stalked their marine prey along the edges of the shore ice, or out on floes. They used fish harpoons and compound leisters in the salmon streams and for char, but the inventory does not include any specific weapons for bird hunting (Figure 3.8). They also seem to have lacked the bow and arrow, a fact which may indicate their greater reliance on summer and fall hunting of caribou with spears at the water-fording places by means of organized drives and ambush techniques. It was formerly believed that the Dorset Inuit did not have domesticated dogs, but the recent discovery of dog bones in two sites on the Belcher Islands proves their limited presence in that phase. They may have been used as hunting aids, or sometimes as food, but they were not employed as traction animals for hauling sledges.

In many Dorset sites we have observed an increased frequency of blubber lamps, either simple rock spalls or soapstone vessels, and this too suggests a greater use of snow houses and more emphasis on winter ice hunting. However, the Dorset people built several kinds of houses and shelters, including simple, round summer tents, and winter dwellings that were round, sometimes rectangular with floors excavated as much as 60 centimeters below the surrounding ground surface. This latter type did not have a cold-trap entrance, but there was usually a central hearth structure and occasionally

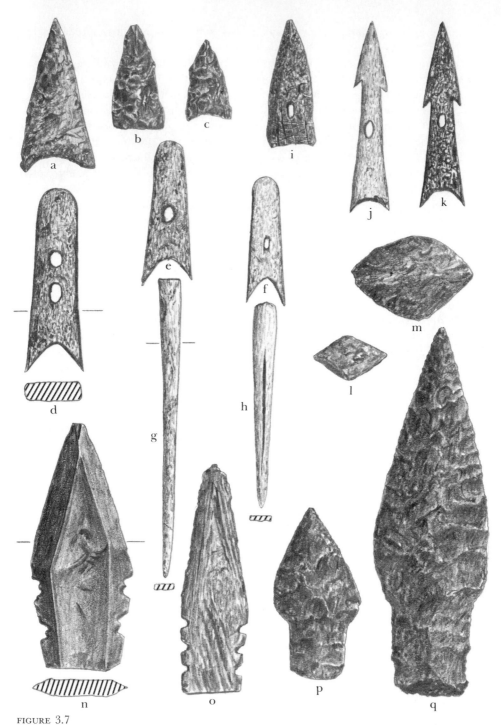

FIGURE 3.7
Dorset Eskimo hunting weapons: *a–c*, flaked chert harpoon points; *d–f*, slotted bone harpoon heads; *g, h*, bone foreshafts; *i*, bone harpoon point, *j, k*, self-pointed bone harpoon heads; *l, m*, chert sideblades; *n, o*, beveled slate lance points; *p, q*, flaked chert spear points.

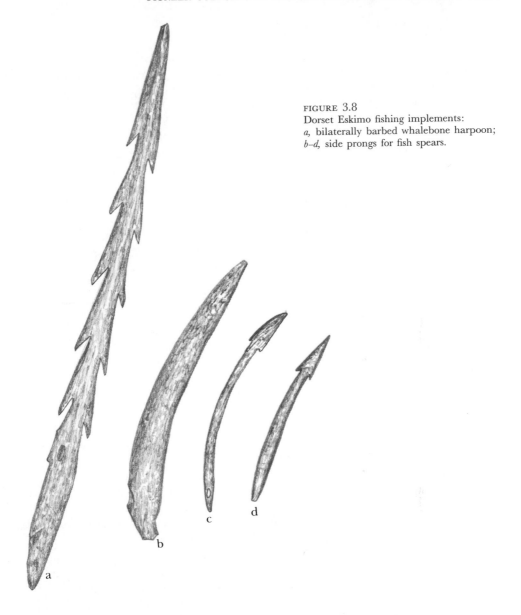

FIGURE 3.8
Dorset Eskimo fishing implements:
a, bilaterally barbed whalebone harpoon;
b–d, side prongs for fish spears.

side benches or a raised sleeping platform in the rear. Superstructures were framed with driftwood or spruce poles, when available, and covered with hides and banked with sod.

Dorset artisans were expert stone flakers, and their basic core and blade technology was clearly related to the Arctic Small Tool tradition and the Denbigh Flint complex in the western Arctic. They introduced a new emphasis on grinding and polishing, however, especially for adzes, knives, skin scrapers, flensing tools, and burinlike gravers. They also favored the practice of side notching as an aid to hafting their knives, scrapers, and burins. Another Dorset innovation was the use of caribou tibia and scapulae as skin scrapers. Curiously, the bow drill was missing in this culture, and all holes in bone or ivory artifacts were laboriously incised with delicate cutting tools, such as microblades of chert or quartz crystal (Figure 3.9).

While some art objects of a magico-religious nature have been found in a few pre-Dorset sites, in the Dorset phase this form of expression was elaborate and highly evolved. The Dorset people conceived and executed a fascinating array of realistic and conventionalized carvings in wood, bone, and ivory, depicting human beings, spirit monsters, and the primary animals of their economy. We interpret these through ethnographic analogy with recent Inuit culture, concluding that Dorset hunters were well aware of a powerful supernatural universe around them. There is a substantial possibility that some of their groups maintained an institutionalized form of shamanism.

The Dorset phase attained its maximum distribution in the period from 200 BC to about AD 400, and for some centuries thereafter it persisted strongly in the core area. Viable outlying colonies were scattered through the Arctic Archipelago as far west as Banks Island, along the shores of Hudson Bay, in Greenland, Labrador, and in Newfoundland, where the Dorset occupation existed farther south than any group of Inuit has ever gone. Then, around AD 1000, their ambient world was disrupted by a totally new immigrant force from the west—the Thules. Confronted with the Thules' superior technology and arctic adaptation, Dorset culture suddenly was at a competitive disadvantage. Unable to meet this challenge, it gradually slipped into decline and ultimately disappeared. The last known representatives of the Dorset phase survived in Richmond Gulf, southeastern Hudson Bay, until AD 1400.

The Thule stage was destined to be ancestral to the present-day Inuit of the central and eastern Arctic. Originating from the Birnirk phase in northern Alaska around AD 900 (see Chapter 2), the Thule culture moved rapidly eastward during a period of warming climate when the distribution of permanent pack ice probably shifted northward in the Archipelago. Thule subsistence activities consisted mainly of the hunting of seals, walrus, and large whales, the latter at first being taken in open water leads during the spring, but later probably in open summer waters. The sealskin-covered kayak and the more substantial umiak were used for this maritime hunting and also afforded means of rapid transportation in the summer. In winter the Thule people used sleds drawn by dogs. The bow and arrow was the chief weapon for hunting caribou and musk ox; birds and fish were taken with bolas, bird darts, nets, and leisters; and a wide variety of specialized harpoons were used, often propelled by a throwing board. In the west, the Thules made a crude, grit-tempered pottery, but this was later supplanted by soapstone vessels in the central region. Thule settlement patterns generally were coastally

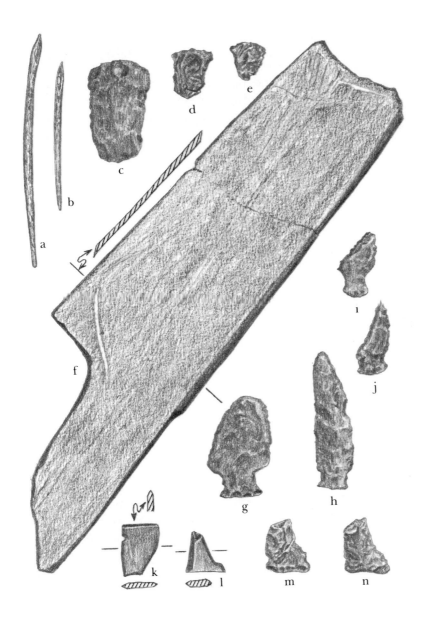

FIGURE 3.9
Manufacturing tools of the Dorset Eskimos: *a, b,* bone needles; *c–e,* flaked chert snub-
nosed end scrapers; *f,* beveled slate flensing knife; *g–j,* asymmetrical flaked chert biface
knives; *k, l,* ground and polished grooving tools with beveled edges; *m, n,* flaked chert
burins.

oriented, and housing consisted of conical, skin-covered tents, temporary snow houses on winter hunting sorties, and permanent winter houses. The latter were often semisubterranean, with frames constructed of driftwood or whale ribs and jawbones, sod coverings, and sloping entrance passages with a cold trap. The size of these settlements proves that the Thule population dominated the thinner densities of the preceding Dorset continuum. Their cultural inventory contains all of the tools, weapons, and other equipment that we customarily see in the Inuit's superb adaptation to the Arctic.

In view of this superiority of numbers and technology, it is not surprising that Dorset culture was forced into a secondary status. The precise reasons for its extinction are still somewhat obscure, but in all probability it did not suffer complete obliteration. We know, in fact, that the two peoples lived more or less side by side in some areas for a period of 200 years, and yet there is no evidence of aggressive conflict between them. Thus, it seems likely that a genetic and cultural blending occurred, a prehistoric example of the overpowering and assimilation of relatively weak indigenous people by relatively powerful invaders. As proof of this acculturation, it has been suggested that several Dorset traits can be seen in later Thule culture: the snow knife and knowledge of snow house construction, the transverse line hole harpoon head, whalebone sled shoes (Figure 3.10), and the use of soapstone for lamps and cooking pots. Also, some authorities claim that vestiges of Dorset culture were perpetuated among the recently extinct Sadlermiut of Southampton Island and the Angmagssalik of East Greenland.

Sometime after AD 1300 there was a reverse movement of Thule culture back toward the west, and for several generations the coastal areas of the central Arctic were abandoned. This development seems in part to have been a response to another cyclical deterioration of the climate; in addition, postglacial isostatic rebound caused a shoaling of the central arctic seas and a consequent retreat of the larger whales to deeper and more distant waters. From that time forward, the various bands of Thule people scattered across the Arctic experienced a generally benign evolution and descent into the local regional components of the historic Inuit. This process has been firmly documented for the Greenlanders, the central Netsilik, and the Caribou Eskimos of the Barren Grounds, all of whose recent origins in the Thule stage can be traced through archeological evidence.

In stark contrast to the contact history of the Indians in the sub-Arctic, most of the Inuit escaped early cataclysmic confrontations with explorers and merchants from the Old World. The Norse episode in Greenland can be dubiously honored as the true beginning of the Europeanization of the New World, and the "skraelings" encountered there by Norsemen, not long after their arrival in AD 985, were Thule people. However, the trauma caused by those foreign colonies, even during a life span of several centuries, was relatively slight, and it exerted a mostly ephemeral influence on native life in Greenland. In any case, the first Norse occupation there died of under-

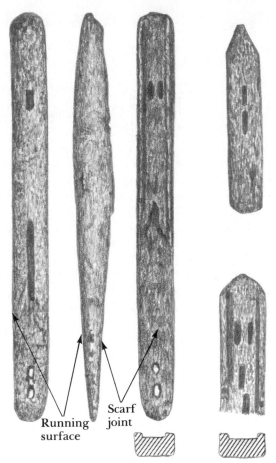

Running surface

Scarf joint

FIGURE 3.10
Whalebone sledge runners of the Dorset Eskimos. These sleds were pulled by people, not dogs, and the runners were fastened to the sled with rawhide lashings.

nourishment, probably by the mid-fifteenth century, and it was the Inuit who survived.

The European whaling industry in North American waters grew constantly through the eighteenth and nineteenth centuries, but after the whalers set up wintering stations on Baffin Island and elsewhere, the exploitation became so severe that the most prized whale species were hunted nearly to extinction by 1910. During this period a few of the Inuit worked aboard the ships or in the seasonal shore stations, and some of the eastern groups suffered painfully from new epidemic diseases introduced from abroad. Most of the people, however, remained inadvertently shielded behind central Arctic bastions, which the Europeans did not fully penetrate until the early decades of the twentieth century.

Now, in a time of modern enlightenment and raised consciousness, the politicized Inuit Brotherhoods are striving for fraternity and equality in the outer world of mankind, and, as a consequence, their ancient lifeways will soon be no more.

CONCLUSION

Prehistoric research in the northeastern quadrant of North America has passed through its childhood of antiquarian curiosity and through an adolescence of ethnographic reconstruction and historiography, and it is now in a more mature phase of true anthropological inquiry. It seems safe to claim that we have managed so far to block in the essential outlines of northern prehistory and to establish a crude chronological framework for its development. However, there are still huge areas in both the sub-Arctic and the Arctic that are physically unknown to archeologists, and until they have been adequately explored our publications must remain spotted with approximations and uncertainties. A tantalizing future of problem solving lies ahead as we face up to such matters as the ethnic identity of our archeological assemblages, the movement of people versus the transference of ideas, cultural exchange in the ecotone of the transitional forest, environmental determinism and cultural adaptation, human biological response to cold, the social dynamics of northern hunting peoples, and perhaps myriad other questions that we do not yet perceive. Thus, the perspectives of northern prehistory are still deep and partially shrouded in mystery. The ultimate telling of mankind's early story in these cold regions remains a worthy cause.

References Cited and Recommended Sources

Baird, Patrick D. 1964 Polar World. New York: John Wiley.

Byers, Douglas S. 1959 The eastern Archaic: some problems and hypotheses. American Antiquity 24:233–256.

Collins, Henry B. 1950 Excavations at Frobisher Bay, Baffin Island, N.W.T. Annual Report of the National Museum of Canada, Bulletin 118:18–43.

――――. 1955 Excavations of the Thule and Dorset culture sites at Resolute, Cornwallis Island, N.W.T. National Museum of Canada, Bulletin 136:22–35.

――――. 1956a Archaeological investigations on Southampton and Coats islands, N.W.T. Annual Report of the National Museum of Canada for 1954–1955, Bulletin 142:82–113.

――――. 1956b The T-1 site at Native Point, Southampton Island, N.W.T. Anthropological Papers of the University of Alaska 4:2:63–89.

――――. 1957 Archaeological investigations on Southampton and Walrus islands, N.W.T. Annual Report of the National Museum of Canada, Bulletin 147:22–61.

————. 1958 Present status of the Dorset problem. Proceedings of the 32nd International Congress of Americanists, 1956, Copenhagen.

Dekin, Albert A., Jr. 1972 Climatic change and culture change: a correlative study from eastern arctic prehistory. Baker Library, Dartmouth College, Polar Notes XII:11–31.

Fitzhugh, William W. 1972 Environmental archaeology and cultural systems in Hamilton Inlet, Labrador. Smithsonian Contributions to Anthropology, No. 16. Smithsonian Institution Press.

Giddings, J. Louis 1956 A flint site in northernmost Manitoba. American Antiquity 21:(3).

————. 1964 The Archaeology of Cape Denbigh. Providence: Brown University Press.

Gordon, Bryan H. C. 1975 Of men and herds in Barrenland prehistory. Archaeological Survey of Canada Mercury Series, Paper No. 28. National Museums of Canada.

Harp, Elmer, Jr. 1951 An Archaeological survey in the Strait of Belle Isle area. American Antiquity 16:203–220.

————. 1958 Prehistory in the Dismal Lake area, N.W.T., Canada. Arctic 11:4:218–249.

————. 1959 The Moffatt archaeological collection from the Dubawnt country, Canada. American Antiquity 24:4:412–422.

————. 1961 The archaeology of the lower and middle Thelon, Northwest Territories. Arctic Institute of North America, Technical Paper No. 8.

————. 1962 The culture history of the central Barren Grounds. In Prehistoric Cultural Relations Between the Arctic and Temperate Zones of North America, ed. J. M. Campbell, pp. 69–75. Arctic Institute of North America, Technical Paper No. 11.

————. 1964 The cultural affinities of the Newfoundland Dorset Eskimos. National Museum of Canada, Bulletin 200.

————, 1970a The prehistoric Indian and Eskimo cultures of Labrador and Newfoundland. Proceedings of the VIIth International Congress of Anthropological and Ethnological Sciences 10:295–299.

————. 1970b Late Dorset Eskimo art from Newfoundland. Folk 11–12:109–124.

————. 1975 A late Dorset copper amulet from southeastern Hudson Bay. Folk 17:33–44.

————. 1976 Dorset settlement patterns in Newfoundland and southeastern Hudson Bay. In Eastern Arctic Prehistory: Paleoeskimo Problems, ed. Moreau S. Maxwell. Memoirs of the Society for American Archaeology No. 31, pp. 119–138.

Harp, Elmer, Jr., and D. R. Hughes 1968 Five prehistoric burials from Port aux Choix, Newfoundland. Baker Library, Dartmouth College, Polar Notes VIII:1–47.

Holtved, Erik 1944 Archaeological investigations in the Thule district. Meddelelser om Grønland 141:(1).

Jenness, Diamond 1925 A new Eskimo culture in Hudson Bay. The Geographical Review 15:428–437.

Johnson, Frederick 1948 The Rogers' collection from Lakes Mistassini and Albanel, Province of Quebec. American Antiquity 14:2:91–98.

Kimble, George H. T., and Dorothy Good (ed.) 1955 Geography of the northlands. American Geographic Society, Special Publication No. 32. New York: John Wiley.

Knuth, Eigil 1952 An outline of the archaeology of Pearyland. Arctic 5:1:17–33.

————. 1954 The Paleo-Eskimo culture of northern Greenland elucidated by three new sites. American antiquity 19:4:367–381.

————. 1958 Archaeology of the farthest north. Proceedings of the 32nd International Congress of Americanists, 1956, Copenhagen.

Larsen, Helge 1938 Archaeological investigations in Knud Rasmussen land. Meddelelser om Grønland 119:(8).

Larsen, Helge, and Jørgen Meldgaard 1958 Paleo-Eskimo cultures in Disko Bugt, West Greenland. Meddelelser om Grønland 161:(2).

Leechman, Douglas 1943 Two new Cape Dorset culture sites. American Antiquity 8:4:363–375.

Lethbridge, T. C. 1939 Archaeology data from the Canadian Arctic. Journal of the Royal Anthropological Institute 69:187–233.

Lloyd, T. G. B. 1874 On the "Beothucs," a tribe of red Indians supposed to be extinct, which formerly inhabited Newfoundland. Journal of the Royal Anthropological Institute 4:21–39.

Lowther, Gordon R. n.d. The archaeology of the Tadoussac area. Unpublished manuscript, National Museum of Canada.

McGhee, Robert 1970 Excavations at Bloody Falls, N.W.T., Canada. Arctic Anthropology 6:2:52–72.

MacNeish, Richard S. 1951 An archaeological reconnaissance in the northwest territories. National Museum of Canada, Bulletin 123:24–41.

———. 1953 Archaeological reconnaissance in the Mackenzie River drainage. National Museum of Canada, Bulletin 128.

———. 1954 The Pointed Mountain site near Fort Liard, N.W.T., Canada. American Antiquity 19:3:234–253.

———. 1955 Two archaeological sites on Great Bear Lake, Northwest Territories, Canada. National Museum of Canada, Bulletin 136:55–84.

———. 1956 The Engigstciak site on the Yukon Arctic coast. Anthropological Papers of the University of Alaska 4:2:91–111.

Mathiassen, Therkel 1927 Archaeology of the central Eskimos, the Thule culture and its position within the Eskimo culture. Report of the Fifth Thule Expedition, 1921–24 4:(1 and 2).

———. 1930a Inugsuk, a medieval Eskimo settlement in Upernavik District, West Greenland. Meddelelser om Grønland 77:145–340.

———. 1930b An old Eskimo culture in West Greenland: report of an archaeological expedition to Upernavik. Geographical Review 20:605–614.

———. 1931a The present stage of Eskimo archaeology. Acta Archaeologica 2:(2).

———. 1931b Ancient Eskimo settlements in the Kangamiut Area. Meddelelser om Grønland 91:(1).

———. 1934 Contributions to the archaeology of Disko Bay. Meddelelser om Grønland 92:(4).

———. 1958 The Sermermiut Excavations, 1955. Meddelelser om Grønland 161:(3).

Maxwell, Moreau S. 1960 "The movement of cultures in the Canadian high Arctic." Anthropologica, n.s. 11:2:1–13.

———. 1972 Archaeology of the Lake Harbour district, Baffin Island. Archaeological Survey of Canada, Paper No. 6, Mercury Series, National Museums of Canada.

Meldgaard, Jørgen 1952 A Paleo-Eskimo culture in West Greenland. American Antiquity 17:3:222–230.

———. 1960 Prehistoric culture sequences in the eastern Arctic as elucidated by stratified sites at Igloolik. Selected Papers, 5th International Congress of Anthropological and Ethnological Sciences, 1956, pp. 588–595.

———. 1962 On the Formative period of Dorset culture. In Prehistoric Cultural Relations Between the Arctic and Temperate Zones of North America, ed. J. M. Campbell, pp. 92–95. Arctic Institute of North America, Technical Paper No. 11.

Morris, Margaret W. 1973 Great Bear Lake Indians: A historical demography and human ecology. Part I: The situation prior to European contact. Institute for Northern Studies, The Muskox 11:3–27.

Nash, Ronald J. 1969 The Arctic Small Tool tradition in Manitoba. Department of Anthropology, University of Manitoba, Occasional Paper No. 2.

Noble, William C. 1971 Archaeological surveys and sequences in the Central District of Mackenzie, N.W.T. Arctic Anthropology 8:1:102–135.

O'Bryan, Deric 1953 Excavation of a Cape Dorset Eskimo culture Eskimo site, Mill Island, West Hudson Strait. National Museum of Canada, Bulletin 128:40–57.

Rogers, Edward S., and R. A. Bradley 1953 An archaeological reconnaissance in south-central Quebec, 1950. American Antiquity 19:2:138–144.

Rogers, Edward S., and M. H. Rogers 1948 Archaeological reconnaissance of lakes Mistassini and Albanel, Province of Quebec, 1947. American Antiquity 14:2:81–90.

Rowley, Graham 1940 The Dorset culture of the eastern Arctic. American Anthropologist, N.S. 42:490–499.

Smith, J. G. E. n.d. The ecological basis of Chipewyan socio-territorial organization. Unpublished manuscript, University of Waterloo, Ontario.

Speck, Frank G. 1916 An ancient archaeological site on the lower St. Lawrence. Washington, D.C.: Holmes Anniversary Volume. pp. 427–433.

Strong, W. D. 1930 A stone culture from northern Labrador and its relation to the Eskimo-like cultures of the northeast. American Anthropologist, N.S. 32:126–143.

Taylor, William E., Jr. 1964 Interim report of an archaeological survey in the central Arctic, 1963. Anthropological Papers of the University of Alaska 12:1:46–55.

———. 1967 Summary of archaeological field work on Banks and Victoria Islands, Arctic Canada, 1965. Arctic Anthropology 4:1:221–243.

———. 1968 The Arnapik and Tyara sites, an archaeological study of Dorset culture origins. Memoirs of the Society for American Archaeology, No. 22.

Terasmae, J. 1961 Notes on Late Quaternary climatic changes in Canada. Annals of the New York Academy of Sciences 96:1:658–675.

Tuck, James A. 1970 An Archaic Indian Cemetery in Newfoundland. Scientific American 222:6:112–121.

Wintemberg, W. J. 1939–1940 Eskimo sites of the Dorset culture in Newfoundland. American Antiquity 5:2:83–102; 5:4:309–333.

———. 1943 Artifacts from ancient workshop sites near Tadoussac, Saguenay County, Quebec. American Antiquity 8:4:313–340.

Wright J. V. 1972a The Shield Archaic. Publications in Archaeology, National Museums of Canada.

———. 1972b The Aberdeen Site, Keewatin District, N.W.T. Archaeological Survey of Canada, Paper No. 2, Mercury Series, National Museums of Canada.

Alternating mountain and valley topograph is characteristic of the Great Basin. Native peoples systematically exploited the resources of different altitudinal zones in the course of their annual round.

During the earlier periods of occupation at Hogup Cave, Utah, the occupants looked out over a shallow lake with fringing marshland. This setting is typical of many Great Basin sites.

CHAPTER FOUR

The Far West

C. Melvin Aikens

Despite the physical diversity of the large region covered in this chapter and the concomitant differences in the adaptations of the prehistoric inhabitants to their environments, there were some remarkable cultural continuities through time and similarities over distance. Dr. Aikens describes some of these similarities as well as discussing the great variety of successful adaptations among the aboriginal populations in California, the Great Basin, and the Columbia-Fraser Plateau.

The area covered by this chapter includes California, the Great Basin, and the Columbia-Fraser Plateau (Figure 4.1). It is a vast and varied country, unified to some extent by cultural and environmental factors. Early ethnologists saw in the simple, unelaborated lifeway of the Great Basin a relic of an ancient cultural substratum that they believed to be very close to that of the earliest occupants of the New World. Similarities in basketry, architectural techniques, puberty rites, folktale motifs, and other traits shared between ethnographic cultures of California, the Great Basin, and the Plateau suggested that a common ancient tradition, from which Basin culture had departed the least, must once have characterized all three areas and provided the ground from which distinctive yet ultimately related regional traditions later sprang. In broadest outline, this conception has been borne out by prehistorians' researches, and it can provide the reader with a general frame of reference for the archeological detail to follow.

Of the three provinces, California is the most diverse. In the south and east, it is desert; on the west, it is seacoast; the great central valley is summer-dry grassland and parkland; and the Coast Range and Sierra Nevada are heavily wooded. Natural foods are abundant, and from quite early times there is evidence of substantial populations living in stable local communities. The Great Basin is a desert by any popular definition, though not to qualify the term would give the impression of a land far less hospitable to

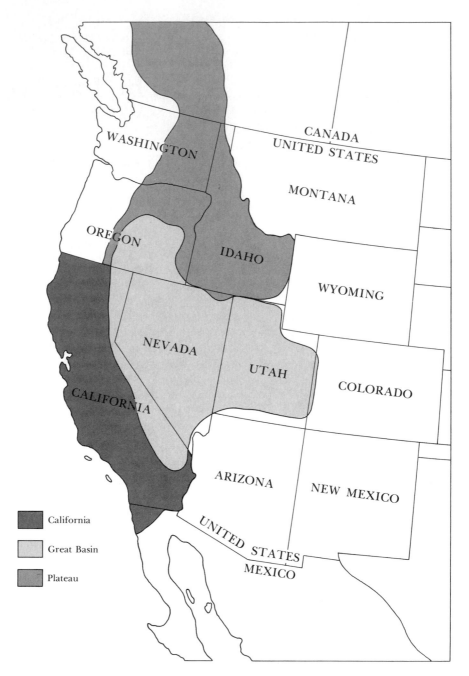

FIGURE 4.1
The Far West.

human occupation than in fact it was. The topography is one of alternating mountain ranges and valley basins, with altitudinal and topographic variation in the occurrence of effective moisture, giving rise to a series of biotically varied microenvironments that the native peoples exploited by ranging between them in a regular annual cycle. The Plateau is dry and open in the south, and wooded to greater or lesser degree in the north, but these characteristics are secondary to the overriding fact of the two major river systems, the Columbia and the Fraser, which dominate the southern and northern portions of the Plateau, respectively. The woods and sagebrush-grasslands were exploited for game and edible roots and plants, but the rivers, with their dependable annual runs of millions of salmon, were the central focus of Plateau settlement and economic life.

The importance of environmental factors to hunting and gathering peoples is great, and California, the Great Basin, and the Plateau give perspectives on hunting-gathering adaptations to three distinctive geographic provinces. The comparison of the three is made the more interesting by the likelihood that their cultures stemmed from a common historical source far back in time.

CALIFORNIA

Aboriginal California was biotically rich, densely populated, and culturally diverse, more so than any comparable area of North America. Its ethnographic population has been estimated at 300,000 to 350,000 people, and within the modern boundaries of the state about 500 separate ethnic groups or independent communities were counted. Kroeber (1925) grouped the hundreds of small California societies into four broad culture provinces, which coincided with broadly defined environmental zones. Northwest California cultures resembled those of the northern Pacific coast of Oregon, Washington, and British Columbia in their maritime-riverine economy, woodworking industry, and wealth emphasis. Central California societies shared similarities in social custom, basketry, houses, and technical processes with cultures of the trans-Sierran Great Basin. Cultures of the southern California coast and the southern deserts were distinctive in society and architecture, but traits such as pottery making, maize agriculture (on the Colorado River), and sand painting are evidence of contact with cultures of the Pueblo Southwest.

These similarities suggest the historical origins and contacts of the native Californians. The fact that northwestern California was dominated by speakers of Athabascan and Algonquian tongues, central California by Penutian speakers, and southern California by Shoshonean and Yuman speakers suggests a general historical stability within each of the major provinces for hundreds, and probably thousands, of years past. The scattered, broken distribution of Hokan speakers throughout the state suggests that they might be remnants of a more ancient people, perhaps the original Californians, intruded upon and displaced by later arrivals.

The first successful synthesis of California prehistory, devised for the Sacramento Delta region of the great central valley, ordered archeological data in terms of the Early, Middle, and Late Horizon (Lilliard et al. 1939). This system is deeply embedded in the literature of California archeology, but since it was developed much new evidence has been discovered, the great complexity of California culture history has been recognized, and the framework has become outmoded. In this summary, a simple chronological approach is used, beginning with the scattered evidence for early occupation over the state as a whole and then considering individually the regional sequences developed for the several archeological subareas.

Paleo-Indian period (? to 6000 BC) finds are so far not adequately dated. Those attributed to this period are believed to be old primarily because of their typological similarity to cultural manifestations dated elsewhere. A number of sites in California have yielded coarsely flaked stone specimens that resemble, sometimes strikingly, the Paleolithic handaxes or pebble tools of Europe, Africa, and Asia. It has been suggested that such sites represent a western lithic cotradition ancestral to all later developments in California and the desert West (Davis et al. 1969:76–77), but a widely supported opposing view is that none of these sites demonstrates truly ancient human activity. Manix Lake and Coyote Gulch in southern California, for example, yielded indisputably man-made artifacts, but all are from the surface and are not reliably dated. Though the artifacts do resemble handaxes known to be ancient in Europe and Africa, a restudy of the Manix Lake industry (Glennan 1976) shows it to be probably a relatively recent quarry-workshop complex, where large stone pieces were flaked and shaped into finished artifacts. Although objections to this study have been raised (Simpson 1976), it remains likely that the coarse paleolithiclike specimens are simply objects broken or abandoned as unpromising early in the process of reducing large lumps of raw material to finished forms. Similar specimens have been found at many sites of no great age, including some so recent as to contain pottery (Wallace 1962). Specimens from other sites, such as Calico Hills and Texas Street, again in southern California, are demonstrably of Pleistocene age but do not exhibit the patterns of consistent form and flaking technique that have been characteristic of human artifacts since earliest times in the Old World. Moreover, in each case it is clear that a small number of specimens fortuitously resembling artifacts were carefully selected from deposits containing hundreds or thousands of pieces of stone or bone broken or abraded by geological forces (Johnson and Miller 1958; Haynes 1973). Buried features in Pleistocene deposits at Texas Street and on Santa Rosa Island, which have been claimed as fire hearths, can equally be attributed to natural causes (Cruxent 1962; Riddell 1969).

Human skulls from Laguna Beach and Los Angeles have been dated to 15,000 and greater than 21,000 BC by carbon-14 determinations on the human bone itself (Berger et al. 1971; Berger 1975), and ages of up to 50,000 BC have been calculated for other California skeletal remains by the aspartic acid racemization technique (Bada et al. 1974; Bada and Helfman 1975). But the aspartic acid racemization dates are calculated from a rate based on the carbon-14 date for the Laguna Beach skull, and carbon-14 dates for the probable context of the skull are in the range of 6000 to 7000 BC, casting doubt on the 15,000 BC date for the skull itself. Independent confirmation of such ages for human presence in California will be required to dispel the skepticism surrounding these dates.

Paleo-Indian sites with distinctive Clovis Fluted points at Borax Lake, north of San Francisco, and at a number of localities in southern California (Figure 4.2) represent more reliable evidence of early occupation. Lake Mohave, Tulare Lake, and China Lake have each yielded a number of specimens, and many more isolated finds are known (Riddell and Olsen 1969). All are undated surface finds, but such points have been securely dated by multiple carbon-14 determinations at several sites in the Great Plains and the Southwest to a period between 9500 and 9000 BC, and obsidian hydration measurements on the Borax Lake specimens, as well as their apparent geological context, are congruent with these dates (Meighan and Haynes 1970). In the Plains and the Southwest, Clovis points occur in kill sites with the bones of mammoth, giant bison, and other now extinct big-game animals. At China Lake, the bones of mammoth, bison, camel, horse, and other mammals and birds have been found eroding out of the lake bed near Clovis points, though the all-important association of bones and artifacts is not clearly established (Davis 1975).

At many of the lake bed sites where Clovis points have been found, there is also evidence of leaf-shaped biface points or knives, crescent-shaped knives, and a variety of heavy scrapers, choppers, and hammerstones. This assemblage, termed the San Dieguito complex (Figure 4.3), has been found in buried context at the C. W. Harris site in San Diego, and there was dated by carbon-14 to approximately 7000 BC (Warren 1967). It thus follows Clovis in time, and appears to be the last manifestation of the Paleo-Indian period in California. The complex has not been formally recognized in more northerly parts of California, but undated artifacts from Borax Lake resemble San Dieguito types very closely, suggesting its presence there.

On the south coast, complexes such as Topanga, Malaga Cove, La Jolla, Oak Grove, and Little Sycamore follow the San Dieguito complex and are probably derivative of it. Warren (1968) has grouped these into the Encinitas tradition, the beginning of which he places about 5500 BC. Manos and metates are abundant; hammerstones and large, crude chopping, scraping, and cutting tools are common; large, crude projectile points, often leaf

TABLE 4.1
Fluted Point Surface Finds in the Far West

Figure 4.2 Location No.	Site	Reference
	California	
1	Cuyamaca Park Pass	Davis and Shutler 1969
2	Pinto Basin	Warren 1967
3	Lake Mohave	Campbell and Campbell 1937; Warren 1967
4	Tiefort Basin	Davis and Shutler 1969
5	China Lake	Davis and Shutler 1969
6	Panamint Basin	Davis and Shutler 1969; Warren 1967
7	Death Valley	Hunt 1960; Warren 1967
8	Owens Lake	Davis 1963; Warren 1967
9	Tulare Lake	Riddell and Olsen 1969
10	Ebbetts Pass	Davis and Shutler 1969
11	Borax Lake	Harrington 1948; Meighan and Haynes 1970
	Nevada	
12	Clark County	Perkins 1967, 1968
13	Beatty	Shutler and Shutler 1959
14	Grrom Dry Lake	Davis and Shutler 1969
15	Caliente	Davis and Shutler 1969
16	Dry Lakes Valley	Davis and Shutler 1969
17	Lowengruhn Beach Ridge, Mud Lake	Tuohy 1968
18	Long Valley Lake	Tadlock 1966
19	Lake Tonopah	Tuohy 1969; Warren 1967
20	Huntoon Valley	Davis and Shutler 1969
21	Fallon Area	Davis and Shutler 1969; Warren and Ranere 1968
22	Reno Area	Davis and Shutler 1969
23	Carson Sink	Warren 1967; Tuohy 1968
24	Lovelock Area	Davis and Shutler 1969
25	Carlin	Davis and Shutler 1969
26	Black Rock Desert	Clewlow 1968; Richards 1968
	Oregon	
27	Guano Valley (Big Springs)	Cressman 1936; University of Oregon Natural History Museum files
28	Coyote Flat	Butler 1970
28	Coyote Flat	Butler 1970
29	Malheur Lake	Strong 1969
30	Glass Buttes	University of Oregon Natural History Museum files; Mack 1975
31	Eastern Oregon Area	Osborne 1956
32	Eugene Area	Strong 1969; Allely 1975
33	Blalock	Strong 1969
34	The Dalles	Osborne 1956
35	Olympia Area	Osborne 1956

Figure 4.2 Location No.	Site	Reference
	Idaho	
36	Lake Channel Locality	Butler 1965
37	Bannock Creek	Butler 1965
38	Big Camas Prairie	Butler 1963
39	Pioneer Basin	Butler 1970
40	Roberts Site	Butler 1965
41	Birch Creek Sinks	Butler 1965
42	Upper Salmon River Area	Butler 1972
43	Birch Creek Area	Swanson and Sneed 1966; Butler 1965
	Utah	
44	Acord Lake	Tripp 1966
45	San Rafael Swell, Silverhorn Wash	Anonymous 1968; Gunnerson 1956
46	Moab Area	Hunt and Tanner 1960

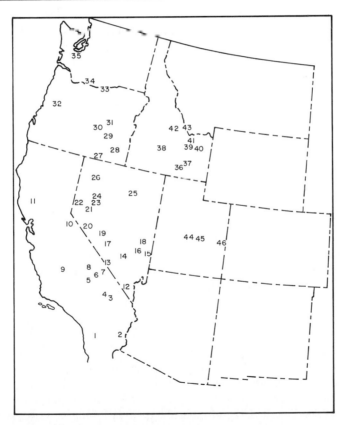

FIGURE 4.2
Fluted point surface finds in the Far West (see Table 4.1).

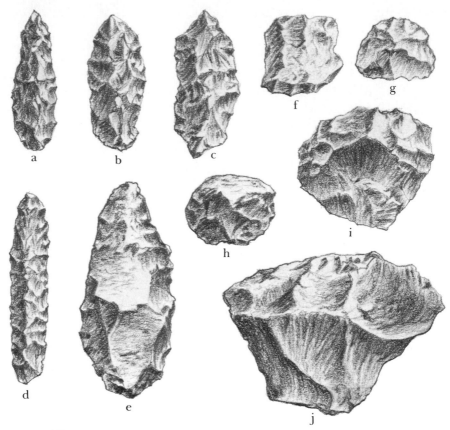

FIGURE 4.3
San Dieguito artifacts: *a–e,* knives; *f–i,* scrapers; *j,* chopper. (From *Prehistory of North America,*
2d ed., by Jesse D. Jennings. Copyright © 1968, 1974 by McGraw-Hill, Inc. Used with
permission of McGraw-Hill Book Company.)

shaped, are present, but relatively rare. Bone awls, flakers, beads, atlatl hooks,
and shell beads and pendants are also characteristic, though of relatively
low frequency. A well-developed collecting economy is indicated by abundant
remains of shellfish and by the characteristic milling stones. Mammal bones,
fish remains, and projectile points are, by contrast, relatively rare, suggesting
that hunting and fishing were less emphasized. The Encinitas tradition is
superseded after about 3000 BC on the Santa Barbara coast, but apparently
lasted until AD 1000 or later in the San Diego area.

The Campbell tradition follows the Encinitas, appearing first on the
Santa Barbara coast and only considerably later as a few site-unit intrusions
on the San Diego coast. Diagnostic artifacts include side-notched, stemmed,
and lanceolate or leaf-shaped points, large knives, and a variety of flake

scrapers and drills. The hopper mortar and stone bowl mortar and pestle appear for the first time, and shell, bone, and stone ornaments of styles different from those of the Encinitas tradition are present. The economic base of the Campbell tradition was heavily oriented toward hunting, as attested by a relative abundance of points, knives, and scrapers and by abundant bones of deer, elk, bear, seal, small land mammals, and fish, as well as shellfish, in the middens at Little Harbor and the Aerophysics site. Warren suggests that the Campbell tradition stemmed from a migration of inland hunters to the coast, where they became amalgamated with the coastally adapted Encinitas people and developed a productive broad-spectrum maritime hunting and gathering economic base. This cultural tradition was always richest in the Santa Barbara region, where the environment was most favorable to maritime developments, and was less developed where it later penetrated the less favorable San Diego coast.

The ethnographic Chumash represent the historical conclusion of this continuum in the Santa Barbara Channel region, where the protohistoric culture has been given the archeological name Canaliño. This was a rich maritime adaptation that emphasized fishing and sea mammal hunting, but broad-spectrum hunting and gathering, both along the coastline and in the interior, was also of major significance. The list of Canaliño artifacts is long and includes small projectile points, drills, scrapers, bone awls, bone and shell fishhooks, abalone shell dishes, stone bowls, mortars, pestles, and an abundance of animal effigies, shell beads, and ornaments. The Canaliño is the climax development of southern California, and apparently represents a society of considerable wealth and complexity.

Archeological antecedents for the Shoshonean and Yuman-speaking peoples who lived south of the Chumash in ethnographic times consist of the Cuyamaca phase, representing the Yuman-speaking Diegueño, and the San Luis Rey I and II phases, representing the Shoshonean-speaking Luiseño. Both phases seem to date within the last 1000 years, although their chronology is not very well established. The Cuyamaca phase may be an outgrowth of the local Encinitas tradition, but the San Luis Rey phases are believed to represent a late Shoshonean migration to the coast from the interior deserts (Meighan 1954; True n.d.).

For central California, a cultural tradition defined principally from excavations in the great central valley around Sacramento includes the Windmiller (3000–1000 BC), Cosumnes (1000 BC–AD 500), and Hotchkiss (AD 500–historic) cultures. All are known almost exclusively from artifacts found with human burials. The nature of the actual settlements is unknown, but the abundance and concentration of human interments in cemeteries suggests that villages were sedentary and occupied over long periods of time.

Windmiller culture sites occur on natural mounds or levees near permanent water. Large, heavy lanceolate, bipointed, and stemmed dart points, along with manos, metates, and mortars, suggest a subsistence economy based on hunting and on the gathering of seeds and acorns (Figure 4.4). Burial finds include distinctive *Olivella* and *Haliotis* marine shell beads, rectangular stone palettes, charmstones in a variety of shapes, and tubular pipes. Burial was by interment; cremation occurred rarely (Ragir 1972).

The subsequent Cosumnes culture is known from many sites, suggesting a relatively dense population. Large, heavy, chipped stone projectile points, bone bipoints and fish spear barbs, and mortars and pestles give evidence of a hunting-fishing-gathering complex; an increased frequency of mortars possibly suggests a growing importance of acorns as a food source. *Olivella* and *Haliotis* beads and ornaments are numerous, and some are of types different from those of the preceding horizon. Perforated coyote teeth and bear claws, fishtail charmstones, and short bird bone tubes appear as burial offerings. A small but significant percentage of burials have embedded projectile points, indicating violent death. Cremation burials were more common than earlier but were still relatively rare.

The late period Hotchkiss culture is also well represented by numerous sites distributed throughout central California. The relative abundance of portable mortars and cylindrical pestles indicates an economy focused on acorn gathering; small side-notched projectile points and barbed bone fish spears suggest the prominence of fishing, hunting, and fowling. Charred remnants of basketry have been found in some graves. There was at this period a great proliferation of ornaments and beads of *Haliotis* shell, clamshell, magnetite, and steatite. Both interment and cremation burial were practiced, with cremations becoming increasingly common. This period culminates in the rich ethnographic cultures of the Wintun, Miwok, and Yokuts (Beardsley 1954).

Earlier formulations treated central coast sites around San Francisco Bay as peripheral to the central valley cultures, but reinterpretation of the Bay Area evidence suggests the existence of a separate coastal cotradition with an integrity of its own and a time depth equal to that of the central valley tradition. The principal site on which this thesis rests is University Village, at the south end of San Francisco Bay. Here many Windmiller-like traits were present, but differences in burial orientation, relative frequencies of shell bead types, flaked stone tools, seed-grinding implements, and quartz crystals, as well as in anthropometric characteristics of the human skeletal remains, are evidence of the site's distinctiveness. Differences between the central coast and central valley traditions are said to be greatest between 2000 and 1000 BC, and to have lessened sufficiently by about 500 BC for a convergence of the originally separate traditions to be postulated (Gerow and Force 1968; Gerow 1974).

For the north coast ranges, a series of "patterns," or phases, has recently been defined. The Post pattern, provisionally dated between 6000 and 10,000 BC, represents the Clovis Paleo-Indian evidence already referred to. A period not yet formally defined for the area follows (San Dieguito hori-

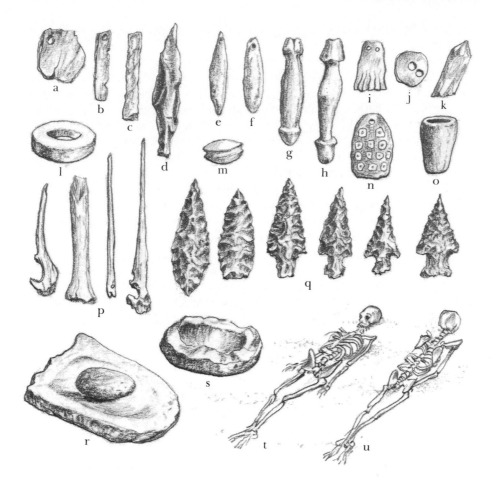

FIGURE 4.4
Artifacts of the central California Windmiller culture: *a,* biotite ornament; *b, c,* slate ornaments; *d,* "bangle;" *e–h,* charmstones; *i,* shell ornament; *j,* shell disk; *k,* worked quartz crystal; *l,* steatite bead; *m,* clay object; *n,* shell-inlaid turtle-carapace ornament; *o,* stone pipe; *p,* bone tools; *q,* projectile points; *r,* metate and mano; *s,* mortar; *t–u,* extended supine and prone burials. (From *Prehistory of North America,* 2d ed., by Jesse D. Jennings. Copyright © 1968, 1974 by McGraw-Hill, Inc. Used with permission of McGraw-Hill Book Company.)

zon?). Then comes the Borax Lake pattern, estimated to date between 5000 and 500 BC, which is characterized by broad-stemmed Borax Lake projectile points, burins, manos, metates, and occasional mortars. The remaining time down to the historic horizon is occupied by the Houx aspect, considered to represent a coalescence of the local Borax Lake pattern with a culture stemming from the San Francisco Bay area. Replacement of the mano and metate by the mortar and pestle and a proliferation of projectile points are the principal artifactual changes described. Burins, present in the Borax Lake pattern, continue into the Houx aspect, suggesting a degree of cultural continuity from the older local pattern (Frederickson 1974a).

The northwest coast of California gives evidence of a distinctive cultural tradition. Excavations at Gunther Island, Patrick's Point, Tsurai, and Point St. George reveal a people living on shell mounds and practicing a lifeway based on fishing, hunting, and collecting. Bone and shell fishhooks, barbed bone harpoons, small barbed arrowpoints, zoomorphic stone clubs, grooved stone and clay sinkers, pestles, and stone bowl mortars, along with actual shell and bone remains, give evidence of economic pursuits and a technology similar in detail to that of the ethnographic Wiyot, Yurok, Karok, and Tolowa inhabitants of the region. The historic lifeway and adaptation to local conditions, which nevertheless shows many similarities to cultures farther north along the Pacific coast, clearly has existed in this region for the past 1000 years. Two millennia or more of occupation are suggested by a carbon-14 date of 300 BC for the Point St. George site, and there are hints of a different cultural complex at that time. Additional older sites are to be expected at locations back from the present shores, but until their potential is exploited and a longer cultural sequence developed, the antecedents and developmental history of the northwestern California cultures will remain obscure (Elsasser and Heizer 1966; Gould 1966).

From the Oroville region of the northern Sierra foothills, Ritter (1970) describes a sequence of four cultural phases spanning the past 3000 years, which suggests a progression from band-level societies focused on the hunting of large game and exploitation of hard seeds to more sedentary tribelets with an economy based on hunting, fishing, and acorn gathering. The Mesilla phase (1000 BC–AD 0) is represented by atlatls and heavy stemmed and side-notched dart points, the mano and metate, and, less common, the bowl mortar and cylindrical pestle. Ornaments are *Olivella* and *Haliotis* shell beads. The Bidwell phase (AD 0–800) saw the introduction of small arrowpoints, which occur with larger dart points. The mano-metate combination continued to predominate over the mortar and pestle as a food-grinding system, implying continued predominance of seed gathering over acorn collecting. Because burials are more abundant and their accompaniments richer than in the Mesilla phase, a more sedentary pattern of occupation is inferred. By the Sweetwater phase (AD 800–1500) cobble pestles and slab mortars dominate the food-processing complex, suggesting a shift of economic focus to the gathering and processing of acorns. New artifacts and types of grave goods suggest an intrusion of peoples from the central valley, and evidence of traumatic deaths may attest to a certain amount of friction accompanying this process. The Oroville phase (AD 1500–historic) represents the ethnographically known Maidu culture, with a well-developed acorn complex, diversified hunting, sedentary villages, and large ceremonial houses. One large archeological site of this period with apparent ceremonial structures seems to have served as a center for a number of nearby smaller villages.

In the southern Sierra foothills, Moratto (n.d.) has described an occupation beginning with the Chowchilla phase (300 BC–AD 300), during which large, heavy, stemmed and side-notched dart points, bone fish spears, slab metates, manos, cobble mortars, and cylindrical pestles were in use. An economy that emphasized hunting, fishing, and seed gathering, with acorn processing less important, is implied. Settlements were small and found only along major streams. During the Raymond phase (AD 300–1500), small corner- and side-notched arrowpoints and bedrock mortars appear, while slab metates and manos continue. A shift to an acorn-processing emphasis is implied, though hunting appears to have still been important. Settlements are more numerous and more diverse. A pattern of centrally based wandering, with seasonal transhumance into the higher Sierra, can be hypothesized. The Madera phase (AD 1500–historic) is marked by small side-notched and unnotched triangular arrowpoints and a proliferation of steatite cylinders, pipes, pendants, earplugs, and the like. The food-processing complex of the Raymond phase continues. An expansion of the local population is indicated by increased numbers of sites. Large settlements with "community houses" appear at key locations on the main streams, and smaller satellite villages or hamlets appear on lesser tributaries. The Madera phase culminates in the historic culture of the Southern Miwok.

Occupation of the high Sierra was apparently always seasonal, controlled by the severe winter cold and snow. There is, however, clear evidence of aboriginal travel into and across the area from a very early period. Obsidian from Sierran or trans-Sierran sources is found in central valley sites as early as 3000 to 2000 BC, Californian shell beads appear in the Great Basin Karlo and Lovelock Cave sites at the same time, and unmodified Pacific coast *Olivella* shells occur at Leonard Rockshelter near Lovelock, Nevada, in a stratum carbon-14 dated to between 6700 and 5100 BC. Evidence of *Olivella* shells at comparably early dates elsewhere in the Great Basin further supports the inference of trans-Sierran travel (Ragir 1972).

California prehistory and ethnology is of great importance for the perspective it offers on the cultural development of hunting-gathering peoples in a rich environment. Whereas such societies are commonly considered to fall low on the scale of sociocultural complexity, the native Californians provide evidence of an impressively high level of cultural elaboration involving dense population, sedentary village life, and political-economic arrangements of some scale and sophistication. This perspective is a relatively new one, however. Traditional ethnological treatises have pictured Californian society as simple and highly fragmented, divided into hundreds of small, autonomous polities with no significant supralocal political integration (Kroeber 1962). But models arguing the existence of more complex sociopolitical structures are now being tested against ethnographic and archeological data, with intriguing results. Ceremonial observances, trade fairs, and confederations or alliances linking a number of local communities are known from ethnographic data, and their importance as aboriginal political and economic institutions is now being emphasized. The culling out and focusing of available ethnographic information on the political functions of high-status individuals makes it appear that California societies were regulated to a significant degree by elite persons whose influence was more than local and who regularly participated in affairs transcending the boundaries of local tribelets. And archeological studies of burial practices are giving evidence that elite groups or lineages may be an old phenomenon in California society, going back perhaps several thousand years in some localities. Widespread trade, especially in marine shells, has long been recognized archeologically, and attempts are being made to comprehend this trade within a model of intersocietal political-economic relationships (Bean and King 1974; Bean and Blackburn 1976).

Excavations at Tiburon Hills, on the northwestern edge of San Francisco Bay, revealed a cemetery carbon-14 dated at approximately the beginning of the Christian era. The site, a small earth and shell midden, yielded 44 burials complete enough for detailed study. In the center of the burial cluster was a concentration of cremation and inhumation burials representing 7 males, 5 females, and 6 children. These 18 individuals were accompanied by 62 percent of all the grave goods from the site. Partly encircling the central concentration was a series of male inhumations with no grave goods. Beyond were scattered males and females with few or no associations and 2 females and an infant with relatively abundant grave goods. Artifacts of symbolic or ornamental value were predominant, including *Olivella* shell beads, abalone and carved bone pendants, and whistles made of mammal and bird bones. On the basis of the observed patterns, a hierarchical social structure was postulated (T. King 1974:38):

. . . the nature of the artifact assemblage, in which non-utilitarian, "sociotechnic-ideotechnic" artifacts predominate, and the distinctly non-random association of elements of this assemblage with the cremated and disarticulated remains of men, women, and children buried in the center of the cemetery, lead me to believe that this cemetery reflects in its structure a form of social organization characterized by ascribed ranking. In other words, I infer that the central cremation zone represents the interment of high-ranking individuals, while persons of lower rank are interred farther and farther from the center. The presence of children and infants in the central area, the slight evidence of sex-based role distinctions, the evidence of social distinctions cross-cutting age/sex divisions, and the "ideotechnic-sociotechnic" weighting of the artifact assemblage all suggest that rank in the society here represented was not achieved on the basis of personal attributes but ascribed on the basis of kin-group membership. Such rank ascription is typical of a "Rank" society in Morton Fried's (1967) terms, or a "Chiefdom" in the words of Elman Service (1962).

Other excavations in the San Francisco Bay region have not exhibited burial patterning of this sort, and King speculates that high-status lineages may have lived somewhat apart from lower-ranking families. A much larger midden about 200 meters from the Tiburon Hills site may have been a commoner's settlement, but it had been badly disturbed and was not examined adequately to provide a test of this hypothesis.

King attempts to explain the appearance of a nonegalitarian, ranked society in this area by a model of population growth and subsequent competition-cooperation. Associating population growth with sedentary residence, he proposes that hunter-gatherer populations would be able, even impelled, to achieve sedentariness where their immediate surroundings contain sufficient natural food resources within one or two hours of travel to see them through an annual round with few periods of food scarcity. Compilation of a map showing potential food resources available within the San Francisco Bay area allowed him to suggest that at localities such as Tiburon Hills sedentariness would be quite possible, while in other places it would be unlikely. As population expanded from more favorable into less favorable localities, competition for resources would grow, and this would have to be resolved either through warfare or through cooperative sharing of resources through trade. Either form of interaction would be facilitated by formal organization of elite leadership cadres of the sort apparently represented at the Tiburon Hills cemetery.

From an analysis of burials at three central California sites near Walnut Creek, Fredrickson (1974b) infers a growth in societal complexity over time there, and other studies suggest comparable developments in southern California (Stickel 1968; L. King 1969; Decker 1969). Additional evidence of growing social complexity might be seen in the increase throughout central and southern California over the past several thousand years of both violent deaths and trade goods. Both trends might be expected as part of the process postulated by King.

Blackburn (1974) has shown from ethnographic information that intervillage trade and political integration in native California were fostered by a system of fiestas and ceremonials that were convened frequently by local chiefs. A fiesta was the occasion for travel and exchange among large numbers of people, while the attendant ceremonies provided an affirmation of social solidarity. Such gatherings enhanced the prestige and wealth of the local leadership cadre; among the Chumash at least, guests were expected to make donations toward the fiesta, and the local chief would save some of the offerings for distribution among his own people in times of stress. Trade was thus fostered and regulated within a system that preserved and enhanced the political power of managerial elites. Moreover, ties between the local elites were evidently far-reaching. When a local chief declared a fiesta, attendance by other local chiefs was considered obligatory. Alliance networks thus maintained, functioning in both trade and conflict, seem to have existed all over California and, interestingly enough, were everywhere laid out in such a fashion that they linked together different environmental zones, making their economic logic perfectly clear (Bean 1974).

Rigorous archeological tests of the proposition that such economic-political integration has great time depth in California have not yet been achieved. But evidence from burials and trade objects suggests its antiquity, and attempts are being made to formulate models in which the trade goods (especially shell beads) increasingly abundant in California sites after about 2000 BC may provide some of the needed tests (C. King 1974). A well-argued ethnographic hypothesis relating food resource management through controlled firing of the landscape to the rich and complex growth of Californian cultures upon a hunting-gathering subsistence base also has archeological implications now being explored (Lewis 1973; Bean and Lawton 1973). California archeology has entered an exciting period.

GREAT BASIN

The Great Basin is a desert land that was, in ethnographic times, sparsely populated by small, far-ranging groups of hunters and gatherers. Most of the historic peoples spoke closely related Numic languages belonging to the great Utaztekan phylum, but in east-central and southeastern California tongues belonging to the Hokan phylum were spoken. The linguistic evidence suggests that several populations may have moved through the area over the long span of prehistoric time, the Numic speakers being the most recent occupants and the peripheral Hokan-speakers perhaps remnants of an earlier population. The principal importance of Great Basin archeology lies in the glimpses it affords of cultural adaptation to a demanding environment, surely one of the most rigorous in native North America. The adjustments made to nuances of environmental variation, both across space and down through time, have long been and continue to be a major focus of interest in Great Basin studies.

In the Great Basin, as in California, great age has been claimed for a pre-projectile point or early lithic tradition considered ancestral to all later manifestations. Artifacts found on high strand lines of a now dry pluvial lake near Fallon, Nevada, were attributed a Pleistocene age (Carter 1958), and putatively culture-bearing deposits at Tule Springs, near modern Las Vegas, were carbon-14 dated at greater than 26,000 BC (Harrington and Simpson 1961). Atlatl parts found with the bones and feces of now extinct giant ground sloth in Gypsum Cave, Nevada, were once claimed as evidence of Pleistocene human occupation there (Harrington 1933). But more recent work has placed the Fallon finds well within postglacial times (Tuohy 1970) and has shown that the maximum demonstrable age for human activity at Tule Springs does not exceed 9000 to 8000 BC (Shutler et al. 1967). The atlatl parts from Gypsum Cave have been carbon-14 dated at 900 and 400 BC, removing them from consideration as evidence for early human occupation (Heizer and Berger 1970). In short, no well-supported evidence of occupation earlier than terminal Pleistocene times has yet been established for the Great Basin.

The earliest carbon-14 date for a Paleo-Indian-period assemblage now known from the Great Basin comes from Fort Rock Cave in south-central Oregon, where a concentration of charcoal lying on Pleistocene lake gravels gave a date of 11,200 BC (Bedwell 1973). Near the charcoal concentration, also resting on lake gravels, were found a milling stone and a mano fragment, two projectile points, several scrapers and gravers, and a handful of flakes. Lack of detailed documentation of the find-spot has prompted questions about the reported association of artifacts and carbon-14 date (Haynes 1969), but the excavator has stated clearly his belief in the association (Bedwell 1970:53–58). Only additional finds of comparable age from other sites will effectively remove all reasonable doubt, though a considerable antiquity for the artifacts is guaranteed by a carbon-14 date of 8200 BC for an overlying level.

It long was thought that fluted projectile points of the Clovis type, common in the Southwest, Plains, and eastern woodlands, were not significantly represented in the West. But sufficient evidence has now accumulated to make it clear that Clovis folk were widespread in the Great Basin and throughout the West as a whole (Figure 4.2). As noted in the preceding discussion of California prehistory, the age of Clovis points in the West remains to be directly established, since all so far reported have been surface finds. Nevertheless, a date of between 9500 and 9000 BC seems likely.

From a time range subsequent to Clovis comes a series of intergrading complexes, also mostly surface finds, which contain large shouldered and stemmed lanceolate projectile points, along with large leaf-shaped knives or points, crescents, flake scrapers, and domed scraper-planes. In southern California and Nevada this horizon is represented by the San Dieguito complex, dated by carbon-14 determinations to 7000 and 6500 BC at the C. W. Harris site in San Diego, and believed by Warren (1967) to date to 8000 BC. In the northern Great Basin comparable types occur in the Fort Rock Valley, carbon-14 dated to between 9000 and 6000 BC (Bedwell 1973). In the eastern Great Basin the earliest level of Danger Cave dates around 9000 BC and contains a small and nondescript assemblage that might conceivably be attributable to the same complex (Jennings 1957). The Sadmat complex of the Fallon area also exhibits San Dieguito-like artifacts, and presumably belongs to the same period.

Warren and Ranere (1968) point out that the Haskett locality in Idaho and the Olcott site in western Washington extend the web of similarity into the Columbia Plateau as well. Hester (1973:65–68) provides a detailed list of the many local complexes or sites representing this unity, which he terms the Western Pluvial Lakes tradition, following Bedwell (1973).

The artifacts of this tradition, like the Clovis Fluted points, occur commonly on the lower strand lines of pluvial lakes. This suggests that their makers were exploiting comparable environments and probably practicing similar lifeways, oriented toward the lakes and marshes common throughout the Great Basin in early postglacial times (Tuohy 1968; Heizer and Baumhoff 1970). It is likely indeed that the San Dieguito-like complexes are derived from Clovis antecedents and represent transitional cultures between the Paleo-Indian period and the early Archaic. This relationship is suggested by general similarities in size, form, and flaking technique shared between some of the western post-Clovis projectile points and such Great Plains types of comparable age as Alberta, Scottsbluff, Hell Gap, and Agate Basin. These latter types are recognized as derivatives of the fluted point tradition on the Plains, and the western points that resemble them may be interpreted as derivatives of the fluted point tradition in the West.

In the southern California deserts and southern Great Basin, the San Dieguito complex gave way to the Pinto Basin complex, characterized by stemmed, indented-base and leaf-shaped dart points, knives, drills, choppers, scrapers, scraper-planes, and the mano and metate (Wallace 1962). Most Pinto Basin sites are known from surface observations and are undated, but at the stratified Rose Spring site near Inyo, California, carbon-14 dates of 1900, 1600, and 1500 BC from the bottom of the sequence may be applicable to the terminal Pinto phase (Hester 1973:71). Estimates for the beginning of the period range between 5000 and 3000 BC, but these dates are not founded on carbon-14 evidence. The lifeway indicated by the artifact assemblage is that of roving hunters and gatherers. However, a series of postmolds, indicative of light pole-and-thatch houses, discovered near the marshy edge of Little Lake in the Owens Valley, suggests a degree of sedentariness, or at least centralized focus within the nomadic wandering pattern (Harrington 1957). Two apparent "house rings" found with a Pinto assemblage at the Cocanour site on the south side of the Humboldt Sink near Fallon reinforce the impression of a certain degree of sedentariness (Stanley et al. 1970).

The Pinto Basin complex is succeeded by the Amargosa complex in the Mohave Desert and by the Rose Spring phase in Owens Valley. Both basically represent a continuation of the older lifeway. The Amargosa complex is known from surface finds of triangular stemmed and notched dart points, drills, flake scrapers, manos, and metates. Small, triangular, stemmed and notched arrowpoints are attributed to the final phase of Amargosa, dated perhaps as late as AD 1000 by Anasazi Pueblo pottery found at the same sites. The Rose Spring phase, known from a stratified open site, contained a similar lithic assemblage, now dated with some carbon-14 support between 1500 BC and AD 500 (Hester 1973:72).

The latest occupation in Owens, Panamint, and Death valleys is identified with the ethnographically known Paiute and related speakers of Numic languages, who are recognized archeologically by their heavy brownware pottery. The beginning date for these cultures is not firmly established, but the pottery is generally assumed to date to approximately AD 1000. Desert side-notched and small, triangular, side- and corner-notched arrowpoints, flake scrapers, manos, metates, mortars, and pestles are also characteristic of the assemblage. Sites are common on dunes, near streams and springs, and in rockshelters. An economy centered around plant-food collecting and the hunting of small game is indicated.

By AD 1000 Paiute brownware pottery appears in several southern Nevada Puebloan sites, and by approximately AD 1400 the bearers of related ceramics had apparently replaced sedentary farming peoples as far north as the Great Salt Lake region and had moved out onto the Snake River Plain beyond (Madsen 1975). By historic times the Numic speakers—Ute, southern Paiute, Shoshoni, Mono-Paviotso, Tubatalabal, and Luiseño—occupied most of the southern California deserts, the northern parts of the Southwest, all of the Great Basin, and much of the northwestern Plains. The remarkable expansiveness of the Numic peoples is one of the striking facts of Great Basin prehistory and has yet to be satisfactorily accounted for.

Along the lower Colorado River in historic times, Yuman-speaking peoples grew maize, beans, and squash on the seasonally inundated floodplains, manufactured a distinctive plainware pottery, and apparently served as a trade conduit between coastal California and the Pueblo Southwest. Their brownware pottery, of Southwestern derivation, is dated to approximately AD 900, and their use of agriculture possibly occurred as early. Although Wallace (1962) emphasizes the gathering aspect of their economy, Rogers (1945) believed that the Yuman-speaking peoples were agricultural, at least in part. Populations occupying the deserts back from the rivers were of course entirely dependent on hunting and gathering. Some historic descendants of this tradition were the Walapai, Yavapai, Yuma, Mohave, and Maricopa. Their ultimate prehistorical origins may be plausibly seen in the older Amargosa complex of the region, though southwestern influences were obviously important in shaping the tradition.

In the eastern Great Basin, a cluster of dry caves in the Great Salt Lake region contain remains spanning most of postglacial time. The earliest level at Danger Cave, carbon-14 dated to 9000 BC, gives only scant evidence of human presence, but after 7000 BC both Danger and Hogup caves offer rich records of human activity (Jennings 1957; Aikens 1970). The Deadman, Black Rock, and Promontory caves appear to have been comparably ancient and long occupied, and exhibit similar if not identical cultural remains (Steward 1937; Smith 1941).

Lanceolate and triangular stemmed and notched projectile points, milling stones, coiled and twined basketry, net fragments, bone awls, and the bones of small and large animals are common to all the Great Salt Lake caves (Figures 4.5, 4.6). At Hogup, detailed analysis of the biota brought into the cave by its human occupants between 6400 and 1200 BC showed that seeds of the pickleweed (*Allenrolfea occidentalis*) were apparently of major importance. Not only were the seeds common in human coprolites, but the early deposits were literally golden with the chaff threshed from them. Bison, antelope, sheep, and deer were well represented in the faunal assemblage, but rabbits,

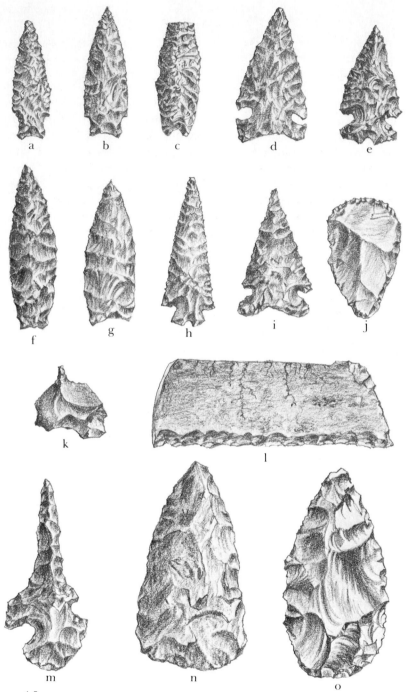

FIGURE 4.5
Lithic artifacts from Danger Cave: *a–i,* projectile points; *j,* scraper; *k,* graver; *l,* knife; *m,* drill; *n,* basalt knife; *o,* obsidian knife. (From *Prehistory of North America,* 2d ed., by Jesse D. Jennings. Copyright © 1968, 1974 by McGraw-Hill, Inc. Used with permission of McGraw-Hill Book Company.)

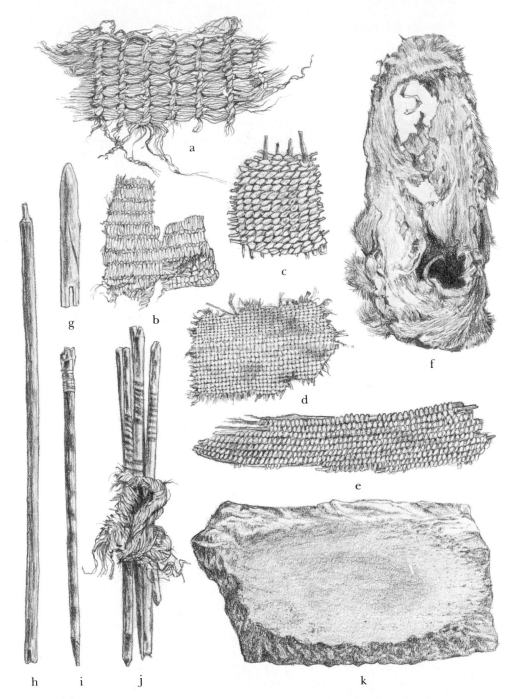

FIGURE 4.6
Artifacts from Danger Cave: *a, b,* twined matting; *c,* twined basketry; *d,* coarse cloth; *e,* coiled
basketry; *f,* hide moccasin; *g,* wooden knife handle; *h,* dart shaft; *i,* arrow shaft with broken
projectile point in place; *j,* bundle of gaming sticks; *k,* milling stone. (From *Prehistory of North
America,* 2d ed., by Jesse D. Jennings. Copyright © 1968, 1974 by McGraw-Hill, Inc. Used with
permission of McGraw-Hill Book Company.)

hares, and rodents were extremely abundant, indicating that catching and gathering small animals was an activity far more common than the bringing down of an occasional large ungulate. Waterfowl and shore birds dominated the avifauna during this period, implying that open water and marshland then covered the now dry flats below the cave. The other sites of the region undoubtedly looked out on comparable scenes, and the same general pattern of hunting and gathering in a lakeshore environment was common to them all.

After 1200 BC evidence of marshland exploitation vanishes at Hogup Cave, and lacustrine deposits in a sediment core from the flats below the site suggest that an abrupt rise in lake level may have completely drowned the marsh at that time (Mundorff 1971). Waterfowl disappear from the later record, and occurrences of pickleweed and of the milling stones used to process it decline radically. Only the mammal-hunting system apparently held up, and it shows a shift to relatively greater emphasis on large animals. Intensity of occupation declined markedly, suggesting that the cave was visited primarily by hunting parties that came infrequently and did not remain long. It is not known whether a comparable episode is represented at the other Great Salt Lake caves, because they were not analyzed in a fashion that might reveal such a change. In any event, it seems unlikely that the changes at Hogup Cave indicate a region-wide shift away from lakeside resources, since marshland environments would have remained available for exploitation at other localities. Places previously unoccupied may have become important in the subsistence cycle, but undoubtedly the same species and the same hunting and gathering techniques continued to be relied upon, with perhaps some shifts in the ranges traversed by individual bands (see Madsen and Berry 1975 for a somewhat different view).

In eastern Utah and western Colorado, part of the Great Basin culture area during the Archaic period, sites such as Hells Midden, Deluge Shelter, Thorne Cave, Clydes Cavern, Sudden Shelter, and the Cowboy Caves give evidence of a long occupation by people with lithic traditions related to those of the Great Salt Lake region. Sudden Shelter (Jennings et al. n.d.) provides an Archaic sequence carbon-14 dated to the period 5800–1300 BC. Within this sequence, change over time in projectile point styles is particularly crisp and well defined. The widespread Pinto Basin, Elko, Humboldt, and Gypsum Cave projectile point types are under closer temporal control here than at any other site yet reported, which will make Sudden Shelter a valuable reference point for regional chronologies. The sequence is essentially duplicated at the Cowboy Caves (Jennings 1975), and an occupation that overlaps it and extends somewhat later in time is present at Clydes Cavern (Winter and Wylie 1974). The occupation of Thorne Cave is carbon-14 dated to 2200 BC (Day 1964), and the Archaic levels of Deluge Shelter are dated between 1600 BC and AD 500 (Leach 1967). Lister (1951) estimates the age of the earliest Hells Midden occupation at about 1500 BC, but it probably is much older, since it contained some Pinto-like points, dated at Sudden Shelter from sometime before 5800 BC up to about 4400 BC. Hells Midden is one location where the Archaic gives way to the Fremont culture, next to be discussed.

Between AD 500 and 1400, a horticulturally based lifeway with Puebloan affinities occurred throughout the eastern Great Basin. This is the Fremont culture. Fremont ceramics and other artifacts appear during this time in most of the Archaic sites already mentioned, which continued to be used as hunting-gathering stations by Fremont people, but small horticultural settlements dominate the period. Fremont culture apparently developed out of related local Archaic traditions as they adopted new elements from different sources at different times (Aikens 1972a). It has recently been suggested that a long period of nonoccupancy—at least 1000 and perhaps 2000 years— intervened between the Archaic and Fremont cultures, but this idea is not well supported and seems unlikely to gain acceptance (Madsen and Berry 1975; Aikens 1976). Corner-notched and side-notched projectile point styles and the distinctive Fremont one-rod-and-bundle coiled basketry type show clear continuity with the later Archaic of the Great Basin, suggesting a direct genetic connection. Maize appears in preceramic Archaic context on the southern fringe of the Fremont area at Cowboy Caves (Jennings 1975). Farther north, at Clydes Cavern, maize occurs just below levels bearing Fremont ceramics. The corn is carbon-14 dated at approximately AD 400 (Winter and Wylie 1974).

Five regional variants of the Fremont culture have been identified north of the Colorado River in Utah, western Colorado, and eastern Nevada (Figures 4.7, 4.8). All were horticulturally based, but the degree of dependence on farming appears to have varied from area to area, and hunting and gathering evidently remained important in all regions. The regional traditions share pithouse and above-ground masonry or adobe architecture, a grayware pottery complex, a distinctive variety of maize, a highly characteristic moccasin type, and the distinctive one-rod-and-bundle Fremont basketry type. An anthropomorphic figurine cult and broad-shouldered anthropomorphic pictographs are also widely shared, but there are distinctive regional differences in style and degree of elaboration of these elements. These shared features indicate a basic cultural unity; at the same time, other evidence shows that the regional traditions were affected by contacts with adjacent non-Fremont areas. The Parowan and San Rafael variants in the south and east, nearest the Anasazi Pueblo area, most closely resemble the Anasazi in painted pottery and architecture. The Sevier, Great Salt Lake, and Uinta Basin variants, farther to the north and west, are less Pueblo-like and more closely resemble the cultures of the western and northwestern Plains (Marwitt 1970; Aikens 1972a).

Between AD 1300 and 1400 the Fremont culture vanished. Decreased effective moisture in a broad region across New Mexico, Arizona, and Utah

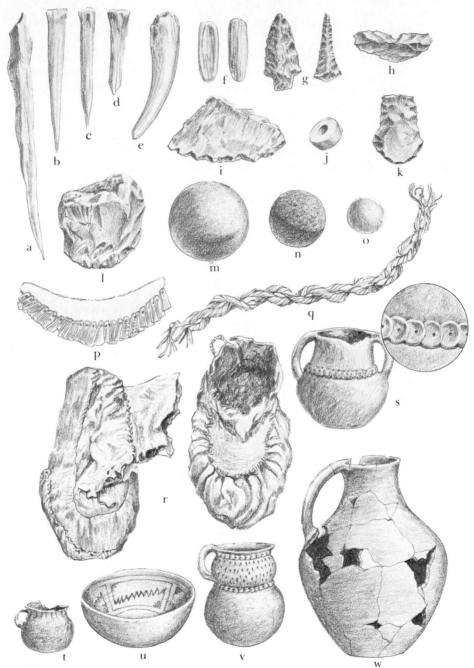

FIGURE 4.7
Fremont culture artifacts: *a,* bone splinter awl; *b–d,* bone awls; *e,* antler flaking tool; *f,* bone gaming pieces; *g,* points; *h,* shaft scraper; *i, k,* scrapers; *j,* perforated clay disk; *l,* rough hammerstone; *m–o,* stone balls (*n* is coated half with red ocher and half with black pigment); *p,* bone necklace; *q,* twisted bark rope; *r,* leather moccasins; *s,* pot and enlarged view of appliqué treatment; *t,* small pot; *u,* Ivie Creek black-on-white bowl; *v,* pot with appliqué at rim and restricted waist; *w,* pottery jar. (From *Prehistory of North America,* 2d ed., by Jesse D. Jennings. Copyright © 1968, 1974 by McGraw-Hill, Inc. Used with permission of McGraw-Hill Book Company.)

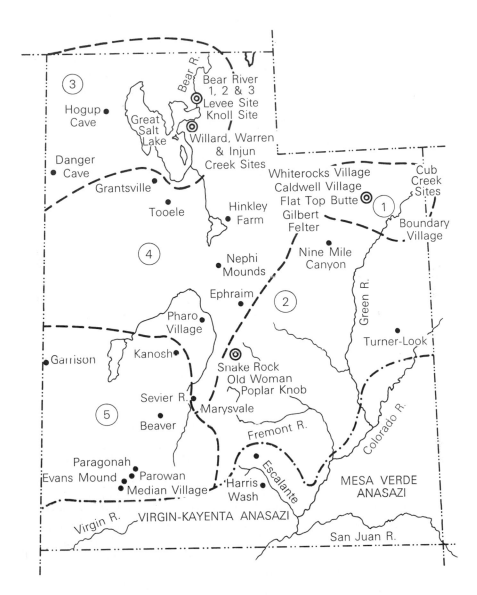

FIGURE 4.8
Fremont culture subareas: *1,* Uinta; *2,* San Rafael; *3,* Great Salt Lake; *4,* Sevier; *5,* Parowan. (From *Prehistory of North America,* 2d ed., by Jesse D. Jennings. Copyright © 1968, 1974 by McGraw-Hill, Inc. Used with permission of McGraw-Hill Book Company.)

is indicated at this time by tree ring evidence, pollen sequences, and other paleoclimatic indicators. Inadequate precipitation may have weakened the horticultural economy and, correlatively, the ability of the people to maintain sedentary villages. The culture that replaced Fremont has been identified with the ethnographic Shoshoni, Ute, and southern Paiute, all of whom were nomadic and nonhorticultural, possessed a pottery tradition clearly distinct from that of the Fremont, and spoke closely related Numic languages. In late prehistoric times, they apparently expanded their range from Death Valley, California, north and east to the High Plains east of the Rockies.

The fate of the Fremont people is uncertain; the idea that they were ancestral Numic-speaking peoples who reverted to a hunting-gathering lifeway, lost their distinctive Fremont traits, and emerged into recent times as the ethnographic Shoshoni, Ute, and southern Paiute (Gunnerson 1962) is appealingly straightforward, but has been cogently challenged on the grounds that no specific continuities in material culture can be traced between the Fremont and the ethnographic groups (Schroeder 1963; Euler 1964). If ethnic continuity was maintained, it is argued, some recognizable cultural continuity ought to have been maintained as well, but there is no evidence of it. Alternatively it has been suggested that, weakened by the collapse of their horticultural economy and driven by Numic-speaking invaders, the Fremont folk straggled south into the Pueblo country or eastward onto the High Plains (Wormington 1955; Aikens 1967). Neither of these theories has gained general acceptance, because unequivocally Fremont artifacts have never been identified in significant numbers outside the original Fremont range of time and place. It is clear that Fremont cultural identity was completely lost; a generally acceptable explanation of what happened to the people themselves is yet to be developed. (For another view of the Fremont culture, see Chapter 8.)

For the south-central part of the Great Basin, carbon-14-dated strata from O'Malley Shelter in southern Nevada suggest that Archaic occupation began there as early as 5000 BC. Occupation at the site was intermittent, with a long hiatus between 4500 and 2600 BC, followed by another occupation similar in character to the first, which lasted until 1000 BC. Projectile points of the Elko, Pinto, and Gypsum series dominated these levels. Occupation resumed at about AD 1100, with projectile points of the Rose Spring, Cottonwood, Desert Side-notched, and Eastgate series, along with Fremont, Anasazi, and Shoshonean ceramics. The pottery types were intermingled, suggesting that the site lay in a boundary zone between three cultural areas and saw use by parties from all three. Conaway Shelter, in the same area, shows evidence of two brief occupations around the beginning of the Christian era and AD 1000, which were similar to those certified for O'Malley Shelter at the same times. Use of these sites as temporary camps for seed collecting and the hunting of mule deer, bighorn sheep, jackrabbits, cottontails, and a variety of smaller mammals is indicated throughout the period of record (Fowler et al. 1973).

Several carbon-14 dates from Deer Creek Cave in northeastern Nevada indicate human occupation there between 8000 BC and AD 1300, but meaningful stratigraphy was lacking at the site, so little more than the fact of human presence is known (Shutler and Shutler 1963). South Fork Shelter near Elko and two sites near Eastgate, in central Nevada, give good records of Archaic occupation after 2500 BC (Heizer and Baumhoff 1961; Heizer et al. 1968). Newark Cave, in the Newark Valley, provides an assemblage for the period between 3000 BC and AD 1200 (Fowler 1968). The lifeway indicated by all these sites is one of hunting-gathering nomadism, with reliance on small game and seed gathering and with the occasional taking of antelope, deer, and mountain sheep. Associated projectile points were predominantly of the Elko series, with small Rose Spring, Cottonwood, Eastgate, and Desert Side-notched arrowpoints representing the latest occupation.

In the Reese River valley, also in central Nevada, systematic archeological survey has disclosed a pattern of archeological site distribution interpreted as indicating seasonal transhumance between stream-side environments of the valley floor and piñon groves on the mountain slopes. This duplicates the historic Shoshoni pattern in the area and supports an extension of the historic occupation pattern at least as far back as 2500 BC (Thomas 1973). Work in progress at the extremely deep Gatecliff Shelter not far away has reached a depth of over 7.5 meters, with cultural deposits carbon-14 dated at 6000 BC and the promise of still earlier dates. Many discrete living floors are represented, and Gatecliff will unquestionably be of major importance to Great Basin prehistory as it is more fully investigated (Thomas n.d.).

In the western Great Basin, early Archaic sites are known from the vicinity of Lovelock, Nevada. Leonard Rockshelter, overlooking the vast Humboldt Sink, contains an early stratum of occupational debris carbon-14 dated at 5100 and 6700 BC. The scanty remains demonstrate the presence of the atlatl and dart, and *Olivella* shell beads give evidence of trans-Sierran contacts at an early date (Heizer 1951). Hidden Cave, not far away, contains dart points and other artifacts in sediments that have been assigned an age of over 7000 years based on geological correlations.

A long period for which no firm dates on cultural remains are available is followed by the Lovelock culture, dated between 2600 BC and AD 500 (Loud and Harrington 1929; Heizer and Napton 1970). This culture extends from the vicinity of Lovelock in west-central Nevada to the Honey Lake area of northeastern California. It was oriented toward life along the shores of lakes and marshes, as shown by very striking tule decoys covered by the feathered skins of real ducks, by the bones of fish, and by the seeds of marsh plants found in human feces at Lovelock Cave (Figure 4.9). A well-developed twined basketry complex and an abundance of milling stones attest to the importance of wild vegetal foods. Semisubterranean houses are said to be present at the Humboldt Lake bed site and are known from another site near the town of Lovelock, indicating a significant degree of occupational sedentari-

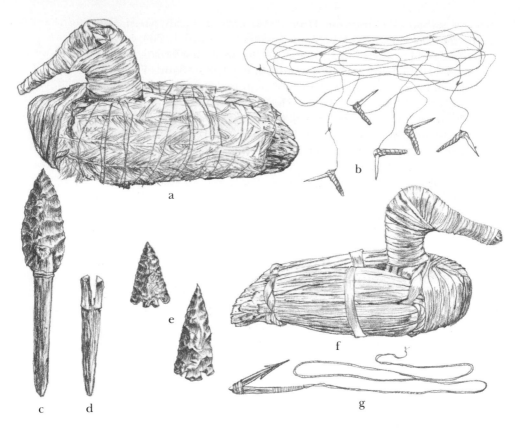

FIGURE 4.9
Lovelock culture artifacts: *a,* duck decoy of tule and duck feathers; *b,* fishhooks on setline; *c,* hafted knife; *d,* knife handle; *e,* projectile points; *f,* tule duck decoy; *g,* bone fishhook with wooden shank and twined line.

ness, based on the rich waterside economy (Cowan and Clewlow 1968). A number of carved effigies of fish, frogs, and monstrous zoomorphs have been found in the Lovelock culture area, and occasional burials containing such goods have been interpreted as the graves of shamans (Tuohy and Stein 1969). Modified and unmodified *Olivella* marine shell beads in some Lovelock culture assemblages indicate trade contacts across the Sierra with California, which further suggests the relative richness of Lovelock culture.

Whether there is historical continuity between the Lovelock culture and the northern Paiute or Washo who occupied the same general area in historic times is disputed. Grosscup (1960) concluded that there was probably a historical discontinuity between the Lovelock and northern Paiute cultures. Heizer and Napton (1970), on the other hand, assert a clear continuity from

Lovelock to historic cultures in the area, pointing out that projectile point and basketry types are similar enough to imply a direct historical connection.

Seasonal occupation of the eastern Sierra Nevada is well indicated by a series of lithic complexes found at the higher altitudes, where snow and cold would effectively prevent any year-round occupation. Best known is the Martis complex, with projectile points of distinctly Great Basin cast, which occurs in the Washo country and is probably ancestral, through the later Kings Beach complex, to the ethnographic Washo (Elsasser 1960). A series of complexes both north and south of the Martis area resemble it and Kings Beach and show widespread occupation throughout the Sierra at approximately the same time levels. A maximum age of 1000 BC has been estimated for the Martis complex (Elston 1971), but a carbon-14 date of 5100 BC from Spooner Lake in the Sierra suggests that it may be older, as does the similarity of some Martis projectile point types to Great Basin types significantly earlier than 1000 BC (Aikens 1972b).

In Surprise Valley, northeastern California, a program of survey and excavation led by O'Connell (1975) discovered five phases of occupation spanning the last 6000 years. The Menlo phase, carbon-14 dated between 4000 and 3000 BC, gives evidence at two sites of substantial semisubterranean earthlodges (Figure 4.10) on the valley floor, it is believed that people ranged out from these to occupy temporary camps found in several different micro-environmental zones from lakeshore to mountain slope. Many such small sites are located within several hours of foot travel from larger villages. Northern Side-notched and other projectile point types, lanceolate knives, T-shaped drills, tanged knives, and the mortar and pestle constitute the hunting and gathering tool complex. Bones of bison, deer, antelope, and mountain sheep are well represented, with jackrabbits, cottontails, and other small mammals being much less important. Waterfowl and such hibernating rodents as marmots and ground squirrels are conspicuously absent. It is believed likely that the pithouse villages were essentially sedentary settlements occupied the year round. The lack of hibernating animals in the food bone debris of the house floors, which suggests that the houses were not occupied in the summer months, may reflect living habits like those of the historic Klamath, who partially dismantled their earth lodges during the summer to dry them out, while living nearby in flimsy structures of brush.

The Bare Creek phase, dated from 2500 to 1000 BC, gives evidence of similar hunting-gathering practices, but the substantial earth lodges were apparently replaced by flimsy saucer-floored structures resembling the brush wickiups of the historic Paiutes of the region. Pinto series dart points (locally called the Bare Creek series) are characteristic of the period, along with ovoid and triangular knives and drills with teardrop-shaped handles. The mortar and pestle persist, and the mano and metate are added to the food-processing inventory. Ungulate bones decline significantly, and jackrabbits, cottontails, marmots, ground squirrels, and waterfowl increase, suggesting a possible

FIGURE 4.10
b

Surprise Valley dwellings: *a*, Menlophase earth lodge plan and reconstruction; *b*, Bare
Creek phase wickiup plan and possible ethnographic analogues. (After O'Connell 1975.)

environmental change. Increasing aridity might have lessened the local concentration of large ungulates and other resources, and this in turn, it is suggested, could account for the shift to smaller, lighter, and apparently more
temporary dwelling structures, reflecting a more extensive, less sedentary
pattern of occupation.

The succeeding Emerson, Alkali, and Bidwell phases, which bring Surprise
Valley occupation up to historic times, represent essentially a continuation
of the Bare Creek pattern, with some stylistic changes in artifact types and the
appearance of the bow and arrow during the Alkali phase, dated between
AD 500 and 1400.

The change in house and artifact types that took place between the Menlo and Bare Creek phases raises the possibility of a population replacement at this juncture. Sedentary villages with earth lodges are old in the Klamath-Modoc area northwest of Surprise Valley, while brush wickiups and less sedentary habitation patterns are characteristic of Great Basin Numic-speaking peoples as a whole. It may be that the cultural change noted around 2500 BC in Surprise Valley reflects a shift in the ranges of ancestral Klamath-Modoc and Surprise Valley Paiute, as the local environment changed from conditions suitable for the Klamath culture to more arid conditions to which Great Basin Numic culture was better adapted. Such a perspective would see the cultural change as a response to environmental change, a response in which migration rather than local readaptation was the solution. Whatever the conclusion to be drawn about this, the Surprise Valley sequence gives the impression of societies a good deal more localized and sedentary than is commonly envisioned for the Great Basin, and the very recent discovery of another village of semisubterranean houses well south of Surprise Valley suggests that such sedentariness may have been relatively common at certain periods in favored locations along the flanks of the northern Sierra (Elston 1976).

In the Klamath Basin, the historic people occupied villages of large semisubterranean earth lodges, not unlike those of the Menlo phase, and a carbon-14 date from a pithouse at Nightfire Island on Lower Klamath Lake shows that such structures were in use ca. 2100 BC. The bottom of the Nightfire Island midden is carbon-14 dated to 4100 BC, and the site was apparently occupied almost to historic times. Projectile point types changed from leaf-shaped and large side-notched dart points in earlier times to small, stemmed, notched, and barbed arrowpoints in later times, but in other respects the contents of the site showed remarkable continuity from the earliest through the latest occupation. Throughout time, the Nightfire Islanders emphasized fowling, fishing, and the gathering of plant foods to be ground with the mortar and pestle (Grayson 1973). Nightfire Island thus supports the concept of Klamath culture as old and stable, with the essentially ethnographic way of life extending deep into the past, as argued by Cressman (1956) on the basis of his excavations at Kawumkan Springs Midden on the Sprague River. Obsidian hydration dates recently determined on projectile points from Kawumkan Springs suggest a date of at least 3000 BC for the earliest level of occupation there (Aikens and Minor n.d.).

From caves of the Fort Rock Valley of south-central Oregon, a complex having leaf-shaped and stemmed projectile points, crescents, scrapers, scraper-planes, manos and metates, and sandals made of sagebrush bark is dated between 9000 and 6000 BC. This represents the San Dieguito-like Western Pluvial Lakes tradition discussed earlier. Thereafter, occupational intensity begins to decline. The period from 6000 to 5000 BC is characterized by leaf-shaped, corner-notched, and side-notched projectile points, knives, scrapers, manos, and twined basketry. Evidence of occupation all but disappears after the eruption of Mount Mazama around 5000 BC blanketed the landscape with a layer of volcanic ash; not until about 3000 BC was there significant reoccupation. The complex that then appears is dominated by small, slender, corner-notched points, knives, and scrapers. Manos and metates, mortars and pestles, and twined basketry increase markedly in frequency, suggesting intensified concentration on plant food resources. The available archeological record terminates at approximately 1000 BC. Occupation of the region surely continued to historic times, as suggested by numerous surface finds of late projectile point types, but digging by relic collectors destroyed the upper cave layers, which might have spanned this period, before they could be studied archeologically (Bedwell 1973).

Dirty Shame Rockshelter, on a small creek in the rolling Owyhee Plateau region of extreme southeastern Oregon, has given evidence of occupation as early as 7500 BC. Projectile points include rare Windust and Lake Mohave forms and more abundant Northern Side-notched, Humboldt Basal-notched, and Pinto series types. These, along with milling stones, twined basketry, and sandals very similar to those known for the Fort Rock Valley, come from three sequent cultural zones carbon-14 dated between 7500 and 3900 BC. After a 3200-year period for which there is no record of human presence, occupation resumed about 700 BC and continued until AD 1600 or later. Characteristic projectile points of the later period include types of the Pinto, Elko, and Rose Spring series. Of considerable interest are the remains of five or six circular pole-and-thatch houses or windbreaks built under the rockshelter between 700 BC and AD 900, which show close resemblance to ethnographic northern Paiute houses in technique of construction (Wheat 1967). Coiled basketry and Desert Side-notched arrowpoints appear only in the uppermost levels of the site, postdating AD 900.

In most functionally defined artifact classes, and in biota recovered from the deposits, the later occupation closely resembles the preabandonment occupation, but an increase in variety within the functional classes suggests a broader range of domestic activities at the shelter, perhaps signifying longer seasonal residence there, lasting into or through the winter. For both early and late periods, the vertebrate, invertebrate, and plant remains demonstrate extensive exploitation of the moist canyon-bottom environment and little reliance on the resources of the sagebrush grassland of the plateau top. Stone alignments elsewhere on the plateau suggest that drive hunting may have been practiced in the uplands, but these sites remain to be investigated (Aikens et al. n.d.).

Hundreds of unexcavated surface sites from the Catlow Valley, Warner Valley, Malheur Lake, Glass Buttes, and Alvord Lake areas have yielded artifacts of all periods from 9000 BC to historic times and give promise of much yet to be learned from them about the prehistory of the northern Great

Basin (Cressman et al. 1940; Cressman 1942; Weide n.d.; Fagan 1974; Mack 1975; Pettigrew 1975).

The series of postglacial fluctuations in temperature and moisture that Antevs (1948) termed the Anathermal (cool, moist conditions: 7000–5000 BC), Altithermal (warm, dry conditions: 5000–2500 BC), and Medithermal (modern conditions: after 2500 BC) have been a major focus of interest among Great Basin prehistorians because of their convinction that, in a desert land of sparse food resources, changes in the environment might require significant changes in the culturally conditioned behavior of the human occupants. Extreme earlier views that a hot, dry Altithermal period rendered the Great Basin largely unfit for human occupation have been tempered by increased knowledge of the archeological and paleoclimatic records. It is now clear that the Ana-Alti-Medi-thermal sequence describes only the broadest outlines of paleoclimatic change in the West, and that prehistorians have to reckon with more complex and local paleoclimatic sequences if they are to meaningfully relate changes in environment to changes in cultural-ecological systems.

The issue now being addressed is not whether there was in fact a period of environmental stress severe enough to drive humanity from the Great Basin (it is clear that there was not), but, rather, how demonstrable changes in local environments might have affected the structured system of interrelated economic activities by which a group maintained itself within a region. O'Connell's (1975) discussion of the possible relationship between climatic and cultural change in Surprise Valley and my summary (Aikens 1970) of the effect that change in the local environment of Hogup Cave had on human use of that site are examples of the current orientation; work elsewhere by others and work now in progress could extend the list of examples.

Great Basin peoples have long been thought of as extremely mobile, with no fixed residences but only a series of temporary stopping places in an annual round of marches between the sparse and scattered food sources of their country. Archeological evidence of fairly substantial house structures at different periods in Surprise Valley, the Humboldt-Carson Sink area, Little Lake, and other places in the Great Basin is beginning to suggest that there were times in the past when occupation in some locales was quite sedentary, especially around the shores of some of the remnant Pleistocene lakes. (The Fremont culture phenomenon is of course in a different class altogether, since it was founded on agriculture.) Great Basin archeology has long focused on the excavation of caves and rockshelters, but the emphasis is now changing. As it continues to shift toward the study of open sites, other such discoveries are probably to be expected.

The Numic-speaking peoples who occupied the Basin in historic times are believed, on both linguistic and archeological grounds, to have spread over the area only recently, perhaps within the last 1000 years, from a homeland in the southern Great Basin and southern California deserts. The impetus behind this spread has never been satisfactorily accounted for, and the Numic expansion remains one of the intriguing problems of Great Basin archeology. It may be that as we learn more about the waxing and waning of local and regional economic systems over time—perhaps with relative sedentariness possible at some times and more atomistic patterns necessary at others—we can offer an explanation for the Numic expansion couched in terms of cultural ecology. As O'Connell's Surprise Valley example shows, cultural adaptation to environmental change in a region can be accounted for by the notion of the in-migration of a people already adapted to similar environmental conditions elsewhere, as well as by the assumption of local *in situ* readaptation by the people living there prior to the environmental change. The Numic people, coming from an arid southern homeland, may have been in a sense preadapted to occupy a country on which the earlier inhabitants' hold had been weakened by unaccustomed economic stress in a deteriorating environment. Such an explanation for the Numic expansion is purely conjectural at present, and surely too simple as stated here, but given the current trend of Great Basin studies, it seems a likely direction for further attempts at explaining this phenomenon.

PLATEAU

Ethnographic Plateau culture was dominated by an orientation to salmon fishing, which concentrated populations along the Columbia River and its tributaries in the south and along the Fraser River and its tributaries in the north. Villages of 5 to 10 earth lodges were situated on the floodplains of major streams, where salmon could be taken during the summer spawning runs and stored for winter consumption. During spring and fall, the villages were largely depopulated as people ranged across the uplands back from the rivers, gathering camas lily and kous roots and hunting.

Salish-speaking people occupied the northern Plateau, reaching as far south as the Columbia at one point, and Penutian speakers were concentrated along the middle and upper Columbia. The concentration of Penutian languages along the Columbia and on the western coast of North America south of the river suggests that Penutian speakers have dominated the southern Plateau for a very long time, while linguistic and archeological evidence suggests that the Salishan peoples spread down from the northern Plateau much later (see Chapter 2).

What is probably the earliest current evidence of human occupation in the Northwest is represented by a few scattered Clovis Fluted points found at The Dalles, at several places in the Puget-Willamette lowland, and on the Snake River plain (Figure 4.2). None of these artifacts has been found in datable context, but if they are assigned an age of 9500 to 9000 BC, based on their dating on the Plains and in the Southwest, they immediately precede the earliest carbon-14-dated occupations at The Dalles and Wildcat Canyon on the middle Columbia, Marmes Rockshelter and the Windust Caves on the lower Snake, Lind Coulee in east-central Washington, and the Milliken site on the lower Fraser River of British Columbia. These related assemblages may be grouped with the loosely defined San Dieguito horizon already referred to for California and the Great Basin, since, like the complexes known further south, they are characterized by large leaf-shaped and stemmed lanceolate projectile points, lanceolate and ovate knives, large scrapers, scraping planes and choppers, and a near if not complete absence of milling stones.

The lower Snake River furnishes the most nearly continuous and best-described cultural sequence currently available for the Plateau (Leonhardy and Rice 1970). It begins with the Windust phase, assigned by 10 carbon-14 determinations from Marmes Rockshelter to the period from 8500 to 5500 BC (Figure 4.11). Diagnostic artifacts are of the types just mentioned. Other items found include large prismatic blades struck from polyhedral cores, single- and multiple-faceted burins, and bone awls, needles, and atlatl spurs. Split and broken food bone refuse represents deer, elk, pronghorn antelope, jackrabbit, cottontail rabbit, and beaver. Shell of the river mussel also occurs. A cremation pit and charred human bones are evidence of burial practices, and *Olivella* shell beads indicate contact with the Pacific coast.

The Cascade phase follows, dated to approximately 5500–3000 BC, although these dates are subject to possible revision. Diagnostic artifacts are medium-sized, finely flaked leaf-shaped Cascade points and edge-ground cobbles. Large side-notched points appear as part of the assemblage after about 5000 BC, but no other changes are noted at that time. Other items are large lanceolate and triangular knives, prismatic blades, tabular and keeled end scrapers, large flake scrapers, polished stone atlatl weights, and bone awls, needles, and atlatl spurs. Manos and small grinding stones of questionable identification also occur. Food remains include the bones of deer, elk, pronghorn antelope, salmon, and steelhead trout. Shell of river mussel also identifies that species as a food source. Burials were both flexed and extended, and in one case capped by a cairn of stones. *Olivella* shell beads were present as burial goods. Recently published evidence shows that semi-subterranean pithouses were also a characteristic of the phase (Brauner 1976).

There is clear historical continuity between the Windust and Cascade phases, as shown by their sharing of many artifact types. Significant new elements also appear in the Cascade phase, however. Manos and grinding stones, providing for the first time substantial evidence of vegetal food processing, and the appearance of pithouse architecture and salmon bones indicate that the subsistence-settlement pattern that dominated ethnographic Plateau culture had its beginnings at least as far back as the Cascade phase.

The following Tucannon phase is dated between 3000 and 500 BC. Triangular contracting-stemmed and corner-notched points, small side and end

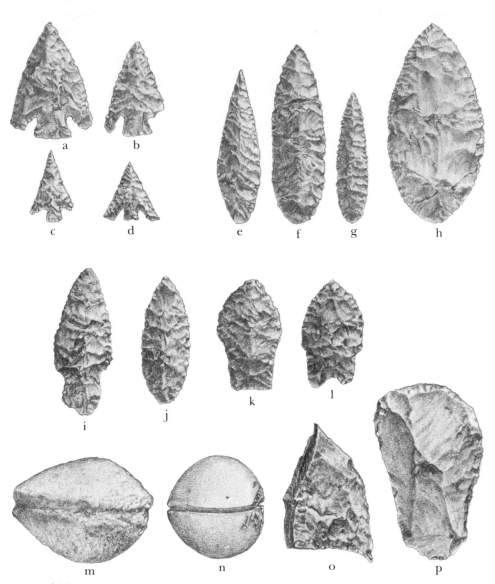

FIGURE 4.11
Diagnostic artifacts of the lower Snake River sequence: *a–d*, Harder phase; *e–h*, Cascade phase; *i–p*, Windust phase. (From *Prehistory of North America*, 2d ed., by Jesse D. Jennings. Copyright © 1968, 1974 by McGraw-Hill, Inc. Used with permission of McGraw-Hill Book Company.)

scrapers, sinker stones, hopper mortar bases, and pestles are characteristic items. Bone and antler awls and wedges and a bone net shuttle have also been found, along with the bones of deer, elk, pronghorn antelope, mountain sheep, small mammals, and a relative abundance of salmonid fishes and river mussels. *Olivella* shell beads occurred with a flexed burial of this phase from Marmes Rockshelter.

A break in cultural continuity between the Tucannon phase and the preceding Cascade phase has been hypothesized, but recent work has identified a possible transitional complex characterized by stemmed, indented-base points (Leonhardy 1975). At Alpowai, a winter village on the lower Snake River that was occupied throughout the past 6000 years, a substantial Tucannon phase component with pithouses and an artifact assemblage linking it to both preceding and succeeding phases evokes a further dimension of cultural continuity (Brauner 1976).

The beginning date for the Harder phase is fixed by several carbon-14 determinations at about 500 BC, and the terminal date is estimated at approximately AD 1300. During this period, villages of substantial semisubterranean earth lodges are common, notably at the Harder site (Figure 4.12). Diagnostic artifacts include both large basal- and corner-notched projectile points and smaller, more finely made points of similar form, indicating that both the atlatl and dart and the bow and arrow were in use. Small end scrapers, lanceolate and pentagonal knives, pestles, hopper mortar bases, sinkers, and bone awls, needles, beads, and gaming pieces are also common. Faunal remains are as in the preceding phase, with continuing importance of salmonids and the first evidence of the domestic dog.

The Piqunin and Numipu phases together span the final 700 years to historic times. Small, finely made corner-notched and stemmed arrowpoints, matting needles, and composite harpoons are added to an inventory that otherwise is essentially identical to that of the Harder phase. The sites of the earth lodge villages Wexpusnime and Alpowai give evidence of cultural continuity between the Harder phase and the historic Nez Perce peoples of the area. The Numipu phase is named to account for the historic end of the cultural continuum. There is abundant evidence of white contact, the adoption of the horse, and cultural influence from the Great Plains (Leonhardy and Rice 1970; Rice 1972).

The Dalles of the Columbia River, a long narrows filled with rapids, was in ethnographic times the most productive salmon fishery on the Plateau and is the locus of a number of archeological sites. The two Five-Mile Rapids sites (Roadcut site, WS-4, and Big Eddy, WS-1) on the Oregon side of the river contain a sequence representing most of the past since 8000 BC (Cressman 1960). The Initial Early period at the Roadcut site, dated by a carbon-14 determination to 7800 BC, contained a few large prismatic blades, scrapers, and bone artifacts. The Full Early, dated before about 5800 BC, yielded large leaf-shaped and shouldered and stemmed projectile points, ovate blades, and

FIGURE 4.12
Artist's reconstruction of a Harder phase pithouse from the lower Snake River region.
(From *Prehistory of North America,* 2d ed., by Jesse D. Jennings. Copyright © 1968, 1974 by
McGraw Hill, Inc. Used with permission of McGraw-Hill Book Company.)

heavy flake choppers comparable to those of the Windust phase on the lower
Snake. Also found were burins, bolas or sinker stones, a rich bone and antler
industry, an enormous number of salmon vertebrae (125,000 were counted,
representing about half the amount observed), and the bones of raptorial
birds, badger, marmot, fox, rabbit, beaver, otter, muskrat, and small rodents.
In the Final Early levels, bone refuse and bone and antler artifacts are no
longer found. The Transitional period is represented at the Roadcut site by
a hardpan layer from which only a few artifacts, mostly choppers, scrapers,
and peripherally flaked cobbles, were recovered.

The Late period, known from deposits in and overlying a level carbon-14
dated at 4100 BC, extends to historic times. Projectile points assigned to this
period belong to a wide range of types, including leaf-shaped points like
those of the Cascade phase on the lower Snake, triangular basal-notched
forms like those of the Harder phase, and small, delicately made basal-
notched and barbed points like those of the Piqunin phase. Edge-ground
cobbles, milling stones, choppers, scrapers, and pestles are also characteristic
of the Late period. The Full Historic period shows white trade goods in addition to aboriginal artifacts.

From sites on the Washington side of the Columbia, Butler (1959) has related the Congdon, Indian Well, Big Leap, Maybe, and Wakemap Mound

sites to infer a continuum of occupation comparable to that known from the Five-Mile Rapids sites. The Wildcat Canyon site, a few miles upriver from The Dalles on the Oregon side, has an important lower component with carbon-14 dates of 7900, 6100, and 5400 BC that contains projectile point forms like those from the Full Early period at Five-Mile Rapids and the Windust phase on the lower Snake. Pithouse villages are known at Wildcat Canyon, Mack Canyon, and other locations near the mouth of the John Day River, with carbon-14 dates spanning the last 3000 years (Cole 1967; 1968a; 1968b).

Cultural developments on the upper Columbia closely parallel those noted for the lower Snake region, except that a microblade complex that appears during the Indian Dan phase (4000–1500 BC) is apparently not represented farther south.

The most northerly Plateau archeological sequence to be mentioned here comes from the Lochnore-Nesikep locality on the Fraser River in British Columbia (Sanger 1967). The Early period there is dated between 5500 and 3000 BC by two carbon-14 determinations. Leaf-shaped and large side-notched points are earliest, with triangular corner- and base-notched points appearing by 4000 BC. Microblades are present though not abundant; antler wedges and rodent incisor chisels also occur. At the nearby Drynoch Slide site, salmon bones dated to 5100 BC give the earliest evidence of fishing, which continues to be important throughout the rest of the Lochnore-Nesikep sequence. The Middle period, 3000 BC to the beginning of the Christian era, exhibits stemmed, indented-base as well as side-notched and basal-notched points. Antler wedges, rodent incisor chisels, ground stone celts, and ground stone mauls indicate a well-developed woodworking complex. Deep semi-subterranean houses first appear shortly after 1500 BC at the Lochnore Creek site, and pithouses may be two centuries older at the Pine Mountain site. Microblades and tongue-shaped microcores were of great importance during the Middle period, being perhaps the dominant artifact class at that time. The Late period, from the beginning of the Christian era to historic times, contains corner- and basal-notched points, with small side-notched arrow-heads making their appearance about AD 1000. Other artifacts continue from the Middle period, with housepits becoming shallower and microblades being gradually phased out.

Farther down the Fraser and not in the Plateau proper, but occupying a site at a juncture between coast and interior analogous to that occupied by The Dalles of the Columbia River, is the Milliken site (Borden 1960). The lowest levels there have been assigned to the Milliken phase, which is carbon-14 dated between approximately 7500 and 6000 BC. Large leaf-shaped points, ovate knives, pebble choppers and scrapers, flake scrapers, and burins constitute an assemblage quite similar to the early ones from The Dalles and lower Snake River. The Milliken site, like those at The Dalles, overlooks a long rapids that was in historic times one of the best salmon fisheries on the Fraser River and a focal point of aboriginal activity. No faunal materials survive in the site deposits, but the location suggests that the site must have been occupied primarily as a fishing station. Subsequent phases continue the local tradition, with evidence of significant influence and elaboration stemming from cultural developments on the Pacific coast appearing after about 1000 BC.

The Snake River plain and northern Rocky Mountains of Idaho belong to the Columbia-Snake drainage system, and both regions provided the salmon and root crops that were the basis of ethnographic Plateau subsistence. Evidence from the Weis Rockshelter and other nearby sites suggests a cultural continuum in the mountains of northern Idaho running from approximately 5500 BC to the historic Nez Perce culture (Butler 1962; 1968). The Craig Mountain phase (5500–1500 BC) is a local equivalent of the Cascade phase on the lower Snake but is believed to have persisted significantly later in the mountains. The Grave Creek phase (1500–100 BC) continues the sequence, with only minor and gradual change. The Rocky Canyon phase (100 BC–AD 1700) is characterized by pithouse villages, hunting of deer, elk, and mountain sheep, and collecting of vegetal foods for processing with edge-ground cobble crushers and with manos and metates. The Camas Prairie phase is represented by Double House Village, a late prehistoric site with evidence of a circular mat lodge and a parallel-sided community structure like those of the historic Nez Perce.

The cultural sequence for southern Idaho begins with a handful of artifacts carbon-14 dated to approximately 12,500 BC from the bottom levels of Wilson Butte Cave on the Snake River plain (Gruhn 1961; 1965). These early dates are controversial (Haynes 1971), and the assemblage is too small to allow meaningful assessment of its relationship to other early manifestations. This site may, however, figure importantly in the regional prehistory when other finds of this period are made. Elsewhere on the Snake River plain surface finds of both Clovis and Folsom Fluted points suggest a Paleo-Indian occupation in the 9000 BC time range, and a sequence developed by Swanson (1972) at Birch Creek, near the northeastern extremity of the plain, carries the evidence of human occupation up to historic times.

The Birch Creek phase, dated between 7000 and 5000 BC, is characterized chiefly by large lanceolate points and otherwise is little known. Large shouldered and stemmed lanceolate points found elsewhere in Idaho (Butler 1967) are apparently of comparable age and are probably associated with the Birch Creek phase. These points, termed the Haskett type, are similar to those found in the San Dieguito-like complexes of the Great Basin and Columbia Plateau and suggest that the Birch Creek phase may have been affiliated with this early western cultural horizon. The Bitterroot phase, spanning the period from 5000 to 1000 BC, is dominated by large side-notched and unnotched points, end scrapers, and coarsely flaked fleshers. During the Beaverhead phase, dated from 1000 BC to AD 400, large side-notched, corner-notched, and stemmed, indented-base points all occur, along with end scrapers and coarse fleshers, as in the preceding phase. The Blue Dome phase, AD 500 to 1200, continues the tradition, with corner-notched points becoming numerically dominant but little other change indicated. The Lemhi phase, dated between AD 1200 and historic times, is characterized by small side-notched and corner-notched arrowpoints. These artifacts are identified with the Lemhi Shoshoni, ethnographic inhabitants of the area. According to Swanson (1972), this archeological continuum carries ancestral Northern Shoshoni culture back over 9000 years, showing these people to have been collectors of plant foods and hunters of mountain sheep, deer, bison, and smaller game, with a way of life essentially identical to that of historic times throughout this whole period.

As a conclusion to this discussion of Plateau prehistory, several areas of uncertainty may be mentioned. Many believe that the early occupants of the Columbia drainage were broad-spectrum hunters and gatherers who made little use of riverine resources, especially the salmon, until 1000 BC or even into the Christian era. Semisedentary villages of substantial earth lodges dated to this period and later are abundantly attested to in the archeological record. This has led to the inference that the pattern of ethnographically known Plateau culture—involving the catching, drying, and storing of salmon as a food reserve to make possible stable wintertime settlement—first emerged at about this time. It has been suggested that this characteristic Plateau pattern is earliest in the north, in the Fraser drainage, and that it expanded southward in relatively recent times, perhaps as a function of the southward spread of Salish-speaking peoples. However, despite the undeniable evidence of cultural influence from the north provided by the appearance of micro-blades on the Columbia, it has not been established that salmon fishing and pithouse architecture spread southward at the same time, or indeed that they had earlier origins along the Fraser than on the Columbia.

On the contrary, current evidence shows that salmon fishing flourished at The Dalles well before 6000 BC and was present on the middle Columbia and lower Snake by the Cascade phase, only slightly later. At the Drynoch Slide site on the Fraser, salmon bones have been dated to 5100 BC, and it has been cogently argued that the Milliken site, lower down the Fraser, was occupied as early as 7000 BC for the express purpose of salmon fishing. In short, the evidence suggests that salmon fishing is as ancient as the first well-established human occupation of the region, which is, after all, what might be expected. It is hardly to be imagined that the most abundant, obvious, and easily taken food resource of an entire geographical province would be neglected by its human inhabitants for some 7000 years before they began to develop a pattern of subsistence and settlement geared to exploiting it.

Surely the ethnographic pattern of summertime fishing along the major streams, spring and fall hunting and gathering in the tributary canyons and uplands, and winter settlement in the sheltered major canyons is older than the Christian era or even 1000 BC. It is true that pithouse villages do not characterize our current archeological record of early times, but this is hardly surprising, considering that the Columbia and Fraser are subject to truly awesome floods. Hammatt (1976) has summarized geological evidence indicating active alluvial cutting and deposition on the Columbia-Snake system between 3000 and 500 BC, and the stratigraphic record at the Sunset Creek site shows that culture-bearing deposits preceding the late pithouse village there were disturbed by fluvial erosion. There were no early pithouses found at Sunset Creek; there is, however, evidence of occupation, consisting of scattered artifacts eroded from their original context and redeposited in sand and gravel lenses, as early as the Vantage phase (Nelson 1969). And evidence that pithouses were in use by this time has recently been demonstrated by the finding of one dated to the Cascade phase on the lower Snake (Brauner 1976). Future archeological work will undoubtedly establish a much greater age for the basic ethnographically known Plateau pattern of subsistence and settlement than is currently accepted.

Almost all discussions of Plateau prehistory comment on cultural influences received from the Great Basin between approximately 5000 and 3000 BC. Triangular side-notched, corner-notched, and stemmed, indented-base projectile points, along with manos and metates, are believed to reflect Great Basin influence. Some have suggested that these traits represent a northward displacement of population from an increasingly arid Basin into the more favorable Plateau, but in fact no convincing evidence has been marshalled that these point types are earlier in the Great Basin than in the Plateau. This evidence is necessary if a direction of movement is to be spoken of. In fact, these general types are known from a vast area, including the Columbia drainage, the northern Great Basin, the Snake River plain, the northern Rocky Mountains, and the northern High Plains. Their appearance in the Plateau area, then, is less likely to be a sign of migrations from the Great Basin than an indication of far-flung contacts, geographical awareness, and sharing of ideas among aboriginal peoples throughout the West as a whole.

Southern Idaho, in certain aspects of both environment and culture an exception to much that might be said of the Plateau, is an exception to the preceding pronouncement about Basin-Plateau relationships as well. Linguistic and other traits of the ethnographic Shoshoni there unequivocally show a close relationship to Great Basin cultures. Swanson (1972), emphasizing ecological similarities between southern Idaho and the Great Basin, saw the region as basically akin to the Basin from very early times, so that in his perspective southern Idaho was always a subarea of the Great Basin rather than of the Plateau. Salmon runs far upstream on the Snake were comparatively meager; without a major abundant resource to depend upon, people were obliged to use sparser resources, as was characteristic of the Great Basin way of life. The historic occupation by clearly Great Basin peoples might be said to bear out Swanson's assessment, but substantial linguistic and archeological evidence (Goss 1968; Gruhn 1961; Madsen 1975) indicates that the northern Shoshoni probably entered the area within the last 1000 years, contrary to what Swanson believed, and it may be that they were successful in doing so because their Great Basin cultural patterns and habits were pre-adapted to the local conditions.

CONCLUSION

The culture history of the Far West may be seen in broadest terms as the development of three major traditions—California, Great Basin, and Plateau—out of a shared early Paleo-Indian culture represented by the Clovis and San Dieguito horizons (Figure 4.13). Within each major tradition, lesser regional or local traditions are indicated, beginning soon after 7000 BC. Cultural diversification closely follows environmental lines and demonstrates the close relationship between culture and environment at the hunting-gathering level of existence.

The divergent economic adaptations and varying levels of societal complexity developed among the three traditions can be seen as closely related to environmental factors. In California, a general biotic abundance and closely juxtaposed microenvironmental zones, making a wide range of resources available within a narrow compass, allowed sedentariness, dense population, and intergroup political-economic intercourse (including both trade and warfare) to develop early. Great Basin societies, by contrast, were much less dense and were farther ranging, as they had to be to make a living from the sparse resources of their land. Archeology is beginning to show, however, that even there societies may not have been so highly atomistic at all times and in all areas as they were when first recorded ethnographically. And where evidence of a richer life and broader social scale has been discovered—in the Lovelock culture, for example—the evidence can be closely tied to the year-round relative biotic richness of the particular area. Plateau societies, much more than those of the other two areas, were shaped by the concentrated abundance of a single major food resource (salmon), which early—how early is yet to be established with certainty—made possible a semisedentary existence, and around the seasonal taking of which societies organized the rest of their year.

The freedom of intercourse and travel that both Basin and Plateau peoples enjoyed, so different from the fear and suspicion that dogged and restricted the movements of native Californians outside their home territories, may also be seen to have environmental correlates. Because of the relatively sparse populations of the Basin and the Plateau, when there was abundance—of salmon in the Plateau, for example, or piñon pine nuts in the Basin—there was usually more than plenty for all comers; it did not profit local societies to control such resources by maintaining strict territorial boundaries. Further, such abundances did not occur everywhere, so that groups regularly traveled long distances across other peoples' usual ranges to participate in the harvest. There was no disadvantage to the people living nearest the sources of

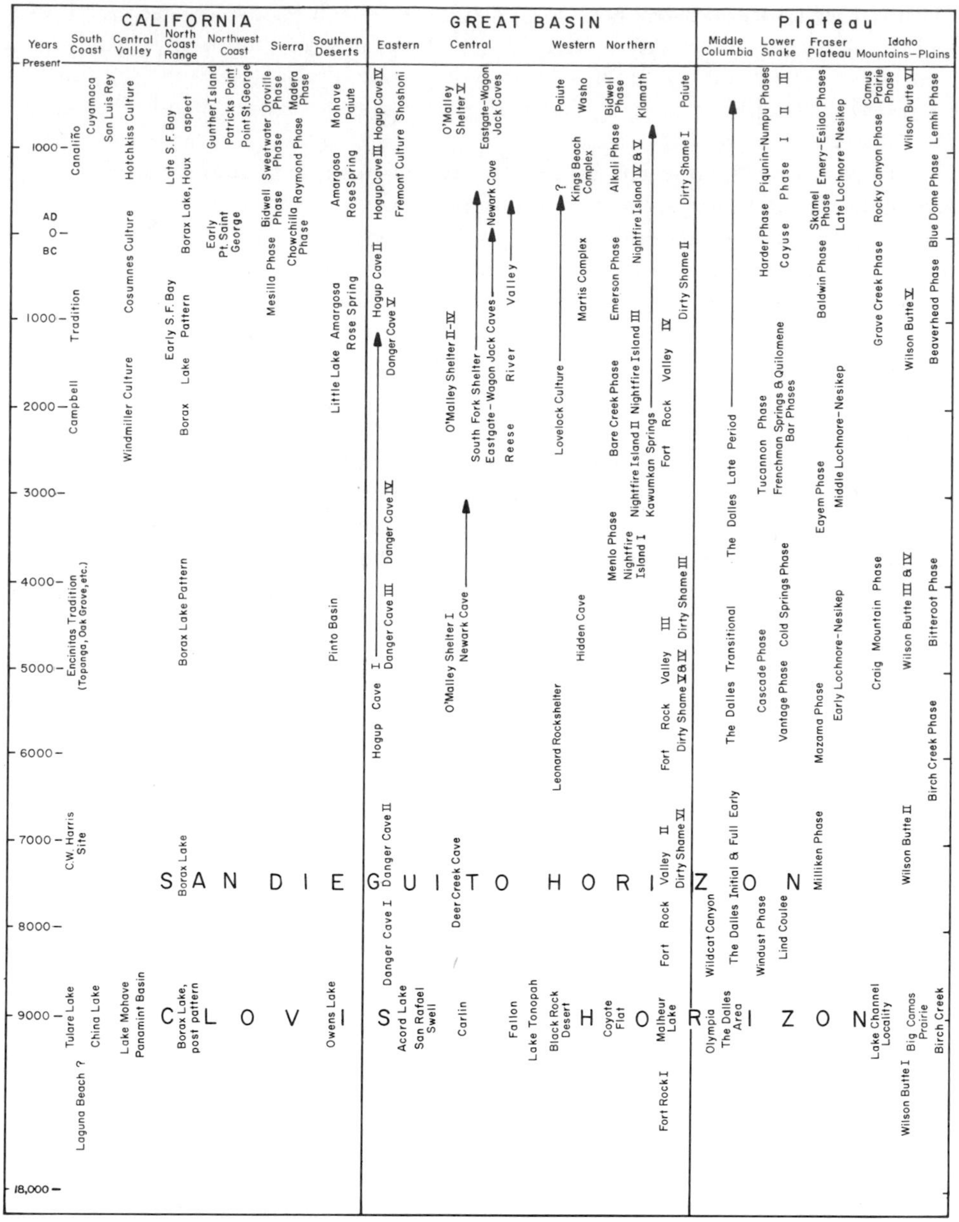

FIGURE 4.13
Regional traditions and local phases or complexes.

abundance, and there was a definite advantage to those who came there from farther away. In California, with its more general biotic richness, populations were much denser, and local societies husbanded their local resources, maintaining territorial boundaries against intruders and regulating distribution of their resources through well-defined trade conventions.

An overview of the prehistory of the Far West shows that many cultural traits, such as projectile point and basketry types and marine shell beads, are shared over vast distances. Some archeologists have seen in the distributions of certain traits evidence of migrations; others have argued for simple group-to-group stimulus diffusion. Undoubtedly both processes were operative in given cases. The point is raised here simply as a comment on the vast scale of cultural awareness on which, this evidence suggests, the prehistoric societies of the West operated. There is a tendency to imagine the known world of aboriginal cultures as small, and to think of the people as isolated and ignorant of events beyond their own narrow compass of time and place. But this is belied by the great distances across which similar concepts of style and form are expressed, and by the evident synchronism and parallelism of changes in such traits as projectile point types over vast areas. Whatever the specific mechanisms of contact, it is clear that in the Far West, throughout the period of record, distant peoples had considerable knowledge of one another. Despite the fact that serviceable and attractive innovations from elsewhere were adopted freely, there was no merging of cultural traditions because, after all, each tradition was maintained within and regulated by a distinctive concatenation of adaptive circumstances specific to its own geographical situation.

ACKNOWLEDGMENTS

I thank Robert F. Heizer, Michael J. Moratto, Thomas F. King, and David A. Fredrickson for their comments on the California section of this chapter.

References Cited and Recommended Sources

Aikens, C. Melvin 1967 Plains relationships of the Fremont culture: a hypothesis. American Antiquity 32:2:198–209.
———. 1970 Hogup Cave. University of Utah Anthropological Papers, No. 93.
———. 1972a Fremont culture: restatement of some problems. American Antiquity 37:1:61–66.
———. 1972b Surface archaeology of southwestern Washoe County, Nevada. Desert Research Institute Publications in the Social Sciences 9.
———. 1976 Cultural hiatus in the eastern Great Basin? American Antiquity 41:4:543–550.

Aikens, C. Melvin, David L. Cole, and Robert Stuckenrath n.d. Excavations at Dirty Shame Rockshelter, southeastern Oregon. Tebiwa. In press.

Aikens, C. Melvin, and Rick Minor n.d. Obsidian hydration dates for Klamath prehistory. Tebiwa. In press.

Allely, Steven 1975 A Clovis point from the Mohawk River valley, western Oregon. *In* Archaeological Studies in the Willamette Valley, Oregon, ed. C. Melvin Aikens. University of Oregon Anthropological Papers 8:549–552.

Anonymous 1968 Bill Mobley does it again. Utah Archaeology 13:1:13.

Antevs, Ernst 1948 Climatic changes and pre-white man. *In* The Great Basin, with Emphasis on Glacial and Post-Glacial Times. Bulletin of the University of Utah 38:(20), Biological Series 10:7:168–191.

Bada, Jeffrey L., and Patricia Masters Helfman 1975 Amino acid racemization dating of fossil bones. World Archaeology 7:2:160–173.

Bada, Jeffrey L., Roy A. Schroeder, and George F. Carter 1974 New evidence for the antiquity of man in America deduced from aspartic acid racemization. Science 184:791–793.

Bean, Lowell John 1974 Social organization in native California. *In* 'Antap: California Indian Political and Economic Organization, ed. Lowell John Bean and Thomas F. King. Ballena Press Anthropological Papers 2:11–34.

Bean, Lowell John, and Thomas C. Blackburn (eds.) 1976 Native Californians: A Theoretical Retrospective. Ramona, Calif.: Ballena Press.

Bean, Lowell John, and Thomas F. King (eds.) 1974 'Antap: California Indian Political and Economic Organization. Ballena Press Anthropological Papers 2.

Bean, Lowell John, and Harry W. Lawton 1973 Some explanations for the rise of cultural complexity in native California, with comments on proto-agriculture and agriculture. *In* Patterns of Indian Burning in California: Ecology and Ethnohistory, ed. Henry T. Lewis. Ballena Press Anthropological Papers 1:V–XI.

Beardsley, Richard K. 1954 Temporal and areal relationships in central California archaeology. Parts I, II. University of California Archaeological Survey Reports 24, 25.

Bedwell, S. F. 1970 Prehistory and environment of the Pluvial Fort Rock Lake area of south-central Oregon. Ph.D. dissertation, University of Oregon Department of Anthropology.

————. 1973 Fort Rock Basin Prehistory and Environment. Eugene: University of Oregon Books.

Berger, Rainer 1975 Advances and results in radiocarbon dating: early man in America. World Archaeology 7:2:174–184.

Berger, Rainer, Reiner Protsch, Richard Reynolds, Charles Rozaire, and James R. Sackett 1971 New radiocarbon dates based on bone collagen of California Paleoindians. Contributions of the University of California Research Facility 12:43–49.

Blackburn, Thomas 1974 Ceremonial integration and social interaction in aboriginal California. *In* 'Antap: California Indian Political Organization, ed. Lowell John Bean and Thomas F. King. Ballena Press Anthropological Papers 2:93–110.

Borden, Charles E. 1960 Djri 3, an early site in the Fraser canyon, British Columbia. National Museum of Canada Bulletin 162:101–118.

————. 1968 Prehistory of the lower mainland. *In* Lower Fraser Valley: Evolution of a Cultural Landscape, ed. Alfred H. Siemens. University of British Columbia, British Columbia Geographical Series 9:9–26.

Brauner, David Ray 1976 Alpowai: the culture history of the Alpowa locality. Ph.D. dissertation, Department of Anthropology, Washington State University.

Butler, B. Robert 1959 Lower Columbia Valley archaeology: a survey and appraisal of some major archaeological resources. Tebiwa 2:2:6–24.

————. 1962 Contributions to the prehistory of the Columbia Plateau. Occasional Papers of the Idaho State College Museum 9.

————. 1963 An early man site at Big Camas Prairie, south-central Idaho. Tebiwa 6:1:22–33.

————. 1965 Contributions to the archaeology of southeastern Idaho. Tebiwa 8:1:41–48.

————. 1967 More Haskett points from the type locality. Tebiwa 10:1:25.

————. 1968 A guide to understanding Idaho archaeology. Special Publication of the Idaho State University Museum.

————. 1970 A surface collection from Coyote Flat, southeastern Oregon. Tebiwa 13:1:34–57.

————. 1972 Folsom points from the Upper Salmon River valley. Tebiwa 15:1:72.

Campbell, Elizabeth W., and William H. Campbell 1937 The Lake Mohave site. *In* The Archaeology of Pleistocene Lake Mohave: A Symposium, ed. Elizabeth W. Campbell et al. Southwest Museum Papers 11:9–24.

Carter, George F. 1958 Archaeology in the Reno area in relation to the age of man and the culture sequence in America. Proceedings of the American Philosophical Society 102:2:174–192.

Clewlow, C. W., Jr. 1968 Surface archaeology of the Black Rock Desert, Nevada. University of California Archaeological Survey Reports 73:1–94.

Cole, David L. 1967 Archaeological research of site 35 SH 23, the Mack Canyon site. Report of the Museum of Natural History, University of Oregon, to the Bureau of Land Management.

———. 1968a Archaeological excavations in area 6 of site 35 GM9, the Wildcat Canyon site. Report of the Museum of Natural History, University of Oregon, to the National Park Service.

———. 1968b Report on archaeological research in the John Day dam reservoir area, 1967. Report of the Museum of Natural History, University of Oregon, to the National Park Service.

Cowan, Richard A., and C. W. Clewlow, Jr. 1968 The archaeology of site NV-PE-67. University of California Archaeological Survey Report 73:195–236.

Cressman, Luther S. 1936 Archaeological survey of the Guano Valley region in southeastern Oregon. University of Oregon Monographs, Studies in Anthropology 1:1–48.

———. 1942 Archaeological researches in the northern Great Basin. Carnegie Institution of Washington, Publication 538.

———. 1956 Klamath prehistory: the prehistory of the culture of the Klamath Lake area. Transactions of the American Philosophical Society 46:4:375–515.

———. 1960 Cultural sequences at The Dalles, Oregon; a contribution to Pacific Northwest prehistory. Transactions of the American Philosophical Society 50:(10).

Cressman, Luther S., Howel Williams, and Alex D. Krieger 1940 Early man in Oregon. University of Oregon Monographs, Studies in Anthropology 3:1–78.

Cruxent, Jose M. 1962 Phosphorus content of the Texas Street "hearths." American Antiquity 28:1:90–91.

Davis, E. L. 1963 The desert culture of the western Great Basin: a lifeway of seasonal transhumance. American Antiquity 29:2:202–212.

———. 1975 The "exposed archaeology" of China Lake, California. American Antiquity 40:1:39–53.

Davis, E. L., Clark W. Brott, and David L. Weide 1969 The western lithic co-tradition. San Diego Museum Papers 6.

Davis, E. L., and Richard Shutler, Jr. 1969 Recent discoveries of fluted points in California and Nevada. Nevada State Museum Anthropological Papers 14:154–178.

Day, Kent C. 1964 Thorne Cave, northeastern Utah: archaeology. American Antiquity 30:1:50–59.

Decker, D. A. 1969 Early archaeology on Catalina Island: problems and potential. University of California, Los Angeles, Archaeological Survey Annual Report 11:69–84.

Elsasser, Albert B. 1960 The archaeology of the Sierra Nevada in California and Nevada. University of California Archaeological Survey Reports 51:1–93.

Elsasser, Albert B., and Robert F. Heizer 1966 Excavation of two northwestern California coastal sites. University of California Archaeological Survey Reports 67:1–150.

Elston, Robert 1971 A contribution to Washo archaeology. Nevada Archaeological Survey Research Paper 2.

———. 1976 Highway archaeology in the territory of the northern Washo, summer 1975. Nevada Archaeological Survey Report for March 1976, pp. 18–24.

Euler, Robert C. 1964 Southern Paiute archaeology. American Antiquity 29:3:379–381.

Fagan, John L. 1974 Altithermal occupation of spring sites in the northern Great Basin. University of Oregon Anthropological Papers 6.

Fowler, Don D. 1968 The archaeology of Newark Cave, White Pine County, Nevada. Desert Research Institute Social Sciences and Humanities Publications 3.

Fowler, Don D., David B. Madsen, and Eugene M. Hattori 1973 Prehistory of southeastern Nevada. Desert Research Institute Publications in the Social Sciences 6.

Fredrickson, David A. 1974a Cultural diversity in early central California: a view from the North Coast ranges. Journal of California Anthropology 1:1:41–53.

————. 1974b Social change in prehistory: a central California example. *In* 'Antap: California Indian Political and Economic Organization, ed. Lowell John Bean and Thomas F. King. Ballena Press Anthropological Papers 2:55–74.

Fried, Morton 1967 The Evolution of Political Society. New York: Random House.

Gerow, Bert A. 1974 Co-traditions and convergent trends in prehistoric California. San Luis Obispo County Archaeological Society Occasional Paper 8.

Gerow, Bert A., and Roland W. Force 1968 An Analysis of the University Village Complex, with a Reappraisal of Central California Archaeology. Stanford: Stanford University Press.

Glennan, William S. 1976 The Manix Lake lithic industry: early lithic tradition or workshop refuse? Journal of New World Archaeology 1:7:43–61.

Goss, James A. 1968 Culture-historical inference from Utaztekan linguistic evidence. *In* Utaztekan prehistory, ed. Earl H. Swanson, Jr. Occasional Papers of the Idaho State University Museum 22:1–42.

Gould, Richard A. 1966 Archaeology of the Point St. George site and Tolowa prehistory. University of California Publications in Anthropology 4.

Grabert, G. F. 1968 North-central Washington prehistory. University of Washington Department of Anthropology, Reports in Archaeology 1.

Grayson, Donald K. 1973 The avian and mammalian remains from Nightfire Island. Ph.D. dissertation, University of Oregon Department of Anthropology.

Grosscup, Gordon L. 1960 The culture history of Lovelock Cave, Nevada. University of California Archaeological Survey Reports 52.

Gruhn, Ruth 1961 The archaeology of Wilson Butte Cave, south-central Idaho. Occasional Papers of the Idaho State College Museum 6.

————. 1965 Two early radiocarbon dates from the lower levels of Wilson Butte Cave, south-central Idaho. Tebiwa 8:2:57.

Gunnerson, James H. 1956 A fluted point site in Utah. American Antiquity 21:4:412–414.

————. 1962 Plateau Shoshonean prehistory: a suggested reconstruction. American Antiquity 28:1:41–45.

Hammatt, Hallett H. 1976 Geological processes and apparent settlement densities along the lower Snake River: a geo-centric view. Paper presented at the 29th Annual Meeting of the Northwest Anthropological Conference, Ellensburg, Washington.

Harrington, Mark R. 1933 Gypsum Cave, Nevada. Southwest Museum Papers 8.

————. 1948 An ancient site at Borax Lake, California. Southwest Museum Papers 16.

————. 1957 A Pinto site at Little Lake, California. Southwest Museum Papers 17.

Harrington, Mark R., and Ruth D. Simpson 1961 Tule Springs, Nevada, with other evidence of Pleistocene man in North America. Southwest Museum Papers 18.

Haynes, C. Vance, Jr. 1969 The earliest Americans. Science 166:709–715.

————. 1971 Time, environment, and early man. Arctic Anthropology 8:2:3–14.

————. 1973 The Calico site: artifacts or geofacts? Science 181:305–310.

Heizer, Robert F. 1951 Preliminary report on the Leonard Rockshelter site, Pershing County, Nevada. American Antiquity 17:2:89–98.

Heizer, Robert F., and Martin A. Baumhoff 1961 The archaeology of two sites at Eastgate, Churchill County, Nevada. I. Wagon Jack Shelter. University of California Anthropological Records 20:(4).

————. 1970 Big game hunters in the Great Basin: a critical review of the evidence. Contributions of the University of California Archaeological Research Facility 7:1–12.

Heizer, Robert F., Martin A. Baumhoff, and C. W. Clewlow, Jr. 1968 Archaeology of South Fork Rockshelter (NV E1 11), Elko County, Nevada. University of California Archaeological Survey Reports 71:1–58.

Heizer, Robert F., and Rainer Berger 1970 Radiocarbon age of the Gypsum culture. Contributions of the University of California Archaeological Research Facility 7:13–18.

Heizer, Robert F., and Alex D. Krieger 1956 The archaeology of Humboldt Cave, Churchill County, Nevada. University of California Publications in American Archaeology and Ethnology 47:(1).

Heizer, Robert F., and Lewis K. Napton 1970 Archaeology and the prehistoric Great Basin lacustrine subsistence regime as seen from Lovelock Cave, Nevada. Contributions of the University of California Archaeological Research Facility 10.

Hester, Thomas Roy 1973 Chronological ordering of Great Basin prehistory. Contributions of the University of California Archaeological Research Facility 17.

Hunt, Alice P. 1960 Archaeology of the Death Valley salt pan, California. University of Utah Anthropological Papers 47.

Hunt, Alice P., and Dallas Tanner 1960 Early man sites near Moab, Utah. American Antiquity 26:1:110–117.

Jennings, Jesse D. 1957 Danger Cave. University of Utah Anthropological Papers 27. (Also released as Society for American Archaeology Memoir 14.)

————. 1974 Prehistory of North America. 2d ed. San Francisco: McGraw-Hill.

————. 1975 Preliminary report: excavation of Cowboy Caves. Submitted in fulfillment of the provisions of permit no. 74-UT-011 issued by Bureau of Land Management and United States Department of the Interior. University of Utah Department of Anthropology.

Jennings, Jesse D., Alan R. Schroedl, and Richard N. Holmer n.d. Sudden Shelter. University of Utah Anthropological Papers. In press.

Johnson, Fredrick, and John P. Miller 1958 Review of "Pleistocene Man at San Diego," by George F. Carter. American Antiquity 24:2:206–210.

King, Chester D. 1974 The explanation of differences and similarities among beads used in prehistoric and early historic California. In 'Antap: California Indian Political and Economic Organization, ed. Lowell John Bean and Thomas F. King. Ballena Press Anthropological Papers 2:75–92.

————. 1976 Chumash inter-village economic exchange. In Native Californians: A Theoretical Retrospective, ed. Lowell J. Bean and Thomas C. Blackburn, pp. 289–318. Ramona, Calif.: Ballena Press.

King, Linda B. 1969 The Medea Creek cemetery: an investigation of social organization from mortuary practices. University of California, Los Angeles, Archaeological Survey Annual Report 11:23–68.

King, Thomas F. 1974 The evolution of status ascription around San Francisco Bay. In 'Antap: California Indian Political and Economic Organization, ed. Lowell John Bean and Thomas F. King. Ballena Press Anthropological Papers 2:35–54.

Kroeber, A. L. 1925 Handbook of the Indians of California. Bureau of American Ethnology Bulletin 78.

————. 1962 The nature of land-holding groups in aboriginal California. University of California Archaeological Survey Reports 56:19–58.

Leach, Larry L. 1967 Archaeological investigations of Deluge Shelter, Dinosaur National Monument. PB 176 960, Clearinghouse for federal and technical information, Springfield, Virginia.

Leonhardy, Frank C. 1975 The lower Snake River culture typology—1975: Leonhardy and Rice revisited. Paper presented at the 28th Annual Meeting of the Northwest Anthropological Conference, Seattle, Washington.

Leonhardy, Frank C., and David G. Rice 1970 A proposed culture typology for the lower Snake River region, southeastern Washington. Northwest Anthropological Research Notes 4:1:1–29.

Lewis, Henry T. 1973 Patterns of Indian burning in California. Ballena Press Anthropological Papers 1.

Lilliard, J. B., Robert F. Heizer, and Franklin Fenenga 1939 An introduction to the archaeology of central California. Sacramento Junior College Department of Anthropology, Bulletin 2.

Lister, Robert H. 1951 Excavations at Hells Midden, Dinosaur National Monument. University of Colorado Studies, Series in Anthropology 3.

Loud, Llewellyn L., and Mark R. Harrington 1929 Lovelock Cave. University of California Publications in American Archaeology and Ethnology 25:(1).

Mack, Joanne M. 1975 Cultural resources inventory of the potential Glass Buttes geothermal lease area, Lake, Harney, and Deschutes counties, Oregon. Final report to the United States Bureau of Land Management. Copy on file, University of Oregon Department of Anthropology.

Madsen, David B. 1975 Dating Paiute-Shoshoni expansion in the Great Basin. American Antiquity 40:1:82–86.

Madsen, David B., and Michael S. Berry 1975 A reassessment of northeastern Great Basin prehistory. American Antiquity 40:4:391–405.

Marwitt, J. P. 1970 Median village and Fremont culture regional variation. University of Utah Anthropological Papers 95.

Meighan, Clement W. 1954 A late complex in southern California prehistory. Southwestern Journal of Anthropology 10:215–227.

——. 1959 California cultures and the concept of an Archaic stage. American Antiquity 24:3:289–305.

Meighan, Clement W., and C. Vance Haynes, Jr. 1970 The Borax Lake site revisited. Science 167:1213–1221.

Moratto, Michael J. 1972 A study of prehistory in the southern Sierra Nevada foothills, California. Ph.D. dissertation, University of Oregon Department of Anthropology.

Mundorff, J. C. 1971 Nonthermal springs of Utah. Utah Geological and Mineralogical Survey, Water Resources Bulletin 16.

Nelson, Charles M. 1969 The Sunset Creek site (45-KT-28) and its place in Plateau prehistory. Washington State University Laboratory of Anthropology Reports of Investigations 47.

O'Connell, James F. 1975 The prehistory of Surprise Valley. Ballena Press Anthropological Papers 4.

Osborne, Douglas 1956 Evidence of the early lithic in the Pacific Northwest. Research Studies of the State College of Washington 24:1:38–44.

Perkins, R. F. 1967 Clovis-like points in southern Nevada. The Nevada Archaeological Survey Reporter 9:9–11.

——. 1968 Folsom and Sandia points from Clark County. The Nevada Archaeological Survey Reporter 2:4:4–5.

Pettigrew, Richard M. 1975 Cultural resources survey in the Alvord Basin, southeastern Oregon. Final report to United States Bureau of Land Management. Copy on file, University of Oregon Department of Anthropology.

Ragir, Sonia 1972 The Early Horizon in central California prehistory. Contributions of the University of California Archaeological Research Facility 15.

Rice, David G. 1972 The Windust phase in lower Snake River region prehistory. Washington State University Laboratory of Anthropology Reports of Investigations 50.

Richards, Brian 1968 A Clovis point from northwestern Nevada. The Nevada Archaeological Survey Reporter 2:3:12–13.

Riddell, Francis A. 1969 Pleistocene faunal remains associated with carbonaceous material. American Antiquity 34:2:177–180.

Riddell, Francis A., and W. H. Olsen 1969 An early man site in the San Joaquin Valley, California. American Antiquity 34:2:121–130.

Ritter, E. W. 1970 Northern Sierra Foothill archaeology: culture history and culture process. Center for Archaeological Research at Davis (University of California), Publications 2:171–184.

Rogers, Malcolm J. 1945 An outline of Yuman prehistory. Southwestern Journal of Anthropology 1:167–198.

Sanger, David 1967 Prehistory of the Pacific Northwest Plateau as seen from the interior of British Columbia. American Antiquity 32:2:186–197.

Schroeder, Albert H. 1963 Comments on Gunnerson's "Plateau Shoshonean Prehistory." American Antiquity 28:4:559–560.

Service, Elman R. 1962 Primitive Social Organization: An Evolutionary Perspective. New York: Random House.

Shutler, Mary Elizabeth, and Richard Shutler, Jr. 1959 Clovis-like points from Nevada. Masterkey 33:1:30–32.

——. 1963 Deer Creek Cave, Elko County, Nevada. Nevada State Museum Anthropological Papers 11.

Shutler, Richard, Jr.; C. Vance Haynes, Jr.; John E. Mawby; Peter J. Mehringer, Jr.; W. Glen Bradley; and James E. Deacon 1967 Pleistocene studies in southern Nevada. Nevada State Museum Anthropological Papers 13.

Simpson, Ruth D. 1976 A commentary on W. Glennan's article. Journal of New World Archaeology 1:7:63–66.

Smith, Elmer R. 1941 The archaeology of Deadman Cave, Utah. Bulletin of the University of Utah 32:(4). Revised and reprinted in 1952 as University of Utah Anthropological Papers 10.

Stanley, Dwight A., Gary M. Page, and Richard Shutler, Jr. 1970 The Cocanour site: a western Nevada Pinto phase site with two excavated "house rings." Nevada State Museum Anthropological Papers 15:1–46.

Steward, Julian H. 1937 Ancient caves of the Great Salt Lake region. Bureau of American Ethnology Bulletin 116.

Stickel, E. G. 1968 Status differentiation at the Rincon site. University of California, Los Angeles, Archaeological Survey Annual Report 10:209–261.

Strong, Emory 1969 Stone Age in the Great Basin. Portland: Binfords and Mort.

Swanson, Earl H., Jr. 1972 Birch Creek: Human Ecology in the Cool Desert of the Northern Rocky Mountains, 9000 BC–AD 1850. Pocatello: University of Idaho Press.

Swanson, Earl H., Jr., and Paul G. Sneed 1966 Birch Creek papers no. 3: the archaeology of the Shoup Rockshelters in east-central Idaho. Occasional Papers of the Idaho State University Museum 17.

Tadlock, W. Louis 1966 Certain crescentic stone objects as a time marker in the western United States. American Antiquity 31:5:662–675.

Thomas, David Hurst 1973 An empirical test for Steward's model of Great Basin settlement patterns. American Antiquity 38:2:155–176.

————. n.d. Preliminary progress report: Gatecliff Shelter, Nye County, Nevada. 1975 Excavations. Unpublished manuscript, Department of Anthropology, The American Museum of Natural History, New York.

Tripp, George W. 1966 A Clovis point from central Utah. American Antiquity 31:3:435–436.

True, Delbert L. 1966 Archaeological differentiation of Shoshonean and Yuman-speaking groups in Southern California. Ph.D. dissertation, Department of Anthropology, University of California, Los Angeles.

Tuohy, Donald R. 1968 Some early lithic sites in central Nevada. In Early Man in Western North America, ed. Cynthia Irwin-Williams. Eastern New Mexico University Contributions in Anthropology 1:4:27–38.

————. 1969 Breakage, burin facets, and the probable linkage among Lake Mohave, Silver Lake, and other varieties of Paleo-Indian projectile points in the desert west. Nevada State Museum Anthropological Papers 14:132–152.

————. 1970 The Coleman locality: a basalt quarry and workshop near Falcon Hill, Nevada. Nevada State Museum Anthropological Papers 15:143–206.

Tuohy, Donald R., and Mercedes C. Stein 1969 A late Lovelock shaman and his grave goods. Nevada State Museum Anthropological Papers 14:96–130.

Wallace, William J. 1962 Prehistoric cultural development in the southern California deserts. American Antiquity 28:2:172–180.

Warren, Claude N. 1967 The San Dieguito complex: a review and hypothesis. American Antiquity 32:2:168–185.

————. 1968 Cultural tradition and ecological adaptation on the Southern California coast. In Archaic Prehistory in the Western United States, ed. Cynthia Irwin-Williams. Eastern New Mexico University Contributions in Anthropology 1:3:1–14.

Warren, Claude N., and Anthony J. Ranere 1968 Outside Danger Cave: a view of early man in the Great Basin. In Early Man in Western North America. ed. Cynthia Irwin-Williams. Eastern New Mexico Contributions in Anthropology 1:4:6–18.

Warren, Claude N., and D. L. True 1961 The San Dieguito complex and its place in California prehistory. University of California, Los Angeles, Archaeological Survey Annual Report for 1960–61:246–337.

Weide, Margaret L. 1968 Cultural ecology of lakeside adaptation in the western Great Basin. Ph.D. dissertation, Department of Anthropology, University of California, Los Angeles.

Wheat, Margaret 1967 Survival Arts of the Primitive Paiutes. Reno: University of Nevada Press.

Winter, Joseph C., and Henry G. Wylie 1974 Paleoecology and diet at Clyde's Cavern. American Antiquity 39:2:303–315.

Wormington, H. M. 1955 A reappraisal of the Fremont culture. Proceedings of the Denver Museum of Natural History 1.

Above: Bison herds near Lake Jessie (North Dakota), sketched by John Mix Stanley, Pacific Railroad surveys, July 10, 1853. (Photograph by Smithsonian Institution.)

Below: Bones of 300 butchered bison from Hell Gap period mass kill ca. 8000 BC, Jones-Miller site, Colorado. (Copyright © National Geographic Society.)

CHAPTER FIVE

The Prehistoric Plains

Waldo R. Wedel

In the nineteenth century the Plains were called the Great American Desert. It was the considered opinion of informed men that the Great Plains constituted a largely uninhabitable region, that even the Indians had been unable to live there before the introduction of horses and rifles. Actually, as Dr. Wedel demonstrates, the Plains were the home of strong, long-lasting lifeways and fairly complex social organizations for many millennia before the invention of firearms or the introduction of the horse.

The Great Plains are visualized here as that portion of the northern temperate grassland lying east of the Rocky Mountains between 32° and 52° north latitude (Wedel 1961). North to south, the region measures nearly 2400 kilometers; eastward, it extends 800 to 1100 kilometers from the mountain front to, or slightly beyond, the 95th meridian west. As thus arbitrarily defined for archeological purposes, it covers approximately two million square kilometers of land whose salient characteristics are low to moderate surface relief; a continental climate featuring cold, dry winters, hot, dry summers, and a scanty and uncertain precipitation regimen; and an original or potential native vegetation of perennial grasses with trees limited to stream valleys, scarp lands, and hilly or mountainous localities (Figure 5.1).

The region has been known to white men since the earliest days of Euro-American exploration of the continental interior (Wedel 1975). Beginning in the mid-sixteenth century, Spanish adventurers who had traversed the dry scrub and desert grasslands of Mexico and the Pueblo Southwest spoke well of the verdant pasturage when they reached the Llano Estacado, of the prodigious numbers of "wild cows," and of the picturesque dog-nomads who followed the herds as they roamed the land. Later and far to the north, British fur traders from the forested lands of eastern Canada had, by the last quarter of the eighteenth century, begun to apply to the treeless grasslands the designation Great Plains (Lewis 1975:32). In contrast, the first American

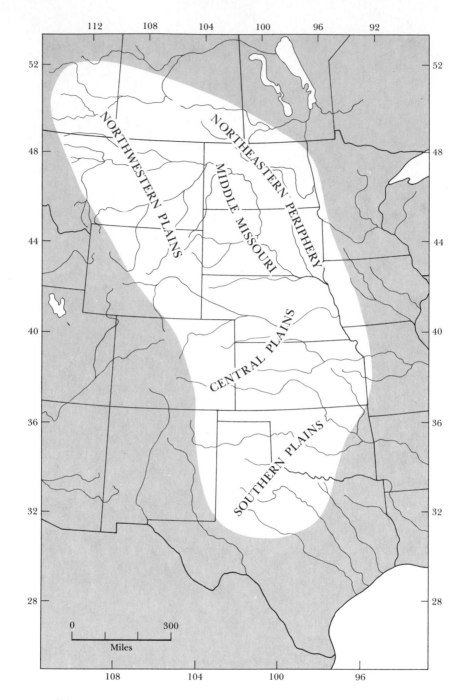

FIGURE 5.1
Map of the North American Great Plains area and its subareas. Subareas recognize the
archeological diversity and specializations that took place in Archaic and later periods.
(After Wedel 1961.)

explorers in the early 1800s called the central portions the Great American Desert, and considered it unfit for human occupation west of the 98th or 99th meridian; most nineteenth-century observers of the native peoples seem to have tacitly accepted the mid-nineteenth-century dictum of Morgan (White 1959:41) that the prairies (read "plains") were only made tolerable to the Indian by his possession of the horse and the rifle. Many years later, Hough (1930:315) saw matters differently and voiced the opinion that "what would appear to have been the most important event in the life of Asiatic tribes assimilating themselves to American environments was getting in touch with the buffalo." At about this same time, expanding archeological fieldwork was providing new perspectives on native American culture history and indicating that the ethnographically conditioned views of man's recent arrival on the Great Plains were out of joint with reality.

Despite the uniformity implied by their usual designation, the Great Plains exhibit much geographical diversity. Topographically, they include flatlands, tablelands, badlands, dunes, hills, stream valleys, and detached mountain masses. Lying in the rain shadow of the Rockies, their climate is produced largely by the interaction of three principal air masses, whose movements, though varying from time to time, are essentially west to east (Borchert 1950). Mild air from the Pacific moving eastward has lost most of its moisture content by the time it crosses the Great Basin and the Rockies, where it meets moist warm subtropical air pushing north from the Gulf of Mexico and cold dry Arctic air flowing south from Canada. A strong flow of westerlies results in an expanding aridity in the Great Plains, which is most pronounced in the west. Changes in circulation patterns that weaken the westerlies and permit the intrusion of moisture-laden tropical air may significantly increase the regional precipitation (see weather system maps in Chapter 1). Such changes in climatic behavior, varying greatly in frequency, intensity, and duration, and the resulting variations in abundance and distribution of plants and animals in the region are a familiar feature of the environmental setting today; there is accumulating evidence that such changes have been going on for a long period of time as measured in terms of the human occupation. For great portions of the Plains region, the moisture available is very often marginal, whether for crop growing in the eastern sections or for grass and pasturage in the western range lands; the vagaries of nature are also reflected increasingly in the archeological record.

The "sea of grass" that greeted the first white men was not always thus, but its origins and its evolution through time are still very imperfectly known. Molluscan evidence (Frye and Leonard 1952:180) suggests a progressive drying of the Kansas-Nebraska region since mid-Pleistocene times, culminating in a biologically severe climate of hot, dry summers and cold, dry winters as far back as 12,000 years ago. There is botanical and pollen evidence that until perhaps 14,000 years ago, when the Des Moines lobe of the continental ice sheet reached its maximum southward extent in present central Iowa, a spruce forest extended from Iowa across northeastern Kansas, Nebraska, and the Dakotas, to merge with the western coniferous forest running eastward from the Rocky Mountains (Wright 1970). The nature of the contemporary vegetation in the present steppe country of western Kansas and eastern Colorado is still unclear. The boreal forest was replaced by deciduous forest and this, in turn, by grassland around 8000 or 10,000 years ago. Thus, by 10,000 years ago, considerable portions of the Great Plains were suited for occupation by large, gregarious herbivores (Bryson and Wendland 1967), and the archeological evidence indicates that such occupation was indeed taking place. Open forests and parklands, varying from time to time in composition and extent, apparently persisted along the southwestern margins (Wendorf and Hester 1975).

Historically, the grasses and other vegetation of the region varied from east to west in accord with the observed precipitation and other climatic factors. In the west, beyond the 100th meridian, there existed a north-south belt of short grasses (chiefly *Bouteloua* and *Buchloe*) peculiarly adapted to dry soils and a short uncertain growing season, with 37.5 centimeters or less of annual precipitation. Eastward, where precipitation rises to 62.5 and finally to 100 centimeters annually, the steppe gave way to mixed grasses and then to tall-grass bluestem prairie. All of this region is included in the *needlegrass-pronghorn-grama grass* biome of Shelford (1963:328). It is also the heart of the former range of the bison, ecologically a dominant in the short-grass and mixed-grass areas and a resource of prime importance to the human inhabitants throughout most of man's residence in the region.

There were other food resources, both plant and animal, to supplement the bison or to serve as substitutes when that animal was unavailable or in short supply. Animals included pronghorn, mule and white-tailed deer, elk, black and grizzly bears, and numerous smaller fur bearers. Birds were of minor importance as food, but feathers and skins were used for ritual paraphernalia (Ubelaker and Wedel 1975) and bones in toolmaking. Fish and shellfish were utilized in varying degrees at some periods and in some sections. Important wild food plants included the prairie turnip (*Psoralea*), groundnut (*Apios*), ground bean (*Amphicarpa*), sunflower and Jerusalem artichoke (*Helianthus*), bush morning glory (*Ipomoea*), and prickly pear (*Opuntia*). In prehorse days, pigweed (*Amaranthus*), ragweed (*Ambrosia*), and various grasses may have supplied seeds, young shoots, and the like. Wild plums and chokecherries (*Prunus*), buffalo berries (*Shepherdia*), serviceberries (*Amelanchier*), and other fruits were gathered; in the south, mesquite (*Prosopis*) beans were available. Excepting the pits of the berries and fruits and occasional charred grass seeds, little of the vegetal material is known from the archeological record; its importance in prehistoric times must be inferred primarily from the ethnographic record for tribes in and adjoining the Plains region.

The vegetational and climatic differences between western and eastern Plains subregions were reflected in the general distribution of native peoples in historic times. The semiarid western steppe has always been primarily an area of hunting and gathering subsistence economies in which human settlement and activities were concentrated along the stream valleys and around the springs and waterholes where the game herds also tended to congregate (Wendorf and Hester 1962; Wedel 1963). The domain of Apachean dog-nomads in the sixteenth century (D. Gunnerson 1956), these lands were taken over, after introduction of the horse in the seventeenth century, by other tribes drawn from surrounding areas by the abundance of bison. The customs of these linguistically and culturally diverse newcomers were reshaped by environmental factors (Oliver 1962) into the more or less uniform lifeway of mobile, horse-using bison hunters. They included the Dakota, Cheyenne, Arapaho, Comanche, Kiowa, and others—the "typical" Plains tribes of Wissler (1922:22).

In the mixed and tall-grass prairies of the eastern Plains, where climate and soils were suited to maize horticulture, there were settled communities of village Indians. Fertile, easily worked valley bottom soils made possible an increasingly productive subsistence economy, often with sufficient crop surpluses to support trade with nonhorticultural bison hunters to the west. The villagers were mainly Siouan and Caddoan speaking. Unlike the horse-nomads, they seem to have had deep roots in the same region where they lived when the whites met them; their way of life, divided between seasonal bison hunting and maize-bean-squash-sunflower cultivation, is now known to have a historical depth of perhaps a half-millennium before the earliest whites arrived. Their way of life, in its horticultural practices and crops, its houses and settlement patterns, its ceramic and other industries, reveals strong relationships with the eastern Woodland cultures of the Mississippi-Ohio valley, whence the culture, and probably in considerable measure the people as well, were apparently derived. By contrast, the nonhorticultural equestrian bison hunters of the short-grass steppe were only the last variants in a long succession of people following a "true" Plains lifeway based on mobility, portability of possessions, and prime reliance on bison hunting.

Among all the natural food resources of the Plains, the bison has been most appropriately termed "the material and spiritual focus of plains life and culture for thousands of years" (McHugh 1972:11). The archeological record indicates that this has been true for at least 10,000 years. To the extent that the animal bone refuse from man's ancient living sites can be regarded as reflecting the associated environmental setting, it appears likely also that over these millennia there have been wide fluctuations in the numbers of bison available to their human predators. Especially suggestive is the work of Dillehay (1974), based on the recorded presence of bison bones at archeological sites in the Southern Plains of Texas, Oklahoma, and New Mexico. On the basis of presence or absence of bison in the faunal lists, which admittedly are too often suggestive or vague rather than definitive, he has proposed the following chart of changing long-term bison populations for the region:

Presence Period I:	10,000 to 6000–5000 BC
Absence Period I:	6000–5000 to 2500 BC
Presence Period II:	2500 BC to AD 500
Absence Period II:	AD 500 to AD 1200–1300
Presence Period III:	AD 1200–1300 to AD 1550

Since the data here are drawn from the archeological record, it could be argued that "absence periods" reflect the incompleteness or inadequacy of that record, rather than actual absence of bison. Equally plausible is the view that the data indicate substantially diminished herds rather than their total disappearance. The periodicity, extent, and intensity of man's utilization of the Plains, at least prior to adoption of cultigens where feasible, more or less directly reflect the abundance and availability of the number-one food product, the bison. It can be further suggested that a study similar to Dillehay's on long-term bison population fluctuations for the northern Plains would be desirable.

This chapter is aimed at updating a summary review of Plains archeology and culture history that was prepared some 12 years ago (Wedel 1964); the same basic outline is followed here. The years since 1962 have witnessed an impressive burgeoning of archeological activity in nearly all parts of the region and the accumulation of much new information. The number of trained workers active today has increased substantially, as has their financial support. Radiocarbon dates in ever-growing numbers have sharply improved our chronological controls. The greater involvement of geologists, palynologists, climatologists, and trained specialists from other disciplines has been highly productive at all time levels from early man to the historic period. Ecological studies utilizing midden leavings once routinely discarded are helping to convert the accumulating knowledge into a measure of better understanding of the significance of our findings. All of this means, of course, that the interpretations of a decade or two ago are now in need of revision, as the updated views of today soon will be. It means also that space limitations here will force the slighting of much of the recently acquired information and its significance (Figure 5.2).

THE EARLY BIG-GAME HUNTERS (10,000–5,000 BC)

Nowhere in the Great Plains have the archeological investigations of the past 15 years produced more exciting results than among the remains of the early hunting cultures of the western steppe lands. These investigations have involved primarily game kills and butchering sites, but attention has in-

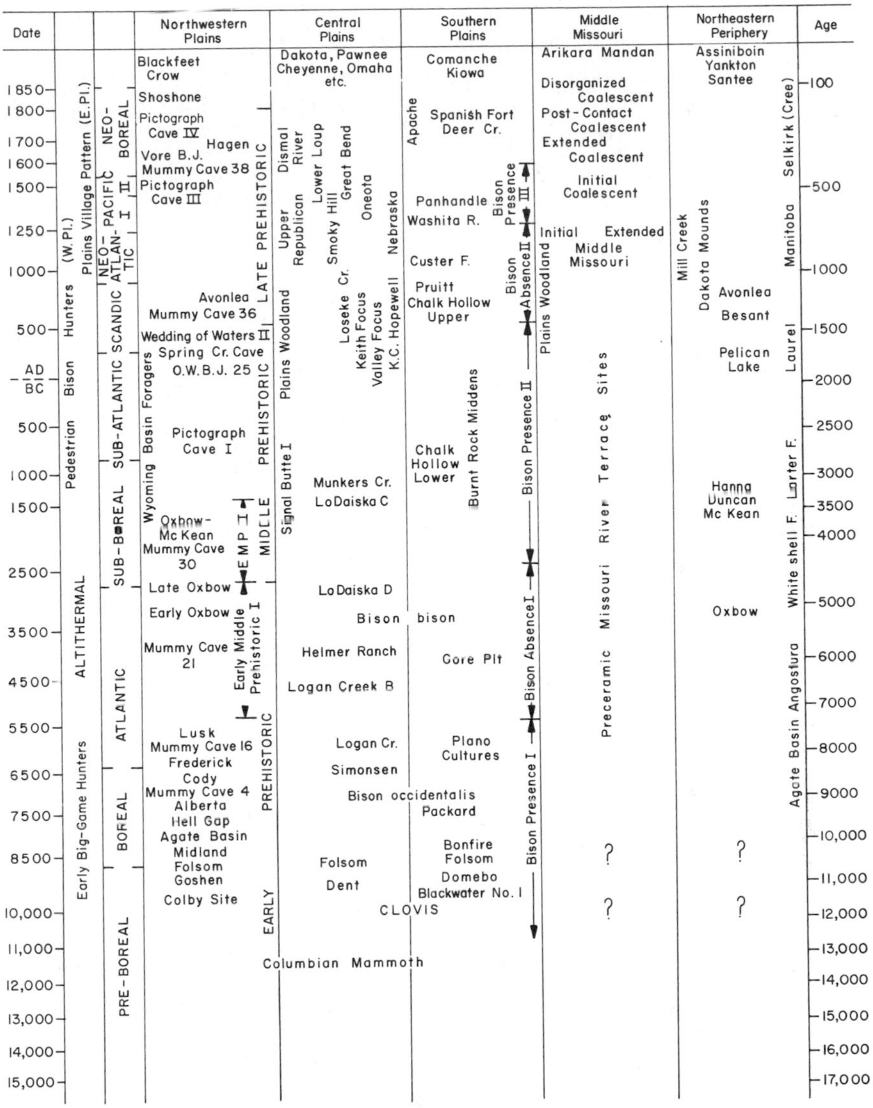

FIGURE 5.2
General time relationships of certain archeological complexes and sites in the Plains area.

creasingly been devoted to camp sites and habitation levels. The sites date fairly consistently between 12,000 and 7,000 years ago and include both complexes that have elsewhere been termed fluted point cultures and materials of the later makers of unfluted lanceolate points. In recent years, meticulously detailed interdisciplinary recovery and analysis techniques have increasingly been brought to bear on these materials. Often the major focus of interest has been less on the artifacts that once titillated amateurs and professionals alike and more on the refuse animal bone and what critical study of it can tell the qualified observer about contemporary animal behavior and biology, ancient hunting and butchering methods, and other possible cultural practices of the early hunters. Inferences and understanding thus generated, when cautiously used, can provide stimulating new insights into the evolving lifeways of human societies operating over thousands of years.

My designation of these groups as early big-game hunters indicates continuing acceptance of Sauer's (1944) observation that this term adequately reflects what we think we know about one of the principal activities of the early Plains people—the food quest. No implication is intended that their subsistence economy did not also include the seasonal or opportunistic use of vegetal products, small game, and perhaps other comestibles that may have been available from time to time but of which neither direct nor indirect evidence has yet been recognized in the material culture inventory as now known. The qualifier "early" distinguishes these ancient Americans from the later bison hunters of post-Altithermal times. In time span they correlate approximately with the Early Prehistoric period of Mulloy (1958:219) and the Late Early Prehistoric of Reeves (1973:1222) in the northern Plains.

The oldest dated materials with clearly established association of men and animals in the Great Plains are still those assigned to the Clovis or Llano complex (Sellards 1952; Wormington 1957). These are mainly in the western and southern sections. They consist of mammoth kills, which may include as well the bones of camel, horse, and giant bison of species now extinct. They cluster between 11,000 and 11,500 radiocarbon years before present (Haynes 1964) and are still without known cultural antecedents. When diagnostic artifacts are associated, they usually involve Clovis or "Clovis-like" Fluted spear points, along with choppers, cutting tools, rare milling stones, and several kinds of bone tools. At the better-known Plains sites, such as Miami (Texas), Dent (Colorado), Domebo (Oklahoma: Leonhardy 1966), and Blackwater No. 1 (New Mexico: Hester 1972), the number of animals killed ranges from one to perhaps a dozen; but where more than one is indicated, it is possible, and sometimes demonstrable, that several killings are involved. The kills are generally associated with waterholes, springs, or stream-side situations, to which a need for water or the presence of better browse or grazing probably drew the animals. Here they were apparently slain by men armed with thrusting or throwing spears, very likely working in groups and perhaps from ambush, and showing some preference for immature animals and females. Butchering was evidently carried out where the animals fell. There is no evidence of dug pits or other constructed traps.

No campsites, dwelling remains, or burials of the mammoth hunters have yet been described from the Plains; but a sparse, scattered, and transient population, probably camping in the neighborhood of springs and waterholes, may be inferred. Little is known of their tool inventory beyond items found in the kills. At Blackwater No. 1, debris believed to have washed from a Clovis campsite included quantities of Alibates chert from quarries approximately 160 kilometers distant. At the same site a grinding stone is regarded as possible indication of use of plant foods to supplement the meat diet, though it could doubtless have served as well for the grinding of dried meat.

Recently discovered but still incompletely reported finds at the Clovis time level include three or more immature mammoths associated with projectile points and butchering tools near Worland, Wyoming (Frison and Wilson 1975), which have been dated at 11,200 years before present, and one or more young animals at former spring sites near Wray, Colorado (Stanford, personal communication), with evidence of man's involvement in the killing or processing. The UP mammoth kill near Rawlins, Wyoming, which had cutting, scraping, and piercing tools in association but no diagnostic projectile points (Irwin 1970), also dates to approximately 11,000 years ago. Somewhat beyond the usual range in time of the dated man-mammoth associations noted above is the lower level of the Lamb Spring site near Littleton, Colorado, where disarticulated mammoth bones underlay a bed of similarly disarticulated bison bone and yielded a radiocarbon bone date of 11,150 ± 1,000 BC (M-1464). Some of the mammoth bones and fragments from this site are now believed to carry butchering marks; others are regarded as possible bone skinning tools; and a *Camelops* phalanx from beneath a pile of mammoth bones was clearly worked by man (Wedel n.d.a).

More abundant and much better known than the sites of the mammoth hunters are the later ones left by people to whom the mammoth was apparently no longer available and who therefore turned their attention to the smaller but more plentiful herd animals that remained. Chief among these were large bison of species now extinct, which seem to have figured to a much lesser extent in the subsistence economy of the preceding elephant hunters. One supposes that these animals, like the mammoth before them, were taken singly or in small groups by stalking, ambush, or other methods available to individual hunters or to small parties, working near waterholes, along game trails, from blinds, with grass fires, or in deep snow where conditions were suitable. Waterholes and the green flats around them, particularly on the drier to semiarid uplands, doubtless attracted bison 10 millennia ago as they did in the nineteenth century. The hazards of hunting bison in such ways may have been reduced somewhat by the seeming tameness of the animals unless they were frightened or aroused (Hammond and Rey 1953:749), a characteristic remarked upon also by Lewis and Clark on the upper Missouri in the spring of 1805 (Thwaites 1904:I, 335; II, 17, 27). Such small-scale efforts, witnessed and reported by the sixteenth- and seventeenth-century Spaniards among the Southern Plains dog-nomads (Hammond and Rey 1953:404; Ayer 1916:55), would have provided a subsistence livelihood, so long as contact was not lost with the herds. The development of effective meat-preserving methods, such as drying, presumably provided stores of food for use in winter or at other times when the bison were not readily available.

The archeological evidence, as was first hinted at Folsom in 1927, has since shown clearly that long before the coming of the Spanish the prehorse Indians had devised highly successful techniques for procuring adequate meat supplies. These exploited the gregarious behavior of the bison and their readiness for headlong flight en masse when they considered themselves threatened, and they featured the mass killing of dozens to hundreds of animals by cooperative efforts. Awareness of the historical depth and wide-spread use of communal drives, brought about particularly by the archeological work of the past 15 years has injected new perspectives into western Plains prehistory by dramatizing the multimillennial antiquity of the prime requirement for native man's occupation of the Great Plains—primary subsistence from the bison and its products.

Neither historical, ethnographic, nor archeological evidence tells us how often attempted communal bison drives were only partially successful or failed entirely. But the early and apparently spectacularly unsuccessful attempts of Mendoza's Spanish cavalry to corral large numbers of bison in the Southern Plains in October of 1598, though they "tried in a thousand ways to drive them inside the corral" (Hammond and Rey 1953:401), as well as Hind's observation nearly three centuries later (Hind 1859:55) among the Saskatchewan Cree that a portion of the stampeding herd broke out of the trap and escaped, remind us that successful mass kills required careful planning, good organization, coordinated execution, and doubtless a measure of good luck insured by ritual sanction—in short, much more than merely chasing a herd of skittish beasts over a bluff or into a pen to its wholesale destruction.

Mass bison kills by such methods as pounding and jumping have been the subject of a voluminous and growing literature, with no end in sight; useful discussions of a general nature are readily available (e.g., Forbis 1962; Malouf and Conner 1962; Kehoe 1967, Frison 1971; 1972; 1974). In historical times, many northern Plains tribes still regularly obtained their winter meat supply by cooperative drives (see Arthur, n.d., for an excellent review). This usually involved the construction of a corral or "pound" from logs and brush, into which up to 200 or more animals were driven through converging lines of piles of brush, sod, stones, or buffalo chips that began wide apart far out on the flats where the herd was gathered. Appropriate rituals to propitiate the animals and help lure them into the trap were celebrated beforehand. In earlier days, before the horse was available to extend the range of gathering operations, the animals were often driven over a cliff or "jump," with or without a corral below, where animals not done in by the fall could be dispatched with lance, dart, or arrow. No jump operation was ever recorded by eyewitnesses, but there are vivid accounts of the scenes at the pound (e.g., Hind 1959:55). For the older prehorse period, we have only the archeological record from which to reconstruct the operation. In broken country, the terrain sometimes provided natural lanes along which the bison could be urged into a man-made enclosure, over a fall, or into a box canyon or escape-proof ravine. With all of these methods, of course, the hunters had to assure themselves that the wind was right, the bison correctly dispersed over the gathering basin, and all participants properly positioned for the drive. If the herd was large enough to stampede blindly and to be unable to turn back before entrapment, and if each hunter did his part well, the chances for success were reasonably good.

The great antiquity of multiple bison kills in the Plains region is indicated by several sites that have been dated either by radiocarbon or by projectile point typology. At least three of these have yielded fluted Folsom points, but only one has also produced carbon-14 dates. At Blackwater No. 1, several pond-side kills of fewer than seven animals each are identified with the Folsom occupation at ca. 8000 years BC (Hester 1972:167). At the original Folsom site, where 19 points were found with 23 large bison in proximity to an ancient bog, no dates are available. There are also no dates for Lipscomb, Texas, where 18 points, plus scrapers, flake knives, and chips, were associated with 23 or more large bison (Schultz 1943), many of whose skeletons were still in articulation.

Much larger numbers of animals, and different projectile point styles, were involved in several other kills that have also yielded dates in the vicinity of 10,000 years ago. At Olsen-Chubbuck (Wheat 1972) in the Big Sandy drainage of eastern Colorado, the systematically butchered remains of nearly 200 bison (*B. occidentalis*) of all ages and both sexes were uncovered in an ancient arroyo into which the beasts had been stampeded and slain by hunters, who left among the debris unfluted points and other artifacts assigned to the Firstview complex. Less than 160 kilometers to the north, on the west bluff line of the Arickaree River, and more than 240 kilometers east of the mountain front, the Jones-Miller site (Stanford 1974) has yielded the remains of some 300 *Bison antiquus* from several fall through winter kills associated with Hell Gap projectile points, cutting and scraping tools of stone, and bone implements. Near Casper, Wyoming, no fewer than 75 *B. antiquus* were trapped in a parabolic sand dune and processed by Hell Gap hunters (Frison 1974). At the extreme southern end of the Great Plains, in the breaks along the Rio Grande 24 kilometers above Pecos River, Bone Bed 2 at Bonfire Shelter, with three radiocarbon dates at ca. 8000 BC (Dibble and Lorrain

1968:51; Dibble 1970), yielded Plainview-like and Folsom points, together with other stone artifacts and the bones of an estimated 120 animals representing a large, now extinct species within the range of both *B. antiquus* and *B. occidentalis*. Olsen-Chubbuck was a single kill; the others listed involve several events over periods of undetermined length.

The kills just listed are of particular significance not only for their high yield to the hunters and as evidence of the antiquity of human history in the region, but also because the meticulous recovery and analytical techniques employed throughout their archeological examination have made possible meaningful reconstructions of the methods followed by the early hunters; of the number, age, and composition of the quarry herd; and of the procedures by which the animals were processed for final human consumption. The details are readily available in the excellent studies cited and in others still to come, and need not detain us here. To those who still hold that hunting bison on foot was an unproductive business (Farb 1968:113) and that the prehorse Indians lived perpetually on the verge of starvation, it may be instructive to reflect on Wheat's (1972:114) calculations that the Olsen-Chubbuck herd probably made available to its destroyers approximately 60,000 pounds of meat, tallow, and other products, most of which seems to have been actually butchered out for use. How this was divided between fresh meat for immediate use and meat to dry for future consumption is not known, but interesting problems that must have confronted the Indians, and possible solutions, are ably discussed. By implication, periods of feasting, even gorging, undoubtedly occurred after the prehorse hunts, as they did following those of historical times.

In addition to the kill sites and bone beds, Folsom and later Paleo-Indian materials also occur at a growing number of sites where domestic and other activities seem to have been carried on. At Blackwater No. 1, for example, hunting and skin-working tools used in processing game from nearby lakeside kills predominate, including fluted points, plano-convex end scrapers, cutting tools, and a few bone artifacts. A much larger range of materials came from the Lindenmeier site, regarded by Roberts (1936) as probably seasonally occupied for periods of several weeks at a time by fairly large groups. The people were perhaps drawn to the spot by water, firewood, and game concentrations near waterholes, which provided opportunities for getting a winter's supply of meat and skins for clothing. Other than the points, few of the tools are of distinctive types. No traces of habitations were found. Some indications of Paleo-Indian settlement patterns are emerging from such studies as Wendorf and Hester (1962) on the Llano Estacado and, somewhat outside the Plains, by Judge and Dawson (1972) in the middle Rio Grande.

Hell Gap, an important series of campsites rather than kills, provides the longest and most complete stratigraphic record in the region for the early bison hunters. Here Plainview-like points were found beneath a Folsom occupation, from which circumstance it has been suggested (Irwin 1971) that this complex, since renamed (Irwin-Williams et al. 1973:46) the Goshen complex, is technologically and chronologically transitional from Clovis to Folsom culture. Viewing the post-Clovis manifestations here as "one culture with variations over time and changes in tool kits, but with basic typological unity," Irwin (1971:48) further proposes the term *Itama culture* for a succession of complexes designated Plainview or Goshen (9000–8800 BC), Folsom (8800–8550 BC), Midland (8650–8350 BC), Agate Basin (8450–7950 BC), Hell Gap (7950–7450 BC), Alberta (7450–6950 BC), and Cody (6750–6350 BC). Throughout this sequence at Hell Gap, the major faunal element in the sites is bison. Subcircular postmold patterns from the Midland level, and again in the following Agate Basin level, are identified as possible house remains. In a later level identified as Frederick complex, a circle of rocks is noted as suggestive of the stone tipi rings of later times; with this complex (6350–5950 BC) are included the bones of deer, small animals, and shellfish, as well as bison. The overlying Lusk complex (5950–5450 BC) has a varied tool kit, including Angostura-like points, and also a varied faunal assemblage perhaps reflecting local cultural adjustments to a changing climatic setting.

In the Southern Plains, environmental fluctuations appear to have been associated with cultural changes during the earlier millennia of human occupation. From molluscan and other evidence, it appears that a drying trend began at least 20,000 years ago and then changed to cooler and moister conditions between ca. 12,000 and 8,500 BC; with the latter came an expansion of boreal forest onto the Llano Estacado. As drier conditions returned, trees again disappeared and lakes and ponds dried up. Concurrently, Folsom man appeared on the scene, to be replaced by carriers of the Agate Basin complex, the first in this locality "of [a] series of related projectile point styles attributed to the Plano horizon (Scottsbluff, Milnesand, Portales, Eden, etc.)" (Wendorf and Hester 1975:275). By ca. 6000–5000 BC, the region was again mostly treeless except along ravines, and the uplands were essentially without surface water.

THE PLAINS ARCHAIC (5000 BC to BC/AD)

In the Northwestern Plains, archeological thinking has been organized for some years around the temporal sequence set up in the early 1950s by Mulloy (1952; 1954a; 1954b; 1958). This included the Early Prehistoric period, prior to 6000 years ago, characterized by small nomadic groups specializing in bison hunting, and involving Folsom and "Yuma" complexes. Following a time span of uncertain length for which there was then no available archeological evidence but which presumably ended more than 3500 years ago, other peoples appeared whose economy featured plant gathering and small-animal hunting, with little or no emphasis on bison hunting. Two similar but sequent complexes evolved, which were designated the Early Middle and Late Middle Prehistoric periods; both were represented at the stratified McKean site in northeastern Wyoming. About AD. 500, the Late Prehistoric period began, involving various groups, some of them from the ceramic-horticultural village people of the eastern Plains, who may have been drawn to a western Plains hunting life by an increasing abundance of bison. Some of these groups were directly ancestral to historical hunting tribes of the region.

This basic chronological outline is still being followed, though with important modifications in light of greatly increased data and more adequate time controls. The thesis that the economies of the Middle Prehistoric period comprised small-game hunting and generalized gathering, with little use of bison, is now regarded as applicable primarily to the Big Horn and Wyoming basins. Ecologically, these are more like the Great Basin than the Great Plains, and such a setting would have fostered a forager type of subsistence economy. Elsewhere in the Northwestern Plains, including the prairie provinces of Canada, the story throughout seems actually to have been one of relatively simple subsistence groups relying heavily on the bison, "of wandering foot nomads almost wholly dependent on buffalo for food, clothing, and shelter" (Forbis 1968:40). A period of putative nonoccupation of the region noted by Mulloy, the Altithermal interval, will be discussed later.

Before the last of the early big-game hunters, as represented by the "Plano" complexes, had left the Plains, cultural complexes based on a differently oriented subsistence economy had established themselves in mountainous and hilly sectors of the region, as well as in the broken country that borders much of the flatlands. Unlike the early hunter sites, with their finely fashioned fluted and unfluted lanceolate points and indications of specialization in the types of big game taken, the later manifestations are visualized as those of hunters and gatherers with a wide spectrum of interests in food acquisition, reflected in the extensive use of a large variety of small animals, seeds and other vegetal products, and occasionally fish, reptiles, amphibians, and the like. Some of these people made use of caves and rock shelters; others utilized stream-side terraces for open campsites. Other than occasional firepits, perhaps used for roasting and baking as well as warmth, there are usually no indications of habitations, storage pits, or other structural features.

There is seldom much evidence of intensive or prolonged residence; but at some sites, such as Mummy Cave (Wedel, Husted, and Moss 1968; McCracken 1971) and Medicine Lodge Creek (Frison 1975) in northwestern Wyoming, there are very considerable accumulations of domestic refuse, some of which precede the time of some early big-game hunter sites in the region. Intermittent residence over long periods of time, perhaps on a seasonal basis, rather than continuous uninterrupted occupation, is inferred. This would result from the sort of lifeway described by Mulloy (1954a) as cyclical nomadism and by Flannery (1968) as scheduling.

At Mummy Cave, the fill consists of 38 distinct cultural levels contained in 8.5 meters of detrital material (Figure 5.3). The lower and middle cultural layers yielded relatively few artifacts. Deposition began before 7300 BC, with

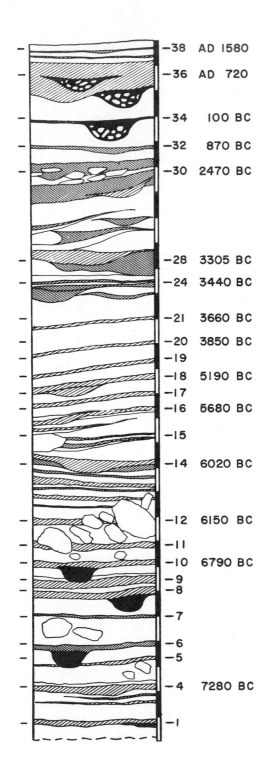

-38 AD 1580
-36 AD 720
-34 100 BC
-32 870 BC
-30 2470 BC
-28 3305 BC
-24 3440 BC
-21 3660 BC
-20 3850 BC
-19
-18 5190 BC
-17
-16 5680 BC
-15
-14 6020 BC
-12 6150 BC
-11
-10 6790 BC
-9
-8
-7
-6
-5
-4 7280 BC
-1

FIGURE 5.3
Stratigraphic section through floor deposits at Mummy Cave, Wyoming. Culture levels numbered 1 to 38. Radiocarbon dates at right. Right-hand margin of column is in 30-centimeter intervals. (After Wedel et al. 1968.)

only medium-sized lanceolate points of mediocre workmanship up to 6000 BC. From 5700 BC, side-notched points reminiscent of eastern Archaic forms were dominant. Other side-notched, stemmed, and shouldered types follow, with cultural layers continuing to be thin. Thicker and more productive layers appear at around 3300 BC. By about the 2500 BC level, McKean and other indented-base points are plentiful, milling stones are present, and there is a considerable inventory of other materials, including both perishables and nonperishables. In cultural layer 30, there are tubular bone pipes, coiled basketry fragments, vegetable fiber cordage and netting, wood trimmings, leather scraps, and many flint chips. Animal bone refuse includes mountain sheep at all levels; rabbit, marmot, porcupine, wood rat, deer, grouse, and waterfowl are present, but there is virtually no trace of bison. Pollen was too poorly preserved for climatic studies and wood-rat nests, from which promising climatic inferences have been made elsewhere in the Wyoming region (Wells 1970), were apparently not investigated or collected. The general impression here is of a mountain-oriented hunting-gathering lifeway rather than a Plains big-game hunter tradition.

Another important deeply stratified site is on Medicine Lodge Creek in the Big Horn Mountains 160 kilometers or so east of Mummy Cave and across the Big Horn Basin (Frison and Wilson 1975). Investigations are still in progress there, and only brief preliminary statements are available. Cultural evidence begins at just under 10,000 years ago and ends with the historic period. Lower levels contain various forms of lanceolate points to about 6500 BC, roughly the same as Mummy Cave. Just above this level, at 6300 BC, Pryor Stemmed points appear. A midden level dated about 7500 BC yielded bones of gopher, wood rat, rabbit, and other small mammals, with deer, sheep, and bison very scarce. Another, at ca. 6500 BC, contained large numbers of small fish, and in some levels simple food-grinding tools appeared. Throughout the entire occupation here, intensive use of plants and small animals was indicated; deer and mountain sheep were of some importance at times, whereas bison were consistently rare.

As these data indicate, local cultural complexes in which bison and other large Plains animals seem not to have been the primary meat source evidently existed along the mountain front zone simultaneously with the bison hunters who were responsible for the kill and butchering at the Horner site, with its complement of Scottsbluff and Eden points, cutting and scraping tools, and other early big-game hunter characteristics. There is no evidence of direct contact or exchange of points or other artifacts between the Horner site hunters and the inhabitants of Mummy Cave, a scant 64 kilometers distant.

In the Northwestern Plains, north of the Yellowstone River and east of the Big Horn and Wyoming basins, archeological sites are very unevenly distributed through the 5000-year period that began about 7000 years ago and ended with the beginning of the Christian era; this apparently holds also for the Central and Southern Plains except on their eastern and western margins.

The first half, roughly from 5000 to 2500 BC, coincides with the Altithermal interval of higher temperatures and increased aridity; from this period there appear to be significantly fewer sites than in later times. At Mummy Cave, cultural levels 18 to 24 or 28 fall within the Altithermal interval, with short-lived occupations suggested before McKean times. Additional investigated sites from this period have been considered by Reeves (1973: Fig. 5 and *pass.*) under the rubric *Early Middle Prehistoric I* (ca. 5500–3000 BC). Included are 38 sites, mostly in Alberta, Montana, and Wyoming. There are at least 3 bison kills, 5 rockshelters, and 21 open stratified campsites. With reference to the Great Plains, most appear to be peripheral, centering in and around the Big Horn Basin and in the broken country to the north and northwest. The impression persists of a largely blank space in the upper Missouri-Saskatchewan region during EMP-I times, where essentially no sites have been reported except in peripheral sectors.

In post-Altithermal times, apparently beginning as early as 3000 BC and multiplying after ca. 2500 BC, the number of known and investigated sites increases dramatically. Reeves's study of 68 components assigned to the Early Middle Period II (3000–1500 BC) includes bison kills, rockshelters, and fishing stations, 31 of which have been dated. On the basis of stone tool technology, "most easily observed in projectile point styles," he distinguishes several complexes: Early Oxbow (3000–2500 BC) and Late Oxbow (2500–2000 BC), Late Mummy Cave (3000–1500 BC), Oxbow-McKean (2500–2000 BC), McKean (2000–1500 BC), and Powers-Yonkee (2500–1500 BC) (Reeves 1973:1237ff., Fig. 6). Early Oxbow, with eared Oxbow and Bitterroot Side-notched points, was putatively derived from the Mummy Cave complex and basically mountain oriented. Other key point types in this model are Oxbow Eared for Late Oxbow; Oxbow, McKean, and Bitterroot Side-notched for Late Mummy Cave; Oxbow and McKean for Oxbow-McKean complex; and McKean points only for the McKean complex. This model raises many provocative questions and requires thorough testing.

Plains Archaic materials in the Central and Southern Plains are not well known. Along the eastern margin, Simonsen, Lungren, and Hill in Iowa and Logan Creek in Nebraska carry radiocarbon dates from ca. 6600 to 4300 BC, in or preceding the early Altithermal range. Simonsen (Frankforter and Agogino 1960) was a bison kill, and bison bone was plentiful also at Lungren and Logan Creek. Somewhat later are Lansing Man, several Flint Hills sites, and the Munkers Creek complex in eastern Kansas. In Oklahoma, Archaic materials are widely scattered as surface finds. Their time span is suggested by such radiocarbon dates (Bell 1968) as 7450 BC for a level at Packard site that yielded lanceolate and side-notched points, 4100 BC for Gore Pit near Lawton, and several levels at Duncan-Wilson Rockshelter (Lawton 1968), where Archaic hunters and gatherers lingered until the third or fourth century AD but left no bison bones in their middens.

Radiocarbon dates from two stratified sites in the Texas panhandle relate to the late Archaic occupancy there. At Chalk Hollow, a small headwater tributary of Palo Duro Canyon about 19 kilometers southeast of Amarillo, 4.7 meters of colluvial terrace fill containing cultural materials included a late midden (ca. AD 440–840) with small Scallorn-like and other side-notched arrow points, potsherds, and so on, and a lower series of relatively thin midden layers containing medium to large stemmed dart points (Castroville-like, Marcos-like, and so on), end scrapers, cutting tools, bone awls and dice (?), and well-built slab hearths. Milling stones and fragments were found at all levels. Associated animal bone suggests a relatively abundant meat diet in some levels, with bison bone especially conspicuous at ca. 850–950 BC. Freshwater snail shells indicate former live water in the now dry creek nearby, but they are identical with forms found in roadside ponds in the general locality today and do not suggest any marked climatic shifts during the Archaic occupancy, which here spanned the period ca. 1650 to 425 BC. A culturally sterile stratum averaging 30 centimeters or more in thickness separates the lower Archaic midden layers from the upper ceramic-small-point midden.

The Canyon City Country Club Rockshelter, a few miles upstream from Chalk Hollow, included two levels dated at 880 BC and 150 BC, which were without diagnostic artifacts but where "faunal and geological evidence suggested drought conditions" (Hughes, personal communication). Such conditions may help to account for the occupation-free zone at Chalk Hollow between 400 BC and 400 AD. There are no known bison kills in the immediate vicinity of these two sites, but several small bone beds at the eastern edge of the Llano Estacado (Hughes, personal communication; Tunnell and Hughes 1955; Dibble and Lorrain 1968:73) east of Palo Duro Canyon have produced stemmed and side- or corner-notched dart points comparable to those from the Archaic levels at Chalk Hollow. The bones are being exposed in the sides and near the heads of rapidly eroding arroyos, suggesting small-group hunts wherein a few animals were corralled at the upper end of a former arroyo that was subsequently filled and is now being reexcavated by erosion. One is reminded here of the apparently similar and approximately contemporaneous Early Middle Prehistoric and post-Altithermal bison traps reported by Frison (1972) in the Powder River Basin of Wyoming.

Texas Archaic sites are generally regarded as representing a hunting-gathering subsistence complex in which bison bone may be present, but only as a relatively minor element in the faunal debris (Dibble and Lorrain 1968:73), rather than as the product of large-scale jumps or other mass kills. A notable exception is Bone Bed 3 at Bonfire Shelter, where an estimated 800 cows and calves of *Bison bison* cascaded over a canyon rim in one gigantic slaughter at around 650 BC. Between the late Archaic bison bone beds in the northern Texas panhandle and the much earlier occurrences of bison at Bonfire and Arenosa shelters nearly 640 kilometers to the south lies a time gap of 6000 or more years, which corresponds roughly to Dillehay's (1974) Absence Period I (6000–5000 to 2500 BC) of bison from the Southern Plains.

Archaic manifestations in eastern Colorado (Breternitz 1969) probably include the Gordon Creek burial dated at 7700 BC, but without diagnostic artifacts; LoDaisKa complexes C and D, at 1450 and 2890 BC, the latter associated with maize samples (Irwin and Irwin 1959); and a number of small sites scattered around the Denver area. Near Kassler, milling stones, points, scrapers, and other tools dated 3500–3800 BC occur in the pre-Piney Creek alluvium, which also contains molluscs suggesting a warmer and drier climate (G. Scott 1962; 1963).

The Archaic time span, here considered to be roughly the period from about 5000 BC to the beginning of the Christian era for the Plains as a whole, presents a number of intriguing problems for the archeologist and his or her coworkers concerned with Plains prehistory. For one thing, the first half of the period includes the Altithermal, whose higher temperatures and lower precipitation were of still undetermined importance in human affairs at the time. The apparent scarcity of archeological sites datable to the Altithermal, as compared with earlier and later periods, has long been regarded by some as evidence that much of the region—at any rate, its western portions—may have been abandoned by man, or nearly so, during this interval (e.g., Krieger 1950:121; Mulloy 1958:200; Davis 1962:11; Wedel 1961:282). Hunt (1966) cites several radiocarbon-dated sites in Wyoming, Montana, and Canada that fall within this period but notes that they occur mostly in mountainous or foothill locations where moisture deficiencies would probably have been less acute than on the lower-lying plains. Accepting the thesis that the climate was warmer and drier, he then suggests that the Plains region as a whole was probably never completely abandoned, that there may still have been favored areas of greater moisture that could have served as natural refuges for men and animals, and that any human populations that remained may have had to expand and diversify the food basis of their economy to include plants and smaller animals in larger proportions than formerly. More recently, in a comprehensive and wide-ranging review, Reeves (1973) has argued that even though the regional climate may have been somewhat drier, resulting in an expanded short-grass area, the survival of a "viable but smaller bison population" would have permitted the "same basic strategy as characterized by subsequent and antecedent prehistoric populations, i.e., communal bison hunting. . . ."

Still more recently, reasoning from firsthand ranching experience and analogy with the recent drought of the 1930s, Frison (1975) has observed that the prolonged moisture deficiencies of the Altithermal would be expected to have materially depleted the amount and quality of the short-grass cover, thereby reducing significantly its carrying capacity and adversely affecting winter survival, spring condition, and general welfare of the herd animals, young and old. In this light, "the main bulk of the bison herds probably abandoned much of the Northwestern Plains during the Altithermal Period, except for some oasis-like areas and followed the expanding shortgrasses as they intruded into the now tall grass areas." He points out further that communal bison hunting, always chancy in terms of escaped animals, was most successful with herds of perhaps several score animals or more, and less successful with smaller herds, such as would be expectable under Altithermal stresses. In sum, there was "a definite reduction of human occupations on the Northwestern Plains during the Altithermal and the ones that remained were centered in areas peripheral to the Plains" (Frison 1975:296).

The nature of Altithermal climate in the short-grass plains is not well known. Considering the length of time and great extent of territory involved, there was undoubtedly a very wide range of variation. Systematic observations made during and since the relatively short drought of 1933–1939, the most serious on record for the region since it became the seat of a major livestock industry, may have some relevance (Ellison and Woolfolk 1937; Weaver and Albertson 1956; Albertson et al. 1957; Coupland 1958). When drought struck, the grasses responded with reduced size and scantier foliage; where it persisted, root damage and finally death resulted. The depleted grass cover resulted in substantial decreases in forage production, amounting in some cases to 80 to 90 percent, or even more, per acre; the amount of range land needed for continued maintenance of grazing cattle rose from 4 or 4.8 to 20, 24, or 28 hectares per animal. At the end of the drought, even with the return of adequate moisture, several years were usually needed to bring forage production and carrying capacity back to normal; in some instances, however, two years of good rainfall increased the forage tenfold or more over that available at the height of the drought. In light of these range-land observations, it would seem likely that the effects of a prolonged period of deficient rainfall and high temperatures, like the conditions postulated for the Altithermal, would almost certainly have been disastrous for the bison on the plains. Herds situated in and around elevated or hilly areas, such as the Black Hills or Cypress Hills, or with access to subirrigated valley bottom lands might have fared better. Abandonment or light population of large sections of the short-grass plains still seems a likely explanation for the apparent scarcity of archeological sites during the time period involved.

Interesting, too, is the question of what was happening physiologically to the Plains bison during the Altithermal period. Prior to ca. 6000–5000 BC, the early big-game hunters from Texas to Montana were in pursuit of bison of larger size than the animals encountered by the white man; after ca. 3000–2500 BC, it appears to be invariably the smaller *Bison bison* with which man was associated. In the Wyoming region, the reduction in size from *Bison occidentalis* to *B. bison* may be even more precisely datable, having occurred possibly between ca. 6500 and 4500 years ago (Wilson 1974:96; Frison 1975). The details of this change and its causes, which may include severe biological stresses associated with worsening environmental conditions and excessive hunting pressures, are among the intriguing questions whose solution may be measurably nearer as a result of ongoing studies of the growing numbers of animal bones being recovered from large kills in the Northwestern Plains.

THE PLAINS WOODLAND (250 BC–AD 950)

In the eastern Plains, the Archaic lifeway—the cyclical or scheduled hunting of small game, the gathering of seeds, tubers, nuts, berries, and other vegetal foods in season, and, when and where the opportunity existed, the hunting of bison—continued into the final centuries of the pre-Christian era and eventually gave rise to a number of locally and temporally distinctive complexes, basically of eastern origin or else strongly influenced by eastern cultures. Archeologically, these complexes are represented by many small sites, often deeply buried, scattered throughout the region from Oklahoma and Texas to North Dakota and the prairie provinces and, apparently in diminishing numbers, westward to the Rockies. During this period, pottery making was introduced into the Plains, as was mound burial; neither practice had been associated with Plains Archaic complexes. The basically eastern orientation of these materials is recognized in their usual designation as the Plains Woodland tradition.

At most sites a simple creek-valley hunting and gathering subsistence economy is inferred. In the Central Plains, the bone refuse suggests that, contrary to the situation in later times, deer and small mammals were a more important source of protein than the bison; but bison hunting seems to have attained greater prominence farther north and west in the region. Maize horticulture is indicated for Hopewellian communities near Kansas City and, more scantily, at a few other sites; only squash remains hint feebly at food-production activities at Sterns Creek in eastern Nebraska (Strong 1935). Several Woodland variants have been identified and characterized (e.g., Wedel 1959:542–557), including the relatively advanced and perhaps more sedentary Kansas City Hopewellian and, mostly farther west and northwest, the Keith, Valley, Sterns Creek, and Loseke Creek complexes in Nebraska and Kansas, and the Parker variant in eastern Colorado. In the Canadian grassland, the linear, conical, and other mounds of southern Manitoba are regarded as Middle Woodland; the Pelican Lake, Besant, and Avonlea complexes are roughly contemporaneous with Plains Woodland. Less well known manifestations occur southward into Oklahoma and Texas.

The Kansas City Hopewellian communities (Wedel 1943; 1959; Johnson and Johnson 1975) include both larger sites of up to 3 or 4 hectares and smaller ones that could scarcely have accommodated more than two or three houses. The larger ones have fairly heavy concentrations of refuse, numerous storage pits, and a varied assemblage of artifacts in pottery, stone, bone, and other materials. The pottery includes plain, rocker-marked, and zone-decorated wares, along with small amounts of cord-roughened ware, and clearly derives from eastern materials, probably in the Illinois River valley. Imitation bear teeth of bone, conical or mammiform objects of stone and clay, native copper, and obsidian reflect both cultural affinities and trade contacts. Large, corner-notched projectile points, three-quarter-grooved axes, stemmed plano-convex scrapers, conical flint disks, beaming tools of deer innominates and metapodials, and tanged antler tip projectile points are locally distinguishing items. The house type is unknown. Stone-chambered earth-covered mounds with cremated and secondary skeletal materials on the nearby bluff tops were probably associated with these villages. A long-headed population is inferred. Maize and beans were grown, but the nature of the cultivating tools used has not been determined. Radiocarbon dates tend to cluster in the first five centuries of the Christian era, with median readings in the third and fourth centuries AD. At least two chambered mound complexes have been radiocarbon dated to the same period.

The Kansas City locale, centering around the junction of the Kansas River and the Missouri, appears to have been a major focus of Hopewellian activity in the region, and a semipermanent residence pattern may be inferred. Related sites about which very little is known occur westward up the Kansas River, north up the Missouri, and south and southwestward into the Arkansas River drainage. In northeast Oklahoma, the Delaware County locale and the Cooper site (Bell and Baerreis 1951:27) appear to have been another center of some importance, but the scatter of seven radiocarbon dates at Cooper from 1460 BC to AD 1270 is unacceptably early and late. Oblong posthole patterns attributed to the Cooper variant in southeast Kansas have been identified as house structures (Marshall 1972).

Other Woodland complexes in the Central Plains usually have a simpler material culture inventory (Hill and Kivett 1941; Kivett 1952; 1953; 1970). The Keith focus and Valley focus variants are characterized by small sites with small basins identified as possible habitations, by stemmed and corner-notched points that include a somewhat varied assortment of medium to large corner-notched and smaller well-made stemmed "Scallorn-like" forms, and by thick, cord-roughened pottery in large, vertically elongate jars, with calcite tempering usually distinguishing Harlan cord-roughened Keith pottery from Valley ware. Loseke Creek ware often has a rim decoration of single-cord impressions. Charred maize has been found in at least one site. Burials are of various kinds. Keith focus connections have been assigned to ossuary pits with secondary burials, unmarked by surface mounds and accompanied by shell disk beads and blanks, shell pendants, and chipped stone artifacts (Kivett 1953). In eastern Nebraska and northeastern Kansas, massed, bundle, and disarticulated burials beneath low inconspicuous earth mounds that commonly contain evidence of fire are thought to be Woodland affiliated (Hill and Kivett 1941; Kivett 1952). The disarticulated bones of multiple burials, some burned, in submound pits in northeastern Nebraska have been attributed to Loseke Creek (Price n.d.). The Taylor mound, with its ritual interment of seven skulls in a slab cist, is identified as Valley focus affiliated and is dated to the first century AD. The possibility that these wide variations in burial methods may reflect class distinctions has been suggested (O'Brien 1971).

The westerly manifestations of Plains Woodland culture in eastern Colorado are becoming better known from several studies. Burial practices and their relationships to Plains complexes elsewhere have been discussed by Breternitz and Wood (1965) and by Scott and Birkedal (1972). Settlement patterns, including rockshelters, mountaintop sites, and open camps, have been analyzed by D. Scott (1973). Hunting and gathering subsistence systems seem generally indicated, with bison procurement in evidence; charred corncob from Culture complex B at LoDaisKa (Irwin and Irwin 1959) is assigned to Woodland, but the nature of the cultivation and processing tools used is unclear. Woodland pottery, milling stones, weapon points, and other materials associated with bison and deer bones have been located in post-Piney Creek alluvium near Kassler, Colorado, and dated at AD 460 (G . Scott 1962; 1963).

In the Southern Plains of Oklahoma and Texas, Woodland materials or their local contemporary complexes have been found in several stratigraphic contexts. At Duncan-Wilson Rockshelter (Lawton 1968) in Caddo County, Oklahoma, some 4 meters of fill included a succession of human occupations dated back to ca. AD 430 by radiocarbon and to ca. AD 220 by extrapolation. Cord-roughened Woodland sherds appear in Levels 15–23 (Level 1 being the top) at ca. AD 520–870, along with first appearance of antelope bone. Various nondiagnostic materials occur sparsely at lower levels, including mostly small animal bones and stemmed projectile points identified as Ellis, Gary, and Bulverde. Immediately above, in Levels 10–12 at ca. AD 827–1070, along with first indications of bison hunting were found plain potsherds, shaft smoothers, and arrow points of Fresno, Washito, Scallorn, and Gary types. These materials impress one as being closer to the Washita focus materials from the later levels of ca. AD 1070–1612.

In the Texas panhandle, rockshelter and campsite locations include complexes dated in the first 10 centuries of the Christian era. Associated with these complexes are small stemmed or corner-notched "Scallorn-like" points, brown plainware pottery apparently related to New Mexico wares, and limited inventories, generally. At Chalk Hollow the upper midden to about 120 centimeters below ground surface, which was radiocarbon-dated between AD 370 and 785, yielded plano-convex scrapers, bifacial chipped knives, milling slabs and mullers of various sizes, split mammal bone awls, bone gaming pieces, obsidian, unformalized hearths with much burned stone, debitage including Alibates agatized dolomite, Tecovas flint, Edwards Plateau chert and so on, and animal bone in highly variable amounts that included bison, an occasional cervid or pronghorn, coyote or wolf, and unidentified small rodents. A sort of transhumance is perhaps to be inferred here, with regular and repeated winter residence in the protected canyon alternating with spring, summer, and fall residence on the nearby wind-swept uplands, including the shores of the many waterholes now represented by mostly dry playas. The Woodland period materials here follow an 800-year break marked by sterile colluvial deposits, beneath which is a series of short-lived Archaic levels. There are other small sites nearby (Hughes, personal communication), recently dated but still unreported, where the changing projectile point forms and sizes from the Archaic to Woodland times are thought to reflect the transition from the Late Archaic dart weapons system to a Middle or Late Woodland bow and arrow system.

The Woodland influences in the eastern Plains, as reflected in the pottery, burial mounds, and incipient horticulture, did not overspread the Northwestern Plains; hunting, gathering, and communal bison driving continued through the final stages of the Late Middle Prehistoric and into the Early Late Prehistoric period. Local variants at this stage are represented in rockshelters at Mummy Cave level 36 (AD 720), Wedding of the Waters Cave (Frison 1962), Pictograph Cave II (Mulloy 1958), Birdshead Cave II and III (Bliss 1950), Daugherty and Spring Creek caves near Ten Sleep, Wyoming (Frison 1965; 1968), and in open stratified campsites at McKean Upper and Signal Butte II. A shift in weapons seems to be indicated at this period, with medium-sized stemmed or corner-notched points giving way to smaller types. Definite evidence of the atlatl has been reported from Spring Creek Cave in the Big Horn Mountains by Frison (1965) at ca. AD 225. Here, in a single-component deposit, associated materials include dart shafts and foreshafts, coiled basketry, bits of sinew, worked bark, tanned skin, porcupine quill work, and several obliquely worn pole butts with wear patterns suggesting use as dog travois frames. The widespread practice of communal bison hunting at this period is indicated by Kobold III and Wardell bison kills in Wyoming (Frison 1970; 1973), at Old Women's Buffalo Jump in Alberta (Forbis 1962), and by a number of sites in Saskatchewan (Kehoe 1973). In and around the Big Horn Basin, bone refuse includes much bison, as well as elk, pronghorn, mountain sheep, rabbit, and vegetal foods. From surface finds, it appears that many sites show strong similarities to the Spring Creek Cave complex, but with significant variations in proportions of tool types. Mountain sites tend to have more weapon points, cutting, scraping, and skin-dressing tools. Badlands and open flatland sites have more milling stones and roasting pits, inferentially for the processing of vegetal foods and small game, both of which were utilized when the larger game in the mountains was not readily available or was seasonally absent.

Widely scattered throughout the eastern Dakotas and southern Manitoba, mostly east and northeast of the Coteau du Missouri but occurring in lesser numbers westward to the Missouri River trench, are mounds and earthworks that differ from those farther south. They vary greatly in size, construction, and contents, with radiocarbon dates ranging from ca. 500 BC to ca. AD 1000. They include linears and conicals, with burials found in both. Log-covered submound pits are common. Particularly noteworthy is the frequent occurrence of bison skeletons or skulls, seldom found in burial mounds farther south. This occurrence suggests that the bison held an extremely important position in the lifeways of the people involved—perhaps more so than among the Woodland people farther south. One wonders whether bison were perhaps more abundant in the northern, northwestern, and western Plains at this time period than they were farther south, where other foods were drawn upon to a greater degree and the bison may never have achieved comparable ritual or economic importance.

The mounds of this subarea are generally related to complexes better known in the Minnesota region, with Blackduck and Arvilla affiliations variously suggested. In a penetrating analysis of southern Manitoba mound materials and data collected by Nickerson in the early 1900s, Capes (1963) has concluded that the Manitoba mounds were the work of closely related peoples operating under influences dating back to Middle Woodland times. Ossenberg (1974:37), using discrete traits in cranial samples from Minnesota and the adjacent Plains, concludes that they represent "a cluster of closely related populations ancestral to the Dakota, Assiniboin, Cheyenne, and possibly Blackfoot," and that their affinity to Illinois Hopewell, sometimes postulated from the log-covered submound burial pits, is weak.

The Besant and Avonlea complexes (Joyes 1970; Kehoe and McCorquodale 1961) are coeval south Canadian equivalents of the Plains Woodland complexes farther south. Cord-roughened pottery in Besant levels at ca. AD 350 has been noted as similar in some respects to Keith focus pottery in the Central Plains (Kehoe 1964). Avonlea sites have been broadly characterized (Kehoe and Kehoe 1968:23) as the earliest evidence for the "complex, ritualized, planned bison drives" in the Late Prehistoric Plains; the same observers regard the Athabascans as probably responsible for introduction into the northern Plains of the bow and arrow, complex ritualized bison drives, and the small-point weapons system.

THE PLAINS VILLAGE INDIANS (AD 900–1850)

From at least the tenth century of the Christian era, and possibly as early as the eighth or ninth, the Woodland complexes of the eastern Plains were giving way to, or perhaps developing into, others of more sedentary character. These involved settlements of substantial structures scattered along the permanent streams throughout much of the tall- and mid-grass prairies from the Dakotas to Texas, and westward into the short-grass plains of eastern Colorado. Throughout, a dual subsistence strategy was followed, involving in varying proportions the horticultural potential of the arable stream bottoms and the game and wild vegetal resources of the wooded bottom lands and the nearby grassy uplands. To these complexes, the term *Plains Village Indians* has been applied (Lehmer 1954a; 1954b); the Plains Village Indians' way of life, with many modifications in time and space, dominated the eastern Plains for nearly a thousand years. Their contemporaries in the western and northwestern Plains were an assortment of foraging and hunting groups, living in transient or portable dwellings, most or all lacking maize, a few with pottery, and many continuing the pursuit of bison by jumps, pounds, and in other ways—in effect continuing the relatively unspectacular, austere, but presumably effective subsistence economies that had been followed since Altithermal times.

Shared by practically all of the Plains Village complexes were (1) the construction of fixed multifamily lodges, generally larger and more substantially built than the inferred habitations of the Woodland peoples; (2) residence for most of the year in permanent settlements, sometimes fortified with dry moats and stockades and usually containing numbers of underground storage pits; (3) pottery of varied character; and (4) a wide range of artifacts in stone, bone, horn, shell, and other materials. The bone hoe, varying in details of manufacture but usually made from a bison scapula, was a particularly characteristic tool, lingering on into the historical period to compete with the iron hoe introduced by the white man. Throughout the Plains generally, the small triangular arrowpoints of this period, with or without side notches, are easily differentiated from the weapons of earlier times; also, the plano-convex end scraper became a common item in this period, judging by the artifact inventory. In the fifteenth or sixteenth century, there seem to have been widespread changes in house form, settlement pattern, and perhaps other aspects of the visible record, dating both before and after arrival of the whites.

The early Village Indian period lacks any evidence of white contact and is everywhere marked by square or rectangular house floors and grit-tempered pottery. On the Middle Missouri, complexes represented by such taxonomic units as the Monroe, Anderson, Thomas Riggs, and Huff foci have been organized by Lehmer (1971) into a Middle Missouri tradition, which consists in turn of two major subdivisions—the Initial Middle Missouri (hereafter cited as IMM) and the Extended Middle Missouri (EMM). Most IMM sites, including the Over, Anderson, and Monroe foci and the Grand Detour phase, are in South Dakota, either on the mainstem or along the James and Big Sioux rivers; EMM variants, including Archaic Mandan, Thomas Riggs, and Fort Yates foci, are in North Dakota. Long, rectangular semisubterranean houses, with floor area not uncommonly exceeding 90 square meters, are characteristic of both; settlement patterns differ mainly in details; burial methods for both are unknown; and artifact types are basically very similar except for minutiae of interest mainly to specialists. Largely on the basis of radiocarbon dates, a time span for IMM of ca. AD 950–1300 was initially proposed (Lehmer 1971:95); for EMM, sites seemed to be bimodally distributed between ca. AD 1100–1250 and again at AD 1450–1550. Tree ring dates from South Dakota sites have been interpreted as indicating markedly different and shorter time spans (Weakly 1971).

With additional dates, it now appears that while IMM may have been present as early as the ninth or tenth century, both major variants of the Middle Missouri tradition coexisted for most of their respective life spans. The IMM people, represented by no fewer than 35 known sites, are thought to have reached the Missouri valley from southwestern Minnesota and northwestern Iowa and may have been "the only village complex in the Middle Missouri for perhaps two centuries" (Lehmer 1971:98). From the same general homeland came the EMM immigrants, who settled farther up the main stem in North Dakota. As both groups expanded, they eventually came into confrontation in the Bad-Cheyenne district, where fortified settlements are seen as reflecting a conflict situation.

In the fifteenth century, people abandoning the Central Plains because of drought moved into the Middle Missouri region, introducing new house forms, such as the four-post earth lodge, and other culture elements. The merging of new ideas and people with local groups gave rise to the Coalescent tradition. This, in turn, spread northward up the Missouri, passing through a series of temporal variants between ca. AD 1450 and 1680; its later stages, termed the Post-Contact Coalescent and involving the Arikara of history, represent the heyday of Village Indian culture on the Middle Missouri. Farther north, the Mandan and Hidatsa can be traced back into the Terminal Middle Missouri, an outgrowth of IMM and EMM that coexisted in part with the later stages of the Coalescent tradition.

The archeological record greatly amplified and enriched since 1946 by the Interagency Salvage Program (Wedel 1967) on the Missouri River, has made clear the lengthy and complex history of the Village Indians in the subregion. Heavily dependent on maize growing and on bison hunting, and living near the northern limits of successful agriculture, these groups would have been particularly susceptible to the well-known vagaries of the Plains climate. Having moved from the woodlands onto the Plains during the Neo-Atlantic climatic episode, when abundant rains would have encouraged corn growing, their varied responses to subsequent fluctuations in terms of the climatic model proposed by Bryson and his coworkers (Bryson and Wendland 1967) have been noted by Lehmer (1970) and others. A thoughtful evaluation of these northern Plains Village cultures is Wood's recent (1974) study.

In the Central Plains, early Village Indian manifestations include the Upper Republican and Nebraska aspects or phases, the Smoky Hill aspect, and a more recently defined Pomona phase in eastern Kansas. Collectively, these comprise the Central Plains tradition, with most radiocarbon dates in the AD 1000–1400 span (Wedel 1961; n.d.b; Brown 1967; Gradwohl 1969). The first three named units are characterized by square or rectangular houses with rounded corners, quite unlike the long, rectangular dwellings of the Middle Missouri people. Villages are generally smaller, unfortified, and less compactly built; houses, especially in the Upper Republican phase, are smaller, commonly from 36 to 67.5 square meters in area. Cord-roughened or plain-surfaced pottery is characteristic, but contacts with a Middle Mississippi complex in northwestern Missouri (Wedel 1943) introduced shell tempering and other exotic traits to nearby contemporary Nebraska aspect and Smoky Hill cultures.

Dating of these complexes is still inadequate, as is knowledge of their taxonomic interrelationships. Most Upper Republican mean dates fall between AD 1100 and 1250; these pertain mainly to a small cluster of sites at Medicine Creek reservoir, Nebraska. Whether these sites truly indicate the life span of Upper Republican throughout their area of occurrence remains to be tested. Time perspective has been injected into the picture by operations at Glen Elder reservoir, Kansas, where Krause (1970) recognizes a Solomon River phase at between the ninth and thirteenth centuries AD and a Classic Republican phase between the eleventh and fifteenth centuries. Seven radiocarbon dates precede AD 900, six follow AD 1250; if validated by further evidence, they suggest a split occupancy of the Solomon River district, one preceding and the other following the dated Upper Republican occupancy at Medicine Creek. They suggest, also, that Village Indian occupancy began about as early in the Central Plains as on the Middle Missouri, and raise again the possibility of late Woodland-Upper Republican contacts or transitional stages. The wide distribution of Upper Republican remains, with most sites showing relatively small quantities of refuse, suggests short occupancies and frequent moves to new localities. Their apparent abundance in Nebraska, northern Kansas, and eastern Colorado may actually reflect a relatively small and scattered population, living mostly in hamlets and single lodges, that moved frequently from one site or district to another, leaving previous habitats essentially unoccupied and unmarked except by decaying earth lodges and trash. Additional radiocarbon dates from other Upper Republican localities, with multiple assays to reduce error, are urgently needed to test this thesis. It has been also suggested (Wood 1969) that the Upper Republican sites were seasonally inhabited by semihorticultural groups who were compelled by limited local food resources to engage in communal bison hunts at more western locales, at which times the earth lodge villages were abandoned in accord with a pattern well established for such historic village tribes as the Pawnee, Omaha, and Kansa; but this thesis still lacks acceptable supporting evidence (Wedel 1970).

Despite some later dates, it seems likely that the western Upper Republican communities were largely abandoned in the thirteenth century, perhaps because of drought (Wedel 1941; 1953). That these drought conditions were real and probably widespread now seems increasingly likely (Bryson et al. 1970); whether the victims migrated to the Middle Missouri, to the Texas-Oklahoma panhandle, or elsewhere, as has been variously postulated, still remains unclear and will continue to be unclear until a great deal more fieldwork is undertaken in the still little-known intervening regions.

In the Southern Plains, there are greatly improved perspectives on the early Village cultures and their interrelationships (Bell and Baerreis 1951; Buck 1959; Pillaert 1963; Bell 1962; 1973; Schneider 1969). The Washita

River and Custer focuses and the Panhandle aspect all share the rectangular house forms, cord-roughened and plain pottery, and various other material culture traits of the contemporary Village complexes of the Central Plains and Middle Missouri subregions. There are significant differences in detail, however, which assume greater significance as more radiocarbon dates provide better chronological controls. Bell (1962), noting that bison bones are much more plentiful in archeological sites after ca. AD 1000–1200, has suggested that the Village Indians may have been attracted to the western grasslands from eastern Oklahoma by the increased bison populations and consequent better hunting to supplement their already well-developed semi-sedentary prairie economy. Population pressures in the east may have been a contributing factor. This movement would have been approximately coincident with the apparent abandonment of the Middle Pecos valley by farming Indians and a shift in subsistence economy to bison hunting on the Plains (Jelinek 1966).

Far too few radiocarbon dates are available for the Oklahoma Village cultures, but it seems likely that the Washita River and Custer focuses were sequent rather than contemporary. The few available Washita dates fall between AD 1100 and 1975, Custer dates between AD 800 and 950. From these figures, Hofman (1975) suggests that out of a Woodland culture base (e.g., Pruitt-like) of pottery use and incipient horticulture, with a continued heavy reliance on hunting and gathering and seasonal change of camps, developed the Custer complex with increased emphasis on horticulture, a shift from cord-roughened to smoothed pottery of more varied kinds, and the appearance of bison scapula hoes and digging stick tips. In the still later Washita River focus sites, there is a marked increase in the number of bone hoes and digging stick tips as well as the first appearance of bison horn core hoes, perhaps implying intensified crop growing. Disappearance from the Oklahoma region of the Washita River focus peoples during the fourteenth century, about the time the Spiro ceremonial center climaxed (AD 1350–1400), has been tentatively attributed to drought conditions (Wedel 1961; Lorrain 1967) and, more recently, to arrival in western Oklahoma of alien peoples who may have been ancestral Apache or Kiowa (Bell 1973).

The Panhandle culture, where an exotic non-Plains or pseudo-Puebloan architectural style has been associated with an otherwise more or less typical Plains Village material culture complex, has been placed in more meaningful perspective largely through an extensive series of radiocarbon dates (Bender et al. 1966; 1967; Pearson et al. 1966). Mean dates range from AD 1120 to 1620; site averages and most individual means run from AD 1250 to 1450. The close correspondence between the beginning date here and the terminal dates of (Medicine Creek) Upper Republican in Nebraska has been noted by Bryson et al. (1970:69), who argue on statistical grounds for a climatic shift after ca. AD 1160–1200 whereby dry conditions unfavorable to maize growing in Nebraska were offset by wetter climate in the panhandle. They also argue that the drought-stricken Upper Republican peoples migrated to the latter area to continue their semihorticultural economy. Despite some attractive features, this thesis has yet to be supported by convincing archeological evidence.

In the late Village Indian complexes of the eastern Plains (those postdating the sixteenth century) can be recognized the archeological manifestations of the major historical tribal entities of the region. In the north, the Mandan, Hidatsa, and Arikara were the final development from the Middle Missouri tradition (Lehmer 1971); farther south, the Pawnees were rooted in the Central Plains tradition through the Lower Loup phase (Wedel 1938; Grange 1968), the relationships of which to the earlier Upper Republican and contemporary Middle Missouri complexes still await clarification; in the Kansas-Oklahoma-Texas area, the Wichita tribes who dominated the western Arkansas River drainage can be traced back to the Great Bend (Wedel 1959; 1968) and Norteño (Jelks et al. 1967) phases and, on an earlier time level, to the Washita River-Custer-Panhandle and perhaps Henrietta complexes. In the western Plains, the Dismal River culture is widely, but not unanimously, regarded as Plains Apache (Gunnerson 1968; Schlesier 1972; Opler 1975). Along the eastern margin, the Oneota materials have been tentatively identified with various Siouan tribes—Fanning site with the Kansa, Leary site with Oto, Stanton site with Omaha. The historical legacy of the easternmost expression of the Central Plains tradition—the Nebraska phase—is still unclear, as are its relationships to the later, or longer lasting, Oneota remains in the same region.

In the western Plains, beyond the erstwhile Village Indian territory, the Late Prehistoric and Historic periods are manifested in the often scantily represented remains of the nomadic bison hunters—late arrivals in the region, of diverse linguistic and cultural origins, who found it most advantageous to operate in accord with bison-hunting systems that were already old in the buffalo country. Who among these groups or their late prehistoric forerunners may have been responsible for the innumerable stone tipi rings, boulder alignments, medicine wheels, and pictographs that add a measure of distinctiveness to the Northwestern Plains is not yet clear. The likelihood that some of these features have astronomical implications is of interest (Eddy 1974). The numerous and widespread bison jumps and pounds, with attendant ritual embellishments, for which archeological evidence is beginning to accumulate at earlier time levels, were quite possibly the response to an accelerated influx of human groups. The influx could have been furthered by introduction of the horse or by a sharply expanding bison population that may have peaked throughout the Plains during the historic period (Gunnerson 1972). It is very possible that climatically favored localities in the northern Plains produced an abundance of animals unmatched at any other period in man's occupation of the Great Plains (Reher n.d.).

Despite enormous spatial and temporal lacunae in our information, archeology is confirming an ever more impressive depth of time for prehistoric man's occupation of the Great Plains. It is clear, too, that this occupation was subject to constant cultural change, reflecting in part adaptations to climatic and other fluctuations in the natural environment. Occupation was certainly underway more than 11,000 years ago by hunters of the last of the mammoths (Martin and Wright 1967) and, later, of giant bison in the western Plains. That bison were utilized in quantity on the eastern margin of the Plains by 7000 or 8000 years ago is clear, too, and a regional pattern may be inferred even for the intervening localities from which evidence is still lacking. In the western short-grass plains, hunting economies centering on bison procurement by individual and communal systems alike seem to have been the mainstay of human existence throughout, although there is an Altithermal interlude when bison and human populations both seem to have declined and of which few archeological sites are known except in the fringing mountain areas.

Farther east, bison were supplemented by other game animals and relatively abundant vegetal foods that were not generally available except in limited quantities in the short-grass country. Here, eventually, under appropriate environmental conditions, food-producing subsistence economies based on a maize-bean-squash triad were developed or introduced, and greater population aggregates and densities resulted. Trade relations between these communities and the western nomads, whereby horticultural products were exchanged for those from the chase, became increasingly important; introduction of the horse greatly accelerated these interactions. The wealth of solid information pertaining to the Village Indians that has accumulated through more than two decades of salvage archeology in the northern Plains can be expected to develop new meaning from the belated recognition of the nature and quality of the archeological record now being pieced together in the bison plains from the Rio Grande to Canada. From the perspectives of archeology, the bison rather than the horse was responsible for native man's successful occupancy of the Great Plains.

References Cited and Recommended Sources

Albertson, F. W., G. W. Tomanek, and Andrew Riegel 1957 Ecology of drought cycles and grazing intensity on grasslands of central Great Plains. Ecological Monographs 27:27–44.

Arthur, George W. n.d. An introduction to the ecology of early historic communal bison hunting among the northern Plains Indians. Ph.D. dissertation, Department of Archaeology, University of Calgary.

Ayer, Mrs. Edward E. (transl.) 1916 The Memorial of Fray Alonso de Benavides, 1630. Chicago: privately printed.

Baerreis, D. A., and R. A. Bryson 1965 Historical climatology and the Southern Plains: a preliminary statement. Bulletin, Oklahoma Anthropological Society 13:69–75.

———. 1966 Dating the Panhandle Aspect cultures. Bulletin, Oklahoma Anthropological Society 14:105–116.

Bell, Robert E. 1962 Precolumbian prairie settlements in the Great Plains. Great Plains Journal 2:1:22–28.

———. 1968 Dating the prehistory of Oklahoma. Great Plains Journal 7:2:1–11.

———. 1973 The Washita River focus of the Southern Plains. *In* Variation in Anthropology, ed. Lathrap and Douglas, pp. 171–187. Illinois Archeological Survey.

Bell, Robert E., and David A. Baerreis 1951 A survey of Oklahoma archeology. Bulletin, Texas Archeological and Paleontological Society 22:7–100.

Bender, Margaret M., Reid A. Bryson, and David A. Baerreis 1966 University of Wisconsin radiocarbon dates II. Radiocarbon 8:522–533.

———. 1967 University of Wisconsin radiocarbon dates III. Radiocarbon 9:530–544.

Bliss, Wesley L. 1950 Birdshead Cave, a stratified site in Wind River Basin, Wyoming. American Antiquity 15:3:187–196.

Borchert, J. R. 1950 The climate of the central North American grassland. Annals of the Association of American Geographers 40:1:1–39.

Breternitz, David A. 1969 Radiocarbon dates: eastern Colorado. Plains Anthropologist 14:44:1:113–124.

Breternitz, David A., and John J. Wood 1965 Comments on the Bisterfeldt potato cellar site and flexed burials in the western Plains. Southwestern Lore 31:3:62–66.

Brown, Lionel 1967 Pony Creek archeology. Publications in Salvage Archeology No. 5. River Basin Surveys. Washington, D.C. The Smithsonian Institution.

Bryson, Reid A., D. A. Baerreis, and W. M. Wendland 1970 The character of late-glacial and post-glacial climatic changes. *In* Pleistocene and Recent Environments of the Central Great Plains, ed. W. Dort, Jr., and J. K. Jones, pp. 53–74. Special Publication No. 3, Department of Geology, University of Kansas.

Bryson, Reid A., and W. M. Wendland 1967 Tentative climatic patterns for some late glacial and post-glacial episodes in central North America. *In* Life, Land, and Water, ed. W. J. Mayer-Oakes, pp. 271–298. Winnipeg: University of Manitoba Press.

Buck, Arthur Dewey, Jr. 1959 The Custer focus of the Southern Plains. Bulletin, Oklahoma Anthropological Society 7:1–31.

Capes, Katherine H. 1963 The W. B. Nickerson survey and excavations, 1912–1915, of southern Manitoba mounds region. National Museum of Canada, Anthropology Papers No. 4.

Coupland, Robert T. 1958 The effects of fluctuations in weather upon the grasslands of the Great Plains. Botanical Review 24:5:273–317.

Davis, E. Mott 1962 Archeology of the Lime Creek site in southwestern Nebraska. Special Publication No. 3, University of Nebraska State Museum.

Dibble, David S. 1970 On the significance of additional radiocarbon dates from Bonfire Shelter, Texas. Plains Anthropologist 15:50:251–254.

Dibble, David S., and D. Lorrain 1968 Bonfire Shelter: a stratified bison kill site, Val Verde County, Texas. Miscellaneous Papers No. 1. Austin: Texas Memorial Museum.

Dillehay, Tom D. 1974. Late Quaternary bison population changes on the Southern Plains. Plains Anthropologist 19:65:180–196.

Eddy, John A. 1974 Astronomical alignment of the Big Horn medicine wheel. Science 184:4141:1035–1043.

Ellison, L., and E. J. Woolfolk 1937 Effects of drought on vegetation near Miles City, Montana. Ecology 18:3:329–336.

Farb, Peter 1968 Man's Rise to Civilization as Shown by the Indians of North America from Primeval Times to the Coming of the Industrial State. New York: E. P. Dutton.

Flannery, K. V. 1968 Archeological systems theory and early Mesoamerica. *In* Anthropological Archeology in the Americas, ed. B. J. Meggers, pp. 67–87. Anthropological Society of Washington.

Forbis, Richard G. 1962 The Old Women's Buffalo Jump, Alberta. National Museum of Canada, Bulletin 180, Contributions to Anthropology, 1960, part I, pp. 55–123. Ottawa: Canada Department of Northern Affairs and National Resources.

———. 1968 Alberta. *In* The Northwestern Plains: A Symposium, ed. W. W. Caldwell, pp. 37–44. Occasional Papers No. 1, Center for Indian Studies. Billings, Mont.: Rocky Mountain College.

Frankforter, W. D., and G. A. Agogino 1960 The Simonsen site: report for the summer of 1959. Plains Anthropologist 5:10:65–70

Frison, George C. 1962 Wedding of the Waters Cave, 48H0301, a stratified site in the Big Horn Basin of northern Wyoming. Plains Anthropologist 7:18:246–265.

———. 1965 Spring Creek Cave, Wyoming. American Antiquity 31:1:81–94.

———. 1968 Daugherty Cave, Wyoming. Plains Anthropologist 13:42:1:253–295.

———. 1970 The Kobold site, 24BH406: a post-Altithermal record of buffalo jumping for the Northwestern Plains. Plains Anthropologist 15:47:1–35.

———. 1971 The bison pound in Northwestern Plains prehistory. American Antiquity, 36:1:77–91.

———. 1972 The role of buffalo procurement in post-Altithermal populations on the Northwestern Plains. In Social Exchange and Interaction, ed. E. N. Wilmsen, pp. 11–19. University of Michigan Museum of Anthropology, Anthropological Papers No. 46.

———. 1973 The Wardell buffalo trap 48SU301: Communal procurement in the upper Green River Basin, Wyoming. University of Michigan Museum of Anthropology, Anthropological Papers No. 48.

———. 1974 The Casper Site: A Hell Gap Bison Kill on the High Plains. New York: Academic Press.

———. 1975 Man's interaction with Holocene environments on the Plains. Quaternary Research 5:2:289–300.

Frison, George C., and Michael Wilson 1975 An introduction to Bighorn Basin archeology. Wyoming Geological Association Guidebook, 27th Annual Field Conference—1975, pp. 19–35.

Frye, John C., and A. Byron Leonard 1952 Pleistocene geology of Kansas. Bulletin 99, University of Kansas State Geological Survey.

Gradwohl, David M. 1969 Prehistoric villages in eastern Nebraska. Publications in Anthropology No. 4, Nebraska State Historical Society.

Grange, Roger T., Jr. 1968 Pawnee and Lower Loup pottery. Publications in Anthropology No. 3. Nebraska State Historical Society.

Gunnerson, Dolores A. 1956 The southern Athabascans: their arrival in the Southwest. El Palacio 63:11–12:346–365.

———. 1972 Man and bison on the Plains in the prehistoric period. Plains Anthropologist 17:55:1–10.

Gunnerson, James H. 1968 Plains Apache archaeology: a review. Plains Anthropologist 13:41:167–189.

Hammond, George P., and Agapito Rey 1953 Don Juan de Onate, Colonizer of New Mexico 1595–1628. Albuquerque: Coronado Cuarto Centennial Publications, 1540–1940, vols. V and VI.

Haynes, C. Vance, Jr. 1964 Fluted projectile points: their age and dispersion. Science 145: 3639:1408–1413.

Hester, James J. 1972 Blackwater Locality No. 1, a Stratified Early Man site in Eastern New Mexico. Dallas: Fort Burgwin Research Center, Southern Methodist University.

Hill, A. T., and Marvin F. Kivett 1941 Woodland-like manifestations in Nebraska. Nebraska History Magazine 21:3:146–243.

Hind, Henry Youle 1859 Northwest Territory. Reports of progress; together with a preliminary and general report on the Assiniboine and Saskatchewan exploring expedition, made under instructions from the Provincial Secretary, Canada.

Hofman, Jack L. 1975 A study of Custer-Washita River foci relationships. Plains Anthropologist 20:67:41–51.

Hough, Walter 1930 The bison as a factor in ancient American cultural history. Scientific Monthly 30:315–319.

Hurt, Wesley R. 1966 The Altithermal and the prehistory of the northern Plains. Quaternaria 8:101–113.

Irwin, Henry T. 1970 Archeological investigations at the Union Pacific mammoth kill site, Wyoming, 1961. National Geographic Society Research Reports 1961–1962:123–125.

———. 1971 Developments in early man studies in western North America, 1960–1970. Arctic Anthropology 8:2:42–67.

Irwin, Henry T., and C. C. Irwin 1959 Excavations at the LoDaisKa site in the Denver, Colorado, area. Denver Museum of Natural History, Proceedings No. 8.

Irwin-Williams, C., H. T. Irwin, G. Agogino, and C. V. Haynes 1973 Hell Gap: Paleo-Indian occupation on the High Plains. Plains Anthropologist 18:59:40–53.

Jelinek, Arthur J. 1966 Correla.ion of archeological and palynological data. Science 152:3728: 1507–1509.

Jelks, E. B. (ed.) 1967 The Gilbert site, a Norteño focus site in northeastern Texas. Bulletin, Texas Archeological Society, vol. 37.

Johnson, A. E., and A. S. Johnson 1975 K-Means and temporal variability in Kansas City Hopewell ceramics. American Antiquity 40:3:283–295.

Joyes, Dennis C. 1970 The culture sequence at the Avery site at Rock Lake. In Ten Thousand Years, Archaeology in Manitoba, ed. W. M. Hlady, pp. 209–222. Manitoba Archaeological Society.

Judge, W. J., and J. Dawson 1972 Paleo-Indian settlement technology in New Mexico. Science 176:1210–1216.

Kehoe, Thomas F. 1964 Middle Woodland pottery from Saskatchewan. Plains Anthropologist 9:23:51–53.

———. 1967 The Boarding School bison drive site. Memoir 4, Plains Anthropologist.

———. 1973 The Gull Lake site: a prehistoric bison drive site in southwestern Saskatchewan. Publications in Anthropology and History No. 1, Milwaukee Public Museum.

Kehoe, Thomas F., and Alice B. Kehoe 1968 Saskatchewan. In The Northwestern Plains: A Symposium. ed. W. W. Caldwell, pp. 21–35. Occasional Papers No. 1, Center for Indian Studies. Billings, Mont.: Rocky Mountain College.

Kehoe, Thomas F., and Bruce A. McCorquodale 1961 The Avonlea Point, horizon marker for the Northwestern Plains. Plains Anthropologist 6:13:179–188.

Kivett, Marvin F. 1952 Woodland sites in Nebraska. Publications in Anthropology No. 1. Nebraska State Historical Society.

———. 1953 The Woodruff ossuary, a prehistoric burial site in Phillips County, Kansas. No. 3, Bureau of American Ethnology Bulletin 154, River Basin Surveys Papers.

———. 1970 Early ceramic environmental adaptations. In Pleistocene and Recent Environments of the Central Great Plains, ed. W. Dort, Jr., and J. K. Jones, Jr. pp. 93–102. Lawrence: University Press of Kansas.

Krause, Richard A. 1970 Aspects of adaptation among Upper Republican subsistence cultivators. In Pleistocene and Recent Environments of the Central Great Plains, ed. W. Dort, Jr., and J. K. Jones, Jr., pp. 103–115. Lawrence: University Press of Kansas.

Krieger, Alex D. 1950 A suggested general sequence in North American projectile points. In Proceedings, 6th Plains Archaeological Conference, 1948, ed. J. D. Pennings, pp. 117–124. University of Utah Anthropological Papers, No. 11.

Lawton, Sherman P. 1968 The Duncan-Wilson bluff shelter: a stratified site of the Southern Plains. Bulletin, Oklahoma Anthropological Society 16:1–94.

Lehmer, Donald J. 1954a Archeological investigations in the Oahe Dam area, South Dakota, 1950–1951. Bureau of American Ethnology, Bulletin 158, River Basin Surveys Papers, No. 7.

———. 1954b The sedentary horizon of the northern Plains. Southwestern Journal of Anthropology 10:2:139–159.

———. 1963 The Plains bison hunt—prehistoric and historic. Plains Anthropologist 8:22: 211–217.

———. 1970 Climate and culture history in the Middle Missouri valley. In Pleistocene and Recent Environments of the Central Great Plains, ed. W. Dort, Jr., and J. K. Jones, Jr., pp. 117–129. Lawrence: University Press of Kansas.

———. 1971 Introduction to Middle Missouri archeology. Anthropology Papers 1, National Park Service, U.S. Department of the Interior.

Leonhardy, Frank C. (ed.) 1966 Domebo: A Paleo-Indian mammoth kill in the prairie-plains. Lawton, Okla: Contributions of the Museum of the Great Plains, No. 1.

Lewis, G. Malcolm 1975 The recognition and delimitation of the northern interior grasslands during the 18th century. In Images of the Plains, ed. B. W. Blouet and M. P. Lawson, pp. 23–44. Lincoln: University of Nebraska Press.

Lorrain, Dessamae 1967 The Glass site. In A Pilot Study of Wichita Indian Archeology and Ethnohistory, assembled by R. E. Bell, E. B. Jelks, and W. W. Newcomb, Jr., pp. 24–44. Dallas: final report to the National Science Foundation.

McCracken, Harold 1971 Mummy Cave (Wyoming) archeological project. National Geographic Society Research Reports, 1965 Projects, pp. 155–160.

McHugh, Tom 1972 Time of the Buffalo. New York: Alfred A. Knopf.

Malouf, Carling, and Stuart Conner 1962 Symposium on buffalo jumps. Montana Archaeological Society, Memoir No. 1.

Marshall, James O. 1972 The archeology of the Elk City reservoir: a local archeological sequence in southeast Kansas. Anthropological Series No. 6, Kansas State Historical Society.

Martin, P. S., and H. E. Wright, Jr. (eds.) 1967 Pleistocene extinctions: the search for a cause. New Haven: Proceedings, VII Congress of International Association for Quaternary Research, vol. 6.

Mulloy, William 1952 The northern Plains. In Archeology of Eastern United States, ed. J. B. Griffin, pp. 124–128. Chicago: University of Chicago Press.

———. 1954a Archeological investigations in the Shoshone Basin of Wyoming. University of Wyoming Publications 18:1:1–70.

———. 1954b The McKean site in northeastern Wyoming. Southwestern Journal of Anthropology 10:4:432–460.

———. 1958 A preliminary historical outline for the Northwestern Plains. University of Wyoming Publications 22:(1, 2).

O'Brien, Patricia J. 1971 Valley focus mortuary practices. Plains Anthropologist 16:53:165–182.

Oliver, Symmes C. 1962 Ecology and cultural continuity as contributing factors in the social organization of the Plains Indians. University of California Publications in American Archaeology and Ethnology, vol. 48.

Opler, Morris E. 1975 Problems in Apachean cultural history, with special reference to the Lipan Apache. Anthropological Quarterly 48:3:182–192.

Ossenberg, N. S. 1974 Origins and relationships of Woodland peoples: the evidence of cranial morphology. In Aspects of Upper Great Lakes Anthropology, ed. Elden Johnson, pp. 15–39. Minnesota Prehistoric Archaeology Series No. 11.

Pearson, F. J., Jr., E. Mott Davis, and M. A. Tamers 1966 University of Texas Radiocarbon Dates IV. Radiocarbon 8:453–66.

Pillaert, E. Elizabeth 1963 The McLemore site of the Washita River focus. Bulletin, Oklahoma Anthropological Society 11:1–113.

Price, Raymond S. n.d. Early ceramic period sites in northeastern Nebraska. M.A. thesis, Department of Anthropology, University of Nebraska.

Reeves, Bryan 1973 The concept of an altithermal cultural hiatus in northern Plains prehistory. American Anthropologist 75:5:1221–1253.

Reher, Charles A. n.d. Buffalo population and other deterministic factors in a model of adaptive process on the short-grass plains. Plains Anthropologist Memoir (accepted for symposium monograph).

Roberts, F. H. H., Jr. 1936 Additional information on the Folsom complex: report on the second season's investigations at the Lindenmeier site in northern Colorado. Smithsonian Miscellaneous Collections 95:(10).

Sauer, Carl O. 1944 A geographic sketch of early man in America. Geographical Review 34:4:529–573.

Schlesier, Karl H. 1972 Rethinking the Dismal River aspect and the Plains Athabascans, AD 1692–1768. Plains Anthropologist 17:56:101–133.

Schneider, Fred E. 1969 The Roy Smith site, Bv-14, Beaver County, Okla. Bulletin, Oklahoma Anthropological Society 18:119–179.

Schultz, C. B. 1943 Some artifact sites of early man in the Great Plains and adjacent areas. American Antiquity 8:3:242–249.

Scott, Douglas D. 1973 Preliminary analysis of location strategies of Plains Woodland sites in northern Colorado. Southwestern Lore 39:3:1–11.

Scott, Douglas D., and Terje G. Birkedal 1972 The archaeology and physical anthropology of the Gahagan-Lipe site with comments on Colorado Woodland mortuary practices. Southwestern Lore 38:3:1–18.

Scott, Glenn R. 1962 Geology of the Littleton quadrangle, Jefferson, Douglas, and Arapahoe Counties, Colorado. U.S. Geological Survey Bulletin 1121-L:L-1 to L-53.

———. 1963 Quaternary geology and geomorphic history of the Kassler quadrangle, Colorado. Geological Survey Professional Paper 421-A. U.S. Geological Survey.

Sellards, E. H. 1952 Early Man in America. Austin: University of Texas Press.

Shelford, V. E. 1963 The Ecology of North America. Urbana: University of Illinois Press.

Stanford, Dennis J. 1974 Preliminary report of the excavation of the Jones-Miller Hell Gap site, Yuma County, Colorado. Southwestern Lore 40:3–4:29–36.

Strong, William Duncan 1935 An introduction to Nebraska archeology. Smithsonian Miscellaneous Collections 93:(10).

Thwaites, R. G. (ed.) 1904–1905 Original Journals of the Lewis and Clark Expedition, 1804–1806. 8 vols. New York: Dodd, Mead and Co.

Tunnell, C. D., and Jack T. Hughes 1955 An Archaic bison kill in the Texas panhandle. Panhandle-Plains Historical Review 28:63–70.

Ubelaker, Douglas H., and Waldo R. Wedel 1975 Bird bones, burials, and bundles in Plains archeology. American Antiquity 40:4:444–452.

Weakly, Ward F. 1971 Tree-ring dating and archaeology in South Dakota. Plains Anthropologist 16:54:(2). (Memoir 8.)

Weaver, J. E., and F. W. Albertson 1956 Grasslands of the Great Plains: Their Nature and Use. Lincoln: Johnsen Publishing Company.

Wedel, Waldo R. 1938 The direct-historical approach in Pawnee archeology. Smithsonian Miscellaneous Collections 97:(7).

———. 1941 Environment and native subsistence economies in the central Great Plains. Smithsonian Miscellaneous Collections 101:(3).

———. 1943 Archeological investigations in Platte and Clay counties, Missouri. Bulletin 183, U.S. National Museum.

———. 1953 Some aspects of human ecology in the Central Plains. American Anthropologist 55:4:499–514.

———. 1959 An introduction to Kansas archeology. Bulletin 174, Bureau of American Ethnology.

———. 1961 Prehistoric Man on the Great Plains. Norman: University of Oklahoma Press.

———. 1963 The High Plains and their utilization by the Indian. American Antiquity 29:1:1–16.

———. 1964 The Great Plains. In Prehistoric Man in the New World. ed. J. D. Jennings and E. Norbeck, pp. 193–220. Chicago: University of Chicago Press.

———. 1967 Salvage archeology in the Missouri River Basin. Science 156:589–597.

———. 1968 Some thoughts on Central Plains-Southern Plains archaeological relationships. Great Plains Journal 7:2:1–10.

———. 1970 Some observations on Two House Sites in the Central Plains: an experiment in archaeology. Nebraska History 51:2:225–252.

———. 1975 Some early Euro-American percepts of the Great Plains and their influence on anthropological thinking. In Images of the Plains, ed. B. W. Blouet and M. P. Lawson, pp. 13–20. Lincoln: University of Nebraska Press.

———. n.d.a Investigations at the Lamb Spring site, Colorado. Unpublished manuscript. Final report to National Science Foundation on Project NSF-G17609.

———. n.d.b The Central Plains Village tradition. Unpublished manuscript. Handbook of North American Indians, vol. 10: Plains.

Wedel, Waldo R., W. M. Husted, and J. H. Moss 1968 Mummy Cave: prehistoric record from Rocky Mountains of Wyoming. Science 160:184–185.

Wells, Philip V. 1970 Vegetational history of the Great Plains: a post-glacial record of coniferous woodland in southeastern Wyoming. In Pleistocene and Recent Environments of the Central Great Plains, ed. W. A. Dort, Jr., and J. K. Jones, Jr., pp. 185–202. Lawrence: University Press of Kansas.

Wendorf, Fred, and James J. Hester 1962 Early Man's utilization of the Great Plains environment. American Antiquity 28:2:159–171.

Wendorf, Fred, and James J. Hester (eds.) 1975 Late Pleistocene environments of the southern High Plains. Ranchos de Taos, N.M.: Fort Burgwin Research Center, Publication No. 9.

Wheat, Joe Ben 1972 The Olsen-Chubbuck site, a Paleo-Indian bison kill. American Antiquity 37:1:2:1–180. (Memoir 26.)

White, Leslie A. (ed.) 1959 Lewis Henry Morgan: The Indian Journals, 1859–62. Ann Arbor: University of Michigan Press.

Wilson, Michael 1974 History of the bison in Wyoming, with particular reference to Early Holocene forms. Geological Survey of Wyoming, Report of Investigations 10:91–99.

Wissler, Clark 1922 The American Indian: An Introduction to the Anthropology of the New World. 2d ed. New York: Oxford University Press.

Wood, W. Raymond 1974 Northern Plains Village cultures: internal stability and external relationships. Journal of Anthropological Research 30:1:1–16.

Wood, W. Raymond (ed.) 1969 Two house sites in the Central Plains: an experiment in archaeology. Plains Anthropologist 14:44:(2) (Memoir 6.)

Wormington, H. M. 1957 Ancient man in North America. Denver: Denver Museum of Natural History, Popular Series No. 4, 4th ed.

Wright, H. E., Jr. 1970 Vegetational history of the Central Plains. *In* Pleistocene and Recent Environments of the central Great Plains, ed. W. Dort, Jr., and J. K. Jones, Jr., pp. 157–172. Lawrence: University Press of Kansas.

Low aerial view of Serpent Mound, showing nearby structures. (Photograph by D. M. Reeves, Smithsonian Institution.)

CHAPTER SIX

The Midlands and Northeastern United States

James B. Griffin

In the resource-rich Northeast, the aboriginal cultures were numerous and varied. Settlements comprising large populations, large complexes of enormous earthworks, abundant evidence of long-range trade networks, and a rich aesthetic tradition are all evidence of the advanced state of many Northeastern cultures. Dr. Griffin gives us a survey of the large numbers of sites and cultures known from this region, where the discipline of archeology has a long history.

PALEO-INDIAN

The earliest reported evidence of early populations in the Northeast is at the Meadowcroft Shelter, some 50 miles southwest of Pittsburgh (Adovasio et al. 1975). Here there are flint knives, flakes, a scraper, and other tools of flint in the lowest stratum, with radiocarbon dates in the 17,000 BC range (see Chapter 1). If these results are supported by future work and if a more adequate assemblage is obtained, this will be by far the oldest acceptable occupation in the area (Figure 6.1).

The oldest widespread prehistoric complex is best identified by fluted projectile points and knives. This early industry is found over the entire area covered by this chapter except on the extreme northern fringe. It is part of a country-wide occupation, and its general similarity over the entire area is a remarkable phenomenon. There is a great deal we do not know about this complex. We do not know with any certainty when the populations came into the New World or what paths they may have followed to reach the Northeast. Many believe that their technological skills were developed in the Old World and adapted to an Arctic environment in northeast Siberia, allowing them to move into northwestern North America and southward along the eastern

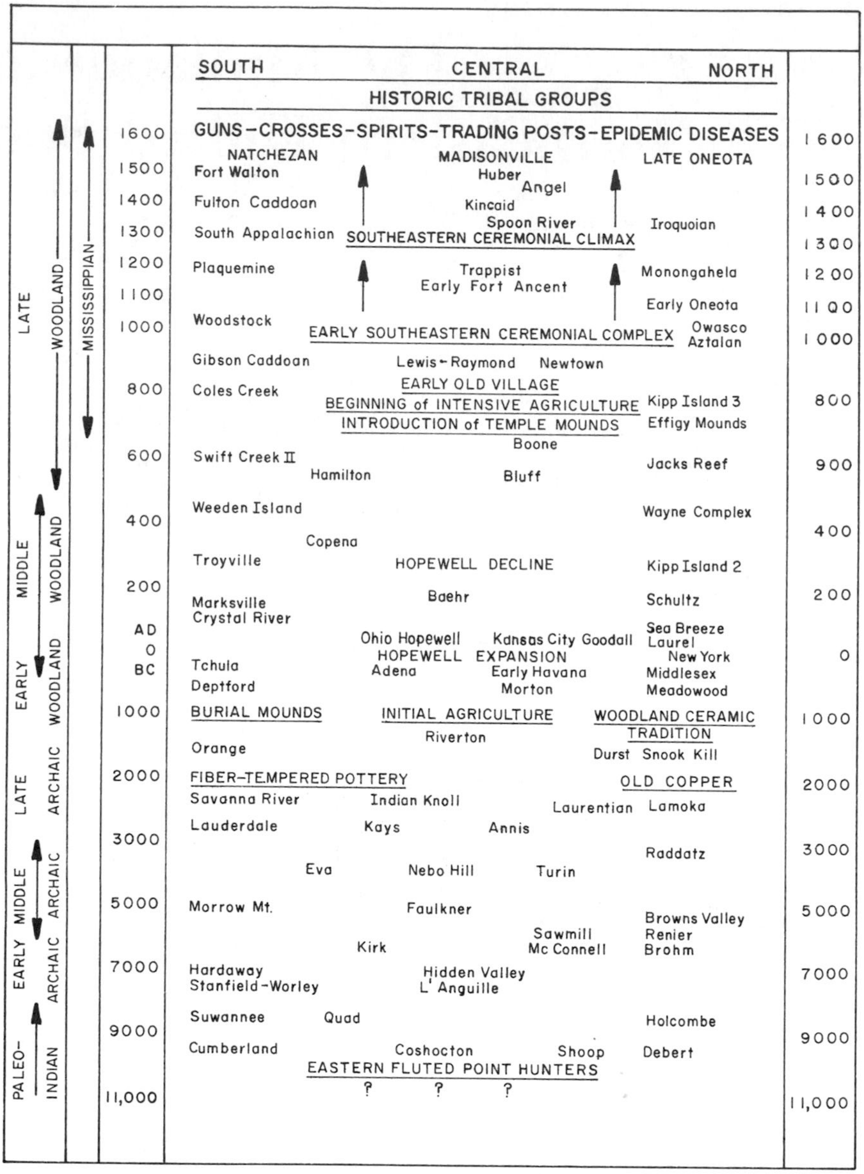

	SOUTH	CENTRAL	NORTH	
	HISTORIC TRIBAL GROUPS			
1600	GUNS – CROSSES – SPIRITS – TRADING POSTS – EPIDEMIC DISEASES			1600
1500	NATCHEZAN	MADISONVILLE	LATE ONEOTA	1500
	Fort Walton	Huber		
		Angel		
1400	Fulton Caddoan	Kincaid		1400
		Spoon River	Iroquoian	
1300	South Appalachian	SOUTHEASTERN CEREMONIAL CLIMAX		1300
1200	Plaquemine	Trappist	Monongahela	1200
		Early Fort Ancent		
1100			Early Oneota	1100
1000	Woodstock	EARLY SOUTHEASTERN CEREMONIAL COMPLEX	Owasco / Aztalan	1000
	Gibson Caddoan	Lewis – Raymond Newtown		
800	Coles Creek	EARLY OLD VILLAGE	Kipp Island 3	800
		BEGINNING of INTENSIVE AGRICULTURE	Effigy Mounds	
		INTRODUCTION of TEMPLE MOUNDS		
		Boone		
600	Swift Creek II		Jacks Reef	900
	Hamilton	Bluff		
400	Weeden Island		Wayne Complex	400
	Copena			
	Troyville	HOPEWELL DECLINE	Kipp Island 2	
200	Marksville	Baehr	Schultz	200
	Crystal River		Sea Breeze	
		Ohio Hopewell Kansas City Goodall	Laurel	
AD 0		HOPEWELL EXPANSION	New York	0
BC	Tchula	Adena Early Havana	Middlesex	
	Deptford	Morton	Meadowood	
1000	BURIAL MOUNDS	INITIAL AGRICULTURE	WOODLAND CERAMIC TRADITION	1000
		Riverton		
	Orange		Durst Snook Kill	
2000	FIBER – TEMPERED POTTERY		OLD COPPER	2000
	Savanna River	Indian Knoll		
		Laurentian Lamoka		
	Lauderdale	Kays Annis		
3000			Raddatz	3000
	Eva	Nebo Hill Turin		
5000	Morrow Mt.	Faulkner	Browns Valley	5000
		Sawmill	Renier	
	Kirk	McConnell	Brohm	
7000	Hardaway	Hidden Valley		7000
	Stanfield – Worley	L'Anguille		
	Suwannee Quad		Holcombe	
9000	Cumberland	Coshocton Shoop	Debert	9000
	EASTERN FLUTED POINT HUNTERS			
	? ? ?			
11,000				11,000

Left margin vertical labels (top to bottom): LATE WOODLAND / MISSISSIPPIAN; MIDDLE WOODLAND; EARLY WOODLAND; LATE ARCHAIC; MIDDLE ARCHAIC; EARLY ARCHAIC; PALEO-INDIAN

FIGURE 6.1
Cultural sequence and chronology.

flank of the Rocky Mountains sometime shortly before or after the climax of the Wisconsin glaciation (see Chapter 1). The distinctive fluting that removed longitudinal flakes from both faces of the projectile points and knives was apparently developed in the United States, but no one knows where or exactly when.

Of the sites associated with this complex, the best dated is located at Debert, Nova Scotia (MacDonald 1968), where a series of radiocarbon dates indicate occupation about 8600 BC. This location is on the northeastern fringe of Paleo-Indian sites and, presumably, represents the furthest extension in that direction. Individual finds have turned up in Maine, New Hampshire, and Connecticut. The New England area's best-known site is Bull Brook (Byers 1954; 1955), which has not been accurately dated but is here assumed to be of approximately the same age as Debert (Figure 6.2). A smaller occupation occurred at Wapanucket 8 in southeastern Massachusetts. In New Jersey, the analysis of the complex from the Plenge site in Warren County in the upper Delaware River drainage (Kraft 1973) is an excellent study of a major eastern site. This site was probably occupied intermittently over an unknown period of time because it was a favorable location for a base camp.

Within a relatively small area may be found the Port Mobil site on Staten Island, the Zierdt site in northwest New Jersey, Dutchess Quarry Cave, West Athens Hills, and Kings Road in the Hudson valley south of Albany. The Reagen site in northwestern Vermont must have been occupied intermittently during the shift from fluted to unfluted projectile points. Only the Potts site in Oswego County, New York, sitting on the former lake bed of glacial Lake Iroquois, has been acceptably identified as a site in that area (Ritchie 1969a: 22–30). This lake bed area would have been available for occupation by vegetation and animal life by shortly after 10,000 BC (Prest 1970:717–718).

In Ontario, scattered finds of fluted points reported by Kidd (1951) suggest that the fluted point sites and activities were above the old Lake Algonquin terrace and that the fluting technique had disappeared before the level of Lake Huron had fallen below the 605 Algonquin level (Griffin 1965). Northwest of London, recent work by William A. Roosa of Waterloo University has produced a series of fluted point sites related to the Barnes complex in central Michigan (personal communication).

As far as I know, there have been no reports of newly discovered fluted point occupations in Pennsylvania since Witthoft's (1952) pioneering paper on the Enterline industry at the Shoop site north of Harrisburg, the first significant analysis and discussion of the Paleo-Indian occupations in the east. Apparently the Susquehanna and Delaware areas had the largest occupations, as shown by subsequent surveys by Mason (1959) and Kinsey (1958; 1959).

Surveys of fluted point distributions in Ohio and in Indiana by Prufer and Baby (1963) and by Dorwin (1966) have pointed out the heavier concentrations of these forms in the southern parts of both states and a considerable

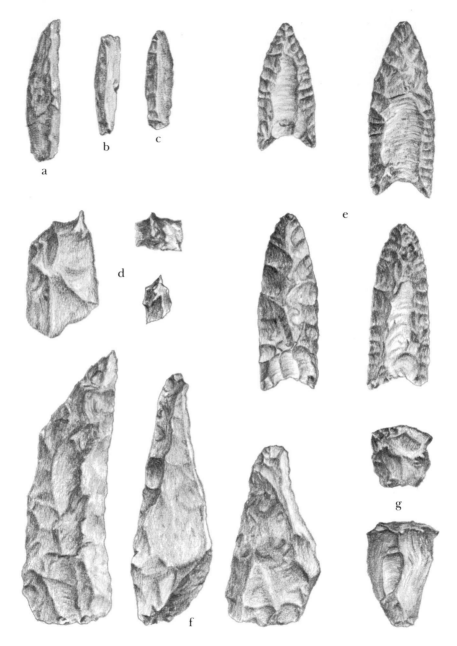

FIGURE 6.2
Flint implements from Bull Brook, representative of eastern fluted point sites: *a, b,* retouched blades; *c,* "twist drill"; *d,* uniface gravers; *e,* fluted projectile points; *f,* side scrapers; *g,* end scrapers with graver spur at edge of blade. (From *Prehistory of North America,* 2d ed., by Jesse D. Jennings. Copyright © 1968, 1974 by McGraw-Hill, Inc. Used with permission of McGraw-Hill Book Company.)

formal variability in artifact shape. The Ohio survey identified almost 500 fluted points in various collections, while the Indiana survey produced nearly 200 with a less intensive review. An even less systematic survey of Illinois identified some 252 specimens from the St. Louis area (Smail 1951), and locations reported by a number of other archeologists from the state add some 130 to the total (Griffin 1968). The Wisconsin distribution (Stoltman and Workman 1969) is primarily in the southern half of the state for a number of reasons; probably that is where most of the population was. The fact that a few fluted points have been found on top of Valders till means that they were deposited after ca. 9500 BC, which is as early as they are known anywhere else.

In Michigan, studies on a correlation of fluted points and geochronology were begun 20 years ago (Griffin 1956; Mason 1958; Quimby 1958). Unfortunately, no sites have been located with the amount of occupational evidence desired for an extensive investigation; the best-known of the sites discovered so far is the Barnes site (Wright and Roosa 1966). In general, the observation made in 1956 that the fluted point occupation was limited to the locations higher than the main Lake Algonquin beach is still valid. The drop in lake levels began between 9500 and 9200 BC because of the opening of the drainage from the Georgian Bay area into the Champlain Sea. One fluted point has also been found on the Valders till south of Grand Traverse Bay (Dekin 1966).

The interpretation adopted in this chapter is that the fluted point hunters moved into the Northeast primarily from the south. By 10,000 BC floral and faunal resources in the Ohio valley and far north into Wisconsin, Michigan, and Ontario were adequate for the support of scattered bands of hunters, each probably comprising from 15 to 20 closely related individuals. The Ontario population probably entered from southeastern Michigan; the New York, New England, and Nova Scotia populations may well have moved up the Susquehanna and Delaware and the coastal area from Virginia and the Southeast.

The considerable homogeneity of tool forms over the entire Northeast, and indeed over much of the United States, allows one to characterize the entire area as possessing essentially one technological complex. From the excavations and careful collections so far undertaken, it appears that some sites, such as Debert, Bull Brook, and Plenge, were probably major camps for either somewhat larger than normal groups or for recurrent occupations or both. Other sites, such as Shoop and Potts, are interpreted as hunting camps, while Kings Road was both a hunting and a workshop location. Some are primarily quarry sites, such as west Athens; briefly occupied locations are the David, Port Mobil, and Wapanucket 8 sites. Many of the locations known from the literature, such as the Kouba site in southern Wisconsin, were probably base camps, though one cannot be sure of this.

The technology of this earliest prehistoric population was adaptable to a wide variety of environments, from coastal plain to upland areas, from river valleys to northern lake environments, from regions in the south with a strong deciduous element in the forest cover to the spruce-pine-dominated areas in the north. Tools included cobblestone choppers; large stone scraping planes; hammerstones and abraders for processing vegetal products for food, shelter, and heat; and the disgnostic fluted or unfluted points and knives for killing and butchering game. Large numbers of end scrapers were made from blades, and some of these have a distinctive spur on each end of the working edge that is almost a diagnostic trait for the period. End scrapers were used in the preparation of leather and perhaps as woodworking or bone-scraping tools. Side scrapers, spokeshaves (used to smooth cylindrical surfaces such as dart or spear shafts), and drills (flakes with a very fine point or multiple points for use as perforators) are characteristic. Flint wedges were employed to split bone, antler, and wood or as grooving tools. Because of unfavorable environmental conditions, no bone tools or ornaments have been found, but we may reasonably suppose that bone awls, needles, knives, flakers, and perhaps shaft straighteners were made.

Poor preservation also affects the faunal assemblages from these early sites. The only animal bone that has been preserved in association with a fluted point in the East is at Dutchess Quarry Cave in Orange County, New York, where bone refuse of a woodland caribou was located and dated to 10,580 BC ± 370 (I-4137). The bones of rodents, deer, and elk were also found. In apparent association was a fluted point identified as a Cumberland type (Funk, Walters, and Ehlers 1969; Funk, Fisher, and Reilly 1970). There is no question that these populations had a heavy emphasis upon hunting and were capable of dealing with anything from caribou and elk to rodents. There are many mastodon and mammoth finds in the Northeast, but there is no evidence that man slew or butchered these beasts. This holds true for the Southeast and for the whole wooded area east of the Plains. We must also recognize that other foods, such as nuts, seeds, berries, fish, and fowl, were available and not beyond the procurement capabilities of these populations.

Analysis of flint sources for these fluted point sites has indicated that favored or known flint from western New York was carried into eastern Pennsylvania, New York, and New England; that Pennsylvania jaspers are known from New York, New Jersey, and New England; and that eastern Ohio sources were used for specimens found in New York and Pennsylvania.

EARLY ARCHAIC

A purely arbitrary division is made between the earlier fluted point hunters and their direct descendants, who are assigned to the time period of about 8000 to 6000 BC. For many years the Early Archaic was not recognized for a variety of reasons, but closer attention to comparisons with Southeastern and Plains assemblages and the opportunity for many more excavations have been productive.

Between 8000 and 6000 BC much of the area acquired a vegetational pattern and an accompanying animal life very like that at the time of European arrival. Although there are no extensive site excavations and none that have well-preserved bone or vegetable material components that can help us directly study the animal and vegetal food supply, certain inferences about subsistence can be made. A continuing strong emphasis on hide working and animal hunting and processing is indicated by a continuation of the gravers, scrapers, knives, and projectile points. The last, particularly, have a much greater variation in form than during the earlier period. Continuity of the basic form used earlier is shown at such sites as Holcombe in southeastern Michigan (Fitting et al. 1966), which produced points similar to the Milnesand and other basally thinned points of the Plains. Similar points can be recognized elsewhere, but they are not satisfactorily isolated as part of a recognizable cultural complex. They seem to be present at the Reagan and Plenge sites discussed earlier and are well represented in Illinois, Wisconsin, and Ohio.

From other excavations in the Northeast we know of the presence of sandstone abraders, of cobbles for grinding vegetable foods or pounding meat, and of mortars. A chipped flint adze makes its appearance and is the first of the heavy woodworking tools. These were important in producing wood for shelter construction, dugout canoes, and wooden containers, and apparently were the prototype for the grooved ax, the gouge, and the celt of later periods.

In southern Illinois and southwestern Indiana there is a sizable proportion of Dalton projectile points, a strong element in Early Archaic levels in the mid-South from about 7500 to 6500 BC. Other lithic forms in this area are the St. Charles, Agate Basin, Quad, and Kirk. In the Miami to Marietta area of Ohio there are indications of points such as Kirk, Kanawha, and LeCroy that have been dated in the lower Kanawha valley and were found in stratigraphic context first in the piedmont of North Carolina. These Kirk and LeCroy forms are now known in stratigraphic excavations in the upper Delaware, from Staten Island, and in the upper Susquehanna valley. Palmer, Kirk, and Charleston projectile forms are now recognized in southeastern Massachusetts, although they have not been excavated within a cultural complex.

One of the best-known sites in the western Great Lakes is the Holcombe site, which is neither located on a beach of glacial Lake Algonquin nor identified as a fluted point occupation. While earlier dates have been given for the draining of Lake Algonquin, the best estimate is now 8600 BC, approximately the time when the shift from spruce parkland to pine and mixed hardwoods (Karow et al. 1975) took place. A toe bone at Holcombe identified as barren ground caribou is hardly enough to formulate either a hunting pattern or an environment. The probabilities are that the site and its artifacts were in existence as one of a series of camps from about 8000 to 7000 BC. There are clear indications in the gravers, scrapers, and projectile forms that the complex was in existence within a few hundred years after the time of the fluted point people.

In Wisconsin the only named phase for this period is the Flambeau, recognized in the north-central part of the state (Salzer 1974:43–44), which is followed in the same area by the Minoqua phase. In form, both are analogous to the Agate Basin to Scottsbluff sequence in the Plains. A burial at the Renier site (Mason and Irwin 1960), originally reported as being in an Algonquin deposit, is probably Early Archaic in age. The fossil beach, which was formed by at least 9000 BC, was probably selected as a burial site because of its favorable elevated position. The burial here is interpreted as dating to about 7000 to 6000 BC. Mason (1963) illustrates a variety of Early Archaic or late Paleo-Indian forms largely from the Neville Museum in Green Bay. Other museums and collections in Wisconsin also contain specimens that show the range from basally thinned lanceolate forms to Scottsbluff. One such collection is from the Kouba site in Dane County (Ritzenthaler 1966); another is from excavations at the Markee site in southwestern Wisconsin (Halsey 1974).

On the northwestern side of Lake Superior, the Brohm complex (MacNeish 1952), which has been duplicated by J. Wright (1972a: Plates 1 and 3) at the Cummins quarry and campsite, is considered Early Archaic. The Cummins finds are on the land side of a fossil Lake Minong beach that was formed about 8000 BC, but the points and scrapers are probably somewhat later because they resemble the western Plainview forms. Most of the specimens from this industry were made from taconite.

Typologically later are the complexes at George Lake, Chickinising, and Sheguiandah in the Manitoulin district of Lake Huron. Here Scottsbluff and Eden-like forms are found with early side-notched points (Greenman 1966; Lee 1954; 1955; 1957). A reasonable estimate of the age of these sites would be from about 7000 to 6000 BC, a time when there is a high pine pollen count from a nearby bog at Sheguiandah. These sites are almost certainly not earlier than the period of the lowest level of Lake Algonquin. George Lake is at an elevation of 97.5 to 90.5 meters above Lake Huron; Sheguiandah is at approximately 65.5 meters; and the Chickinising I site is midway between the two. The artifacts at these sites are primarily fabricated from quartzite from the local deposits. A fine, narrow, lanceolate form, also made of quartzite but found near Flesherton, Ontario, southeast of Owen Sound, has been described by Storck (1972). Different forms, closely similar to those from the Holcombe site but somewhere in the 8000 to 7000 BC range, are illustrated by Storck from his survey of the Bronte Gap just to the north of Hamilton, Ontario (Storck 1973).

In Ohio the largest number of sites with projectile forms equivalent to the Plains types from the period 8000 to 6000 BC are in the north (Prufer and Baby 1963: Figure 20; Prufer 1963; 1966). Such types are also present south of the Ohio River, but they are not well dated in that area. Plano forms should also be present in the lowland area of western and north-central New York, which had been occupied during the earlier period.

The interpretation adopted here is that the appearance of the Plano forms is the result not of a movement of people abandoning the western Plains but rather of gradual changes taking place in conjunction with changes on the Plains by means of the same social mechanisms or group interactions that allow new ideas and technical developments to move with fair speed over considerable areas. The strength of the Plano forms in the northern part of the Northeast may have been aided by the prairie extension into Minnesota, Iowa, and Illinois; but there were large areas where the eastern Plano forms are found which were not and have never been prairies. The prairie development was later than the presence of these points. The hypothesis that the relative absence of sites is due to the closed pine forest is rejected partly on the ground that from 8000 to 6000 BC in most of the Lake Forest area there was not a closed pine forest (Brown and Cleland 1968). Moreover, the scarcity of sites in some states may be due to a failure to devote adequate time and resources to the search for them.

MIDDLE ARCHAIC

During the next 2000 years of adaptation to the environment in the Northeast, 6000 to 4000 BC, not only did the vegetational pattern acquire a completely modern appearance over most of the area, but Indian expansion reached about as far north as it would ever go both in the interior and along the Atlantic coast. Sea level came within about 9 meters of its present height, and land uplift almost ceased in the New England area. A number of new technological developments appeared during this period, including the grinding and polishing of stone implements. Bone tools appear in a few locations, and there are some early indications of increasing status differentiation among the band members.

In southern New England, the Neville complex has been identified by Dincauze (1971; 1974). She includes in this complex large, straight-based Neville points, perforators, and small end scrapers. The Stark complex follows in time and includes a more pointed stemmed form. These complexes are associated with choppers, full-grooved axes, and a bipinnate winged bannerstone. At 6000 to 5000 BC, the Neville and Stark complexes have the earliest ground and polished stone forms. The Neville to Stark succession is similar to the succession from Stanly to Morrow Mountain II in North Carolina, according to Dincauze. Some of the sites are spring fishing stations where spawning anadromous fish could easily be caught. There are other indications of a diversification of activities exploiting seasonal resources, and indeed it would be difficult to postulate any other subsistence base in the Northeast Probably the sea-oriented sites are now under water; we have records only of the riverine and lake border sites.

Prehistoric Indian populations moved north into the Strait of Belle Isle and southern Labrador and occupied coastal sites from 20 to 27 meters above the sea. The area was forested, and the people were hunting caribou, sea birds and mammals, and fish. The sites are small and were probably reoccupied many times over the years. At the L'Anse Amour site a mound contained the extended burial of a 12-year-old about 100 centimeters below the surface. The upper part of the mound was composed of piled boulders. There was a small amount of red ocher in association. The burial was accompanied by a walrus tusk, three socketed bone points, a stemmed bone point, six stone projectiles or knives, modules of graphite with red ocher stains, an antler point grinder or applicator, a bone pendant, a bone whistle or flute, a decorated ivory toggle, and what is said to be the earliest toggling harpoon head in the world. The present radiocarbon dating is 7530 BC ± 140 (Tuck 1975a: 85–93). The projectile forms in this early period range from triangular to a stemmed point related to the Neville forms to the south. By ca. 5000 to 4500 BC narrow-stemmed forms have appeared along with ground slate points and knives and ground gouges. The Belle Isle development is aptly called the Maritime Archaic and is now known to have a time depth, originality, and versatility that were hardly suspected ten years ago. These early sites are known because the rebounding land kept them above sea level; presumably, comparable coastal sites to the south were submerged.

On Staten Island the Hollowell Old Place and Ward's Point sites have occupations from just before 6000 BC to about 5,000 BC. Artifacts include points equated with Stanly, Morrow Mountain, and Kirk Stemmed, giving typological support to the time range set by radiocarbon dates (Ritchie and Funk 1973:38–39).

At the Sheeprock Shelter in the Zone 4 level there are small stemmed forms called Raystown Stemmed that are regarded as a regional variant of the Kanawha to Stanly type (Bebrich 1968:323–324). These are also found at the Workman site in Bedford County, Pennsylvania, about 48 kilometers upstream from Sheeprock. Here a wide variety of a few points are believed to represent short occupations during Early and Middle Archaic times. Unfortunately, good contextual associations are not present (Bebrich and Morgan 1968).

There are not many data from the period between 6000 and 4000 BC in the western part of the Northeast. There may well have been some occupation at Modoc Rockshelter in Illinois, but it is difficult to determine just what the occupation was. Perhaps the winged bannerstone and the Hidden Valley and side-notched forms belong here. A dog burial at the Koster site probably belongs to the same general level.

In north-central Wisconsin, a primarily hunting tool complex of end and side scrapers, large and small biface points and knives, bifacially flaked flake knives, wedges, and bipolar cores is identified as the Menocqua phase by

Salzer (1974). His estimated age for the assemblage is between 6000 and 5000 BC. Unit B at the Markee site in southwestern Wisconsin might be slightly later (Halsey 1974).

LATE ARCHAIC

While there were relatively few sites for the preceding periods for which a cohesive complex could be represented, the situation is vastly different for the final 3000 years of the Archaic. In many areas successive units are recognized; in some areas contemporary groups in different types of locations had significantly different behavioral patterns. The arbitrary time period of 4000 to 1000 BC dates the most complex and diversely developed pre-Woodland societies. Specialized adaptations to broad regional and even local environments are recognized. Plants were important for their food, medicinal, and magical properties. The manufacture of many tools and implements from forest and plant materials was probably common. In favorable localities a rich bone industry has been preserved, and this too must actually have been widespread. The wide variety of faunal remains is testimony to skill in hunting, fishing, fowling, and trapping. Transportation by dugout and birchbark or elmbark canoe was almost certainly in existence from the mouth of the St. Lawrence to the Ohio and Mississippi valleys. The path of distribution of copper and copper implements into the eastern Great Lakes follows the water routes. The best evidence for early houses appears at this time. The ground and polished stone industry reached a high development.

There is considerable evidence for the long-distance movement of goods, some as raw materials but some apparently already in final form. Much of this transported material was eventually placed with burials, a practice interpreted as evidence of both personal and magical power. The importance of burial offerings and their association with red ocher, which was seen at such separated localities as Renier and Belle Isle Strait during the Early and Middle Archaic, is accentuated in this period. Relatively few of the burials have such grave goods, and the total amount per year per individual in the society is probably quite small. Toward the close of the period, the first pottery makes its appearance, as do the first tropical agricultural plants—squash, and perhaps gourds.

Sites are of larger size and represent recurrent habitation, sometimes over long periods of time. Many more areas were occupied than in earlier times. Closely related complexes can be identified in rather restricted geographical areas; they represent band or tribal hunting areas. All the evidence during this period points to a population expansion.

One good reason for beginning the Late Archaic about 4000 BC in New England is that the sea then began to invade the Charles River valley west of

Boston, setting in motion environmental changes, including the covering of the freshwater peat deposits. These bogs have proved to be of great value in the analysis of environmental conditions in an area where several fish weirs were buried ca. 2500 BC. These weirs are remains of an exploitation of sea resources by the Indians at or near river mouths. This practice could well be part of an even older (beyond 2500 BC) tradition that lasted into the historic period. The Boston Back Bay weirs are attributable to the Squibnocket complex (Dincauze 1973:31).

About 32 kilometers north of Bangor, excavations by the University of Maine have identified Neville points in the lower levels of excavations at the Hirundo site. At higher levels there is an occupation associated with Otter Creek Side-notched points that also includes ground slate blades and bayonets, bannerstones, ground stone adzes, gouges and full-grooved axes, plummets, and cigar-shaped stone rods, perhaps used as whetstones. This complex is estimated to belong to the period between 4500 BC and somewhat after 4000 BC. It is related to the Vergennes complex of northern New England, where the earliest radiocarbon date is on the Sylvan Lake Rockshelter (Funk 1966).

One of the common occupation identification markers during the Late Archaic in the Northeast is the narrow-stemmed-point complexes, which cover a time span from the mid-third millennium into the first millennium BC. These include the Bare Island phase in the lower Susquehanna, the Lamoka of the central Finger Lake area and the Taconic and Sylvan Lake complexes of the lower Hudson valley in New York, the Squibnocket complex in Massachusetts, and the Wading River complex of Long Island and Connecticut. These complexes are regarded as representative regional groups engaged in a variety of maritime-oriented activities throughout the year, such as collecting oysters and other mollusks and taking sea, stream, and freshwater fish by weir, net, traps, lines, spears, and harpoons. Many game animals and birds were also harvested, with heavy emphasis on deer. A wide selection of vegetal foods were available; mortars and mullers, nutting stones, and preserved nut hulls attest to a significant but difficult-to-measure vegetal food intake.

Site sizes range from small groups of 10 to 15 individuals living in rockshelters to sites at favorable processing locations, which show evidence of recurrent occupations by as many as 50 or more individuals over the years. There are indications of house floors on many sites, but there are remains of very few structures. The Wapanucket 6 site (Figure 6.3) in southeastern Massachusetts has six circular domestic structures from 9 to 14 meters in diameter and a much larger structure 20 meters in diameter; the latter was presumably employed in group ceremonial activities (Robbins 1959). Presumably associated with the village is the Assawompsett II 8 burial complex; both have dates of 2300 BC and overlapping cultural content. Burials are cremations in belowground, carefully made pits, some with red ocher deposits. With the burials are included intentionally shaped stone slabs (some with sharpening grooves),

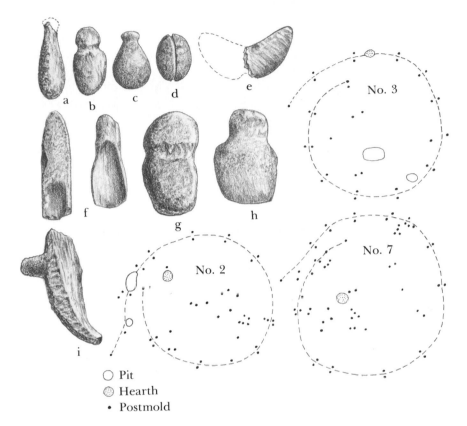

FIGURE 6.3
Lodge floor plans and selected artifacts found at Late Archaic Wapanucket No. 6. Note southwesterly entry common to all lodges. *a–c*, plummets; *d*, bolas stone; *e*, atlatl weight; *f*, gouges; *g*, grooved ax; *h*, maul; *i*, steatite pottery fragment. Copyright © 1968, 1974 by McGraw-Hill, Inc. Used with permission of McGraw-Hill Book Company.)

gouges and their sharpening stones, plummets, strike-a-light sets, celts, bannerstones, choppers, bone beads, ground hematite, narrow-stemmed points, quartz scrapers, and bone awls (Robbins 1968). A burial at Bear Swamp I dated some 250 years earlier contains red ocher and charcoal, small stemmed points, a winged atlatl weight, an atlatl blank, and a piece of graphite. The emphasis on burial ceremonialism that appears in eastern New England is not so prominent in other narrow-stemmed-point cultural complexes.

From about 2000 to 1000 BC, there are several regional complexes from Maryland into southern New England that are associated with broad-bladed stemmed projectile points and knives. These are known as Perkiomen, Susquehanna, Lehigh, and Koens-Crispin Broad Spear, types that have minor variations in form. They are associated with steatite bowls, bannerstones, adzes, celts, gorgets, flint drills, gravers, and scrapers. Burial practices include cremation, the use of red ocher, and ceremonial destruction of grave goods. This complex forms a significant element of the Watertown phase of New England (Kinsey 1972:343–355).

In eastern Massachusetts, by the middle of the second millennium BC, a group of cremation cemeteries is associated with distinctive broad-bladed stemmed points and knives of the Susquehanna tradition of eastern Pennsylvania and the Snook Kill phase of southeastern New York. Most of the artifacts in these cremations are broken. The cemeteries are often associated with gravel knolls; some of the graves have red ocher. There are full-grooved axes, pecked and flaked adzes, pounding pestles, steatite bowls, strike-a-lights, and an incised antler comb (Dincauze 1968). This complex is regarded as having contributed to the later Orient complex of Long Island.

North into the Maritime Provinces and Labrador, there is a major sequence of Indian cultural succession, recently delineated by Tuck (1975a; 1975b) and Fitzhugh (1972), among others, which has provided a hitherto unsuspected time depth and continuity for the predecessors of the northeastern Algonquin hunters. Between 4000 and 3000 BC, hunters with a kit of polished stone celts, ulus, and slate points and knives were in the area between Newfoundland and Sandy Cove in Labrador. By 3000 BC these Indians had pushed north along the coast to the Ramah-Saglek area of northeast Labrador. The typical contracting-stemmed and straight-stemmed projectile forms occur from Maine into Labrador.

For a few centuries on either side of 2000 BC, the burial ceremonialism and quantity of grave goods in some sites in Newfoundland parallel that of Massachusetts and Maine. The spectacular burial associations at Port aux Choix, where preservation of skeletal material and bone artifacts was remarkably good, reflect a high development of hunting equipment. The burials were of adults and children of both sexes. All were liberally accompanied by red ocher, and all had artifacts associated with the occupations of both sexes. There were ground slate spears and knives and long bayonets and counterparts of these implements made of bone. There were large whalebone lances, short toggle-type antler harpoons, three or four barbed bone points, large multiple-barb leister points startlingly like European forms of 10,000 years earlier, foreshafts of whalebone, bone effigy combs, effigy hairpins, stone gouges, adzes, celts, long-bone beamers, bone scrapers, needles for sewing, beaver incisor chisels in antler handles, and shell beads and pendants (Tuck 1971). The full report of the finds at this site has not been published, but special adaptations to sea mammal hunting, fishing, birding, and similar subsistence activities were obviously highly developed.

When the early Indians arrived in Labrador at the Ramah area, a trade and exchange activity soon began, with the Ramah chalcedony as a nonperishable remainder of an interaction that stretched from northern Labrador to New England. The arrival of Eskimo groups in Labrador and Newfoundland resulted in interesting fluctuating occupation shifts during the last three millennia. Some of the changes in areas of occupation may have been caused by climatic fluctuations, with Eskimos moving south under colder conditions and returning north during warmer episodes.

The Vergennes phase, regarded as one of the earliest "Laurentian" complexes, is best known from Lake Champlain to the Ottawa River and adjoining areas and evinces strong connections to the Maritime Archaic. The side-notched, concave-base Otter Creek points are the distinctive projectile form; stemmed slate knives or points, slate ulus, chipped ovate and lanceolate knives, winged drills, chipped celts, gouges, plummets, and bannerstones of lunate and trapezoidal forms are also common. Vergennes seems to date from about 4000 to 3000 BC.

The Lamoka complex of central New York is apparently an offshoot of the northward spread of the cultural items, such as the narrow-stemmed points, up the Susquehanna or the Hudson into the Finger Lakes district. This complex, with its well-balanced hunting and gathering economy, can be documented at a series of stations and was a dominant complex from about 2500 to 1800 BC. There was a well-developed bone industry consisting of tools for working hides, mats, and nets; fishhooks, spears, daggers, chisels, and whistles were also common. Beveled adzes, celts, mortars, pestles, and bannerstones are the most common ground and worked stone tools. The people did not adopt the grooved axes or the gouge or use atlatl weights. Of the animal remains identified from one site, mammal remains were by far the most common and comprised about 99 percent of the estimated dressed meat, with deer furnishing by far the highest proportion. Some sites show a heavy dependence on acorns and freshwater fish. Site size varies from small camps to ones covering more than 1.2 hectares with deep refuse. These latter sites Ritchie (1965:76) believes were occupied throughout the year by as many as 150 to 200 persons.

The Brewerton sites in central New York have the same basic economic structure as Lamoka but differ in the presence of bannerstones and the absence of fishhooks, in an emphasis on corner-notched and side-notched projectile forms, and in the use of a small amount of copper tools, some plummets, the ulu, and the gouge. These and other features indicate connections with eastern Canada and New England as well as with the Maritime Archaic. The Frontenac phase of central New York has been interpreted as a blend of Lamoka and Brewerton. It continues many of the tools of Brewerton and has many bone implements similar to those of both Lamoka and Brewerton (Figure 6.4). In central New York there are some copper tools (primarily awls), a few marine shell pendants, antler bird effigy combs, turtle shell rattles, flutes, and whistles. Burial goods are much more common with adult males than with females. The grave goods are personal belongings; apparently some individuals were hunters and others shamans. Dog burials were sometimes placed with males. Some burials were extended, others were flexed, and

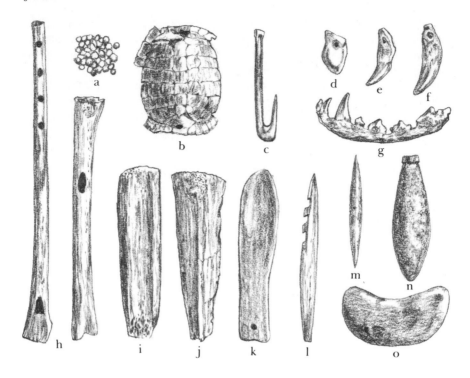

FIGURE 6.4
Artifacts from the Frontenac phase of central New York: *a, b,* terrapin-carapace rattle with pebbles; *c,* bone fishhook; *d–f,* perforated elk, wolf, and black bear canines; *g,* wolf mandible with ground-off base; *h,* bone whistles; *i,* bone gouge; *j,* deer scapula scraper; *k,* antler spoon; *l,* barbed bone point; *m,* bone gouge; *n,* stone plummet; *o,* atlatl weight. (From *Prehistory of North America,* 2d ed., by Jesse D. Jennings. Copyright © 1968, 1974 by McGraw-Hill, Inc. Used with permission of McGraw-Hill Book Company.)

there were some bundle burials and cremations. Trade or exchange for marine shells and copper was well established although not extensive. The earliest strike-a-light set in New York, of flint and iron pyrites, is from this complex (Ritchie 1969a:101–125).

In southern and eastern Ontario there are materials in museums and private collections that can be ascribed loosely to Laurentian complexes (J. Wright 1962). Two islands, Allumette and Morrison's Island, contain sites excavated by Kennedy (1966) that are of considerable significance. The first of these has material related to Vergennes, including some copper tools, and a radiocarbon date of about 3300 BC on human bone. Morrison's Island is more closely connected with the Brewerton complexes and probably belongs in the latter half of the third millennium BC.

James V. Wright (1972a) developed the concept of the Shield Archaic to encompass occupations in the boreal forest between Great Bear and Great

Slave lakes southeastward to an interfingering with the Lake Forest formation of the Great Lakes, and eastward as far as Labrador. This area forms a great arc, or "infertile crescent." The very large territory and the considerable time span (from before 4500 BC almost to the historic period) means that it can hardly be a homogenous assemblage. The economy was based on hunting and fishing, with caribou used as a major animal protein source and presumably also for bone tools, although the forest soils are not favorable to preservation. The projectile points have seven different hafting or base treatments, and within each category, such as side-notched points, there is great variation. Scrapers are the most common class of stone tools, exhibiting considerable range in size and form. The complex includes end and side scrapers, with a few small "random" scrapers, and two types of scrapers with graver spurs at Keewatin sites in Manitoba and Ontario. Biface blades were general utility tools. There are uniface blades, large wedges, and a few flake knives. Some of the sites on the southern and southeastern borders of the Laurentian shield also include items of copper—spears and ornaments—and slate forms (Wright 1972b). It is debatable whether these are correctly included within the Shield Archaic. One reasonable postulation included in Wright's model is that the hunting-fishing groups who occupied this territory were descendants from Paleo-Indian groups and eventually became the northern Algonquian speakers from the Montagnais-Naskapi on the east to the central and western Cree.

In the lower Illinois valley, the Helton phase of Cook (1974) at the Koster site Horizon 6 ends just before 2000 BC. The people of this phase were engaged in the hunting and gathering of the rich natural resources and participated in some long-distance trade and exchange. Besides the usual debris indicating chert and ground stone tool manufacture, there are also worked shell fragments. Many of the tools indicate hide and leather working, bone and antler tool fabrication, and probably mat and cloth manufacture. There are large roasting areas, baking pits or earth ovens, and a rectangular house pattern. Some mound burials have been attributed to this period, but the evidence is questionable or at least not fully published.

At the Godar site, north of Hardin in the Illinois valley, over 400 projectile points forms are said to have been recovered, including biface preforms for the Godar Side-notched and the larger Hemphill forms. There were 40 well-made T-shaped drills, 35 full-grooved and three-quarter-grooved axes, 6 drills, hematite plummets, and 3 rhyolite beads. Twenty-four bannerstones are tubular, rectanglar, bar, and geniculate forms (Titterington 1950). This complex has analogies to the burials beneath the Hemphill Mound in Brown County up the Illinois River (Griffin 1941; Knoblock 1939; Titterington 1950), and there is strong cultural continuity into the Early Woodland levels in the Illinois area.

The Titterington phase as it is now interpreted by Cook (1974) belongs in the 1500 to 2000 BC range. It has a distinctive burial complex and evidence of a well-adjusted economy. The Titterington phase is found in Horizon 4 at the Koster site, where there is evidence from tools and debris of the manufacture of chert and ground stone tools and wood items, of hide preparation and leather working, and of bone and antler tool manufacture. The inhabitants of this area utilized resources in about equal proportion from the Illinois floodplain, the upland area, the base of the bluffs, and from the secondary valleys.

While the excavator of groups of extended burials covered with red ocher and limestone slabs at the Etley site claimed these were in two low mounds on a high bluff overlooking the Illinois River north of Hardin, I am skeptical that they were artificial mounds; more likely they were low natural rises into which the burials were intruded. At this location the 27 to 64 burials (or whatever the exact number was) were accompanied by 75 Sedalia points, 13 Etley Barbed points, 25 full-grooved and three-quarter grooved axes, 3 saddle-back bannerstones, 3 small copper celts, and a long copper awl, square in cross-section. Another burial area, in Marquette State Park, is also on a bluff and was covered with limestone slabs. It contained a compound burial of two individuals extended on their backs. Grave goods consisted of 2 Sedalia knives, 1 Etley Barbed point, 2 grooved axes, 2 unique engraved shell ornaments, and a brown diorite awl. Near the south end of the park, the Hartford Church location had "several" burials with 6 three-quarter and 1 full-grooved ax, 4 Sedalia points, 5 Hardin Stemmed points, 1 Etley Barbed point, 3 Hemphill spears, and 3 Godar points.

In Indiana the best-known Late Archaic site is the McCain site in Dubois County (Miller 1941), although more recent work along the Ohio near Louisville by Donald Jansen and east of Cincinnati by Kent Vickery will add another variant of the Late Archaic comparable to Indian Knoll (see Chapter 7). The McCain site has engraved bone pins or needles that are similar to those from Koster, Indian Knoll, and other sites on this time horizon in the Southeast as far as the Georgia coast.

The populations in the upper Great Lakes area obtained a considerable amount of copper by extensive mining in the Lake Superior area (Griffin 1961). During the Late Archaic the copper was shaped into various utilitarian forms of spears, knives, ulus, adzes, celts, gouges, awls, and fishhooks, which are similar to their bone and stone counterparts (Figure 6.5). These have a wide distribution but are concentrated in Wisconsin and Michigan. Worked and unworked copper moved over considerable distances, following water routes where possible. Both in eastern Ontario and in the "heartland" of the distribution, the copper is found in the village sites and occasionally in burials as the personal possessions of the deceased. The copper forms are present in burials associated with the so-called Glacial Kame, Laurentian, Shield Archaic, and other such constructs. It is best to discontinue thinking of the Old Copper culture as a distinct ethnic entity.

The Glacial Kame complex of Ohio, Indiana, Michigan, and adjacent areas is known from a series of burials in gravel knolls. These feature orna-

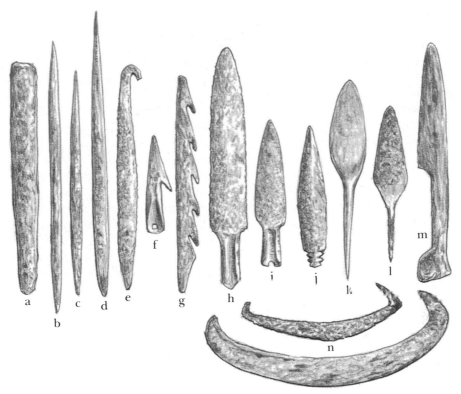

FIGURE 6.5
Utilitarian copper artifacts of Late Archaic, primarily from upper Great Lakes area:
a, chisel; *b, c*, awls; *d, e*, punches; *f, g*, harpoons; *h–l*, spear points; *m*, knife; *n*, "women's"
knives, similar to Eskimo ulu. (From *Prehistory of North America*, 2d ed., by Jesse D. Jennings.
Copyright © 1968, 1974 by McGraw-Hill, Inc. Used with permission of McGraw-Hill
Book Company.)

ments made from marine shell, circular or rectangular gorget forms, beads,
and the sandal-sole gorget. The complex is interconnected with "Old Copper"
and is a forerunner of the so-called Red Ocher local complex (Cunningham
1948; Ritzenthaler and Quimby 1962). From the latter half of the second
millennium BC, Winters (1969) has identified a Riverton complex. These
people in the lower Wabash valley followed a seasonal round of activities with
some attention to mussel collection. Band size of around 50 people is a reasonable figure. Winters sees strong connections to the west Tennessee Big Sandy
complex, but there are also strong ties throughout the Ohio valley and Great
Lakes area. The report is an excellent analysis of Late Archaic activity patterns and such new features as the presence of tubular pipes of the "Cloud-
blower" shape.

THE EARLY WOODLAND COMPLEXES

In the Middle Atlantic area near the beginning of the Early Woodland period, the people began to fashion pottery, perhaps following the lead of Late Archaic groups in the south. The earliest form is a simple, flat-bottomed, flaring-sided container, which often has lug handles. This form is similar to the earlier steatite bowls of the same area; indeed, the first pottery is actually tempered with crushed steatite. Apparently this concept of vessel manufacture, but without steatite temper, spread rapidly, and local names such as Fayette, Marion, and Vinette I are given to this earliest pottery of the Northeast. I do not consider hypotheses of Asiatic and European origin for pottery or for any other features of Woodland culture viable (Griffin 1966).

The complex that most clearly shows the transition from Archaic to Early Woodland in the New York area is the Meadowood phase (Ritchie 1965) (Figure 6.6).

Squash is known in Early Woodland sites in Michigan (H. Wright 1964) by 500 BC; considering its presence in Kentucky and Missouri before 2000 BC, one can assume that it was probably widely spread in the Midwest by 2000 to 1500 BC. Ethnobotanists believe that such native plants as sunflowers and sumpweed were cultivated, a practice perhaps suggested by squash growing (Ford 1974; Yarnell 1972). If corn was truly a part of the Late Adena (200 BC) food supply as suggested by Murphy (1971), it would probably have been more widespread than it evidently was.

The burial ceremonialism that has been noted in Late Archaic, particularly in the far Northeast, reached a high point in Early Woodland times. During this period, construction of mounds for the dead became an important part of the mortuary activities from west of the Appalachians to west of the Mississippi and north into Wisconsin and Michigan. While mounds may occur sporadically before 500 BC, they become common after that date. The most notable culture practicing this burial ceremonialism was the Adena complex of the central Ohio valley. There are no major cultural intrusions into the area. The common gift exchange, the movement of valued exotic materials or, more rarely, finished items, and the inevitable cultural diffusion accompanying such activities is, along with local developments, sufficient to account for the observed changes.

The western and central parts of the Northeast exhibit a number of distinctive features in the production and utilization of large leaf-shaped spears or knives of a variety of forms; some of them are "turkey tails," while others are bipointed or ovoid or have a squared haft. They are often made of a bluish grey hornstone from southern Indiana or from similar formations in Illinois (Didier 1967). These spears or knives are found in mound burial associations from Illinois to Ohio or, sometimes, in caches without burials. They may have moved as gifts and must have been of considerable value. While they were at least initially roughed out at quarries, we do not know whether

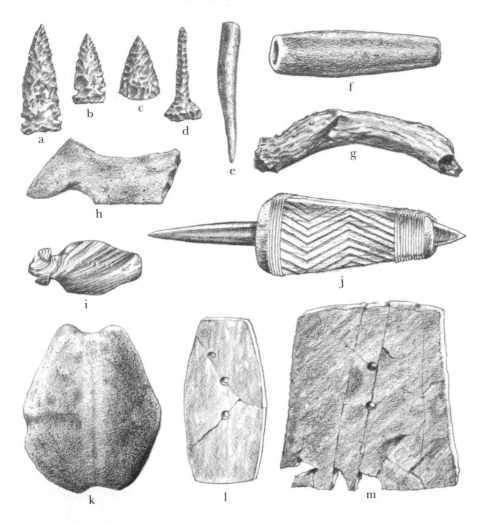

FIGURE 6.6
Artifacts of the Meadowood culture: *a–c,* projectile points; *d,* flint drill; *e,* antler awl; *f,* tubular pottery pipe; *g,* cut section of deer antler; *h, i,* birdstones; *j,* copper flaking tool in wooden handle (restored); *k,* ovate pebble net sinker with imprint of double-cord attachment to net; *l, m,* stone gorgets. (From *Prehistory of North America,* 2d ed., by Jesse D. Jennings. Copyright © 1968, 1974 by McGraw-Hill, Inc. Used with permission of McGraw-Hill Book Company.)

secondary shaping took place at villages or camps near the quarries or closer to their find areas, since relatively few village sites have been studied.

Another common burial accompaniment with an even wider distribution is the cache of small triangular points or preforms. These are made of local materials and occur with burials in cemeteries and, rarely, in mounds. Occasionally they appear in a cache not associated with mounds or burials.

While a wide variety of chert sources were used, some caches were apparently exchanged over considerable distances. Both the large and small points are found from Illinois and Wisconsin to New England (Willoughby 1935:126) in association with copper beads and awls, marine shell ornaments, and stemmed points such as the Kramer type in Illinois.

Some artifact types show marked changes in this period. The pipe form became strongly cylindrical, often with a blocked end or a cigar holder end. Many of these were made from Ohio pipestone from the lower Scioto valley. Such pipes were exchanged into Indiana, Michigan, Killarney Bay, Ontario, New York, New England, and Maryland. The bannerstone disappeared, to be replaced by birdstones and boatstones during the late Archaic and Early Woodland (Figure 6.7). The three-quarter-grooved axe and the celt are the most widely found woodworking tools. The slate gorget of the Late Archaic is also found in this period, exhibiting a variety of forms and made of different materials in different areas.

New pottery types appeared. In the Illinois area Marion Thick is followed by the Black Sand pottery, which develops into the Morton complex by about 400 to 200 BC. Not too much is known of possible comparable developments in Michigan, Wisconsin, and northern Indiana, although there is some evidence of a thinner, cord-marked ware with incising that is comparable to Black Sand. In southern Illinois and Indiana, this period saw the early phases of the Baumer complex, with thick, wide-warp, fabric-impressed pottery; parallel developments appeared in the Tennessee valley.

The most widely known, if poorly understood, Early Woodland expression is the Adena complex in the Ohio valley, discussed earlier in terms of burial ceremonialism. This complex is found from the Whitewater River valley of Indiana on the west to the upper Ohio valley as far as Pittsburg on the east, and from the Blue Grass region of the Licking and the Big Sandy and Kanawha Rivers on the south and east to the upper reaches of the Scioto and Muskingum of Ohio on the north. Adena as a mound-building complex may well have not begun until about 500 BC, but many of the artifacts and behavior patterns common after that date originated in the area with Early Woodland complexes. There were once at least 300 to 500 sites in this area that were Adena. Most of the known sites are mounds representing considerable variation, with area and time, in burial practices and grave goods (Greenman 1932; Webb and Snow 1974; Webb and Baby 1957; Dragoo 1963). When village sites are excavated and connected to the burial complexes, local river valley groupings will almost certainly be recognized. Serpent Mound, the burial mound near it, and the lower levels of the village site are Adena. A village site from Perry County, Ohio, has recently been reported and assigned to this complex (Bush 1975). The site produced Montgomery Incised pottery, but one radiocarbon date of 235 BC seems a bit early for this pottery style.

The Adena burial complex was an accentuation of earlier and contemporary burial patterns. The Adenans developed circular earth enclosures that

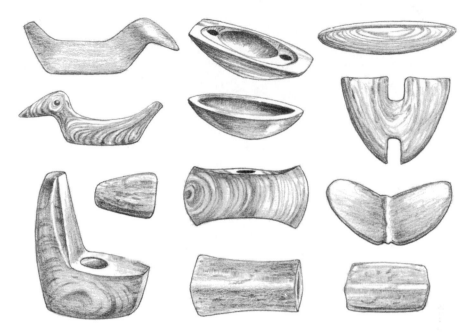

FIGURE 6.7
Polished stone atlatl weights. The birdstones (*upper left*) are Late Archaic and Early
Woodland, the boatstones (*upper center*) are Early and Middle Woodland, and the banner-
stones are Middle to Late Archaic. (From *Prehistory of North America*, 2d ed., by Jesse D.
Jennings. Copyright © 1968, 1974 by McGraw-Hill, Inc. Used with permission of McGraw-
Hill Book Company.)

were certainly socio-religious and that sometimes encircle burial mounds.
Many of the mounds covered circular dwellings with or without burials on
the floor of the dwelling. Burials were made in a number of forms. Many in
village sites were cremated, and some cremations were in mounds. Most of
the mound burials were extended in a central area, and in late Adena this
was often in a carefully prepared log tomb. There were also flexed burials,
bundle burials, multilated or decapitated burials, and burials of separate
skulls or other skeletal parts. Cranial deformation by purposeful modification
was common. There was no marked preference in orientation of burials.
While an adult male often received preferential treatment in terms of grave
location and high-status objects, children more often had grave goods.

Grave items were both useful and ornamental. Mica from North Carolina
appears shaped into crescents or sheet fragments. Bracelets, beads, gorgets
(Figure 6.8), crescents, celts, and adzes were made from Lake Superior copper.
There are tubular pipes, including some late effigy forms in Ohio and West
Virginia. Highly distinctive of Adena are engraved stone tablets, probably
used during ceremonies for preparation of paints. There is some marine shell,

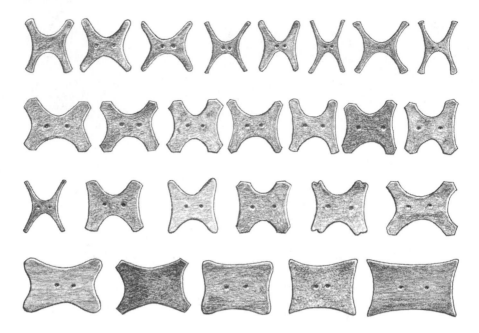

FIGURE 6.8

Adena reel-shaped gorgets. Seriation: oldest forms are at lower right, the most recent are top row. (From *Prehistory of North America,* 2d ed., by Jesse D. Jennings. Copyright © 1968, 1974 by McGraw-Hill, Inc. Used with permission of McGraw-Hill Book Company.)

but it is not extensive. The pottery in the first half-millennium or so before the Christian era was Fayette Thick; during the major Adena expression it was Adena Plain, with regional variants of Montgomery Incised now known from Indiana, Kentucky, Ohio, and West Virginia. A number of the projectile point styles, such as Adena and Robbins, are local expressions of similar eastern forms of this period.

House size varies from small, single-family units to larger structures capable of holding 40 people. There are groups of 10 or more structures at some sites; other, possibly transient camps have from 2 to 4. A central communal hearth and interior storage pits are usually found (Figure 6.9). The Adena people almost certainly did not occupy any one village all year long. Population density would have been less than 0.39 per square kilometer. There was some occupation of shelters in Ohio, but it is doubtful that Adena populations lived in caves or shelters to any degree, although their contemporaries elsewhere did.

The diversity within what has been called Adena is considerable; "Adena" is probably a grouping by archeologists of local complexes in the central Ohio valley that were contemporaneous, contiguous, and participating in

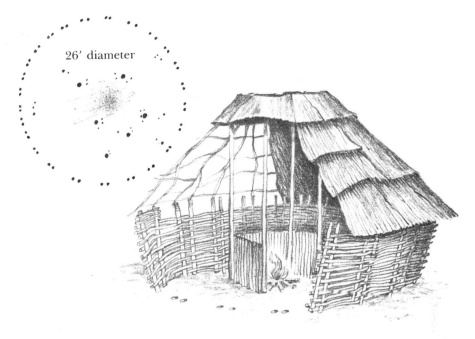

26' diameter

FIGURE 6.9
Postmold plan and cutaway view of restored Adena house, showing probable construction. (From *Prehistory of North America*, 2d ed., by Jesse D. Jennings. Copyright © 1968, 1974 by McGraw-Hill, Inc. Used with permission of McGraw-Hill Book Company.)

both widespread and highly localized developments. The blend is unique and occurs nowhere else as a functioning interacting macrosociety or as a series of local societies.

In the eastern part of the Northeast, Kinsey (1974) sees a series of closely related complexes stretching from the tidewater area to southern New England and displaying a strong regional continuity during the period from ca. 800 BC to AD 600. Some of these were coastal adaptations such as the Lagoon phase (Ritchie 1969b) on Martha's Vineyard and coastal New England and New York; others were river valley adaptations such as the Bushkill and Byram in the Delaware valley and the Fox Creek complex in southeastern New York. Abbott Farm near Trenton, New Jersey, has representative material of these inland complexes. Pottery ranges from the early plain and cord-marked to net-impressed types; the latter are particularly prevalent in coastal and tidewater areas. Projectiles are primarily medium-sized stemmed forms. There are celts, narrow two-hole gorgets, net sinkers, bola stones, and milling stones and mortars. At some time during the Delaware valley occupations the dentate stamped decorative technique made its appearance.

While the eastern New England area is not very well known in this period,

Dincauze (1974) has proposed that after 1000 BC there was a marked shift of populations toward the coast and a breakdown of the older established trade patterns of the Late Archaic.

MIDDLE WOODLAND: HOPEWELL AND RELATED CULTURES

During a period of time from approximately 100 BC to AD 300, the Middle West was occupied by local regional complexes that can be recognized as participating in a wide range of behavioral patterns inherited from preceding groups and augmented by local progress and by exchange and diffusion from group to group over short or long distances. These Middle Woodland complexes had two dominant areas, one, known as the Hopewell culture, in southern Ohio from Marietta to the Miami River, and the other comprising Havana societies of the Illinois valley and adjacent areas. Of these, the Ohio area was by far the more dramatic, marking a culmination of many cultural trends of the Archaic and Early Woodland periods. Both the Ohio and the Illinois variants are regarded as Hopewellian societies.

Six major Hopewell sites have been excavated in Ohio, and there are probably well over a hundred little-known or unreported sites. Many other complex earthworks and mound groups have not yet been excavated or have been destroyed. Although there have been other presentations of the cultural material from the six major sites, the careful summary by Morgan (1952) is still one of the best. Some of the other, lesser mounds and sites that have been excavated and reported (Magrath 1945; Starr 1960:23–24, 97; Lee and Vickery 1972) are often ignored. The major excavated earthwork sites range from some 5.25 hectares with 21 mounds at Mound City northeast of Chillicothe (Mills 1922) to the Hopewell site of 45 hectares and 38 mounds (Moorehead 1922; Shetrone 1926).

At the six major sites there were over 1150 burials; the exact number will never be known. At Tremper, all of the burials were cremated, and the estimate there is 375 individuals (Mills 1916). Other burial sites, such as those at Hopewell, also yielded extended, bundle, flexed, and partial skeletal remains (Figure 6.10). The mound, depending on size, often covered single- or multiple-mortuary structures or charnel houses. There were also specially prepared basins or "altars" of puddled clay that contained cremated burial offerings, with or without evidence of cremated human bone. The burial groupings found in mortuary structures probably represent kin groups. Some of the most significant burials were in small mounds, such as that of the cremated male in Mound 11 at Hopewell. In addition to two mica sheets, a few pearl beads, and a polished piece of green chlorite, the grave goods included some 136 kilograms of worked obsidian fragments. This burial I regard as being that of the individual who produced the magnificant Hopewell obsidian

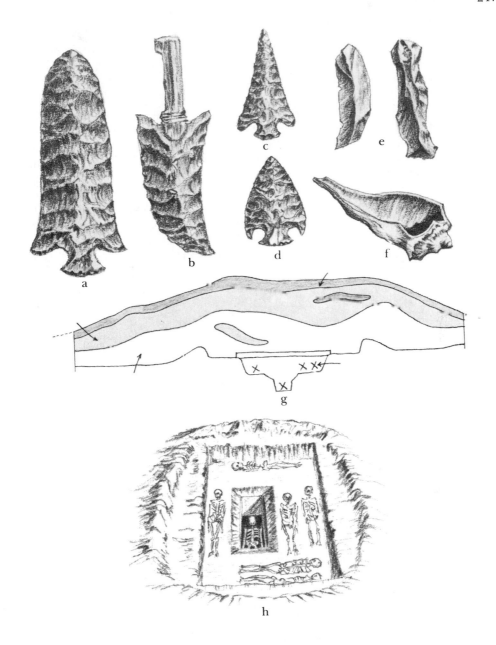

FIGURE 6.10
Hopewell artifacts and diagram of burial mound: *a*, obsidian knife or spearhead; *b*, obsidian knife, wooden handle (restored); *c, d*, spearheads; *e*, flake knives; *f*, conch-shell dipper; *g*, cross-section of Wh6 burial mound; *h*, view of central tomb in Wh6 mound. *a–c, e*, and *f* are from Ohio; *d* is from Illinois. (From *Prehistory of North America*, 2d ed., by Jesse D. Jennings. Copyright © 1968, 1974 by McGraw-Hill, Inc. Used with permission of McGraw-Hill Book Company.)

spears of which there were between 250 and 500 in altar 2 in Mound 25 at Hopewell. These vary in shape and size, but an estimated 95 percent of all the Hopewell period obsidian in the Middle West was in these two caches; the source of this obsidian is in what is now Yellowstone National Park (Griffin 1965; Griffin et al. 1969).

Another instance of a concentration of items made from an exotic raw material is the presence of 30 to 40 chlorite disks in Mound 1 at Hopewell, found by Squier and Davis (Stevens 1870:438). The same author mentions that the only other object of this material in the Squier and Davis collection was a gorget from Mound 8 at Mound City, but a few chlorite objects subsequently were discovered in other mounds. It appears that some of the exotic raw materials gathered and brought to Ohio were the property of an individual to utilize as he wished or to have buried with him—the 3000 sheets of mica and 90.5 kilograms of galena from Mound 17 of the Hopewell site, for example. From a small mound in the northeastern part of the Newark group, one-half to three-quarters of a cubic meter of mica plates were removed along with 14 human skeletons when a lock was constructed on the canal in 1828 (Squier and Davis 1848:72n). Each of the many items in these long-distance exchanges will have to be studied and interpreted as an individual case. No single model will handle the entire remarkable activity.

The large, complex geometric earthworks are unique to Hopewell and vary from site to site. They were probably constructed over a period of time at any of the large sites, and the large mounds were probably built over a period of several generations. The fill of the mound and of the earthworks contained considerable quantities of village debris, and the areas within the earthworks or near them were village sites. Recent excavations at Mound City and at the Seip group are uncovering the house sites and village debris. At Seip the houses vary somewhat in shape, but they are basically rectanguloid with rounded corners and vary in size. Typical houses are 10.5 to 12 meters long by 9 to 10.5 meters wide. While it might be possible to house an extended family of perhaps 30 to 40 people in such a structure, the interior activities and furnishings would take up much of the space. Large refuse and storage pits occur in the floors; there is evidence of various craft activities involving mica, leather, and wood; and cord-marked, plain, and Hopewell-style pottery appear (Baby 1976). When these earthwork areas are intensively excavated, we will learn more of the local settlement system. In addition to the major village areas, there probably were other, smaller loci not only for smaller related groups but also for use in the procurement of food and other supplies during the year.

We cannot now recognize the temporal differences between the major sites. There was certainly temporal overlap between them, but the exact time spans of the sites are not very well known, in spite of valiant attempts by several interpreters to place the sites in time. Nor are accurate estimates of population available. The best estimate of the number of burials at the six major sites is about 1150+. This is certainly not the total number of the people who participated in the life of these sites. Somewhat more accurate demographic figures for the lower Illinois valley Hopewellian occupation give a figure of a bit less than 0.39 per square kilometer. The figure probably could not have been much more than that.

We have evidence of more foreign goods in Ohio than of Ohio goods exported to other areas. At least six species of marine shell from the Atlantic and Florida Gulf coasts appear; other Florida items are barracuda jaws, ocean turtle shells, and shark and alligator teeth. Other exotics and their sources include large quantities of mica from southwestern North Carolina and chlorite from the southern Appalachians, meteoric iron from a number of sources, cobble-size chunks of galena from unknown sources, hundreds of pounds of copper from the Lake Superior deposits, and silver that may have been from near Cobalt, Ontario. Nodular bluish flint, probably from Harrison County, Indiana, occurs in great quantities—over 8000 pieces were found at one small mound. In addition to the obsidian mentioned before, Knife River chalcedony from North Dakota has been recovered. It is reasonable to postulate that certain items, such as the copper ear spools and breastplates, were made in and distributed from Ohio, but the same is not as likely for the panpipes or celts and adzes. The major direction of exchange for platform pipes of Ohio pipestone was into the Illinois valley, which perhaps received from 100 to 150 pipes. Much smaller numbers reached the Davenport area of southwestern Wisconsin, and there are practically no Ohio platform pipes in Michigan, New York, or in the Southeast. A small amount of Flint Ridge, Ohio, flint moved into western New York and down the trade routes through east Tennessee to Florida.

This trade reflects the wide geographical knowledge of much of the eastern United States that some of its aboriginal inhabitants possessed. Trade helps to explain the apparent speed with which new ideas and techniques moved across long distances. Some of the trade or acquisition was probably done by long-distance travel, but other materials or finished goods may have been exchanged locally and moved from group to group. Each type of good or produce will have to be studied to determine its exchange pattern.

Ohio Hopewell art expression was highly developed in both naturalistic and geometric styles. Animal and human effigies were skillfully sculptured in Ohio pipestone, and human figurines were made from baked clay (Figure 6.11). Copper and mica sheets were cut into geometric and effigy forms. Some of the copper plates have embossed designs of eagles, turkeys, buzzards, and parrots (Figure 6.12). Cut-out designs may have been stencils for painting designs on finely woven cloth of native bast fibers. The Ohio Hopewell people also made fine engravings on animal and human bone, with representations of shamans in ceremonial dress and many other designs.

While exchange activities were being carried on in different ways by the Ohio Hopewell people, they were neither colonialists nor expansionists. In the Illinois area the development from late Early Woodland into early local Havana-Hopewellian patterns that occurred around 200 BC seems to have

250

FIGURE 6.11
Hopewell ceramic figurines from the Knight site, Illinois. (From *Prehistory of North America*, 2d ed., by Jesse D. Jennings. Copyright © 1968, 1974 by McGraw-Hill, Inc. Used with permission of McGraw-Hill Book Company.)

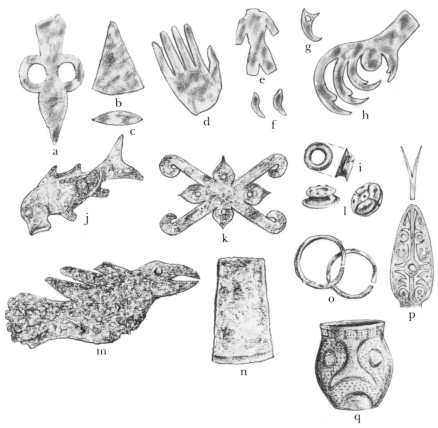

FIGURE 6.12
Hopewell artifacts from Ohio: *a–h*, ornaments of sheet mica (*f* representing bear claws and *g* a bird talon); *i*, stone ear ornament; *j–p*, copper artifacts (*j*, fish, probably a sucker; *k*, robe ornament; *l*, ear ornaments; *m*, bird with pearl eye; *n*, ax head; *o*, bracelets; *p*, ornament, probably a serpent's head); *q*, pot. (From *Prehistory of North America*, 2d ed., by Jesse D. Jennings. Copyright © 1968, 1974 by McGraw-Hill, Inc. Used with permission of McGraw-Hill Book Company.)

taken place somewhat earlier than did the Adena to Hopewell shift in Ohio. The use of log tombs and pits below the mound floor is a practice related more to the late Adena than to Hopewell. There is an almost total absence of cremation in the Illinois area burial practices. In Illinois there are no really comparable geometric earthworks, no mounds comparable to the major tumuli in Ohio, and few striking caches of goods. Only in the great deposits of flint disk preforms at a number of sites in the Illinois valley, totaling some 20,000 specimens, does this area outdo the spectacular Ohio Area.

Although the two regions vary in the details of such items as projectile and knife point forms, lamellar blades, the variants of the celt, the use of mollusk shell spoons, marine shell containers, bone awls, the use of beaver and other incisors, and basic ceramic vessel forms, the overall manufacturing and decorative techniques of these items indicate their contemporaneity and participation in a widespread lifestyle adaptation. These techniques are at the core of the interrelationships of these northern Hopewellian groups; specific examples of exchange and trade are a reflection of the basic similarities. Such examples are a result not a cause; they did not initiate but rather helped to maintain connections within and between societies.

From Illinois there were either strong interaction and exchange at all levels of behavior with resident groups in southern Wisconsin, northern and eastern Iowa, northeastern Illinois, northwestern Indiana, southwestern Michigan, and the Saginaw Valley of Michigan, or there were population movements into these areas, or both. This expansion took place around the time the Havana pottery style had developed and the Hopewell pottery style had recently appeared. Somewhere around AD 1 to 100 would be a reasonably close estimate of the time (Griffin 1967). There was also cultural expansion west into central and western Missouri, eastern Kansas, and northeastern Oklahoma. Mound burial practices similar to those of the Illinois area appear in southeast Missouri, eastern Arkansas, and northwestern Mississippi. A little locally made pottery of the Havana Zone-stamped style is known from west-central Mississippi. The Illinois area seems, naturally, to have had closer relations with the lower Mississippi valley than did Ohio Hopewell, while the lower Wabash populations had connections up the Tennessee. Because of its geographic and physiographic difference from the northern glaciated area, southern Illinois, as usual, had a much different series of Middle Woodland societies. Those with the closest affinities to the Illinois valley area are along the Mississippi valley or in the lower reaches of its tributaries.

Burials among the western groups were primarily in mounds, although some village burials are known. Mound size varies from only a meter or so high and 6 to 9 meters in diameter to the two or three structures found at Ogden-Fettie in Fulton County that were 61 by 53 by 4 meters and 30 by 24 by 2 meters. The other 32 mounds of the latter group were much smaller (Cole and Deuel 1937).

There are many more Middle Woodland sites than Early Woodland sites. They are closer together and have deeper village site deposits, and many more burial areas can be attributed to them. The villages, though averaging from 0.4 to 1.2 hectares, may be as small as a 0.1 hectare or as large as 6 or more hectares. At one site in southwest Wisconsin there were 14 circular to rectangular houses (Freeman 1969) on about 0.1 hectare of land, and, like the Illinois sites, it had many refuse pits. At some of the larger sites, however, we are not certain that the entire area was occupied contemporaneously. There probably would not have been more than a few hundred people in the largest villages. Subsistence was primarily by hunting and gathering and quite effective utilization of the game in the broad Mississippi and Illinois valleys. Maximum return from local seeds, nuts, and tubers was also evident (Struever 1968). There is some evidence of corn in Ohio, Illinois, and Louisiana; but there is not much of it, and continued, more careful excavation and recovery techniques have not produced new significant amounts. Summaries of this data need to be critically evaluated (Griffin 1960; Yarnell 1964; Struever and Vickery 1973).

To the north in Minnesota, northern Wisconsin, Michigan, southeastern Manitoba, and western Ontario, a ceramic, mound-building complex is identified as Laurel (Stoltman 1973; 1974; J. Wright 1967). This complex has some similarities to Hopewell in pottery and projectile point styles, but the total complex is distinctive from those of other areas. The time range is about 50 BC to AD 800–900. In northern Wisconsin, Saltzer (1974) has briefly described a Nokomis phase with some ceramic traits close to Illinois Hopewellian, but his sites and their complex are noticeably different from those of the Trempealeau populations in the southwestern part of the state and the contemporary groups in the southeastern part of Wisconsin. Some eastern expressions of Laurel can be found at Naomikong Point (Jansen 1968) on the south shore of Lake Superior west of Sault Ste. Marie, at Summer Island (Brose 1970), and around the north shore of Lake Superior as far as the mouth of the Michipicoten.

Another northern stamped pottery tradition stands between Laurel and Point Peninsula on the east. This is the Saugeen complex of southwestern Ontario discussed by J. Wright (1967; 1972b). He suggests a beginning date of 500 BC for Saugeen, which is difficult to accept on a comparative basis. The Saugeen burials are in small cemeteries. Villages are on the lower reaches of tributaries of southeastern Lake Huron and northwestern Lake Erie. Fishing was a common activity. House postmolds outline structures about 5.2 meters by 7 meters, containing hearths and pits. They are single-family units. Artifacts include celts and adzes, stemmed and corner-notched points and scrapers, slate gorgets, copper awls, axes, and at least one panpipe. I would estimate the time span of Saugeen from about the beginning of the Christian era to AD 800 or 900.

Thus, both Laurel and Saugeen and, as will be pointed out, Point Peninsula culture ceramics with dentate-stamped decoration last until AD 800–1000. Since stamping of this type was the hallmark of the Middle Woodland cultures in the Middle West, the archeologists in New York and adjoining areas have referred to all of their stamped pottery complexes as Middle Woodland. This terminology was applied even though the northeastern Middle Woodland lasted 600 years or so after Hopewellian had disappeared in the area where the terminology was instituted. The Middle West was in the Late Woodland and Early Mississippi time periods at the time that Point Peninsula is still being called Middle Woodland.

There are many regional Point Peninsula complexes from Pennsylvania, New York, Ontario, Quebec, and New England. Their long duration is reflected in a number of temporal variants from Canoe Point to the Hunters Home phase (Ritchie 1969a; Ritchie and Funk 1973). There are some indications of Hopewell exchange and trade up the Allegheny into western New

York during the Squawkie Hill phase (Ritchie 1969a). These have been known for some time, but the data are mostly from mounds; the village complex is unknown. In Ontario, the Trent waterway has a series of sites reported upon by Ritchie (1949) and the Levesque Mound, some 1.2 meters high and 9 by 12 meters in diameter, which contained 4 copper and 4 silver panpipe covers. These were excavated by W. A. Kenyon of the Royal Ontario Museum. One of the better-known Point Peninsula sites is that of Serpent Mounds, where extensive excavations in the mounds and in the village uncovered a striking degree of similarity in content to locations in the lake district of New York. One unusual feature was the considerable frequency of mollusks from Rice Lake (Johnston 1968). There are strong indications of exchange about AD 1 in the St. Lawrence complex of Spence (1967) in the form of late Adena tubular pipes and large corner-notched point forms. Point Peninsula extends as far north as Killarney Bay, Frank Bay, Lake Abitibi, and the Nottaway River, which flows into James Bay. There is very little of Point Peninsula culture, however, in these far northern sites within the Shield Archaic area. The complex also extends into eastern Ontario, well into southern and eastern Quebec (Mitchell 1966), and into New England where Ritchie (1969b:226–227) believes much of the pottery compares to the late Kipp Island phase of New York. Among items excavated long ago are a number of platform pipes, of a variety of forms, from Massachusetts. The pottery extends north into Maine (W. Smith 1926) and Nova Scotia. There are many regional adaptations from the coast to inland lakes and waterways and from the hardwood forests of New England and New Jersey to the mixed boreal and hardwood forests to the north.

LATE OR TERMINAL WOODLAND AND MISSISSIPPIAN COMPLEXES

The factors that resulted in the gradual disappearance of the broad spectrum of activity characterizing Hopewell in the East and Northeast are not known. We can see the results of this change in the rather drab appearance of many of the products in the Ohio and Mississippi valley and in the almost total disappearance of the interregional exchange of raw materials and of finished goods. (In spite of this, however, it should be noted that there were many cultural changes in ceramics, projectile styles, house types, and settlement pattern, spread over wide areas.) Projectile points tend to become smaller, and by about AD 700 to 900 small stemmed, triangular, or triangular notched forms imply use of the bow and arrow. The greater fire power of the bow could have affected hunting techniques, and its effectiveness in warfare or raids may have stimulated the development of early Late Woodland stockades with open central courtyards, which are known from the upper Monongahela River and northeastern Lake Erie area by AD 800 to 950. The discovery of significant amounts of corn at sites from this time period indicates that

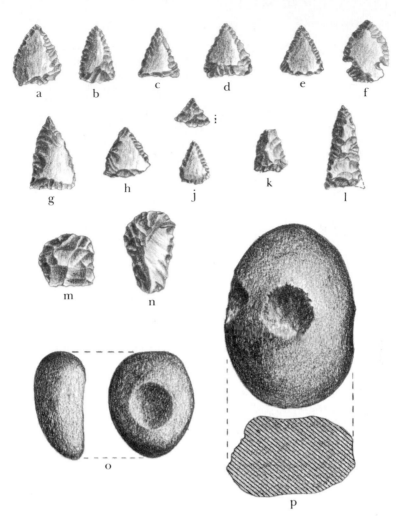

FIGURE 6.13
Late Woodland Effigy Mound artifacts: *a, c–e*, Sanders Triangular quartzite points; *b*, Triangular (A) point; *f*, corner-notched quartzite point; *g, i–l*, Triangular (B) quartzite points; *m, n*, quartzite end scrapers; *o*, pecked stone; *p*, pecked hammerstone.

skills in handling corn had increased. The importance of corn would also have been a factor encouraging village permanence and protection against raids. These are some of the discoveries that are causing reevaluation of the idea that many of the late prehistoric developments were diffused from Middle Mississippi centers.

In the upper Mississippi valley there was a gradual shift from Late Hopewellian into a number of interacting societies. These societies developed a cord-impressed decoration on the rim of vessels, later placing this on a collared rim; changed some of their artifact styles along with the rest of the Northeast; and began to construct effigy mounds (Figures 6.13 and 6.14). The basic way of life of the Effigy Mound cultures was much the same as that of

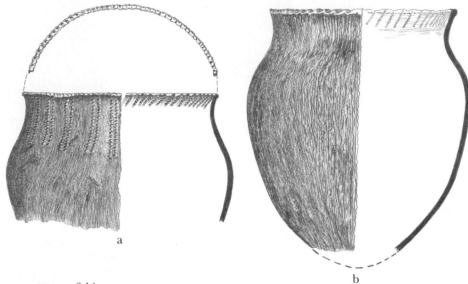

FIGURE 6.14
Madison ceramics: *a*, Madison Punctated jar; *b*, Madison Plain (cord-marked) jar.

the Middle Woodland period (Hurley 1974; 1975; Rowe 1956). The shifts in behavior are a part of a widespread exchange and interaction activity in the Lake Forest area that was clearly recognizable in Late Archaic times, emphasized by Middle Woodland times (Mason 1969; J. Wright 1972), and carried over into Late and Terminal Woodland (Figure 6.15). Developments in the Great Lakes area of Wisconsin, Michigan, and Ontario during this time were similar to the changes that took place in New York, producing the Owasco complexes and finally the Iroquoian that developed from them.

Middle Mississippi

A significant dependence upon maize agriculture developed over a wide area from AD 700 to 1200, and many of the societies involved became a part of what is broadly conceived of as a Mississippian pattern over much of the Mississippi-Ohio valley and the Southeast (see Chapter 7). Much of the Northeast did not participate in the full Mississippian pattern, although the Northeast did achieve some dependence upon agriculture and pushed the limits of maize growing into Lake Superior, the middle Ottawa River valley, and the Maritimes. The increased dependence on agriculture (up to about 50 percent) and the resultant increased populations are reflected in the marked dominance of the societies that lived in favorable geographic locations on or near major alluvial valleys or other agricultural soils that were in

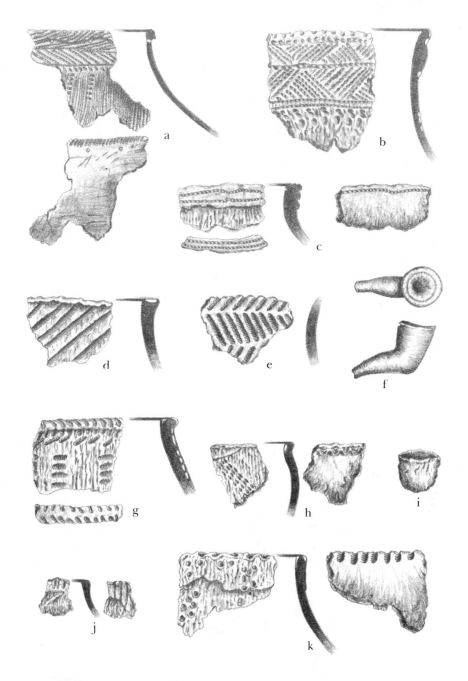

FIGURE 6.15
Late Woodland pottery from Wisconsin: *a, b,* Point Sauble Collared; *c, k,* Aztalan Collared; *e, e, g, h,* Heins Creek Corded Stamped; *f,* clay pipe; *i,* child's pot; *j,* Leland Cord-marked. (After Hurley 1975)

a good climatic area with a dependable rainfall and temperature regime. At no previous period in eastern prehistory had these factors been so important or so clearly reflected in the cultural pattern on the landscape.

Much attention has been and should be given to the Cahokia area, for it was the scene of important developments from about AD 700 to 1700 that produced a major center of Mississippian culture and probably the largest number of mounds of the platform type. These mounds, located on both sides of the Mississippi River, were never accurately counted. This was probably one of the most densely populated areas in the eastern United States from about AD 900 to 1600, which leaves some 700 years for mound and house construction.

There are scattered indications in the flood plain and immediately adjacent area of complexes comparable to other post-Hopewell Woodland groups in the Middle West, such as Weaver and Fox Creek and White Hall to the north, and Raymond (Figure 6.16), early Lewis, and most of the La Motte complex to the south in Illinois. By AD 700 one can recognize that significant changes have taken place in Cahokia; the ceramic complex, house forms, and early platform (?) mounds of the Fairmount phase represent the earliest expressions of Mississippian culture. The available evidence strongly suggests that this is a local development from the Patrick phase through an unnamed phase that lasted about 300 years (Griffin and Spaulding 1951). Fairmount is followed by the Stirling and Moorehead phases of AD 900 to 1050 and 1050 to 1250, respectively (Fowler and Hall 1972; Fowler 1969; 1974). Toward the end of this period, the Cahokia area reached a climax in known cultural growth, complexity of products, and indications of far-flung direct contact, the last ranging as far north as the mouth of the Minnesota River, the Strait of Mackinac (by way of Aztalan and the Fox River valley); northwest to Iowa and southeastern South Dakota; northeast to around Danville, Illinois; southeast to the Kincaid site; and south to the Memphis area and near Vicksburg. (Similar exchange between the lower Mississippi valley Coles Creek and Caddoan area to the west has been recognized for some time.) I would suggest, however, that recent estimates of population size for Cahokia are overly generous and that the complexity of social and economic organization that has been postulated may also be exaggerated.

Mississippian towns at Cahokia, along the Mississippi to Cairo, at Kincaid (Figures 6.17–6.20), Angel (Figures 6.21 and 6.22), and sites in the lower Wabash, and up the Illinois River as far as Peoria were fortified permanent locations for multilineage societies living in single-family rectangular structures that were rebuilt many times. Houses were arranged in an orderly fashion and surrounded an open central courtyard or plaza. Larger towns had one or more earthen platform mounds, which increased in size through periodic rebuilding. Because of the difficulty of assessing contemporaneity of structures and the total span of time of a given site, it is difficult to give the

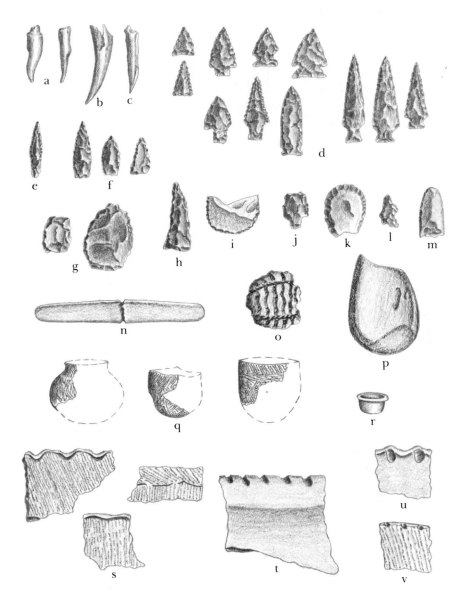

FIGURE 6.16

Raymond complex of Late Woodland: *a,* cut antler tips; *b,* antler awl; *c,* split bird bone awl; *d,* projectile points of various types; *e,* drill or reamer; *f,* ovoid knives; *g,* side scrapers; *h,* trianguloid knife; *i,* flake knife; *j,* hafted scraper; *k,* thumbnail scraper; *l,* graver; *m,* chisel; *n,* grooved bar—possibly an atlatl weight; *o,* pebble celt of basalt; *p,* clay disk ornamented with impressed cords; *q,* shapes of Raymond Cord-marked jar; *r,* miniature bowl of plain ware; *s,* exterior views of rim and lip treatment of Raymond Cord-marked; *t,* interior view of notched inner lip edge on Raymond Cord-marked; *u,* inner rim notching with cord-wrapped-stick impressions; *v,* exterior lip edge notching or nicking.

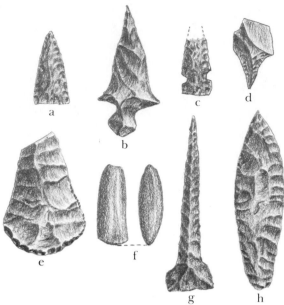

FIGURE 6.17
Flint implements from the Kincaid complex: *a*, Madison Triangular point; *b*, stemmed point; *c*, Cahokia Side-notched; *d*, flake drill; *e*, flint hoe; *f*, polished stone celt; *g*, flint drill; *h*, flint knife. (After Cole 1951.)

FIGURE 6.18
Miscellaneous ornaments and implements from the Kincaid complex: *a*, stone discoidal; *b*, small stone figure; *c*, baked clay elbow pipe; *d*, pottery trowel; *e, f*, shell beads; *g*, clay labret; *h*, cannel coal gorget; *i*, cannel coal ring (ca. 4 centimeters). (After Cole 1951.)

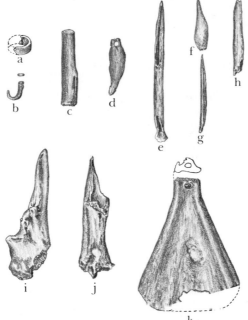

FIGURE 6.19
Miscellaneous bone implements of the Kincaid complex: *a,* bone ring; *b,* broken fishhook segment; *c,* antler punch; *d,* perforated bear canine; *e,* turkey bone awl; *f, g,* bone splinter awls; *h,* broken bone needle; *i,* deer ulna awl; *j,* deer radius awl; *k,* deer scapula hoe. (After Cole 1951.)

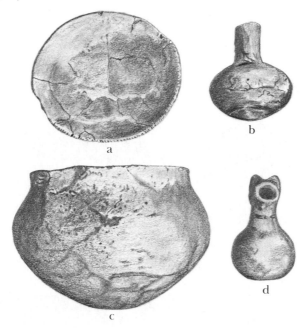

FIGURE 6.20
Representative pottery vessels of the Kincaid complex: *a,* flaring-sided bowl; *b,* cylindrical neck bottle; *c,* large cooking jar; *d,* small hooded bottle. (After Cole 1951.)

FIGURE 6.21
Representative pottery vessels from the Angel site: *a*, jar with rim nodes; *b*, large
Mississippi jar with loop handles; *c*, low rim bowl with notched lip; *d*, negative pointed
carafe neck bottle; *e*, short-neck, wide-mouth bottle; *f*, short-neck, constricted-mouth storage
bottle. (After Black 1967, Vol. II.)

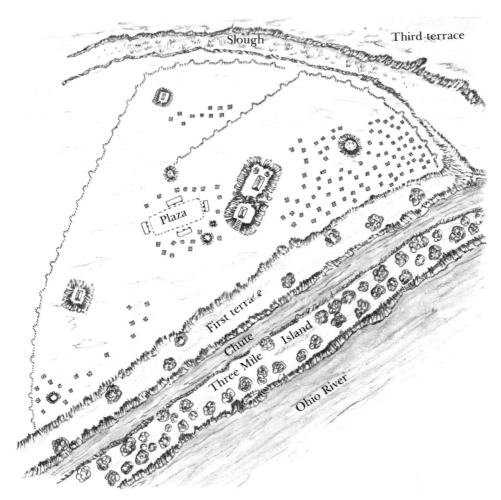

FIGURE 6.22
Sketch of Angel stockaded town with civil and religious buildings on large mounds, the town plaza, and house of the inhabitants. (After Black 1967, Vol. II.)

population figure. In the Spoon River area of Illinois, the larger towns would probably have had from 500 to 1000 people. Large sites such as Kincaid in southern Illinois and the Angel site in southwestern Indiana would have had populations of 1000 or slightly more. It is unlikely that the central Cahokia area was as much as five times this size.

These river valley societies developed a variety of vessel forms, including large to modest-sized cooking and storage jars with rounded bases and handles, bowls, plates, bottles, beakers, and large, flat evaporating pans for salt manufacture. Regional and local decorative styles reflect intersocietal connections, as does the common possession of many similar bone and stone tools for working hides and making them into clothing and of shuttles and weaving tools, drills, flakers, flutes, and awls. There were both shell and flint hoes, and at Cahokia a very large number of these were produced for construction as well as agriculture. Many of them were made of local flints, but some were from southwestern Illinois Mill Creek deposits, evidently procured through a trade and exchange network. The most common pipe form is an elbow of clay smoked with a stem, although stone pipes also occur.

The Middle Mississippi societies participated in varying degrees in the art and insignia of the Southeastern Ceremonial complex. The Angel site, for instance, was a center for the manufacture of a distinctive plate with a negative painted rim utilizing designs of this complex. Cahokia received large effigy bauxite pipes, presumably from the Spiro area, and Spoon River sites have many shell gorgets and painted vessels that fit into the pan-southeastern ceremonial art motifs.

Oneota and Related Complexes

In the upper Mississippi valley, following the Effigy Mound and other early Late Woodland societies, there was a strong shift toward adoption of the behavioral patterns associated with Mississippian societies to the south. There is evidence for population spread from Cahokia to northwestern Illinois and southern Wisconsin sometime between AD 1000 and 1100. One theory is that these groups and others from Cahokia became the Oneota societies (Figures 6.23–6.28). It has also been suggested that Oneota developed from the Effigy Mound complex or that Oneota was a blend of Woodland and Mississippian. Some ceramic features in northeastern Wisconsin show signs of such influences, but that location is on the northeastern periphery of both Oneota and Effigy Mound.

Oneota sites vary in size from little more than 0.5 hectare to 14 to 16 hectares; in the latter, the whole site was probably not occupied contemporaneously. Many of the sites were fortified. Houses were wigwam types, either oval or, in northern Illinois and northeastern Iowa, subrectangular with rounded ends. Houses vary from about 7.5 to 21 meters in length and may well have been multifamily dwellings. There were also smaller, single-family, oval-house patterns. The pottery is primarily shell tempered, with plain surfaces, rounded body and base, and a straight rim sloping outward from the neck. The normal weapon was the bow with a small triangular arrow point. At some sites, many end scrapers, perforators, knives, and other lithic tools, such as abrading stones, were found. At sites with good preservation, many bone and shell tools for processing and manufacturing activities have been recovered.

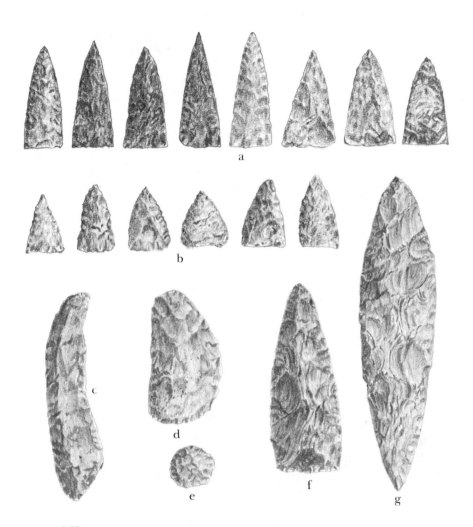

FIGURE 6.23
Lithic implements from northeast Iowa Oneota: *a, b,* triangular arrow points; *c–e,* scrapers; *f, g,* knives. (After M. Wedel 1959.)

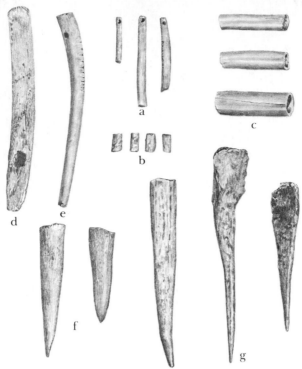

FIGURE 6.24
Bone implements and ornaments from northeast Iowa Oneota: *a*, needle fragments; *b*, beads; *c*, cylinders or beads; *d*, arrowshaft straightener; *e*, unidentified perforated and notched bone; *f*, worked antler tips; *g*, scapula spatulate awls. (After M. Wedel 1959.)

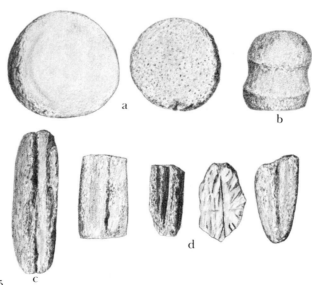

FIGURE 6.25
Stone implements from northeast Iowa Oneota: *a*, mullers; *b*, grooved maul; *c*, shaft smoothers; *d*, abraders. (After M. Wedel 1959.)

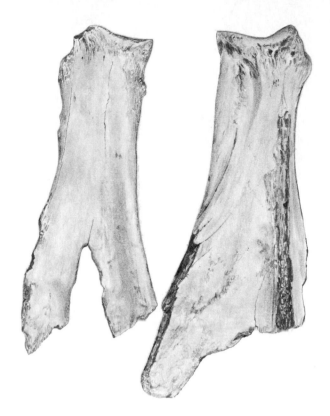

FIGURE 6.26
Bison scapula hoes from northeast Iowa Oneota sites. (After M. Wedel 1959.)

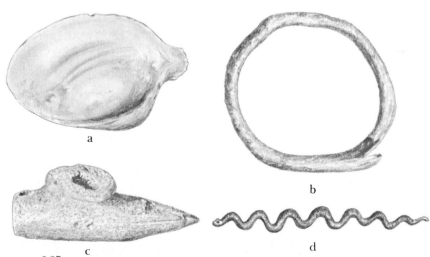

a

b

c

d

FIGURE 6.27
Miscellaneous artifacts from northeast Iowa Oneota sites: *a*, shell spoon; *b*, metal (brass?) bracelet; *c*, Oneota pipe with narrow disk; *d*, metal (brass?) serpent. (After M. Wedel 1959.)

a   b

FIGURE 6.28
Representative burial vessels from northeast Iowa Oneota sites: *a*, Allamakee Plain;
b, Allamakee Trailed. (After M. Wedel 1959.)

For many years, Oneota in Wisconsin has been divided into a number of subgroups, one of which reached the historic period as the Winnebago and another, presumably, as the Ioway Indians, who were also residents of the adjacent northeast Iowa-southeast Minnesota area.

In northern Illinois, northwestern Indiana, and southeastern Michigan, there are occupations of Late and Terminal Woodland that seem to represent ancestral groups to such Central Algonquian-speaking people as the Potta-wattomie, Kickapoo, northern Miami, and Illinois. In their material culture products, some of these are very close to the Oneota Chiwere groups, although they belong, of course, to a different language family.

Lower Michigan Late Woodland

The Late Woodland occupations in Michigan began with complexes similar to that of the Fort Wayne Mound, with a strong infusion of concepts and items also found in the post-Hopewell Mound Instrusive culture of Ohio. This similarity is most evident in the southeastern half of the lower peninsula. This area also participated in the developments that produced the Glen Meyer in Ontario in a series of steps represented at such sites as Riviere aux Vase and the Younge site. There are even suggestions that this area of Michigan was occupied by Iroquoian speakers, and there are maps by linguists and eth-nologists that show this. I suspect the situation here was much like that of the northern, eastern, and southern borders of the Five Nations and the Hurons, where Algonquian-speaking groups shared ceramic and utilitarian tool de-velopments with their neighbors.

The western and northern sections of the lower peninsula were interacting with developments in Wisconsin; from about AD 700 to 1100 the ceramic treatment reflects connections with the Late Woodland, Mississippi, and

Oneota styles. There are other similarities as well, for this area is part of the Lake Forest environment, which has produced a strong east-west cultural belt for at least 4500 years. The Juntunen site (McPherron 1967) is perhaps the best known of the typical sites, and probably reflects the developments in adjoining areas not yet delimited in any detail. The populations in these sections were primarily hunters and gatherers who engaged in some agriculture. Their descendants appear on the historic horizon as the Ottawa and Chippewa (Fitting 1970).

The Fort Ancient Societies

Fort Ancient covers an area nearly equivalent to that occupied by the Adena-Hopewell occupations before it. The several Fort Ancient societies date from somewhere before AD 700 to close to AD 1000. They represent regional groupings in the valleys of the tributaries of the Ohio and along the Ohio River, and over time they became increasingly dependent upon agriculture and increasingly close to Middle Mississippi cultural configurations (Griffin 1943). In the Miami and Scioto valleys, the earlier Fort Ancient sites clearly are derived both culturally and genetically from Late Woodland societies. Early houses are circular; later ones are rectangular. Some sites have evidence of a central courtyard, and a platform mound was excavated at the Baum site. These sites range from 1.2 to 4 hectares and probably had populations of a few hundred people at a time. A wide variety of burial positions were practiced, but single, extended burials are most common. The late, large Fort Ancient sites along the Ohio often had palisades and large rectangular house patterns 15 by 21 meters as well as the more normal 5.5 by 7.5 meter houses. The houses had circular fire basins and two center posts. The later pottery is all shell-tempered Mississippi jar forms, bowls, pans, and a few rare plates (Figure 6.29). By at least AD 1400 shell gorgets of styles normally associated with central and eastern Tennessee make their appearance in Fort Ancient sites—the result of trade and exchange along the old paths of the past, indicating new religious integrating devices between these two areas. The trade goods are of a period that coincides with suggestive but hardly precise references to Shawnee groups in the Ohio valley (Hanson 1966:171–175, 197).

Monongahela Woodland

In the contiguous area of eastern Ohio, northern West Virginia, and western Pennsylvania from a short time before AD 1000 to the protohistoric period, a partially agricultural complex emerged with significant areal and temporal variations. In marked contrast to most Fort Ancient sites, the Monongahela locations are usually on saddles between hills. Many of the sites are known to

FIGURE 6.29

Artifacts of the Fort Ancient aspect: *a,* pitted hammerstone; *b,* ungrooved ax; *c,* mussel-shell hoe; *d,* conoidal tobacco pipe; *e,* elbow tobacco pipe; *f,* grooved abrading stone; *g,* shell pendant; *h,* perforated wolf tooth; *i,* bone fishhook; *j,* discoidal stone; *k,* drill; *l,* triangular projectile point; *m,* disk-shaped shell bead; *n,* mussel-shell spoon; *o,* beamer (deer metapoidal bone); *p,* bone needle; *q,* bone awls—ulna (*top*), raccoon penis, splinter, turkey metatarsal; *r,* bone (bird) bead; *s,* flaking tool (antler); *t,* projectile point (antler); *u,* hairpin; *v,* pottery rim sherd, Feurt focus; *w,* rim sherd, Anderson focus; *x,* pottery vessel, Baum focus; *y,* pottery vessel, Madisonville focus.

have oval to circular stockades and circular house patterns. The houses are arranged around an open central courtyard. Village size is from about 0.5 to 2 hectares; stockade diameters range from nearly 61 meters to 137 meters. The circular houses are about 6 meters in diameter. The refuse pits had originally been used for food storage. At some sites there is a "Big House," which was probably the council house. A few Monongahela sites are reported to have rectangular, single-family units. Population was from somewhat less than 100 to about 150. Many of the utilitarian tools and weapons are similar to those of Fort Ancient or Owasco-Iroquois groups. The vessel forms and treatment are simpler than in Fort Ancient; the simple wide-mouth jar is almost the only form, although it shows variation in lip and rim shape and decoration. It is estimated that there are well over 500 Monongahela sites, but it is clear that they were not comparable to Fort Ancient in population density. A number of attempts have been made to identify a historic people whose ancestors were responsible for this culture, but none of them are convincing.

Terminal Woodland in Eastern Pennsylvania and Northern New Jersey

In eastern Pennsylvania and New Jersey some of the Late Woodland developments are known to terminate in the several groups of the Susquehannocks and the several Algonquian groups called Delaware by the early colonists. Following the Early Woodland Bushkill complex, there is still very little evidence of a Middle Woodland occupation during the period from 200 BC to AD 300. There is even very little evidence for Point Peninsula-like complexes. The newly proposed Fox Creek occupation in the Delaware valley fills some of this void (Kinsey 1974), and undoubtedly some part of the mélange at the Abbott Farm dates to this period (Cross 1956).

In the upper Susquehanna there are a number of sites with occupations around AD 1000 to 1300 that parallel the Owasco groups in New York. These probably lead into the proto-Andaste Iroquois sites of the 1500s to 1600s in that area. The Shenks Ferry complex of this area has many features indicating its participation in the trend toward sedentary villages and its adoption of decorative techniques common first to Owasco and then to Iroquoian pottery. The village plan is circular with a palisade, and house form changes from circular to rectanguloid with rounded ends (Kinsey and Graybill 1971; Heisey 1971), apparently wigwam-type structures. What happened to these people when the Susquehannocks arrived is a matter of conjecture. The latter group came from the north into the Safe Harbor, Pennsylvania, area and were attacked there by the Five Nations.

In the upper Delaware, also, there is a progression from a period equivalent to Owasco into the historic period, during which the populations become increasingly sedentary. As Kraft (1975) and others have demonstrated, the

Pahaquarra phase gradually moves toward the Munsee complex, which is almost certainly Delaware. In some features, such as ceramics, this late pre-historic assemblage is, distressingly for archeologists, very like Iroquois, but as we now know, all the articles of Iroquois style in the Northeast were not necessarily made by Iroquois speakers.

A few excavated houses in the upper Delaware have been round-ended long houses with one doorway. They are about 6 meters wide and range from 8.5 to 18 meters long. So far no palisaded villages have been found. Instead, there appear to have been many small farmsteads located along the main river, utilizing the resources from the river and the surrounding land area.

New York and the Upper St. Lawrence

The Point Peninsula complexes in New York developed, through a series of steps, from the Hudson to the Niagara River. The cultural changes included the adoption and spread of the elbow pipe, the appearance of the triangular arrow point, a diminution of projectile point size, the gradual abandonment of gorgets, and the replacement of dentate stamping and rocker stamping by cord-wrapped stick decoration on the rim of vessels. In the Owasco period from about AD 1000 to about 1350 or 1400, villages were increasingly pali-saded. The house form shifts from rounded or somewhat ellipsoidal to good-sized long houses up to 27.5 meters or so in length. Village size varies around 1.2 hectares. Some of the late Owasco houses are multifamily long houses over 61 meters in length (Ritchie and Funk 1973:165–173).

In the several areas occupied by the Five Nations a fine sequence is being worked out for the development from local Owasco into early Iroquois vil-lages and for the periodic moves as the villages were changed by the Onon-daga (Tuck 1971) and others. The movements of the Mohawk, Oneida, Cayuga, and Seneca are not as carefully documented, but such documen-tation is possible. Iroquois sites range in size from 0.5 to 4 hectares. Most of them are palisaded, but I believe that none have been completely excavated to obtain the village plan. The Iroquois material culture may be seen in the illustrations of the cited publications and their sources; Iroquois pottery and pipe styles are relatively well known. It perhaps should be mentioned in passing that archeological work of the past 30 years has conclusively demon-strated that the Iroquois were in their historic homeland for a long time—at least 1500 years before the arrival of the French, Dutch, and Spanish.

Huronia

In Ontario there is a parallel development to that which has been outlined for New York. The still largely unreported Princess Point complexes of the northeastern side of Lake Erie and western Lake Ontario are regional repre-sentatives of Point Peninsula. They followed the Hopewellian period in that area and developed into the Glen Meyer sites, which in turn probably developed into the Erie and Neutral western Iroquois groups. In the western Lake Erie area, a series of sites with some holdover of burial practices from the Hopewellian period is known, but the cord-wrapped-stick-decorated pottery and isosceles triangular points clearly indicate the sites' correct time period. They gradually change from hunting-fishing-gathering campsites to some dependence upon agriculture by AD 800 or 900, and that development and the appearance of the triangular point and palisaded village were coeval.

The Pickering people of southeastern Ontario also developed out of Point Peninsula, eventually becoming the Huron and Petun Iroquoian-speaking villages in Ontario. With the development of these Ontario Iroquois there arose recognized regional "tribal" ceramic and pipe styles that have enabled Canadian archeologists to trace Iroquois movements and locations with some confidence (J. Wright 1966; 1969; 1972; Pendergast 1966).

The Huronian cultures also seem to have acquired palisades early, and many of their villages were located in defensible positions. They too had long houses with multiple fireplaces, perhaps reflecting an extended matrilineal organization. Many of the sites are about 2 hectares in size and contained fewer than 20 houses. Some of the sites, however, are considerably larger. In the early 1600s Cahiague was said by Champlain to have over 200 long houses, representing perhaps 5000 people. The early historic population of the Huron-Petun branch is estimated to have been close to 45,000 (Pendergast 1966:81). The large number of clay pipes on many Iroquois sites is a strong indication that pipe smoking had become more common than would be required for ritual communication with the spirit world.

Iroquoian towns existed along the St. Lawrence from the Thousand Islands to Montreal. The village of Hochelaga, seen by Cartier in 1535 at Montreal, contained Iroquois speakers; yet these groups had left before Champlain arrived in 1603. It is estimated that Hochelaga had a population of 2000. Culturally, the Hochelaga inhabitants were very close to the Pickering complex. Like the Hurons, for many years they practiced cannibalism and burial in a flexed position; they also had long houses in a palisaded village. It is now believed they may have been absorbed by the Huron clans along the Trent River system (J. Wright 1972b).

Bordering the Huron from the northwest to the east were Algonquian speakers, including the Chippewa, Ottawa, Algonquin, and many named northern bands. As in earlier millennia, the southern Ontario and the cultural trends they participated in were dominant. As the historic period approached, the northern neighbors of the Huron-Petun groups adopted ceramics and pipe styles of their trading and exchange partners to the south while maintaining their older traditions in terms of such utilitarian items as bone and stone tools. Somewhat to the north of these partially Iroquoianized bands were others whose ceramic ties were west along the north shore of Lake Superior to the Selkirk tradition of Manitoba (Wright 1972b).

In southern New England and Long Island a basic sequence was presented by Rouse (1947) and C. Smith (1950) and has been modified by subsequent workers, such as Ritchie (1969a; 1969b), Salwen (1969), and Salwen and Ottesen (1972). Developing out of a series of Windsor traditions, occupations in this area up to about AD 700 are attributed to the Sebonac phase of Windsor (AD 700–1000). During this period, wide-base triangular points appear, as do wide-mouth jars, a variety of surface finishes and decorative styles and techniques, and shell tempering. These people were primarily hunters, gatherers, and fishers; however, they gradually changed as the later Shantok complex developed, and they adopted maize and beans, as did most of their neighbors. Their pottery takes on an "Iroquois" look, but, as we now know, this was actually a widespread ceramic development not limited to Iroquoian speakers. This general sequence is valid except in eastern New England, where there is little evidence of participation in "Iroquois" ceramic styles. Groups along the coast continued to acquire a significant part of their food supply from fish and mussels as well as from game animals. Ceramic occupations in northern New England are not well known, but a pattern similar to that of their neighbors to the south and west can be expected.

The preceding pages describe in minimal detail the complex interrelationships of the aboriginal populations of northeastern America and their ecological adjustments to the resources of that area. In addition to varied natural resources, the cultures reacted to influence from distant cultures in other areas, making the Northeast one of the most intricate and difficult areas of study for the archeologist.

References Cited and Recommended Sources

Adovasio, J. M., J. D. Gunn, J. Donahue, and R. Stuckenrath 1975 Excavations at Meadowcroft Rockshelter, 1973–74: a progress report. Pennsylvania Archaeologist 45:1–30.

Baby, R. S. 1976 Research continues at Seip Mound Memorial. Echoes Ohio Historical Society 15:1–3.

Baby, R. S., and M. A. Potter 1965 The Cole complex. Papers in Archaeology of the Ohio Historical Society No. 2.

Baby, R. S., M. A. Potter, and A. Mays, Jr. 1966 Exploration of the O. C. Voss Mound, Big Darby Reservoir area, Franklin County, Ohio, Papers in Archaeology of the Ohio Historical Society No. 3.

Bebrich, C. A. 1968 A supplementary report on the lithic artifacts from the Sheep Rock Shelter. In Archaeological Investigations of Sheep Rock Shelter, Huntingdon County, Pennsylvania, ed. J. W. Michels and J. S. Dutt. Department of Anthropology, Pennsylvania State University Occasional Papers in Anthropology No. 5.

Bebrich, C. A., and T. Morgan III 1968 A preliminary report on the lithic artifacts from the Workman site (36 Bd 36), Bedford County. In Archaeological Investigations of the Workman Site, Bedford County, Pennsylvania. Department of Anthropology, Pennsylvania State University Occasional Paper No. 4.

Black, Glenn A. 1967 Angel Site: an archaeological, historical, and ethnological study. Indiana Historical Society.

Brose, D. S. 1970 The archaeology of Summer Island. University of Michigan Museum of Anthropology, Anthropological Paper No. 41.

Brown, J. A., and C. Cleland 1968 The late glacial and early postglacial faunal resources in Midwestern biomes newly opened to human habitation. *In* The Quaternary of Illinois. University of Illinois College of Agriculture Special Publication No. 14.

Bush, D. E. 1975 A ceramic analysis of the Late Adena Buckmeyer site, Perry County, Ohio. Michigan Archaeologist 21:9–23.

Byers, D. S. 1954 Bull Brook—a fluted point site in Ipswich, Massachusetts. American Antiquity 19:343–351.

———. 1955 Additional information on the Bull Brook site, Massachusetts. American Antiquity 20:274–277.

Cole, F.-C. 1951 Kincaid: A Prehistoric Metropolis. Chicago: University of Chicago Press.

Cole, F.-C., and T. Deuel 1937 Rediscovering Illinois. Chicago: University of Chicago Press.

Cook, T. G. 1974 Koster: an artifact analysis of two Archaic phases in west-central Illinois. Ph.D. dissertation, University of Chicago.

Cross, D. 1956 Archaeology of New Jersey, Vol. 2. Trenton: Archaeological Society of New Jersey and New Jersey State Museum.

Cunningham, W. M. 1948 A study of the Glacial Kame culture in Michigan, Ohio, and Indiana. Occasional Contributions from the Museum of Anthropology of the University of Michigan No. 12.

Dekin, A. A., Jr. 1966 A fluted point from Grand Traverse County. The Michigan Archaeologist 12:37–39.

Didier, M. E. 1967 A distributional study of the Turkey-Tail point. Wisconsin Archaeologist 48:3–73.

Dincauze, D. 1968 Cremation cemeteries in eastern Massachusetts. Papers of the Peabody Museum of Archaeology and Ethnology, Harvard University 59:1.

———. 1971 An Archaic sequence for southern New England. American Antiquity 36:194–198.

———. 1972 The Atlantic phase: a Late Archaic culture in Massachusetts. Man in the Northeast 4:40–61.

———. 1973 Prehistoric occupation of the Charles River Estuary: a paleogeographic study. Bulletin of the Archaeological Society of Connecticut, Inc., No. 38.

———. 1974 An introduction to archaeology in the Greater Boston area. Archaeology of Eastern North America 2:39–67.

Dorwin, J. T., 1966 Fluted points and Late-Pleistocene geochronology in Indiana. Indiana Historical Society, Prehistory Research Series 6:3:141–188.

Dragoo, D. W. 1963 Mounds for the dead: an analysis of the Adena culture. Annals of the Carnegie Museum, Vol. 37.

Fitting, J. E. 1970 The archaeology of Michigan. New York: Natural History Press.

Fitting, J. E., J. DeVischer, and E. J. Wahla 1966 The Paleo-Indian occupation of the Holcombe Beach. University of Michigan Museum of Anthropology, Anthropological Paper No. 27.

Fitzhugh, W. W. 1972 Environmental archaeology and cultural systems in Hamilton Inlet, Labrador. Smithsonian Contributions to Anthropology No. 16.

Ford, R. I. 1974 Northeastern archaeology: past and future directions. Annual Review of Anthropology 3:384–413.

Fowler, M. L. 1969 Explorations into Cahokia archaeology. Illinois Archaeological Survey Bulletin No. 7.

———. 1974 Cahokia: Ancient Capital of the Midwest. Menlo Park, Calif.: Addison-Wesley Publishing Company.

Fowler, M. L., and R. L. Hall 1972 Archaeological phases at Cahokia. Illinois State Museum Papers in Anthropology No. 1.

Freeman, J. 1969 The Millville site, a Middle Woodland village in Grant County, Wisconsin. Wisconsin Archaeologist 50:37–67.

Funk, R. E. 1966 The significance of three radiocarbon dates from the Sylvan Lake Rockshelter. New York State Archaeological Association Bulletin No. 36.

Funk, R. E., D. W. Fisher, and E. M. Reilly, Jr. 1970 Caribou and Paleo-Indian in New York state: a presumed association. American Journal of Science 268:181–186.

Funk, R. E., G. R. Walters, and W. F. Ehlers, Jr. 1969 A radiocarbon date for early man from the Dutchess Quarry Cave. New York State Archeological Association Bulletin 46:19–21.

Greenman, E. F. 1932 Excavation of the Coon Mound and an analysis of the Adena culture. Ohio Archaeological and Historical Quarterly 41:369–523.

———. 1966 Chronology of sites at Killarney, Ontario. American Antiquity 31:540–551.

Griffin, J. B. 1941 Additional Hopewell materials from Illinois. Indiana Historical Society, Prehistory Research Series 2:165–223.

———. 1943 The Fort Ancient aspect: its cultural and chronological position in Mississippi valley archaeology. Ann Arbor: University of Michigan Press. Reissue 1966 as Anthropological Paper No. 28, University of Michigan Museum of Anthropology.

———. 1952 Archaeology of Eastern United States. Chicago: University of Chicago Press.

———. 1956 The reliability of radiocarbon dates for Late Glacial and Recent times in central and eastern North America. University of Utah Anthropological Papers 26:10–34.

———. 1960 Climatic change: a contributory cause of the growth and decline of northern Hopewellian culture. Wisconsin Archeologist 41:21–33.

———. 1961 Lake Superior copper and the Indians: Miscellaneous Studies of Great Lakes Prehistory. University of Michigan Museum of Anthropology, Anthropological Paper No. 17.

———. 1965 Late Quaternary prehistory in the northeastern Woodlands. In The Quaternary of the United States, ed. H. E. Wright, Jr., and D. G. Frey, pp. 655–667. Princeton: Princeton University Press.

———. 1965 Hopewell and the dark black glass. Michigan Archaeologist 11:115–155.

———. 1966 The origins of prehistoric North American pottery. Atti del VI Congresso Internationale della Scienze Preistoriche e Protostoriche, Sezioni V–VII:267–271.

———. 1967 Eastern North American archaeology: a summary. Science 156:3772:175–191.

———. 1968 Observation on Illinois prehistory in Late Pleistocene and Early Recent times. In The Quaternary of Illinois. University of Illinois, Urbana, College of Agriculture Special Publication 14:123–135.

Griffin, J. B., A. A. Gordus, and G. A. Wright 1969 Identification of the sources of Hopewellian obsidian in the Middle West. American Antiquity 34:1–14.

Griffin, J. B., and A. C. Spaulding 1951 The central Mississippi valley archaeological survey, season 1950: a preliminary report. Journal of the Illinois State Archaeological Society (New Series) 1:74–81.

Halsey, J. R. 1974 The Markee site (47–VE-195): an Early Middle Archaic campsite in the Kickapoo River valley. The Wisconsin Archaeologist 55:42–75.

Hanson, L. H. 1966 The Hardin Village site. University of Kentucky Studies in Anthropology No. 4.

———. 1975 The Buffalo site: a late 17th century Indian village site (46 Pu 31) in Putnam County, West Virginia. Report of Archeological Investigations No. 5, West Virginia Geological and Economic Survey.

Heisey, H. 1971 An interpretation of Shenk's Ferry ceramics. Pennsylvania Archaeologist 41:44–70.

Hurley, W. M. 1965 Archeological research in the projected Kickapoo Reservoir, Vernon County, Wisconsin. The Wisconsin Archeologist 46:1–114.

———. 1974 Silver Creek Woodland sites, southwestern Wisconsin. Report 6, Office of State Archaeologist, University of Iowa.

———. 1975 An analysis of Effigy Mound complexes in Wisconsin. University of Michigan Museum of Anthropology, Anthropological Paper No. 59.

Jansen, D. E. 1968 The Naomikong Point site and the dimensions of Laurel in the Lake Superior region. University of Michigan Museum of Anthropology, Anthropological Paper No. 36.

Johnston, R. B. 1968 The archaeology of the Serpent Mounds site. Royal Ontario Museum, Art and Archaeology Occasional Paper No. 10.

Karow, P. F., T. W. Anderson, A. H. Clarke, L. D. Delorme, and M. R. Sreenivasa 1975 Stratigraphy, paleontology and age of Lake Algonquin sediments in southwestern Ontario, Canada. Quaternary Research 5:49–87.

Kellar, J. H. 1973 An introduction to the prehistory of Indiana. Indiana Historical Society.

Kennedy, C. C. 1966 Preliminary report on the Morrison's Island 6 Site. National Museum of Canada Bulletin 206:100–124.

Kidd, K. E. 1951 Fluted points in Ontario. American Antiquity 16:260.

Kinsey, W. F. 1958 A survey of fluted points found in the Susquehanna Basin. Report No. 1. Pennsylvania Archaeologist 28:103–111, 126.

———. 1959 A survey of fluted points found in the Susquehanna Basin. Report No. 2. Pennsylvania Archaeologist 29:73–79.

———. 1972 Archaeology in the upper Delaware valley. Pennsylvania Historical and Museum Commission Anthropological Series No. 2.

———. 1974 Early to Middle Woodland cultural complexes on the Piedmont and Coastal Plain. Pennsylvania Archaeologist 44:9–19.

Kinsey, W. F. and J. R. Graybill 1971 Murry site and its role in Lancaster and Funk phases of Shenks Ferry culture. Pennsylvania Archaeologist 41:7–43.

Knoblock, B. W. 1939 Bannerstones of the North American Indians. La Grange, Ill. privately printed.

Kraft, H. C. 1973 The Plenge site: a Paleo-Indian occupation site in New Jersey. Archaeology of Eastern North America 1:56–117.

———. 1975 The archaeology of the Tucks Island area. South Orange, N.J.: Archaeological Research Center, Seton Hall University Museum.

Kuttruff, L. C. 1972 The Marty Coolidge site, Monroe County, Illinois. Southern Illinois University Museum Research Records. Southern Illinois Studies No. 10.

Lee, A. M., and K. D. Vickery 1972 Salvage excavations at the Headquarters site, a Middle Woodland village burial area in Hamilton County, Ohio. Ohio Archaeologist Vol. 22.

Lee, T. E. 1954 The first Sheguiandah expedition, Manitoulin Island, Ontario. American Antiquity 20:101–111.

———. 1955 The second Sheguiandah expedition, Manitoulin Island, Ontario. American Antiquity 21:63–71.

———. 1957 The antiquity of the Sheguiandah site. The Canadian Field Naturalist 71:117–137.

MacDonald, G. F. 1968 Debert: a Paleo-Indian site in central Nova Scotia. National Museum of Canada Anthropology Papers No. 16.

MacNeish, R. S. 1952 A possible early site in the Thunder Bay District, Ontario. In National Museum of Canada Bulletin 126:23–47.

McPherron, A. 1967 The Juntenen site and the Late Woodland prehistory of the upper Great Lakes area. University of Michigan Museum of Anthropology, Anthropological Papers No. 30.

Magrath, W. H. 1945 The North Benton Mound: a Hopewell site in Ohio. American Antiquity XI:40–47.

Mason, R. J. 1958 Late Pleistocene geochronology and the Paleo-Indian penetration into the lower Michigan Peninsula. University of Michigan Museum of Anthropology, Anthropological Paper No. 11.

———. 1959 Indications of Paleo-Indian occupations in the Delaware valley. Pennsylvania Archaeologist 29:1–17.

———. 1962 The Paleo-Indian tradition in eastern North America. Current Anthropology 3:227–278.

———. 1963 Two late Paleo-Indian complexes in Wisconsin. The Wisconsin Archeologist 44:4:199–211.

———. 1969 Laurel and North Bay: diffusional networks in the upper Great Lakes. American Antiquity 34:295–302.

Mason, R. J., and C. Irwin 1960 An Eden Scottsbluff burial in northern Wisconsin. American Antiquity 26:43–57.

Maxwell, M. S. 1951 Woodland cultures of southern Illinois. Excavations in the Carbondale area. Logan Museum Publications in Anthropology, Bulletin No. 7.

Miller, R. K. 1941 McCain site, Dubois County, Indiana. Prehistory Research Series, Indiana Historical Society, Vol. 2.

Mills, W. C. 1916 Exploration of the Tremper Mound. Ohio Archaeological and Historical Quarterly 25:262–398.

———. 1922 Exploration of the Mound City group. Ohio Archaeological and Historical Quarterly 31:423–584.

Mitchell, B. M. 1966 Preliminary report of a Woodland site near Deep River, Ontario. National Museum of Canada Anthropological Paper No. 11.

Moorehead, W. K. 1922 The Hopewell Mound group of Ohio. Field Museum of Natural History Publication 211. Anthropological Series Vol. 6.

Morgan, R. G. 1952 Outline of cultures in the Ohio region. In Archaeology of Eastern United States, ed. J. B. Griffin. Chicago: University of Chicago Press.

Murphy, J. L. 1971 Maize from an Adena mound in Athens County, Ohio. Science 171:897–898.

Pendergast, J. F. 1966 Three prehistoric Iroquois components in eastern Ontario: the Salem, Grays Creek, and Beckstead sites. National Museum of Canada Bulletin No. 208, Anthropological Series No. 73.

Potzger, J. E. 1946 Phytosociology of the primeval forest in central-northern Wisconsin and upper Michigan, and a brief post-glacial history of the Lake Forest formation. Ecology Monographs 16:211–250.

Prest, V. K. 1970 Quaternary geology of Canada. Geological Survey of Canada Economy Geology Report Series No. 1.

Prufer, O. 1963 The McConnell site: a late Palaeo-Indian workshop in Coshocton County, Ohio. Scientific Publications of the Cleveland Museum of Natural History (New Series) 2:1–51.

———. 1966 The Mud Valley site: a late Paleo-Indian locality in Holmes County, Ohio. Ohio Journal of Science 66:1:68–75.

Prufer, O., and R. S. Baby 1963 Paleo-Indians of Ohio. Columbus: Ohio Historical Society.

Prufer, O., and O. C. Shane 1970 Blain Village and the Fort Ancient Tradition in Ohio. Kent, Ohio: Kent State University Press.

Quimby, G. I. 1958 Fluted points and geochronology in the Lake Michigan Basin. American Antiquity 23:247–254.

Ritchie, W. A. 1949 An archaeological survey of the Trent Waterway in Ontario, Canada. Researches and Transactions of the New York State Archeological Association, Vol. 12.

———. 1965 The Archaeology of New York State. Garden City, N. Y.: Natural History Press.

———. 1969a The Archaeology of New York State. Rev. ed. Garden City, N. Y. Natural History Press.

———. 1969b The Archaeology of Martha's Vineyard. Garden City, N. Y.: Natural History Press.

Ritchie, W. A., and R. E. Funk 1973 Aboriginal settlement patterns in the northeast. Memoir 20, New York State Museum and Science Service.

Ritzenthaler, R. E. 1966 The Kouba site: Paleo-Indians in Wisconsin. The Wisconsin Archeologist 47:171–187.

Ritzenthaler, R. E., and G. I. Quimby 1962 The Red Ochre culture of the upper Great Lakes and adjacent areas. Chicago Natural History Museum 36:243–275.

Robbins, M. 1959 Wapanucket No. 6: an Archaic village in Middleboro, Massachusetts. Cohannet Chapter Massachusetts Archaeological Society, Inc.

———. 1968 An Archaic ceremonial complex in Assawompsett. Massachusetts Archaeological Society, Inc. Attleboro: Bronson Museum.

Rouse, I. 1947 Ceramic traditions and sequences in Connecticut. Bulletin of the Archaeological Society of Connecticut. 21:10–25.

Rowe, C. W. 1956 The Effigy Mound culture of Wisconsin. Milwaukee Public Museum Publications in Anthropology No. 3.

Salwen, B. 1969 A tentative "in situ" solution to the Mohegan Pequot problem. In An Introduction to the Archaeology and History of the Connecticut Valley Indian, ed. W. R. Young. Springfield Museum, Science New Series 1:81–87.

Salwen, B., and A. Ottesen 1972 Radiocarbon dates for a Windsor occupation at the Shantok Cove site, New London County, Connecticut. Man in the Northeast No. 3:8–19.

Salzer, R. J. 1974 The Wisconsin north lakes project. In Aspects of Upper Great Lakes Anthropology, ed. E. B. Johnson, pp. 40–54. St. Paul: Minnesota Historical Society.

Sanger, D. 1971 Passamaquoddy Bay prehistory. Summary Bulletin of the Maine Archaeological Society 11:14–19.

Shetrone, H. C. 1926 Explorations of the Hopewell Group of Prehistoric earthworks. Ohio Archaeological and Historical Quarterly 35:1–227.

Smail, W. 1951 Some early projectile points from the St. Louis area. Journal of the Illinois Archaeological Society (New Series) 2:1:11–16.

Smith, C. S. 1950 The archaeology of coastal New York. Anthropological Papers of the American Museum of Natural History No. 43.

Smith, W. B. 1926 Indian remains of the Penobscot valley and their significance. The Maine Bulletin, Vol. XXIX.

Spence, M. W. 1967 A Middle Woodland burial complex in the St. Lawrence valley. National Museum of Canada Anthropology Paper No. 14.

Squier, E. F. and E. H. Davis 1848 Ancient monuments of the Mississippi valley. Smithsonian Contributions to Knowledge, Vol. 1.

Starr, F. 1960 The archaeology of Hamilton County, Ohio. Journal of the Cincinnati Museum of Natural History XXIII.

Stevens, E. T. 1870 Flint Chips. London: Bell and Daldy.

Stoltman, J. B. 1973 The Laurel culture in Minnesota. Minnesota Prehistoric Archaeology Series No. 8. Minnesota Historical Society.

———. 1974 An examination of within-Laurel cultural variability. *In* Aspects of Upper Great Lakes Anthropology: Papers in Honor of Lloyd A. Wilford, ed. E. Johnson. St. Paul: Minnesota Historical Society.

Stoltman, J. B., and K. Workman 1969 A preliminary study of Wisconsin fluted points. The Wisconsin Archaeologist 50:189–214.

Storck, P. L. 1972 An unusual late Paleo-Indian projectile point from Grey County, Southern Ontario. Ontario Archaeology 18:27–45.

———. 1973 Two Paleo-Indian projectile points from the Bronte Creek Gap, Halton County, Ontario. Archaeology Paper 1. Royal Ontario Museum 1–4.

Struever, S. 1968 Woodland subsistence systems in the lower Illinois valley. *In* New Perspectives in Archeology, ed. S. R. and L. R. Binford, pp. 285–312. Chicago: Aldine Press.

Struever, S., and K. D. Vickery 1973 The beginnings of cultivation in the Midwest-Riverine area of the United States. American Anthropologist 75:5:1197–1220.

Titterington, P. F. 1950 Some non-pottery sites in the St. Louis area. Illinois State Archaeological Society (New Series) 1:19–30.

Tuck, J. A. 1971 Onondaga Iroquois Prehistory: A Study in Settlement Archaeology. Syracuse: Syracuse University Press.

———. 1975a An archaic sequence from the Strait of Belle Isle, Labrador. National Museum of Man Mercury Series. Archaeological Survey of Canada. Paper No. 34.

———1975b Prehistory of Saglek Bay, Labrador; Archaic and Paleo-Eskimo occupations. Archaeological Survey of Canada Paper No. 32. Mercury Series. National Museum of Man.

Webb, W. S., and R. S. Baby 1957 The Adena People No. 2. Columbus: Ohio Historical Society.

Webb, W. S., and C. E. Snow 1974 The Adena People. Knoxville: University of Tennessee Press.

Wedel, Mildred M. 1959 Oneota sites on the upper Iowa River. Missouri Archaeologist 2:(2–4).

Willoughby, C. C. 1935 Antiquities of the New England Indians. Cambridge: Peabody Museum of American Archaeology and Ethnology.

Winters, H. D. 1963 An archaeological survey of the Wabash valley in Illinois. Illinois State Museum Report of Investigations, No. 10.

———. 1969 The Riverton culture. Illinois State Museum Report of Investigations, No. 13, Illinois Archaeological Survey Monograph No. 1.

Witthoft, J. 1952 A Paleo-Indian site in eastern Pennsylvania. Proceedings of the American Philosophical Society 96:464–495.

Wittry, W. L. 1959a The Raddatz Rockshelter, Sk 5, Wisconsin. The Wisconsin Archeologist 40:33–69.

———. 1959b Archaeological studies of four Wisconsin rockshelters. The Wisconsin Archeologist 40:137–267.

Wright, H. T. 1964 A transitional Archaic campsite at Green Point (20SA1). Michigan Archaeologist 10:17–22.

Wright, H. T., and W. B. Roosa 1966 The Barnes site: a fluted point assemblage from the Great Lakes region. American Antiquity 31:850–860.

Wright, J. V. 1962 A distributional study of some Archaic traits in southern Ohio. National Museum of Canada Bulletin 180:124–141.

———. 1966 The Ontario Iroquois tradition. National Museum of Canada Bulletin 210, Anthropological Series No. 75.

———. 1967 The Laurel tradition and the Middle Woodland period. Bulletin 217. National Museum of Canada.

———. 1969 The archaeology of the Bennett site. *In* National Museum of Canada Bulletin 229, Anthropological Series 85:3–115.

———. 1972a The Shield Archaic. Publications in Archaeology No. 3. National Museum of Man. Ottawa: National Museum of Canada.

———. 1972b Ontario Prehistory. Archaeological Survey, National Museum of Man. Ottawa: National Museum of Canada.

Yarnell, R. A. 1964 Aboriginal relationships between culture and plant life in the upper Great Lakes region. University of Michigan Museum of Anthropology, Anthropological Paper No. 23.

———. 1972 *Iva Annua* var. *Macrocarpa:* extinct American cultigen? American Anthropologist 74:335–341.

An early aerial view of the site of Cahokia. In the foreground are three large truncated pyramidal mounds; in the background is the largest aboriginal earth mound structure in the United States, Monk's Mound. Its size can be appreciated by comparing it with the farmhouses to the right. (Photograph by D. M. Reeves, Smithsonian Institution.)

CHAPTER SEVEN

The Southeast

Jon D. Muller

In an attempt to avoid the pitfalls and irrelevancies of arguments about complex archeological systems of terminology and classification, Dr. Muller emphasizes in this chapter "the dynamics of social and cultural development." He feels that it is time for those studying the archeology of the Southeast "to concern themselves more directly with testing hypotheses about the kinds of social relationships between one society and another," and less with "creating area-wide classifications of dubious explanatory value."

THE SETTING

The Southeast largely corresponds physiographically to the Coastal Plain and the southern half of the Appalachians, but, from the archeological viewpoint, the dominant features of the last 6000 to 8000 years have been the valleys of the major rivers, such as the Tennessee and the Mississippi. These valleys were the setting for the development of the most complex social and political organizations north of Mexico. The climate of the Southeast is temperate, with long, frost-free seasons that ensure rich vegetation and, as a result, rich animal resources. Rainfall is plentiful, and the soils are relatively drought resistant. Originally, much of the Southeast was forested, and even the uplands had rich resources. At the time of the European invasion, the plentiful wild foods were very important in the diet of native Southeastern Indians, even though cultivated plants had become increasingly important as the economic basis for complex chiefdoms. Limitations on both the technology and the fertility of the soils in these later times led to increasing concentration in the river valleys.

There are, of course, very great differences in the local plant and animal life within the Southeast that are important in understanding the nature of human settlement. Different kinds of strategies and scheduling were required for exploitation of these differences, and the densest populations in the Southeast generally occurred at those locations where the most diverse natural resources were present.

THE PEOPLE

The indigenous peoples of the Southeast were, without exception, American Indians. These and no other were responsible for the massive earthworks and mounds of the Southeast. While human occupancy of the area is not clearly established before 10,000 BC, it is possible and even likely that humans occupied the area even before that time. Physically, the later populations of the Southeast were similar to other people east of the Rocky Mountains, although they may have had slightly larger heads and broader skulls than some neighboring people. Attempts to establish racial classifications of eastern North American populations (e.g., Neumann 1952) have not proved to be particularly useful in understanding the archeology of the Southeast. Present evidence, both of physical type and of other characteristics, such as relationships among the languages spoken in the Southeast, is consistent with a view of relative continuity of population through time.

It would be useful to have a clearer picture of what environmental limitations on population growth existed in the Southeast in prehistoric times. One of the major puzzles is why population was not higher. Endemic disease might have been one factor, but traditional explanations have emphasized widespread warfare. Since population density appears to have much to do with forcing social change, this factor remains a matter of importance for future work. A major difficulty in investigating aboriginal population here, however, is the considerable impact of European diseases between the time of first contact and the period for which good records exist. As a result of epidemics, the early French and English records are not particularly useful in population estimates. For the same reasons, there are problems in using these historic records as a source of analogy for prehistoric social and political organization.

ARCHEOLOGICAL PERIODS

Literally hundreds of local archeological phases and complexes have been defined for this large and diverse province. At the same time, most of these complexes are based on fine distinctions between one locality and another that are not very significant for a general picture of developments. In some areas there have been more general classifications that are useful for the nonspecialist, but in other areas not even a culture-historical chronicle has been agreed upon. Even the areas that are well known, however, are still understood primarily in terms of historical chronicle rather than in terms of the dynamics of social and cultural development.

The traditional discussion of the Southeast has generally been in terms of four stages—Paleo-Indian, Archaic, Woodland, and Mississippian. While these terms are reasonably useful for discussion of the eastern United States as a whole, there are certain difficulties in their application to the Southeast proper. One of the difficulties is that these are stages implying an evolutionary classification, which is fairly accurate for the central eastern United States but is not very appropriate for much of the Southeast. For example, the Early Woodland stage is usually defined as including cultures with the earliest ceramics with cord-roughened exteriors. Such pottery in the Southeast, however, is relatively unimportant as a marker and occurs much later than the first pottery made in the area. Similar problems exist in the use of the term *Mississippian,* since it is a moot question whether some of the most developed cultures of the Southeast can be usefully or even properly described by that term.

For these reasons, these terms will be avoided in this description and neutral period names will be employed in their place as follows:

Paleo-Indian	ca. 10,000 BC–6000 BC
Archaic	6000 BC–700 BC
Sedentary	700 BC–AD 700
Late Prehistoric	AD 700–AD 1540

The duration of these periods is arbitrary, and inclusion in a period is primarily a matter of convenience. At the same time, there are different subsistence bases for most of the cultures in each period that can be characterized for the Southeast as a whole, even if this characterization does not apply to all of the individual archeological complexes (Figure 7.1). For example, both Paleo-Indian and Archaic are periods during which basic subsistence was obtained by hunting and gathering wild foods. The Sedentary period was probably also a time when the major food resources were wild; some domesticated plants were well established, but it is not known how important these were. Although populations were larger and more settled, seasonal movements were probably still very common. During the Late Prehistoric period, most of the people in the Southeast were dependent upon agricultural produce for a major part of their livelihood.

The Paleo-Indian Period

In terms of projectile point and other lithic technology, the Paleo-Indian pioneers of the Southeast used the same tools and weapons as did those of the Great Plains and the Northeast. While projectile points of the Clovis form are

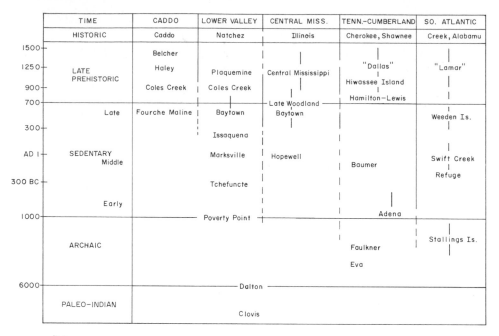

TIME		CADDO	LOWER VALLEY	CENTRAL MISS.	TENN.-CUMBERLAND	SO. ATLANTIC
HISTORIC		Caddo	Natchez	Illinois	Cherokee, Shawnee	Creek, Alabamu
LATE PREHISTORIC		Belcher / Haley / Coles Creek	Plaquemine / Coles Creek	Central Mississippi / Late Woodland	"Dallas" / Hiwassee Island / Hamilton–Lewis	"Lamar"
SEDENTARY	Late	Fourche Maline	Baytown / Issaquena	Baytown		Weeden Is.
	Middle		Marksville / Tchefuncte	Hopewell	Baumer	Swift Creek / Refuge
	Early		Poverty Point		Adena	
ARCHAIC					Faulkner / Eva	Stallings Is.
			Dalton			
PALEO–INDIAN			Clovis			

Time scale (left axis): 1500, 1250, 900, 700, 300, AD 1, 300 BC, 1000, 6000

FIGURE 7.1
Representative archeological complexes in the Southeast. Many regional complexes throughout the Southeast are not included.

not uncommon in the eastern woodlands, the number of actual living or kill sites known is quite small, although it is increasing. As a result, it is difficult to determine the exact character of the Paleo-Indian use of the eastern woodlands environment. Some distributional studies do suggest a concentration on river valley resources, but this finding may also reflect the greater attention these areas have received from both professional archeologists and amateur collectors.

Despite the similarities in technology, the economic basis of the eastern Paleo-Indians may have been different from the big-game-hunting pattern proposed for the Great Plains. In fact, the apparent river valley emphasis may even be taken as an indication that the Paleo-Indian peoples of the East started early to move toward the highly efficient gathering economy usually associated with the following Archaic period.

In any case, both the nature of the sites and the distribution of Clovis projectile points are consistent with the view that the usual Paleo-Indian form of social organization was that of small groups of people moving about an area in response to local availability of plant and animal foods. The number of people living in the Southeast during this period was probably quite small.

Toward the end of the Paleo-Indian period, many areas within the Southeast saw the development of a complex known as Dalton. The Dalton projectile point form and its relatives are somewhat similar to the earlier Clovis points, and it seems likely that the Dalton complex in this and other ways was a development of the earlier Paleo-Indian pattern in response to the particular needs of the Southeastern environment. In some areas, Dalton findspots and sites appear to be more widely distributed than Clovis locations (Morse 1973) and to have less concentration in the river valleys, but the evidence is far from conclusive that this is a general pattern.

As in the Clovis complexes of earlier times, the Dalton peoples utilized a broad range of animals, with major emphasis on the hunting of deer. It is probable that a wide variety of plant foods were eaten as well. At the same time, the evidence shows little indication of specialization of the sort believed to have existed in the later Archaic period.

The Brand site in northeast Arkansas is one of the better-known Dalton sites (Goodyear 1974). Although evidence of diet was unfortunately not directly preserved, it seems that the pattern of exploitation may have been somewhat broader than that suggested by the Dalton levels at the Stanfield-Worley Bluff Shelter in Alabama (DeJarnette et al. 1962). The artifacts at the Brand site show that a number of different kinds of activities were undertaken. Larger Dalton sites in the region are interpreted by Goodyear and Morse as base camps from which parties went out for specialized hunting and gathering activities (Goodyear 1974:106). These larger sites are up to 500 meters across; as with other large sites of hunting and gathering peoples, however, there are problems in determining whether this entire area was occupied at one time. Moreover, it is not known whether these possible larger sites were occupied for much of the year or whether they might represent larger seasonal groupings dependent upon the local availability of some rich food source (as in the case of the large groups that gathered prickly pear in Texas at the time of earliest European contact [Cabeza de Vaca 1972]). It is equally possible that the larger sites may simply be areas that were used over and over again by smaller groups.

One of the important results of the work at the Brand site is that there is strong reason to believe that the Dalton point form was used as a knife as well as a projectile point. The many different "types" of Dalton points thus appear to result, at least partly, from the different wear as well as the resharpening of this class of artifact. This possibility should serve as a caution in the use of such typologies for the definition of social groupings.

The Archaic Period

While not well known by comparison with later times in the Southeast, the Archaic period has been studied extensively in a number of regions. Since one of the outstanding characteristics of the period is the ability of the populations to adapt skillfully to a broad range of local conditions, it is not surprising that there are often considerable differences in Archaic period societies

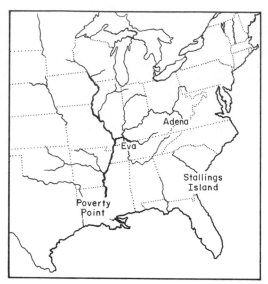

FIGURE 7.2
Archaic and early Sedentary complexes.

from one locality or region to another (Figure 7.2). In most cases, however, the basic strategies employed by Archaic peoples appear to have been similar, despite the differences in technique required for particular locations. The most common pattern of life in this period appears to have been seasonal, with movement from one part of the home range of a band to another area, according to the local availability of resources such as fruits, nuts, fish, and game. In many cases, Archaic peoples in the Southeast made use of a very wide range of plant and animal species—a practice that probably spread and minimized risk by allowing choice in tactics for any given season.

The evidence from Archaic period sites throughout the Southeast makes it clear that the population was usually organized into quite small groups of the sort called bands by political theorists (Service 1962). More recent treatment of this level of social organization by Service (1975) has emphasized the egalitarian nature of such social organizations. In such societies, differences in social status are slight, and decision making is informal and diffuse, at least in comparison with more centralized political systems. Exchange and reciprocity are basic to all social systems, but these relationships are nongovernmental in bands (Service 1975:60–61), despite their importance in interband relationships.

Dispersal of population in small bands would have allowed any given group to react quickly to variation in the local availability of any food resource, at least as long as total population density over the Southeast was fairly low. This flexibility in response would have been particularly important to people who were faced with variation in local food resources from one year to another, and it is known that many of the nut-bearing trees of the area have cycles of high and low yield over periods of two to five years. For peoples who were mobile, who had relatively little capacity or need for long-term storage, and for whom exchange of food and other goods was fairly informal, the ability to shift to other resources or to move to other areas was very important. As population increased throughout Archaic times, however, there would have been increasing pressure upon groups with restricted mobility to develop local resources subject to less annual variation. There would also have been a need to increase the efficiency of exchange and distribution of goods or to improve storage systems to allow carry-over from good year to bad— or all of these pressures could have applied to some degree (see Sahlins 1972). At the same time, the development of such responses also requires more in the way of administration and organization than the simple band organization of most of Archaic times could provide. In Late Archaic, particularly, differences in burial patterns suggest increasing social status differences (for explicit recognition of this farther north, see Binford [1972;388]; for the Southeast, examine the differences in quantity of grave goods from Indian Knoll, Webb [1946]; see also Chapter 6, this volume).

Studies of modern peoples who follow ways of life like those of the Archaic period show that this pattern can be extremely successful so long as population growth does not restrict mobility. However, the seasonal movements in the Southeast at this time did involve some areas, especially along the coasts and rivers, that offered rich opportunities for the development of more sedentary ways of life.

One site that illustrates this shift away from mobility is the Eva site in Tennessee (Lewis and Lewis 1961). Eva is an inland riverbank site with a mound of refuse or midden made up of river clam shells. Such shell midden sites often show evidence of considerable population or, at least, evidence of long-term periodic reuse of the same site. Not all sites of the Eva complex are shell middens, however, and it seems likely that there was still some seasonal movement even for the most settled Archaic period peoples. As suggested by the refuse at some Eva sites, freshwater mussels were an important part of the diet. These people also made full use of the other resources of the area, ranging from deer to nuts. The Eva site itself actually had several archeological phases represented, and later phases such as the Three Mile and Big Sandy phases do show some minor variation in diet. The basic pattern, however, was similar throughout the thousands of years of use of the Eva site area. Deer appear to have been very important as a food animal, and this suggests that upland areas were also important for these riverside people, even though sites in the uplands are rare. The Eva people built structures of some size, but the mass of postholes found at the Eva site made it impossible to tell the size or shape.

The materials used at the Eva site were available in the region (Figure 7.3). Only with the later Three Mile Phase do exotic, imported items such as marine shell and copper objects begin to appear in burials. Thus, between the earlier and later Archaic in the Southeast, there is evidence of the establishment of far-reaching exchange relationships. As shall be seen, these relationships of exchange persisted throughout the remainder of the prehistoric record. The means by which these materials were exchanged were probably informal in Archaic times. But the social situation that had created the need and desire for such materials was very likely part of the cause of status differences that culminated in more systematic exchange or trade networks in the highly stratified societies of the Late Prehistoric period.

Another of the well-known Archaic sites in the same part of the Southeast is the Indian Knoll site in Kentucky (Webb 1946). The settlement of the site was similar to the Eva site, although the nature of the shelters used by the Indian Knoll people is even less certain. Two areas of clay "floor" were found that had hearths and that may have been the floors of structures. These areas were 4.6 meters in diameter and had an area of approximately 14 square meters. If this was a "house," it is likely that only a nuclear family (mother, father, and offspring) lived there. The knoll at Indian Knoll was a shell midden some 1.5 meters high and 120 by 60 meters in dimension. In addition to the shellfish whose remains made up the midden, there were also the bones of a great number of animal species. Substantial amounts of hickory, walnut, and acorn shells were also found.

One of the more striking features of the site, however, was the large number of burials found there. In various excavations at the site, more than 1100 burials were found. Of these, some 31 percent had surviving grave accompaniments (Figure 7.4). Depending upon how "exotic" is to be defined, between 1 and 4 percent of the graves contained exotic items. Among these items were copper objects and decorated pieces made of conch shell from the Gulf or South Atlantic coasts. It is also interesting to note that these valuable (in the archeological sense of requiring greater investment of time to acquire or transport) goods do not seem to be restricted to one particular sex or age group. It has been argued that the presence of grave goods with young children, for example, may be one indication of status distinctions (Binford 1971). To the degree that grave goods represent the fulfillment of social obligations toward the dead person, it is very likely that the existence of such obligations to the young may indicate some social distinctions that are ascribed rather than attained by an individual's own achievements. Much caution is needed in interpreting such remains, but it is likely that the egalitarian societies of the earlier Archaic period were becoming more organized.

By 1700 bc, at least, there were well-established and relatively settled societies along the South Atlantic coast that were quite similar to the Indian Knoll and Eva societies inland. Social groups appear to have been small, and sites generally consist of shell middens on rivers or in coastal swamps. In

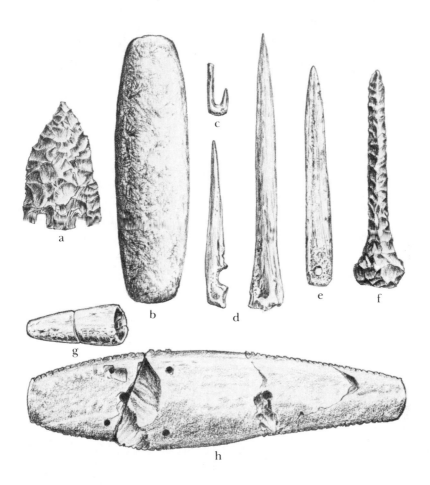

FIGURE 7.3

Artifacts from the Eva site. These artifacts show the specialized tool kit that was characteristic of the Archaic peoples. *a,* Eva point or knife; *b,* pestle; *c,* bone fishhook; *d,* bone awl; *e,* bone needle; *f,* drill; *g,* tubular pipe; *h,* gorget. (From *Prehistory of North America,* 2d ed., by Jesse D. Jennings. Copyright © 1968, 1974 by McGraw-Hill, Inc. Used with permission of McGraw-Hill Book Company.)

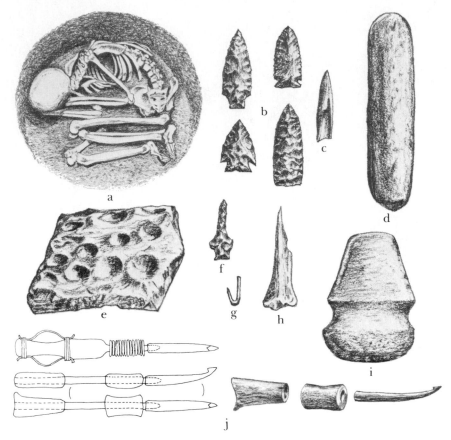

FIGURE 7.4

Materials from Indian Knoll, Kentucky. Like the Eva complexes, the Archaic peoples of Indian Knoll had a complex kit of tools. Large numbers of burials were found at the site, and some beginnings of social stratification may be seen in differences in grave accompaniments. *a*, flexed burial at Indian Knoll; *b*, projectile points and knives; *c*, bone projectile point; *d*, pestle; *e*, nutting stone; *f*, drill; *g*, bone fishhook; *h*, bone awl; *i*, grooved ax; *j*, atlatl (spear thrower). (From *Prehistory of North America*, 2d ed., by Jesse D. Jennings. Copyright © 1968, 1974 by McGraw-Hill, Inc. Used with permission of McGraw-Hill Book Company.)

fact, aside from some engraved bone not unlike material from Indian Knoll, there would be nothing remarkable about these sites at all, were it not for the very early manufacture of pottery there. The pottery itself is fairly simple, consisting of round bowls with occasional drag-and-jab decoration in the wet clay. Fiber was added to the clay before the vessel was formed; accordingly, the appearance of such pottery has led to the "fiber-tempered pottery horizon" designation (Figure 7.5). Both in form and in the addition of fiber temper, the South Atlantic early pottery is very like the earliest pottery of northern South America, and it is quite possible that there is some direct re-

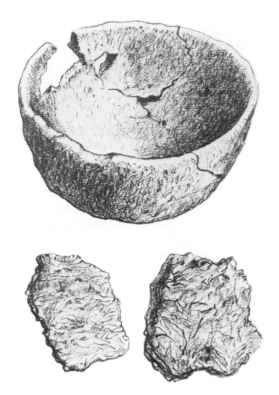

FIGURE 7.5
The earliest pottery of the Southeast is simple in form and has various kinds of fiber inclusions added to the clay. (From *Prehistory of North America,* 2d ed., by Jesse D. Jennings. Copyright © 1968, 1974 by McGraw-Hill, Inc. Used with permission of McGraw-Hill Book Company.)

lationship between the two areas as proposed by James A. Ford (1969). At the same time, there is considerable debate over just how similar phases such as Stalling Island in Georgia and others in northern Florida really are to supposed South American antecedents. Many of the comparisons presented by Ford become less convincing when examined closely either from a structural point of view or in terms of the nature of the complexes from which the comparisons are drawn.

The Sedentary Period

The definition of archeological periods is always arbitrary, but the distinction between the societies of the later Archaic period and the earlier Sedentary period is an exceptionally good example of the problems of constructing such units. While there are important and major differences between, say, 2000 BC and 200 BC, it is not clear just where the line between these two times should be drawn. Fortunately, the definition of periods is merely a terminological problem, so 700 BC is used, being as good a starting date as any for the Sedentary period.

By 700 BC, moreover, societies in the Southeast and along the southern border of the Northeast had already changed in some significant, and some not so significant, ways. Perhaps the most widespread of the changes from the Archaic period was the wide acceptance of ceramic technology over most of eastern North America. This new technology had, of course, been developed in the Southeastern Archaic some 1000 years before; but it was only with the coming of the Sedentary period that it came to be accepted over the entire area. It is not likely that this acceptance indicated any great changes in the lifeway of the Southeast, but it may be that the spread of pottery making was a reflection of greater permanence of settlement. In the Southeast, some, but not all, of the pottery by this time had cord-roughened exteriors and was of the sort called Woodland in the Northeast. Even though pottery probably made little difference in lifeways, pottery making is important because it provides archeologists with a diverse, "sensitive," and virtually indestructible set of artifacts. After the beginning of the Sedentary period, virtually all of the archeological "phases" in the Southeast are based more on ceramic similarities and differences than on any other one thing.

Another of the major innovations of the early Sedentary is far more impressive to the nonspecialist than pottery. The construction of earthen mounds in the lower Mississippi valley may actually have started in later Archaic times, but both in the lower valley and on the northern border of the Southeast, in the Ohio valley, quite large mounds were being constructed by the start of the Sedentary period. The two outstanding examples of these developments are the Poverty Point culture of Louisiana and the Adena culture of the Ohio valley. The dating of the Poverty Point complex is still somewhat unsettled, but it probably started after 1300 BC and persisted well into the Sedentary period. To the north, many Adena sites are outside the Southeast, but the Adena complex as a whole is as much a part of Southeastern prehistory as it is of Northeastern. In the remainder of the Southeast, mound building did not appear quite so early as it did on the periphery, but mounds were common by 300 BC.

In the northern areas, early mound building was often linked to the burial of what seem to have been very high-status people. Even at the beginning, however, mound constructions such as those at Poverty Point were not primarily burial mounds, and, by the end of the Sedentary period in the Southeast, some areas seem to have developed platform and perhaps even substructure mounds that foreshadow the developments of the Late Prehistoric. Some later Sedentary mounds may have been more oriented toward literal and figurative elevation of the living than toward the honorable disposal of the dead.

The early mound building of the Southeast was often truly monumental. At Moundsville, West Virginia, the Grave Creek Mound built by the Adena people is over 20 meters high. At Poverty Point, the diameter of the whole mound complex is some 1200 meters. Moundbuilding on this scale probably means greater sedentism, and it certainly implies greater organization.

As might be guessed, the most significant changes between the Sedentary and Archaic periods were the alterations of social organization and settlement. The social system did not become more complex overnight, even though the archeological evidence seems to show dramatic and rapid development in areas of the technology that were related to social status. Mound building was the most dramatic of all of these, but the production of "ceremonial" items of all kinds increased in ways that required extensive exchange networks tying all of eastern North America together. In the north, the most developed center for this exchange has come to be called the Hopewellian Interaction Sphere. The Southeast was directly involved in this interaction (read "exchange") sphere, and some Southeastern peoples had access to materials such as conch shells and galena that appear to have been highly prized in the value system of the time. In the lower Mississippi valley, there was a direct participant in the Hopewellian "culture" called Marksville. In other areas of the Southeast, there were societies that participated less completely in the Hopewellian system but that show many resemblances to Marksville and Hopewell.

The causes of all of these developments are difficult to identify. In the earlier years of modern Southeastern archeology it was believed that the construction of large mounds was a direct reflection of surplus productive capacity, which was thought to have been a result of the introduction of maize agriculture (for example, J. Ford 1969:45). Archeologists found it difficult to believe that nonagricultural people could have built such substantial and impressive monuments without some means of growing their food. Since the obvious center of mound construction in the New World was Mexico, and since maize and the other produce of New World agriculture were also Mexican, it was thought that mound construction and agriculture were both introduced as a package from Mesoamerica. But recent work in the eastern United States has created some problems for this theory of development and diffusion. While Mesoamerican crops are definitely the basis for developments in the Late Prehistoric period, maize simply does not appear to have been an exceptionally important food plant for the Sedentary period peoples, even though some maize was grown. Furthermore, the Mesoamerican food complex of maize, beans, and squash was not introduced all at one time into the Southeast. Domesticated cucurbit appears to have been used well back into the Archaic period, maize begins to show up in small quantities around 300 BC, and beans were not important until the Late Prehistoric period.

Faced with the lack of evidence for intensive growing of Mesoamerican crops, some archeologists have suggested that native crops may have been

domesticated in eastern North America. Thus, it was thought that the cultivation of the sunflower, goosefoot (*Chenopodium*), sumpweed (*Iva*), and other
plants along river bottoms might have formed the economic basis for sedentism and social development in the Sedentary period (Struever 1964:96–103).
Even earlier, however, it had been suggested that the rich environment of the
Southeast might have allowed development of fairly complex societies without an agricultural basis through what was called primary forest efficiency
(Caldwell 1958:30). All of these theories about the origins of the Sedentary
and its northern relatives, Early and Middle Woodland, share the same emphasis on the idea that the "cause" of complex social organization is surplus
economic production. Of the three, Caldwell's theory comes closest to appre-
ciating the degree to which social organization itself can have a major part
to play in the economic life of a people. Richard I. Ford has suggested a
model for a nonagricultural system requiring complex social organization for
the northern Hopewell. Ford's idea is that the complex social status differences in Middle Woodland may have been part of a method of ensuring
intraarea exchange that would allow relatively permanent settlement and
dense population despite the variability in production of wild foods within
an area from year to year (R. I. Ford 1974:403ff).

The importance of Ford's suggestion is that it emphasizes the organizational and distributive aspects of Sedentary life, rather than focusing all of
the attention on means of production. Taken as a whole, the Southeast was
probably capable of supporting much larger populations of humans than it
actually did, even at the peak of the Sedentary period. Many of the limitations that are placed on a collecting economy in an area are due to the
variability of yield of various resources from one year to another. As already
discussed, this variability was probably a major factor in maintaining relatively low populations in Archaic times. Malthusian principles suggest,
however, that it is common for a species to outbreed the carrying capacity of
its environment. There are several possible responses to such population pressure: reduction of population through famine or other causes, an increase in
the economic "production" of the population, or an increase in the efficiency
of distribution of food within the population. If human beings take this last
course, it usually becomes necessary to create a "bureaucracy" to administer
the distribution system. It would be too strong to say that this administrative
function was the sole purpose of the high-status leadership that seems to have
developed in Sedentary times; nevertheless, even if new production capa-
bility eventually proves to have been the main impetus behind the Early
Sedentary florescence, the archeological evidence shows that an administrative mechanism also proved necessary.

In all, probably no one cause was responsible for all of the developments
throughout the whole area; but the most impressive developments seem to
have come in areas that had not seen much elaboration in the Late Archaic
of ca. 2000 BC. This may indicate that the causes of the Adena and Poverty

Point complexes are to be found in the interplay and feedback of new sources of food and increasing organization of population. The existence of such relatively highly organized societies would have had considerable impact upon their neighbors, who might have found themselves with the choice of being absorbed, driven out of their territories, or organizing themselves along similar lines. Thus, it comes as no surprise to learn that by 300 BC many societies in the Southeast had either become part of the Hopewell Interaction Sphere or had organized similar, if smaller, networks of their own.

The Sedentary period as a whole may be divided into several equally arbitrary subdivisions. The early Sedentary can be taken to refer to the time from 700 BC to 300 BC, corresponding to the later part of Adena and Poverty Point. Middle Sedentary would be from 300 BC to AD 300, corresponding to the Marksville (Louisiana) and Santa Rosa-Swift Creek complexes (Florida). The late Sedentary (AD 300–AD 700) is represented by the Weeden Island complex of Florida and southern Georgia.

The Adena complex is the best known and most obvious of the early Sedentary complexes, but because it is covered more fully in Chapter 6, the discussion here will focus on the Poverty Point complex of Louisiana (Broyles and Webb 1970). As already indicated, the Poverty Point complex started before the arbitrary beginning of the Sedentary period, but it did continue into the early Sedentary. Unfortunately, the dating of the Poverty Point complex as a whole still presents some problems to archeologists, and the actual time of construction of the impressive earthworks at the Poverty Point site has not been firmly determined. Radiocarbon dates from Poverty Point "period" sites have ranged from 1700 to 870 BC, with an average of radiocarbon dates and thermoluminescence dates being close to 1200 BC. However, these dates do not provide us with the critical information of when Poverty Point people began to build massive mounds and earthworks.

The Poverty Point site itself consists of a large semi-circular earthwork of concentric ridges, one large mound, and some other smaller features (Figure 7.6). James Ford and Clarence Webb, who excavated the site, felt that the ridged mounds had accumulated through occupation by a planned and organized village. This semicircular pattern of settlement is characteristic of Poverty Point sites that have mound construction, but only at the Poverty Point site did mound construction actually achieve such scale that it seems likely that something more than an "Archaic" form of social organization was present. Other Poverty Point sites are not so impressive.

Sites of the Poverty Point and closely related Jaketown phases occur along tributaries of the Mississippi River and in other locations where wetland resources are available. Other similar complexes are found in similar environments throughout the lower Mississippi valley. What are known as Poverty Point objects—lumps of baked clay in various shapes—are found over this area at the same time as the Poverty Point complex, but this should not be taken as an indication of some vast network of social relationships (Figure

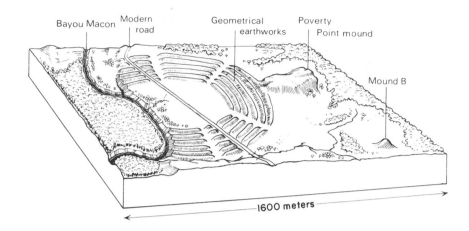

FIGURE 7.6
Poverty Point, Louisiana. The enormous earthworks at Poverty Point are among the earliest large-scale construction in the New World. It is thought that the geometrical banks may be debris from occupation. (From *Prehistory of North America*, 2d ed., by Jesse D. Jennings. Copyright © 1968, 1974 by McGraw-Hill, Inc. Used with permission of McGraw-Hill Book Company.)

7.7). The wide valley floor of the lower Mississippi has very little rock; and people who wished to use the technique of "stone boiling" had to make their own "stones" out of clay in order to cook their food. Even the more tightly defined microlithic stone tool industries of the Poverty Point "culture" are of little help in pinning down the limits of Poverty Point social and political units.

The large mound at Poverty Point is nearly 23 meters high and has a diameter of approximately 200 meters. As already indicated, this is many times larger than other Poverty Point mounds and, in fact, is at least twice the size of the more or less contemporary Olmec mound at La Venta in Mexico, even though the La Venta mound is somewhat taller. The scale of this construction and the far-reaching exchange relations of the Poverty Point sites suggest that this Southeastern society had developed social institutions that were qualitatively different from those of earlier times. In fact, the Poverty Point society was probably the first "chiefdom" of the eastern United States and may have been as early as such developments anywhere in the New World. The importance of Poverty Point as an early mound center, however, should not obscure the relative lack of success of the system in this area. After Poverty Point times, nearly a thousand years were to pass before such a level was once again reached. The reasons for this decline are not known, but any theory of the formation of such units will have to account for this failure.

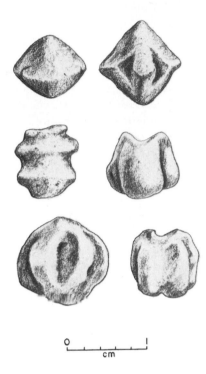

0 ⌞___⌞___⌞___⌟ 1
cm

FIGURE 7.7

So-called Poverty Point objects are widely found in the lower Mississippi valley. These baked clay lumps are known in many shapes and were probably used as substitutes for "boiling stones." Although they are very common in the Poverty Point complex, they are also found elsewhere in the area. (From *Prehistory of North America*, 2d ed., by Jesse D. Jennings. Copyright © 1968, 1974 by McGraw-Hill, Inc. Used with permission of McGraw-Hill Book Company.)

Not much is known of the life of the ordinary Poverty Point person. Methods of house construction in Poverty Point sites are poorly understood; house size appears to have been small. The presence of stone hoes that show distinctive polish patterns has led to the suggestion that Poverty Point peoples were agricultural, but it can also be suggested that people who are building large earth mounds will need digging tools whether they are agricultural or not. Domesticated squash is known to be present in Poverty Point (R. Ford 1974:401), but the present evidence and the evidence from later complexes in the same area suggest that domesticated plants did not play an important role in the diet of the early Sedentary peoples. As discussed above, it is likely that these and other early Sedentary peoples were highly efficient hunters and gatherers whose complexity of social organization was a means of improving distribution of goods.

Poverty Point sites do have some pottery that is similar to the fiber-tempered pottery of the South Atlantic coast, but steatite bowls are equally common. Neither form of vessel seems to have been important. Crude pottery figurines also occur. James Ford has described some of these traits of the Poverty Point complex as being indicative of Mesoamerican or South American influence on the early Southeast. Actually, even if it were to be accepted that the Poverty Point and Mesoamerican complexes were connected, the direction of influence would be uncertain. The presence of domesticated squash and the later introduction of maize do represent influence from Mesoamerica, but this is no indication of the direction of flow for other kinds of relationships. In any case, the entire question of "influence" and "direction" is largely irrelevant to any attempt to understand the development of societies. The mere introduction of a technology or an "idea" does not explain or cause developments. The local society, whether innovating or accepting, still can develop only so far as the local social and environmental conditions permit. People do not form chiefdoms because someone has told them how wonderful chiefdoms are but because such organizations are necessary to cope with local problems. In any case, the similarities that are cited by James Ford— circular settlements, crude figurines, fiber-tempered pottery, and so on—are not very specific; to see similarity in these traits depends upon the examiner's conviction that external contacts are necessary to account for the development of societies. Regardless of these possible external connections, it is the lack of good information about the local reasons for chiefdom organization that is the greatest weakness of Poverty Point studies. It simply is not known what features of early Sedentary life led to the organization of the centralized societies implied by the mounds at Poverty Point.

The times immediately after Poverty Point were characterized by complexes that were much less organized. The lifeways of the Tchula, Tchefuncte, Refuge, and other "Early Woodland" phases in the Southeast seem little different from those of Archaic times and are certainly not comparable to Poverty Point or Adena societies. A major marker for this time period is the spread of surface-textured (usually cord-marked) pottery. In the northern part of the Southeast, the Adena complex continued and is connected with the later Hopewellian developments of the middle Sedentary. There are some ceramic continuities in the coastal ceramic complexes, such as Bayou La Batre, and later techniques in other areas of the Southeast; in general, however, the main development in the Southeast during the period between Poverty Point and Marksville was the return to less centralized, presumably more egalitarian social structures.

The middle Sedentary period developments in the Southeast proper began once again to show signs of greater organization, largely as an echo of the Hopewellian Interaction Sphere of the Northeast (Figure 7.8). The mechanisms explaining these developments in the Southeast are not entirely clear, but it seems certain that exchanges of raw materials and finished goods played

FIGURE 7.8
Middle and late Sedentary complexes.

an important part in the stimulation of ranked societies in the area. The best example of a direct relationship between the Southeast and the Northeastern Hopewellian is the Marksville culture of the lower Mississippi valley. For this middle Sedentary period, the similarities of Marksville pottery, mound construction, and other features of those of the Hopewell are very strong (Figure 7.9). In fact, the similarities are so strong that it is even possible that actual movement of populations was partly responsible for the development of Marksville. The best present evidence suggests that Marksville is somewhat later than Illinois Hopewell, so the temporal relationships are consistent with such an idea. At the same time, the stylistic connections of Marksville art and Hopewell art may rather suggest that local complexes in the Mississippi valley adopted a Hopewell way of life. It is interesting to note that it is only in the lower part of the Mississippi valley that "Hopewellian markers" are commonly found in association with village debris (Phillips 1970:901), while in most Hopewellian complexes such goods are largely restricted to mortuary contexts.

Settlement in the lower Mississippi valley during the middle Sedentary showed much the same pattern as in earlier times, an increase in the density

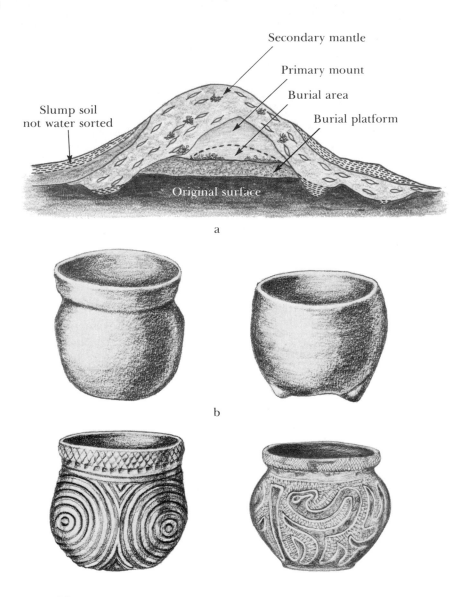

Secondary mantle

Primary mount

Burial area

Burial platform

Slump soil
not water sorted

Original surface

a

b

FIGURE 7.9
Marksville complex. This Hopewell-related complex in the lower Mississippi valley has
many similarities to the Hopewell of Illinois and of Ohio. *a,* a Marksville burial mound;
b, Marksville pottery. (From *Prehistory of North America,* 2d ed., by Jesse D. Jennings.
Copyright © 1968, 1974 by McGraw-Hill, Inc. Used with permission of McGraw-Hill
Book Company.)

of settlement being the major change. But this is largely a reflection of the limited range of choices for settlement sites in this area if one wished to keep his feet dry. Elsewhere in the Southeast, settlement of the middle Sedentary showed an increasing emphasis on riverine locations, a trend that began in the later Archaic and continued up to the European invasion. Examples of middle Sedentary groups that were less directly linked into the Hopewellian Interaction Sphere include Copena in Alabama, so called because of the frequency with which copper and galena are found in the area, and the Santa Rosa and Swift Creek complexes of northern Florida and southern Georgia. In these areas, burial mounds occur, and the ceramics show some similarities to Illinois and Ohio Hopewell; but the scale of the societies seems to have been smaller. Thus, while it might be suggested that the northern Hopewell "leaders" achieved their positions through their social roles in local distributive networks, it seems likely that the high status of individuals in many parts of the Southeast was more directly a result of the position of those individuals in externally oriented networks of exchange.

Although maize is known to have been present in Hopewellian times in the Southeast and Northeast, the evidence still suggests that cultivated plants played a relatively small part in the diet. Outside of the Marksville complexes, there is little indication that redistribution of foodstuffs may have been important for survival, if indeed such was the case in Marksville itself. Population pressure in the Southeast was steadily increasing, but local productive capacities seem to have kept ahead of economic needs through much of this time. The distribution of exotic materials throughout the Southeast in middle Sedentary times appears to find closer analogies with the nature of status and distribution of goods in Melanesia than with the more highly centralized and ranked societies of Polynesia. That is to say, the possession of exotic goods and of status itself may have been more often *achieved* by Southeastern "leaders" than inherited by them through membership in chiefly or royal lineages. This, of course, must remain a moot point until more effort is expended in the Southeast on archeological testing of such hypotheses.

So far, the Southeast has been seen as rather less developed in terms of social organization than the southern Northeast. Ironically, this may be a reflection of the greater carrying capacity of the Southeastern environment. It may simply be that the Southeastern swamps, river valleys, and woodlands were so rich in resources that a relatively high density of population was possible without the need for the centralized bureaucracies discussed earlier. When the cubic volumes of burial mounds in the Southeast are examined, it will be seen that the amount of labor involved in such constructions is usually not greater than that which might be locally available as a result of reciprocal obligations to important persons or Big Men (Service 1975:72–73). Increasing population pressure, requiring more efficient production and distribution systems as well as creating an increased need for maintenance of order, may sometimes have caused such societies to become "chiefdoms" characterized by an increasing emphasis on inheritance of authority, economic redistribution, and centralization of power (Service 1975).

The decline of Hopewell in the Northeast has been attributed to many causes, ranging from "peasant revolt" (very unlikely) to climatic shifts that lowered the carrying capacity of the environment below that point for which efficiency of distribution could compensate (possible). One of the problems in the climatic interpretation, however, is that the population of eastern North America may have actually increased following the decline of Hopewell. Population estimates for such large areas are bound to be uncertain at best, but northern Late Woodland phases often seem to be represented by more and larger sites than the earlier phases in the areas. To some extent this is a reflection of the greater mobility of late Sedentary peoples, but it may also be true that this increase was caused by some new breakthrough in productive capacity that caused the redistributive mechanisms of Hopewellian times to become redundant. It would be pleasing if it could be shown that this development toward greater local autonomy and more egalitarian organization was related to an increasing importance of cultivated plants. This does not seem to have been the case, however. R. I. Ford (1974:402–403) has suggested that these changes may be due in some part to the introduction of the bow and arrow. As attractive as this interpretation is, it unfortunately does not explain why mound building and other features of the Hopewellian time period survived in the Southeast long after the decline of Hopewell in the Northeast. While the culture of the northern part of the Southeast during late Sedentary times was very similar to that of the Northeastern Late Woodland, the southern Southeast in late Sedentary times was characterized by a continuation of extensive mound building and by the development of platform and even substructure mounds. Even though the distribution of exotic goods did not cease in the north, it was much curtailed; the southern area appears to have experienced increased exchange of such goods during this period.

The direct continuity between the late Sedentary and the Late Prehistoric periods is very clear in a late Marksville phase known as Issaquena (Greengo 1964; Phillips 1970). Although it is true that ceramic discontinuities exist, it is apparent that the Issaquena construction of platform mounds of some size (Phillips 1970:544–545) indicates the persistence of more centralized organization. By the earlier part of the Late Prehistoric period, the Baytown period phases of the southern Mississippi valley already showed many of the characteristics of the later Mississippian complexes of the northern Southeast. This is not to say that the Mississippian cultures developed from Baytown, but merely to observe that the many continuities between middle Sedentary and Late Prehistoric make the Mississippian "renaissance" much less spectacular when viewed from the south than when viewed from a northern perspective. Moreover, the lower Mississippi valley is not the only place where

▲ Kolomoki
⚊ Weeden Island
⚊ Lamar

FIGURE 7.10
Kolomoki site, Georgia. A large Weeden Island site with evidence of complex site planning.
(After Sears 1953.)

there was no decline following the middle Sedentary. In Florida and in southern Georgia, the Weeden Island complex is, if anything, more impressive than
the Marksville-Baytown developments. Most Weeden Island sites are not
enormously complex, but the Kolomoki site in southern Georgia is a clear
example that the post-Hopewellian decline of the north was not a pan-eastern
phenomenon.

The Kolomoki site is located on a small creek tributary of the Chattahoo-
chee River in an area with good water sources and a diverse local environment
(Figure 7.10). The site covers some 1.2 million square meters and has numerous small "burial" mounds and a large mound nearly 17 meters in height
that is square with a relatively flat top. In short, this mound is very much like
the (probably) later substructure mounds of the Late Prehistoric in general
and the Mississippian culture in particular. The mounds at Kolomoki and at
other Weeden Island sites, however, are possibly platform mounds rather
than clearly substructure mounds, although it may be that structures were
erected atop the mounds. At Kolomoki it was difficult to find any trace of
structures of any kind, although areas of refuse about 9 meters in diameter
and scattered postholes were found (Sears 1956:9). In any case, many of the
mounds did have burial functions like those of the earlier Sedentary. The
ceramics that were found associated with the burials are extremely elaborate

FIGURE 7.11
An elaborate mortuary vessel from Kolomoki.
(After Sears 1953.)

vessels of the sort which are clearly "nonfunctional" in terms of ordinary activities such as cooking or eating (Figure 7.11).

The scale and overall organization of the Kolomoki site suggests that it was based on some effective economic system, but, unfortunately, very little information as to its nature is available. Because Sears mistakenly thought that the Kolomoki materials were from the same time as the Mississippian developments farther north, it was suggested that an agricultural basis for the society was likely (1956:95). However, no charred vegetal materials were recovered by the techniques used at the time of the excavation, so this question must await further work before it can be resolved. As has already been seen, squash and maize had been introduced into the Southeast much earlier, but present evidence still does not suggest heavy dependence on these or other cultigens.

If the size of midden areas is related to the size of residential units, it would be likely that a residential group here consisted of no more than 15 to 20 persons. Sears suggests that the construction of one mound stage of Mound D was completed in one season and that this implies a work group of about 1000 persons (1956:93). Actually, the volume of the mound in question is only about 700 cubic meters; even given a very conservative figure of 0.5 cubic meters per person per day, the volume of the mound could be accounted for by some 350 people working for four days. Since the mound has at least four building stages, it may be that the labor force was even less. The mounds are large, but that may imply more about the organization of the workers than about the extraordinary size of the labor force. In this case, as in so many others, Southeastern archeologists have come to realize that population size is not the only critical variable in mound-building activity. The size of the mounds at Kolomoki does not necessarily imply a resident or subject population exceeding that known for the area in the time of early European intrusion. On the basis of estimates of village area, however, a population of 1000 people at Kolomoki is not unreasonable. Indication of some complexity of social organization is provided not only by the size of the population, the size of the mounds, and the layout of the site, but also by the probable practice of retainer sacrifice at the death of important persons and by the impressive amount of energy expended on grave goods. While none of these traits by itself is necessarily indicative of a society organized on a level above that of a tribe, the total picture does suggest that Kolomoki was a chiefdom at a time when most societies in the eastern woodlands of North America were socially and politically much less organized.

The causes of the Kolomoki florescence at a time when most eastern and even Weeden Island peoples possessed a less elaborate social organization are not clear. The "fall" of the Hopewell Interaction Sphere of the middle Sedentary did not mean a cessation of all exchange of exotic goods, but this exchange was reduced enough in volume to make it unlikely that Kolomoki is to be explained in terms of control of trade. It may even be that the relative complexity of societies on and near the Gulf coast and in the lower Mississippi valley during this period is partly a reflection of greater need for centralized authority in order to maintain the population there. Resolution of this problem is impossible with the present information about the nature of the economic bases for these societies.

In general, the Sedentary period is of enormous interest. The elaborate earthworks and beautifully executed art objects of the Sedentary peoples of the Southeast, like those of the Northeast, are evidence of increasing political and social complexity. Unlike developments in the Northeast, however; in the Southeast the development of centralized and status-oriented societies did not falter in the late Sedentary period. The factors that led to the technological developments of the Sedentary have not been learned from the archeological record. It can be suggested that population pressure played an important part in encouraging these developments, but the reasons for supposing that sedentism led to increased population in one area and not in another have not been fully explored, much less tested.

The development of platform mounds, and probably of substructure mounds as well, in the late Southeastern Sedentary is only one of a number of indications that link the Southeastern Sedentary period very closely to the developments of the Late Prehistoric period. It would be too strong a statement to say that the late Sedentary complexes like Weeden Island and Issaquena somehow "caused" the development of Late Prehistoric cultures like the Mississippian. Nonetheless, it is likely that many of the iconographic and technical continuities that exist between middle Sedentary complexes like the Hopewell and the Late Prehistoric Mississippian are at least partly due to the continuity of complex social organization in the Southeast. Even in ceramics, the similarities that led to the mistaken idea that Kolomoki was on the Mississippian time level are an indication of the extent to which Weeden Island and similar complexes are precursors of later developments. The possible origin of the substructure (so-called temple) mound in Weeden Island and Issaquena is also of considerable importance. It is possible that the substructure mound is an introduction from Mesoamerica, but in the Mississippi valley and in southern Georgia and northern Florida there is what appears to be a sequential development from the conical burial mound to the platform mound to the substructure mound. Whether this is a purely local development or whether it was introduced from outside, the substructure mound (like the earlier mounds) is an artifact reflecting increased social complexity and organization. As such, the introduction, development, and acceptance of mound construction in a given culture has to be related to changes in the organization of that culture, regardless of the origin of the trait itself.

In other areas of the Southeast, the later Sedentary period was much less impressive in terms of material remains and, not surprisingly, has often received less archeological attention. In the Tennessee and Cumberland drainages, the archeological cultures of the time were generally similar to the Late Woodland of the Northeast. Here and there in the Southeast there were some survivals of burial mound construction as in the Hamilton phase of eastern Tennessee. Some status goods such as shell from the coast continued to be exchanged, but as these features were even found in the Late Archaic, it is not surprising that they are found in Late Woodland complexes.

The usual explanation of the Late Woodland has been that it was a period of decline following the high achievements of the Hopewellian. It should be understood that this is more an assumption than a view that is supported by empirical evidence. While it is true that monumental construction and elaborate works of art are uncommon in the Late Woodland, it is possible that population may actually have increased in many areas. On the northern fringes of the Southeast, at least some Late Woodland complexes are known from large numbers of sites in a great variety of local environments. The number of Late Woodland sites is no doubt partly due to a seasonal pattern of population movement, but to some extent it does appear that larger populations may have been present in Late Woodland times than in Hopewellian times. The reasons for this are difficult to sort out. It would be tempting to suggest that the increase in population resulted from new production capabilities. As already indicated, R. I. Ford has suggested that the bow and arrow may have played a part in severing the exchange relations of the East (1974: 402–403). Perhaps even more important than the "severing" of the routes would have been the effect of improved hunting tools, which could have made the local community more independent of both those routes and the local redistributive network. It would also be tempting to suggest that agriculture became more important after the fall of Hopewell, but the best present evidence seems to show even less evidence of agriculture in Late Woodland than in Hopewell (R. I. Ford 1974; Kuttruff n.d.).

Whatever the causes, the central part of the North American East, including both areas in the Northeast and in the Southeast, was less organized socially than in the preceding part of the Sedentary. By the traditional criteria this means that the people were less "advanced," but it may be that the real advancement of the period was in finding ways to survive well on a local level without surrendering local authority to centralized tyrants and chiefs.

The Late Prehistoric Period

An increasing dependence upon agriculture for livelihood was the most significant change of the Late Prehistoric period. While earlier peoples had domesticated plants, some imported from Mesoamerica and others native, present information suggests that basic foodgetting did not depend primarily on domesticated plants until the beginning of the eighth or ninth century of the Christian era. It may be that this change did begin earlier in complexes like Weeden Island, but most of the Late Woodland complexes to the north seem still to have depended primarily on wild foods. Granted that the evidence on this problem is incomplete, the change to an agricultural economic base seems to have taken place very rapidly, as these things go. The causes of the change are also not clear. New varieties of maize do seem to have been introduced about this time, and it is likely that the bean (*Phaseolus vulgaris*) appeared in the Southeast about this time. Whatever caused Southeastern peoples to become more agricultural, the process, once started, was largely irreversible. The more important agriculture became, the more necessary it would be to have centralized, redistributive authorities. The more centralized the economic controls and population were, the more agriculture was necessary for survival (cf. R. I. Ford 1974:406–407).

At the same time, it must be remembered that the Southeastern peoples never became totally dependent on agriculture in the strictest sense. The best evidence shows that some wild foods, especially nuts of various kinds, were important sources of protein and fats. Techiques such as flotation have dramatically increased our knowledge of prehistoric diet, and these data tend to correct for earlier viewpoints that agriculture was all important. Indeed, if the historic record for the Southeast is examined, it will be seen that the earliest European accounts of the interior Southeast, in 1539 and 1540, indicate that nuts were important then (account of the Gentleman of Elvas, Buckingham Smith translation 1866: 43, 47, 131, and elsewhere). A diet of maize, beans, squash, and nuts, especially if supplemented with greens, would be well balanced even without the game that appears to have been plentiful.

If hunting became less important for survival, warfare seems to have become more important. Late Prehistoric sites throughout the Southeast were often well fortified. It is tempting to see the rise of fortified centers, and to some degree even the growth of centralized and stratified societies, as a result of competition for scarce agricultural land in the face of growing population. Such situations have been seen by some as directly responsible for the origins of the political units known as states (Carneiro 1970; Service 1975:43–44). It is also important to remember that the Southeast does not present the same opportunities for agriculture to hoe cultivators that it did to European farmers with draught animals and plows. American Indian agriculture in the area was largely restricted to the fertile river valleys.

These restrictions on aboriginal agriculture, together with the use of rivers as transportation avenues, meant that Southeastern settlement patterns became even more river oriented in the Late Prehistoric than previously. Not only did the river valley environments offer rich wild resources in plants and animals; they also offered considerable areas of rich soils that were continually renewed by alluviation.

It is likely that a major function of the high-status individuals of Late Prehistoric societies was to control the operation of the economy. Most archeological attempts (e.g., Sears 1968) to deal with the sociology of the Late Prehistoric have assumed that the form of economic structure was that known as redistribution (Sahlins 1972:188), but very little has been done to test this idea.

An increase in the widespread exchange of goods is another important feature of Late Prehistoric life; the quantity of imperishable goods exchanged may even have exceeded that of the middle Sedentary. It is likely that many perishable goods that have not been recovered by archeologists were also exchanged, but the importance of the goods that have been found was undoubtedly very great. These goods were almost certainly not money in anything like our sense of the term, but the desire for such items was probably both a stimulus for and a result of exchange of other goods more necessary for survival.

There are at least two divergent views of the level of political organization in the Southeast in Late Prehistoric times. One view has been that the peoples of the Southeast were organized on the political level known as the state (Sears 1968), while others have seen the dominant political form in the area as being like the chiefdoms of the historic Southeast. It must not be forgotten that even the earliest records from the Southeast do describe societies that had already felt the impact of European influences, including diseases; even so, most present definitions of *state* would not apply to Southeastern Late Prehistoric societies, with perhaps a few exceptions, such as Cahokia.

Possibly the most important question in Southeastern archeology is why states did not develop in the Southeast. The conditions of environmental limitations on agricultural land ("circumscription"), limited routes of exchange, and chiefdoms ready to make the transition are all present. Why, then, did only a few, at best, of these societies develop into states (or even into "Archaic civilizations"), and why did the few examples of possible states in the area not survive? Perhaps climate is some part of the answer; it is notable that the temperate north of Europe was late in developing states. More likely, population pressure was just not high enough to force the development of such organizations, but the reasons for relatively low population are not known. Warfare has been suggested as a cause of low population, but warfare has led toward the formation of state more often than away. Cases like those of eastern North America show that there are factors in the development of states that are not well understood and that must be dealt with in any comprehensive theory of political and social development.

The complex called Mississippian dominated the Late Prehistoric period in the Southeast (Figure 7.12). Even so, many areas in the Southeast did not see the development of Mississippian proper. Moreover, some of the largest Mississippian sites are outside of the Southeast as it is usually defined. All the same, it should be noted that these sites in Illinois and Indiana, for example, are in riverine extensions of the Southeastern environments, as shown by their location just inside the northern limits of the area where cypress trees grow.

The problem of defining *Mississippian,* unfortunately, is much more complex than deciding that it is predominantly a Southeastern phenomenon. Some archeologists tend to see all of the Late Prehistoric societies of the Southeast as having been Mississippian to one degree or another, pointing to the widespread construction of substructure mounds and certain other technical features as indications of unity within the area. Others have tended to define the Mississippian complex very narrowly as a specific ceramic tradition characterized by particular vessel forms such as the bottle and hooded effigy vessel. The first view stresses area unity; the second emphasizes local diversity. In order to find a way out of these differences of interpretation, a recent conference has suggested naming the broader concept the Mid-South Tradition. I am not sure what practical use such a term will have, but it will be beneficial if it can move archeologists away from fruitless discussions over the classifications of cultures in the Southeast. For example, most archeologists seem to agree that the Coles Creek culture of the lower Mississippi valley had a complex social organization, and they would probably agree on what

FIGURE 7.12
One view of Mississippian and other Late Prehistoric complexes. (From *Prehistory of North America*, 2d ed., by Jesse D. Jennings. Copyright © 1968, 1974 by McGraw-Hill, Inc. Used with permission of McGraw-Hill Book Company.)

FIGURE 7.13
Late Prehistoric complexes as discussed in this section. Note
that the concept of single origin and diffusion is not employed.

is generally known about Coles Creek; so it seems fruitless to expend much
energy debating whether the complex should be called Coles Creek Mississippian or not. It is hard to see what important theoretical and practical
issues are served by such discussion.

The term *Mississippian* will be used here to describe those Late Prehistoric
societies along the major river valleys in the area from Natchez to St. Louis
and from Memphis to Knoxville that built substructure mounds and made
pottery with crushed shell added to the clay (Figure 7.13). Outside of the
area of the Tennessee, Cumberland, and Mississippi Rivers, these criteria are
much less useful, even though many complexes there have been described as
being Mississippian-influenced. Recent work has made it clear that the development of these "peripheral" societies was largely coeval with Mississippian. It seems more accurate, therefore, to look upon these developments—
Lamar, Fort Ancient, and others—as being caused by the same processes and

events as Mississippian itself. In each case, the local conditions and potentials seem to have been more important than some unspecified "influence."

Even within Mississippian there does not seem to be much internal unity. The Mississippian of the Dallas phase in eastern Tennessee, for example, is probably as different in most nonceramic traits from the Fairmount phase of the Cahokia area as either of these are from Coles Creek or Plaquemine in the lower Mississippi valley. It should be clear by now that ceramic similarities and differences may not be the most significant measure of cultural differences and relationships, despite the undoubted usefulness of such traits to the archeologist as horizon markers. In fact, it seems that the time has come for Southeastern archeologists to concern themselves more directly with testing hypotheses about the kinds of social relationships between one society and another in the area and less with creating area-wide classifications of dubious explanatory value. The term *Mississippian* originated as a name for a ceramic tradition, and it may be time to return it to that status (Holmes 1903).

As in the case of other Late Prehistoric complexes, Mississippian settlement in general and central Mississippi settlement in particular was mostly in the river valleys. Upland sites do occur, but these sites often seem to have been used for special functions. In some cases these upland sites appear to have been hunting camps. In other cases, salt springs and other natural resources appear to have been exploited by groups of Mississippians. To some extent, earlier societies in the Southeast also had special-purpose sites, but in Mississippian areas and times it sometimes seems that whole settlements were involved in relatively specialized activities on a scale previously seen only at the very peak of the middle Sedentary Hopewellian complexes. The distribution and apparent functions of Mississippian sites in many regions make it extremely likely that individual sites were organized into a specialized hierarchy of purpose and function in the broader society. Large, centralized sites with many substructure mounds appear to have functioned as administrative centers where bureaucrats and priests (more than likely the same persons) coordinated the collection and redistribution of food and materials and supervised the ceremonial and ritual celebrations of the social system (Figures 7.14 and 7.15). In smaller centers of population, a similar but lower-ranked group of administrators probably conducted the affairs of local areas. Still smaller settlements were scattered around local centers, and these in turn were surrounded by farmsteads where the basic unit of population was very likely a small family group of some sort.

As might be expected, the vast majority of archeological work on Mississippian has been concentrated on the large and spectacular mound centers. In the last few years, however, increasing attention has been paid to the smaller sites, and a much more complete picture of Mississippian life has been emerging. It seems that most Mississippian people were farmers, and that a substantial proportion of the population at even the larger sites was directly engaged in agriculture. Some specialization of labor did apparently occur,

a

b

c

FIGURE 7.14
Various large Late Prehistoric sites. *a*, Moundville, Alabama; *b*, Etowah, Georgia;
c, Kincaid, Illinois, speculative reconstruction. (From *Prehistory of North America*, 2d ed., by
Jesse D. Jennings. Copyright © 1968, 1974 by McGraw-Hill, Inc. Used with permission of
McGraw-Hill Book Company.)

FIGURE 7.15
Late Prehistoric ceramics. These are examples of Mississippian shell-tempered pottery.

however, although it remains an open question whether there were many full-time specialists other than the administrators themselves. Some indication of local specialization may be found, even though the individuals in each case may not have been full-time specialists. In Union County, Illinois, for example, there were extensive chert quarries that appear to have been a major source for cherts used in making stone hoes. In other locations in southern Illinois, salt springs appear to have been a focus for settlements that specialized in the production of salt. The existence of specialization on this level, combined with the evidence of the large central sites, very strongly supports the idea of some form of centralized distribution system. Although a suggestion has been made that this distribution was by actual market mechanisms (Porter 1969:159) in the case of the largest center at Cahokia, there have been criticisms of this view (R. I. Ford 1974:406). Even if Cahokia did have a market economy (an economic system that implies the existence of a state), it is not likely that other Mississippian economies were organized in this fashion. In most cases, the economic system of the Mississippian complexes appears to have been redistributive. This means that goods from the areas of production were controlled and distributed by central authorities. The historic literature gives good examples of this kind of economic system (e.g., Gentleman of Elvas 1866:52, 55, 58, 69), but little has been done to prove clearly the existence of such systems in prehistoric times.

Mississippian peoples in the Southeast depended upon agriculture combined with products of gathering and hunting, very like the lifeway already described for Southeastern peoples in general in this time period. The largest centers of settlement of Mississippian peoples are found in areas where there are broad, fertile river bottoms suitable for agriculture as well as highly diverse wild resources. In addition, these large centers often are in locations that would have afforded easy control of routes of exchange of goods. At the same time, it is likely that most Mississippian people lived outside of the important political-religious centers, with their "palaces" and "temples." The typical Mississippian site, as opposed to those that are most spectacular, was probably a small group of only a few structures consisting of several households directly engaged in agriculture and in the gathering of wild resources.

The houses themselves were constructed of vertical poles set in trenches and covered over with mud plaster. The roof was thatched. In some areas, the walls were more often mats or other covering than plastered, but the basic house was similar throughout the Southeast. The form was generally square, and there was a hearth in the center of the floor of the structure. This design not only was used for the houses of the farmers but, in larger sizes, was also used for mortuary temples for the bodies of the local aristocracy and for the palaces of the living chieftains and their followers. Occasionally, some structures with different shapes were built for special purposes, but the dominant architectural form in the Late Prehistoric Mississippian was the square, vertical-post structure.

To some extent, larger Mississippian sites appear to have been conglomerations of settlement units not unlike those found at the small farmsteads and hamlets. Large Mississippian sites were not exactly "empty ceremonial centers," but neither were they usually completely packed with houses tightly pushed up against one another. The large sites do often have fortifications that are very extensive and militarily well planned. At the same time, however, many smaller sites show no traces of defensive works. Many Mississippian burials do show signs of injury, but it is not clear how much of this can be laid to warfare.

The clustering of small numbers of houses together may indicate that the basic residential unit was some form of extended family, perhaps a lineage segment. It seems likely, then, that basic activities of food getting operated on a level that was not unlike that of Late Woodland late Sedentary peoples, even though agriculture represented a change in strategy from earlier food gathering and collecting. What made Mississippian and similar cultures different from their predecessors was that these local producers became only the lowest level in a highly stratified society. Although Mississippian times have sometimes been called the Temple Mound period, it is actually likely that the majority of mounds were platforms for the houses, even palaces, of the community leaders. The highly organized and planned character of Mississippian centers, built in some cases over the course of several centuries of work, very strongly supports the hypothesis that the leadership of these societies was marked by continuity. Coupled with the very strong likelihood that many of the nonresidential platform structures were mortuary temples honoring the ancestors of the leadership, the conclusion that Mississippian leaders were hereditary chieftains of "royal" kinship groups is almost inescapable. Much more archeological work needs to be done to verify this; but at least the direction such investigations should take is relatively clear, unlike many other sociological problems faced by archeologists.

The distinction between politics and religion may not have been very clear in Mississippian times. The great central sites consist of enormous substructure mounds arranged around open spaces that were probably used as meeting places and locations for major ceremonies. These ceremonies probably played both political and religious roles in Mississippian society. One of the markers of chiefdoms, in fact, is that the separation between politics and religion is often indistinct.

The content of Mississippian religions is difficult to define, although some attempts at understanding by analogy with historic Southeastern beliefs have been made (Waring 1968; Howard 1968). There is no doubt that there were direct relationships between the beliefs of historic and modern Indians in the Southeast and those of the prehistoric residents. At the same time, considerable caution is necessary in the use of such analogies to "interpret" archeological materials. Most of the religious practices and beliefs for which we have good ethnographic evidence are either modern or go back little further than the early eighteenth century. The archeological complexes with which we are concerned date as far back as the ninth century. Thus, the ethnographic data refer to societies that are from 200 to 1000 years later than the archeological evidence. The best use of the ethnographic evidence here is as a source for hypotheses than can be tested rather than as a source for interpretations. One fact does stand out from the ethnographic data on the Southeast; the Southeastern rituals "differ significantly from any aspects of southwestern or Mexican ceremonialism" (Witthoft 1949:82). Although largely true, this statement is rather too strong, since all New World religious beliefs share certain basic features, including emphasis on four-part division of the world and universe with stress on cardinal directions and celestial objects.

One of the most striking features of the Late Prehistoric period is the widespread occurrence of certain artistic themes and objects over almost all of the Southeast. This complex of themes and objects has been variously known as the Southern Cult and the Southeastern Ceremonial Complex (Waring and Holder 1945; Waring 1968; Howard 1968; Muller 1966; 1970; 1973). The usefulness of this concept has been somewhat weakened by efforts to describe all elaborate art and artifacts from the Late Prehistoric period as being Southern Cult. In fact, there appear to have been several different horizons with widespread distributions of this kind during the Late Prehistoric period, and it seems most useful to call only the largest and most highly organized of these *the* Southern Cult. There is not the slightest evidence that the complex was, in sociological terms, a "cult." Even *Southeastern Ceremonial Complex,* quite aside from its awkwardness, is not very satisfactory, for it has become increasingly obvious that archeologists are really describing networks of exchange and interaction in this case rather than "ceremonies" or cults.

Whatever it is called, the Southern Cult extends far beyond the limits of any one complex or archeological unit. So-called Cult materials are known from Mississippi to Minnesota, from Oklahoma to the Atlantic coast. The greatest concentrations of such materials occur in mortuary "temple" mounds at some of the major sites of the Late Prehistoric period—Moundville, Alabama; Etowah, Georgia; and Spiro, Oklahoma (Figure 7.16). Other large sites, such as Cahokia itself, seem to have very little in the way of Southern Cult artifacts, but it is likely that in some cases this reflects the uncertainties of archeological recovery, since Cult artifacts are usually found in only a few kinds of archeological contexts. The network of exchange involved in the Southern Cult was very extensive, with raw materials and finished goods moving long distances. Shell gorgets, for example, that must have been made in northern Georgia or eastern Tennessee have been found at Spiro in Oklahoma. It is very tempting to suggest that this exchange may not have been restricted solely to long-distance exchange of small and "expensive" items but that the exchange routes may also have played an important role in the movement of primary economic goods and materials, such as food and salt. In any case, the peak of the Southern Cult proper seems to have come within

FIGURE 7.16

Materials associated with the so-called Southern Cult or Southeastern Ceremonial complex of ca. AD 1250. Such materials occur very widely in many different phases on this time level. The major centers of the cult were Moundville, Alabama; Spiro, Oklahoma; and Etowah, Georgia. Each of the many different areas participating in this exchange network had its own distinctive art styles, even though certain art motifs are widespread. *a, b,* repousse copper plates; *c,* "bi-lobed arrow" motif in copper; *d,* copper ax; *e,* monolithic ax; *f,* polished stone "mace;" *g,* shell gorget from Etowah; *h,* design from an engraved shell cup from Spiro. (From *Prehistory of North America,* 2d ed., by Jesse D. Jennings. Copyright © 1968, 1974 by McGraw-Hill, Inc. Used with permission of McGraw-Hill Book Company.)

a short period around AD 1250. Similar but more localized exchange networks grew up in the central Cumberland valley around AD 1350 and again in the eastern Tennessee drainage shortly after AD 1500. Valuable goods such as marine shell, of course, had been exchanged throughout the Southeast from Late Archaic times on. What concepts like Southern Cult and even the earlier Hopewell actually represent are periods in which similarities of theme, motif, and medium are sufficiently strong to suggest social interaction as well as trade. Two features of the Southern Cult should be strongly emphasized. Southern Cult goods are most common in Mississippian sites but are also found in areas that can be called Mississippian only by the broadest definitions possible for that term. Moreover, although the themes and motifs of the Cult probably did have politico-religious significance in many cases, the Southern Cult and its relatives should not be considered solely or even primarily as religious.

When sites like Cahokia and Moundville are considered, Mississippian complexes in the central Southeast were the most complex societies of the Late Prehistoric period. At the same time, many other peoples in the Southeast developed highly complex social systems that correspond to the Mississippian developments in many ways. In the Ouachita physiographic province of Arkansas and eastern Oklahoma, for example, there were societies that archeologists have called Caddoan. In the lower Mississippi valley below present-day Greenville, Mississippi, continuity of development can be seen from the Sedentary complexes such as Marksville into the early Late Prehistoric Coles Creek and the later Plaquemine cultures. On the eastern Coastal Plain and in the mountains of the southern Appalachians, there are still other societies that have sometimes been grouped together in the later part of the Late Prehistoric period under the name Lamar. All of these complexes share certain basic features. It is likely that all of them, like the Mississippian, were socially organized into ranked societies. All of these societies also participated to a greater or lesser degree in Southeast-wide exchange networks, such as the Southern Cult and its later analogues. In addition, high social rank in such societies was reflected by substructure mound construction and elaborate mortuary practices.

At this time it seems much better to treat these complexes on regional terms rather than to subsume them all under *Mississippian.* The distinctive characteristics of the Plaquemine, Caddoan, or even Lamar complexes are direct reflections of the developments toward greater complexity that mark the entire Southeast in Late Prehistoric times. The use of *Mississippian* to describe all of these gives the false impression that the central Mississippi societies had priority in these developments and that they "influenced" other peoples throughout the Southeast. Present evidence shows that, regardless of where shell-tempered pottery may have developed, the complex social structures that are the true markers of Late Prehistoric life in the Southeast developed at pretty much the same time throughout the area. If priority must be sought for some one area, however, it would certainly not be found in central Mississippi but rather in the Coles Creek or Weeden Island areas further south. The problem of the Coles Creek to Plaquemine developments in the lower Mississippi valley below Greenville, Mississippi, exemplifies some of the problems in terminology and classification. The Late Prehistoric period is important as the time of maximum development; the following sections, therefore, briefly deal with the Lower Valley, Caddoan, and Lamar complexes of the Late Prehistoric.

The Coles Creek and Plaquemine complexes in the Lower Valley represent direct developments from the late Sedentary complexes described in the previous section. Coles Creek is one of the earliest Southeastern societies in which platform, substructure mound construction is known, given some ambiguity about the character of some of the earlier mound building. Even in Coles Creek, the exact chronology of substructure mound building is far from firmly established. The scale of mound construction in Coles Creek is generally modest. At the Greenhouse site in Louisana, for example, the total volume of the mounds is some 7500 cubic meters, and not all of the mound construction can be dated to Coles Creek times. When compared with the 95,000 cubic meters of mound construction at a Tennessee-Cumberland (Mississippian) site like Kincaid, it can be seen that Coles Creek organizations were probably not on the same scale as the Mississippian. At the same time, the complexity of the Coles Creek site layout and the continuity of planning needed for such sites do suggest that chiefdomlike societies may have been present.

The Caddoan societies of the Ouachita Province have largely been distinguished from Mississippian complexes by their elaborately engraved, polished pottery. It is true that many workers in the Caddoan area (e.g., Hoffman 1970:160) do see the Caddoan complexes as Mississippian, but, as indicated above, the similarities seem to be those shared by most Late Prehistoric peoples in the Southeast. At least *some* Caddoan societies were organized on a chiefdom level, although many may not have been. Caddoan centers rarely show the kind of centralized planning over time that appears to be characteristic of central Mississippi, Dallas, Tennessee-Cumberland, and other "true" Mississippian complexes (Hoffman 1970:160). There also appears to have been a relatively greater emphasis on burial than was the case in other Late Prehistoric areas. Centralization of power is suggested by what appears to have been retainer sacrifice and by almost incredible amounts of grave goods accompanying the dead. For example, there are nearly as many engraved shell artifacts from Spiro as are known from the rest of the Eastern Woodlands altogether. Unlike the Lower Valley complexes, Spiro and other Caddoan sites were directly involved in the Southern Cult exchange network. Another indication of the complexity of Caddoan social organization may be seen in the large mounds in the area, even though these are not common.

The Battle Mound, for example, has a volume of nearly 180,000 cubic meters. While this is only a third of the size of Monks Mound at Cahokia, it is still one of the largest platform mounds in the Southeast.

In the eastern section of the Southeast there are other distinctive cultures. In this area, many of the later Late Prehistoric groups have been called Lamar and defined as a kind of backwoods, Mississippian-influenced complex. In its later phases, Lamar is identified by the presence of pottery shaped and decorated with elaborately carved paddles, a trait that began very early along the South Atlantic coast. Like the more northerly Oneota complex, however, the Lamar concept has been poorly defined, and too little investigation of its development has been carried out for much to be said about it. At the same time, some complexes from the area that are clearly not "Mississippian" and are presumably "pre-Lamar" are apparently at least as old as Mississippian developments elsewhere.

In all of the preceding cases, the major point to be noted is that the development of highly organized and ranked societies is largely contemporaneous throughout the Southeast. The old picture of central Mississippi priority and subsequent "influence" upon other areas has been steadily collapsing as more is discovered about other areas. The combination of increased population, new technology, and new forms of social organization developed in many areas throughout the Southeast. In some areas these developments led to "Mississippian" societies, in other areas to complexes like Caddoan or Plaquemine. The major impediment to understanding these developments has been the concentration on tracing the history of traits like shell-tempered pottery and substructure mounds rather than on understanding the social and ecological processes that caused these developments.

The decline of the Late Prehistoric societies was directly related to the beginning of the historic period. The earliest historic records from the sixteenth century describe actual chiefdoms, and a few groups in the Southeast, such as the Natchez, did maintain this form of organization into the historic period. Given the instability of chiefdoms in general, however, the decline in population that resulted from European contact led, at the very least, to a collapse of the political structure to smaller "chiefdoms" based on the immediate settlement. The subsequent redevelopment of larger-scale chiefdoms and even states in the Southeast occurred under other circumstances—pressure from European settlers and conflicts between various European states that caught up the indigenous populations (Service 1975: Chap. 8; Gearing 1962). The large-scale disruption of the political and social organization that followed the spread of European disease and power makes analysis of the historic situation fraught with peril. Archeological evidence from the Southeast suggests that earlier, prehistoric peoples of the area had more complex political and social systems than those described in the eighteenth century. For these and many other reasons, attempts to link prehistoric, archeologically defined societies with the historic "tribes" of the Southeast are inadvisable. It is probable, for example, that the present-day Creek Indians include many whose ancestors were members of the Dallas (Mississippian) society of eastern Tennessee, but this is not the same as saying that the Dallas complex is prehistoric Creek.

The Historic Period

The beginnings were scarcely notable: a few European ships along the coast and a few cursory attempts at exploration. Although there were Indian settlements along the coast, the majority of the Indian population was inland. All the same, the peoples along the coast showed many of the features of the inland chiefdoms. By 1539 or 1540, when Hernando de Soto's expedition penetrated inland, there were numerous accounts of what appear to have been small chiefdoms. The account by Alvar Nuñez Cabeza de Vaca of the ill-fated Narvaez expedition of 1527 describes the village of Appalachen as consisting of "forty small and low houses" (1972:22). At the same time, the country is described as having houses scattered all over (1972:23), so it is unlikely that population in the area along the coast can be estimated from the small village size. Even in Cabeza de Vaca's account the affect of European contact may be seen in the account of some disease of the "stomach" which killed half of a group of Indians who had helped the stranded Spanish (1972:53).

By de Soto's time, the Indians in many areas had learned to flee at the approach of Europeans. In one deserted town, the account of the Gentleman of Elvas described a situation that sounds familiar to the preceding account of the Late Prehistoric: "The town was of seven or eight houses, built of timber, and covered with palm leaves. The Chief's house stood near the beach, upon a very high mount made by hand for defense . . ." (Gentleman of Elvas 1866:23–24). Later, it is mentioned that this small village paid "tribute" to a chief some 30 leagues away (1866:33). The sixteenth-century Spanish league may be taken as approximately 3 English miles, so even discounting for some misunderstanding, this suggests sizable political entities in an area that was not nearly so complex as the inland societies described earlier.

As the de Soto expedition went inland, it encountered plastered walled houses like those known archeologically from the Southeast. The houses of the chiefs were described as larger than those of the other people "and about are many large barbacoas [described as a house with wooden sides raised aloft on four poles], in which they bring together the tribute their people give them of maize, skins of deer, and blankets of the country" (1866:52). Although the role of the chief may not have been fully understood by the Spanish chroniclers, this description of centralized storage strongly suggests the redistributive function of the chief. But even in 1539 or 1540, there were indications that European disease may have outraced the European explorer. The Gentleman of Elvas describes large vacant towns grown up with grass, and the Spanish were told of a major epidemic some two years earlier (1866:63).

De Soto was after wealth, but he did not find it in the Southeast. There were some attempts at settlement of more permanent kinds, but these were predominantly coastal and do not throw much light on the upheavals of the late sixteenth and seventeenth centuries.

A recent history by Francis Jennings has drawn attention to the ideological background for the European claims to have discovered an "empty land" inhabited only by savages and wild beasts (1975). The "civilization" brought to eastern North America by the Europeans consisted mainly of the kinds of repressive force that are characteristic of a *state*, especially efficiency of military and other forms of control. Firearms in this period were not the source of critical technical superiority over the weapons of the Indian. Rather, the main source of European military superiority was organization. Faced with this organizational superiority, some Indian tribes and chiefdoms did manage to restructure their societies into true states; but by that time the European bridgehead on the east coast was too firmly established. The native Americans in the Southeast were not completely destroyed. Today there are over 190,000 people of Indian descent in the Southeast, but over half of them live in Oklahoma and nearly half of those remaining live in North Carolina. Although many of these Indians no longer seem very different from their neighbors of European descent in their dress and behavior, some of the old beliefs and patterns survive. Even so, generations of repression have left their mark so that it is very difficult to connect contemporary beliefs and behavior with their prehistoric origins.

References Cited and Recommended Sources

Binford, Lewis R. 1971 Mortuary practices: their study and their potential. Society for American Archaeology, Memoir 25:6–29.

———. 1972 An archaeological perspective. New York: Seminar Press.

Broyles, Bettye J., and Clarence Webb (eds.) 1970 The Poverty Point culture. Southeastern Archaeological Conference, Bulletin 12.

Cabeza de Vaca, Alvar Nuñez 1972 The Narrative of Alvar Nuñez Cabeza de Vaca. Translated by Fanny Bandalier. Barre, Mass.: The Imprint Society.

Caldwell, Joseph H. 1958 Trend and tradition in the prehistory of the eastern United States. American Anthropological Association, Memoir No. 88. (Illinois State Museum, Scientific Papers, Vol. 10.)

Carneiro, Robert L. 1970 A theory of the origin of the state. Science 169:3947:733–738.

DeJarnette, David L., Edward Kurjack, James Cambron, and others. 1962 Stanfield-Worley Bluff Shelter excavations. Journal of Albama Archaeology 8:(1–2).

Ford, James A. 1969 A comparison of Formative cultures in the Americas: diffusion or the psychic unity of mankind. Smithsonian Contributions to Knowledge, Vol. 11. Washington, D.C.: Smithsonian Institution Press.

Ford, Richard I. 1974 Northeastern archaeology: past and future directions. *In* Annual Review of Anthropology 3:385–413.

Gearing, Fred 1962 Priests and warriors. American Anthropological Association, Memoir 93.

Gentleman of Elvas 1866 Narratives of the Career of Hernando de Soto . . . As Told by a Knight of Elvas. Translated by Buckingham Smith. New York: Bradford Club. (Reprint edition, 1968, Gainsville, Fla.: Palmetto Books.)

Goodyear, Albert C. 1974 The Brand site: A techno-functional study of a Dalton site in northeast Arkansas. Arkansas Archaeological Survey, Research Series No. 7.

Greengo, Robert E. 1964 Issaquena: an archaeological phase of the Yazoo Basin in the lower Mississippi valley. Memoirs of the Society for American Archaeology, No. 18. American Antiquity 30:2:(2).

Griffin, James B. 1967 Eastern North American archaeology. Science 156:3772:175–191.

Hoffman, Michael P. 1970 Archaeological and historical assessment of the Red River Basin in Arkansas. Part IV of Archaeological and Historical Resources of the Red River Basin, ed. Hester A. Davis. Arkansas Archaeological Survey, Publications on Archaeology, Research Series No. 1:135–194.

Holmes, W. H. 1903 Aboriginal pottery of the eastern United States. Bureau of American Ethnology, 20th Annual Report (1898–1899), pp. 1–237.

Howard, James H. 1968 The Southeastern Ceremonial complex and its interpretation. Missouri Archaeological Society, Memoir 6.

Jennings, Francis 1975 The invasion of America: Indians, colonialism, and the cant of conquest. Chapel Hill: University of North Carolina Press.

Kuttruff, L. C. n.d. Late Woodland and Mississippian settlement systems in the lower Kaskaskia river valley. NSF report summary and longer, unpublished dissertation, Southern Illinois University at Carbondale, Department of Anthropology.

Lewis, T. M. N., and M. K. Lewis 1961 Eva and Archaic Site. Knoxville: University of Tennessee Press.

Morse, Dan F., Jr. 1973 Dalton culture in Northeast Arkansas. The Florida Archaeologist 26:1:23–38.

Muller, Jon 1966 Archaeological analysis of art styles. Tennessee Archaeologist 22:1:25–39.

———. 1970 The Southeastern Ceremonial complex and its interpretations by James H. Howard. Review in American Anthropologist 72:1:182–183.

———. 1973 Structural studies of art styles. IXth International Congress of Anthropological and Ethnological Sciences 1036, Chicago. (Will be reprinted as a part of the volumes of the Congress on Art in World Anthropology.)

Neumann, Georg K. 1952 Archeology and race in the American Indian. *In* Archaeology of the Eastern United States, ed. James B. Griffin, pp. 13–34. Chicago: University of Chicago Press.

Phillips, Philip 1970 Archaeological survey in the lower Yazoo Basin, Mississippi, 1949–1955. Peabody Museum Papers No. 60.

Porter, James W. 1969 The Mitchell site and prehistoric exchange systems at Cahokia: AD 1000 ± 300. *In* Explorations into Cahokia Archaeology, ed. M. L. Fowler, pp. 137–164. Illinois Archaeological Survey, Bulletin 7.

Sahlins, Marshall 1972 Stone Age Economics. Chicago: Aldine Publishing Company.

Sears, William 1968 The state and settlement patterns in the New World. *In* Settlement Archaeology, ed. K. C. Chang, pp. 134–153. Palo Alto, Calif.: National Press Books.

———. 1953 Excavations at Kolomoki—Season III and IV, Mound D. Athens: University of Georgia Press.

———. 1956 Excavations at Kolomoki, final report. University of Georgia Series in Anthropology, No. 5.

Service, Elman R. 1962 Primitive Social Organization: An Evolutionary Perspective. New York: Random House.

————. 1975 Origins of the State and Civilization: The Process of Cultural Evolution. New York: W. W. Norton.

Struever, Stuart 1964 The Hopewell Interaction Sphere in Riverine-Western Great Lakes culture history. *In* Hopewellian Studies, ed. J. R. Caldwell and R. L. Hall, pp. 85–106. Illinois State Museum Scientific Papers XII.

Waring, Antonio J., Jr. 1968 The Waring papers: the collected works of Antonio J. Waring, Jr., ed. Stephen Williams. Papers of the Peabody Museum of Archaeology and Ethnology, Harvard University, Vol. 58.

Waring, Antonio J., Jr., and Preston Holder 1945 A prehistoric ceremonial complex in the southeastern United States. American Anthropologist 47:1:1–34. (Reprinted in Waring 1968.)

Webb, W. S. 1946 The Indian Knoll, site Oh 2, Ohio County, Kentucky. University of Kentucky Reports in Anthropology and Archaeology 4:3:1:111–365.

Witthoft, John 1949 Green corn ceremonialism in the Eastern Woodlands. Occasional contributions from the Museum of Anthropology, University of Michigan, No. 13.

Inscription House ruin. (Photograph by Marc Gaede.)

CHAPTER EIGHT

The Southwest

William D. Lipe

As was the case in many of the areas discussed in this volume, the picturesque nature of the archeological remains in the Southwest led to an early (and sometimes unfortunate) interest in the prehistoric inhabitants of the region. Who built the great cliff dwellings? Why were they constructed in such difficult and sometimes nearly inaccessible locations? How did the people live? Where did they come from? Where did they go? Why did they leave so abruptly? As the sequence of events in the prehistoric Southwest unfolds in this chapter, it becomes plain that some of these questions are easily answered; some are the subject of much debate among Southwesternists; and some may be unanswerable.

The archeology of the Southwest caught the fancy of the American public and scholars alike in the late nineteenth century, an infatuation that endures, generation after generation. The masonry cliff dwellings (brooding ageless under sheltering rock), the stylized yet always fresh designs of pottery and pictographs, the spectacular natural settings—all produce in the visitor a sense of heightened awareness and communication with man's past. But this basic humanistic appeal, though powerful, does not alone explain the continuing interest in the Southwest. The Southwest has been fortunate in the archeologists and ethnologists who have chosen to work there; over the past century they have given us an increasingly sophisticated understanding of the prehistory of the region. Pottery vessels can now be appreciated not only aesthetically, but also as documents in the history of peoples; the ruins can be seen not only as architectural monuments, but also as solutions to specific environmental problems faced by particular groups at known times.

THE SOUTHWESTERN REGION

The Southwest can be variously defined (e.g., Kroeber 1939; Kirchoff 1954; Reed 1964), but it is impossible to arrive at boundaries that neatly coincide with the boundaries of major geologic, biotic, climatic, and cultural units.

The regional definition we shall use corresponds to the extent of maize-growing, pottery-making, village- or rancheria-dwelling cultures of about AD 1100, which for most of them was the time of maximum geographic extent. This boundary is necessarily fuzzy everywhere, but it is especially so in the south, where relationships with northern Mexico are poorly known. This vagueness to the south is in part due to lack of research in this area, and in part to the failure of most Southwesternists, including the author, to become sufficiently informed about the work that has been done.

The Southwest is an area of great topographic variety, of elevations that range from near sea level in the lower Colorado River valley to over 3600 meters atop some of its mountains. Much of the region's biotic diversity is related to this variation in elevation and land form, and it is no accident that the concept of altitudinal life zones (Merriam 1890; 1898) was developed in the Southwest. Rainfall rises with elevation, while temperatures decrease; superimposed on these local controls are general geographic trends in the amounts and seasonal distribution of rainfall. One of the most rewarding areas in current Southwestern research is the analysis of the adaptation of cultures to the possibilities and challenges of this environmental diversity.

Although there were substantial changes in Southwestern climate, flora, and fauna at the end of the Pleistocene (8000 to 10,000 BC), environments since that time have approximated present conditions. Some of the climatic variations that have taken place since the Pleistocene may have been great enough to affect prehistoric cultures, but they were probably not sufficient to alter the major environmental zones or regions that exist today. An understanding of these geographic subdivisions (Figure 8.1) is therefore a logical starting point for understanding the environmental settings to which the prehistoric cultures adapted.

The Colorado Plateau

Most of the northern Southwest consists of this extensive highland of uplifted but relatively undeformed sedimentary formations—sandstones, shales, and limestones. A few isolated mountains of igneous origin have been thrust up through the Plateau, and at a number of locations, especially around its edges, sheets of lava have spilled out of fissures to cover the underlying sedimentary rocks. Nearly all the Plateau is drained by the Colorado River and its tributaries; the drainage system has everywhere cut into the land, producing a complex topography of mesas, buttes, canyons, and valleys. Because of extensive erosion, soils tend to be thin, and in some parts there are extensive exposures of bare rock. The deepest soils, and the ones generally most suited to agriculture, are alluvial fills in the valleys and patches of aeolian or windblown silts in the uplands. Only the major streams are permanent; the others flow only briefly after rainfall or to carry away snow melt from the

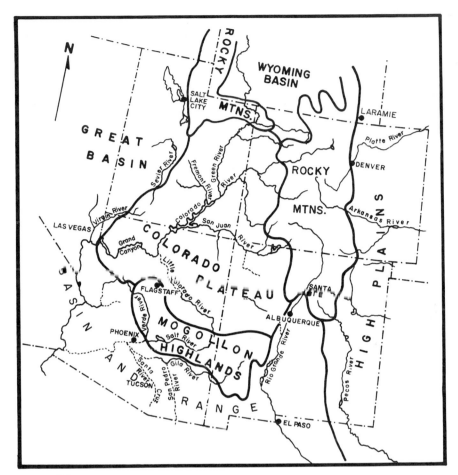

FIGURE 8.1
Southwestern geographic regions.

highlands. Some of the sedimentary formations are good aquifers, and springs are abundant in canyons cut into them.

Plateau vegetation and climate are roughly zoned by altitude, although the rugged topography provides much opportunity for local variation due to exposure, slope, and so on. The few highest peaks have alpine shrubs above the treeline. Coniferous forests of spruce and fir on the upper slopes give way to Ponderosa pine at lower elevations.

The dominant vegetation between 1500 and 2100 meters, where most of the Plateau surface lies, is the piñon-juniper forest. In parts of the southern interior of the Plateau, woodland is replaced by grasslands at this elevation. Wherever they occur, patches of deep soil tend to support shrubs and grasses rather than woodland. Of the shrubs, big sage is most common, but saltbush and greasewood take over on the more alkaline soils. Rainfall at this elevation ranges from about 25 to 38 centimeters and the frost-free period from about 120 to 160 days.

Below 1500 meters, shrubs and grasses predominate, with extensive areas of sage, greasewood and saltbush, and blackbrush. In both the piñon-juniper zone and the lower shrublands, riparian communities of cottonwood, willow, and other water-loving plants occur along drainages and around seeps and springs, especially in the narrower canyons.

The Plateau is a transition zone between two major precipitation patterns. On the northwestern edge of the region, the majority of the moisture comes from the Pacific in the form of broad frontal storms, concentrated in the winter and spring, with only a small rainfall peak in late summer. On the region's southeastern edge, the wettest season is late summer, with a lesser peak in late spring, and winters are dry. The summer rains come from thunderstorms, which are often quite localized and tend to be triggered by highland masses. The moisture source is the Gulf of Mexico. Between these two extremes, at approximately the Four Corners point, rainfall is about equally divided between winter and late summer.

The Basin and Range Area

To the west, south, and southeast of the Plateau are numerous more or less parallel mountain ranges, separated by broad basins deeply filled with alluvial material eroded from the mountains. The narrow highlands have been uplifted by complex block faulting, and their rock formations, of both sedimentary and igneous origin, have generally been deformed. The flat-topped mesas so characteristic of the Plateau skyline are here replaced by the jagged profiles of eroded mountains.

The highest and coolest part of the Basin and Range area lies in western Utah and Nevada and is called the Great Basin because it is a region of interior drainage. Much of the Great Basin is above 1350 meters, but it is in the rain shadow of the Sierra and is drier than the Plateau. Annual precipitation is generally below 25 centimeters, with a peak in the winter and spring. Basin vegetation resembles that of the Plateau, except that shrubland (predominantly big sage, greasewood, and saltbush) is much more extensive. The mountains have piñon-juniper woodland, and the highest ones are topped by pine forests.

South of the Great Basin and the Colorado Plateau, the elevations are lower, the climate hotter and drier, and the mountain ranges older and more eroded. In the lowest areas, the more level surfaces often are covered by desert pavement, an armor of pebbles and cobbles left after wind and water have removed the intervening fine soil particles. Drainage is better developed, and such water as does run off the predominantly desert landscape finds its way into the Gila River system or, in the extreme east, into the Rio Grande. The only flowing streams in the area bring water in from adjacent highlands, most located to the north.

The vegetation of the southern Basin and Range area contrasts strongly with that of the Plateau. The low deserts have a monotonous cover of creosote bush and bursage on the valley floors, with sparse cacti and shrubs such as hill palo verde on the higher areas. As elevation rises to the east, the valley sides and upland support a rich, diversified flora of shrubs and cacti, including the giant saguaro, organ pipe and barrel cacti, cholla, and various species of prickly pear. Dense growths of tree legumes, such as mesquite and acacia, occur in the washes. East of Tucson, the broad valleys are covered by a shrub-steppe vegetation, including creosote bush and abundant grasses (predominantly grama and tobosa), while the highlands support oak-juniper woodland, with pine forest on the highest peaks.

From the extremely hot, near-sea-level deserts along the lower Colorado, the southern Basin and Range area gradually rises to the east, until elevations over 1200 m are reached on the valley floors of the Arizona–New Mexico borderlands. As one moves from west to east, rainfall patterns change strikingly. In addition to increasing with elevation from less than 12 to more than 25 centimeters annually, the seasonal distribution changes from winter dominant with a lesser summer peak in the west to a strong summer concentration in the east.

The Mogollon Highlands

The rock layers of the Colorado Plateau are gently uptilted toward its southern edge, which, as a result, generally rises above 2100 meters. In central Arizona, the prominent escarpment formed at the Plateau's edge is called the Mogollon Rim. Eastward, the Rim becomes a less definite cliff line and merges with the volcanic mass of the White Mountains.

This high southern edge of the Plateau, and the extremely rough mountainous area just south of it I have called the Mogollon Highlands. Sloping land predominates, and there are few broad valleys or flat-topped mesas. The area is transitional between the Plateau and Basin and Range, both geologically and ecologically. At the higher elevations, pine forest is typical, trending in the east to pine-Douglas fir forest. Intermediate elevations have piñon-juniper woodland or oak-juniper woodland transitional to mountain mahogany-oak scrub. Desert shrub-steppe occurs in some of the lower valleys. The intergradation of Plateau and Basin-Range vegetation gives the area an extremely rich and varied flora.

The Mogollon Highlands are well watered. Rising abruptly from lower desert areas, they receive precipitation as air masses from the south, southwest, or southeast rise over them, are cooled, and release their moisture. On the Plateau, north of the Rim, points at comparable elevations receive considerably less moisture. For example, Cibecue, Arizona, in the Mogollon Highlands near the New Mexico border, at 1590 meters, receives nearly 48 centimeters of precipitation a year. About 64 kilometers to the northeast, Snowflake, Arizona, on the Plateau, receives less than 30 centimeters at 1680 meters. Both have similar temperatures, with Snowflake slightly cooler. Farther to the north, well into the Plateau interior, Petrified Forest National Monument has less than 25 centimeters of rainfall at an elevation intermediate between Snowflake and Cibecue.

The Rocky Mountains

The southern Rockies, just east of the Plateau, are part of an uplifted and complexly folded mountain chain that forms the highest and generally most rugged portion of the North American continent. Although well watered, their cool temperatures made most of this area marginal for aboriginal Southwestern farming cultures. Some of the lower areas in the mountains of southwestern Colorado and northern New Mexico—particularly around the upper Rio Grande valley—were fairly heavily occupied. The vegetation in these areas resembles that of the Plateau, although a greater portion of the land surface is given over to coniferous forest.

THE EARLY CULTURES

Plains-Oriented Big-Game Hunters

The Southwest has yet to produce remains that are demonstrably older than the Clovis horizon of about 9000 to 9500 BC. The Sandia Cave materials, once candidates for an earlier position, cannot be credibly interpreted (Stevens and Agogino n.d.), leaving their true age unknown. That the widespread Clovis horizon extended throughout the Southwest is documented from excavations in southern Arizona and from sparse surface materials elsewhere. The Clovis groups were oriented toward hunting mammoths, as demonstrated at the Naco, Lehner, and Murray Springs sites in the San Pedro valley of Arizona (Figures 8.2 and 8.3). This last site has also produced evidence that now-extinct forms of bison and perhaps the horse were hunted as well. The distinctive Clovis horizon is not confined to the Southwest and is described in Chapter 1, as is the controversy over whether these early men played a role in the extinction of the terminal Pleistocene megafauna in North America.

Irwin-Williams and Haynes (1970) paint a picture of gradual retreat eastward for the plains-based big-game hunters after the Clovis period, presumably as increasing desiccation led to the replacement of grasslands by shrubs

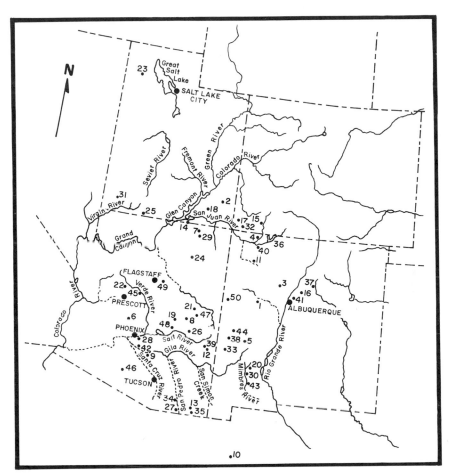

FIGURE 8.2
Sites and locations referred to in the text: *1*, Acoma Pueblo; *2*, Alkali Ridge; *3*, Armijo
and En Medio shelters; *4*, Aztec ruins; *5*, Bat Cave; *6*, Beardsley Canal site; *7*, Betatakin
and Kiet Siel; *8*, Bluff site; *9*, Casa Grande; *10*, Casas Grandes; *11*, Chaco Canyon;
12, Cienega Creek site; *13*, Double Adobe site; *14*, Dust Devil and Sand Dune caves;
15, Durango Basketmaker sites; *16*, Galisteo Basin; *17*, Gilliland site; *18*, Grand Gulch;
19, Grasshopper site; *20*, Harris site; *21*, Hay Hollow Valley; *22*, Henderson site; *23*, Hogup
Cave; *24*, Hopi Pueblos; *25*, Kanab Basketmaker sites; *26*, Kinishba; *27*, Lehner site;
28, Los Muertos site; *29*, Marsh Pass; *30*, Mattocks ruin; *31*, Median Village; *32*, Mesa
Verde; *33*, Mogollon Village; *34*, Murray Springs site; *35*, Naco site; *36*, Navajo Reservoir;
37, Pecos site; *38*, Pine Lawn Valley and Reserve area; *39*, Point of Pines; *40*, Salmon
ruin; *41*, Sandia Cave; *42*, Snaketown; *43*, Swarts ruin; *44*, Tularosa Cave; *45*, Tuzigoot;
46, Ventana Cave; *47*, Vernon area; *48*, Walnut Creek Village; *49*, Winona site; *50*, Zuni
Pueblo.

334

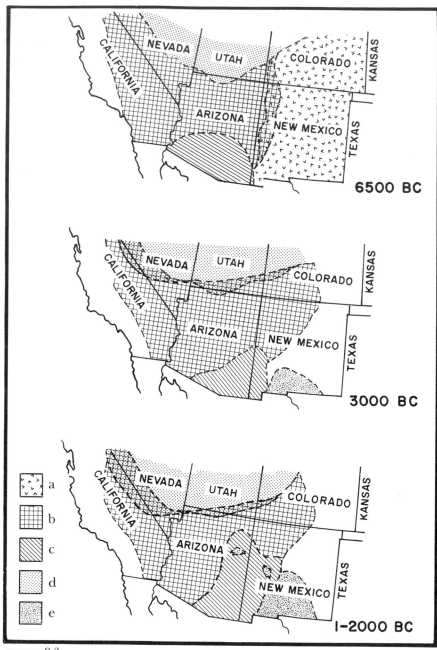

FIGURE 8.3

Distribution of early cultures at various points in time: *a*, Plains-oriented big-game hunters; *b*, Western-based Archaic cultures (with Oshara as a local tradition); *c*, Cochise tradition; *d*, Great Basin Archaic cultures (with Desha as a local manifestation); *e*, poorly known Archaic cultures based in northern Mexico. (After Irwin-Williams and Haynes 1970.)

and as surface water became scarcer. Folsom and early Plano sites, dating ca. 9000 to 7500 BC, tend to be found primarily east of the Arizona–New Mexico border. Plano materials from the period ca. 7500 to 6500 BC occur only rarely in the Southwest. The late Plano Cody complex of about 6500 to 6000 BC is, however, fairly well represented in the eastern and northern Southwest, perhaps because herds and hunters moved back into the area from the Plains in response to a temporary increase in effective moisture.

The Folsom and Plano groups were oriented toward exploiting bison herds. In the central Rio Grande valley of New Mexico, Judge (1973) has reconstructed from survey data some aspects of what he calls the "settlement technology" of these groups. Their sites tend to occur at the northeast ends of plains, which the bison presumably favored for grazing. Sites were located in general proximity to water—first near playas and then near streams as continuing desiccation reduced the number and importance of playas.

Judge identifies three kinds of sites. *Preparatory,* or armament, sites were located at overview points not necessarily close to water but having a good view of hunting areas. The principal activity at these locations was the flaking of projectile points, presumably by groups of hunters waiting for game. *Processing* sites were generally quite near water; tool types and wear patterns on them suggest that soft materials, such as hides, were being processed, perhaps by cooperative work groups of women. *Base camps* were strategically located with respect to major hunting areas, water sources, and overlooks; artifacts are most abundant and varied here, indicating that numerous activities occurred.

The Archaic

The term *Archaic* covers a quite varied group of American archeological cultures that exhibit neither a specialized big-game-hunting adaptation nor a sedentary-horticultural adaptation. The various poorly documented manifestations that may predate the Clovis horizon cannot, however, be called Archaic. If they existed at all, these are manifestations of cultures that had a very generalized subsistence technology, the adaptations of which are poorly understood.

The American Archaic cultures, on the other hand, can be amply demonstrated to have had a close adaptation to a large variety of local plant, animal, and inorganic resources. Tool kits, paleoecological data, and settlement patterns suggest that several food and raw material procurement systems were ordinarily employed, and that these often required precise scheduling of activities, commonly within a seasonal round of movement. Because of the variety of resources exploited, these adaptations tended to be stable, and slow to change. There was substantial interregional variation because of regional differences in resources and procurement systems and local accumulations of stylistically distinctive traits.

Turning from the Archaic in the abstract to a more concrete level of analysis, we find that the Southwestern Archaic displays substantial regional and temporal diversity in material culture and inferred adaptive strategy. This can be documented by a review of the better-known local sequences.

VENTANA CAVE AND SAN DIEGUITO □ At Ventana Cave, a stratified site in southwestern Arizona (Haury 1950), the lowest occupational stratum yielded stone tools, a carbon-14 date of 9300 BC ± 1200 years, and bones of now extinct horse, tapir, ground sloth, jaguar, and four-pronged antelope. Modern forms also occurred: jackrabbit, prairie dog, badger, peccary, and deer. A crudely made lanceolate point was likened by Haury (1950) to Folsom and by Haynes (1964) to Clovis, but Irwin-Williams (n.d.) doubts both assignments. Other artifacts include scraper-planes, choppers, scrapers, and cutting tools made by percussion techniques on side-struck flakes, plus a single discoidal mano. Although probably contemporaneous with Clovis or Folsom, these materials imply a more generalized hunting pattern and the possibility of plant resource exploitation; they may indicate the very early emergence of a generalized Archaic pattern.

The Ventana complex resembles the widespread but as yet rather poorly defined San Dieguito complex (see Chapter 4) of California, southwestern Nevada, and western Arizona. Diagnostic artifacts include Lake Mohave and Silver Lake points, bifacial leaf-shaped knives, and a variety of percussion-flaked scrapers and choppers. Grinding tools are absent. Warren (1967) suggests that San Dieguito dates between about 8000 and 6500 BC and represents an early generalized hunting culture with relationships in the Northwest.

The next cultural materials to be deposited at Ventana Cave follow an erosional hiatus and are dated on geologic grounds as post-5000 BC. Grinding tools are still absent; Haury notes affinities of the chipped stone to California-centered late San Dieguito-Amargosa materials. Manos and grinding slabs do not appear until subsequent levels, when assemblages increasingly resemble the Cochise tradition farther east, but with strong elements of the western Pinto Basin-Amargosa tradition remaining.

THE COCHISE TRADITION □ In 1926, the same year that a Folsom point was found *in situ* with extinct bison remains (Figgins 1927), Dr. Byron Cummings of the University of Arizona and three students (Lyndon Hargrave, Emil Haury, and John McGregor, all of whom later became prominent archeologists) observed artifacts lying stratigraphically below mammoth remains in alluvial deposits at the Double Adobe site, southeastern Arizona (Whalen 1971). Sayles and Antevs (1941) excavated here and at other sites in the area and defined a long sequence they named the Cochise Culture, with three stages or phases: Sulphur Springs, Chiricahua, and San Pedro.

The origins of this tradition are obscure, but it appears throughout to manifest evidence of an Archaic style of adaptation. Percussion-flaked choppers, planes, scrapers, and knives—all made on large flakes—and food-grinding implements are present throughout the tradition (Figure 8.4). Although the Sulphur Springs stage is known only from a small cluster of sites in southeastern Arizona, the later materials occur widely in the southern desert and Mogollon Highlands, where San Pedro appears to have evolved into the Mogollon tradition. The Sulphur Springs stage has yielded carbon-14 dates falling between 7300 and 6000 BC, dates for Chiricahua cluster between 3500 and 1500 BC, and San Pedro extends to ca. 200 BC (Whalen 1971:67–68). The lack of dated materials between 6000 and at least 4000 BC may be due to vagaries of preservation and discovery or may reflect a sparse occupation during the Altithermal.

Fossils of now extinct animals such as mammoth, camel, horse, and dire wolf, as well as modern forms such as antelope, jackrabbit, mallard, and coyote, have been found at Sulphur Springs sites. The association of the extinct mammals with the cultural materials has been questioned, but Haury (1960) strongly argues that it is authentic. Split and burned bones at the Sulphur Springs sites indicate that at least some of the animals were hunted, but the artifactual assemblage, lacking projectile points and heavily dominated by cobble manos and thin grinding slabs (Figure 8.4), is more suggestive of plant-food processing. Whalen (1971:69) proposes that nearby occurrences of the poorly known Cazador complex, which does include projectile points, may represent Sulphur Springs hunting activities, but Irwin-Williams (n.d.) questions both the stratigraphic and the typological bases for this assignment.

Projectile points, some resembling the widespread Pinto type, are definitely present in the Chiricahua stage, and San Pedro sites yield a variety of stemmed points, including distinctive narrow side-notched types (Figure 8.4). Large base camps with storage pits, outlying special-activity sites, small mortars, and heavy basin milling stones can be documented by Chiricahua times. San Pedro sites tend to be larger and more numerous, and simple pithouses have been found at several of these sites.

Late Cochise contexts at Bat Cave (Dick 1965), Tularosa Cave (Martin et al. 1952), and Ventana Cave (Haury 1950) demonstrate that a large variety of seed foods and small to medium game animals were being exploited. Evidence from Bat Cave shows that by 2000 BC primitive maize was being cultivated in small quantities. Squash was apparently introduced about the same time, but beans do not appear until the San Pedro stage (Whalen 1973). These early cultigens occur in highland sites along the Arizona-New Mexico border, just north of the Sierra Madre Occidental, which extends southward into central Mexico. Haury (1962) makes a good case for the gradual early diffusion of farming from Mexico into the Southwest along this mountain chain.

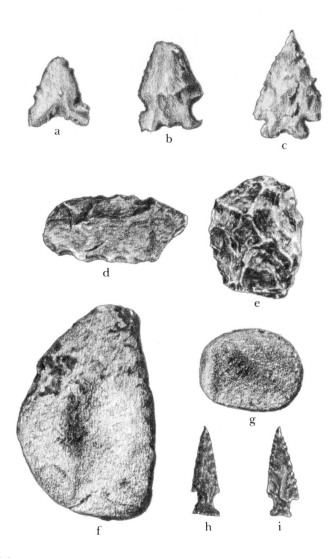

FIGURE 8.4
Artifacts of the Cochise tradition: *a–c*, projectile points of general Pinto Basin type;
d, flake knife with retouch on one edge; *e*, plano-convex chipping-scraping tool; *f*, shallow
basin grinding slab; *g*, one-hand cobble mano; *h, i*, narrow side-notched projectile points
of the San Pedro stage. *a–g* are all Chiricahua stage. (After Sayles and Antevs 1941.)

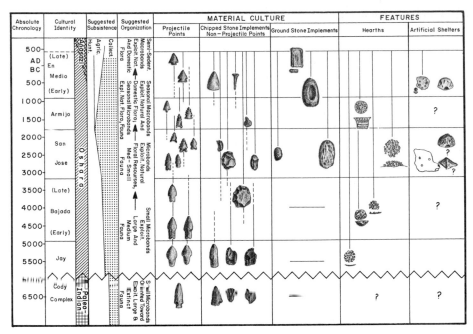

Absolute Chronology	Cultural Identity	Suggested Subsistence	Suggested Organization	MATERIAL CULTURE			FEATURES	
				Projectile Points	Chipped Stone Implements Non–Projectile Points	Ground Stone Implements	Hearths	Artificial Shelters

FIGURE 8.5
Synopsis of the Oshara tradition. (After Irwin-Williams 1973.)

THE OSHARA TRADITION □ Recent work by Irwin-Williams (1968; 1973; n.d.) in northwestern New Mexico has defined a long Archaic sequence (Figure 8.5) locally ancestral to Anasazi. The earliest Archaic manifestation (the Jay phase) is so different from the Paleo-Indian Cody complex that preceded it that Irwin-Williams sees no connections. Instead, there are resemblances to San Dieguito, leading her (n.d.) to postulate slow demographic movements from the west, which spread into the niche left by the withdrawal of the Paleo-Indian groups.

The Jay phase (5500–4800 BC), which lacks grinding tools, has large projectile points reminiscent of the Lake Mohave type, along with well-made side scrapers and bifacial knives. Sites and populations were small. Irwin-Williams thinks the economic cycle was not strongly seasonal or transhumant. Small limited-activity sites record hunting, foraging, and quarrying activities that probably were staged from base camps established at environmentally favored canyon-head locations.

The succeeding Bajada phase (4800–3200 BC) resembles the Jay phase. Projectile points, though still large and long stemmed, have concave bases and more definite shoulders. Crude flake scrapers and chopping tools become more abundant and may indicate increased use of coarse plant foods, while the introduction of cobble-filled hearths and earth ovens suggests technical improvements in food processing as well. Although this phase coincides with the Altithermal, population may actually have increased slightly.

In the San Jose phase (3200–1800 BC), base camps are larger and more numerous, with more debris. Posthole patterns at one site suggest simple surface structures. Increased use of seeds and other plant foods is indicated by the appearance of shallow grinding slabs and cobble manos and an increase in chopping tools and coarse flake scrapers. The formation of larger special-activity groups is indicated by one hunting site with 15 hearths. Projectile point forms and the assemblage in general parallel the Pinto Basin materials to the west. Irwin-Williams thinks that population increased during this period, probably in response to the onset of slightly moister conditions after the Altithermal and to more effective resource exploitation brought about by improved technology.

In the Armijo phase (1800–800 BC), primitive maize began to be raised on a small scale, and the frequency of ground stone tools continued to increase. The pattern of canyon-head base camps and distant special-activity sites continues, but a new settlement type appears—a fall or winter camp that joined several small bands into a seasonal macroband of perhaps 30 to 50 people. Irwin-Williams thinks this development was based on the small horticultural surplus, which was coincident with a seasonal abundance of wild food resources. Typologically, the Armijo assemblage continues to show resemblances to the late Pinto Basin complexes to the west.

The En Medio phase (800 BC–AD 400) shows continued regional population increase and greater seasonality of the annual economic cycle. The number of fall-winter macroband camps increased, while the canyon-head locations were depopulated in the summer in favor of a new type of limited-activity site—gathering camps located on upland dune ridges. The tool kit shows continuities with the preceding phase, with the addition of greater numbers of bifacially flaked knives and drills and the predominance of corner-notched projectile points. The latter part of this phase is what has commonly been classified as Basketmaker II (originally one of the Pecos Classification stages) of the Anasazi tradition.

THE DESHA COMPLEX □ Excavations in Dust Devil and Sand Dune caves in southeastern Utah (Lindsay et al. 1968) resulted in definition of the Desha complex, dating in those sites to 5000 to 6000 BC. This as yet poorly known complex is quite different from the Jay phase of that date in northeastern New Mexico and from the general Lake Mohave-Silver Lake materials to the west. Instead, relationships are with the Great Basin and the southern Rockies (Irwin-Williams 1970). The Desha materials include numerous shallow basin grinding slabs and one-hand manos and infrequent but distinctive elongate, shallowly side-notched points. Distinctive techniques of basketry and sandal construction also occurred among the perishable items.

In more recent cave excavations in south-central Utah, Jennings (1975) has found Desha-related materials extending much later in time. In the late Desha or Terminal Archaic levels was a cache of maize. Also associated were split-twig figurines—small animal effigies. Evidently not confined to the Desha complex, these figurines have been found in northern Arizona, southern Nevada, and southeastern California and have consistently dated between 2000 and 1000 BC (Schwartz et al 1958; Euler and Olson 1965; Fowler 1973). Some have been pierced by what are probably effigy spears, and many have been found cached in remote caves, especially in the Grand Canyon; these facts suggest they were used in hunting rituals.

THE TRANSITION TO SETTLED LIFE

As previously noted, domesticated plants were being cultivated on a small scale in the Southwest by 2000 BC, if not earlier, and the Late Archaic was also a time of gradual population growth and increasing cultural complexity. At various times between 300 BC and AD 700, regionally distinctive cultural traditions emerged (such as Hohokam, Mogollon, Anasazi, Fremont, Patayan, and Sinagua), and the pace of change markedly quickened. Although during this period the timing and intensity of change varied locally, in general, pithouse villages became numerous across the Southwest, population grew more rapidly than before, pottery became widely used, and cultigens came to dominate subsistence in most areas. Changes in settlement pattern, social organization, technology, and the organization of work can also be recognized.

A series of basic and fascinating questions arise concerning this transition from an Archaic lifestyle to one that can be called incipient Formative (Willey and Phillips 1958) or Neolithic. What made the presumably stable, well-adapted Archaic cultures susceptible to change, why did it take cultigens 2000 years or more to become basic to subsistence, what processes brought about the transformation of culture and society, and why did the rate of change vary from place to place? Although these problems are not unique to the Southwest, their solution is essential to understanding the Southwestern transition. All we can say at this point is that work on these topics has begun.

That corn, beans, and squash were initially domesticated in Mexico and transferred to the Southwest seems well established (Mangelsdorf, et al. 1967). A favorable milieu for this sort of cultural transmission was established by about 3000 BC with the emergence of what Irwin-Williams (1967) has called

Picosa or the Elementary Southwestern culture. This was based on a wide-spread communications network that permitted the rapid sharing of information among diverse local cultures. Irwin-Williams and Haynes (1970) suggest that this development was made possible by increases in population and cultural complexity that were in turn related to increased effective moisture and, presumably, increased wild food resources at the close of the Altithermal.

That the adaptively sophisticated Archaic peoples would have been receptive to information about new plant foods seems likely. Already keen students of natural history, they would not have needed to be taught that plants would grow if seeds were put in the ground. And their seed-processing technology was preadapted to the addition of a new cereal food such as maize. Ethnographic accounts of Basin peoples having an essentially Archaic lifestyle indicate that they sometimes manipulated the environments of wild food plants by irrigation and weeding and that some groups cultivated small patches of true domesticates. Yet these activities were fited in only as permitted by the demands of the larger round of foraging and contributed relatively little to total subsistence. "Incipient cultivation" of this sort must have characterized the Late Archaic in the Southwest.

What changed the old pattern of exploiting environmental diversity to a new one of concentration on a few crop plants? One answer could be that the Mexican Formative frontier pushed north into the Southwest, and that the Archaic peoples were replaced or absorbed by groups that had made the transition farther south. If Haury (1976) is right, and his argument is persuasive, the early Hohokam Vahki phase settlements of about 300 BC in southern Arizona do represent just such a colonization by village-dwelling irrigation farmers. Outside the riverine Hohokam area, however, the data suggest a more gradual transformation of *in situ* Archaic cultures. Certainly the proximity of Hohokam villages might have hastened this process by providing trade items and information, but juxtaposition and contact cannot in themselves account for the changes. The Southwestern ethnographic literature provides abundant examples of stable and even symbiotic relationships between adjacent Formative and Archaic groups. Explanations must be sought within the changing cultures themselves, as well as in the broader regional context of information availability and flow.

Flannery's (1968) model of the transformation of the Mesoamerican Archaic provides insights that may help illuminate the Southwestern case. His analysis treats seasonal scheduling of food collecting as a device that not only enabled groups to adapt to variable and scattered resources but that also acted as a regulatory mechanism countering tendencies to concentrate on any single food procurement system. This was altered, however, when the conditions under which early domesticates were grown selected for genetic changes that increased their food value and hence their attractiveness. This triggered positive feedback or deviation-amplifying processes, such as population growth and investment in fixed facilities, which led to increasing dependence on cultigens, radical alteration in food procurement scheduling, and changes in the social organization.

Somewhat similar processes may have been operating in the Southwest. Adaptation of cultigens to local environments was undoubtedly important, but there is also evidence of continuing introduction of more productive strains of maize, presumably from the south (e.g., Dick 1965:92–99; Galinat and Gunnerson 1963). Even at the level of incipient cultivation in a basically Archaic subsistence pattern, this new food energy source may have triggered cultural change of the sort described by Flannery. Irwin-Williams (n.d.), for example, interprets the shift to winter macroband camps and the associated increase in ceremonial activity in the late Oshara tradition as being based on a food surplus generated by cultigens.

A somewhat different tack is taken by Glassow (1972) in his study of the transformation of Anasazi Basketmaker culture in the Plateau area. Adapting a general model promulgated by Binford (1968), Glassow emphasizes the role of population growth, seeing the Southwest as a region that received external population from areas such as coastal California, where successful sedentary fishing-foraging adaptations were generating population increase. He argues that early Basketmaker groups—having an essentially Archaic subsistence pattern with some use of cultigens—occupied a limited number of favorable ecotone situations, giving them access to the resources of both canyon and mesa environments. When these situations became fully occupied, less favored settings received more population. In these environmentally less diverse locations, adaptive alternatives, such as increased dependence on farming and the construction of larger storage facilities, were favored, setting off positive feedback processes of the sort described by Flannery. In a frequently parallel analysis of the evolution of Basketmaker culture, Lipe and Matson (1971b) speculate that even in the absence of population increase a period of environmental deterioration might have had similar effects by reducing the number of most favored areas, thus forcing some groups to readapt to conditions of diminished resource availability.

In the most ambitious study of the Archaic-Formative transition to date, Plog (1974) makes a case study of Mogollon-Pueblo data from the upper Little Colorado area in the southern Plateau. He does not try to identify the precise mechanisms triggering the transition but instead focuses on the processes operating during its unfolding in the period between AD 850 and 1050. He develops a model having population, differentiation, integration, and technology as its critical, measurable variables and attempts to define their interrelationships through time in the study area.

Plog recognizes that many aspects of the analysis remain speculative or data deficient, and he is properly cautious about extrapolating his conclusions to other Southwestern regions. Nevertheless, the study is a pioneering attempt to come to grips with the organizational as well as the ecological aspects of this important step in the evolution of Southwestern cultures.

THE LATE CULTURES

The Hohokam

The term *Hohokam*, a Pima Indian word meaning "all used up," has been applied to the settled prehistoric agriculturalists who occupied much of the southern Basin and Range province in what is now Arizona (Figures 8.6 and 8.7). If, as is generally believed, the Pima and Papago are the cultural heirs of the Hohokam, their cultural tradition can probably be traced back as many as 2300 years in this arid region.

GENERAL CHARACTERISTICS □ Several traits are generally accepted as being diagnostic of Hohokam culture. Hohokam pottery was generally thinned and smoothed by the paddle-and-anvil method, and was of gray to brown paste color. Most of the painted vessels were first coated with a buff-colored wash or slip, on which the red design was then applied (Figure 8.8). Cremation of the dead was practiced throughout the Hohokam sequence, but inhumations came increasingly to be used in the latest phases. Hohokam houses were generally oblong in plan and built in shallow pits (Figure 8.9). They were not true pithouses because the pit wall was not used as the lower part of the house wall; instead, the structure's jacal walls were footed at the floor level. Late in the cultural sequence, these sunken houses were largely replaced by surface structures. Settlements varied in size from a few houses to over 100 and generally displayed little evidence of a village plan until the late phases, when walled compounds appeared.

Specialized structures that may have served community integrative functions included ball courts and platform mounds. The former were large, bowl-shaped depressions, which have generally been interpreted as being related to the Mesoamerican structures in which ceremonial ball games were played (cf. Gladwin et al. 1937:36–49). Ferdon (1967) has argued, however, that in the Hohokam area these structures may have been dance courts instead. The platform mounds are low but often large, flat-topped features, generally built of trash midden material stabilized by an adobe cap. Such mounds have been interpreted as being of ceremonial or socio-political function.

On the basis of Bohrer's (1970) pioneering study of the Snaketown botanical remains, it appears that the Hohokam subsistence adaptation resembled the ethnographic Pima-Papago pattern. This strategy consisted of a flexible single or dual cropping of maize, beans, cucurbits, cotton, and possibly tobacco and amaranth. Plantings were scheduled to correspond to the biannual rainfall and flooding pattern in the Hohokam area (Figure 8.10). In locations where irrigation from flowing streams could be practiced, that technique was favored; elsewhere, the Hohokam employed floodplain farm-

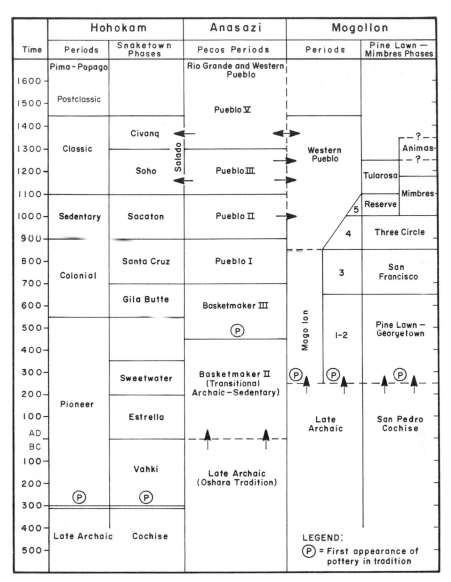

FIGURE 8.6
Correlation of Hohokam, Mogollon, and Anasazi cultural sequences.

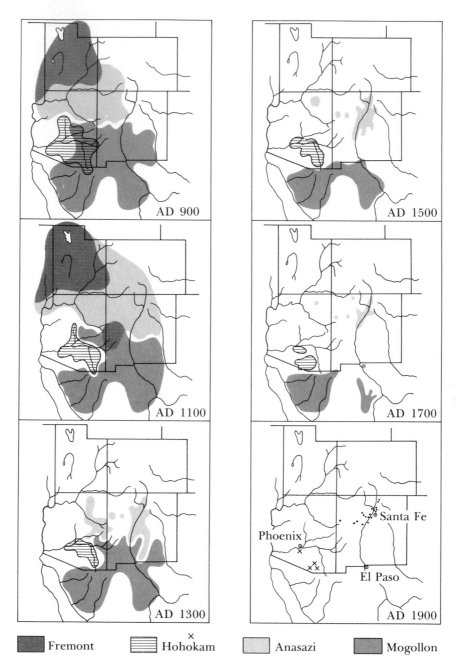

AD 900

AD 1500

AD 1100

AD 1700

AD 1300

Phoenix

Santa Fe

El Paso

AD 1900

Fremont   Hohokam   Anasazi   Mogollon

FIGURE 8.7
Approximate distribution of principal late cultures, AD 900–1900. (From *Prehistory of North America,* 2d ed., by Jesse D. Jennings. Copyright © 1968, 1974 by McGraw-Hill, Inc. Used with permission of McGraw-Hill Book Company.)

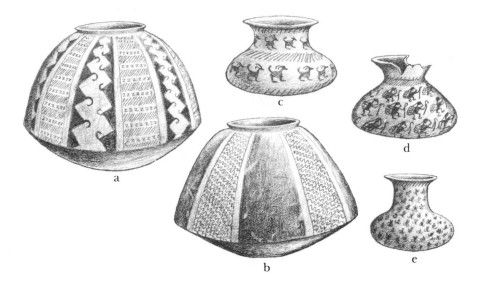

FIGURE 8.8
Examples of Hohokam decorated pottery: *a, b,* Sacaton Red-on-Buff; *c–e,* Santa Cruz Red-on-Buff. (From *Prehistory of North America,* 2d ed., by Jesse D. Jennings. Copyright © 1968, 1974 by McGraw-Hill, Inc. Used with permission of McGraw-Hill Book Company.)

ing, or the construction of stone grids, terraces, or check dams to catch runoff after local storms. The cultivation of domesticates was complemented by the seasonally scheduled exploitation of a wide range of wild biotic resources. Especially important were the fruits of cacti such as saguaro, organ pipe, and prickly pear and the seed-bearing pods of tree legumes such as mesquite. Harvesting of these foods allowed the Hohokam to compensate for fluctuations in the production of domestic crops.

The archeological evidence for this subsistence strategy, primarily in the form of a subsistence-related technology and settlement pattern, does not change markedly throughout the length of Hohokam culture history. Thus, the adaptive strategy provides a consistent base from which to describe Hohokam stability and change. Although relatively little paleoenvironmental work in the Hohokam area has been focused on the time period of interest here, such evidense as exists (for example, the latter part of the record studied by Mehringer et al. 1967) does not indicate major environmental change during this time. It may be, then, that environmental stability contributed to Hohokam adaptive stability.

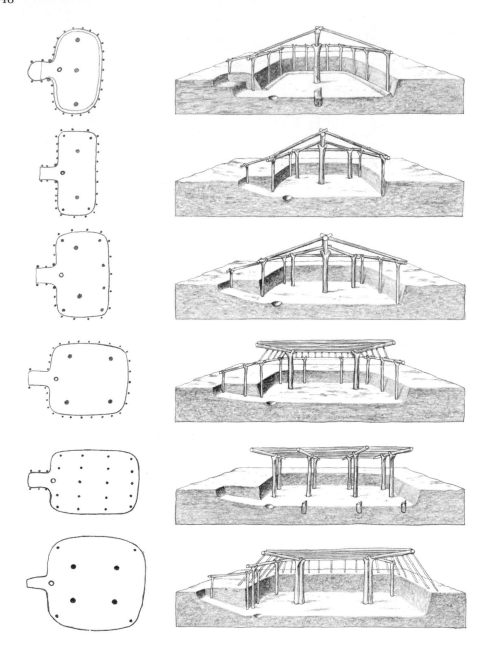

FIGURE 8.9
Floor plans and cross-sections (postulated roof constructions) of Hohokam houses at
Snaketown, arranged in temporal sequence. (From *Prehistory of North America,* 2d ed., by
Jesse D. Jennings. Copyright © 1968, 1974 by McGraw-Hill, Inc. Used with permission of
McGraw-Hill Book Company.)

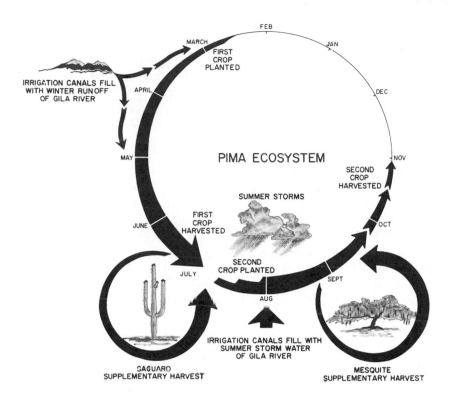

FEB

MARCH
FIRST
CROP
PLANTED

JAN

DEC

IRRIGATION CANALS FILL
WITH WINTER RUNOFF
OF GILA RIVER

APRIL

MAY

PIMA ECOSYSTEM

NOV

SECOND
CROP
HARVESTED

SUMMER STORMS

JUNE

FIRST
CROP
HARVESTED

OCT

SECOND
CROP PLANTED

SEPT

JULY

AUG

IRRIGATION CANALS FILL WITH
SUMMER STORM WATER
OF GILA RIVER

SAGUARO
SUPPLEMENTARY HARVEST

MESQUITE
SUPPLEMENTARY HARVEST

FIGURE 8.10
The Pima ecosystem, which was probably similar to that of the Hohokam. (After Bohrer 1970.)

THEORIES OF HOHOKAM CULTURAL DEVELOPMENT □ Until recently, most Southwesternists have seen early Hohokam culture as an essentially *in situ* development, the result of local Cochise groups having gradually adopted traits of Mexican origin, such as agriculture and pottery, either directly or through a Mogollon intermediary (cf. Gladwin et al. 1937; Haury 1945a). A special formulation of this general position was developed by DiPeso (1956), who labeled the indigenous agriculturalists the Ootam. Schroeder (1957; 1960; 1965) included the early Hohokam as part of the Hakataya tradition, which he believed to be a very widespread indigenous cultural pattern that occupied parts of the central and western Arizona uplands as well as the desert areas.

Although Haury long favored an *in situ* theory of Hohokam origins, his 1964–1965 excavations at the important site of Snaketown in the Gila River valley led him to change this view (Haury 1965; 1967; 1976). He now believes that the earliest Hohokam (ca. 300 BC) were migrants from northern Mexico, who came to Arizona with an already formed, sedentary, pottery-using culture supported by intensive irrigated agriculture. He also postulates that such river valley-based colonies would have quickly influenced the native hunter-gatherers of the hinterlands, a process that would have contributed to the development of a nonriverine or desert variety of the Hohokam lifeway.

Such reservations as exist about Haury's conclusions appear to be because most of the evidence is from a single site, because a specific north Mexican ancestor has not been identified, and because there is no convincing theory of why and how such a migration and rapid readaptation might have occurred. These concerns speak to the state of research in southern Arizona and northern Mexico for this time period rather than to the quality of Haury's work. The majority of Southwesternists appear to have accepted his conclusions as the best reading of the evidence currently available.

There is general agreement that the Colonial and Sedentary periods of the Hohokam tradition (about AD 550–1100) saw a heightened influx of traits of Mexican origin (Figure 8.11). The evidence (Haury 1976:347) includes new varieties of maize, the appearance of platform mounds and ball courts, trade goods such as copper bells, mosaic mirrors, and exotic pottery, and the use of decorative motifs employing Mesoamerican symbolic themes (Figure 8.12). As reflected in their use of the term *Colonial* in the Hohokam period sequence, the Gladwins (1934) initially viewed such traits as having been brought by migrants from the south.

In a more explicit theory, DiPeso (1956) argues that disruptions in Mesoamerican centers had forced the dispersion of small groups of the elite stratum of Mesoamerican society. Some of these entered southern Arizona, subjugating the indigenous Ootam peoples. DiPeso prefers to reserve the label *Hohokam* for these Mexican intruders. His dating of these events at about AD 900 reflects a radical and not widely accepted shortening of the Hohokam chronology; culturally, the postulated migration equates with the beginning of the Colonial period.

Schroeder (1947; 1960; 1965; 1966) has proposed a somewhat different migration theory. He suggests that at approximately AD 700 an organized mercantile group (similar to the *pochteca* of the Aztecs) moved from the Tarascan region of western Mexico and subjugated the indigenous Hakataya of the Salt and Gila river valleys. From this base, the group conducted extensive trading activities, which resulted in the widespread diffusion of Hohokam-Mexican traits in the Southwest. Like DiPeso, Schroeder reserves the title *Hohokam* for the cultural intruders.

Others, notably, Haury (1976:343–348), view the appearance of additional Mexican elements in Hohokam sites at this time as a result of a variety of continuing contacts rather than of actual migrations, as occurred at first.

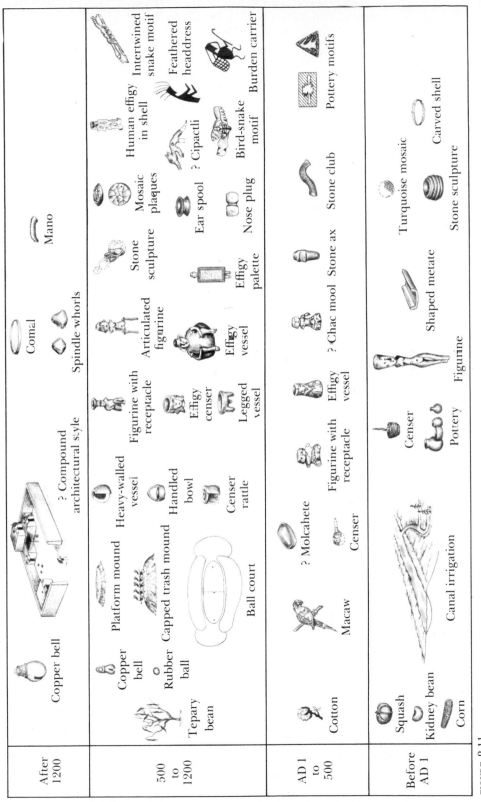

FIGURE 8.11
Hohokam cultural elements exhibiting Mesoamerican influence. (After Haury 1976.)

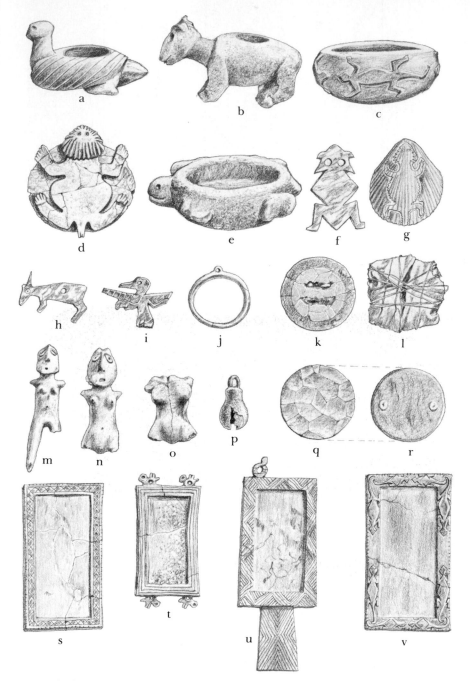

FIGURE 8.12
Nonutilitarian Hohokam artifacts: *a–e,* zoomorphic stone bowls and censers; *f–j,* zoomorphic shell ornaments; *k, l, q, r,* pyrite mirror in wrapping; *m–o,* clay anthropomorphic figurines; *p,* copper bell; *s–v,* stone palettes. (From *Prehistory of North America,* 2d ed., by Jesse D. Jennings. Copyright © 1968, 1974 by McGraw-Hill, Inc. Used with permission of McGraw-Hill Book Company.)

This theory of primarily *in situ* development for this portion of Hohokam prehistory appears to be the currently dominant position among Southwesternists.

A third recurring issue in the interpretation of Hohokam culture history is the role of migrations during the Classic period (ca. AD 1100–1450). A frequent entry into this debate is the postulated intrusion of a group called the Salado; they have been variously characterized as an Anasazi, Mogollon-Pueblo, or Western Pueblo group. The Tonto Basin-Globe area located in the higher country northeast of Phoenix, Arizona, has been frequently mentioned as the probable Salado homeland. The Salado hypothesis seems to have developed as an explanation for the appearance of multistoried pueblo-like structures, polychrome pottery, and inhumations in Classic period sites. In his study of the Los Muertos site near Phoenix, Arizona, Haury (1945b) interpreted the evidence as indicating that both Hohokam and Salado maintained some degree of ethnic identity and lived side by side in an amicable way. This remains the "standard" formulation of the Salado concept, but alternative interpretations abound. For example, a recent symposium on the Salado (Doyel and Haury 1976) produced a number of new hypotheses and reviewed new data, but little consensus emerged.

Schroeder (1960) also sees an intrusion from the north during the Classic period, but identifies it as Sinagua, not Salado. Basically Hakataya in tradition, Sinagua culture had been strongly shaped by Anasazi contacts, as well as by Hohokam expansion northward into the Verde valley and the Flagstaff area during the preceding periods.

As an alternative to the northern-intrusion theories, DiPeso (1956), following out his model of Hohokam-Ootam relationships, sees some Classic period characteristics as resulting from an overthrow of the dominant Hohokam by the now acculturated Ootam. He subsequently may have modified or at least added to this position, for he has recently interpreted aspects of Classic period Hohokam and of the Salado phenomenon as being the result of the activities of *pochteca* housed at the site of Casas Grandes, located southeast of the Hohokam area (DiPeso 1974:314; 1976).

Wasley (1966; see also Wasley and Johnson 1965) rejected migration theories in favor of an *in situ* theory of Classic Hohokam development. Citing the presence in earlier phases of most of the diagnostic traits that have been used as evidence of intrusions, Wasley concluded that continuing diffusion of ideas from Mexico was the only extraneous influence during this period. More recently, others (e.g., Doyel 1972; Weaver 1972; Grady 1976) have also emphasized *in situ* cultural and ecological processes in attempting to account for cultural change during the Classic period. Although perhaps not currently dominant, such theories seem to be gaining ground.

Proper assessment of the role of external versus internal factors in Hohokam cultural continuity and change continues to be hampered by (1) insufficient data on the range of cultural variability in the Hohokam core area, particularly for the Pioneer and Classic periods; (2) insufficient data on areas suggested as donors of population or culture, particularly northern Mexico and the Tonto Basin; and (3) an insufficient understanding of the organization and dynamics of Hohokam society. As research progresses in these three areas, we may see continuing progress in the solution of the problems raised earlier in this section.

THE PIONEER PERIOD (300 BC–AD 550) □ The earliest stage of Hohokam development, the Vahki phase, is dated on the basis of the latest chronological interpretations at about 300 BC to AD 1. These Hohokam already had a sophisticated material culture that included relatively large pithouses and a subsistence-related artifact assemblage containing pottery vessels, grinding implements, projectile points, and a range of scraping and cutting tools. Nonutilitarian implements include turquoise mosaic plaques, stone bowls, marine shell ornaments, and ceramic anthropomorphic figurines, all having a strong Mexican caste. The most striking Vahki accomplishment is canal irrigation. Haury (1976) documents a sophisticated irrigation technology, including a canal of about 5 kilometers in length.

By the Vahki phase the Hohokam were cultivating a primitive strain of maize as well as beans. The dog had been domesticated. Wild resources in the form of at least saguaro and prickly pear fruits and seeds, legume seeds (mesquite and screw beans), and some aquatic plants (sedge) were exploited. A wide range of faunal resources was used, including relatively high percentages of deer and rabbits. Birds do not seem to have been an important aspect of the animal resource base, and aquatic life was evidently of only marginal significance (Greene and Mathews 1976; McKusick 1976; Minckley 1976).

The Vahki phase was probably one of considerable experimentation. Data available from the few securely identified Vahki phase sites indicate that the variability in such trait constellations as houses, burials, and technological inventories is greater within the Vahki phase than it is for the rest of the Pioneer period (Gladwin et al. 1937; Haury 1976; Morris 1969).

By the beginning of the Estrella phase, the stable adaptive pattern that was to characterize most of the rest of the Hohokam cultural sequence had been developed. Conjointly, house forms became smaller and more uniform. Painted pottery emerged, and other decorating practices, such as surface grooving, were implemented. Stylized palettes and similar items of stonework are found, and the numbers of carved marine shells increases.

In the late Pioneer phases, no basic changes in the adaptive pattern occurred, though some elaboration on the Vahki phase strategy has been detected. Mexican macaws and cotton were added to the list of domesticates, and a superior strain of maize was being cultivated. The faunal records indicate that some increase in the use of deer and avifauna may have occurred—a change perhaps attributable to the more extensive use of the bow and arrow. Amaranth, tansy mustard, and other annuals were exploited in addition to the wild plants used during the Vahki phase (Bohrer et al. 1969; Greene and Mathews 1976; McKusick 1976).

By the end of the Pioneer period, Hohokam territory had increased considerably. From a core locality in the central Salt, Gila, and Santa Cruz river basins, the Hohokam had moved up these drainages, as well as into adjacent basins. Their settlements, generally smaller than those of succeeding periods, were usually located on the stabilized terraces above the river floodplains. The expansion of Pioneer period settlements into the Papagueria, west of the Santa Cruz River, attests to the Hohokam capacity to exploit locations lacking permanent surface water (Raab 1976).

THE COLONIAL PERIOD (AD 550–900) □ The Colonial period includes two phases: Gila Butte and Santa Cruz. These phase distinctions, based primarily on changes in ceramic styles, obscure the fact that very few modifications in the overall Hohokam lifeway occurred. During this period, ball courts and platform mounds, indicative of a degree of social integration, appeared. Elaboration of ground and chipped stone, shell artifacts, effigy ceramics, and other nonutilitarian items continued. Pottery designs were executed with greater technical skill. As previously noted, indications of Mesoamerican influence increase, particularly after AD 700.

Although the subsistence economy remained essentially the same, the appearance of cultivated tepary beans during the Colonial period provided an additional crop, one more resistant to drought than many other cultigens. Exploitation of deer continued to increase, as did the use of varieties of fowl, particularly riparian species (Haury 1976; Greene and Mathews 1976; McKusick 1976).

Hohokam expansion continued in the Colonial period. Not only did site size increase, but by the end of the Santa Cruz phase the Hohokam had pushed up the Salt, Verde, and Agua Fria rivers well into the Mogollon Highlands (Weed 1972; Weed and Ward 1970; Morris 1970). They also had moved east into the San Simon drainage (Gladwin and Gladwin 1935; Sayles 1945), south at least as far as the lower reaches of the Santa Cruz and San Pedro rivers (Greenleaf 1975; DiPeso 1956; Kelley 1960), and west to the Gila Bend vicinity on the Gila River (Wasley and Johnson 1965; Vivian 1965). Although the Hohokam population had not peaked by its end, there is little doubt that the Colonial period saw the greatest expansion of the Hohokam sphere of influence.

THE SEDENTARY PERIOD (AD 900–1100) □ The original Snaketown report identified two phases in the Sedentary period—a Sacaton phase and a later Santan phase (Gladwin et al. 1937:170). Subsequent research in the Hohokam region has failed to confirm the existence of the latter phase, however. Thus, the current literature does not include this phase, although Haury believes that it remains to be identified (Haury 1976:39).

The transition from the Colonial to the Sedentary period is less marked than the Pioneer-Colonial distinction. The subsistence technology remained virtually unchanged. The embellishment of nonutilitarian material culture continued, particularly within the realm of shell ornament manufacture. Copper bells, a Mexican trade item, appear. Platform mounds became a common aspect of Sedentary period architecture, sometimes appearing as large, isolated structures (Wasley 1960).

The Hohokam strains of maize continued to be improved during this period, becoming more and more drought resistant. Amaranth may well have been domesticated by this time (Bohrer et al. 1969). A notable increase in the amount of bighorn sheep bone over deer bone in the Sedentary period trash suggests more dependence upon the former animal (Greene and Mathews 1976)—a situation that might reflect overexploitation of the deer population.

The overall Sacaton phase settlement pattern bears a strong resemblance to that of the Colonial period. Although some territorial contraction appears to have occurred, site size had increased. Some intrasite organization in the form of clusters of pithouses is evident in a few sites (DiPeso 1956; Tuthill 1947). Site abandonment took place mainly in the north and northeast, where such Colonial period settlements as the Henderson site (Weed and Ward 1970), the Beardsley Canal site (Weed 1972), and Walnut Creek Village (Morris 1970) were abandoned by the Sacaton phase. Although the Hohokam site distribution contracted somewhat during the Sedentary period, the actual number of sites continued to increase.

THE CLASSIC PERIOD (AD 1100–1450) □ The Classic period, subdivided into the Soho and Civano phases, is probably the most widely speculated upon aspect of the Hohokam cultural sequence. Despite the fact that a considerable amount of research has centered around the study of the Classic period, it remains enigmatic. Of particular importance was the relatively abrupt development of a constellation of traits that had not previously been widespread in the Hohokam archeological record. Manifestations viewed as most significant are the appearance of contiguous-room surface pueblos, *cerros de trincheras,* the practice of inhumation, and the Salado polychrome ceramic series. Above-ground simple pueblo structures appear during the Soho phase and develop into large edifices, often surrounded by a compound wall, by the Civano phase. *Cerros de trincheras*—hilltop or hillside sites characterized by stone terraces and other features—also appear during the Soho phase and continue into the Civano. They are seemingly an adjunct to the Classic period Hohokam settlement pattern rather than a pattern in their own right (Stacy 1974:190–193).

Although the general subsistence pattern did not change, there is evidence for the intensification of cultivation, as manifested in increases in canal irrigation and the appearance of *cerros de trincheras.* The latter have been interpreted as having functioned in part as dry-farming features (Stacy 1974:194). There may also have been an increase in the emphasis on wild biotic resource exploitation (Grady et al. 1973; Grebinger 1971; Schroeder 1952; Weaver 1972), though this has not been substantiated (Doyel 1972; Grady 1976).

Classic period sites occur in the same environmental settings as Preclassic Hohokam sites. In many cases they are stratigraphically superimposed over Sedentary and older sites, though occupational continuity has not been demonstrated (Schroeder 1940). Generally larger than earlier settlements, Classic period sites are believed to have been formally planned and structured before being built. Such a transition represents an important modification in residence group relationships. The incorporation of habitation units within activity spaces that included platform mounds, often topped by edifices, suggests that community organization had become more integrated and probably more centralized.

THE POSTCLASSIC PERIOD (AD 1450–1700). □ The 250-year time span between the end of the Classic period and documentation of the indigenous Pima-Papago lifeway by the first Spanish explorers has not, so far, been the subject of archeological investigation. Due in large part to Pima-Papago sensitivity about disturbing protohistoric sites, archeologists have not studied these manifestations. Available evidence indicates that the protohistoric Indians encountered by the Spanish did not follow the Classic period lifeway. Although their settlement-subsistence strategy was very similar to that determined archeologically for the Classic period Hohokam, other aspects of their lifestyle were much more like those of the Preclassic period peoples. The territory inhabited by the Pima and Papago did not extend as far north and east as had that of the Hohokam (Ezell 1961), but those localities occupied by the protohistoric Indians were utilized in fashions similar to those of their prehistoric predecessors; in some cases historic villages were located at or near Classic or earlier sites. Yet both the Pima and Papago lived in spatially separate houses, which were often semisubterranean. They did not make polychrome pottery, nor construct platform mounds or compound walls. Despite this apparent hiatus in cultural tradition, many authors have presented a strong case for genetic continuity between the Hohokam and the Pima-Papago (Haury 1975; 1976; Ezell 1963; Niswander and Brown 1970).

Many diffuse and often speculative suggestions as to the fate of the Classic period Hohokam have been advanced. Ideas range from demise due to earthquakes (Cushing 1890:186–187), crop failure (Haury 1945b:211; Hayden 1957:196), Athapaskan invasions (Gladwin et al. 1937:101–102), and the withdrawal of intrusive groups (DiPeso 1974:321; Schroeder 1947), to population pressure (Grady 1976) and climatic deterioration (Grebinger 1971:203; Weaver 1972:9–10). Some, such as the Athapaskan raider and earthquake propositions, have been adequately debunked (e.g., Haury 1945b:210–211 and Wilcox n.d.). Others, such as the departure of a population segment responsible for Classic period culture, lack credible evidence. Internal factors, such as climatic change, agricultural problems, and population stress, are most amenable to confirmation or rejection as casual mechanisms. Although one factor may be responsible for such change in certain circumstances, it is more likely that combinations of variables will be found to have been responsible for inducing change within the Postclassic period in specific and throughout the Hohokam cultural sequence in general.

The Mogollon

At the time of its maximum extent—probably about AD 800 or 900—the Mogollon tradition occupied not only the mountainous Mogollon Highlands but also portions of the Basin and Range province lying to the south, southwest, and east. The tradition emerged from Late Archaic antecedents sometime between about 300 BC and AD 300 and disappeared as a separate entity between about AD 900 and 1100, when increasing Anasazi influence led to its incorporation into Western Pueblo culture. Although Bullard (1962:184–185) considers the Mogollon "nuclear area" to have been in the lower and more southerly parts of its range, the tradition's "natural habitat" has traditionally been thought of as the more northerly, higher, and topographically rugged mountain area we have labeled the Mogollon Highlands. If we consider it to include the Mimbres drainage, which extends south from the mountains into the lower elevations, the Highland area is certainly better known and consequently is the source of most of our information about the Mogollon. We incline to the traditional view of the Mogollon as a culture adapted to mountain environments.

GENERAL CHARACTERISTICS □ Although domesticated plants became well established in the Mogollon area in Late Archaic times, hunting and gathering remained substantial contributors to Mogollon diet throughout the tradition. We have the impression that hunting, in particular, played a larger role here than among either the Anasazi or Hohokam. The abundance and diversity of wild food resources in the highlands and the limitations on farming in some areas because of steep slopes or high altitudes must have contributed to the persistence of a generalized subsistence pattern.

Mogollon farming appears to have depended primarily on direct rainfall, runoff from slopes, or natural flooding in washes. Simple water-control devices such as check dams and lines of boulders transverse to slopes are reported for the late Mogollon and Western Pueblo periods (Woodbury 1961). Although Plog (1974:40) reports prehistoric ditch irrigation from the Hay Hollow Valley on the Mogollon-Anasazi border, and LeBlanc (1976) posits it for the Mimbres Valley, Mogollon farming in general appears to have resembled Anasazi practice more than it did Hohokam.

Mogollon sites typically are small, although a few sites of over 50 houses have been noted. The dwellings are pithouses, arranged in unsystematic fashion. The larger villages generally have an oversized, nondomestic pithouse that probably functioned as a place of community assembly and ritual; these have often been labeled great kivas. The smaller true kivas typical of the Anasazi tradition do not occur. Mogollon villages lacked definite trash disposal areas; consequently, refuse is found distributed as a thin sheet throughout the site. Special cemetery areas were also lacking; the dead were generally interred in flexed position in scattered extramural pits. In the later periods, there was a tendency for burial to be under house floors.

Utilitarian objects dominate the artifact assemblage. Marine shell ornaments and other decorative items appear to have been rarer than in Anasazi or Hohokam contexts. Simple flake tools and heavy chopping and pounding tools are common, and numerous notched and stemmed projectile points were used. Simple basin grinding slabs persist throughout the tradition but are increasingly augmented by troughed metates. Despite the amount of woodworking that must have been done in house construction, grooved axes are rarely found and appear to increase proportionally with increasing Anasazi and Hohokam influence. Throughout the tradition, pottery was of brown and red ware, built up by coiling and finished by scraping. The earliest painted pottery was produced by adding designs in red to plain brown pottery. In later periods, a white slip was added to some vessels. Designs on these were at first painted in red; as Anasazi influence increased, black designs were used.

At any point in time, Mogollon culture seems to have displayed considerable variability, not only between regional subdivisions but within regions or even within a single site. The preponderance of plain pottery and the relatively few dendrochronological dates have led to much ambiguity in chronology, particularly in the early periods. Finally, the general absence of surface architecture has made it difficult for site sizes and numbers of houses to be estimated. For these reasons, attempts to develop temporal and regional subdivisions or trends for the Mogollon tradition as a whole have usually been subject to much debate.

Wheat's (1955) scheme is no exception, but it remains the most comprehensive attempt at synthesis. Most of his six proposed regional variants are still generally accepted. Wheat labeled as Mimbres the Mogollon culture of the central region, which includes the Gila River headwaters as well as the Mimbres drainage. The northernmost part of this subdivision has sometimes been treated separately as the Pine Lawn or Reserve region. To the southeast, between the Mimbres region and Hohokam territory, is the hot, low-lying region of the San Simon branch or variant. North of this, back in the highlands and largely in the headwaters of the Salt River, are the territories of the Black River (Point of Pines) and Forestdale Mogollon. East of the central Mimbres region are the poorly known Eastern Peripheral and Jornada regions, which extend through the lower Rio Grande valley to the edge of the

Plains. At the northern edge of the Mogollon area, Wheat distinguished the Cibola region, most of which I consider to have been more Anasazi than Mogollon.

The dating and phase correlations of Wheat's five tradition-wide periods have sparked extensive criticism (e.g., Bullard 1962:68–87); this is especially true for the two early periods. Because of uncertainties such as this and the previously mentioned variability within the Mogollon tradition, the discussion of Mogollon cultural development below relies primarily on the phase sequence of the Mimbres-Pine Lawn area, where most work has been done (Figure 8.13). Wheat's periods are, however, followed as a chronological outline.

MOGOLLON 1 AND 2 (PINE LAWN AND GEORGETOWN PHASES), ca. AD 250–650 □ Excavations at Tularosa Cave in the Reserve area (Martin et al. 1952), at Bat Cave, also in southwestern New Mexico (Dick 1965), and at the Cienega Creek site in the Point of Pines region (Haury 1957) have provided good evidence for the *in situ* development of the Mogollon tradition from an Archaic San Pedro Cochise ancestry. Primitive strains of maize were being grown by Cochise groups at least by 2000 BC, and beans and squash were also added to the diet in Late Archaic times. Shallow, oval pithouses were in use, but villages comparable to those of later Mogollon times probably had not developed.

Application of the label *Mogollon* begins when pottery appears in this continuum of cultural development. This distinction is perhaps not entirely arbitrary, for substantial pithouse villages seem to have developed at about the same time, probably indicating population growth or increased sedentism. The earliest pottery is a plain brown called Alma Plain and a slipped and polished plain red called San Francisco Red. Origins are unclear, but transmission of ceramic technology from Mexico along a highland corridor is a reasonable possibility (Haury 1962), as is diffusion from the Vahki phase Hohokam, who probably were making pottery as early as 300 BC (Haury 1976).

Martin (Martin et al. 1952; Martin and Plog 1973) would place the earliest Mogollon pottery at 200 or 300 BC, on the basis of several carbon-14 dates from Pine Lawn phase deposits stratified in Tularosa Cave. A generally early placement is also supported by the appearance of a few Mogollon trade sherds in Vahki phase contexts at Snaketown (Haury 1976:327–331); most Mogollon intrusives at Snaketown are, however, considerably later. Bullard (1962) disagrees with an early dating of initial Mogollon on a variety of grounds. So far, the Mogollon tree ring dates tend to support his position, since none are earlier than about AD 300 (from the Bluff Ruin in the Forestdale area: Haury and Sayles 1947; Bannister et al. 1966). In the central area, the situation is complicated by the fact that Martin (Martin et al. 1952 and elsewhere) recognizes both a Georgetown and an earlier Pine Lawn phase, while workers in the Mimbres drainage to the south (e.g., Haury 1936) recog-

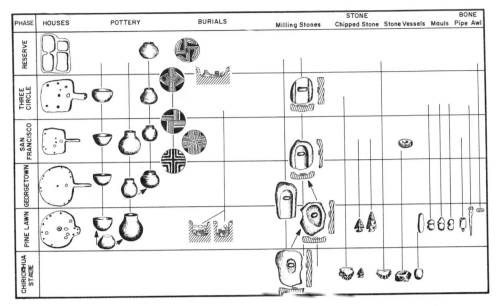

FIGURE 8.13
Synopsis of Mogollon cultural development in the Pine Lawn Valley area. (After Martin et al. 1949.)

nize only a Georgetown phase. So far, tree ring specimens attributed to both Georgetown and Pine Lawn contexts have dated in the AD 400s through early 600s (Bannister et al. 1970). I prefer to lump Pine Lawn and Georgetown together into a general early Mogollon unit and to date it conservatively at ca. AD 250 to 650. In this way, Wheat's Periods 1 and 2 are collapsed and their dates revised upward. The dating of early Mogollon is clearly an area where more work needs to be done.

The early Mogollon villages tend to be located on mesas or high promontories, generally close to cultivable valley-bottom lands. Because access to some villages is restricted by walls, Martin and Plog (1973:182) suggest that these locations were defensive and speculate that the increasingly sedentary villagers may have disrupted the adaptive patterns of as yet unidentified nomadic groups.

The pithouses of this period tend to be round or D-shaped in plan, with lateral ramp entries (Figure 8.14). A common roof support system relied on a single central and multiple sidewall posts. Great kivas are round or bean-shaped in plan and two or three times as spacious as the dwellings. Villages of several tens of houses occur, but most are smaller. In Pine Lawn Valley, Bluhm (1960) estimates average village size at 6 houses, with a range from 1 to 26.

At Tularosa Cave, Martin found evidence indicating an adaptive shift around AD 500 to 700; cultivated plants decreased and wild foods increased

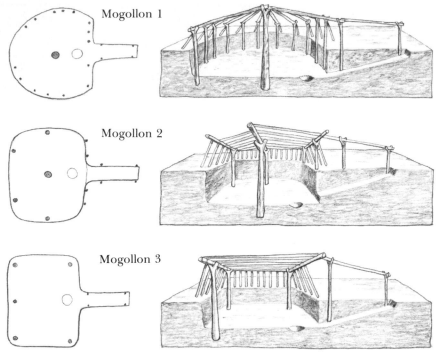

Mogollon 1

Mogollon 2

Mogollon 3

FIGURE 8.14
Floor plans and cross-sections (postulated roof constructions) of Mogollon houses at the Harris village site. (From *Prehistory of North America*, 2d ed., by Jesse D. Jennings. Copyright © 1968, 1974 by McGraw-Hill, Inc. Used with permission of McGraw-Hill Book Company.)

in relation to both earlier and later periods (Martin et al. 1952; Martin and Plog 1973). At approximately the same time, house size in the Pine Lawn Valley decreased (Martin and Rinaldo 1950; Bluhm 1960), a change that Martin attributes to a shift from extended family to nuclear family residence. During this 200-year period, the number of dwelling units in Pine Lawn Valley remained about the same as earlier and then increased rapidly after AD 700 (Bluhm 1960). Bullard (1962) accepts these general trends but questions whether the early Pine Lawn-Reserve area sites can be dated precisely enough to support the temporal correlations noted above.

In the Mimbres Valley, LeBlanc (1976) describes a shift in settlement from high knolls or ridges to locations noticeably lower and closer to the river probably before AD 600. Northeast of Tularosa Cave in the Hay Hollow Valley, Plog (1974:157–158) reports the abandonment of large sites in favor of small dispersed settlements about AD 500. He attributes this shift to the failure of larger communities to develop adequate integrative mechanisms.

The functional relationships, if any, between these settlement changes and the subsistence changes inferred by Martin at Tularosa Cave remain problematical. Graybill (1975:149–150) is skeptical of generalizing from the cave data, pointing out that the plant materials recovered there are "only a sample from a context that is apparently not the most common mode of habitation that is associated with agricultural pursuits, and would not necessarily be expected to contain a representative sample of economic plant foods. . . ."

MOGOLLON 3 (SAN FRANCISCO PHASE), AD 650–850 □ Alma Plain and San Francisco Red continued as major pottery types throughout this period; new types were Mogollon Red-on-Brown, a plainware variant called Alma Neck-Banded, and "smudged" bowls having a blackened, polished interior surface. These types may actually have begun late in the preceding period, but they became characteristic of the ceramic assemblage in San Francisco times. By the end of this phase, a white-slipped type, Three Circle Red-on-White, was beginning to appear.

Although a few circular-plan houses continued to be built, San Francisco phase pithouses were generally rectangular, with a gable-roof construction. Lateral ramp entries continued to be used. Great kivas were more variable, but with rounded and D-shaped plans predominating over rectangular. Martin and Rinaldo (1950) see the continuing trend to fewer metates and other artifacts per dwelling during this phase as supporting their inference of an earlier shift from extended to nuclear family residence units.

In the Pine Lawn Valley, there was a substantial increase during San Francisco and Three Circle times in numbers of dwelling units and in site size; the average village had nine rooms (Bluhm 1960). High, "defensive" locations had been largely abandoned, and sites were located close to arable soil and water. In one part of the valley, there was some tendency for sites to cluster, suggesting greater intervillage integration than previously. The Mimbres Valley seems to have had similar settlement trends at this time, although the maximal village there may have been somewhat larger (LeBlanc 1976).

MOGOLLON 4 (THREE CIRCLE PHASE), AD 850–1000 □ Although Alma Plain and San Francisco Red continued to decline in frequency, they remained ubiquitous in pottery assemblages. Three Circle Red-on-White peaked in popularity and was supplemented and then replaced by Mimbres Bold-Face, a black-on-white type indicative of increasing Anasazi influence. Alma Neck-Banded gave way to another Anasazi-related type, Alma Neck-Corrugated, and smudged pottery continued to be made.

Pithouses were rectangular and most often had flat roofs supported by a four-post framework. Lateral ramp entries continued to be common, but the use of a roof entry and a lateral ventilator tunnel was not unknown. Masonry was increasingly used to line pithouse walls. Great kivas were predominantly rectangular in plan. Population and site size probably continued to increase during this period, which is transitional between Mogollon and Western Pueblo.

MOGOLLON 5 AND WESTERN PUEBLO, AD 1000–1450 ☐ Mogollon 5 (AD 1000–1100) witnessed the full emergence of the Western Pueblo pattern and the eclipse of Mogollon as a separate tradition. During this period, surface pueblos of the general Anasazi type became the standard form of housing, and population increase was beginning to accelerate, probably as a result of immigration as well as of local growth. By the late 1200s, pueblos of several hundred rooms had developed in a few areas. Planning was evident in pueblo construction, and some were built around plazas. Great kivas continued in use, and some appear to have served clusters of smaller pueblos. Small kivas resembling those of the Anasazi, but with square floor plans, were being used. Although the old Mogollon plain brown and polished red pottery continued in small frequencies, the ceramic assemblages were dominated by a variety of black-on-white, polychrome, and corrugated types.

In the Pine Lawn-Reserve area, the Reserve (AD 1000–1100) and Tularosa (AD 1100–1250) phases have been defined. Population declined rapidly during the Tularosa phase, and the area was abandoned by AD 1250. Elsewhere in the northern Mogollon area, population was clustering into a few large pueblos, such as Point of Pines Ruin, Kinishba, and Grasshopper. Although people began to leave these sites in the late 1300s, a few areas were occupied until perhaps AD 1450. Much of the population that left the northern Mogollon Highlands probably moved to Hopi, Zuni, Acoma, and perhaps other pueblos. It seems clear that the Western Pueblo contribution was important in the formation of these surviving Pueblo cultures and societies.

Farther south in the Mimbres Valley, a distinctive and unparalleled development took place in the Mimbres phase; LeBlanc (1976) tentatively dates this development about AD 1050 to 1150 or 1200. There was an explosive growth of population, much of it probably due to immigration from the surrounding area, and numerous large pueblos (e.g., the Swarts and Mattocks ruins) were established, each housing probably several hundred persons. Spaced between these centers were smaller pueblos of approximately 100 persons or less.

Mimbres phase pottery has received attention for many years because of the attractive human and animal depictions on some of the black-on-white bowls. As the demand among collectors for these aesthetically appealing artifacts has increased, so has the destruction of Mimbres sites. The pictorial bowls were usually placed with burials made beneath room floors. Looters seeking these trophies have badly damaged virtually all Mimbres phase sites and have totally obliterated some. Many questions about the cultural context of this important art tradition must now remain forever unanswered.

LeBlanc (1975; 1976) is attempting to study the Mimbres culture before it is totally destroyed. Among the hypotheses he hopes to test is a model of Mimbres phase development suggesting that it is related to the rise of Chacoan trade with Mexico and that the strategically located Mimbrenos played some intermediary role. Production of the special pictorial pottery may have been supported by groups or individuals who had acquired power and rank by virtue of their role in the trade system.

Casas Grandes

Since the early days of Southwestern archeology (e.g., Bandelier 1892; Kidder 1924), the Casas Grandes district in northern Chihuahua (not to be confused with the Classic Hohokam site of Casa Grande in Arizona) has commanded attention as being potentially of great importance. It was not until 1958, however, when DiPeso began three years of fieldwork for the Amerind Foundation and Mexico's Instituto Nacional de Anthropologio y Historia, that extensive scientific excavations were carried out there. The monumental eight-volume report of this work (DiPeso 1974) has only recently appeared, and Southwesternists are still digesting its contents.

In this work, DiPeso demonstrates the existence, between about AD 1060 and 1340, of a city that he calls Paquimé, and he posits it to have been the economic and administrative center of the approximately 30,000-square-mile Casas Grandes region. Integrated systems of check dams and other devices to control runoff and hold the soil, thereby increasing agricultural productivity, were developed in this region. There also were systems of fortresses, trails, wayhouses, and signal towers. All of these are indicative of central planning and administration.

At its height during the Paquimé phase (ca. AD 1200–1260), the city of Paquimé covered approximately 36.5 hectares, had about 1600 rooms, and probably housed over 2200 people. The builders demonstrated sophisticated planning and technical skills in the construction of multistory and single-story apartment buildings, a marketplace, ceremonial mounds of various types, ball courts, public plazas, and an internal water supply and drainage system.

There is abundant evidence that the Paquimeans engaged in widespread trade with the Southwestern hinterlands to the north and the Mexican cities to the south. Items traded were primarily marine shell and decorative items made from shell, ceramics, minerals (especially turquoise), and exotic birds.

It is DiPeso's thesis that Paquimé was built and maintained as a trading center by *pochteca* or merchant groups from the south, who derived a good part of their influence over local indigenous populations from their roles as bearers of attractive Mesoamerican religious cults. From this perspective,

Casas Grandes is an outpost of Mexican civilization, and the Southwest is part of the Gran Chichimeca, Mesoamerica's northern frontier.

With some exceptions, Southwesternists have tended to treat Mesoamerica as a vague presence, both geographically and culturally remote. The new Casas Grandes data, plus Haury's (1976) strong case for Mexican origins of the Hohokam tradition, have made this "isolationist" view unsupportable. It would be premature to assess the wider impact of the new data and interpretations here, but it seems certain they will lead to many new perspectives on Southwestern cultural development.

The Anasazi

Although the precise linkages in most cases remain to be demonstrated, the Anasazi tradition was, in varying degrees, ancestral to the cultures of the modern Pueblo Indians—the Hopi, Zuni, and Rio Grande groups. This historical continuity has resulted in numerous parallels between archaeological and recent Pueblo cultures that have greatly enriched our understanding of the archeological record (cf., Anderson 1969). This valuable source of inference must, however, be used judiciously; historic and prehistoric pueblos differed in some major ways, and cultural forms that have continued into the ethnographic present do not necessarily retain the functions they had prehistorically.

The Anasazi tradition appears to have emerged from local Archaic antecedents, such as Oshara and Desha. As these continuities have become better known, the customary 1 AD date for the beginning of the Anasazi tradition appears increasingly arbitrary.

Traits generally considered as distinctively Anasazi come from the main part of the sequence, between ca. AD 500 and 1300. Predictably, not all last throughout this span or appear in all subareas. Nevertheless, the following constitute convenient markers for the tradition.

Anasazi pottery was built up by coiling, finished by scraping, and fired in an oxygen-poor or reducing atmosphere that gave it a gray to white color. In some areas, an oxidized red or orange ware was also made. The gray vessels are often decorated with black geometric designs over a white slip. By about AD 1000, unpainted "utility" pots exhibit a textured surface called corrugation, a systematic pinching of the unsmoothed coil marks. Full-grooved stone axes and flexed inhumations are typically Anasazi, as are stone masonry "apartment houses" or pueblos and semisubterranean ceremonial rooms called kivas.

Although wild plant foods continued to be used and were undoubtedly relied on heavily at times, the Anasazi made a serious commitment to maize-bean-squash horticulture by about AD 500. Ditch irrigation from perennial streams was developed in the Rio Grande area in late prehistoric times, but, in general, the Anasazi depended on dry farming and floodwater farming. The former refers to primary dependence on direct rainfall; the latter encompasses techniques of planting in areas where runoff from showers augments precipitation (Bryan 1929; 1941); both rely on soil moisture accumulated during winter and spring to germinate the plants and carry them through the May–June dry period and on additional water from July and August thunderstorms to mature the crops.

Under these conditions, Anasazi farming was often an uncertain venture. At elevations high enough for dry farming, the growing season is often less than 130 days, too short for unirrigated maize. Floodwater farming based on small watersheds is risky because of the spotty distribution of summer storms. Larger valleys flood more reliably and hold moisture in alluvial flood plains, but they also are more subject to violent floods, silting, and arroyo-cutting erosion, all of which can destroy crops.

By Basketmaker III times, several regional variants of Anasazi culture can be recognized. These local traditions are most distinctive in the Pueblo II and III periods. They include the Rio Grande, the Chaco of northwestern New Mexico, the Cibola of the upper Little Colorado drainage, the Mesa Verde of southwestern Colorado and southeastern Utah, the Kayenta of northeastern Arizona, and the Virgin of the "Arizona strip" north of the Grand Canyon.

Anasazi chronology is well understood because dendrochronology is applicable over most of the area and has been used to date many pottery types (Breternitz 1966) and sites. The 1927 Pecos Conference periods (Kidder 1927) have generally agreed-upon dates and are still widely used as convenient temporal units, a practice followed here. Their original developmental descriptions have been largely discarded in favor of local phase sequences on the one hand and more analytical approaches to cultural evolution on the other.

BASKETMAKER II (AD 1–450) □ Communities of this period are thinly scattered over the southern Plateau. Best known are the Durango shelters of southwestern Colorado (Morris and Burgh 1954), the Los Pinos and En Medio phases of northwestern New Mexico (Eddy 1961; Irwin-Williams 1973), the Marsh Pass caves of northeastern Arizona (Guernsey and Kidder 1921), the Grand Gulch and Kanab regions of southeastern Utah (Pepper 1902; Lipe and Matson 1971a; Nusbaum et al. 1922), and the Moapa phase of the Virgin River area in Arizona and Nevada (Shutler 1961).

The considerable diversity among these sites suggests variation both in cultural antecedents and in environmental adaptation. For example, the river flood plain-oriented small villages of the Los Pinos and Moapa phases may indicate rather more sedentary adaptations than do the other manifestations.

In general, Basketmaker II appears adaptively transitional between the Archaic and later patterns. Maize and squash were cultivated to some extent, but beans apparently were not. Wild plant foods, including seeds of grasses, chenopods, amaranths, composites, and piñon, were important, as was hunting. Settlements were generally established in areas having soil and water adequate for farming but also giving easy access to several different environmental zones for hunting and gathering. Typical settlement patterns include large base camps near canyon-head springs (probably used in fall and winter) and numerous scattered (and probably seasonal) limited activity sites. Natural shelters were often used for storage and burial of the dead and sometimes for camps. Storage was in large jar-shaped unlined cists dug into hard cave floors or in slab-and-mortar cists placed in soft fill or among boulders. Simple circular-plan houses, ranging from deep pithouses in the west to surface structures in the east, occur sporadically, but villages as such are very rare and quite small.

Pottery is lacking except at a few eastern locations, and here it is a Mogollon-influenced brownware, rather than the grayware characteristic later on. Containers are more typically those suited to a mobile lifestyle and to exploitation of wild plant foods—well-made twined bags and a variety of coiled baskets. The latter include winnowing trays, conical collecting baskets, and bowls. Hunters employed the atlatl and compound darts with hardwood foreshafts and large side- or corner-notched points. Curved throwing sticks, large rabbit nets, and various types of snares were also used. Milling equipment consists of Archaic-style basin grinding slabs and cobble manos; heavy milling stones approaching troughed metates occur at some base camps. Domestic dogs were present. Remains of turkeys appear, but it is not clear that they were domesticated.

BASKETMAKER III (AD 450–700/750) □ A shift in settlement pattern, and probably in adaptation, marks this period in most Anasazi areas. Sites tend to be near deep, well-watered soils, both in the alluvial valleys and the uplands, regardless of ease of access to diverse environments. The obvious inference is that agriculture had become more important.

Villages are common; most are small, but some containing more than 50 structures are known. At the Gilliland site in southwestern Colorado, Rohn (1975) has excavated an encircling stockade. It is not known whether or not this was a regular feature because the extensive excavations that would test for it have generally not been done at other sites.

The typical dwelling is a circular-to-rectangular-plan pithouse, from 2 to

7 meters in diameter. Small surface storage structures of wattle and daub with slab wall footings usually occur north or northwest of the pithouse. Exceptionally large pithouses, probably having a group assembly or ceremonial function, appear in the east and may have been early "great kivas." Arrangement of structures in the village does not appear to follow an obvious overall plan.

Beans were added to the domesticated plant list, and turkeys were definitely kept. By the end of the period, the bow and arrow begin to replace the atlatl and dart. Coiled baskets and twined bags continue, but pottery was universally used as well. The common types are plain gray jars and bowls, some decorated with simple black designs. In southeastern Utah red-on-orange pottery, reminiscent of some Mogollon types, is abundant (Brew 1946). Troughed metates begin to replace grinding slabs, and larger, "two-hand" manos appear.

PUEBLO I (AD 700–850/900) □ It is our impression that population was less uniformly distributed during this period than in Basketmaker III; some areas gained population, while others were abandoned. Most villages are small, but some, such as Alkali Ridge in Utah (Brew 1946) have over 100 structures. Great kivas appear at a few settlements in the east. DeBloois (1975) reports numerous high-altitude one-room surface structures from southeastern Utah—probably seasonally occupied farmhouses.

Diversity characterizes dwelling arrangements as well as settlement types. Domestic activities appear to have been increasingly removed from pithouses, the latter assuming the role and formal characteristics of kivas. Surface structures are larger and were used for habitation as well as for storage. Most surface construction was done with jacal (wattle and daub), but by the end of the period, masonry is being used in some areas.

Pottery is better finished and more diversified. Decorated vessels have been carefully polished and often slipped before being painted. On utility vessels, the upper coils of clay have often been left unsmoothed to produce a "neck-banded" effect.

Cotton was added to the list of domesticated plants during this period, and true loom weaving appears. Finger-woven items such as twined bags and sandals decrease in quantity and quality. Small coiled baskets continue, but the large carrying baskets and winnowing trays apparently were no longer made.

Some early workers thought that a long-headed Basketmaker population was replaced by a different, short-skulled, Puebloan one. This physical difference was found to be due instead to a cultural practice that started in Pueblo I times—the artificial flattening of infants' skulls by placing a wooden "pillow" in their cradle boards.

PUEBLO II (AD 900–1100/1150) □ Many unoccupied or previously abandoned areas were settled at this time; the Anasazi reached their maximum geographic distribution and, probably, their population peak. The increasingly Anasazi character of the Mogollon tradition during this period may have been caused by a southward drift of Anasazi groups, but this has not been fully demonstrated.

The Pueblo II peak may well have been the cumulative result of the successful integration of a horticultural adaptive strategy during the preceding few centuries, but there may have been other "kickers" as well. Galinat and Gunnerson (1963) argue that a more productive highland maize was introduced to the Plateau between about AD 700 and 1000. The tree ring record indicates that the period between AD 850 and 1150 was generally stable, with few profound droughts and several relatively wet periods. There is also some evidence that summer rains were exceptionally strong between about AD 800 and 1100 or 1200 (Schoenwetter and Eddy 1964; Baerreis and Bryson 1965).

Certainly the Pueblo II site distribution suggests favorable climatic conditions. The larger sites, which generally had been founded earlier, tend to be near the best-watered soils, but many of the smaller new sites are in upland areas where farming is marginal or impossible today, and where even domestic water supplies are now rare. Implied is a substantial dependence on dry farming or on runoff from small watersheds, which occurred under conditions more favorable than today's. Various water-and-soil-control systems, which would have increased the farming potential in some of these areas, appear here and there by mid-Pueblo II. These include check dams in washes, terraces and stone grids on slopes, and reservoirs and ditches for household water (cf., Rohn 1963).

Although jacal continues as a structural alternative in many areas, masonry is increasingly dominant. Small unit pueblos, which appeared in Pueblo I, become very common in this period; these consist of a small block of habitation and storage rooms with a kiva and trash area to the south or southeast. The larger pueblos, some of which had over 100 rooms, generally appear to be agglomerations of such units.

Kivas have circular floor plans, are fully masonry lined, and display all or most of the "typical" kiva features: central fire pit, deflector, ventilator shaft, encircling bench, pilasters, southern recess, sipapu, and wall niches (Figure 8.15). In the east, great kivas continue. Their locations in the largest sites, or as isolated structures within site clusters, suggest community integrative functions. Grebinger (1973) and Plog (1974) suggest that one such function may have been economic redistribution and that the small rooms sometimes built around the kiva were storehouses.

Pottery styles continue their florescence; painted designs are more varied and complex, and corrugation textures the outsides of utility vessels (Figure 8.16). Ring baskets of twilled yucca leaves increasingly supplant the more durable but harder to make coiled baskets.

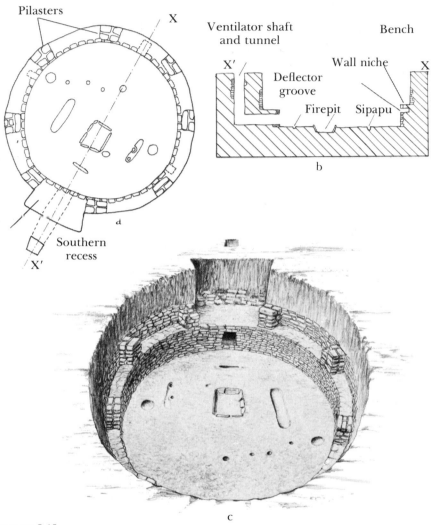

Pilasters

X

Ventilator shaft
and tunnel

Bench

X′

Deflector
groove

Wall niche

X

Firepit

Sipapu

b

d

Southern
recess

X′

c

FIGURE 8.15
Pueblo II kiva at Mesa Verde National Park: *a*, plan view; *b*, cross-section; *c*, view of excavated kiva. (From *Prehistory of North America*, 2d ed., by Jesse D. Jennings. Copyright © 1968, 1974 by McGraw-Hill, Inc. Used with permission of McGraw-Hill Book Company.)

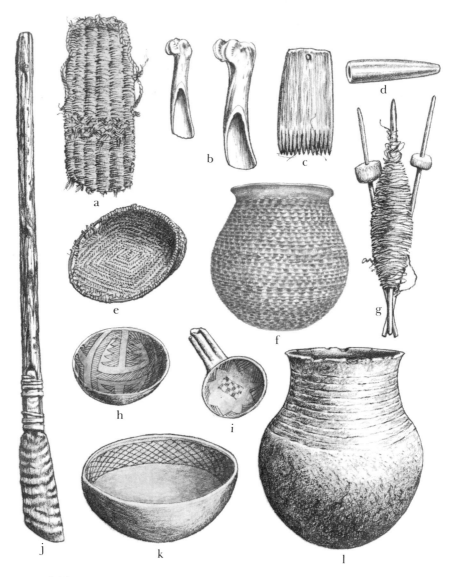

FIGURE 8.16
Pueblo II and III artifacts: *a*, wickerwork sandal of yucca leaves; *b*, bone scrapers; *c*, wooden comb; *d*, stone pipe; *e*, ring basket of twilled yucca leaves; *f*, fully corrugated utility vessel; *g*, spindles with whorls and a distaff of spun yarn; *h*, black-on-white bowl; *i*, black-on-white ladle; *j*, digging stick with sheep-horn blade (restored); *k*, black-on-orange bowl; *l*, partially corrugated utility vessel. (From *Prehistory of North America*, 2d ed., by Jesse D. Jennings. Copyright © 1968, 1974 by McGraw-Hill, Inc. Used with permission of McGraw-Hill Book Company.)

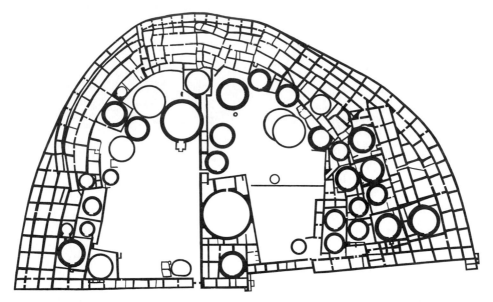

FIGURE 8.17
Ground plan of Pueblo Bonito. (From *Prehistory of North America*, 2d ed., by Jesse D. Jennings. Copyright © 1968, 1974 by McGraw-Hill, Inc. Used with permission of McGraw-Hill Book Company.)

THE CHACO PHENOMENON □ Anomalous in the general context of Pueblo II development is Chaco Canyon in northwestern New Mexico. Between about 850 and 1150, this broad, alluvium-filled canyon supported a dozen or so large "town" pueblos of several hundred rooms each (Figures 8.17 and 8.18), plus several hundred contemporaneous "villages" or typical small to medium-sized unit pueblos (Vivian 1970). In the latter part of this period, the towns were built according to a predetermined plan. They have great kivas, and are associated with fairly complex runoff water-control systems, as well as broad roadways, which lead to other town sites or even outside the Chaco Canyon area. These large sites have also yielded luxury goods such as turquoise, copper bells imported from Mexico, and parrot and macaw remains (Vivian 1970; Grebinger 1973).

Vivian (1970) argues that the two settlement types reflect different organizational principles, the villages being localized corporate lineages and the towns having localized nonexogamous moieties. By analogy with the eastern Pueblos, he suggests that the dual division principle was more effective in organizing work on the water-control systems and in generating the social cohesion that permitted the town-sized populations to stay together.

Grebinger (1973) notes that the towns are all in locations with access to abundant flood runoff from side canyons and argues that their populations

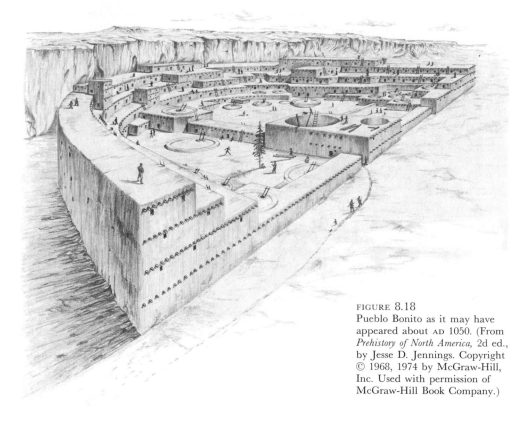

FIGURE 8.18
Pueblo Bonito as it may have appeared about AD 1050. (From *Prehistory of North America,* 2d ed., by Jesse D. Jennings. Copyright © 1968, 1974 by McGraw-Hill, Inc. Used with permission of McGraw-Hill Book Company.)

controlled the most productive farming areas. He then builds a model of the towns as ranked societies, with the founding lineages controlling the economic efforts of the rest of the population and maintaining their favored status through control of productive land, ceremony, and water-channeling structures and by economic redistribution.

DiPeso (1968, 1974), in his model of Mesoamerican mercantilism, sees Mexican *pochteca* groups moving into the hinterlands to obtain supplies of turquoise, shell, slaves, and so on. Bearers of attractive religious cults as well, such groups could have organized native populations in locations such as Chaco.

Whatever the reasons for its development, Chaco was a powerful influence in the northern Southwest. Town pueblos built on the Chacoan plan are known at a number of locations, such as the Aztec and Salmon ruins in New Mexico (Morris 1928; Irwin-Williams 1972), and Chaco ceramic styles are widespread in Pueblo II times.

DiPeso (1968) suggests that the Chaco decline in the middle 1100s may correlate with internal disruptions in the Mexican mercantile system. There also appears to have been arroyo cutting at Chaco in the 1100s (Bryan 1954), which might have destroyed its agricultural base. Major research projects now under way at Chaco and Salmon ruins promise to shed much new light on these and other fascinating problems raised by the Chaco phenomenon.

PUEBLO III(AD 1100/1150–1300) □ This period saw the aggregation of population into fewer but larger pueblos in fewer but more densely settled locations. In many areas, the people moved from open locations to shelters and ledges in canyon walls (Figure 8.19). Some such "cliff-dweller" sites are difficult to reach and appear to have been located for defensive purposes. In addition, features that suggest defense are fairly common: loopholes in walls flanking entries, walls restricting access to ledges, and large towers. The last are often attached by tunnels to kivas and may have had ceremonial functions instead of, or in addition to, defensive ones. Despite these indications of anxiety, there is little evidence of actual hostilities.

In some areas, pottery reaches a peak of technical and artistic quality. Corn-grinding equipment was improved, as flat metates set in mealing bins generally replace troughed metates.

Social changes were occurring in concert with the formation of larger villages. In the Tsegi phase (1250–1300) of the Kayenta area, Dean (1970) notes the lack of association between kivas and habitation units in the large sites of Betatakin and Kiet Siel. He proposes that kivas had by this time lost their association with localized lineage segments and had come to serve larger, nonlocalized groups, such as clans or ceremonial sodalities; this is the case in modern Hopi society, to which the Tsegi phase is in part ancestral. Such new associations for kivas may have been promoted by need in the larger communities for institutions to crosscut the diverse, small, kin-based groups that had moved into the village and thereby help tie them together. Dean's analysis lends support to Eggan's (1950) earlier reconstruction of the evolution of Hopi society.

During Pueblo III, Anasazi groups were gradually moving south and southeast; by AD 1300, their original Plateau homeland had been largely abandoned except for its southern margins. Gaining population in the 1200s were the Hopi mesas, the Cibola area near what are now the Zuni and Acoma towns, parts of the Mogollon Highlands, and the Rio Grande valley.

PUEBLO IV (AD 1300–1600) □ Cliff dwellings became less common as groups moved away from canyon areas. Some sites of this period occur on defensible outcrops or mesas, but the size of communities had increased to the point where this alone probably gave protection. By late Pueblo IV, towns of 200 to 2000 were the norm, and the small villages that typify most of Anasazi prehistory are found no more.

The southward and eastward shift of population continued, and by 1450 the Mogollon highlands had been abandoned along with virtually all of the Plateau. By the end of Pueblo IV, the Pueblo peoples occupied approximately

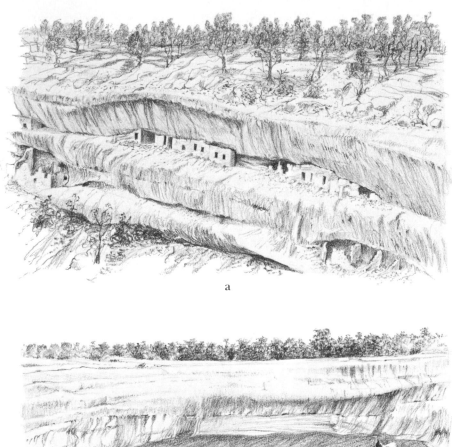

a

b

FIGURE 8.19
Pueblo III cliff dwellings, Mesa Verde: *a*, Double House; *b*, Cliff Palace. (From *Prehistory of North America*, 2d ed., by Jesse D. Jennings. Copyright © 1968, 1974 by McGraw-Hill, Inc. Used with permission of McGraw-Hill Book Company.)

their present locations, except for the lower Rio Grande settlements, which declined somewhat later (Kelley 1952). Tracing Pueblo III and Pueblo IV population movements and identifying the cultural ancestry of historic Pueblo groups has occupied much scholarly energy (e.g., Ellis 1967; Ford et al. 1972). Although some partial correlations have been made (e.g., the strong Kayenta contribution to Hopi), it is apparent that there were no simple one-to-one transformations of Pueblo III groups into historic Pueblos.

Extensive kiva wall murals (Smith 1952; Dutton 1963) give evidence of great ceremonial elaboration during Pueblo IV. The kachina cult probably developed its present complexity at this time (Brew 1944; Schaafsma and Schaafsma 1974). Mexican influences appear strong, but the ceremonial system itself appears to be a Pueblo product, not a total import. New pottery styles that spread during Pueblo IV also show southern influences, including curvilinear stylized parrot motifs.

THE WESTERN PUEBLO TRADITION □ Sometime during late Pueblo II or Pueblo III, the Mogollon tradition ceased to exist as a separate cultural entity. Some (e.g., Rouse 1962) consider it to have been absorbed into the Anasazi tradition, while others (e.g., Reed 1950) see the emergence of a new entity—Western Pueblo culture—in the Cibola-Mogollon Highlands area as a result of the Anasazi-Mogollon merger. Johnson (1965) argues for Hohokam contribution to Western Pueblo as well. The archeological marker traits of this new tradition include organization of sites around plazas or multiple courtyards, rectangular small kivas, brownware pottery (often slipped with red or white), three-quarter grooved stone axes, and extended supine inhumation (Johnson 1965:vi). Western Pueblo culture is thought to have contributed heavily to the development of historic Hopi and Zuni-Acoma culture and perhaps to some of the Rio Grande groups as well. Other Rio Grande groups were direct inheritors of the Anasazi tradition, stemming largely from the Mesa Verde and Chaco areas. Johnson (1965) also sees Western Pueblo as contributing to the Salado phenomenon in the Hohokam area.

PUEBLO ABANDONMENT OF THE PLATEAU: A CONTINUING PROBLEM □ The Plateau's empty ruins have stirred the imaginations of generations of travelers and scholars. Many theories have been advanced to account for the abandonment of this once populous region (Jett 1964). The principal ones are reviewed below.

Perhaps the earliest theory to be proposed was that "hostile nomads" had driven the Puebloans from their homes. Presumably these were the ancestors of the nomadic peoples who were occupying much of the northern Southwest when the Spanish explorers arrived: the Athapaskan-speaking Navajo and Apache, the Numic-speaking Paiute and Ute, and the Yuman-speaking Havasupai and Walapai. Although this theory would account for the defense nature of Pueblo III sites, so far little archeological evidence to support it has been forthcoming. It is becoming increasingly clear that the Athapaskans did not come into the area until a century or more after the Puebloans had left (Hester 1962; Wilcox n.d.). The Numic peoples were in contact with the westernmost Anasazi by 1100 (Shutler 1961; Madsen 1975), but there is no evidence for contact in the Anasazi heartland farther east. Eastward Numic expansion seems to have followed Anasazi abandonment. The post-1150 northeastward movement of upland Yumans of the Cerbat Branch (Euler and Gumerman 1974:303) did not actually reach Anasazi territory.

Interpueblo warfare has been suggested to account for defensive sites (Linton 1944), but it is difficult to see how small-scale raiding and feuding could have led to depopulation of a large region (Jett 1964:296). More plausible is Davis's (1965) suggestion that disruptions of whatever sort on the margins of the Anasazi area might have had a snowball effect as refugees put pressure on previously unaffected communities.

Climatic change has often been invoked as a cause. Early tree ring workers (Douglass 1929) recognized a series of very narrow rings, thought to represent a "Great Drought" in the late 1200s, coincident with abandonment of the large cliff dwellings of Mesa Verde and the Tsegi canyons. The general explanatory power of this widespread drought faded, however, when it became clear that most Plateau areas had already been abandoned by this time. The tree ring record (Fritts et al. 1965) also reveals several serious earlier droughts that were not accompanied by widespread abandonment.

The discovery that arroyo cutting in alluvial valleys was probably widespread during Pueblo III times (Bryan 1941; 1954; Hack 1942) sparked hope that a general explanation was at hand. Further work, however, showed that many Pueblo groups did not depend on alluvial soils and that Hopi country was receiving population at a time when arroyos were active there.

It might be argued that the organizational shift toward larger communities required the support of intensified agriculture. This could be provided through stream irrigation—hence, the move to the Rio Grande. Most of the Pueblo III population gain in the central Rio Grande was not, however, in areas where irrigation could easily have been practiced (Dickson 1975), nor was stream irrigation feasible in most other areas that were receiving population.

In conclusion, it appears that no one of these theories is, in itself, sufficient to account for the population movements that occurred. Joining the numerout other students of this problem, we offer below a speculative model based on a combination of factors.

A MODEL OF PUEBLO RELOCATION □ During Pueblo III times a relatively stable climate and ample summer moisture supported population increase and the occupation of marginal uplands on an essentially dryfarming basis. An additional inch or two of summer precipitation might not have greatly improved floodwater farming in the larger drainages, but it could have opened up large areas of the Plateau to dry-farming or small-watershed floodwater techniques. Unfortunately for the farmers, such areas can also be suddenly closed off by small losses of moisture. In previous periods of climatic difficulty, groups exploiting these marginal lands had been able to move back into more favored areas, including the larger alluvial valleys. When moisture patterns became more variable at 1100 or 1150, however, populations in both marginal and favored locations were too great for all to be supported in the latter locations. Furthermore, the alluvial valleys were being affected by arroyo cutting, which lowered their ability to support population.

The resulting squeeze on land and water led to competition and, probably, to some raiding. One response was defensive structures and site locations, but a more effective one was increased community size, which was also favored by the concentration of population in the remaining habitable areas.

A more direct response to the adaptive stress was movement out of the Plateau to areas where summer rainfall had always been heavier and more reliable—to the south and east. This process was already under way and was probably only accelerated by the Pueblo III adaptive difficulties.

Increasing community size may also have promoted movement. Because of the Plateau's topographic complexity, arable soils and other resources are often distributed in an extremely discontinuous, patchy way. This circumstance would be intensified by drought. Such environments are not very amenable to the support of large, nucleated communities. The locations where the Puebloans finally settled tend to have good water supplies and relatively broad, open valleys where fairly large expanses of arable soil lie close to settlements and where surveillance of fields from a distance is often possible. These conditions are rare in most parts of the Plateau.

In addition to defensive needs, a variable that may also have promoted increased community size was the ceremonial elaboration that occurred in late Pueblo III and Pueblo IV times. The adaptive difficulties they were experiencing would have made Pueblo groups receptive to adopting or developing new ceremonies in search of supernatural assistance. In this context, the Tlaloc (Mexican water deity) elements in the emerging Pueblo IV kachina cult (Brew 1944) are not surprising. Successful operation of an elaborated ceremonial system required more personnel and social categories than were ordinarily available in small villages; hence, community growth was promoted. Pueblo ceremonies may also have aided adaptation directly by providing a certain amount of food redistribution and by regulating the scheduling of economic activities (Ford 1972). And the integrative functions of ceremonial systems in helping tie together politically fragmented communities has long been recognized (Eggan 1950). Whatever its contribution to promoting formation of larger communities, the Pueblo IV ceremonial elaboration probably helped maintain them.

The Hakataya

This tradition (Schroeder 1957) consists of a number of often poorly known archeological manifestations in the southwestern part of the Plateau, the lower Colorado River valley and adjacent low deserts, and the transition zone between these lowland and highland areas. The appearance of pottery between AD 500 and 800 in the highlands, and probably several hundred years earlier in the lowlands, marks the emergence of the tradition. Ancestry in local Late Archaic cultures is likely but remains to be demonstrated. Most of the area occupied prehistorically by the Hakataya was, in historic times, the territory of Yuman-speaking peoples. Although physical continuity between the archeological Hakataya and the historic Yumans can be demonstrated or seems highly probable in some cases, it has been considered unwise to give the archeological materials a linguistic or ethnographic label (Colton 1938).

The Hakataya tradition is characterized by pottery finished by paddle-and-anvil techniques. Primarily a brownware, it had regional gray or buff variants as well. Most pottery is plain, but simple painted designs appear in some areas, generally in the later periods. Subsistence adaptations ranged from primary dependence on a mix of farming, gathering, and fishing in the riverine areas to primary dependence on hunting and gathering in some of the highland situations (e.g., among the Cerbat). The mortar and pestle were commonly used in food processing in the western areas; grinding slabs and troughed metates appear more frequently in the east. Stone-lined pits or ovens were widely employed in cooking, especially in the western and lower-lying areas. In the villages, rubbish was scattered unsystematically rather than being accumulated in trash mounds. Disposal of the dead was by cremation in some groups, inhumation in others.

Schroeder (1960 and elsewhere) has argued that the earliest Hohokam developments should be considered Hakataya, with the Hohokam proper coming in from the south at a later date to dominate the indigenous populations. Haury's (1976) recent findings at Snaketown appear to eliminate this possibility.

THE RIVERINE HAKATAYA □ Because these groups on the lower Colorado River usually occupied flood plains or low terraces, their archeological traces have frequently been lost to erosion or alluviation. The evidence we have suggests that their villages were composed of individual houses widely scattered along the river. The houses were typically brush or jacal structures, square in plan and built on the surface or in shallow pits. Large community-assembly structures were also sometimes present.

Pottery is a buff or brownware; a few vessels are decorated with simple designs in red. Schroeder (1960) sees the buff and red-decorated pottery as indicating influence from the neighboring Hohokam.

Maize, tepary beans, and squash were grown on the broad river flood-plains; the success of the crops depended on natural flooding, as ditch irrigation was not practiced. The Mohave, a Yuman group that occupied part of the lower Colorado River valley in historic times. derived 40 to 50 percent of their subsistence from flood-plain farming; most of the remainder came from harvesting wild plants of the flood plain, especially mesquite, and from fishing (Castetter and Bell 1951). Such ethnographically documented Yuman subsistence patterns can probably be extrapolated into at least the latter part of the archeological record in this area.

THE UPLAND OR PATAYAN HAKATAYA □

The Cohonina This group occupied the area south of the Grand Canyon between about AD 700 and 1150. Their sites are small, often consisting of only an artifact scatter or a single house. The houses range in form from shallow pithouses to surfact structures outlined with boulders or a few courses of masonry; superstructures were probably of jacal. Troughed metates and two-hand manos are more common than basin grinding slabs, indicating that maize was an important subsistence item (McGregor 1951). The typical Cohonina pottery is a plain paddle-and-anvil grayware; a few vessels have Anasazi-like designs painted in black. More commonly, decorated pottery was obtained in trade with the Anasazi.

After reaching a peak about AD 900 to 1100, Cohonina population declined precipitously (Schwartz 1956). Schwartz (1959) and McGregor (1967) have argued that the remaining Cohonina migrated to the Grand Canyon and were ancestral to the Yuman-speaking Havasupai, who still occupy the area. Euler (Euler and Gumerman 1974) argues that instead another Hakataya group—the Cerbat—moved in from the west shortly after the Cohonina decline, and that these people were the ancestors of both the Havasupai and the closely related Walapai. To date, the bulk of archeological, historical, and linguistic evidence favors Euler's theory; the fate of the Cohonina remains unknown.

The Cerbat Before expanding into the Cohonina area, the Cerbat lived in the mountainous Basin and Range country just to the west, near the Colorado River. Both before and after their move eastward, they occupied rockshelters or simple brush wickiups, made undecorated brown pottery, and used distinctive, small, side-notched projectile points. They probably relied largely on hunting and gathering for subsistence, except in a few well-watered locales such as Havasu Canyon, a Grand Canyon tributary that is still occupied by their probable descendents, the Havasupai.

The Prescott Branch This group occupied the highlands south of the Cohonina area. Although some work has been done in this area (e.g., Spicer and

Caywood 1936; Euler and Dobyns 1962; Barnett 1970; 1974), its archeology is not yet well understood. There does appear to have been an architectural shift from early pithouses to surface masonry pueblos (Euler and Gumerman 1974); some of the late pueblos were as large as 25 rooms (Barnett 1974). The numerous masonry hilltop "forts" or lookouts found in the area may indicate that the Prescott people were concerned about possible hostilities.

Subsistence patterns evidently included both maize agriculture and hunting and gathering. Local ceramics consist of plain brown and graywares, sometimes enhanced by simple designs in red or black paint. Pottery was also traded in from the Anasazi, Sinagua, and Hohokam areas (James 1974). The Prescott area seems to have been abandoned sometime between 1200 and 1300, but the fate of the population is unknown.

The Sinagua   This tradition occupied the area around Flagstaff, Arizona, and the upper Verde Valley. Although Colton (1939) originally classed Sinagua with the Mogollon tradition, subsequent research and comparative studies led him to conclude tentatively that its earliest relationship was with Patayan (and hence Hakataya) cultures (Colton 1946), a position that has received further backing from Schroeder (1960; 1961) and Euler and Gumerman (1974).

About AD 1075, the eruption of Sunset Crater east of Flagstaff spread a blanket of volcanic cinders and ash over a large part of the northern Sinagua area. This event provides a convenient marker for separating the substantially different preeruptive and posteruptive Sinagua patterns (Schroeder 1961).

The preeruptive Sinagua occupied small pithouse villages. The earliest houses—ca. AD 500 to 700—tend to be shallow and round in plan, while the later ones are generally rectangular and deeper, with strong timbered walls lining the pit interior. Maize farming was probably the major subsistence pursuit, with hunting and gathering secondary. The dominant pottery is Alameda Brown Ware, a plain paddle-and-anvil-finished ceramic that remains characteristic of the Sinagua tradition throughout. Decorated vessels were obtained in trade with neighboring groups; for the northern Sinagua, the source was usually the Anasazi, while the Verde Valley Sinaguans traded with both the Anasazi and Hohokam (Breternitz 1960).

After it produced a brief disruption, the Sunset Crater cinder fall is thought to have provided a moisture-conserving mulch that made the area more attractive to dry farmers (Colton 1945b; 1949; 1960; Breternitz 1967). The larger number of sites in the immediate posteruptive period and the appearance of more Anasazi, Mogollon, and Hohokam traits have been used to suggest that there was in-migration from neighboring areas at this time (e.g., McGregor 1965:298). These hypotheses about the relationship between the cinder fall, population growth, and migration remain subjects of debate. It is clear, however, that the posteruptive Sinagua culture was both variable and rapidly changing. In the northern area, a shift to masonry pithouses and

Anasazilike small surface pueblos occurred early in posteruptive times. Concurrently, there was strong Hohokam influence. At Winona Village east of Flagstaff, McGregor (1937; 1941) found Hohokam-style houses, as well as other types, local copies of Hohokam red-on-buff pottery, a relative abundance of shell ornaments, cremations, and a ball court. Further south, the Verde Valley was essentially an extension of Hohokam culture in the late 1000s and early 1100s (Breternitz 1960).

By the late 1100s, however, Hohokam influence was receding and the Sinagua were coming under increasing Anasazi or Western Pueblo dominance. In the 1200s and 1300s, population increasingly aggregated in a few large pueblos, and there was a general shift southward into the Verde Valley, where large sites such as Tuzigoot seem to have been occupied until the early 1400s. When European explorers first arrived, the Verde Valley was peopled by the Yuman-speaking Yavapai. Their relationship—or lack of it—to the earlier Sinagua-Western Pueblo population is entirely unknown.

The Fremont

The Fremont tradition takes its name from the Fremont River drainage of east-central Utah, where Morss recognized a "peripheral culture" related to but outside the "main stream of Southwestern development" (Morss 1931: 76–77). Judd's pioneering work had earlier demonstrated that the numerous village sites of central and western Utah differed from those of the San Juan Anasazi, although certain general characteristics, such as gray pottery and maize agriculture, were held in common (e.g., Judd 1919; 1926). The label *Fremont* has gradually been extended to include all post-Archaic manifestations north of the Anasazi area.

The Fremont tradition, as now defined, occupied the northern half of the Plateau and the eastern portion of the Great Basin in Utah and westernmost Nevada. Morss's reference to Fremont as "peripheral" is characteristic of the thinking of most of the early workers in the area, who saw it as a hinterland or marginal expression of a basic Anasazi culture. As both the Fremont and the Anasazi areas have become better known, Fremont has increasingly come to be treated as a separate tradition, related to Anasazi in various ways but not a subdivision of it.

FREMONT ORIGINS ☐ Several models of Fremont cultural origins have been proposed. The earlier ones generally postulated various waves of Anasazi influence or migration to account for Fremont development. The most recent of these is Gunnerson's (1962; 1969) hypothesis that the Fremont culture resulted from the northward movement of people from the Anasazi Virgin branch area about AD 950, as part of the general Anasazi Pueblo II expansion, and that these Anasazi migrants merged with or displaced sparse

Archaic-level foraging populations. The numerous carbon-14 dates now available for Fremont sites (summarized in Marwitt 1970; see also Madsen and Berry 1975:401), although not without their problems of interpretation (cf., Ambler 1969), do appear to show that the Fremont tradition was established in a number of areas several centuries before AD 950. Furthermore, most of the traits cited by Gunnerson as indicating Virgin branch relationships could have come from the Kayenta Anasazi, or from earlier sources in the Anasazi area in general.

A quite different source for Fremont was proposed by Aikens (1966:11), who argues that "the proto-Fremont people were bison hunters of Northwestern Plains origin, probably Athapaskans . . . [who] expanded westward and southward into Utah at approximately 500 AD." He cites as evidence for his theory the existence in Fremont of Plains-oriented traits, such as bison hunting, and the use of tipis, moccasins, shields, and shield pictographs. He believes that, after entering Utah, the proto-Fremont acquired a number of traits from the Anasazi, with the resultant synthesis giving Fremont its distinctive character.

Although Aikens's hypothesis is intriguing and recognizes certain elements in Fremont culture that may well result from Plains contacts (see also Wormington 1955), it has not been generally accepted. Aikens has not abandoned it, but he now prefers to emphasize the local components in Fremont development (Aikens 1970; 1972). A number of other workers have also stressed the *in situ* development of Fremont from Archaic antecedents (e.g., Rudy 1953; Wormington 1955; Jennings and Norbeck 1955; Jennings 1966; 1974; Marwitt 1970). While recognizing outside influences, they relegate them to secondary roles and depend little or not at all on migration.

The most recent formulations of the *in situ* hypothesis suggest that several distinctive Fremont culture elements can be traced back to Archaic horizons, as can the roots of some of the regional variation observed later (Aikens 1970; 1972). In the early centuries of the Christian era, the Archaic societies ancestral to both Anasazi and Fremont were affected by the rapid diffusion out of the Mogollon area of the cultural complex including pottery, pithouse architecture, and, perhaps, improved varieties of maize (Marwitt 1970; Jennings 1966; 1974). Later developments were largely based on local processes, although Anasazi influences were felt, particularly in the Pueblo II and early Pueblo III periods and in the southern part of the Fremont area.

The evidence for Archaic-Fremont continuity has recently been questioned by Madsen and Berry (1975). After reexamining and in some cases reinterpreting the sequences from Hogup Cave and other sites in the northeastern Great Basin, they posit a hiatus of 1000 to 2000 years between Late Archaic and early Fremont. If their interpretation is correct, it does not disprove the theory that Fremont developed out of Late Archaic antecedents somewhere in the Fremont area, but it shows that the case is not yet proved and that such a transition is not likely to have taken place in the northeastern Basin.

Madsen and Berry note that the few data we have for the northern Plateau suggest a smaller Archaic-Fremont hiatus there; it seems likely that the gap will eventually be closed in this area.

GENERAL CHARACTERISTICS AND REGIONAL VARIABILITY □

Marwitt (1970) has documented five regional Fremont variants. Three were centered in the Basin area of Utah and extended into adjacent portions of Nevada—Great Salt Lake (ca. AD 400–1350), Sevier (ca. AD 780–1260), and Parowan (ca. AD 900–1300). The other two, centered in the Plateau portion of Utah and extending into adjacent parts of Colorado, were the Uinta Fremont (ca. AD 650–950) and San Rafael Fremont (ca. AD 700–1200). This last variant was Morss's (1931) original "Fremont culture." The Fremont tradition as a whole can be defined by a number of traits and cultural emphases that occur widely; almost none, however, are universal.

Fremont sites tend to be small and widely scattered; where villages exist, they generally have only a few houses. An exception may be the Parowan Fremont in southwestern Utah, where a few sites each cover a hectare or more. Marwitt's (1970) excavations in Median Village in this area showed, however, that such sites may have had smaller populations than might be expected. Of the 16 houses he excavated, no more than 5 could have been occupied simultaneously, and he estimated the maximum life of a house at 20 years.

Fremont subsistence patterns appear to have emphasized hunting and gathering more than did the Anasazi. The Great Salt Lake Fremont sites excavated so far seem to have been oriented toward exploiting lakeside and river estuary resources rather than farming, and most of the Nevada sites seem to reflect hunting and gathering activities. Numerous village sites in other areas, however, have yielded evidence that maize-beans-squash agriculture was important in subsistence. A distinctive maize variety, Fremont Dent, was commonly grown; Winter (1973) thinks it probably developed in the Fremont area in response to the conditions of agriculture there. These must have been somewhat harsh, for growing seasons are short in most regions and the summer thunderstorms characteristic of the southern Plateau weaken rapidly as one moves north through Utah. Dry summers may account for the location of many Fremont villages at places along valley sides where mountain streams debouch onto alluvial fans. The natural storage of soil moisture and the possibilities for ditch irrigation in such locations may have provided solutions to the problems of unreliable late summer rainfall. No actual evidence of ditch irrigation has yet been found, however.

Although masonry surface structures occur in the later phases of the eastern Fremont variants, pithouses were used everywhere and probably continued alongside masonry dwellings in the east. Kivas are absent everywhere. House and granary superstructures were frequently built of jacal or of adobes called turtlebacks, laid in courses while still wet.

Fremont pottery (Figure 8.20) is a grayware, constructed by a coil-and-scrape technique. Plain gray is overwhelmingly the most abundant, but textured variants also occur, including scored, incised, and appliquéd treatments. Corrugated pots are found late in the San Rafael and Parowan traditions, presumably in imitation of Anasazi types. Painted vessels also display motifs probably derivative from Anasazi models. Anasazi trade pottery has been found at many sites, particularly in the south, but never abundantly. Unfired clay figurines (Figure 8.20) occur widely and are especially elaborate in the San Rafael area.

Utah metates, troughed forms having a small depression or shelf at the closed end, are common, as are well-shaped stone balls of enigmatic function. Large, well-executed pictographs of anthropomorphs, often with elaborate headdresses and bodily ornamentation, are found in eastern and central Fremont area shelters; certain horned and shield-bearing figures have been likened to Northwest Plains pictographs (Wormington 1955; Aikens 1966). Leather moccasins are reported from several areas and contrast sharply with the ubiquitous fiber sandals of other Southwestern traditions.

WHAT HAPPENED TO THE FREMONT? □ The Fremont tradition as characterized above did not last much if at all past AD 1300, and it probably was contracting and consolidating after AD 1150. Several theories as to what happened to the Fremont have been proposed, but none is very satisfactory.

Gunnerson (1962; 1969) has attempted to link the Virgin branch, western Fremont, and eastern Fremont with ethnographically known Numic-speaking groups—respectively, the northern Paiute, the Shoshone-Comanche, and the southern Paiute-Ute. Schroeder (1963) and Euler (1964) effectively criticized this theory on archeological grounds, pointing out the essentially complete lack of cultural continuity between the Numic groups and their putative ancestors. Schroeder and Euler also cite evidence that groups having traits of the ethnographic Paiute were already present in the eastern Great Basin and in contact with the Fremont and Virgin peoples by the 1100s; hence, the former could not be descended from the latter. Miller (1964) and Goss (1968) also criticized Gunnerson's theory on linguistic grounds.

Aikens's hypothesis that the Fremont moved to the Northwestern Plains, where they founded the Dismal River culture (cf., Gunnerson 1960) and eventually became Plains Apache, has not fared much better (cf., Wedel 1967; Husted and Mallory 1967; Fry and Dalley 1970). Sharrock (1966, quoted in Marwitt 1970) has recorded probable Fremont sherds in association with tipi rings in southwestern Wyoming, outside the Dismal River area. This may lend some tentative support to a Plains dispersal route for the Fremont.

A third possibility is that the Fremont drifted south during the 1200s and 1300s, much as the Anasazi did, perhaps in response to similar pressures.

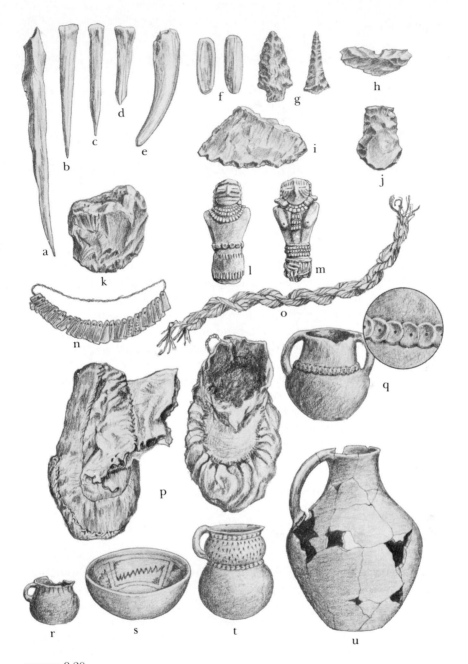

FIGURE 8.20
Artifacts of the Fremont culture: *a*, bone splinter awl; *b–d*, bone awls; *e*, antler flaking tool; *f*, bone gaming pieces; *g*, projectile points; *h*, shaft scraper; *i, j*, scrapers; *k*, rough hammerstone; *l, m*, clay figurines; *n*, bone necklace; *o*, bark rope; *p*, leather moccasins; *q*, pot and enlarged view of appliqué treatment; *r*, small pot; *s*, black-on-white bowl; *t*, pot with appliqué at rim and restricted waist; *u*, plain grayware vessel. (From *Prehistory of North America*, 2d ed., by Jesse D. Jennings. Copyright © 1968, 1974 by McGraw-Hill, Inc. Used with permission of McGraw-Hill Book Company.)

Positive evidence of their incorporation into either Rio Grande or Western Pueblo is, however, lacking. The fate of the Fremont culture remains a mystery. [Editor's note: For another view of the Fremont culture, see Chapter 4.]

CONCLUDING COMMENTS

In preparing an introduction to the prehistoric Southwest, we judged it best to define regional traditions and discuss their changes and interrelationships through time. We might instead have organized this paper around Southwest-wide stages of development or particular cultural changes of widespread impact. The brief comments below are directed toward such a pan-area perspective.

During the early stage of Plains-based big-game-hunting cultures, many parts of the Southwest were used little or not at all. In addition, the Southwest appears to have been marginal to a larger culture area centered to the east. In the Archaic stage, the Southwest was also a participant in developments that extended, and may often have originated, outside the area. Such relationships appear generally to have been stronger to the west than to the east. During the Archaic, new areas of the Southwest were settled, and the beginnings of distinctively Southwestern traditions, adapted to particular geographic areas, can be distinguished.

In the Late Archaic, population growth and intensified interareal communication set the stage for a transition to adaptations based on cultivated plants. It was during this period that cultigens originating in Mexico entered the Southwest and spread, initially as a minor dietary item, to some and perhaps most parts of the area's highland and plateau zone. The Mogollon Highlands appear to have been an important center for the adaptation of the southern cultigens to Southwestern upland climate and for their dispersal to the Plateau region. Whether the lowland desert areas participated in this early argicultural development is not clear.

In the thousand years between 300 BC and AD 700, a number of regional traditions emerged from this transition phase. Their growing populations now lived in villages of substantial pithouses, made pottery and other new items of equipment, and increasingly depended on increasingly productive varieties of maize, beans, and squash. The first such tradition to appear was the Hohokam of the Arizona desert river valleys. Unlike the other Southwestern sedentary traditions, which evolved largely in place, the Hohokam culture, in the opinion of many Southwesternists, may have been imported in developed form by a migrant group from the south. Although the mechanisms and pathways remain to be traced, this intrusion may have acted as a catalyst for change among Southwestern groups already in a transitional state. The next tradition to emerge was one neighboring the Hohokam—the Mogollon. During the period ca. AD 300 to 700, the Mogollon tradition appears to have functioned again as a center for the integration of new elements—whether derived from the Hohokam or elsewhere—and their transmission through the upland zone, in particular to the developing Anasazi and Fremont traditions. During the emergence of the various Southwestern sedentary traditions, interregional information transfer seems clearly to have been an important process. Of course the actual changes that took place in each locality were the results of local evolutionary processes that selected for or against locally generated as well as imported information.

The period from about AD 500 to 1050 or 1150 was apparently one of population growth, with elaboration and consolidation of sedentary-agricultural adaptations. Most settlements remained small, evidently egalitarian, and economically isolated. A few, such as those in Chaco Canyon, developed relatively large and concentrated populations, probably had more complex and possibly stratified social organizations, and participated in widespread trading networks. The role of such centers in cultural change and population distribution in the Southwest is just beginning to be studied.

The period between about 1100 and 1350 or 1400 was one of increasing consolidation of population into fewer but larger settlements and of the abandonment of territory once occupied, particularly in the northern Southwest. Although the number of sites decreased dramatically, it is not clear that population decreased, although it may have. Most of the unoccupied or lightly used areas left by the consolidation or retreat of the agricultural traditions were sparsely filled by the immigration of small groups of Numic, Upland Yuman, and Athapaskan speakers practicing mobile adaptations that emphasized hunting and gathering. The causes of this period of turbulence and change remain obscure. Processes of economic and organizational change that had been set in motion in the previous period may account for the changes observed at this time. Or these changes may only have been the response to some rather severe climatic-environmental shifts that affected the whole Southwest. More likely, the changes were the result of interrelated environmental, organizational, and adaptive shifts, most of which we are barely beginning to study and understand.

The latest prehistoric period (ca. 1350–1550) is poorly known in most areas. Although links between Anasazi-Western Pueblo and historic Rio Grande and Western Pueblo seem fairly well documented, those between the Hohokam and Pima-Papago rest more on general cultural similarities than on actual evidence of continuity. The fate of groups such as the Fremont, Virgin Anasazi, Cohonina, and Prescott remains unknown.

In conclusion, although our knowledge of the culture history of the Southwest is as good as that for any similar-sized area of the New World and better than for most, there is an abundance of culture historical problems yet to be solved. And our understanding of the paleoenvironmental and cultural processes that lie behind culture history is rudimentary, to say the least. The odds appear good that the Southwest will continue to be a vital topic of study in its own right, as well as serving as an important laboratory for the development of method and theory in archeology.

ACKNOWLEDGMENT

With gratitude I acknowledge the considerable help I received from Dr. Mark Grady in preparing the Hohokam section of this chapter, for which I take full responsibility but not full credit. Dr. Grady spent much time discussing with me current issues in Hohokam archaeology and also generously contributed, for use as working drafts, condensed versions of several portions of his doctoral dissertation. [Editor's note: Dr. Grady is the assistant director of the Archaeology Research Program at Southern Methodist University. He has done fieldwork in the Central Valley of California and the Sierra foothills and in several areas of Arizona; he has been head of the Cultural Resource Management Section of the Arizona State Museum.]

References Cited and Recommended Sources

Aikens, C. Melvin 1966 Fremont-Promontory-Plains relationships. University of Utah Anthropological Papers 82.

————. 1967 Excavations at Snake Rock Village and the Bear River no. 2 site. University of Utah Anthropological Papers 87.

————. 1970 Hugup Cave. University of Utah Anthropological Papers 87.

————. 1972 Fremont culture: restatement of some problems. American Antiquity 37:1:61–66.

Allen, William L., and James B. Richardson, III 1971 The reconstruction of kinship from archaeological data: the concepts, the methods, and the feasibility. American Antiquity 36:1:41–53.

Ambler, J. Richard 1966 Caldwell Village. University of Utah Anthropological Papers 84.

————. 1969 The temporal span of the Fremont. Southwestern Lore 34:4:107–117.

Anderson, Keith M. 1969 Ethnographic analogy and archeological interpretation. Science 163:133–138.

Antevs, Ernst 1955 Geologic-climatic dating in the West. American Antiquity 20:4:317–335.

Baerreis, David A., and Reid A. Bryson 1965 Climatic episodes and the dating of Mississippian cultures. The Wisconsin Archeologist 46:206–220.

Bandelier, Adolph F. 1892 Final report of investigations among the Indians of the southwestern United States, carried on mainly in the years from 1880 to 1885, part II. Archaeological Institute of America Papers, American Series IV.

Bannister, Bryant, Elizabeth A. M. Gell, and John W. Hannah 1966 Tree-ring dates from Arizona N-Q, Verde-Show Low-St. Johns area. Laboratory of Tree-Ring Research, University of Arizona.

Bannister, Bryant, John W. Hannah, and William J. Robinson 1970 Tree-ring dates from New Mexico M-N, S, Z, southwestern New Mexico area. Laboratory of Tree-Ring Research, University of Arizona.

Barnett, Franklin 1970 Matli Ranch ruins: a report of excavation of five small prehistoric Indian ruins of the Prescott culture in Arizona. Museum of Northern Arizona Technical Series 10.

————. 1974 Excavation of main pueblo, Fitzmaurice Ruin. Museum of Northern Arizona.

Berry, Michael n.d. Excavations at Evans Mound. University of Utah Anthropological Papers, in press.

Binford, Lewis R. 1962 Archaeology as anthropology. American Antiquity 28:2:217–225.

———. 1968 Post-Pleistocene adaptations. *In* New Perspectives in Archeology. ed. Lewis R. Binford and Sally R. Binford, pp. 313–341. Chicago: Aldine Publishing Company.

Bluhm, Elaine A. 1960 Mogollon settlement patterns in Pine Lawn Valley, New Mexico. American Antiquity 25:4:538–546.

Bohrer, Vorsila L. 1970 Ethnobotanical aspects of Snaketown, a Hohokam village in southern Arizona. American Antiquity 35:4:413–430.

Bohrer, Vorsila H., Hugh C. Cutler, and Jonathan D. Sauer 1969 Carbonized plant remains from two Hohokam sites, Arizona BB:13:4 and Arizona BB:13:50. The Kiva 35:1:1–10.

Bradfield, Wesley 1931 Cameron Creek Village. School of American Research Monographs 1.

Brand, Donald D. 1938 Aboriginal trade routes for sea shells in the Southwest. Association of Pacific Coast Geographers Year Book 4:3–10.

Breternitz, David A. 1957 A brief archaeological survey of the lower Gila River. The Kiva 22:2–3:1–13.

———. 1959 Excavations at Nantack Village, Point of Pines, Arizona. University of Arizona Anthropological Papers 1.

———. 1960 Excavations at three sites in the Verde Valley, Arizona. Museum of Northern Arizona Bulletin 34.

———. 1966 An appraisal of tree-ring dated pottery in the Southwest. Anthropological Papers of the University of Arizona 10.

———. 1967 The eruption(s) of Sunset Crater: dating and effects. Plateau 40:2:72–76.

———. 1970 Archaeological excavations in Dinosaur National Monument, Colorado-Utah, 1964–1965. University of Colorado Studies, Series in Anthropology 17.

Brew, J. O. 1944 On Pueblo IV and the Katchina-Tlaloc relations. *In* El norte de Mexico y sur de Estados Unidos. Sociedad Mexicana de Antropologia, Mesa Redonda 2.

———. 1946 Archaeology of Alkali Ridge, southeastern Utah. Harvard University, Peabody Museum of American Archaeology and Ethnology Papers 21.

Bryan, Kirk 1929 Flood-water farming. Geographic Review 19:444–456.

———. 1941 Pre-Columbian agriculture in the Southwest, as conditioned by periods of alluviation. Association of American Geographers Annals 31:4:219–242.

———. 1954 The geology of Chaco Canyon, New Mexico, in relation to the life and remains of the prehistoric peoples of Pueblo Bonito. Smithsonian Miscellaneous Collections 122:7.

Bullard, William, Jr. 1962 The Cerro Colorado site and pit house architecture in the southwestern United States prior to AD 900. Harvard University, Peabody Museum of American Archaeology and Ethnology Papers 44:2.

Caldwell, Joseph R. 1958 Trend and tradition in the prehistory of the eastern United States. American Anthropological Association Memoir 88.

Canouts, Veletta, John Beezley, Gordon Fritz, Mark Grady, Timothy Kearns, Michael Polk, and Lynn Teague 1975 An archaeological survey of the Orme Reservoir. Arizona State Museum Archaeological Series 92.

Canouts, Veletta, Edward Germeshausen, and Robert Larkin 1972 An archaeological survey of the Santa Rosa Wash project. Arizona State Museum Archaeological Series 18.

Castetter, Edward F., and Willis H. Bell 1951 Yuman Indian agriculture. Albuquerque: University of New Mexico Press.

Colton, Harold S. 1938 Names of the four culture roots in the Southwest. Science 87:251–252.

———. 1939 Prehistoric culture units and their relationships in northern Arizona. Museum of Northern Arizona Bulletin 17.

———. 1941 Prehistoric trade in the Southwest. Scientific Monthly 52:308–319.

———. 1945a The Patayan problem in the Colorado River valley. Southwestern Journal of Anthropology 1:1:114–121.

———. 1945b Sunset Crater. Plateau 18:1:7–14.

———. 1946 The Sinagua: a summary of the archaeology of the region of Flagstaff, Arizona. Museum of Northern Arizona Bulletin 22.

———. 1949 The prehistoric population of the Flagstaff area. Plateau 22:2:21–25.

———. 1960 Black Sand: Prehistory in Northern Arizona. Albuquerque: University of New Mexico Press.

Colton, Harold S., and Lyndon L. Hargrave 1937 Handbook of northern Arizona pottery wares. Museum of Northern Arizona Bulletin 11.

Cosgrove, H. S., and C. B. Cosgrove 1932 The Swarts Ruin, a typical Mimbres site of south-western New Mexico. Harvard University, Peabody Museum of American Archaeology and Ethnology Papers 15:1.

Cummings, Byron 1927 Ancient canals of the Casa Grande. Progressive Arizona 3:5:9–10.

Cushing, Frank H. 1890 Preliminary notes on the origin, working hypothesis, and primary researches of the Hemenway Southwestern Archaeological Expedition. Congres International des Americanistes, Compte-rendu de la septieme session, pp. 151–194.

Daifuku, Hiroshi 1952 A new conceptual scheme for prehistoric cultures in the southwestern United States. American Anthropologist 54:2:191–200.

Davis, Emma Lou 1963 The Desert culture of the western Great Basin, a lifeway of seasonal transhumance. American Antiquity 29:2:202–212.

———. 1965 Small pressures and cultural drift as explanations for abandonment of the San Juan area, New Mexico and Arizona. American Antiquity 30:353–354.

Dean, Jeffrey S. 1970 Aspects of Tsegi phase social organization: a trial reconstruction. *In* Reconstructing Prehistoric Pueblo Societies. ed. W. A. Longacre, pp. 140–174. Albuquerque: University of New Mexico Press.

DeBloois, Evan 1975 The Elk Ridge archeological project: a test of random sampling in archeological surveying. USDA Forest Service Intermountain Region Archeological Reports 2.

Dick, Herbert W. 1965 Bat Cave. Monographs of the School of American Research 27.

Dickson, Bruce 1975 Settlement pattern stability and change in the middle northern Rio Grande region, New Mexico: a test of some hypotheses. American Antiquity 40:2:159–171.

DiPeso, Charles C. 1951 The Babocomari Village site on Babocomari River. Amerind Foundation Publications 5.

———. 1953 The Sobaipuri Indians of the upper San Pedro River valley, southeastern Arizona. Amerind Foundation Publications 6.

———. 1956 The upper Pima of San Cayetano del Tumacacori. Amerind Foundation Publications 7.

———. 1958 The Reeve Ruin of southeastern Arizona: a study of a prehistoric western pueblo migration into the middle San Pedro Valley. Amerind Foundation Publications 8.

———. 1968 Casas Grandes and the Gran Chichimeca. El Palacio 75:4:45–61.

———. 1974 Casas Grandes, A Fallen Trading Center of the Gran Chichimeca, I, II, III. Dragoon and Flagstaff: Amerind Foundation, Inc., and Northland Press.

———. 1976 Gila Polychrome in the Casas Grandes region. The Kiva 42:1:57–63.

Doelle, William 1974 Prehistoric resource exploitation within the CONOCO Florence Project. Arizona State Museum Archaeological Series.

Douglass, A. E. 1929 The secret of the Southwest solved by the talkative tree-rings. National Geographic Magazine 54:737–770.

Doyel, David E. 1972 Cultural and ecological aspects of Salado prehistory. Unpublished master's thesis, California State University at Chico.

———. 1974 Excavations in the Escalante Ruin Group, southern Arizona. Arizona State Museum Archaeological Series.

Doyel, David E., and Emil W. Haury (eds.) 1976 The 1976 Salado Conference. The Kiva 42:1:1–134.

Dutton, Bertha 1963 Sun Father's Way. Santa Fe: School of American Research.

Eddy, Frank W. 1961 Excavations at Los Pinos phase sites in the Navajo Reservoir district. Museum of New Mexico Papers 4.

———. 1966 Prehistory in the Navajo Reservoir district, northwestern New Mexico, with sections by Thomas Harlan, Kenneth A. Bennett, and Erik K. Reed, Museum of New Mexico Papers in Anthropology 15:I–II.

Eggan, Fred 1950 Social Organization of the Western Pueblos. Chicago: University of Chicago Press.

Ellis, Florence Hawley 1967 Where did the Pueblo people come from? El Palacio 74:3:35–43.

Euler, Robert C. 1964 Southern Paiute archaeology. American Antiquity 29:3:379–381.

Euler, Robert C., and Henry F. Dobyns 1962 Excavations west of Prescott, Arizona. Plateau 34:3:69–84.

Euler, Robert C., and George Gumerman 1974 A resume of the archaeology of northern Arizona. *In* The geology of Northern Arizona with Notes on Archaeology and Paleoclimate, ed. Thor Karlstrom. Proceedings Twenty-seventh Annual Meeting, Rocky Mountain Section, Geological Society of America.

Euler, Robert C., and Alan P. Olson 1965 Split-twig figurines from northern Arizona, new radiocarbon dates. Science 148:368–369.

Ezell, Paul H. 1961 The hispanic acculturation of the Gila River Pimas. American Anthropological Association Memoirs 90.

———. 1963 Is there a Hohokam-Pima continuum? American Antiquity 29:1:61–66.

Ferdon, Edwin N., Jr. 1955 A trial survey of Mexican-Southwestern architectural parallels. School of American Research Monographs 21.

———. 1967 The Hohokam "ball court": an alternative view of its function. The Kiva 33:1:1–14.

Fewkes, Jesse W. 1892 A report on the present condition of a ruin in Arizona called Casa Grande. Journal of American Ethnology and Archaeology 2:177–193.

———. 1912 Casa Grande, Arizona. Annual Report of the Bureau of American Ethnology 28:25–180.

Figgins, J. D. 1927 The antiquity of man in America. Natural History 27:3:229–239.

Fitting, James E. 1971 The Burris Ranch site, Dona Ana County, New Mexico. Southwestern New Mexico Research Reports 1.

———. 1972 Chipped stone from the 1967 Mimbres area survey, parts I and II. Southwestern New Mexico Research Reports 8.

———. 1973 Four archaeological sites in the Big Burro Mountains of New Mexico. Center of Anthropological Study Monograph 1.

Flannery, Kent V. 1968 Archaeological systems theory and early Mesoamerica. In Anthropological Archeology in the Americas, ed. Betty J. Meggers, pp. 67–87. Washington, D.C.: Anthropological Society of Washington.

Ford, Richard I. 1972 An ecological perspective on the eastern Pueblos. In New Perspectives on the Pueblos, ed. Alfonso Ortiz, pp. 1–17. Albuquerque: University of New Mexico Press.

Ford, Richard I., Albert H. Schroeder, and Stewart L. Peckham 1972 Three perspectives on Puebloan prehistory. In New Perspectives on the Pueblos, ed. Alfonso Ortiz, pp. 19–39. Albuquerque: University of New Mexico Press.

Fowler, Donald D. 1973 Dated split-twig figurine from Etna Cave, Nevada. Plateau 46:2:54–63.

Fritts, Harold C., David G. Smith, and Marvin A. Stokes 1965 The biological model for paleoclimatic interpretation of Mesa Verde tree-ring series. Contributions of the Wetherill Mesa archeological project. Society for American Archaeology Memoirs 19:101–121.

Fritz, John M., and Fred T. Plog 1970 The nature of archaeological explanation. American Antiquity 35:4:405–412.

Fry, Gary F., and Gardiner F. Dalley 1970 The Levee site and the Knoll site. Unpublished manuscript. Department of Anthropology, University of Utah.

Fulton, William S. 1934 Archeological notes on Texas Canyon, Arizona. Museum of the American Indian, Heye Foundation, Contributions 12:1–2.

———. 1941 A ceremonial cave in the Winchester Mountains, Arizona. Amerind Foundation Publications 2.

Fulton, William S., and Carr Tuthill 1940 An archaeological site near Gleeson, Arizona. Amerind Foundation Publications 1.

Galinat, Walton C., and James H. Gunnerson 1963 Spread of 8-rowed maize from the prehistoric Southwest. Harvard University, Botanical Museum Leaflets 20:5.

Gladwin, Harold S. 1928 Excavations at Casa Grande, Arizona. Southwest Museum Papers 2.

———. 1937 Excavations at Snaketown, II. Medallion Papers 26.

———. 1942 Excavations at Snaketown III: revisions. Medallion Papers 30.

———. 1948 Excavations at Snaketown IV: review and conclusions. Medallion Papers 38.

Gladwin, Harold S., Emil W. Haury, E. B. Sayles, and Nora Gladwin 1937 Excavations at Snaketown, material culture. Medallion Papers 25.

Gladwin, Winifred, and Harold S. Gladwin 1929a The Red-on-Buff culture of the Gila Basin. Medallion Papers 3.

———. 1929b The Red-on-Buff culture of the Papagueria. Medallion Papers 4.

———. 1930a The western range of the Red-on-Buff culture. Medallion Papers 5.

———. 1930b An archaeological survey of the Verde Valley. Medallion Papers 6.

———. 1934 A method for designation of cultures and their variations. Medallion Papers 15.

———. 1935 The eastern range of the Red-on-Buff culture. Medallion Papers 16.

Glassow, Michael 1972 Changes in the adaptations of Southwestern Basketmakers: a systems perspective. *In* Contemporary Archaeology, ed. Mark P. Leone, pp. 289–302. Carbondale: Southern Illinois Press.

Goodyear, Albert C. III 1975 Hecla II and III: an interpretive study of archeological remains from the Lakeshore Project, Papago Reservation, southcentral Arizona. Arizona State University Anthropological Research Papers 9.

Goss, James A. 1968 Culture-historical inference from Utaztekan linguistic evidence. Occasional Papers of the Idaho State Museum 22:1–42.

Grady, Mary A. 1976 Aboriginal agrarian adaptation to the Sonoran Desert: a regional synthesis and research design. Ph.D. dissertation, University of Arizona.

Grady, Mark, Sandra Kemrer, Sandra Schultz, and William Dodge 1973 An archaeological survey of Salt-Gila Aqueduct. Arizona State Museum Archaeological Series 23.

Graybill, Donald A. 1975 Mimbres-Mogollon adaptations in the Gila National Forest, Mimbres District, New Mexico. USDA Forest Service Archeological Report 9.

Grebinger, Paul 1971 Hohokam cultural development in the middle Santa Cruz Valley, Arizona. Ph.D. dissertation, University of Arizona Microfilms.

———. 1973 Prehistoric social organization in Chaco Canyon, New Mexico: an alternative reconstruction. The Kiva 39:1:3–23.

Grebinger, Paul F., and David P. Adams 1974 Hard times? Classic Period Hohokam cultural development in the Tucson Basin, Arizona. World Archaeology 6:2:226–241.

Greene, Jerry L., and Thomas W. Mathews 1976 Faunal study of unworked mammalian bone. *In* The Hohokam, Desert Farmers and Craftsmen, ed. Emil W. Haury, pp. 367–373. Tucson: University of Arizona Press.

Greenleaf, J. Cameron 1975 Excavations at Punta del Agua in the Santa Cruz Basin, southeastern Arizona. University of Arizona Anthropological Papers 26.

Guernsey, Samuel J., and A. V. Kidder 1921 Basket Maker caves of northeastern Arizona, report on the explorations, 1916, 1917. Harvard University, Peabody Museum of American Archaeology and Ethnology Papers 8:2.

Gumerman, George, and S. Alan Skinner 1968 A synthesis of the central Little Colorado Valley, Arizona. American Antiquity 33:2:185–199.

Gunnerson, James H. 1960 An introduction to Plains Apache archeology: the Dismal River aspect. Bureau of American Ethnology Bulletin 113.

———. 1962 Plateau Shoshonean prehistory: a suggested reconstruction. American Antiquity 28:1:41–45.

———. 1969 The Fremont culture: a study in culture dynamics on the northern Anasazi frontier. Harvard University, Peabody Museum of Archaeology and Ethnology Papers 59:2.

Hack, John T. 1942 The changing physical environment of the Hopi Indians of Arizona. Harvard University, Peabody Museum of American Archaeology and Ethnology Papers 35:1.

Hargrave, Lyndon L. 1938 Results of a study of the Cohonina branch of the Patayan culture in 1938. Museum of Northern Arizona Museum Notes 11:6.

Haury, Emil W. 1932 Roosevelt 9:6, a Hohokam site of the Colonial period. Medallion Papers 11.

———. 1936 The Mogollon culture of southwestern New Mexico. Medallion Papers 20.

———. 1940 Excavations in the Forestdale Valley, east-central Arizona. University of Arizona Bulletin 11:4.

———. 1943 The stratigraphy of Ventana Cave. American Antiquity 8:3:218–223.

———. 1945a The problem of contacts between the southwestern United States and Mexico. Southwestern Journal of Anthropology 1:1:55–74.

———. 1945b The excavation of Los Muertos and neighboring ruins in the Salt River valley, southern Arizona. Harvard University, Peabody Museum of American Archaeology and Ethnology Papers 24:1.

———. 1950 The Stratigraphy and Archaeology of Ventana Cave, Arizona. 1st ed. Tucson and Albuquerque: University of Arizona Press and University of New Mexico Press.

———. 1956 Speculation on prehistoric settlement patterns in the Southwest. *In* Prehistoric Settlement Patterns in the New World, ed. Gordon R. Willey. Viking Fund Publications in Anthropology 23:3–10.

———. 1957 An alluvial site on the San Carlos Indian Reservation, Arizona. American Antiquity 23:1:2–27.

————. 1960 Association of fossil fauna and artifacts of the Sulphur Springs stage, Cochise culture. American Antiquity 25:4:609–610.

————. 1962 The greater American Southwest. In Courses Toward Urban Life, ed. Robert J. Braidwood and Gordon R. Willey, pp. 106–131. Chicago: Aldine Publishing Company.

————. 1965 Snaketown: 1964–1965. The Kiva 31:1:2–27.

————. 1967 The Hohokam, first masters of the American desert. National Geographic Magazine 131:670–695.

————. 1975 The Stratigraphy and Archaeology of Ventana Cave, Arizona. 2d ed. Tucson: University of Arizona Press.

————. 1976 The Hohokam, Desert Farmers and Craftsmen: Excavations at Snaketown, 1964–1965. Tucson: University of Arizona Press.

Haury, Emil W., Ernest Antevs, and J. F. Lance 1953 Artifacts with mammoth remains, Naco, Arizona. American Antiquity 19:1:1–24.

Haury, Emil W., and E. B. Sayles 1947 An early pit-house village of the Mogollon culture, Forestdale Valley, Arizona. University of Arizona Bulletin 18:4.

Haury, Emil W., E. B. Sayles, and William W. Wasley 1959 The Lehner mammoth site, southeastern Arizona. American Antiquity 25:1:2–30.

Hawley, Florence 1937 Kokopelli of the prehistoric southwestern pueblo pantheon. American Anthropologist 39:4:644–646.

————. 1938 The family tree of Chaco Canyon masonry. American Antiquity 3:2:247–255.

Haynes, C. Vance, Jr. 1964 Fluted projectile points: their age and dispersion. Science 145: 1408–1413.

Hayden, Julian D. 1957 Excavations, 1940, at University Indian Ruin, Tucson, Arizona. Southwestern Monuments Association Technical Series 5.

Hester, James J. 1962 Early Navajo migrations and acculturation in the Southwest. Museum of New Mexico Papers in Anthropology 6.

Hibben, Frank C. 1941 Evidences of early occupation of Sandia Cave, New Mexico, and other sites in the Sandia-Manzano region. Smithsonian Miscellaneous Collections 99:23.

Hill, James N. 1966 A prehistoric community in eastern Arizona. Southwestern Journal of Anthropology 22:1:9–30.

————. 1970 Broken K Pueblo: prehistoric social organization in the American Southwest. University of Arizona Anthropological Papers 18.

Hough, Walter 1907 Antiquities of the upper Gila and Salt river valleys in Arizona and New Mexico. Bureau of American Ethnology Bulletin 35.

Husted, Wilfred M., and Oscar L. Mallory 1967 The Fremont culture: its derivation and ultimate fate. Plains Anthropologist 12:222–232.

Irwin-Williams, Cynthia 1967 Picosa: the elementary Southwestern culture. American Antiquity 32:4:441–455.

————. 1968 Archaic culture history in the southwestern United States. Eastern New Mexico University Contributions in Anthropology 1:4:48–53.

————. 1970 Review of survey and excavations north and east of Navajo Mountain, Utah, 1959–1962. American Anthropologist 72:6:1549–1550.

————. 1972 The structure of Chacoan society in the northern Southwest: investigations at the Salmon site, 1972. Eastern New Mexico University Contributions in Anthropology 4:3.

————. 1973 The Oshara tradition: origins of Anasazi culture. Eastern New Mexico University Contributions in Anthropology 5:1.

————. n.d. Paleo-Indian and Archaic cultural systems in the southwestern United States. Manuscript to be published in Handbook of North American Indians, ed. W. Sturtevant.

Irwin-Williams, Cynthia, and C. Vance Haynes, Jr. 1970 Climatic change and early population dynamics in the southwestern United States. Quaternary Research 1:1:59–71.

James, Kathleen 1974 Analysis of potsherds and ceramic wares. In Excavation of Main Pueblo at Fitzmaurice Ruin, ed. Franklin Barnett, pp. 106–129. Flagstaff: Museum of Northern Arizona.

Jennings, Jesse D. 1953 Danger Cave: a progress summary. El Palacio 60:5:179–213.

————. 1956 The American Southwest: a problem in cultural isolation. In Seminars in Archaeology: 1955, ed. Robert Wauchope. Society for American Archaeology Memoirs 11:61–127.

————. 1966 Glen Canyon, a summary. University of Utah Anthropological Papers 81.

————. 1973 The short useful life of a simple hypothesis. Tebiwa 16:1:1–9.

————. 1974 Prehistory of North America. 2d ed. New York: McGraw-Hill.

————. 1975 Preliminary report: excavations of Cowboy Caves. Unpublished manuscript, Department of Anthropology, University of Utah.

Jennings, Jesse D., and Edward Norbeck 1955 Great Basin prehistory: a review. American Antiquity 21:1:1–11.

Jett, Stephen C. 1964 Pueblo Indian migrations: an evaluation of the possible physical and cultural determinants. American Antiquity 29:3:281–300.

Johnson, Alfred E. 1964 Archaeological excavation in Hohokam sites of southern Arizona. American Antiquity 30:2:145–161.

————. 1965 The development of western Pueblo culture. Ph.D. dissertation, University of Arizona Microfilms.

Johnson, Alfred E., and William W. Wasley 1966 Archaeological excavations near Bylas, Arizona. The Kiva 31:4:205–253.

Judd, Neil M. 1919 Archaeological investigations of Paragonah, Utah. Smithsonian Miscellaneous Collections 70:3:1–22.

————. 1926 Archaeological observation north of the Rio Colorado. Bureau of American Ethnology Bulletin 82.

Judge, W. James 1973 Paleoindian Occupation of the Central Rio Grande Valley, New Mexico. Albuquerque: University of New Mexico Press.

Kelley, J. Charles 1952 Factors involved in the abandonment of certain peripheral Southwestern settlements. American Anthropologist 54:356–387.

————. 1960 North Mexico and the correlation of Mesoamerican and Southwestern cultural sequences. In Selected Papers of the Fifth International Congress of Anthropological and Ethnological Sciences, ed. Anthony F. C. Wallace, pp. 566–573. Philadelphia: University of Pennsylvania Press.

Kidder, Alfred V. 1924 An Introduction to the Study of Southwestern Archaeology, with a Preliminary Account of the Excavations at Pecos. New Haven: Yale University Press.

————. 1927 Southwestern Archaeological Conference. Science 66:1716:489–491.

Kirchoff, Paul 1954 Gatherers and farmers in the greater Southwest. American Anthropologist 56:4:529–550.

Kroeber, A. L. 1916 Zuni potsherds. American Museum of Natural History Anthropological Papers 18:1:1–37.

————. 1939 Cultural and natural areas of native North America. University of California Publications in American Archeology and Ethnology 38.

Leach, Larry L. 1966 The archeology of Boundary Village. Miscellaneous Paper 13, University of Utah Anthropological Papers 83:85–129.

LeBlanc, Steven A. 1975 Mimbres Archeological Center: Preliminary Report of the First Season of Excavation, 1974. Los Angeles: Institute of Archaeology, University of California.

————. 1976 Mimbres Archeological Center: preliminary report of the second season of excavation, 1975. Journal of New World Archaeology 1:6:1–23.

Leone, Mark P. 1968 Neolithic economic autonomy and social distance. Science 162:1150–1151.

Lindsay, Alexander J., Jr., J. Richard Ambler, Mary Ann Stein, and Philip M. Hobler 1968 Survey and excavations north and east of Navajo Mountain, Utah, 1959–1962. Museum of Northern Arizona Bulletin 45.

Linton, Ralph 1944 Nomad raids and fortified pueblos. American Antiquity 10:1:28–32.

Lipe, W. D., and A. J. Lindsay, Jr. (eds.) 1974 Proceedings of the 1974 cultural resource management conference, Federal Center, Denver, Colorado. Museum of Northern Arizona Technical Series 14.

Lipe, W. D., and R. G. Matson 1971a Human settlement and resources in the Cedar Mesa area, southeast Utah. In The Distribution of Prehistoric Population Aggregates, ed. George J. Gumerman, pp. 126–151. Prescott College Anthropological Reports 1.

————. 1971b Prehistoric cultural adaptation in the Cedar Mesa area, southeast Utah. Research proposal submitted to the National Science Foundation.

Longacre, William A. 1964 Archeology as anthropology: a case study. Science 144:1454–1455.

————. 1966 Changing patterns of social integration: a prehistoric example from the American Southwest. American Anthropologist 68:1:94–102.

————. 1970 Archaeology as anthropology: a case study. University of Arizona Anthropological Papers 17.

Longacre, William A., and J. Jefferson Reid 1974 The University of Arizona archaeological field school at Grasshopper: eleven years of multidisciplinary research and teaching. The Kiva 40:1–2:3–38.

McGregor, John C. 1937 Winona Village. Museum of Northern Arizona Bulletin 12.

————. 1941 Winona and Ridge Ruin, Part I. Museum of Northern Arizona Bulletin 18.

————. 1951 The Cohonina Culture of Northwestern Arizona. Urbana: University of Illinois press.

————. 1965 Southwestern Archaeology. 2d ed. Urbana: University of Illinois Press.

————. 1967 The Cohonina culture of Mount Floyd, Arizona. University of Kentucky Studies in Anthropology 5.

McKusick, Charmion R. 1976 Avifauna. In The Hohokam, Desert Farmers and Craftsmen, ed. Emil W. Haury, pp. 374–377. Tucson: University of Arizona Press.

Madsen, David B. 1975 Dating Paiute-Shoshoni expansion in the Great Basin. American Antiquity 40:1:82–86.

Madsen, David B., and Michael S. Berry 1975 A reassessment of northeastern Great Basin prehistory. American Antiquity 40:4:391–405.

Mangelsdorf, Paul C., Richard S. MacNeish, and Walton C. Galinat 1967 Prehistoric wild and cultivated maize. In The Prehistory of the Tehuacan Valley, Vol. 1: Environment and Subsistence, ed. Douglas S. Byers, pp. 178–200. Austin: University of Texas Press.

Martin, Paul Snyder 1940 The SU site, excavations at a Mogollon village, western New Mexico, 1939. Field Museum of Natural History, Anthropological Series 32:1.

————. 1943 The SU site, excavations at a Mogollon village, western New Mexico, second season, 1941. Field Museum of Natural History, Anthropological Series 32:2.

Martin, Paul Snyder, James N. Hill, and William A. Longacre 1967 Chapters in the prehistory of eastern Arizona, III. Fieldiana: Anthropology 57.

Martin, Paul Snyder, and Fred T. Plog 1973 The Archaeology of Arizona. New York: Doubleday Natural History Press.

Martin, Paul Snyder, and John B. Rinaldo 1947 the SU site: excavations at a Mogollon village, western New Mexico, third season, 1946. Field Museum of Natural History, Anthropological Series 32:3.

———— —. 1950 Sites of the Reserve Phase, Pine Lawn Valley, western New Mexico. Fieldiana: Anthropology 38:3.

————. 1960 Excavations in the upper Little Colorado drainage. Fieldiana: Anthropology 51:1.

Martin, Paul Snyder, John B. Rinaldo, and Ernst Antevs 1949 Cochise and Mogollon sites, Pine Lawn Valley, western New Mexico. Fieldiana: Anthropology 38:1.

Martin, Paul Snyder, John B. Rinaldo, Elaine A. Bluhm, Hugh C. Cutler, and Roger Grange, Jr. 1952 Mogollon cultural continuity and change: the stratigraphic analysis of Tularosa and Cordova caves. Fieldiana: Anthropology 40.

Martin, Paul Snyder, John B. Rinaldo, William A. Longacre, Constance Cronin, Leslie G. Freeman, Jr., and James Schoenwetter 1962 Chapters in the prehistory of eastern Arizona I. Fieldiana: Anthropology 53.

Martin, Paul Snyder, John B. Rinaldo, William A. Longacre, Leslie B. Reeman, Jr., James A. Brown, Richard H. Hevly, and M. E. Cooley 1964 Chapters in the prehistory of eastern Arizona II. Fieldiana: Anthropology 55.

Martin, Paul Snyder, Ezra B. W. Zubrow, Daniel C. Bowman, David A. Gregory, John A. Hanson, Michael B. Schiffer, and David R. Wilcox 1975 Chapters in the prehistory of eastern Arizona, IV. Fieldiana: Anthropology 65.

Marwitt, John P. 1968 Pharo Village. University of Utah Anthropological Papers 91.

————. 1970 Median Village and Fremont culture regional variation. University of Utah Anthropological Papers 95.

Mehringer, Peter J., Jr., Paul Schultz Martin, and C. Vance Haynes 1967 Murray Springs: a mid-postglacial pollen record from southern Arizona. American Journal of Science 265: 786–797.

Merriam, C. Hart 1890 Results of a biological survey of the San Francisco Mountains region and desert of the Little Colorado in Arizona. USDA North American Fauna 3:1–136.

————. 1898 Life-zones and crop-zones of the United States. USDA division of the Biological Survey Bulletin 10:1–79.

Miller, Wick R. 1964 Anthropological linguistics in the Great Basin. Paper presented at the Symposium on the Status of Great Basin Research, Great Basin Anthropological Conference, September 1964.

Minckley, W. L. 1976 Fishes. *In* The Hohokam, Desert Farmers and Craftsmen, ed. Emil W. Haury, p. 379. Tucson: University of Arizona Press.

Mindeleff, Cosmos 1896a Casa Grande Ruin. Annual Report of the Bureau of American Ethnology 13:295–319.

————. 1896b Aboriginal remains in Verde Valley, Arizona. Annual Report of the Bureau of American Ethnology 16.

Morris, Donald H. 1969 Red Mountain: an early Pioneer period site in the Salt River valley of central Arizona. American Antiquity 34:1:40–53.

————. 1970 Walnut Creek Village: a ninth century Hohokam-Anasazi settlement in the mountains of central Arizona. American Antiquity 35:1:49–60.

Morris, Earl H. 1928 The Aztec Ruin. American Museum of Natural History, Anthropological Papers 26:1–5.

Morris, Earl H., and Robert F. Burgh 1954 Basket Maker II sites near Durango, Colorado. Carnegie Institution of Washington Publication 604.

Morss, Noel 1931 Ancient culture of the Fremont River in Utah. Harvard University, Peabody Museum of American Archaeology and Ethnology Papers 12:3.

Nelson, Nels C. 1916 Chronology of the Tano ruins, New Mexico. American Anthropologist 18:2:159–180.

Nesbitt, Paul H. 1931 The ancient Mimbrenos. Logan Museum Bulletin 4.

Niswander, J. D. et al. 1970 Population studies on Southwestern Indian tribes I, culture history and genetics of the Papago. American Journal of Human Genetics 22:7–23.

Nusbaum, Jesse L., A. V. Kidder, and Samuel J. Guernsey 1922 A Basket Maker cave in Kane County, Utah. Heye Foundation Indian Notes and Monographs 29.

Pepper, George H. 1902 Ancient Basket Makers of southern Utah. American Museum Journal 2:4(Supplement).

Plog, Fred T. 1974 The study of prehistoric change. New York: Academic Press.

Raab, L. Mark 1973 AZ AA:5:2: a prehistoric cactus camp in Papagueria. Journal of the Arizona Academy of Science 8:116–118.

————. 1974 A report of archaeological investigations at Santa Rosa Wash, southern Arizona, Phase I. Master of Science thesis, University of Arizona.

————. 1976 The structure of prehistoric community organization at Santa Rosa Wash, southern Arizona. Ph.D. dissertation, Arizona State University.

Reed, Erik K. 1950 Eastern-central Arizona archaeology in relation to the Western Pueblos. Southwestern Journal of Anthropology 6:2:120–138.

————. 1964 The greater Southwest. *In* Prehistoric Man in the New World, ed. Jesse D. Jennings and E. Norbeck, pp. 175–191. Chicago: University of Chicago Press.

Rodgers, James B. 1974 An archaeological survey of the Cave Buttes Dam alternative site and reservoir, Arizona. Arizona State University Anthropological Research Papers 8.

Rohn, Arthur H. 1963 Prehistoric soil and water conservation on Chapin Mesa, southwestern Colorado. American Antiquity 28:441–455.

————. 1975 A stockaded Basketmaker III village at Yellow Jacket, Colorado. The Kiva 40:3:113–119.

Rouse, I. 1962 Southwestern archaeology today. *In* An Introduction to the Study of Southwestern Archaeology, ed. A. V. Kidder, pp. 1–53. 2d ed. New Haven: Yale University Press.

Rudy, Jack R. 1953 Archeological survey of western Utah. University of Utah Anthropological Papers 12.

Sayles, Edward B. 1945 The San Simon branch excavations at Cave Creek and in the San Simon Valley, I, material culture. Medallion Papers 34.

Sayles, E. B., and Ernst Antevs 1941 The Cochise culture. Medallion Papers 29.

Scantling, Frederick H. 1939 Jackrabbit Ruin. The Kiva 5:3:9–12.

Schaafsma, Polly, and Curtis F. Schaafsma 1974 Evidence for the origins of the Pueblo Katchina cult as suggested by Southwestern rock art. American Antiquity 39:4:535–545.

Shiffer, Michael B. 1976 Behavioral Archeology. New York: Academic Press.

Schoenwetter, James, and Frank W. Eddy 1964 Alluvial and palynological reconstruction of environments, Navajo Reservoir district. Museum of New Mexico Papers in Anthropology 13.

Schroeder, Albert H. 1940 A stratigraphic survey of pre-Spanish trash mounds of the Salt River valley, Arizona. Master's thesis, University of Arizona.

––––––. 1947 Did the Sinagua of the Verde Valley settle in the Salt River valley? Southwestern Journal of Anthropology 3:3:230–246.

––––––. 1952 The bearing of ceramics on developments in the Classic Hohokam period. Southwestern Journal of Anthropology 8:4:320–335.

––––––. 1953 The problem of Hohokam, Sinagua, and Salado relations in southern Arizona. Plateau 26:2:75–83.

––––––. 1957 The Hakataya cultural tradition. American Antiquity 23:2:176–178.

––––––. 1960 The Hohokam, Sinagua, and Hakataya. Archives of Archaeology 5.

––––––. 1961 The pre-eruptive and post-eruptive Sinagua patterns. Plateau 34:2:60–66.

––––––. 1963 Comment on Gunnerson's "Plateau Shoshonean prehistory." American Antiquity 28:4:559–560.

––––––. 1965 Unregulated diffusion from Mexico into the Southwest prior to AD 700. American Antiquity 30:3:297–309.

––––––. 1966 Pattern diffusion from Mexico into the Southwest after AD 600. American Antiquity 31:5:683–704.

Schwartz, Douglas 1956 Demographic changes in the early periods of Cohonina prehistory. In Prehistoric Settlement Patterns in the New World, ed. Gordon R. Willey, pp. 26–31. Viking Fund Publications in Anthropology 23.

––––––. 1959 Culture area and time depth: the four worlds of the Havasupai. American Anthropologist 61:1060–1070.

Schwartz, Douglas, Arthur L. Lange, and Raymond deSaussure 1958 Split-twig figurines in the Grand Canyon. American Antiquity 23:2:264–274.

Scoville, Douglas, Garland J. Gordon, and Keith M. Anderson 1972 Guidelines for the preparation of statements of environmental impact on archaeological resources. Unpublished document. National Park Service Western Archeological Center.

Sharrock, Floyd W. 1966 Prehistoric occupation patterns in southwest Wyoming and cultural relationships with the Great Basin and Plains culture areas. University of Utah Anthropological Papers 77.

Sharrock, Floyd W., and John P. Marwitt 1967 Excavations at Nephi, Utah, 1965–1966. University of Utah Anthropological Papers 88.

Shields, Wayne F., and Gardiner F. Dalley n.d. The Bear River no. 3 site. Miscellaneous Paper 22, University of Utah Anthropological Papers, in press.

Shutler, Richard, Jr. 1961 Lost City: Pueblo grande de Nevada. Nevada State Museum Anthropological Papers 5.

Smith, Watson 1952 Kiva mural decorations at Awatovi and Kawaik-a, with a survey of other wall paintings in the Southwest. Harvard University, Peabody Museum of American Archaeology and Ethnology Papers 37.

Spicer, Edward H., and L. P. Caywood 1936 Two Pueblo ruins in west central Arizona. University of Arizona Bulletin 7:1, Social Science Bulletin 10.

Spier, Leslie 1917 An outline for a chronology of Zuni ruins. American Museum of Natural History Anthropological Papers 18:3:209–331.

––––––. 1919 Ruins in the White Mountains, Arizona. Anthropological Papers of the American Museum of Natural History 18:5:363–386.

Stacy, V. K. Pheriba 1974 Cerros de Trincheras in the Arizona Papagueria. Ph.D. dissertation, University of Arizona.

Stanislawski, Michael 1973 Review of archaeology as anthropology: a case study by William A. Longacre. American Antiquity 38:1:117–122.

Stevens, Dominique E., and George A. Agogino n.d. Sandia Cave: a study in controversy. Eastern New Mexico University Contributions in Anthropology 7:1.

Steward, Julian 1937 Ecological aspects of Southwestern society. Anthropos 32:87–104.

––––––. 1938 Basin-Plateau aboriginal socio-political groups. Bureau of American Ethnology Bulletin 120.

Steward, Julian, and F. M. Setzler 1938 Function and configuration in archaeology. American Antiquity 4:1:4–10.

Taylor, Walter W. 1948 A study of archeology. American Anthropological Association Memoir 69.

———. 1954 Southwestern archeology, its history and theory. American Anthropologist 56:4:561–575.

Thompson, Raymond H., and William A. Longacre 1966 The University of Arizona archaeological field school at Grasshopper, east-central Arizona. The Kiva 31:4:255–275.

Tuohy, Donald R. 1960 Archaeological survey and excavation in the Gila River channel between Earven Dam site and Buttes Reservoir site, Arizona. Manuscript on file with the Western Archeological Center of the National Park Service.

Turney, O. A. 1929a Prehistoric irrigation. Arizona Historical Review 2:5:1–4.

———. 1929b Prehistoric irrigation, Part II. Arizona Historical Review 2:2:11–52.

Tuthill, Carr 1947 The Tres Alamos site on the San Pedro River, southeastern Arizona. Amerind Foundation Publications 4.

Vivian, R. Gwinn 1965 An archaeological survey of the lower Gila River, Arizona. The Kiva 30:4:95–146.

———. 1970 An inquiry into prehistoric social organization in Chaco Canyon, New Mexico. In Reconstructing Prehistoric Pueblo societies, ed. William A. Longacre, pp. 59–83. Albuquerque: University of New Mexico Press.

Warren, Claude N. 1967 The San Dieguito complex: a review and hypothesis. American Antiquity 32:2:168–186.

Wasley, William W. 1960 A Hohokam platform mound at the Gatlin site, Gila Bend, Arizona. American Antiquity 26:2:244–262.

———. 1966 Classic Period Hohokam. Master's thesis, University of Arizona.

Wasley, William W., and Blake Benham 1968 Salvage excavation in the Buttes Dam site, southern Arizona. The Kiva 33:4:244–279.

Wasley, William W., and Alfred E. Johnson 1965 Salvage archaeology in Painted Rocks Reservoir, western Arizona. University of Arizona Anthropological Papers 9.

Weaver, Donald E. 1972 A cultural-ecological model for the Classic Hohokam period in the lower Salt River valley. The Kiva 38:1:43–52.

Wedel, Waldo R. 1967 Review of Fremont-Promontory-Plains relationships in northern Utah, by C. Melvin Aikens. American Journal of Archeology 71:426–427.

Weed, Carol S. 1972 The Beardsley Canal site. The Kiva 38:2:57–94.

Weed, Carol S., and Albert E. Ward 1970 The Henderson site: Colonial Hohokam in north central Arizona: a preliminary report. The Kiva 36:2:1–12.

Wendorf, Fred 1950 A report on the excavation of a small ruin near Point of Pines, east central Arizona. University of Arizona Bulletin 21:3.

Whalen, Norman 1971 Cochise culture sites in the central San Pedro drainage, Arizona. Ph.D. dissertation, University of Arizona.

———. 1973 Agriculture and the Cochise. The Kiva 39:1:89–96.

Wheat, Joe Ben 1954 Crooked Ridge Village (Arizona W:10:15). University of Arizona Bulletin 25:3.

———. 1955 Mogollon culture prior to AD 1000. American Anthropological Association Memoirs 82.

Wilcox, David R. n.d. The entry of Athapascans into the American Southwest: the problem today. Unpublished manuscript.

Willey, Gordon R., and Philip Phillips 1958 Method and Theory in American Archaeology. Chicago: University of Chicago Press.

Winter, Joseph 1973 The distribution and development of Fremont maize agriculture: some preliminary interpretations. American Antiquity 38:4:439–451.

Winter, Joseph C., and Henry G. Wylie 1974 Paleoecology and diet at Clydes Cavern. American Antiquity 39:2:303–315.

Withers, Arnold M. 1944 Excavations at Valshni Village, a site on the Papago Indian Reservation. American Antiquity 10:33–47.

———. 1973 Excavations at Valshni Village, Arizona. Arizona Archaeologist 7.

Woodbury, Richard B. 1961 Prehistoric agriculture at Point of Pines, Arizona. Society for American Archaeology Memoirs 17.

Woodward, Arthur 1931 The Grewe site. Los Angeles Museum of History Science and Art Occasional Papers 1.

Wormington, H. Marie 1955 A reappraisal of the Fremont culture. Denver Museum of Natural History Proceedings 1.

Zubrow, Ezra B. W. 1971 Carrying capacity and dynamic equilibrium in the prehistoric Southwest. American Antiquity 36:2:127–138.

———. 1975 Prehistoric carrying capacity: a model. Menlo Park, Calif.: Cummings Publishing Company.

Teotihuacán. (Copyright © 1973 by René Millon. All rights reserved.)

CHAPTER NINE

Mesoamerica

T. Patrick Culbert

It is well known that the arrival of the Spanish brought an abrupt end to a group
of native high civilizations in Mesoamerica. What is not as often realized is that
these high civilizations were only the latest (and in some ways not the highest)
in a series of such civilizations stretching back for centuries in the Mexican and
Guatemalan highlands and lowlands. Dr. Culbert traces the evolution of these
civilizations from their simple hunting-gathering and agrarian village pasts through
their rises and declines until the arrival of the Spanish brought the cycle to an end.

Mesoamerica is a culture area characterized by a set of shared cultural characteristics that indicate long-standing communication and interrelatedness
among the prehistoric inhabitants. Together, the Mesoamerican people forged
one of the two civilizations of native America. Because of the continual
interaction, it is impossible to understand the cultural development of any
specific part of the area without reference to the whole.

The boundaries of Mesoamerica are delineated in Figure 9.1. The northern
boundary corresponds to a sharp break in both ecology and culture. To the
north lies desert, where agricultural possibilities are limited to scattered,
oasislike areas of available water. Culturally, this is a frontier where, at least
in some areas, representatives of Mesoamerican high cultures directly confronted peoples who still lived by hunting and gathering. This confrontation
was emphasized—perhaps overemphasized—by the native Mesoamericans
themselves; their illustrated texts depict northern barbarians clad in skins
and armed with bows and arrows. The fact that groups of farming peoples
not very different from those within Mesoamerica lived in favored areas
beyond the northern frontier was less romantic and received less notice. On
the south, the limits of Mesoamerica are far less pronounced. Environmental
conditions like those of Mesoamerica continue into Central America, and
the peoples who occupied neighboring territories had well-developed hierarchical societies that lacked only the more elaborate features of Mesoamerican cultural complexity.

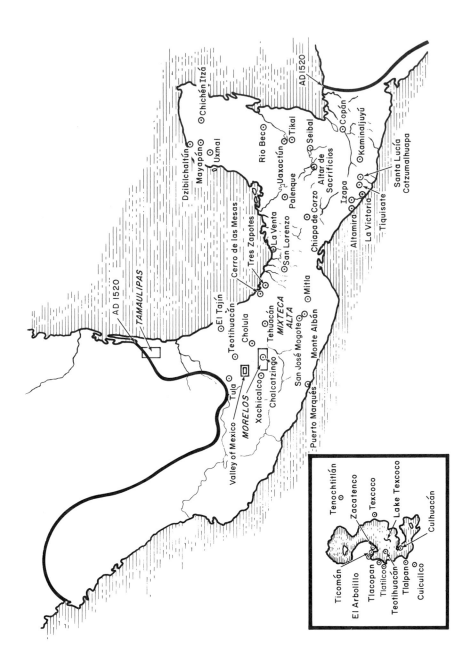

FIGURE 9.1
Mesoamerica.

GEOGRAPHY AND ENVIRONMENT

Mountains are the primary geographic fact of Mesoamerica, and the variety of altitudinal, climatic, and vegetational zones associated with the precipitous topography of the region has deeply influenced human adaptation. Physiographically, Mesoamerica can be described as a series of major mountain masses separated and bounded by relatively limited areas of lower elevation (West 1964).

Northern and Central Mexico is occupied by a vast, U-shaped tableland defined on the east and west by mountain ranges (the Sierra Madre Oriental and the Sierra Madre Occidental) and on the south by the geologically recent Neovolcanic Axis. The northern part of this upland is the parched desert of northern Mexico that lies outside the boundaries of Mesoamerica. To the south lies the Mesa Central, dotted with a profusion of volcanic features between and among which a series of ancient highland lake basins provide the choice areas for human habitation.

Below the precipitous southern escarpment of the Neovolcanic Axis lies the Balsas Depression, a land of low hills among which the Balsas River finds a sinuous passage to the Pacific. One of the few major river basins in Mesoamerica, the Balsas Depression has suffered from a paucity of archeological investigation that makes it impossible to evaluate its role in Mesoamerican development.

Rising to the south of the Balsas Depression are the highlands of Oaxaca. Incredibly dissected by erosion over much of their surface, the Oaxacan Highlands offer few substantial flat areas for human occupation, and in many places the modern Indian populations still live in scattered households and hamlets that cling to narrow ridges or perch on steep slopes above tiny valley floors. The Valley of Oaxaca offers the only major area of valley floor and was the site of important cultural centers from very early times. North and west of the Valley of Oaxaca lies the Mixteca Alta, whose tiny, lofty valleys are the homeland of the Mixtec culture.

To the south of the Oaxacan Highlands, the continent narrows to 192 kilometers in breadth at the Isthmus of Tehuantepec, which has long been a corridor of migration and culture contact. The isthmus is usually considered to be the division between northern and southern Mesoamerica.

The highlands of Chiapas and Guatemala constitute the major mountain mass of southern Mesoamerica. A geologically complex set of ranges that parallel the Pacific coast, the Chiapas-Guatemalan Highlands are characterized by recent vulcanism close to the coast and uplifted sedimentary rocks further inland. Between and crosscutting the mountain ranges are a number of highland basins, the most important of which archeologically is the Valley of Guatemala. The Chiapas section of the highlands is split by the Central Depression of Chiapas in which the Grijalva River drains the highland massif in an extensive, semiarid basin.

To the north of the Guatemalan Highlands lie the Maya Lowlands, a limestone platform that provides the only large mass of low-elevation land in Mesoamerica. The northern third of the platform, in the Yucatan Peninsula, is almost flat; to the south, there are a series of low but steep-sided ridges separated by swampy areas. The porosity of the underlying limestone provides an opportunity for rapid underground drainage, so most of the Maya Lowland area is devoid of rivers.

The remaining lowland areas of Mesoamerica are the Pacific and Gulf coasts. From the southern border of Mesoamerica as far as the Isthmus of Tehuantepec, the Pacific coast combines a flat, narrow, coastal plain with a rainy piedmont crossed by myriad rivers that drain the heavy rainfall of the coastal mountain ranges into the Pacific. The Gulf coast is generally broader and is crossed by several meandering rivers that discharge huge amounts of water into the Gulf of Mexico.

The climate of Mesoamerica is characterized by a summer rainy season and a winter dry season. The rainy season is longest (May–November) in southern Mesoamerica, becoming progressively shorter by a month or more at each end as one moves to the northern frontier. In general, rainfall is moderate to heavy in lowland areas. Most of the highlands are semiarid, and in many parts of northern Mesoamerica the rains are so scanty that rainfall farming is a high-risk proposition. Temperatures are dependent upon elevation. Regions below 1500 meters are essentially frost free, while those above 2100 meters suffer from frost that is severe enough to curtail the growing season.

The contrast between the arid highland and moist lowland environments in Mesoamerica has profound effects upon native farming patterns. Of equal importance, however, are microenvironmental variations within each limited zone (Coe and Flannery 1964); gross generalizations, based upon the assumption of very large homogeneous areas within which adaptation was everywhere identical, have not proved profitable as a tool for analysis. Detailed consideration of microenvironments is now an indispensable part of any research that stresses ecological considerations.

ARCHEOLOGICAL RESEARCH IN MESOAMERICA

The beginnings of an orderly interest in the archeological remains of prehistoric Mesoamerica date back to the mid-nineteenth century when explorers and travelers began to attract public attention to the marvels that had long lain forgotten. Probably the most influential of the early explorers was John Lloyd Stephens, who, accompanied by the artist Frederick Catherwood, visited Yucatan and Central America and published accounts (1841; 1843) that achieved instant popularity. By the turn of the century, explorers' accounts had become both more numerous and more scientific, and initial excavations and reconstructions had begun. The period until 1940 was largely devoted to archeological basics—locating and mapping sites, establishing sequences, and excavating and reconstructing some of the more impressive structures. The Mexican government sponsored projects at major sites like Teotihuacán and Monte Albán, while the Carnegie Institution, under the leadership of A. V. Kidder, was the most important research organization in the Mayan area. The questions asked tended to be ones of origins and diffusion—where did things start and by what routes did they spread?

After World War II, archeologists took new directions. Settlement pattern studies became of importance in both the Mayan area and Central Mexico, with Gordon R. Willey and William T. Sanders among the pioneers. Ecological interests awakened, with Richard S. MacNeish focusing upon the problem of plant domestication and a number of people, including Sanders, Angel Palerm, and Eric Wolf, considering the effect of subsistence systems upon cultural development. The primary theoretical framework was neoevolutionary and strongly influenced by the ideas of Julian Steward and Elman Service. The directions in which research has been moving in the past ten years is a primary focus in this article and will be the topic of much of the material that follows.

CHRONOLOGICAL PERIODS

Mesoamerican cultural development may be conveniently summarized by using a scheme of five major periods: Paleo-Indian, Food Collecting or Archaic, Preclassic or Formative, Classic, and Postclassic. In earlier, more naive days, when there were few data to handicap the imagination, the last three periods were envisioned as having additional significance as area-wide cultural stages. As data accumulated, so many instances of precocious or laggardly development became known in individual regions that the position that "periods = stages" became untenable. Here, the periods and subdivisions are used in a strictly chronological sense. My particular version of the periods and their subdivisions appears in Figures 9.2 and 9.3.

The treatment in this chapter will be chronological, following the development of culture, period by period. I have eschewed division by geographical sections such as Maya-Mexican or highland-lowland, hoping thus to keep the focus on Mesoamerican unity and the problems that were Mesoamerica-wide at particular times. At the same time, I have tried to bring out the importance of geographical and ecological contrasts.

As noted in Chapter One, evidence of the Paleo-Indian period in Mesoamerica is so spotty that reconstruction of cultural patterns must depend heavily upon the introduction of data from North America. That early man lived in Mesoamerica is clear; to say more in a summary of this length is impossible.

408

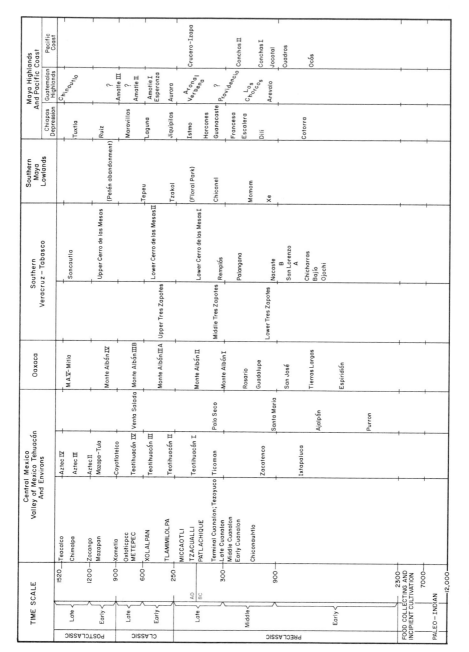

FIGURE 9.2
Chronological chart.

Postclassic	Late	AD 1200 – 1520
	Early	AD 900 – 1200
Classic	Late	AD 600 – 900
	Early	AD 250 – 600
Preclassic	Late	300 BC – AD 250
	Middle	900 – 300 BC
	Early	2300 – 900 BC
Archaic		7000 – 2300 BC
Puleo – Indian		12,000 (?) – 7000 BC

FIGURE 9.3
Periods of Mesoamerican prehistory.

THE TRANSITION TO FOOD PRODUCTION

A critical factor in the emergence of the Mesoamerican lifestyle and all later cultural developments was the transition in subsistence from the collecting of wild foods to food production based upon the native American plant trilogy of corn, squash, and beans and a few not very important domestic animals. This transition was illuminated in admirable detail in the Tehuacan Valley of Central Mexico by Richard S. MacNeish and a team of interdisciplinary experts (MacNeish 1964; Byers 1967).

The Tehuacan Valley, 240 kilometers southeast of Mexico City, lies at an elevation of 1800 meters. The climate is exceedingly dry, with valley-floor rainfall averaging less than 50 centimeters per year. Aridity is a critical factor in the preservation of plant remains, which in turn is necessary to the study of the origins of domestication. Of 392 prehistoric sites discovered in a survey, MacNeish conducted excavations at 30. A sequence of nine cultural phases was delineated; the first six phases, beginning before 7000 BC and lasting until 900 BC, demonstrate the transition from post-Pleistocene hunting and gathering to full-scale agriculture. By the end of the Ajureado phase (6500 BC), climatic conditions were identical to those of the present, and subsistence depended upon hunting, especially of deer and rabbit, and gathering a variety of wild plant foods including maguey, mesquite beans, roots, and a number of tree and cactus fruits. The first domestic plants—chili peppers, amaranth, and squash—appear in the succeeding El Riego phase (6500–4800 BC), but these domesticates provided only a tiny fraction of the diet. The three following phases, between 4800 BC and 1500 BC, show a continually increasing variety of domestic plants and slow increments in the percentage of the diet derived from cultivation. Important introductions include the first domestic common beans and either wild or domestic maize during the Coxcatlan phase (4800–3500 BC). In spite of steady growth in the techniques of food production, the Tehuacan inhabitants at the end of the Abejas phase at 2300 BC still derived 70 percent of their diet from wild foods and still followed a seasonal round in which sizable groups (macrobands) aggregated in summer camps but split into tiny microbands during the lean months of winter and early spring. It is not until the Ajalpan phase, beginning at 1500 BC, that there is evidence for year-round sedentary villages, which presupposes dependence upon agriculture for a major part of the foodstuffs.

Data from the highlands of the state of Tamaulipas at the northeastern edge of Mesoamerica show a different sequence of domestic plants (MacNeish 1958). In Tamaulipas, the cultivation of pumpkins and bottle gourds is earlier than at Tehuacan, but domestic corn and beans are later. As in Tehuacan, several millennia of incipient cultivation precede the appearance of sedentary villages.

The foregoing data suggest important conclusions about the rate and origins of domestication in the highlands of Mesoamerica. First, domestication is, as Coe and Flannery note, an evolution, not a revolution (1964:650). In other words, there is a long period of gradual growth in cultivation and change in domestic plants before the transition to full-scale agriculture. Second, since plants appear in domestic forms in varying sequences at different locations, there seem to have been multiple centers for domestication rather than a single center.

But what have we learned about the *processes* of domestication? Analyses of the Tehuacan data by Kent Flannery (1968a; 1973) provide useful insights. Flannery notes that, although the wild resources utilized by the Tehuacanos include a large variety of edible plants and animals, a relatively small number of species were consistently the most important. Some of the major resource species are strictly seasonal in availability. Cactus fruit and mesquite seed pods, for example, are available at the beginning of and during the rainy season. In good years, these seasonal foods are present in great abundance, but they must be harvested rapidly to prevent spoilage or consumption by birds and animals. It is the seasonal abundance of such resources that favors large macroband camps during the rainy season. Other resources are available all year but are less abundant at any single place or time. These year-round resources support the scattered microbands of the dry season. Making the picture more complicated is the fact that the Tehuacan Valley is divided into a number of environmental microzones. Although the most important resources crosscut microzones, they may be more abundant in some than in others, so that maximum food recovery demands movement from one zone to another.

The subsistence routine was not a hit-or-miss proposition but a *strategy* that involved careful scheduling of activities and a series of deliberate choices about where to be at any given time and how to allocate energy among a series of possible alternatives. A number of factors of availability and scheduling militated against overexploitation of any single resource. In other words, the system was strongly conservative (or deviation counteracting) and tended to favor continuation of a strategy emphasizing a variety of different resources with only such variation as was necessitated by year-to-year fluctuations in the quantities of the different resources.

Why, then, would people have abandoned a stable system of wild food collecting to embark upon a career in cultivation? The answer may lie in the fact that the routine of cultivation has potentialities that do not exist in simple collecting. When a particular wild resource is heavily utilized, the yield it produces will either remain constant or, if reaping exceeds the replacement rate, will diminish. Cultivation, on the other hand, given the right conditions, can reward increased attention with continually increasing yields as the nature of the cultivated plants changes under man's care. Most of the plants that became important domestic food sources underwent a series of genetic changes that greatly increased their productivity. A specific example may serve to illustrate the importance of this point.

Maize was by far the most important food plant in native Mesoamerica. It existed prehistorically in a dazzling array of varieties that grew under a great diversity of climatic conditions. Yet maize has been so changed by the process of domestication that its ancestry remains a matter of hot debate (see Flannery 1973 for an excellent review of the problem). Paul Manglesdorf (1974) believes that the domestic strain is descended from a wild maize that is now extinct. Several other specialists (Galinat 1971; Beadle 1972) have vigorously reasserted an older viewpoint that maize is descended from teosinte, a weedy wild grass that grows over a wide area in the semiarid highlands of Mexico. The earliest maize from Tehuacan (Coxcatlan phase, 4800–3500 BC) can fit either viewpoint, since it can be interpreted as the hypothesized wild ancestor or as an early stage in the transition from teosinte to maize.

Whatever the ancestor, it must have been a most unattractive food source. Ears and kernels were tiny—the Coxcatlan cobs are little larger than a strawberry. The axis (rachis) that bears the fruit was extremely brittle, making harvesting difficult. The fruit case enclosing the kernels was hard, and separating fruit from chaff was a slow, arduous process. Several mutations were necessary to improve these unappealing characteristics. Genetic change to a less brittle rachis both made harvesting easier and made way for further mutations to increase size, for a more durable rachis could support larger ears. A single mutation to a soft fruit case made separation of fruit and chaff a much easier process. Once some of these basic changes had occurred, the door was open for a series of mechanisms that might promote further favorable change, such as hybridizing strains from different areas or moving the plant outside of its natural environmental zone to areas where selective pressures were different.

Once the process of improvement in maize or other domestic plants was underway, a self-stimulating (deviation-amplifying) cycle could promote an increase in food production. Improvement in the yield of cultivated plants would lead to greater investment of time in cultivation, which would increase opportunities for further improvement in plants, and so forth. Additional time spent in cultivation would be taken from food collecting, and eventually the expansion of cultivated areas would destroy areas of wild food resources, making the commitment to food production irreversible.

The foregoing reconstruction remains untested, but it seems plausible and does not invoke either climatic change, which is unlikely at the time when food production rose to importance, or an undemonstrated population increase great enough to *force* people to change subsistence patterns. Rather, the mainspring consists of human choices among alternative routines. These choices may have been influenced by such diverse factors as return for labor investment, the desire to maintain large groups in a single location, or an interest in providing security against periodic fluctuations in wild resources.

It should be noted, however, that current information about the transition to food production in Mesoamerica comes almost entirely from the Tehuacan Valley, a marginal environment in which only a few areally limited microzones are suitable for cultivation without irrigation. It is quite possible that the marginality of Tehuacan (and Tamaulipas as well) is responsible for the very slow transition to full-scale food production in these areas. It would not be surprising the find that processes and rates of change differed considerably in other parts of Mesoamerica, particularly in the humid lowland zones where rainfall is plentiful enough to permit two crops per year in many locations.

THE BEGINNINGS OF SOCIAL COMPLEXITY

This section will combine consideration of the Early (2300–900 BC) and Middle (900–300 BC) Preclassic periods, an arrangement that permits uninterrupted tracing of important phenomena that crosscut the border between the two periods. The Early Preclassic marks the appearance of pottery and sedentary village life in most parts of Mesoamerica. Shortly thereafter the first signs of increasing cultural complexity appear, and these were followed by the swift development of an incredibly sophisticated Olmec culture on the Gulf coast.

The earliest known pottery in Mesoamerica currently seems to be either the Purron phase of the Tehuacan Valley or the Pox phase known from shell mounds at Puerto Marques on the coast of Guerrero. Both phases begin somewhat before 2300 BC. Purron and Pox ceramics are quite similar; both are crude in technique and nearly devoid of decoration. The earliest vessel shapes have precedents in stone bowls in Tehuacan, and Purron-Pox pottery may well represent the independent invention of ceramic techniques somewhere in Mexico.

Most other ceramic sequences in Mesoamerica start around 1500 BC. Among the most interesting of these somewhat later phases are those from the Pacific coast. Here, the earliest pottery, the Barra phase (1600?–1500 BC), was discovered at the site of Altamira in Chiapas, Mexico. Barra is followed by the Ocos phase (1500–1000 BC), best known from La Victoria in coastal Guatemala and also reported from neighboring Chiapas. Both Barra and Ocos ceramics are very well made and decorated with both incised and painted designs. The pottery shows similarities to early pottery from Panama, Colombia, and Ecuador; most archeologists accept the idea of coastal sea travel connecting Mesoamerica and points south (Coe 1960), but I remain somewhat skeptical that the connections were as direct as some claim.

The data from Pacific coast sites raise interesting questions about subsistence and sedentism. Many Early Preclassic sites are shell mounds close to the sea that reveal a sophisticated utilization of estuarine and marine resources (Coe and Flannery 1964). Although there are clear indications of cultivation by Barra and Ocos times, there are unexcavated preceramic shell mounds that may represent a period when sedentary life was based entirely upon exploitation of the sea without supplementary cultivation.

The data from Altamira also pose problems about what crops were grown in Barra and Ocos times. Although close to the shore, Altamira shows no evidence of a sea-oriented economy and presumably was supported by cultivation. Yet manos and metates, the grinding implements generally taken to be indicative of maize cultivation, are absent, and Lowe (1967) has suggested that an abundance of tiny obsidian flakes found at the site may be parts of graters used to shred manioc, a root crop staple of probable South American origin. If it can be substantiated that manioc cultivation began this early in Mesoamerica, there will be important implications for theories of subsistence development.

By the end of the Early Preclassic, sedentary villages and efficient farming techniques had been established in most parts of Mesoamerica (see Figure 9.2 for phase names in various areas). A striking characteristic of Mesoamerican cultural development after the establishment of village life is the rapid appearance of public or ceremonial structures and of communities that are large enough to presuppose that they served as centers for integration of smaller surrounding communities. Such evidences of social complexity, labor coordination, and economic integration occur within a few centuries after the first known villages in most parts of Mesoamerica. Since many of the finds of the earliest phases are too deeply buried beneath later remains to indicate community patterns, and since still earlier phases may yet be discovered in many areas, the evidence is too slim to draw very firm conclusions. At the moment, however, it appears that the period of simple, egalitarian, and self-sufficient villages was short-lived in Mesoamerica.

A giant step in social complexity was taken by the enigmatic Olmec culture in a homeland in the swampy Gulf coast lowlands of Veracruz and Tabasco. In this area, the earliest known ceramic phases (Ojochi, 1500–1350 BC, and Bajio, 1350–1250 BC) show little relationship to later Olmec material. By the next phase, Chicharras (1250–1150 BC), sculpture in the Olmec style was being produced, and massive construction efforts were underway at the site of San Lorenzo. By the San Lorenzo phase (1150–900 BC), Olmec culture was in full flower (Coe 1968). Some remarks on Olmec origins are perhaps worthwhile in the light of Jett's comments (Chapter Thirteen) on the subject. There seems to me to be no reason to believe that Olmec culture was other than an *in situ* development on the Gulf coast. Several centuries of previous occupation precede the Olmec in this area, and at the moment no other area in Mesoamerica is known to have an early complex culture that seems a likely Olmec source. As a nondiffusionist who believes in human inventiveness and, in general, evolutionary processes that are likely to carry cultures along similar paths of development, I consider the probability of significant interhemispheric input to the Olmec to be diminishingly remote. As Jett notes, however, differences of opinion about diffusion rest far more upon basic assumptions about the nature of culture and human inventiveness than upon any specific evidence, either positive or negative.

The Olmec hallmark is an art style that is most dramatically expressed in stone carving (Figure 9.4). Undoubtedly the most spectacular carvings are great stone heads nearly 3 meters tall and weighing up to 18 metric tons. The heads depict humans with unusually thick-lipped physiognomies wearing what look like football helmets. Additional in-the-round and bas-relief carvings show a variety of themes and scenes, many of which seem to be ceremonial. In addition, small carvings of Olmec origin are scattered to the four corners of Mesoamerica, as are Olmec clay figurines. The most undeniably Olmec theme is the "were-jaguar"—human representations infused with feline characteristics to show snarling, downturned mouths, toothless gums, and, occasionally, jaguar fangs. The were-jaguars have an infantile appearance and are not infrequently depicted as babies carried in the arms of equally feline adults.

Two major Olmec sites, San Lorenzo and La Venta, are known from archeological excavations (Coe 1968; Drucker et al. 1959). The sites are ceremonial centers, not towns or cities; they contain clusters of public buildings and a concentration of sculpture but only limited areas of residential structures. The entire site of San Lorenzo is a construction, a huge, man-made platform surmounted by a number of smallish buildings. The site of La Venta

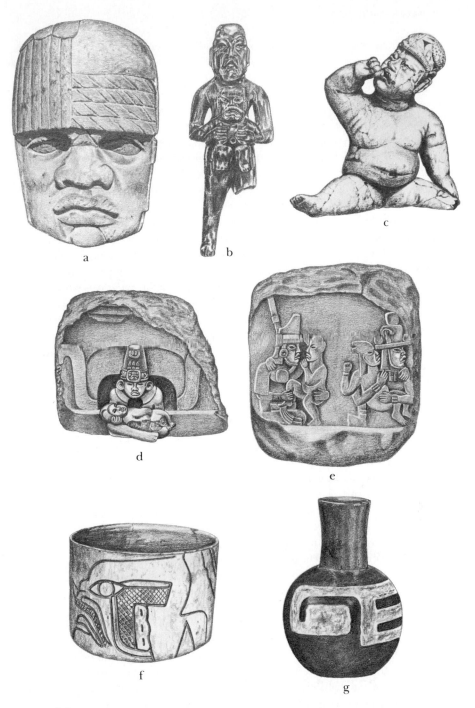

FIGURE 9.4
Olmec art: *a,* great stone head; *b,* jade figurine; *c,* ceramic figurine; *d, e,* LaVenta Altar 5;
f, g, Olmec pottery. (From *Prehistory of North America,* 2d. ed., by Jesse D. Jennings.)

is crammed onto a tiny island in the Tonala River. It contains a series of public structures arranged along a north-south axis, over which towers a single large pyramid.

Surprisingly little is known of the nature and workings of Olmec society. Where the supporting farming population lived and the density of occupation remain mysteries for lack of archeological surveys. The structure of Olmec elite society is equally unknown. It has been suggested that the great stone heads were portraits of rulers, but they could equally well be gods, symbols of idealized beauty, or famous players of the Mesoamerican ball game. Almost no burials have been recovered at Olmec sites, so we are unable to point to the tombs of kings and princes. No elite residential complexes or administrative buildings have been recovered, so it is impossible to infer societal organization from such sources. Olmec society is not infrequently pictured as a chiefdom in Elman Service's (1962) evolutionary scheme or as a theocracy ruled by priest-leaders. Although such reconstructions are not illogical, they are based almost entirely upon presuppositions about what Olmec society *should* have been rather than upon anything in the nearly nonexistent archeological evidence. A more cautious view could stress only that Olmec society must have had organized formal leadership, that religious enterprises probably consumed a healthy percentage of the "gross national product," and that there must have been a class of specialists carefully trained in the production of the famous art objects. The ability of the Olmec leaders to concentrate labor is demonstrated in the importation of vast quantities of volcanic stone for carvings and offerings from sources in the Tuxtla Mountains more than 80 kilometers distant.

That the Olmec were engaged in long-distance exchange is undeniable. Exotic materials including obsidian, jade, and magnetite are found in Olmec heartland sites; conversely, portable Olmec art is found to the borders of Mesoamerica and even beyond. Large boulder sculptures of unmistakable Olmec workmanship occur in Morelos and El Salvador, and Olmec cave paintings have been found in Guerrero. Moreover, Olmec motifs were widely imitated in stone carving and pottery in a number of areas of Mesoamerica.

The great spread of Olmec influence and the splendor of Olmec sites in comparison with those known in other areas have generated a lively debate about the role of the Olmec in the rise of civilization elsewhere in Mesoamerica. One viewpoint, propounded most forcefully by Michael Coe (1962), pictures the Olmec as a "mother culture," the first civilization in Mesoamerica and the primary source of all later civilizations. The alternative stance, asserted by Kent Flannery (1968b), is that Olmec civilization crystallized at a point in time when a number of areas had independently reached the point of incipient class stratification. Olmec influence, then, was made possible by, rather than being causative to, the increasing complexity of other areas. I lean toward the latter viewpoint, but since resolution of the question demands much fuller information about both the Olmec and the other societies in question, the fun of the debate is not likely to be lost in the near future.

Although Olmec civilization persisted for some seven centuries, there is little detailed information about changes within that time span. The mantle of Olmec leadership seems to have passed from San Lorenzo to La Venta about 900 BC. At that time, huge numbers of sculptures at San Lorenzo were defaced and buried at great expense of labor. The site was occupied by people using new kinds of ceramics, who stayed there for two centuries and then left the site empty and lifeless. One thinks easily of intra-Olmec power struggles, but the facts needed to determine exactly what happened still lie buried beneath the silts of the Gulf coast. After the 900 BC trauma at San Lorenzo, La Venta continued to flourish for three or four centuries until it, too, was abandoned, and Olmec culture came to an end.

A series of sites and cemeteries in highland Central Mexico exhibits a mixture of ceramics and figurines identical to those of the Gulf coast with a second ceramic style known variously as Tlatilco, Rio Cuautla, or "Highland Olmec" (Figure 9.5). Work by Grove (1974) and Grennes-Ravitz and Coleman (1976) in Morelos, where this manifestation is particularly strong, leads, despite disagreement in details, to two important conclusions. First, the Tlatilco-style ceramics are of highland origin and are considerably more common in the highlands than true Olmec material. Second, the Tlatilco style was established in Morelos by the fourteenth or fifteenth century before Christ, *before* the arrival of strong Olmec influence. The Olmec ceramic influence arrived in the highlands after 1200 BC, at the time when San Lorenzo was the Olmec center. The famous Olmec rock carvings at the site of Chalcatzingo are even later and are contemporary with Middle Preclassic La Venta.

The Early and Middle Preclassic periods in the Valley of Mexico have long been a source of confusion. A series of simple villages along the shores of the lakes that occupied a large section of the valley floor provide a ceramic sequence beginning with El Arbolillo and running through Zacatenco to a Late Preclassic Ticoman, with little evidence of outside contact. Juxtaposed with these villages is the fabulous cemetery of Tlatilco where rich burials include an incredible array of Tlatilco-style and Olmec offerings. The relationship of Tlatilco to the lakeside villages is uncertain. Tlatilco could not be later, since the village sequence is continuous through the Late Preclassic, and it seems impossible that such a rich site could have been earlier. If the two were coeval, what sort of social relationship existed between them, and why is there so little evidence of interaction? The most popular conclusion is that the Tlatilco graves are those of Olmec lords who had migrated to the valley and established themselves as an elite, ruling the humble local peasants who were not allowed to participate in Tlatilco elegance. Recent work by Tolstoy and Paradis (1970) has done much to clarify the situation. They have established an Early Preclassic occupation of the Valley of Mexico called Ixtapaluca, which shows strong Olmec influence and relates to the most Olmec-like burials at Tlatilco. Ixtapaluca is followed by the Arbollillo-Zacatenco sequence. This solution raises new questions in relation to the Morelos data. If Ixtapaluca was the first sedentary life in the Valley of

FIGURE 9.5
Tlatilco-style ceramics: *a–c*, pots; *d*, *e*, figurines; *f*, mask. (*a–c*, after Coe 1965; *d–f*, after Ekholm and Bernal 1971.)

Mexico, Olmec influence was crucial in the area from the beginning; Tolstoy and Paradis seem to favor the idea of actual Olmec intrusion. But the Morelos researchers believe that Olmec influence affected already well established village life and probably did not involve actual population intrusions. There is no reason, of course, why the higher and cooler Valley of Mexico should not have followed a different path from that of Morelos, but it is also possible that there are still-undiscovered earlier ceramic phases within the valley.

The Valley of Oaxaca is another major area in highland Mexico for which there are substantial data for the Early Preclassic. A good-sized highland valley at an intermediate elevation of 1500 meters, the Valley of Oaxaca suffers from a scanty rainfall that makes rainfall farming difficult. In parts of the valley, the water table lies no more than 2 to 3 meters below the surface, making possible a technique of pot irrigation accomplished by digging wells to the water table and irrigating individual plants by hand. In addition, a series of streams that emerge at the top of the piedmont zone can be used for small-scale canal irrigation.

Extensive settlement pattern survey by a team of investigators led by Kent Flannery (Flannery et al. 1967) has produced invaluable information about the location and nature of early sites. Early and Middle Preclassic phases are Espividion (1700–1400 BC), Tierras Largas (1400–1150 BC), San José (1150–850 BC), and Guadalupe (850–600 BC). Almost all of the Early Preclassic sites are located close to the high water-table zone, suggesting that pot irrigation was utilized by even the earliest farming inhabitants. During the Middle Preclassic, earlier sites increased in size and occupation spread upward along the larger streams into the piedmont, where a canal irrigation system has been recovered at the site of Hierve el Agua. A most significant feature of the Oaxaca data is the very early development of a large community at San José Mogote. Even in Tierras Largas times, San José Mogote was several times larger than any other village in the Etla arm of the valley, and by the San José phase it had expanded to an impressive size of nearly 20 hectares. In addition, San José phase remains at San José Mogote show signs of social and occupational diversity. The site consisted of three zones: one of small, lower-class residences, one with better-made public buildings, and a third that seems to have been an area of specialized manufacture, since the debris contained both worked and unworked fragments of magnetite, mica, and shell. Olmec influence is apparent during the San José phase, and Flannery (1968b) believes that the Valley of Oaxaca and the Olmec heartland were in a trade relationship that involved the exchange of ceremonial and elite items. The Oaxacan elite aped their more elegant trade partners and adopted Olmec styles, particularly in ceremonialism.

In the Guatemalan Highlands, the Early Preclassic is represented by the enigmatic (and perhaps nonexistent) Arevalo phase and the first half of the Las Charcas phase. The Middle Preclassic includes the latter half of Las Charcas and the Providencia-Majadas phase. Information about all of these phases is scanty.

Few archeological remains dated to the Early Preclassic have as yet been discovered in the Maya Lowlands, although the existence of corn pollen dated to 2000 BC hints at some early occupation, and the newly reported Swazey ceramics from Belize (Hammond et al. 1976) may date as early as 2050 BC (radiocarbon years). During the Middle Preclassic, ceramics appear in the

Xe phase at Altar de Sacrificios and Seibal on the Pasión River. By the Mamom ceramic horizon (600–300 BC), most parts of the Maya Lowlands show evidence of occupation (Willey et al. 1967).

THE SPREAD OF CIVILIZATION

This review will adopt a generalized scheme that lumps together all of the time between 300 BC and AD 250 as the Late Preclassic. Although some authorities prefer separating the period between AD 1 and AD 250 as the Proto-classic, the summarizing nature of this article makes the simpler, single-period classification more desirable.

The Late Preclassic was a period of regional growth in which almost all areas in Mesoamerica underwent a rapid rise in cultural complexity accompanied by population increase, the development of great cities or ceremonial centers, and the crystallization of highly class stratified societies. By the end of the Preclassic, a number of regional centers had developed into massive sites that far outstripped earlier settlements in both size and grandeur. The most impressive of all these centers was Teotihuacán, which by AD 150 had become the dominant center of all Mesoamerica.

Because of Teotihuacán, the Valley of Mexico deserves first consideration. The valley is a large highland basin at an elevation of 2200 meters. Five shallow, often coalescing lakes that offer both resources, such as fish and waterfowl, and easy canoe transportation cover an extensive area of the valley floor. Rainfall varies considerably within the valley from a slim 50 centimeters in the north to as much as 100 centimeters in the south. Frosts may occur as early as October and as late as early April. The combination of scanty rainfall and frost offers a double danger for agriculturalists, for maize planted in May to permit harvesting before fall frosts may not germinate if the rains are delayed. Irrigation obviates this danger by permitting early planting. In prehistoric times there was fairly extensive canal irrigation from streams and especially from numerous springs located just outside of Teotihuacán. Settlement surveys at the southern and eastern sides of the lake system provide a good picture of population development (J. Parsons 1974). At the start of the Late Preclassic, the densest populations were found at the rainier southern end of the valley. Several substantial sites occurred in this area, favoring either locations where sloping land came close to the lakeshore or higher elevations where rainfall exceeded 75 centimeters. The largest site was Cuicuilco, which Parsons estimates to have housed 7500 people at this time.

In the next two centuries there was a rapid growth of population along the eastern shore of the lakes, particularly at the northeastern corner where Teotihuacán is located. Sanders's (1965) data from the Teotihuacán Valley show a shift in settlement location from sites at high elevations, where rainfall would have been greater, to locations at the juncture of the piedmont and valley floor. He believes that this shift indicates the beginning of techniques of water control, including irrigation from the Teotihuacán springs. By the Patlachique phase (150–1 BC), Teotihuacán already had a population of 30,000, while Cuicuilco at the other end of the lakes may have had a population of 20,000. The two giant sites faced each other, probably uncomfortably, until at some time in the first century BC the volcano Xitle erupted, covering Cuicuilco with lava and destroying large amounts of the valuable farming land upon which the site had relied. Although it would be unwise to attribute the success of Teotihuacán to this natural accident, the volcanic eruptions must, indeed, have smoothed the road to glory for the Teotihuacanos.

Although the major structures at Teotihuacán have long been studied, the extent of the site and density of its population are recent archeological revelations. Not until Millon's survey started in the 1960s did it become clear that the site contained nearly 21 square kilometers of almost continuous structures (Millon 1973). Another revelation was the early date of the city's growth. Recent reestimates (Cowgill 1974) of population suggest that by the end of the Tzacualli phase (AD 150), after only three centuries of existence, Teoti huacán was already near its peak population.

Why should Teotihuacán have become such an immense city and with such rapidity? Part of the answer must lie in the location and environment of the Valley of Mexico, for the valley was a focal point throughout prehistory. The size of the valley, the relative richness of its environment once techniques of intensive agriculture had been adopted, the possibilities for communication and transportation offered by the lake system, and the relative isolation from outside threats must all have been factors. Yet these factors do not explain the location of Teotihuacán at the least favorable end of the valley nor the concentration of power and population in a single center rather than in multiple centers. To explain these phenomena, William Sanders (Sanders and Price 1968) has suggested that the irrigation system at the Teotihuacán springs created a need for control of labor and centralization of authority that triggered the concentration of population and power in the city. Thomas Patterson (1973) has recently proposed that the control of obsidian was a principal factor in Teotihuacán's development. One of the largest obsidian sources in Mesoamerica lies at Otumba near the head of the Teotihuacán Valley, and the sources of the famous green obsidian of Hidalgo are easier to reach from Teotihuacán than from any other center of its time. Patterson sees a near monopoly in obsidian production and trade as the keystone of a great economic empire centered at Teotihuacán. The current trend among archeologists to admit that complex phenomena merit complex, multicausal explanations allows acceptance of both irrigation and control of obsidian as important factors in the rise of Teotihuacán.

In the Valley of Oaxaca, as in the Valley of Mexico, the most important trend in the Late Preclassic was the rapid growth of a single site that came to dominate the entire area. In Oaxaca, this site was Monte Albán, located on a steep hill at the point where the three arms of the valley come together. Monte Albán was first occupied during the Middle Preclassic Monte Albán I phase (600–200 BC). During Monte Albán II (200 BC–AD 300), the site expanded considerably, and some of the structures in the main plaza area on top of the hill were already established. A series of glyphic inscriptions date from Monte Albán II; some glyphs resemble later symbols used to indicate conquests. Already, then, Monte Albán may have been in the process of establishing an empire.

On the Gulf and Pacific coasts, the collapse of La Venta and dissolution of Olmec power initiated a vigorous development of regional sites. On the Gulf coast, Tres Zapotes, a site that had already been occupied in Olmec times, continued to be of importance. Carved stone stelae from Late Preclassic Tres Zapotes show richly garbed individuals quite like the Maya rulers depicted so magnificently a half millennium later. One Tres Zapotes stela bears a date in a calendrical system believed to be the same as that used by the Classic Maya. If this is so, the date reads 31 BC, and the inhabitants of the Gulf coast or the Pacific coast (where dated stelae also occur) get credit for the invention of the remarkably accurate Mesoamerican calendar and the astronomical computations that made it possible.

On the Pacific coast, Izapa was a major Late Preclassic center with dozens of large structures and an important collection of stone carvings. The Izapa style of carving, which spread along the Pacific coast and even into the Guatemalan Highlands, is a possible stylistic link between Olmec and Classic Maya art (Figure 9.6). Izapa compositions include complex mythological themes that must have to do with the life and labors of gods or culture heroes but also include naturalistically rendered humans who may be rulers. Izapa is by no means the whole story of the Pacific coast, for a series of large and important Late Preclassic sites cover the area from the Isthmus of Tehuantepec far into Guatemala. Many of the sites are located in the rainy piedmont zone on the slopes of the volcanic highlands. This suggests that cacao, the source of chocolate, which grows only at these elevations, may already have become a crop of major value.

The Central Depression of Chiapas is also lined with a series of Late Preclassic sites. The best known, and probably the largest, is Chiapa de Corzo, located in a semiarid zone on the banks of the Grijalva River. Excavations at Chiapa de Corzo show that the site was subject to constantly changing influences and had trade contacts with a large number of regions in Mesoamerica.

The Guatemalan Highlands were also the focus of important Late Preclassic developments. The best known site is Kaminaljuyú, a vast adobe ruin now being rapidly engulfed by the growth of Guatemala City. Kaminaljuyú consisted of several separate ceremonial precincts, each with a small residential population. Rich tombs show the splendor of the site's rulers, and evidence of

FIGURE 9.6
Izapa stelae. (After Willey 1966 and Norman 1973.)

extensive trade contacts demonstrates its importance in the wider Mesoamerican sphere. Even before the end of the Preclassic, influences from the growing power of Teotihuacán began to work drastic changes at Kaminaljuyú.

After a late start in initial occupation, the Lowland Maya "caught up," with a surge in population and complexity during the Late Preclassic Chicanel horizon. The temple center, which was always to be the characteristic form of Maya settlement, became established during this time. Rich tombs provide a clear sign of social stratification, and fragmentary murals at Tikal indicate that the symbols and finery that were to mark Classic period rulers were already in use.

In the first century AD, the Maya Lowlands were strongly influenced by outside contacts from the Salvador-Honduras area to the southeast. The hallmark of this influence is a new set of ceramics called Floral Park, which replaces local Chicanel horizon complexes in Belize and along the Pasión River near the southern border of the lowlands. Several investigators feel that the Floral Park intrusion is strong enough to suggest actual population influx. In the central and northern part of the Maya Lowlands, local Chicanel complexes persisted, although there is evidence of trade with the Floral Park zone. The role that Floral Park influences had in the crystallization of the Maya

Classic period is uncertain, but Floral Park ceramic traits, such as polychrome painting, became an integral part of Classic tradition.

Why civilization should have arisen in the unlikely rain forest homeland of the Lowland Maya has always proved difficult to understand. Most early civilizations occupied arid regions, and explanations devised to account for civilization in these regions fit very poorly in the humid tropical forest. Two attempts to grapple specifically with the Maya situation deserve mention. William Rathje (1971; 1973) has stressed that the impetus for Maya complexity lies in the desire for certain resources, such as salt, obsidian, and volcanic stone for grinding implements, that are lacking in the Maya Lowlands. There is solid archeological evidence that these items were imported into the Maya Lowlands from great distances even by the early occupants, and by the Late Preclassic and Classic periods the volume of trade and transport would have been very large. In competing for these external resources, the central area of the lowlands (the Core Zone) is at a disadvantage in relation to outlying lowland areas (the Buffer Zone), since it lies farther from the sources and has no trade products not also available in the Buffer Zone. Consequently, Rathje believes that the Core Zone must have competed by developing a high level of organization and creating artificial scarce resources—a ceremonial cult and its paraphernalia. One would expect, then, that the Core would show a more rapid development of organization and ceremonialism, a situation that fits the archeological facts.

Recently, an alternative explanation stressing population pressure and warfare has been advanced to explain Maya civilization. This viewpoint, advocated by Webster and Ball (in Adams 1977), calls for an initial colonization of the Maya Lowlands by people using a system of slash-and-burn farming. This adaptation was highly productive but necessitated a large amount of land per individual because much of the land was in fallow at any given time. As population expanded, the area of virgin forest available for exploitation was depleted. Competition for land led to warfare, which favored an increase in cultural complexity. Although many Mayanists seem to favor this reconstruction, I remain skeptical because neither high population densities nor warfare are solidly attested to for the Late Preclassic, the period during which the process should have been in operation.

THE FIRST PERIOD OF PROSPERITY

The Classic period in Mesoamerica was in many ways the kind of culture implied by its name—prosperous, cosmopolitan, and given to great height of achievement. The major fact of the Early Classic (AD 250–600) was the commanding position of Teotihuacán, which was felt in one way or another in every corner of Mesoamerica. At the end of the Early Classic, Teotihuacán influence began to decline. Other major centers continued to flourish for a while until one by one they too fell upon evil days. Very few areas in Meso-america escaped culture change of cataclysmic proportions in the years from AD 700 to 1000.

Teotihuacán, of course, had already become one of the great cities of the world by the end of the Tzacualli phase at AD 150. Current analysis (Cowgill 1974) suggests that much of the city's population growth occurred during the Late Preclassic Patlachique and Tzacualli phases and that later growth rates were much reduced. By the Xolalpan phase (AD 450–650), the population had reached a peak that was probably around 125,000, although a figure as high as 200,000 is not beyond reason (Millon 1974). In the process of amassing so many people in a single urban conglomeration, the city attracted population from surrounding rural areas, reducing the occupation in a large territory to a tiny fraction of what it had been earlier. Much of the land in the Teotihuacán and Texcoco regions must have been farmed by "walk-out" farmers who resided within the urban zone. Elsewhere, in more distant parts of the Valley of Mexico, the Early Classic population was less affected by "urban drift," but Teotihuacán had no rivals; the next largest settlements were no more than small towns with a few thousand inhabitants.

As a city, Teotihuacán was a masterpiece of urban planning (Figure 9.7). Major thoroughfares, straight and obviously carefully engineered, cross near the center of the city. Structures are arranged in careful blocks that utilize a standard unit of measurement. The largest structures, the temples of the Sun and Moon, were religious in function, as were many other structures along the Street of the Dead. At the intersection of the two major avenues lie the Ciudadela, presumed by many to have been an administrative center, and the Great Compound, which was probably a central market. Many of the other structures in the central part of the city appear to have been residential. They show a great love of luxury and the lavish expenditure of skilled labor in careful construction and elaborate decoration.

The careful planning of the city, the problems of provisioning so large a populace, and the amount of specialization and trade that must have gone on presuppose a complex administrative structure. Yet, again, as with the Olmec, crucial kinds of information that bear upon social structure are lacking. Most art at Teotihuacán is religious (Figure 9.8). It shows gods and priests repeated monotonously; George Kubler (1967) has likened it to a litany in which the gods were placated by the repeated recitation of their attributes and gifts. Informative though this may be about religious beliefs, the art says little about secular life; missing completely are representations of bureaucrats at work or of elite Teotihuacanos living the good life they had created. Since cremation, unaccompanied by offerings, was the favored burial practice, graves provide no key to social status. The best sorts of information about social arrangements will probably come from comparisons of the apartment-like building complexes to determine variation in room size, features, and positioning. Although too few such complexes have been excavated to pro-

426

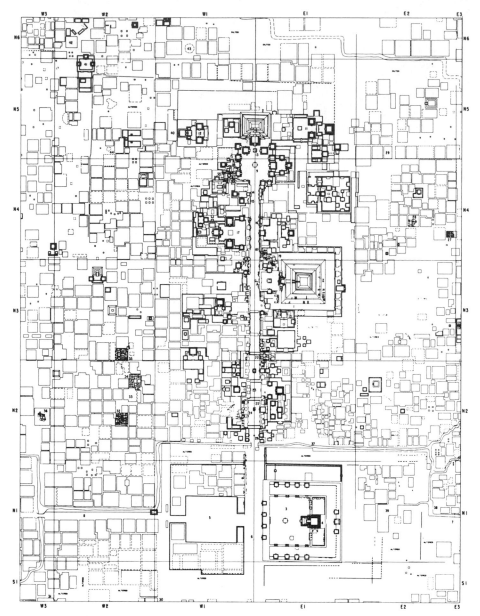

FIGURE 9.8
Murals from Teotihuacán. (After Ekholm and Bernal 1971.)

vide much of a comparative base, it is already evident that contrasts such as that between the formal and luxurious complex of Xolalpan and the chaotic jumble of small rooms at Tlamimilolpa must have social significance (Figure 9.9).

There is much more substantial information about the role of Teotihuacán as a highly specialized center for manufacture and trade. Surface collections provide evidence of workshop areas devoted to such specialized products as obsidian tools, ceramics, figurines, and items of shell. Workshops of a single kind cluster together to create a pattern suggestive of the craft wards or *barrios* found in Aztec cities. It is undoubtedly indicative of Teotihuacán's special status that specialization at other Classic period centers is scattered and lacks this barriolike character.

The Teotihuacán manufacturing specialty best studied to date is the obsidian industry (Spence 1975). More than 400 workshops have already been discovered, some dating as early as the Patlachique phase (150–1 BC). By the time the city reached its apogee, there was a clear division of obsidian workshops into two kinds: "local" shops that produced a variety of tools commonly used within the city itself and "export" shops that produced specialized items at least some of which were widely traded throughout Mesoamerica.

Teotihuacán goods were desired throughout Mesoamerica. The most easily identified are objects of Central Mexican green obsidian, which are found in abundance in areas as far distant from Teotihuacán as the Maya Lowlands. Thin Orange pottery, a ware produced somewhere in Puebla but undoubtedly peddled by Teotihuacán, also has a wide distribution, despite obvious problems in transporting it without breakage (Figure 9.10). The desirability of Teotihuacán products also led to copious imitation and local potters everywhere in Mesoamerica borrowed Teotihuacán vessel shapes, especially the cylindrical tripod.

Millon (1973; 1974) stresses that the economic functioning of Teotihuacán was intimately interwoven with its religious system. He pictures Teotihuacán as a great pilgrimage center, attracting people and trade through theological as well as technological sophistication. That gods and goods were indeed compatible seems demonstrated by the wide diffusion of Central Mexican deities, such as the rain god Tlaloc, whose goggle-eyed visage occurs throughout Mesoamerica and who seems to have been accepted into other pantheons as eagerly as Teotihuacán vessels were accepted into households.

The degree to which Teotihuacán's economic strength may have been accompanied by political or military adventurism probably varied from area to area. In some areas, Teotihuacán influence is so overwhelming that outright conquest seems a possibility. Close to the Valley of Mexico, the site of Cholula in the Valley of Puebla was probably ruled by Teotihuacán. At a far greater distance, Kaminaljuyú in highland Guatemala shows strong Teotihuacán influence in elite graves and so slavishly copied Teotihuacán architecture in its central precincts that most Mesoamericanists feel that here also conquest is a likelihood.

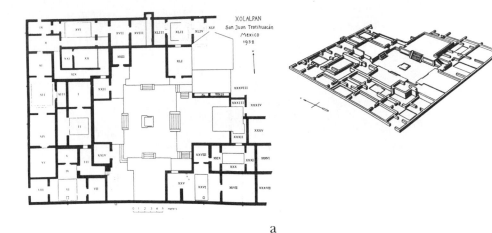

a

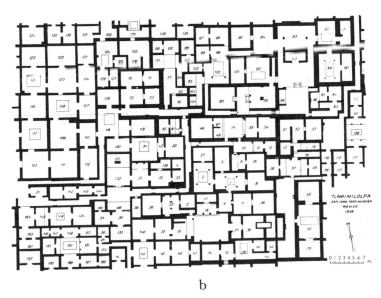

b

FIGURE 9.9
Residential complexes at Teotihuacán: *a*, Xolalpan; *b*, Tlamimilolpa. (from Gordon R. Willey, *An Introduction to American Archaeology:* Vol. I, © 1966, pp. 112, 113. Reprinted by permission of Prentice-Hall, Inc., Englewood Cliffs, New Jersey.)

In Oaxaca, Monte Albán developed strong ties to Teotihuacán in its period IIIa. The obvious strength of Monte Albán and the fact that it always expressed Teotihuacán architectural innovations in its own way suggest some kind of alliance or working relationship rather than outright subservience. This special relationship is underlined by the discovery of a Oaxacan barrio at Teotihuacán (Millon 1974). For more than two centuries beginning at

FIGURE 9.10
Teotihuacán pottery. (After Coe 1962.)

AD 400 the people of this barrio either imported or manufactured locally pottery that was identical to that in use at Monte Albán. In addition, they constructed a tomb built in typical Oaxacan style that contained a Oaxacan-type carved stela. At the same time, barrio inhabitants lived in buildings that were of pure Teotihuacán style and worshiped in a temple that followed Teotihuacán architectural conventions. That a colony of Oaxaqueños resided in Teotihuacán for several hundred years and continued to maintain their native customs provides evidence of continuing strong interaction between Oaxaca and Central Mexico.

The nature of interaction between Teotihuacán and the Lowland Maya raises interesting questions. Teotihuacán trade goods are present in the Maya Lowlands, as are occasional representations of Tlaloc, but the architectural manifestations of contact are very weak. One might conclude that interrelationships were restricted to fairly remote trade contacts except for the presence of Stela 31 at the great Maya site of Tikal, which portrays an armed individual from Teotihuacán and a hieroglyphic inscription that seems to refer to a Mexican or Mexicanized ruler. The implications of this fact will be discussed at greater length in the section on the Lowland Maya.

It used to be thought that the city of Teotihuacán flourished only until the end of the Xolalpan phase at AD 650 and that the succeeding Metepec phase (AD 650–750) represented a greatly diminished population living among the ruins of the city. Current evidence (Cowgill 1974), however, suggests that the population of Metepec Teotihuacán was little less than that for Xolalpan and that the population decline occurred only late in the Metepec phase. Teotihuacán's wide-ranging power, however, seems to have been lost far earlier, for at most of the sites where Teotihuacán influence was strong the impingement on local culture seems to have stopped not long after AD 600.

Understanding the decline of Teotihuacán is a critical problem for Mesoamerican archeology, since it may be the key factor in the several centuries of cultural reformulation that mark the end of the Classic period. The earlier hypothesis that the site succumbed to barbarian invaders is far too simplistic in the light of present data about its size and power. The problem is immensely complex; its elucidation will demand far more detailed information about the political and economic integration of Teotihuacán itself as well as a presently unavailable fund of data on regional interaction. So far, the problem, perhaps because of its magnitude, has not been thoroughly discussed by those who have the most detailed knowledge of Central Mexico at this time period.

The Gulf coast was the site of vigorous but little known Classic cultures. In the southern part of Veracruz, the important Preclassic sites of Tres Zapotes and Cerro de las Mesas continued to thrive in the Classic. They show a blend of influences with carved monuments bearing calendrical dates in the Maya system at Cerro de las Mesas and abundant Teotihuacán imports at both sites. It is likely that the area was of importance to Teotihuacán both as a source of lowland resources and as a route to and point of contact with the cultures of southern Mesoamerica. To the north, in central Veracruz, the influential Classic Veracruz culture and art style centered at the site of El Tajín. Located in a rain forest-covered valley near the town of Papantla, El Tajín was a massive site only the ceremonial core of which has as yet been investigated archeologically. Influenced by Teotihuacán during the Early Classic, El Tajín survived the Teotihuacán demise to be one of the centers contesting for power in Central Mexico during the Late Classic. Classic Veracruz was an important center of the Mesoamerican ball game, and much of its art is devoted to the decoration of stone yokes, *palmas,* and *hachas,* which are thought to have been ball game accoutrements.

Monte Albán was undoubtedly the dominant site in Oaxaca during the Classic period. The entire top of the hill upon which the site is located was leveled to create a gigantic complex of structures around a central plaza. Construction in the plaza area started as early as Monte Albán II, but the site was repeatedly remodeled, and the bulk of the visible structures date from the Classic. Below the summit of the site, terraced hillsides held a substantial population that gives the site urban status. The Classic period is divided into

Monte Albán IIIa (Early Classic), during which Teotihuacán influence was prominent, and IIIb (Late Classic), after the cessation of Teotihuacán contacts. The withdrawal of Teotihuacán had no apparent effect upon the prosperity of the site, and period IIIb was a time of heavy occupation and feverish building activity.

The Highland Guatemalan center of Kaminaljuyú was profoundly influenced by Teotihuacán. The brief Aurora phase that opens the Early Classic was before Teotihuacán influence, but in the succeeding Esperanza phase an initial period of trade goods from Teotihuacán and copying of Teotihuacán forms gave way to much deeper influences that affected architecture and settlement patterns as well as artifact inventories. From the scattered ceremonial precincts described for Late Preclassic Kaminaljuyú, the site became a single, densely nucleated center at the heart of which was a concentration of buildings and courtyards designed in nearly pure Teotihuacán style. Burials of the time show a great concentration of Teotihuacán-inspired objects, and a number of Mexican gods appear in the iconography. Sanders and Price (1968) feel that such drastic changes are likely to have been the result of an outright conquest of Kaminaljuyú, which may have been motivated by the desire to control the abundant obsidian resources located near the Valley of Guatemala. On the Pacific coast, the region around the modern town of Tiquisate also shows a heavy concentration of Teotihuacán goods and architecture and might well be another colonial outpost of Mexican conquerors.

The Late Classic Amatle-Pamplona phase in the Valley of Guatemala witnessed the end of Teotihuacán inspiration and the decline of Kaminaljuyú. There were a number of Late Classic sites in the valley, but none of them seem to have had the concentration of power suggested by Early Classic Kaminaljuyú.

Archeology in the Maya Lowlands has developed different emphases from those characteristic of Mesoamerican highland archeology. Although partly a result of historic events and personages, these differences are even more strongly shaped by environmental factors and the kinds of data that are most readily available in the two zones. The ecological and settlement pattern studies that have proved so fruitful for highland archeologists have been badly neglected in the Maya Lowlands. Both the difficulty of conducting large-scale surveys in the rain forest and the long-standing assumption of lowland ecological homogeneity have been involved in the neglect. On the other hand, the presence in the Maya area of rich and diversified burial offerings, artistic depictions of elite life, and hieroglyphic inscriptions giving historical data provides a wealth of information about social and political arrangements that is unmatched in any of the highland areas. That Mayanists talk eagerly of priests, princes, and politics while their Mexican colleagues discuss population densities and subsistence practices is more a reflection of available data than of any contrast between historical and scientific temperaments.

Several generations of archeological research provide a solid outline of Classic period development, at least for the southern half of the Maya Lowlands in the Peten district of Guatemala and neighboring Belize and southern Mexico. Recent discoveries that reveal the solid Preclassic base of Maya civilization make the transition to the Classic appear less a sudden flowering or possible import than a reformulation—the coming together of a set of features, most of which were present, or at least presaged, in earlier times. But the change from Preclassic to Classic was drastic, ceramically and architecturally, and especially in the appearance of stone carving and hieroglyphic inscriptions including dates in the long-count calendrical system. Some of the Classic features seem to have been indigenous developments in the lowlands; others were imported from surrounding areas. Whatever the sources, the blend of these characteristics produced an unmistakable constellation that was uniquely and forever Mayan.

The easiest trend to follow within the Early Classic is the spread of carved stone monuments that include dated inscriptions. The earliest such calendrical inscription in Maya territory, which almost certainly follows the calendar used earlier on the Gulf and Pacific coasts, occurs on Stela 29 at Tikal. The date is 8.12.14.8.15 in the Maya calendar, which corresponds to 6 July AD 292 in the Christian calendar. In the first century and a half after the date on Stela 29, Maya calendrical dates occur only within a restricted region near the heart of the Maya Lowlands. But between AD 435 and 534 the calendrical custom expanded explosively to the corners of the Maya Lowlands. Associated with carving and calendrics, although by no means in a one-to-one correlation, was the Maya temple, placed on a towering pyramidal substructure and vaulted by use of the Maya-invented corbeled arch.

Data on population distribution suggest varying patterns from region to region. Sites in the heart of the lowlands show substantial Early Classic populations that represent an increase over those of the Late Preclassic. Sites on the Usumacinta and Pasión rivers, on the other hand, seem to have been sparsely occupied during the Early Classic, even though sites on the Pasión had been heavily populated during the Late Preclassic. These variations in regional patterns suggest that many more data are needed before we can speak with confidence about population trends for the Maya Lowlands as a whole.

Although it was once thought that there was a period at the start of the Early Classic before Teotihuacán influence was felt in the Maya Lowlands, more recent work suggests that Teotihuacán contacts, at least in some sites, began at the very start of the Early Classic, if not in the Late Preclassic. Teotihuacán influence included imported items such as green obsidian and the imitation of vessel shapes and portrayal of Mexican gods, but Teotihuacán architectural forms had little impact in the Maya Lowlands. Those who emphasize the role of trade in Maya development tend to believe that contact with Teotihuacán commercialism may have been a critical factor in shaping the Maya destiny. Others would grant Teotihuacán an even more forthright and aggressive role in the lowlands. Stela 31 at Tikal (AD 445) shows an inscription that may refer to a ruler with a Mexican name and depicts an important individual garbed in Teotihuacán style; many take this as indicative of Mexican conquest in the lowlands. Although I have long resisted the idea of direct military intervention in the Maya Lowlands and am still dubious, I must admit that my resistance is beginning to feel like a rear-guard action. Perhaps Teotihuacán meddling in internal Maya Lowland politics might represent a viable intermediate position.

Between 9.5.0.0.0 and 9.8.0.0.0 in the Mayan calendar (AD 534–593) there is a curious gap in dated monuments that may be associated with a slowdown in construction. In a recent consideration of this hiatus, Willey (1974) terms it a "rehearsal" for the later collapse at the end of the Classic and attributes it (agreeing with Rathje 1973) to a loss of symbiotic relationships between the Maya and other Mesoamerican cultures occasioned by the decline of Teotihuacán influence.

Maya recovery from the hiatus was successful, and with the start of the Late Classic period around AD 600 the Maya Lowlands began a period of unparalleled prosperity. The prosperity was marked by striking population growth, both in the central area and in the peripheral areas that had been less populated during the Early Classic. Population growth was everywhere accompanied by heightened construction efforts that included both new temples and an ever-increasing number of the administrative or residential structures that have traditionally been termed palaces. As the number of important centers escalated, there is clear inscriptional evidence of warfare and conquest as well as suggestions of increasing rigidity in the class structure of Maya society. By about AD 800 Maya Classic vigor had run its course, and the lowland area underwent a spectacular decline that in little more more than a century resulted in the near total depopulation of most of the southern lowlands.

Starting from this brief outline of Maya Classic development, it is possible to flesh out the picture with more specifics about the operation of society. The reconstruction of Lowland Maya culture that most Mayanists would propose today is very different from that of a generation ago (see Willey and Shimkin 1973; Culbert 1974). The changes in viewpoint are the result both of increased data from recent projects and of the infiltration of more systemic ideas from other areas of anthropology.

Maya subsistence adaptation is one of the areas that has received serious reconsideration. The lowland environment offers challenges for farming quite different from those which exist in the highlands. In the lowlands, frost is unknown, rainfall is ample for a single summer crop, and the lack of surface water makes irrigation impossible. On the other hand, soil fertility is a serious problem; cleared lands are rapidly leached, and the recovery of soil nutrients is a slow process. For many years it was assumed that the only practical means of lowland farming was a long-fallow, slash-and-burn system. Since few variations were possible and since all farmers knew the best routine, maximum potential was achieved without management, and the elite had no necessary role in the system.

The logical result of this assumed system would be severe limitations on population density and on the number of people that could live in a single community. But as house mound counts at an increasing number of pre-historic sites provide estimates of population, a paradox arises; there were more people than could have been supported by slash-and-burn farming. The likely conclusion is that the slash-and-burn routine does *not* provide maximum yield per unit of available land. Instead, it is a labor-conservative system that maximizes yield per man-hour. Given appropriate pressure or incentives, greater productivity per unit of land could be achieved through a whole series of alternatives that might include shortened fallow cycle, root cropping, ramon-tree cultivation, double cropping, terracing, and raised-field agriculture in swampy areas (see Turner 1974). It is not unlikely that all of these measures may have been practiced by the prehistoric Maya in a complicated subsistence mix that would have implications quite different from those of slash-and-burn farming for both population densities and managerial requirements.

Recent projects in the Maya Lowlands that have sampled whole sites rather than just ceremonial precincts have transformed our knowledge of Maya centers. It is now clear that at major sites like Tikal (Haviland 1970) tens of thousands of people lived within easy walking distance of the site center. At the same time, the density of population, even in the heart of Maya sites, numbered no more than a few hundred inhabitants per square kilometer—far below the several thousand persons per square kilometer at the ultimate urban center of Teotihuacán. In Maya sites, house groups were separated by patches of open land, presumably devoted to trees and gardens, in contrast to the wall-to-wall construction at Teotihuacán (Figure 9.11). Another important difference, however, was that while Teotihuacán had obvious borders beyond which there was almost no population, the lower-density concentrations of people around Maya centers spread over a much larger area. Teotihuacán at its greatest extent covered fewer than 25 square kilometers. Haviland's survey data show that the population core at Tikal was scattered over an area exceeding 60 square kilometers. Even beyond this area, population did not cease but was simply reduced to a lower density; scattered house groups and small ceremonial centers occur throughout the territory between Tikal and neighboring major centers. Central Mexico and the Maya Lowlands show two quite different patterns of arranging people in space. The interesting questions for research are the causes and consequences of the different patterns rather than the much discussed (but largely semantic) question of whether both or only one of these patterns may be called urban.

436

FIGURE 9.11
Map of Tikal. (Courtesy of the University Museum, University of Pennsylvania.)

Ideas about the economic organization of the Classic Maya have also changed in the light of recent archeological data. That elite goods, cult paraphernalia, and carving were the products of specialized and highly skilled craftsmen has long been evident. It is now known that some consumer products, such as pottery and stone tools, were also produced by specialists, although the concentrated craft barrios noted at Teotihuacán seem to be lacking at Maya centers (Figure 9.12). Since ecological diversity is a spur to village specialization and trade in highland Mesoamerica, it has often been suggested that the greater homogeneity of the lowlands should have resulted in a weak development of specialization among the Maya. This inference, however, is based upon two assumptions: first, that the lowlands really *are* homogeneous enough to minimize local differences in the availability of raw materials, and second, that ecological diversity is the only factor that is likely to promote specialization. I tend to believe that neither of these assumptions is accurate.

The emphasis upon Maya trade has been revitalized by the work of Webb (1964; 1973) and Rathje (1971; 1973). In addition to elite goods, it now seems clear that the Maya imported from long distances a large volume of raw materials (or products) for the use of all segments of Maya society. Maintaining the flow of these materials must have demanded massive efforts in organization, transportation, and distribution, as well as a sizable outflow of exports. Since most lowland resources are perishable, the nature of Maya exports is not clear; we are uncertain whether the Maya depended heavily upon export of forest products or whether they specialized in processing activities, such as the production of textiles. I have recently suggested (Culbert n.d.) that we must also consider the possibility that there was substantial trade in foodstuffs and specialized consumer goods *within* the Maya Lowlands.

The Maya were ruled by a hereditary aristocracy, and considerable information on ruling families has been amassed since the time of Proskouriakoff's (1960) breakthrough in identifying records of rulers in the inscriptions. Rathje's (1970) work with burial offerings suggests decreased social mobility between the Early and Late Classic, and a number of authors have found evidence for a widening social gulf between elite and commoners (see especially Willey and Shimkin 1973). That the Maya elite were involved in elaborate ceremonialism and were the sponsors of esoteric studies in astronomy and calendrics has long been obvious. Recent trends in thinking about ecological and economic patterns have added an increased administrative responsibility for the management of subsistence, manufacturing, and trade to the tasks of the elite. This would suggest that there were rewards to the lower echelons of society in the form of imported goods and manufactured items—a tangible supplement to the oft-mentioned joys provided by ceremonials and fiestas.

The size of political units in the Maya Lowlands is a matter of uncertainty. For a long time a model of independent city-states prevailed, but recent

a

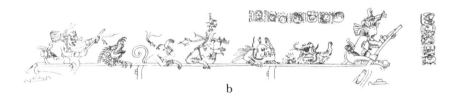

b

FIGURE 9.12   c

Mayan art: *a*, Bonampak mural; *b*, boatload of Mayan gods; *c*, throne scene from a painted vessel. (*a*, courtesy of the Peabody Museum, Harvard University; *b*, after Culbert 1974; *c*, courtesy of the University Museum, University of Pennsylvania.)

research suggests that some half-dozen sites were as much as an order of magnitude larger than average ceremonial centers, and there has been increasing consideration of the possibility of regional political units headed by these "supersites." Inscriptions and art show that warfare was commonplace, especially in Late Classic times, and that major sites claimed campaigns of conquest. Whether these conquests forged lasting empires, however, is not indicated by present evidence.

One can hardly write of the Maya without noting their achievements in writing and calendrics. The Maya hieroglyphic script was the only full system of writing invented by Native Americans. The script still cannot be translated into its original language, but the meaning of many individual signs has been determined, so that considerable passages of the texts can be interpreted. Recent research shows that, in addition to information of calendric and sacred nature, Maya writing includes a strong historical component that celebrates the births, deaths, and doings of important leaders.

The Maya calendrical system is a marvel of complexity. Not satisfied, in their passion for time, with a single calendar, the Maya had two calendars that operated simultaneously. One was a 365-day calendar, the closest whole-day approximation to the solar year (which the Maya knew with great accuracy). The second was a 260-day calendar of great sacred significance, although of unknown origin. Each day was designated by its position in both calendars. For example, the day 4 Ahau 18 Zotz occurred when the 260-day calendar had reached 4 Ahau at the same time that the 365-day count stood at 18 Zotz. The combined cycle of the calendars was such that any given day, such as 4 Ahau 18 Zotz, occurred only once each 52 years. This 52-year cycle was known as the Calendar Round. To be an accurate record of time, a calendar must count from some fixed staring point. This point for the Maya calendar was a day in the year 3113 BC—undoubtedly the date of some mythical event of great importance. Elapsed time from the starting point was recorded in a five-place notation that included periods of 400 years, 20 years, single years, months, and days to give a figure such as 8.16.9.3.0. This full five-place notation, called the long count, was unfortunately abandoned around 900 AD in favor of an abbreviated system subject to the same kinds of ambiguities that would occur if we began to record dates as '78 rather than 1878 or 1978. Because of this uncertainty, the exact correlation of the Maya and Christian calendars has been a matter of debate, although most Mayanists now accept a correlation known as the Goodman-Martinez-Thompson correlation.

Although the Maya carried the use of the calendar to its greatest extremes, the basics of the system seem to have been worked out outside the Maya area, perhaps by the Olmecs. Nor were the Maya the only users of the system, for varieties of the same calendar were used throughout Mesoamerica until the time of the conquest. Everywhere the calendar was tied to religion and feast days of the gods and was used to predict the omens of good or ill luck related to particular days.

Among Mayanists it is becoming common to distinguish the Late Classic (AD 600–800) from the Terminal Classic (AD 800–900 or 950). The Late Classic was the pinnacle of Maya Lowland success—population was at a peak, the amount of civic and ceremonial construction was immense, and carving and other arts flourished. Yet disaster lurked in the near future, and the Maya soon underwent a collapse that has few parallels in the history of early civilizations. The first realization of the collapse came from turn-of-the-century work on Maya-dated inscriptions. The inscriptions showed that a record 40 sites commemorated the Maya date 9.18.0.0.0 (AD 790). Only 40 years later, the date 10.0.0.0.0 was noted at only 3 sites, and within another 60 years the Maya long-count system of calendrical notation had passed from existence. Early research also showed that construction of major buildings at Maya sites in the southern lowlands had ceased and existing structures had fallen into ruin. But the extent of the tragedy was not established with certainty before research projects at major sites in the last two decades. These projects showed that the fate of total Maya populations was as drastic as that of the stone carvers and temple builders. In less than a century after AD 790, Maya population had declined by as much as 90 percent. The remaining inhabitants survived for another century; then they too disappeared from all but a few sites.

This succession of events was not simultaneous everywhere in the lowlands. Sites at the eastern edge of the lowlands succumbed first, probably followed by the sites in the central zone. Meanwhile, sites on the Pasión River to the south persevered for a while, and the site of Seibal even underwent a brief flourish of construction during the Terminal Classic.

Signs of intrusion are also associated with Terminal Classic events. Fine Orange pottery from centers of production on the Gulf coast was widely traded and late stelae at Seibal show foreigners with waist-length hair and bones in their noses. These strangers were certainly not Classic Maya, although they may well have been speakers of Maya languages from peripheral areas in the northern or northeastern lowlands.

What caused this spectacular disintegration of a civilization that seems to have been at the peak of its power and glory? A recent conference of Mayanists reconsidered this question (Culbert 1973; see Willey and Shimkin 1973 for a summary of conclusions). That there was neither complete agreement nor a final solution is hardly surprising, but directions for future research were clearly delineated. There was agreement that a complex concatenation of circumstances must have been involved in the Maya collapse, some of them external to the Maya Lowlands. Outside invasion seems to have occurred along the Pasión River, although there is disagreement about whether the invasion was the cause of the collapse or a result thereof. Competition in trade that cut the Maya off from outside markets may have been more important than actual intrusions in weakening the Maya structure.

Internal factors within the lowlands must have been involved as well. The heavy population of Late Classic times probably strained the capacity of the subsistence adaptation, and some kinds of environmental degradation that might have resulted from overexploitation would have been almost irreversible. The increasing gap between elite and commoners and possibly increased warfare could have strained the social adaptation of the Maya. In addition, the administrative capabilities of the Maya may have been overtaxed by the steep rise in population and economic activity of the Late Classic and left without the flexibility to respond to emergencies.

At the moment, there is some polarity between those who see external factors, such as invasion or stifling of trade, as the initial point of stress and those who believe that the collapse was initiated by internal stresses within the fabric of Maya environmental or social adaptation; but there are as many shades of opinion and mixtures of scenarios as there are Mayanists who have considered the question. Future research must aim at providing greater detail about the chronology and events of the collapse and a better understanding of the organization and operation of Maya Lowland society in the frantic period of growth that immediately preceded the collapse.

POSTCLASSIC SOLDIERS AND STATESMEN

The fall of so many Classic centers in the eighth and ninth centuries opened the door for a new order in Mesoamerica—an order that emerged in the Early Postclassic period (AD 900–1200). This transition is traditionally pictured as a shift from peace-loving, religiously oriented Classic centers devoted to serving the gods, to militaristic and far more secular Postclassic ones in which soldiers were the men of power and in which empire by conquest was the aim of society. Although this picture is sometimes overdone, there are still strong elements of validity in it. Even though we now know that leaders of the Classic period were less benign and peaceful than it was once thought, the degree of preoccupation with military matters *does* seem to have increased in Postclassic times. Prowess in war was obviously admired in both gods and men in the Postclassic, and the route to the top of the social ladder was one of arms. Expansion of political units by conquest was also a major theme in Postclassic times, culminating in the nearly pan-Mesoamerican empire of the Aztecs.

Whether there really was a trend from a more religious to a more secular emphasis in society seems less certain than before. The notion of such a trend was based upon the idea that most Classic cultures were theocracies in which priests were the principal leaders and the religious hierarchy was the same as the governmental hierarchy. Religious ferver was clearly portrayed in Classic art—probably more so than in later times—but one can hardly doubt that cities like Teotihuacán were filled with the same bureaucrats and administrators that peopled Aztec centers.

To turn from this general picture to specifics, it will be useful once again to start with Central Mexico, where both archeological and ethnohistorical data are rich. In Central Mexico the reorganization of power actually began in the Late Classic, when the decline of Teotihuacán's·dominance opened a power vacuum in which several contenders struggled to assume the mantle of Mesoamerican supremacy. At least four centers were involved in this rivalry: El Tajín on the Gulf coast; Xochicalco, southwest of the Valley of Mexico in a fortified location guarding access to the Balsas Depression; Cholula, Teotihuacán's one-time satellite in Puebla, which now emerged as a power center in its own right; and Tula, located toward the northern periphery of Mesoamerica. All of these centers seem to have been involved in trade, and there are indications in both art and architectural defenses that relationships between them were not always amicable.

From this hodgepodge of contending powers, the Toltecs of Tula emerged triumphantly in control of a large section of Early Postclassic Mesoamerica. Documentary accounts credit them with 40 tributary pueblos stretching from the Gulf coast into western Mexico. In addition, Chichén Itzá in Yucatan so faithfully copied the art and architecture of Tula (Figure 9.13) that it too must have been occupied by Toltec conquerors. In their success, the Toltecs must be credited with one of the most powerful public relations compaigns in the history of Mesoamerica. When the Spanish conquistadores arrived—centuries after the site of Tula had fallen to ruin and its exact location had been forgotten—the Toltecs were still credited with legendary accomplishments as artists, craftsmen, and rulers, and kings scattered throughout Mesoamerica proudly traced their descent from Toltec ancestors (many of whom were probably apocryphal).

Archeological Tula is a disappointment in the wake of such public acclaim. The ceremonial precincts are minuscule in comparison with Teotihuacán, and the architecture is far from outstanding. But a recent survey by Diehl (1971) shows that the site was the center of a very sizable urban area; in population, if not in splendor, it can lay claim to importance.

The location of Tula is suggestive. The farthest north of any major Mesoamerican center, it lies athwart likely routes of travel to the frontier of Mesoamerica. A line of frontier fortress sites still farther north suggests an important focus of Toltec trade and commerce in that direction. Armillas (1964) long ago suggested that the northerly position of Tula might be related to a period of increased rainfall that temporarily extended the area of successful farming into the northern desert country and provided the agricultural base for warlords who supported, with their resources, the rise of Tula.

FIGURE 9.13
Early Postclassic art: *a*, Tula warrior statues; *b*, artist's reconstruction of Pyramid B at Tula; *c*, bas-relief from Pyramid B; *d*, a "Chac-Mool" from Tula. (*a*, after Weaver 1972; *b*, after Ekholm and Bernal 1971; *c*, *d*, after Coe 1962.)

The idea is interesting, for this northern country is climatically such that shifts of only a few inches in annual precipitation could open or shut large areas for farming, but this theory has never been followed by the detailed paleoclimatological work necessary to prove or disprove the hypothesis.

Like other centers before it, Tula was destroyed and abandoned, probably at some time around AD 1160. The legendary accounts of Tula's demise speak of weak rulers and factionalism, and the condition of the site suggests violent destruction.

Meanwhile, the Valley of Mexico underwent a period of eclipse. Jeffrey Parsons (1974) notes that between AD 700 and 950 dispersion of population from Teotihuacán created a series of small nucleated centers in areas of the valley most suitable for irrigation. Between AD 950 and 1200 population declined still further, and even these small centers were lost, leaving only a dispersed rural population in the valley.

With the fall of Tula, the natural advantages of the Valley of Mexico reasserted themselves and population began a rapid resurgence. New centers were established and contested for power. Some of these centers claimed ties with the fallen Tula and may well have housed some of the dispersed Tula population. Others were founded by immigrant Chichimecs from the north and west. Known in the legendary accounts as barbarians of awesome military accomplishments but with distinct shortcomings in the social graces, the Chichimecs soon learned from local inhabitants the adaptations required of Mesoamerican heartlanders. Between AD 1200 and 1450, a period covered with some accuracy by historical sources, the Valley of Mexico was the scene of remarkable political turmoil in which the growing cities vied with each other. Their tactics ranged from marriage alliances to assassination to open warfare. There were few winners and many losers. One of the less impressive groups of immigrants to arrive during this period was the Mexica, better known as the Aztec. For some time after their arrival in the thirteenth century, the Aztec served an apprenticeship in deviousness as mercenaries and allies of more important powers. How they used this training will be described in the final section on the Aztec Empire.

Postclassic coverage for the Maya Lowlands must shift to the northern half of the area, for after the Classic collapse the south remained nearly abandoned while the north went on to vigorous new developments. The earliest of these developments occurred in a hilly zone paralleling the eastern coast of the Yucatan Peninsula. This zone, known as the Puuc, contains a number of very large and important sites, including Uxmal, Labna, Sayil, and Kabah. The data of the major occupation of the Puuc sites has long been debated between those who believed they were fully equivalent in time to the Late Classic in the southern lowlands and those who believed the entire development to be Postclassic. An intermediate dating of the principal period for the Puuc as having been equivalent to Terminal Classic (AD 800–1000) now seems likely. Terminologically, the period of the Puuc sites is known as the Pure Florescent, avoiding any equation with the term *Classic*. The architectural style of the Puuc sites is characterized by a sophisticated use of veneer masonry and decoration made by setting standardized precut blocks into patterns. Large palace buildings dominate the sites, and pyramid-temples are less common than at sites in the southern lowlands. Since no full site surveys have been done in the area, the size of resident populations in the Puuc area is uncertain; remains of small structures, however, seem to be common. At the same time as the Puuc florescence, the site of Dzibilchaltún, not far from the ocean at the northern edge of the Yucatan Peninsula, was a huge population center with a density of house mounds considerably greater than that which is typical of Maya Lowland sites (Andrews 1965). The monumental construction at Dzibilchaltún is not nearly so impressive as one might expect from its high population, and the site may have been a center devoted primarily to trade and exploitation of sea resources.

After a few centuries of success, the Puuc sites underwent a rapid collapse, and Chichén Itzá became the primary seat of power in the Yucatan Peninsula. Located in the drier thorn forest in the northern part of the peninsula, Chichén had a long history that began in the Preclassic and included an important Classic (Early period) occupation that provided the structures in the section of the site known as Old Chichén. The dominant period at Chichén Itzá was that known as the Modified Florescent or Mexican period extending between AD 1000 and 1250. In this period, the site fell under the sway of the Toltecs, who remodeled it after their capital at Tula. Under its Mexican overlords, Chichén Itzá seems to have ruled most of the Yucatan Peninsula. Some of the documentary histories from later times contain historical material bearing upon this period (Roys 1962). A great Mexican leader, Kukulcan (a Mayan translation of the Mexican name Quetzalcoatl), came to the site. This may well be the same Quetzalcoatl who, according to Toltec histories, was expelled from Tula after a factional dispute. The Itzá for whom the site is named were a group of immigrants who were said to speak Maya brokenly. They were probably Putun Maya from the coast of Campeche and Tabasco who had already been partly Mexicanized in their homeland (Thompson 1970). A number of confused and conflicting accounts speak of migrations of the Itzá before their arrival at Chichén, and a reconstruction of the event involved is a matter of considerable debate. After Chichén Itzá had dominated Yucatan for two and a half centuries, the site fell to military strife and internal intrigue, and Mexican power in Yucatan began to decline.

Yucatan leadership was seized by Mayapan, a walled city of some 12,000 inhabitants. The Cocoms, an offshoot Itzá lineage from Chichén Itzá, established themselves as rulers at the site and proceeded to subjugate most of the peninsula. As a means of controlling their territory, they are said to have required all lords of subsidiary towns to reside at Mayapan. With such a concentration of nobility, one might expect Mayapan to have been a luxurious site. In fact, it is exactly the opposite. The structures were shoddily built, and the public precincts appear impoverished in comparison with earlier sites. Intrigue and civil war plagued the rulers of Mayapan; in 1441 the site was destroyed, and Yucatan fell into a period of fragmentation. The region was divided into a number of petty states, some unified under strong central leadership, others so weakly centralized that individual communities were almost autonomous. Bickering and disputes were continuous, and until the Spanish Conquest a century later the Maya made no serious gestures toward regaining their former glory. The time between 1250 and the Spanish Conquest is usually called the Decadent period in reference to declining architectural techniques. Sabloff and Rathje (1975), as a result of their research at the trade center on Cozumel Island, believe that the process involved was not cultural decay but a reordering of priorities in which a rising merchant elite invested their capital and concern in production and trade rather than in conspicuous consumption.

For the Postclassic period in Oaxaca, one can speak with some confidence about the archeological remains of the Zapotecs and Mixtecs, the two major ethnic groups of the area at the time of the conquest. The Valley of Oaxaca, which was traditionally Zapotec territory, lacked a really major site after the death of Monte Albán at the end of the Classic. Mitla, the best known Postclassic site in the valley, was much smaller than Monte Albán. Most of the population, especially in the Late Postclassic, lived in settlements of hamlet or village size.

The Mixtecs are best known from the Mixteca Alta, a rugged, mountainous country north and west of the Valley of Oaxaca where populations are confined to a series of tiny highland valleys. Postclassic occupation of the area seems to have been high, but none of the sites approach the size of those in larger valleys. A fine ethnohistoric reconstruction by Spores (1967) shows that the contact period Mixtecs were split into a series of petty kingdoms whose rulers were tied together by intricate alliances based upon intermarriage. Despite the small size of their political units, the Mixtecs were the most famous craftsmen in Late Postclassic Mesoamerica. Metallurgy, which had spread throughout Mesoamerica by this time, was one Mixtec specialty; polychrome pottery was another (Figure 9.14). Finally, the Mixtecs were expert in the recording of history and genealogy in pictographic manuscripts, some of which have survived to the present.

The Postclassic period in the highlands and on the Pacific coast of Guatemala was a time of political fragmentation and intense warfare. At the end of the Classic, highland sites were shifted from valley-floor locations to defensible eminences; in the course of the Postclassic, architectural defensive works became more and more impressive. Contact period sources show the

FIGURE 9.14
Mixtec art: *a*, from Codex Nuttal; *b*, *c*, pectorals from Monte Albán. (After Willey 1965.)

Guatemalan Highlands to have been divided among a series of small king-doms, constantly bent on conquest and at war with one another. This part of Guatemala was the scene of several waves of Mexican influence. The impact of Teotihuacán has already been noted, and it has now been demon-strated (L. Parsons 1967) that Mexican-influenced sculpture from the Santa Lucía Cotzumalhuapa area on the coast dates between AD 400 and 900. In the Postclassic, the Toltecs were undoubtedly active in the area, and sev-eral highland Guatemalan kingdoms proudly traced their origin to Toltec ancestors. Scattered pockets of people speaking Mexican languages still resided in the area at the time of the conquest, indicating that one or more of the waves of Mexican influence were accompanied by immigration.

THE AZTEC EMPIRE: CULMINATION OF MESOAMERICAN CULTURE

To return to the Valley of Mexico, Aztec prospects looked far from bright through the thirteenth and fourteenth centuries. Although occasionally successful in warfare as allies of established city-states, they continued to darken their own future by overagression and lack of diplomacy. A famous legend illustrates the point. The Aztecs are said to have asked for and been granted a daughter of the ruler of Culhuacan. This was a great boon, for the Culhuacan dynasty was directly descended from the Toltecs, and to incorporate Toltec blood into one's lineage was a key step in gaining social prestige. Instead of honoring the Toltec princess by marriage into their royal house, however, the Aztecs sacrificed her to their god Xipe Totec, and when her father arrived for what he thought was to be a wedding ceremony he was greeted instead by a priest dancing in the skin of his slain daughter. This was neither polite nor politic, and the Aztecs were expelled from their homes and forced to flee the wrath of Culhuacan.

The location that the Aztecs chose for refuge was amidst the reeds in the swamps that bordered the west side of Lake Texcoco. According to their legends, they were to select a spot at which they saw an eagle sitting on a cactus eating a snake. The eagle and the snake, if they were there, were there for the same reason as the Aztecs—the area was remote and desolate and avoided by sensible men. In this unlikely location, the Aztecs founded the city of Tenochtitlán about 1345. By hard work they turned the disadvantages of the spot to their favor. The shallow lake bed was converted into *chinampas*—fabulously productive gardens formed by piling up mud from the lake bottom to make artificial islands. Isolation from the shore was advantageous; the causeways that were built to connect the city to the mainland could be easily defended. The lake location and the canals that interlaced the city provided easy water transport for goods and people, eventually aiding the growth of Tenochtitlán as a center of commerce.

From this point, the fortunes of the Aztecs continually improved. Gaining strength by judicious alliances with larger powers and rapidly shifting sides at propitious moments, they emerged by the fifteenth century as a member of the famous Triple Alliance with the cities of Texcoco and Tlacopan. After the death of the remarkable lawgiver-poet king, Nezahuacoyotl of Texcoco, the Aztecs were soon to be in essential control of the entire Valley of Mexico. Serious Aztec expansion outside of the valley did not start until ca. 1450, however, so that the magnificent empire that greeted the Spanish was less than a century old when it met its sudden and inglorious end.

The territory amassed by the Aztecs during their surge of conquest was impressive. Almost all of Central Mexico and the Gulf coast was under their dominion as were sizable parts of southern Mexico in Oaxaca and along the Pacific coast. Theirs was not, however, a tightly controlled and heavily administered empire like that of the Incas in Peru. Instead, many local rulers retained much of their power under the Aztecs and were bound to the empire only by oaths of loyalty and the payment of tribute to Tenochtitlán. The threat of the Aztec armies kept these arrangements alive, but, even so, revolts were frequent and each Aztec ruler seems to have spent a considerable amount of time suppressing rebellions and pacifying areas already within the empire.

The many first- and second-generation accounts by both the Spanish and persons of native descent provide a richness of information about the operation of Aztec society that can hardly be hinted at in a survey of this length. The most interesting questions for research involve detailed analysis of the intricate variety that can be glimpsed from these sources. Social arrangements both varied from place to place and changed rapidly through time; even book-length treatments are insufficient for complete analyses of the intricacies involved. The brief summary that follows can do no more than touch a few very general considerations. See Weaver (1972) for a lengthier summary and Soustelle (1964) for a detailed treatment.

Economically, the Late Postclassic Valley of Mexico developed a complex pattern of specialization and trade in which Tenochtitlán played the dominant role. The great market at Tenochtitlán, estimated to have attracted 60,000 people daily, seemed a thing of wonder to the sixteenth-century Spanish. (See Bernal Diaz del Castillo 1963 for a fascinating eyewitness account.) Intensive specialization in which whole barrios of the city were devoted to individual craft products supplied both this market and the export trade to other parts of Mesoamerica. Goods from outside the Valley of Mexico were brought into Aztec hands by the tribute agreements with conquered territories. Tribute lists that survived into Colonial times show the amazing variety and volume of both raw materials and finished products procured in this manner. Exotic materials from outside the area of Aztec conquest were brought to Tenochtitlán by long-distance trade. This trade was in the hands of the *pochteca,* a group of professional traders who occupied a special status within Aztec society (Acosta Saignes 1945).

A basic social unit of the Aztec was the *calpulli.* The exact nature of the *calpulli* has been a matter of anthropological debate for generations. A few facts, however, seem clear. *Calpulli* were territorially defined units that possessed land and had hereditary leaders. They may have originated as kin groups and still seemed to possess at least some kin functions in Aztec times.

Aztec society was divided into social classes that included slaves, commoners, and nobility. The structure of noble society was extremely complicated and is blurred by variation through time. An important distinction existed between a hereditary nobility and a nobility by achievement consisting of those who had been given grants of land for a lifetime as reward for prowess in war. Although in theory these grants reverted to the Aztec ruler at the death of the holder, they seem to have had a tendency to become hereditary as well. Wolf (1959), whose summary of Aztec social structure is excellent, feels that there was increasing tension between the two kinds of nobility.

In 1519, this entire structure was to disintegrate within a few months under the impact of a handful of men from an alien culture. The enmities that the Aztecs had created in the process of ruling served the Spanish well, and the power of the Aztec rulers crumbled almost overnight. The loss of leadership and the disastrous consequences of European-introduced disease that decimated native Mesoamerican populations destroyed the elite culture. But the peasants of Mesoamerica persisted. Fragments of native Mesoamerican culture persevere until the present, although whether they can—or should—survive the impact of modernization remains to be seen.

References Cited and Recommended Sources

Acosta Saignes, Miguel 1945 Los pochteca. Acta Antropologica, Epoca I 1:(1). Mexico: Sociedad de Alumnos, Escuela Nacional de Antropologia e Historia.

Adams, Richard E. W. (ed.) 1977 The origins of Maya civilization. Albuquerque: University of New Mexico Press.

Andrews, E. W., IV 1965 Progress report on the 1960–1964 field seasons: National Geographic Society-Tulane University Dzibilchaltun program. Middle American Research Institute, Tulane University, Publication 31:23–67.

Armillas, Pedro 1964 Northern Mesoamerica. *In* Prehistoric Man in the New World, ed. J. D. Jennings and E. Norbeck, pp. 291–330. Chicago: University of Chicago Press.

Beadle, George W. 1972 The mystery of maize. Field Museum Natural History Bulletin 43:10:2–11.

Byers, Douglas S. (ed.) 1967 Prehistory of the Tehuacan Valley, Vol. 1. Austin: University of Texas Press.

Coe, Michael D. 1960 Archaeological linkages with North and South America at La Victoria, Guatemala. American Anthropologist 62:3:363–393.

———. 1962 Mexico. New York: Praeger Publishers.

———. 1965 The Jaguar's Children: Pre-Classic Central Mexico. New York: Museum of Primitive Art.

———. 1968 San Lorenzo and the Olmec civilization. Dumbarton Oaks Conference on the Olmec, ed. E. P. Benson, pp. 41–71. Washington, D.C.: Dumbarton Oaks.

Coe, Michael D., and Kent V. Flannery 1964 Microenvironments and Mesoamerican prehistory. Science 143:3607:650–654.

Cowgill, George L. 1974 Quantitative studies of urbanization at Teotihuacán. In Mesoamerican Archaeology: New Approaches, ed. N. Hammond, pp. 363–396. Austin: University of Texas Press.

Culbert, T. Patrick 1974 The Lost Civilization: The Story of the Classic Maya. New York: Harper and Row.

———. n.d. Maya development and collapse: an economic perspective. In Social process in Maya Prehistory: Studies in memory of Sir Eric Thompson, ed. N. Hammond. London: Academic Press, in press.

Culbert, T. Patrick (ed.) 1973 The Classic Maya Collapse. Albuquerque: University of New Mexico Press.

Diaz Del Castillo, Bernal 1963 Conquest of New Spain. Translated by J. M. Cohen. New York: Penguin Books.

Diehl, Richard A. 1971 Preliminary report, University of Missouri archaeological Project at Tula, Hidalgo, 1970–1971 field seasons. Unpublished manuscript. University of Missouri.

Drucker, Philip, R. J. Squier, and R. F. Heizer 1959 Excavations at La Venta, Tabasco, 1955. Bureau of American Ethnology Bulletin 170. Washington, D.C.: Smithsonian Institution.

Ekholm, Gordon F., and Ignacio Bernal (eds.) 1971 Archaeology of northern Mesoamerica. Handbook of Middle American Indians, Vol. 10, Part 1. Austin: University of Texas Press.

Flannery, Kent V. 1968a Archeological systems theory and early Mesoamerica. In Anthropological Archeology in the Americas, ed. B. J. Meggers, pp. 67–87. Washington, D.C.: Anthropological Society of Washington.

———. 1968b The Olmec and the Valley of Oaxaca: a model for interregional interaction in Formative times. In Dumbarton Oaks Conference on the Olmec, ed. E. P. Benson, pp. 79–110. Washington, D.C.: Dumbarton Oaks.

———. 1973 The origins of agriculture. Annual Review of Anthropology 2:271–310.

Flannery, Kent V., Anne V. T. Kirkby, Michael J. Kirkby, and Aubrey W. Williams, Jr. 1967 Farming systems and political growth in ancient Oaxaca. Science 158:3800:445–453.

Galinat, W. C. 1971 The origin of maize. Annual Review of Genetics 5:447–478.

Grennes-Ravitz, Ronald A., and G. H. Coleman 1976 The quintessential role of Olmec in the Central Highlands of Mexico: a refutation. American Antiquity 41:2:196–206.

Grove, David C. 1974 The Highland Olmec manifestation: a consideration of what it is and isn't. In Mesoamerican Archaeology: New Approaches, ed. N. Hammond, pp. 109–128. Austin: University of Texas Press.

Hammond, Norman, Duncan Pring, Rainer Berger, V. R. Switsur, and A. P. Ward 1976 Radiocarbon chronology for early Maya occupation at Cuello, Belize, Nature 260:5552:579–581.

Haviland, William A. 1970 Tikal, Guatemala, and Mesoamerican urbanism. World Archaeology 2:2:186–97.

Kubler, George 1967 The iconography of the art of Teotihuacán. Dumbarton Oaks Studies in Pre-Columbian Art and Archaeology 4.

Lowe, Gareth W. 1967 Discussion. In Altamira and Padre Piedra, Early Preclassic Sites in Chiapas, Mexico, ed. Dee. F. Green and Gareth W. Lowe, pp. 53–79. New World Archaeological Foundation Publication No. 15.

MacNeish, Richard S. 1958 Preliminary archaeological investigations in the Sierra de Tamaulipas, Mexico. Transactions, American Philosophical Society 48, pt. 6.

———. 1964 Ancient Mesoamerican civilization. Science 143:531–537.

Manglesdorf, Paul 1974 Corn: Its Origin, Evolution and Improvement. Cambridge: Belknap Press.

Millon, René 1973 The Teotihuacán map: text. Urbanization at Teotihuacán, Mexico. Vol. 1. Austin: University of Texas Press.

————. The study of urbanism at Teotihuacán, Mexico. In Mesoamerican Archeology: New approaches, ed. N. Hammond, pp. 335–362. Austin: University of Texas Press.

Norman, V. G. 1973 Izapa sculpture. Papers of the New World Archaeology Foundation, No. 30.

Parsons, Jeffrey R. 1974 The development of a prehistoric complex society: a regional perspective from the Valley of Mexico. Journal of Field Archaeology 1:81–108.

Parsons, Lee A. 1967 Bilbao, Guatemala: an archaeological study of the Pacific coast Cotzumalhuapa region. Milwaukee Public Museum, Publications in Anthropology 11.

Patterson, Thomas 1973 America's Past: A New World Archaeology. Glenview, Ill.: Scott, Foresman and Company.

Proskouriakoff, Tatiana 1960 Historical implications of pattern of dates at Piedras Negras, Guatemala. American Antiquity 25:4:454–475.

Rathje, William L. 1970 Socio-political implications of lowland Maya burials: methodology and tentative hypotheses. World Archaeology 1:3:359–375.

————. 1971 The origin and development of Lowland Classic Maya civilization. American Antiquity 36:3:275–285.

————. 1973 Classic Maya development and denouement: a research design. In The Classic Maya Collapse, ed. T. P. Culbert, pp. 405–456. Albuquerque: University of New Mexico Press.

Roys, Ralph L. 1962 Literary sources for the history of Mayapan. In Mayapan, Yucatan, Mexico, ed. H. E. D. Pollock, Ralph L. Roys, Tatiana Proskouriakoff, and A. L. Smith. Carnegie Institution of Washington Publication, No. 619.

Sabloff, Jeremy A., and William L. Rathje (ed.) 1975 A study of pre-Columbian commercial systems: the 1972–1973 seasons at Cozumel, Mexico. Monographs of the Peabody Museum, Harvard University, No. 3.

Sanders, William T. 1965 The Cultural Ecology of the Teotihuacán Valley. State College: Pennsylvania State University.

Sanders, W. T., and Barbara J. Price 1968 Mesoamerica: the Evolution of a Civilization. New York: Random House.

Service, Elman 1962 Primitive Social Organization. New York: Random House.

Soustelle, J. 1964 The Daily Life of the Aztecs. London: Pelican Books.

Spence, Michael W. 1975 The development of the Teotihuacán obsidian production system. Unpublished manuscript. Department of Anthropology, University of Western Ontario.

Spores, Ronald 1967 The Mixtec Kings and Their People. Norman: University of Oklahoma.

Stephens, John L. 1841 Incidents of Travel in Central America, Chiapas, and Yucatan. 2 vols. New York: Dover. (Reprinted in 1969.)

————. 1843 Incidents of Travel in Yucatan. Norman: University of Oklahoma Press. (Reprinted in 1962.)

Thompson, J. Eric S. 1970 Maya History and Religion. Norman: University of Oklahoma Press.

Tolstoy, Paul, and Louise I. Paradis 1970 Early and Middle Preclassic culture in the Basin of Mexico. Science 167:3917:344–351.

Turner, William L., II 1974 Prehistoric intensive agriculture in the Maya Lowlands. Science 185:4136:118–124.

Weaver, Muriel Porter 1972 The Aztecs, Maya, and Their Predecessors. New York: Seminar Press.

Webb, Malcom C. 1964 The Post-Classic decline of the Peten Maya: an interpretation in the light of a general theory of state society. Ph.D. dissertation, University of Michigan.

————. 1973 The Peten Maya decline viewed in the perspective of state formation. In The Classic Maya Collapse, ed. T. P. Culbert, pp. 367–404. Albuquerque: University of New Mexico Press.

West, Robert C. 1964 Surface configuration and associated geology of Middle America. In Natural Environment and Early Cultures, Handbook of Middle American Indians, Vol. 1, ed. R. C. West, pp. 33–83.

Willey, Gordon R. 1965 Archaeology of southern Mesoamerica. Handbook of Middle American Indians, Vol. 3, Part 2. Austin: University of Texas Press.

————. 1966 An Introduction to American Archaeology, Vol. 1. Englewood Cliffs, N.J.: Prentice-Hall.

————. 1974 The Classic Maya hiatus: a "rehearsal" for the collapse? *In* Mesoamerican Archaeology: New Approaches, ed. N. Hammond, pp. 417–430. Austin: University of Texas Press.

Willey, Gordon R., T. Patrick Culbert, and Richard E. W. Adams (eds.) 1967 Maya Lowland ceramics: a report from the 1965 Guatemala City conference. American Antiquity 32:3:289–315.

Willey, Gordon R., and Demitri B. Shimkin 1973 The Maya collapse: a summary view. *In* The Classic Maya Collapse, ed. T. P. Culbert, pp. 457–501. Albuquerque: University of New Mexico Press.

Wolf, Eric 1959 Sons of the Shaking Earth. Chicago: University of Chicago Press.

View across the Callejon de Huaylas from the mouth of Guitarrero Cave, Peru.

CHAPTER TEN

The South American Paleo-Indians

Thomas F. Lynch

Dr. Lynch surveys the evidence of early man in South America. The date of his arrival, the environment into which he moved, the animals and plants upon which he subsisted, the tools he used—these are the important facts to be dealt with in any discussion of early man, and each is explored here. Dr. Lynch also discusses the probable nature of the postglacial climate and its effect on the environment and hence on the Paleo-Indians who were exploiting that environment. What emerges is a fascinating picture of ever-adaptable man entering and flourishing in unfamiliar landscapes, often populated by strange creatures and covered with unknown vegetation.

BACKGROUND

While in principle this chapter treats the first human occupation of all South America, in practice this means only the long Andean chain—with its high plateaus, intermontane valleys, steep mountain flanks, and adjacent pied-monts—which stretches along the western edge of the continent (Figure 10.1). To the east of this highland region only a few sites, principally in the far north and far south, give reasonable evidence of initial postglacial cultural adapta-tion. The lack of convincing evidence of early man in most of the eastern, lowland parts of South America is usually attributed to the difficulties of modern reconnaissance or poor site preservation. But it is probably equally significant that much of the lowland zone was heavily forested and disadvan-tageous for Paleo-Indian exploitation in postglacial times. The southeastern highlands of Brazil are more promising, to judge by new reports of stemmed and lanceolate points, bones, and early dates at the Alice Boer site (Beltrão 1974).

FIGURE 10.1

Key sites for the reconstruction of Central and South American subsistence and ecology:
1, Rio Pasion sloth; *2,* Totonicapan and Guatemala City fluted points; *3,* Lago de
Managua mudflows; *4,* Guanacaste fluted point; *5,* Madden Lake fluted points; *6,* Taima-
Taima and Muaco; *7,* El Abra and Laguna de Fuquene; *8,* El Inga; *9,* Chobshi Cave;
10, Talara tar seeps; *11,* La Cumbre, Quirihuac, and Pampa de los Fosiles; *12,* Guitarrero
and Lauricocha caves; *13,* Quiqche, Tres Ventanas, and Ayacucho caves; *14,* Toquepala;
15, Cerca Grande 6; *16,* San Pedro de Atacama; *17,* Ayampitin; *18,* Gruta del Indio;
19, Tagua-Tagua; *20,* Los Toldos; *21,* Palli Aike and Fell's caves; *22,* Marazzi.

YEARS BC	LAURENTIDE SEQUENCE (North America)	FUQUENE SEQUENCE (Colombia)	SOUTH AMERICAN PALEO-INDIANS (Elary Postglacial Hunters)
			WILLOW LEAF or AYAMPITIN HORIZON (Andean Hunting-Collecting Tradition) Diversified economy based on modern game
8,000	– – – – – Postglacial Boundary – – – – –		
9,000	Valders Event	El Abra Stadial	
			FISHTAIL POINT HORIZON (Old South American Hunting Tradition) Empasis on Pleistocene large game
10,000	Two Creeks Interval	Guantiva Interstadial	
11,000			
	Woodfordian Glacial (Mankato, Cary, and Tazewell substages)	Upper Pleniglacial (last full glacial)	HYPOTHETICAL PREPROJECTILE POINT STAGE (e. g., various Chopper, Burin, Biface, and Edge-retouched collections)
24,000			

FIGURE 10.2
Late Wisconsin time-stratigraphic and cultural correlations.

The first certain human adaptation, some 10,000 to 12,000 years ago, was apparently to more "open" habitats, suitable for communal hunting techniques. As in North America, horses and elephants figured prominently among the first game animals, only to become rapidly extinct soon after their world was disturbed by man. Huge ground sloths, some nearly the size of elephants, and various deer and camelids (much like the modern llama) were also hunted. The latter became increasingly important through time, as the resource base was widened to include many smaller animals. The early use of birds (especially ground nesters), aquatic resources, land mollusks, and plants has probably been insufficiently appreciated, for it is difficult to detect archeologically.

I have identified this first South American hunting and gathering horizon with the Paleo-Indian culture of North America as a result of correspondences in chronology, economic orientation, and technology. However, the reader should be aware that it has been widely known as the Fishtail Point horizon and, more recently, as the Old South American Hunting tradition (Willey 1971:43–50). Much as the Paleo-Indian culture of North America can be seen to flow, as a tradition, into the Plano and perhaps other Western Archaic cultures, there is clear continuity between the earliest South American hunters and their descendants in Willey's Andean Hunting-Collecting tradition. In this latter adaptation, which I have previously labeled the Willow Leaf or Ayampitín horizon, there is more emphasis on smaller game and plant foods. At this point regional differentiation becomes obvious, and there is reason to consider the adaptations separately under the names given in local sequences, such as Los Toldos, Lauricocha, Puente, El Abra, and El Jobo, to name just a few beyond Ayampitín. In a general sense, all may be considered Paleo-Indians, insofar as hunting and a high degree of mobility characterized their life styles. The term *Early Postglacial Hunters,* coined by Lumbreras, with its lack of either ethnic or areal connotations, might be preferred, at least until these peoples and cultures are better understood (Figure 10.2).

THE QUESTIONABLE PREPROJECTILE POINT STAGE

There is much dispute as to whether South American Paleo-Indians were preceded by earlier peoples, perhaps related through the typology of their stone tools to the European Paleolithic (Le Paige 1971). Over the last 20 years, there has been a flurry of activity, chiefly by North Americans and Europeans, who claim to be able to find man in South America even before he can be identified in the northern continent. It appears that the spirit of Florentino Ameghino, a pioneering Argentine paleontologist and archeologist, is still with us some 65 years after his death. Ameghino went so far as to try to prove the pampean origin of mankind by the simple expedient of "seriating" Pleistocene fauna, artifacts, and human skeletal remains throughout the Tertiary period. At one time, it was even proposed that people might have come first to South America by way of Antarctica.

In recent years, starting with Krieger (1964), there have been more serious proposals of great antiquity, based at first on the primitive quality of some artifact collections (chiefly selective surface and quarry "industries") but also based increasingly on new dating techniques. A few radiocarbon and thermoluminescence dates, of suspect association and accuracy, may be taken to indicate human presence in South America as early as 29,000 years ago. Some archeologists, with great confidence in their abilities to predict typological succession in artifacts, would use these to date a preprojectile point stage of generalized food collecting. Sometimes the hypothetical preprojectile point stage is even subdivided, most typically into Chopper, Burin, and Biface industries, as in a highly speculative presentation by Lanning and Patterson (1967). See also Lanning (1970) and Patterson (1973) for their Edgeretouched tradition. Given the nature of the archeological data, I take this to be largely an exercise of faith, while acknowledging the remote possibility of some such sparse population of the continent in Wisconsin times. The bulk of the evidence (a series of stratified camp and kill sites with projectile point industries, datable charcoal, and sometimes fossil fauna) indicates that hunters related to North American Paleo-Indians quickly adapted their culture to the major unforested habitats of South America during the tenth and ninth radiocarbon millennia BC. A few apparently trustworthy dates suggest human penetration of South America in the eleventh millennium, but these are in cultural associations that suggest a hunting economy rather than generalized gathering or foraging (Lynch 1974).

The only serious support for a South American preprojectile point stage comes from the Pacaicasa and Ayacucho phase deposits in Pikimachay Cave, Peru. However, MacNeish (1975:13–15; 1971:44) disagrees with his consulting geologists as to which levels represent periods of glacial advance or retreat, an issue extremely critical to the dating of the cultural remains. MacNeish prefers to accept the anomalously early bone dates at face value, despite the awkwardness of having glaciation in the Andes out of phase with that of Europe and North America.

There are additional problems with MacNeish's Pacaicasa complex. All dates (18,250 ± 1,050 BC, 17,650 ± 3,000 BC, 14,100 ± 1,200 BC, and 12,750 ± 1,400 BC) were determined from samples of bone of Pleistocene sloths. The giant sloths had been inhabitants of American caves long before men invaded their habitat and, probably, contributed to their extinction about 10,000 BC. As best one can tell from MacNeish's sometimes contradictory reports, all but 4 of the 71 items he identifies as lithic artifacts are pieces of the rock that composes the walls of the cave itself. Since it is possible that the sloth bones were a natural occurrence, there is good reason to question the likelihood of man's use of this fractured tuff, or solidified volcanic ash, an unlikely raw material in an area where better rocks are readily available and universally used for indubitable artifacts. (Most recently, MacNeish has referred to this rock as tufa, a precipitate of calcium carbonate from spring or lake water, an equally unusual material for flint knapping.) My own inclination, following that of other archeologists who have inspected the Pacaicasa "artifacts" or even their casts, is to maintain reservations on the validity of the industry until better artifacts are located in firm association with definitively cultural, dated materials. The four artifacts and flakes of exotic stone could easily be intrusive or have fallen from above, despite care taken in excavation.

The Ayacucho complex, similarly lacking in stone projectile points, is much more firmly established, although there is doubt about some of the bone and tuff artifacts. Many of the 209 tools are made of exotic stone appropriate for the purpose, and the faunal collection is composed of modern rodents, cats, skunks, deer, and camelids as well as now extinct sloth and horse. There is a single problematical date on sloth bone of 12,200 ± 180 BC for the Ayacucho deposit, followed by roof fall and an improbable 5,000-year gap before the overlying Puente-Jaywa industry, dated by charcoal to 6,910 ± 125 BC at the Puente site.

Forbis (1974:15) has recently summarized the argument against a South American preprojectile point stage as follows:

1. Frequently the sites are in surface locations, where reliable dating is impossible.

2. Some sites are dated, but the putative artifacts may not be man-made.

3. Some sites are firmly dated to an early period but have yielded such a small sample of artifacts that they cannot convincingly be demonstrated to lack projectile points.

4. Some sites are workshops or quarries. Crudeness of the waste debris left at these stations cannot be accepted as proof of antiquity.

5. Some sites lie in situations suggesting antiquity but have not as yet been dated precisely.

Numerous putatively ancient collections, particularly in the high desert regions of northwest Argentina, northern Chile, and the Bolivian Puna, fit into Forbis's category 1. Having been selectively collected or later subdivided, some may not even be complete industries. Forbis's second argument, along with the problem of suspect associations, covers the claim of 14,000 years for Rancho Peludo and Manzanillo in Venezuela, as well as the Pacaicasa controversy. Category 3 applies to the basal Tagua-Tagua industry in Chile ($9,430 \pm 320$ BC), the lowest level at Los Toldos in Argentina ($10,650 \pm 600$ BC), and perhaps to the Guitarrero I industry ($10,610 \pm 360$ BC). Great age has been attributed to numerous workshops and quarries (category 4) in Peru and Argentina, but, owing to their very nature and purpose, such sites are hard to assess. Sources of good stone characteristically remain in use through many periods, while digging and quarrying activities destroy any useful stratigraphy. At quarries, datable organic material is rare, for these were neither living sites nor kill sites, and their use was short-term and sporadic. Finely worked artifact types, characteristic of later periods, are generally absent, because the artifacts were finished elsewhere after the crude blanks (often large bifaces) and cores were removed from the quarry. Category 5 pertains to a multitude of sites, but especially to those situated on old river and marine terraces in Argentina and to Cruxent's extraordinarily idealized Rio Pedregal terrace sequence in Venezuela. At the Alice Boer site the lower part of Bed III, which lacks projectile points, is undated but may also be early (Beltrão 1974).

All in all, it is my opinion that the case for a horizon of crude bifaces and choppers is not much stronger in South America than it was in North America several decades ago, when the Trenton gravels and the surface collections from Black's Fork were the latest word on the "American Paleolithic." In a recent article (Lynch 1974), after an extensive review of the published data, I concluded that the very number of poor sites that have been put forward, in the context of a total lack of convincing cases, speaks against the notion of preprojectile point man rather than for it. Taken as a whole, the evidence from radiocarbon dating, river terrace successions, stratigraphic associations, and intercontinental climate correlations does not support the presence of man in South America before terminal Pleistocene times.

PALEO-INDIAN ANTECEDENTS IN CENTRAL AMERICA

In terms of stone tool technology, if not economy, one can no longer argue against extension of the North American Paleo-Indian horizon to Central America. The similarity of artifact types suggests that there are close cultural and chronological relationships (Figure 10.3). Early identifications of "Clovis Fluted" points from Central America were open to question, in that they were from the surface or had been excavated without attention to the deposits in which they were located. This reservation applies to the point from the Hart-

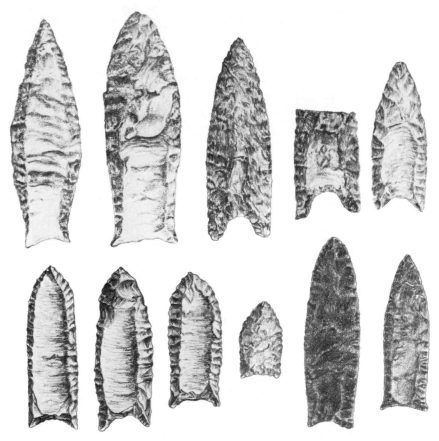

FIGURE 10.3
Fluted and fishtail points from North America. (From *Prehistory of North America*, 2d ed.,
by Jesse D. Jennings. Copyright © 1968, 1974 by McGraw-Hill, Inc. Used with permission
of McGraw-Hill Book Company.)

man collection, said to have been excavated in northwestern Guanacaste,
Costa Rica, in 1903 but not reported until 1952. It is undeniably of the general Clovis class of fluted points. Another point with classic Clovis "ears" and
constricted "waist," fluted on one side only, was found by a child in an erosion gully just west of Guatemala City and reported by Coe. Four fluted
points, two of them quite similar to the fishtail types from Fell's Cave in
Patagonia, have been recovered from surface contexts on the shores of Madden Lake in the Panama Canal Zone. All four probably were derived from
the south bank of the Chagres River when the artificial lake was impounded.
In 1976 in Costa Rica, Michael Snarkis collected a good Paleo-Indian industry with classic fluted points from a shallow site overlooking the Rio Reven-
tazón on the eastern slopes of the Cordillera Central.

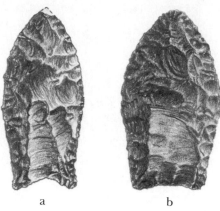

FIGURE 10.4
Central American points: *a*, fluted point from San Rafael, Guatemala; *b*, Costa Rican point.

The sole stratified Central American site with a Paleo-Indian component is located at the remarkable elevation of 3,150 meters (10,400 feet) in the Totonicapan mountains of Guatemala (Figure 10.4). Gruhn (n.d.) reports the base of a fluted point (without prominent ears or constricted waist, but with Paleo-Indian edge grinding), a channel flake from the fluting process, 14 fragments of other bifacial tools (possibly knives), 20 flake scrapers, 5 burins, 7 gravers, 1 unifacial point, 8 blades, and 25 retouched flakes. It is possible that, in these highland temperate zones, Paleo-Indians maintained their basic North American adaptation as far south as Guatemala. Soil conditions did not permit preservation of bone, but pooled samples of charcoal yielded results from 5600 to 8760 BC.

Other than what can be inferred by analogy with North and South America, we cannot yet say much about the nature of Paleo-Indian subsistence in Central America. Even massive bone deteriorates rapidly in the wet tropics; associations with stone artifacts are uncommon. Nevertheless, a mineralized sloth bone, incised while still green, is supposed to have been found with stone flakes in the Pasión drainage of the southern Petén.

In exceptional circumstances other unusual fossilizations of cultural activity occur, such as the human footprints preserved in solidified volcanic mudflows from several exposures in Nicaragua and El Salvador. Difficult though they are to fix in time, Bryan has done us a service by dating the soil directly beneath a buried mudflow near Lake Managua to 3995 ± 145 BC. From this he calculates an age of about 3000 BC for that series of footprints. Evidence from other discoveries, made as many as 85 years ago, has disappeared, but the prints may have been of equal or greater age. The human footprints, although emotionally satisfying, tell us little by themselves, but sometimes the mudflows have included prints made by contemporary animals, such as white-tailed deer and bison, the latter no longer found in Nicaragua. I am aware of only one associated artifact—the imprint of leather-soled footgear worn by an adult. Woven agave-fiber sandals are typical of the recent inhabitants of the Southwest and most of Mesoamerica, while leather footwear speaks to us of the hunting peoples of north-central North America. It is tempting to assume that the footprints might have been made by an early moccasin-shod hunter of Paleo-Indian derivation, but it is perhaps more likely that they were left by a recent inhabitant of lower Central America, where leather sandals are known from historic times.

MAN ENTERS SOUTH AMERICA

As the first concrete signs of human occupation of South America follow so closely upon the well-studied Paleo-Indian exploitation of North America, many students would adopt the Haynes-Martin model of a rapid, wavelike expansion of a specialized hunting culture out of the North American Arctic. The Haynes-Martin thesis fits nicely with the rapid extinction of many large game animals; in terms of yield relative to energy expended in the hunt, these were the most rewarding and efficient source of food on either continent. Bryan (1973; 1975) emphasizes the difficulties of this model in terms of such a rapid expansion of hunters through the Central American bottleneck, and he proposes an essentially coeval but independent evolution of hunting culture and bifacial projectile points in northern South America. His hypothesis has the merit of providing an explanation for a few marginally pre-Clovis dates in South America, and it allows traversal of the now lushly forested Darien Isthmus under different and hopefully drier full Wisconsin conditions; but I prefer a simpler interpretation of the available data.

It is by no means certain that an ice-free corridor between the Laurentide and Cordilleran ice sheets appeared precisely at the Two Creeks Interval, allowing Arctic elephant hunters to move suddenly against the untouched herds of the Great Plains. The ice gap may have opened some 2000 or 3000 years earlier than is usually calculated or, I would think, it is even possible that big-game hunters followed their prey across dead-ice ablation moraines. These would have begun to acquire their characteristic surface cover of clastic debris soon after the climax of classic Wisconsin glaciation, about 20,000 years ago. Where the ice has lain stagnant for many years, vegetation becomes established on the surface debris, to the extent that an ice-cored moraine may merge almost imperceptibly into the proglacial moraine and outwash field.

There is increasing evidence from Fort Rock Cave, Wilson Butte Cave, and Meadowcroft Rockshelter (see Chapter 1) that the Clovis mastodon specialization was preceded, for perhaps several thousand years, by a somewhat more generalized hunting and gathering adaptation. In fact, Judge argues that even Clovis culture should be viewed as transitional from a broad-spectrum, generalized subsistence strategy to the specialized bison exploitation of Folsom times. A somewhat more generalized hunting strategy could be more easily accommodated to the difficult transitional zone of lower Central America.

When did the South American glacial stage end, and when did conditions in the Panamanian-Darien Isthmus begin to approach those of the present, so that a crossing by Paleo-Indians would have been difficult if not impossible? Fortunately, this question is now close to a definite answer. From north to south, the latest studies of glaciation and vegetational succession show that, contrary to MacNeish's pronouncements from Ayacucho, Upper Pleistocene glacial events in South America were closely synchronous with those in North America, Europe, and even Africa (van der Hammen 1974; Heusser 1974; Mercer 1972). In general, it seems from data analyzed in the CLIMAP project that Ice Age cooling over South America, Africa, and Australia averaged about 5°C at 16,000 BC.

Extensive studies by van der Hammen and his colleagues show clearly that the first part of the last glacial stage in the Colombian Andes was both cold and wet, with interstadials and stadials comparable to those of the northern temperate latitudes. Some 20,000 years ago conditions became progressively dryer, culminating about 11,000 BC when annual precipitation was less than half what it is now. Snow line and treeline were lowered drastically, and the surface area occupied by *páramo* (a high-altitude, tall-grass formation) became much greater than its present extent. After a short interstadial interval, cool, dry conditions returned during the El Abra stadial, which correlates with the European Younger Dryas and North American Valders (now Greatlakean) events—about 9000 to 7500 BC. Van der Hammen's data come from several field stations where long pollen histories have been obtained; he also has direct evidence of reduced precipitation from lower stands of the Laguna de Fuquene, in spite of synchronous contrary effects of lower temperature (some 6° or 7°C) and evaporation.

Similarly, Heusser's recent work in the southern Chilean Lake District places the end of the last major Llanquihue (Wisconsin) stage at 8000 BC. The pollen record shows as increasing midelevation montane forest; Heusser estimates that for the late glacial advances average January temperatures were 4°C cooler than now and effective precipitation was greater. Studies throughout the Southern Hemisphere demonstrate the essential equivalence of late Quaternary patterns of temperature, glaciation, and vegetation sequence (Porter 1975).

There is evidence of marked climate changes, as late as 8000 or 9000 BC, in both North and South America. It is probable that corresponding, but as yet unrecorded, variations in climate and vegetation occurred over the Isthmus of Panama. It is very likely that these changes would have made the currently inhospitable land bridge more congenial to either generalized hunting and gathering folk or Paleo-Indians. Oxygen isotopic and micro-paleontological analysis of deep-sea cores in the Gulf of Mexico show that Caribbean waters remained cold during the Valders episode (Emiliani et al. 1975). This resulted, perhaps, as much from the release of glacial meltwater through the Mississippi River as from general atmospheric conditions, but the Caribbean waters (some 2°C cooler than now, as recorded by the CLIMAP project) evidently exerted a powerful influence on the precipitation and vegetation patterns of the surrounding shorelands. Van der Hammen (1974) calculates a 3°C lowering of glacial stage temperatures over the tropical lowlands of northern South America. From pollen sequences he has established that dry savanna vegetation existed in the coastal lowlands of Guyana to the east during at least a part of the last glacial stage, while extrapolations of shorter cores suggest very dry conditions in the Colombian Llanos Orientales. Dry, open conditions also existed somewhat inland in the Rupununi savannas of Guyana.

Damuth and Fairbridge (1970; Fairbridge 1976) argue that an arid to semiarid climate extended over most of lowland and northeastern South America during glacial times, in stark contrast to present humid interglacial conditions. Their position is based on paleobotanical and sedimentological studies of cores off the Argentine and Brazilian coasts, coastal geomorphology, and especially their own analyses of cores from the Guiana Basin and Amazon Delta. During Wisconsin times, an abundance of largely unweathered feldspar sands were derived from the continental shield rocks and deposited at sea. Under the present humid climate, this would not be possible without extremely rapid uplift, erosion, and seaward transport, all of which are contradicted by the geological record. The unweathered sediments, washed off the continental margin in late Wisconsin times, constitute evidence of a much drier and/or colder climate, with rapid erosion probably aided by deforestation. Damuth and Fairbridge attempt to explain climate changes on a continental scale by postulating changes in atmospheric circulation that would deflect the South Atlantic trade winds off the northeast coast and bring cold, dry, southerly winds up across the continent. Whatever the meteorological mechanisms, there is little doubt that large parts of South America were more hospitable to Paleo-Indians at the end of the last glacial stage than they would be today.

Modern and paleontological distributions of plants and animals, of direct relevance to today's environment-oriented archeologists, also indicate Pleistocene changes in the landscape of Central America and northern South America. As early as 1944, Sauer pointed out that many plants and animals incapable of surviving in tropical forests had been exchanged, during the Pleistocene, between North and South America. Notable among the animals were edentates and ground sloths from the south and horse, deer, mastodon, cottontail, and jack rabbit from the north. At some point in Pleistocene time, these animals must have found a suitable habitat, perhaps a westward extension of the savannas of northern Colombia, in the Colombian-Panamanian Isthmus. I find it suggestive that horses and various genera of deer were among the most abundant and consistent Paleo-Indian prey in South America. Botanists believe that the Costa Rica-Panama highland vegetation was once an extension of the similar montane forest of the Colombian Andes. Lower glacial-stage temperatures and an extension of the present dry season, rain shadow effect on the Pacific side of the isthmus may have brought the two plant communities together.

The application of modeling techniques in paleoclimatology also supports the hypothesis of aridity in northern South America at the end of the last glacial age. Some years ago Lamb and others observed that in several parts of the world, but especially West Africa and South Asia, the climate of the 1960s differed markedly from that of the first half of the twentieth century; it apparently resembled the climate of the "Little Ice Age," which began in the thirteenth century, and is known from historical records. With this in mind, Sánchez and Kutzbach (1974) examined Central and South American temperature and precipitation records from 1961 to 1970, looking for departures from the 1931-to-1960 averages. Through the "glacial" regime of the 1960s, there was less rainfall in Central America below Mexico, especially along the Pacific coasts of Guatemala and El Salvador. Much of South America also received decreased precipitation, and this was most pronounced over northern South America and the western slopes of the Andes. Lake levels dropped in Nicaragua, Guatemala, El Salvador, and the central Andes (Lake Titicaca), confirming the direct evidence from rainfall records. Lower average temperatures, although of less magnitude and significance, also characterized the "glacial" conditions of the 1960s for lower Central America, northern South America, and the western side of the northern and central Andes. Paleoclimatologists insist that computer-assisted modeling has hardly begun and that all results are less than definitive; yet it seems that the climatic patterns of the 1960s may serve as a useful model for conditions during the Little Ice Age. It is another long step back to the end of the last major glaciation, but it is particularly interesting that in Colombia and northern Brazil rainfall began to decrease only near the *end* of the Little Ice Age, that is, near the end of the nineteenth century.

Previously, archeologists had assumed that, to take advantage of improved conditions along the Central American land bridge, hunter-gatherers should have made their crossing as early as possible in classic Wisconsin times. It now seems from both climate modeling and van der Hammen's studies of Colombian paleoclimates that a relatively late crossing, near the climax or even end of the last glacial stage, would have been better.

Glacially lowered sea level is a final mechanism that might have provided a better corridor for Paleo-Indian hunters. After a comprehensive study of glacial-eustatic and isostatic controls of later Quaternary sea level, Bloom (1971) calculated that 88 percent of the area that had been glaciated was still covered at 12,000 BC and that at 10,000 BC, just before the Valders surge, 70 percent of the ice area remained. He accepts Emery's figure of 13,000 BC for the minimum sea level stand. On the Bering Shelf, lowered sea level, together with extreme climatic conditions, provided a broad, grassy plain for the herds that Paleo-Indians followed. This would not have been the situation in Panama, but lower sea level is still a desideratum because it would have temporarily incised the river and stream channels on the Pacific side of the isthmus. Much of that coast has a dry season of up to five months. As streams responded to the lower base (sea) level by incising their channels and bringing down the water table in the interfluves, they would have created a seasonally dry landscape susceptible to fire damage. It seems to me that, even without major climate changes, after each major glacial advance there would have appeared a strip of savanna, cut by gallery forest in the incised river bottoms, along the Pacific coast of lower Central America. In this model a broad and gently sloping continental shelf, as under the Bering Sea, would have been a detriment, for it would have slowed (and thus made less effective) the incision process by moving the mouths of the rivers rapidly seaward. It would seem that any glacial advance, and perhaps best of all the last one, would have permitted Paleo-Indian hunters to expand their range from Central America into a temporarily more open habitat along the Pacific side of the isthmus. (Here I must parenthetically admit that Bloom, Emiliani, and some others now think that the Valders surge raised, rather than lowered, sea level. Perhaps, from their point of view, a crossing postulated as occurring just before the Two Creeks Interval is preferable.) Having crossed into open habitats of northern and Andean South America, they would have continued to hunt deer, horses, and occasional mastodons, but their descendants would also have quickly acquired a taste for South American novelties such as megatherium, glyptodon, and the camelids.

EARLY TECHNOLOGICAL AND CULTURAL ADAPTATION IN SOUTH AMERICA

Technological continuity between the stone tool industries of North American Paleo-Indians and those of their South American descendants is evident beyond any reasonable doubt. It is unlikely that simple, bifacially worked, stone projectile points would have been independently invented, by chance, within a period of a few hundred years, on both continents. It is simply inconceivable that this would have happened with the fluted, eared, and waisted points of the eastern United States (see Figure 10.3), on the one hand, and the fluted fishtail points of South America (Figure 10.5), on the other. Rather than representing cultures divergent on a major time scale, the early Paleo-Indian industries in South America are fairly closely and obviously tied to North

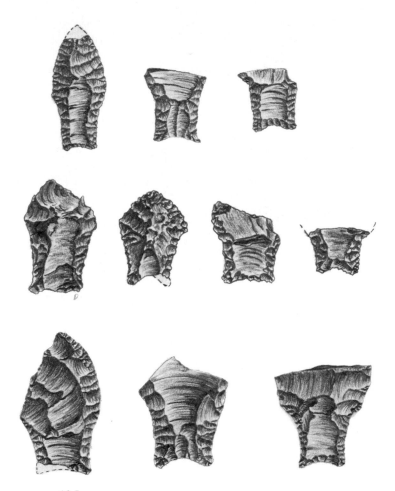

FIGURE 10.5
El Inga fishtail points.

American antecedents. Other specialized artifacts of the early industries are also nearly identical, such as snub-nosed end scrapers, thumbnail scrapers, gravers, notched tools, bifacial knife-scrapers, and flake scrapers with retouch from alternate sides. Whatever the exact nature of their subsistence strategies, these people were clearly using a very similar and closely related tool kit.

The occurrence of South American fishtail points has been intensively discussed by Bird (1969) and, more recently and adventurously, by Schobinger (1972). The latter speculates on the nearly complementary distribution of fishtail points in relation to that of foliate and lanceolate points in the Andean area, especially Peru, Bolivia, northern Chile, and northwest Argentina (Figure 10.6). Bryan (1975), although less familiar with the South American materials, states that the thick lanceolate points (for example, the El Jobo series he knows from Venezuela) are made from a different "mental template" than the thin fluted and fishtail points, and that they must come from totally different cultural traditions. This is admittedly possible and even likely, but I cannot follow him in his insistence that the El Jobo type is earlier than the fluted points of either continent and that bifacial projectile points were invented in South America. (But, given his Alberta address, neither can I accuse him of southern chauvinism!) The argument for the priority of El Jobo points is precariously based on controversial radiocarbon assays from Taima-Taima, which the geochronologist Haynes (1974) and I have criticized in tiresome detail.

The evidence is insufficient for a definitive judgment, but it is probably preferable to take the simple course of following Schobinger in seeing the two traditions as largely complementary in distribution and possibly coeval. Many have observed that the El Jobo points bear a strong resemblance to the Lerma type of Texas and associated types in Mexico, where there are at least two possible associations (Santa Isabel Iztapan and Hueyatlaco) with extinct fauna. The Western North American Cordilleran complex, proposed first by Butler and then by MacNeish, might also provide antecedents, except that typologically it resembles the Plano industries of the eighth or ninth millennium, and thus is not sufficiently early.

The large, triangular-bladed, long-stemmed points of the Paiján type may mark a third early complex (Figure 10.7). First identified at the Pampa de los Fósiles, these have a quite restricted distribution, chiefly in northern Peru. They usually lack the fine workmanship and finish of the fishtail points, and they are never fluted; but the rough similarity of outline and their very size have suggested to some that they might be Paleo-Indian in age and purpose (Figure 10.8). Like the large lanceolate points, the Paiján points would have required a different hafting technique. Radiocarbon dates from Quirihuac Rockshelter and superficial associations with now extinct megafauna support the Paleo-Indian hypothesis, but the dates and the modern fauna associated with similar stemmed points in southern Ecuador (see Chobshi Cave, below) do not lend credence to the idea (Figure 10.9).

470

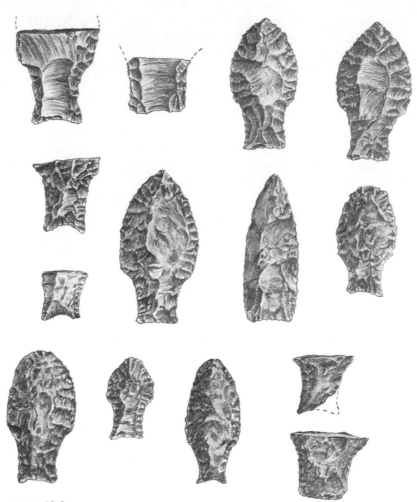

FIGURE 10.6
Magellan I points from Fell's Cave.

FIGURE 10.7
Paiján points.

FIGURE 10.8
Long-stemmed points from El Inga.

FIGURE 10.9
Chobshi stemmed points.

Happily, all archeologists seem to agree that the fishtail points—as found in Fell's Cave I, Toldense I, and El Inga contexts—are Paleo-Indian in date and technological relationship. To the well-known examples described by Bird, Bell, Mayer-Oakes, and Menghin, Ossa would add a surface find from the Moche Valley of Peru. Whether this isolated example, and all of the multitude of finds brought to our attention by Schobinger, belong in the same type is open to question. Nevertheless, Schobinger strives to make sense of their distribution by postulating a dispersal along the eastern flank of the Andes and adjacent lowlands before the establishment of the closed postglacial Amazon forest.

There is some general support for Schobinger's thesis in the Damuth and Fairbridge model of glacial stage aridity in Amazonian South America, reviewed above. Specific corroboration of the former existence of savannas in the thickly forested southwestern Amazon basin has now been provided by van der Hammen (1972; 1974). Palynological data from Rondonia (Brazil), only 160 kilometers west of the northern tip of Bolivia, demonstrate the replacement of rain forest by a "dry" vegetation type during one or more of the as yet undated, but most probably glacial, periods of the Pleistocene. Simpson-Vuilleumier (1971), reviewing the differentiation and speciation of lizards and birds in the forested eastern Andean slopes and Amazon basin, also concludes that arid cycles and fragmentation of the heavy forest are required to explain Pleistocene evolutionary patterns. Apparently the Amazon lowlands have been consistently hot, humid, and heavily forested only during parts (probably interglacial) of the Quaternary period. Finally, geomorphologists have identified landforms in humid areas of central Brazil that must have had their origins in arid cycles of the Pleistocene epoch.

I can only conclude by observing that the complete absence of signs of early man along the forested eastern flank of the north and central Andes and the adjacent Amazon lowlands cannot be attributed solely to the difficulties of access and preservation. If men were present in South America significantly before postglacial environmental changes closed the area to Paleo-Indian exploitation, surely they would have left some traces.

For many years it has been recognized that topography and environmental zonation favored north-south cultural expansion along the Andean chain, once the continent was entered. Whatever the adaptation, and whatever the date of arrival, "Romer's Rule" suggests that mankind, at least until carrying capacity was approached, would have tried to maintain a familiar way of life and eschew hazardous experimentation. Ranere (n.d.) thinks that early man might already have adapted to the tropical forest in Panama, and that this indeed was his primary strategy as he moved through the isthmus; Ranere's thesis, however, is unsupported by archeological evidence. Many have observed that the relatively scarce, solitary prey animals of the tropical forest are hard to hunt. Life in Ranere's forest would have been difficult without substantial reliance on fishing or agriculture, both unknown in the Americas at 10,000 BC.

I follow my more conventional predecessors, then, in supposing that the Andean highlands of western South America, with their rather uniform and altitudinally zoned flora and fauna, favored a rapid penetration of the continent from north to south. In one form or another, Sauer (1944), Lothrop (1961), and Hester (1966) all favored such an interpretation, Hester going a bit further to propose a rapid postglacial florescence of hunting culture on the cold steppe and tundra zones of the central and southern Andes. South American scholars (e.g., Fernandez 1971; Le Paige 1970) have been most helpful in bringing together the field data on specific regional adaptations. For my own part, I have argued that, at least in the central Andes, hunter-gatherers adapted to seasonal use of lower-altitude zones and to characteristic features of the montane environment; this seasonal transhumance quickly masked the Paleo-Indian flavor of the initial adaptation, but it may have been an important mechanism in the development of Andean pastoralism, agriculture, and "verticality."

In recent years some North Americans, such as Bryan, have selected the coastal zone as perhaps the most favorable habitat for early man. This preference undoubtedly relates to their disposition to find a gathering economy well back into the Wisconsin stage, when the subequatorial coast might have been less arid. However, with loss of faith in the early dates of many of these "preprojectile point" collections (e.g., Grove's demonstration of the modern origin of the Chuquicamata complex of northern Chile and the fourth millennium BC radiocarbon date on undisturbed Manantial deposits in Ecuador), Lanning's proposals have found fewer supporters.

The Pacific coast remains a promising zone for investigation, as a result of recent tectonic activity and strategic uplift that has preserved old beaches and marine terraces. Over a number of years, Richardson (1973; 1975) has investigated the prehistoric occupation of this barren environment, beginning with two sites at the foot of the Amotape Mountains, overlooking the famous Talara Tar Seeps, now dated (on marine shell) to 9250 ± 115 BC and 6175 ± 80 BC. Presumably the Amotape hunters preyed upon the terminal Pleistocene fauna that became mired in the seeps. The types of birds and mammals extracted from the Talara Seeps indicate a local environment of savanna woodland or grassy savanna broken by river bank woodlands. Richardson believes that a southward shift on the intertropical convergence zone would have brought winter rainfall during the Late Pleistocene, as it does sporadically today, but there is no evidence that the desert coasts of southern Ecuador, Peru, and northern Chile were once lush meadows. It is generally believed that the coastal fauna was localized in oasis and river bank situations and dependent on surface water originating as rain and snow in the high mountains to the east.

Most workers believe that the Pleistocene climate of the coastal strip was much like that of the present, although perhaps with somewhat more extensive fog-fed *lomas* vegetation and some localized but important changes in southern Ecuador and northern Peru. But even these moderate increases in local atmospheric moisture are hard to reconcile with the most recent and convincing assessment of the problem. Simpson (1975) argues that during the glacial regime the western coast would have received even more vigorous upwellings of Antarctic waters than now. A cooling on the order of 5° or 6°C is estimated from changes in carbonate composition and distributions of foraminifera. Since the depression of land surface temperatures would have been only half as great, the modern summer pattern of arid lowlands with precipitation at higher elevations would have been intensified and continued during most of the year. Simpson stresses that most climate changes in the tropics probably occurred near the beginnings and ends of the glacial cycles, when ocean and land surface temperature contrasts were greatest, causing repetitive cycles of aridity and humidity. My proposal for timing the environmental changes on the Panamanian isthmus at the glacial-postglacial juncture conforms to her model.

It is further evident that the most important changes along the whole central Andean coast should have been those brought about by fluctuating precipitation and depressed snow line in the western Andes. Meltwater runoff, higher water table, subterranean flow, and springs should have maintained themselves for a time into the postglacial period. Although there is evidence of later preceramic use of the coastal lowlands and now nearly dry stream courses, there are no absolute indications that Paleo-Indians hunted Pleistocene megafauna on the relatively well surveyed coastal lowlands. The possible association of mastodon and horse with artifacts at La Cumbre, on the Peruvian north coast, has been carefully qualified by Ossa and Moseley (1972), and the Paleo-Indian use of the Talara Tar Seeps is also only a probability. There are gaps today of up to 64 kilometers between freshwater sources along the Peruvian coast, while along the north coast of Chile one may travel 300 kilometers between the few streams that regularly reach the ocean. It seems most likely to me that the first hunting peoples extended their range south as they sought new and unwary game along the Andean Cordillera itself. In my tentative reconstruction, the coastal occupations represent lateral excursions into habitats that could hardly have provided, even at 9,000 or 10,000 B0, game and vegetal food resources comparable to those of the montane zones.

I have a subjective feeling that "openness" ranked high on the Paleo-Indian list of desirable habitat characteristics. Of course, given the limitations of most of our field and laboratory procedures, we are usually able to identify only the *hunting* aspect of Paleo-Indian culture in South America. Archeologists themselves take more pleasure in surveying open landscapes than closed thickets and forests, and the first object of a reconnaissance in archeologically unknown territory is to get results by finding sites. Still, it is remarkable that virtually all early sites in South America are found in environmental zones that would have been tundra, puna, páramo, steppe, savanna, or perhaps open thorn-forest landscapes. In addition, the early Andean sites are characteristically found near water, not only in the dry south-central Andes and at lower elevations but also where freshwater is readily available.

The distribution of sites is clearly related to the habits of the game animals and the hunting methods employed. South America lacks an equivalent to the Olsen-Chubbuck and Casper sites of the North American Plains, but it is reasonable to presume collective hunting, drives, and surrounds for herding and semigregarious animals. If we can extrapolate anything from the culture of the north Eurasian antecedents of American Paleo-Indians, communal hunting was a distinctive attribute, and possibly an innovation, of the Upper Paleolithic. Nevertheless, I must admit that there are no direct indications of Paleo-Indian hunting procedures in South America, beyond scattered charcoal flecks, suggesting fire drives, in the deposits of the lakeside Tagua-Tagua kill site (Chile) and suspicious concentrations of bone and artifacts at the Taima-Taima and Muaco "miring places." Perhaps the Talara Tar Seeps, with the Amotape campsites overlooking them at a distance of several hundred yards, were also used in that way. Then, too, there is some slight reinforcement from the drives and surrounds characteristic of much later Inca state hunts. In the end, our most useful indication of hunting procedure is probably the location of sites near and overlooking freshwater. Inasmuch as the hunters had effective long-range weapons, large game must have been stalked at watering places or perhaps hunted from stands situated along paths to and from water. At the relatively low-altitude Guitarrero Cave site, the predominance of foot bones of brocket deer suggests that the killing and butchering took place some distance away. Useless bones were left behind, while the meat was perhaps carried home in a hide bundle with the feet still attached; also, the feet may have been valued for their tendons or sinews. It is quite likely that hunting parties sometimes separated themselves from the rest of the group at base camps, to seek game at the lusher higher elevations. There the more open terrain and treeless landscape might well have encouraged group efforts. At the same time I am forced to admit that the high-altitude hunters' rockshelters, at least those with which I am familiar in Peru, are hardly spacious. Most could have protected only a few persons.

PALEO-INDIAN SUBSISTENCE

Few remains of game animals are known from early South American sites. Of those sites that are unequivocally early, there are a number which have yielded no faunal remains, or none which could be recovered or identified. Some such sites, with radiocarbon-dated occupations preceding 7000 BC and no reported fauna, include El Abra (Colombia), El Inga (Ecuador), Quiqche and Toquepala (Peru), Marazzi (Tierra del Fuego, Chile), and possibly Chivateros (Peru). There are, in fact, so few sites where faunal remains are accompanied by both a firm date and unquestionable stratigraphic association with cultural material that I must include in this survey some cases where either the association or the date is questionable.

Let us begin, then, in the north, with Venezuela. It is generally agreed that the apparently sealed association of mastodon and horse with artifacts in the gray-sand stratum at Taima-Taima must precede our cutoff date of 7000 BC, whatever the true age may be. The fauna collection from Taima-Taima is said to resemble that from the badly disturbed Muaco assemblage—much of which may be either earlier than any human activity or later than the Paleo-Indian use of Muaco. For whatever the list is worth, the Muaco fauna is said to include elephants (mastodon and stegomastodon), large extinct sloths (megatherium and mylodon), glyptodon (another large edentate with armadillolike carapace), toxodon (a rhinoceros-sized herbivore), extinct bear (arctotherium), extinct horse, a camelid, dire wolf, jaguar, lynx, rabbits, and a mustelid (Figure 10.10). The Garzón site in Colombia represents another

FIGURE 10.10
Pleistocene mammals hunted by Paleo-Indians in South America: *a*, paleolama; *b*, camelid; *c*, hippidium; *d*, arctotherium; *e*, mylodon; *f*, toxodon; *g*, capybara; *h*, megatherium; *i*, glyptodon.

reported association of megatherium and mastodon with man, but the authenticity of the chopper tools, the association, and the pre-Wisconsin date have all been questioned.

In Ecuador there are only two sites with radiocarbon ages greater than 7000 BC. Bone was not preserved at El Inga, most unfortunately, for that is the northernmost site with fishtail points. At Chobshi Cave the fauna is modern, and only one (8060 ± 430 BC) of the dates precedes 7000 BC. Nevertheless, the Chobshi collection, identified by Wing (personal communication) is interesting as one of the very few early South American archeological faunas to be described. White-tailed and pudu (*Pudu*) deer predominate, with brocket deer (*Mazama*) also possibly present. Rabbit (*Sylvilagus brasiliensis*) and paca (*Agouti taczanowski*) are fairly common, with opossum, porcupine, tapir, spectacled bear, a canine, and tinamou also identified.

On the north coast of Peru various workers have reported surface associations of artifacts (sometimes including pottery) with extinct mastodon, horse, armadillo, and capybara (Figure 10.10). Some of these cases inspire no more confidence than the early claims of mastodon in association with pottery and obsidian artifacts in northern Ecuador, but the recently discovered mastodon at La Cumbre, dated by the bone apatite method to 10,410 ± 700 and 8,585 ± 280 BC, is more credible. Some horse teeth were also found. However, it should be noted that all the artifacts were found on the surface, except for the base of a single, stemmed point, which was buried only 4 centimeters into the bone-bearing deposit. Ossa and Moseley (1972:14) caution that "the possibility of a legitimate stratigraphic association between artifacts and extinct fauna at La Cumbre exists but is tenuous. . . . The faunal and lithic remains found in the riachuelo must be considered a secondary association and nothing more." La Cumbre constitutes the only "proof" of Paleo-Indian status for the stemmed Paiján points.

On the other hand, at the nearby Quirihuac Shelter there is no question of the association of snail shells with simple artifacts and human skeletons dating, by a weighted average of six assays, to 8700 ± 180 BC. (The average date does not include the anomalous result of 2790 ± 210 BC on one sample.) Ossa speculates that the Quirihuac people may have consumed the snails as much for their high moisture content as for the slight food value.

We recovered three genera of snails from early preceramic contexts of Guitarrero Cave, but Thompson, our expert on terrestrial mollusks, warns that some of these may be natural inhabitants that chose to burrow in the loose deposits. Additional animals found in the Guitarrero I stratum (five dates from 10,610 ± 360 to 7,190 ± 90 BC) are brocket and possibly white-tailed deer, viscacha (a rabbit-sized high-altitude rodent), rabbit, hog-nosed skunk, small rodents, and tinamou. From the Guitarrero II strata (eight dates from 8585 ± 290 to 5625 ± 220 BC), Wing identified the bones of the same animals plus opossum, mouse opossum, a feline, duck, and frog or toad.

The major fauna from Lauricocha I and II, where Cardich conducted his pioneering excavations of the Peruvian Preceramic, includes llama and/or guanaco (the large camelids), the smaller vicuña, and taruca or huemal deer (*Hippocamelus antisensis*). Only the taruca is specifically mentioned as having been found in Lauricocha I, which has a date of 7575 ± 250 BC, but the implication is that all of the aforementioned species were found as well. Engel reports camelids, deer, small to medium-sized mammals, fish, and marine shellfish from Tres Ventanas I (8080 ± 170 BC), a cave on the western slopes of the Peruvian Andes.

The similar Huanta and Puente occupations in levels K to H at Jaywamachay (Ayacucho, Peru) have dates of 7510 ± 145, 6695 ± 140, and 7030 ± 140 BC. MacNeish reports horse, deer, and llama from these cultural contexts. MacNeish's Pacaicasa and Ayacucho levels at the Pikimachay site, which by all reckonings assuredly date well before 7000 BC, are said to include the megatherium, the rhinoceros-sized *Scelidotherium,* lesser *Scelidotherium,* and Andean horse. Modern elements include a camelid, deer, canid (*Dusicyon*), puma, skunk, viscacha, and another Andean rodent (*Phylotis*).

González wrote long ago of the surface find of a glyptodon carapace at the Ayampitín-type site in northwest Argentina. Eight dates on sloth dung, bone, sticks, and charcoal from Gruta del Indio (Mendoza) range from 21,540 ± 1,040 to 6,095 ± 55 BC and cluster around 9000 BC, according to Lagiglia. If the sloth dung were not so plentiful, and *Mylodon listai* were not a cave dweller himself, one would be happier about trusting the association with artifacts. Still, it seems safe to join Long and Martin (1974) in viewing this Argentine cave as an example of Paleo-Indian "overkill." Recent work by Lagiglia, Long, and Martin suggests, alternatively, that human occupation might have followed upon, or at least might not have been entirely contemporary with, that of the mylodons. Martin points out that sloths may have brought in sticks, later to be used as convenient dry firewood by human inhabitants—and as radiocarbon samples by archeologists.

Only preliminary reports are available for Tagua-Tagua I, a lakeside hunting and possibly camping site in central Chile. The small industry from the lowest level lacks projectile points, but the major game animals (mastodon, horse, and deer) suggest that this is a result of chance. Some of the bones show clear butchering scars, and the charcoal date (9430 ± 320 BC) is appropriate for the Paleo-Indian orientation. Montane also records the recovery of canid, rodent, bird, frog, and fish bones.

The association of now extinct fauna with stone tools in the caves at Hacienda Los Toldos (Patagonia) was originally problematical in that Menghin had extracted only a single horse tooth. However, in his 1973 and 1974 excavations in Cave 3, Cardich found horse, guanaco, canid, rodent (*Cavidae*), rhea, and tinamou (*Eudromia*) bones in the Toldense levels, which have a terminal date of 8750 ± 480 BC. Cardich (1973) specifically mentions only guanaco for the underlying level II, which carries a determination of 10,650 ± 600 BC. No cultural association with the sloth and horse remains from Eberhardt (Mylodon) Cave is claimed today; in fact Saxon's recent excavations indicate alternating occupations by sloths and guanaco hunters.

Nevertheless, the ninth millennium BC dates are still suggestive of Paleo-Indian hunting.

Finally, no review of Paleo-Indian sites in South America would be complete without mention of Bird's initial proof of the contemporaneity of Pleistocene fauna and fishtail points in Tierra del Fuego. Since the Fell's Cave I deposit was sealed by a roof fall, the Fell's Cave I association of artifacts with dates of 9050 ± 170 and 8770 ± 300 BC on charcoal, together with bones of horse (*Parahipparion*), mylodon, and guanaco, is beyond question. Palli Aike Cave is a similar, somewhat less certain, case.

Although the evidence is meager and at times controversial, a few generalizations about Paleo-Indian subsistence are possible. Whatever their dietary importance, elephants were hunted in South America as well as in North America, to judge by the evidence from Tagua-Tagua, Taima-Taima, and maybe La Cumbre. Bones of horse occur at the same sites, but also at Pikimachay, Jaywamachay, Los Toldos, Fell's Cave, and, in less certain association, at Palli Aike. Horse, then, is the most nearly ubiquitous of the now extinct Paleo-Indian game animals. It is found at seven of the sites with secure or reasonably probable associations. Perhaps horses were the last of the major Pleistocene animals to be driven to extinction, or, equally likely, they were numerous, relatively easy to hunt, and no great problem to butcher and eat.

Solitary ground sloths occur with surprising frequency, but they were probably slow, stupid, and unused to predation. Even so, the elephant-sized megatheriums from Taima-Taima and Pikimachay and the not much smaller *Scelidotherium* from the latter site would have been formidable opponents. The lesser *Scelidotherium* from Pikimachay and the mylodons at Taima-Taima, Fell's Cave, and Gruta del Indio must have been easier game in many ways.

If the sample were larger, I would argue strongly that horse and ground sloth were proportionately more important than elephants to South American Paleo-Indians. Surely, mylodons and horses were easy game compared with the proboscidians and the North American bison; in any event, native horse and giant sloth became extinct almost as soon as we have proof that they were hunted. If giant armadillos survived until the end of the Pleistocene, they were likely prey too, but there are no certain associations with men.

Deer or camelids were apparently hunted concurrently with the Pleistocene megafauna in the central and southern Andes (Pikimachay, Jaywamachay, Tagua-Tagua, Los Toldos, and Fell's Cave). Our meager data suggest that as the major postglacial extinctions progressed Paleo-Indians were forced to reorient their economy increasingly towards deer, camelids, and other more diverse resources. Wing (1975) has begun to demonstrate this nicely for the animal food sources through her studies of species diversity and equitability or degree of dependence on a single species. In a preliminary comparative analysis of the bones from sites in the Peruvian Andes, she computes high values for both species diversity and equitable spread of dependence at, for example, Guitarrero Cave and Rosamachay (a late preceramic site in the Ayacucho Valley). In later sites, as the camelids are domesticated and bred for wool, meat, and burden bearing, these values tend to drop. More complete studies on more reliable data should show that intensive specialization is a characteristic of both the initial Paleo-Indian adaptation and sedentary agriculture but not of the period of transition.

At any rate, several species of deer (which live in the central Andes above 2000 meters) and the various camelids (whose natural range is characteristically above 3000 meters) became the major big-game animals in the latter part of the Paleo-Indian tradition, or what Willey calls the Old South American Hunting tradition (9000 to 7000 BC). Where soil conditions allow the preservation of bone, virtually all sites from this period include the remains of cervids and camelids. The camelids became progressively more important; two forms (llama and alpaca) were eventually domesticated, but, as in North America, deer have remained important up to the present.

In fortunate situations where smaller and more fragile bones have escaped destruction, and where specialized zoological study has been possible, it is apparent that Paleo-Indians used a wide variety of animals. However, a degree of caution is indicated here; some rodents, cats, and especially skunks from Guitarrero and Pikimachay cannot be proved to have been game rather than coincidental cave dwellers. Wing's intensive zooarcheological analyses may establish that the proper ratios of bones within species that would indicate natural site inhabitants, living and dying in the cave, are not present. Butchering techniques can also be determined not only from scars on bone but also by the conspicuous absence of certain bones from the faunal sample. If some bones are more regularly charred than others, this will tell us something about cooking habits. Other elements of the small mammal fauna identified at late Paleo-Indian sites were surely hunted or trapped and eaten. These include rabbit, viscacha, and tapir, which are still considered to be good game in the central Andean zone. Opossum and especially porcupine are so easy to take that they must have been utilized occasionally.

My favorite Paleo-Indian game animal is the tinamou bird, found in Guitarrero I and II deposits and at Chobshi and Los Toldos Caves (Figure 10.11). Members of the Tinamidae range in size from "quail" to "chicken," and they are all equally delectable. Considering how poorly small and fragile bird bones normally fare in site deposits, and observing the frequency with which tinamou bones have been recovered and identified, I conclude that these birds constituted a relatively important meat source. Beyond the issue of taste, this is understandable since all tinamous are ground nesters and most are reluctant fliers. These birds typically prefer to run for cover when alarmed by predators, although Weeks (1973 and personal communication) has found that they are easily flushed by dogs. (It is noteworthy that canid bones were found at Chobshi and Los Toldos, along with tinamou, as well as at Tagua-Tagua where fire drives are suspected.) Like North and Central

American turkeys, which similarly prefer to evade danger on foot, tinamous may have been flushed into trees where they would have provided stationary targets. American Indians also lured turkeys with decoys and calls. This would have been especially effective with the tinamous, for they can be easily "whistled" by mimicking their simple calls. Finally, like rabbits, tinamous habitually run paths through the grass and low brush, and thus they are easily snared and trapped. The incomplete remains of snares and traps are not easy to identify archeologically, but we have collected knotted cordage, spiral interlinking, and twined basketry from secure ninth millennium BC contexts (Complex II a) at Guitarrero Cave. It is evident that Andean Paleo-Indians had the technological capacity to construct snares and game nets.

It is obviously less than coincidental that the Tinamidae occur chiefly in the same grasslands habitats in which early South Americans and their major game were at home. The much larger, ostrichlike rhea (identified at Los Toldos I) is also a grasslands bird, similar to the flightless moa hunted to extinction by the first inhabitants of New Zealand (Figure 10.11). Perhaps the simple but effective *bolas* weapon was used against the rhea, as it was in later times. Archeologists have probably underemphasized birds (a duck was also identified in Guitarrero II), and especially ground-dwelling birds, as potential early game animals.

On either continent, Paleo-Indians were clearly gatherers as well as hunters, but the evidence of early gathering in South America is minimal. Snails are documented in Peru at Quirihuac Rockshelter and Guitarrero Cave, but aside from Engel's isolated reference to Tres Ventanas there are no signs that people resorted to freshwater and marine mollusks until later times. If they were indeed collected, bird eggs would be less likely to find their way back to occupation sites, and the shell fragments would be less likely to be recognized by archeologists. Nevertheless, bird eggs are an obvious and widely available, if largely seasonal, food; the abundant, shiny, and brightly colored tinamou eggs are one such prominent possibility.

The role of plant foods is not yet known. Many wild tuberous plants that characteristically mature in July and August just before the coldest weather of the dry austral winter can be easily dug in the central Andes (Figures 10.12–10.17). Engel claims to have recovered potato, jiquima, sweet potato, and perhaps olluco in all levels of the Tres Ventanas Caves; however, he also extracted agave, or maguey, which botanists and historians believe was introduced from Mexico in colonial times, from all levels of the deposits. Grinding stones were found in the lowest levels too, and these are not otherwise known in Paleo-Indian contexts (except, possibly, at Lauricocha and Guitarrero). These uncertainties notwithstanding, many Andean seed and fruit crops are available during the sunny austral winter at varying intervals after the heavy rains cease in April.

a

b

FIGURE 10.11
Ground-dwelling birds hunted by Paleo-Indians in South America: *a*, tinamou; *b*, rhea.

FIGURE 10.12
Common native South American tuber and root plants—olluco: *a*, plant; *b*, tuber; *c*, branch.

FIGURE 10.13
Common native South American tuber and root plants—achira: *a*, plant; *b*, corm; *c*, branch.

FIGURE 10.14
Common native South American tuber and root plants—jiquima or jícama: *a*, plant; *b*, root; *c*, branch.

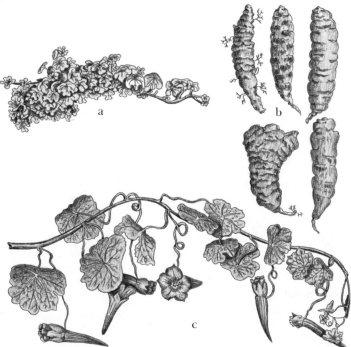

FIGURE 10.15
Common native South American tuber and root plants—añu: *a*, branch; *b*, tubers; *c*, flowering branch.

486

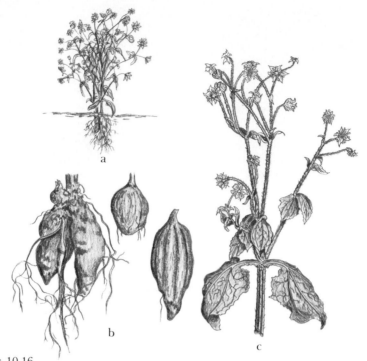

FIGURE 10.16
Common native South American tuber and root plants—yacón or jiquima: *a*, plant; *b*, tuberous roots; *c*, flowering branch.

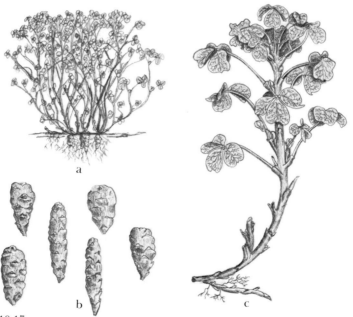

FIGURE 10.17
Common native South American tuber and root plants—oca: *a*, plant; *b*, tubers; *c*, branch.

The end of the Paleo-Indian horizon can be somewhat arbitrarily set at 7000 BC. At about this time numerous domestic beans and pods appear in firmly documented Guitarrero II contexts that are entirely free of signs of contamination or mixture with more recent material. These common beans, as well as the "hot" Andean pepper (*Capsicum*), were probably cultivated as early as 8500 BC. By the same date the inhabitants of Guitarrero Cave were also digging tubers and rhizomes, some related to the modern cultivar oca (*Oxalis*) and others possibly to olluco (*Ullucus*). According to C. Earle Smith, who has studied the remains, the morphology of these plants is insufficiently known to allow confident identification of genus and species. Neither is it possible to tell whether they were wild or cultivated. The same qualifications apply to Smith's identifications of fruits related to lulo or cocona (*Solanum hispidum*).

To both Smith and me, it is remarkable that the Andean utilization of tuberous and rhizomatous plants for carbohydrates appears so early in the sequence. Peppers and other fruits contributed vitamins, minerals, and flavor to the diet, then as now. Primitive Indian corn, or maize, comes from Complex III at Guitarrero Cave, which probably dates sometime after 4000 BC, and corn is a carbohydrate supplement rather than replacement for the root crops and beans.

I should note in conclusion that by 4000 BC agriculture was well underway throughout nuclear America; thus, it is clear that before 7000 BC Paleo-Indians must already have been paying considerable attention to the plants as well as to the animals in their environment. The abundant, efficiently hunted, and largely predatorless megafauna must have been basic to the rapid expansion of Paleo-Indian culture and peoples. Somewhat like the North American fur hunters of colonial times, they rapidly crossed continental expanses in the search of virgin resources. Inevitably, the large Pleistocene mammals were quickly overhunted, and attention soon shifted to lesser and more readily available sources of food. Finally, I might add that one encouraging new trend in archeology, which may be observed in many of the works cited herein, is a movement away from arbitrary isolative cultural categorizations and toward serious investigation of the transition to a more diversified subsistence base.

ACKNOWLEDGMENT

Portions of this chapter were adapted from a paper presented at the IXth International Congress of Prehistoric and Protohistoric Sciences. Additional bibliographic references are cited in that article (Lynch 1976).

References Cited and
Recommended Sources

Beltrão, Maria C. M. C. 1974 Datacões arqueológicas mais antigas do Brasil. *Anales da Academia Brasileira de Ciencia* 46:211–251.

Bird, Junius B. 1969 A comparison of south Chilean and Ecuadorian "fishtail" projectile points. Kroeber Anthropological Society Papers 40:52–71.

Bloom, Arthur L. 1971 Glacial-eustatic and isostatic controls of sea level since the last glaciation. *In* The Late Cenozoic Glacial Ages, ed. K. K. Turekian. New Haven: Yale University Press.

Bryan, Alan L. 1973 Paleoenvironments and cultural diversity in Late Pleistocene South America. Quaternary Research 3:237–256.

———. 1975 Paleoenvironments and cultural diversity in Late Pleistocene South America: a rejoinder to Vance Haynes and a reply to Thomas Lynch. Quaternary Research 5:151–159.

Cardich, Augusto, Lucio A. Cardich, and Adam Hajduk 1973 Secuencia arqueológica y cronologia radiocarbónica de la cueva 3 de Los Toldos (Santa Cruz, Argentina). Relaciones (Sociedad Argentina de Antropologia) (New Series) 7:85–123.

Damuth, John E., and R. W. Fairbridge 1970 Equatorial Atlantic deep-sea arkosic sands and ice-age aridity in tropical South America. Geological Society of America Bulletin 81:189–206.

Emiliani, Cesare et al. 1975 Paleoclimatological analysis of late Quaternary cores from the northeastern Gulf of Mexico. Science 189:1083–1087.

Fairbridge, Rhodes W. 1976 Effects of Halocene climatic change on some tropical geomorphic processes. Quaternary Research 6:529–556.

Fernández, Jorge 1971 La edad de la piedra en la Puna de Atacama. Revista del Instituto de Antropología (Tucumán) (New Series) 1:9–136.

Forbis, Richard G. 1974 The Paleoamericans. *In* Prehispanic America, ed. S. Gorenstein. New York: St. Martin's Press.

Gruhn, Ruth n.d. A preliminary report on the finds at Los Tapiales, a Paleo-Indian site in the mountains of Totonicapán, Guatemala. Unpublished manuscript. Department of Anthropology, University of Alberta, Edmonton.

Haynes, C. Vance 1974 Paleoenvironments and cultural diversity in Late Pleistocene South America: a reply to A. L. Bryan. Quaternary Research 4:378–382.

Hester, James J. 1966 Late Pleistocene environments and early man in South America. The American Naturalist 100:377–388.

Heusser, Calvin J. 1974 Vegetation and climate of the southern Chilean Lake District during and since the last interglaciation. Quaternary Research 4:290–315.

Krieger, Alex D. 1964 Early man in the New World. *In* Prehistoric Man in the New World, ed. J. Jennings and E. Norbeck. Chicago: University of Chicago Press.

Lanning, Edward P. 1970 Pleistocene man in South America. World Archaeology 2:90–111.

Lanning, Edward P., and T. C. Patterson 1967 Early man in South America. Scientific American 217:5:44–50.

LePaige, Gustave 1970 Industrias líticas de San Pedro de Atacama. Santiago de Chile: Editorial Orbe.

———. 1971 Paleolitico en el sureste del Salar de Atacama: Tulan. Actas del VI Congreso de Arqueología Chilena, pp. 151–161.

Long, Austin, and Paul S. Martin 1974 Death of American ground sloths. Science 186:638–640.

Lothrop, S. K. 1961 Early migrations to Central and South America: an anthropological problem in the light of other sciences. Journal of the Royal Anthropological Institute 91:97–123.

Lynch, Thomas F. 1974 The antiquity of man in South America. Quaternary Research 4:356–377.

———. 1976 The entry and postglacial adaptation of man in Andean South America. Proceedings of the IXth International Congress of Prehistoric and Protohistoric Sciences, Section IV, Colloque XVII.

MacNeish, Richard S., T. C. Patterson, and D. L. Browman 1975 The Central Peruvian Prehistoric Interaction Sphere. Andover, Mass.: R.S. Peabody Foundation for Archaeology.

Mercer, J. H. 1972 Chilean glacial chronology 20,000 to 11,000 carbon-14 years ago: some global comparisons. Science 176:1118–1120.

Ossa, Paul, and M. E. Moseley 1972 La Cumbre: a preliminary report on research into the early lithic occupation of the Moche Valley, Peru, Ñawpa Pacha 9:1–16.

Patterson, Thomas C. 1973 *America's Past: A New World Archaeology*. Glenview, Ill.: Scott, Foresman and Company.

Porter, Stephen C. 1975 Equilibrium-line altitudes of late Quaternary glaciers in the Southern Alps, New Zealand. Quaternary Research 5:27–47.

Ranere, Anthony J. n.d. Early human adaptations to New World tropical forests: the view from Panama. Ph.D. dissertation, University of California, Davis.

Richardson, James B., III 1973 The preceramic sequence and the Pleistocene and post-Pleistocene climate of northwest Peru. *In* Variation in Anthropology. ed. D. W. Lathrop. Urbana: Illinois Archaeological Survey.

———. 1975 Early man on the Peruvian north coast. early maritime exploitation and the Pleistocene and Holocene environment. Paper presented at the 13th Pacific Science Congress, Vancouver.

Sánchez, W. A., and J. E. Kutzbach 1974 Climate of the American tropics and subtropics in the 1960's and possible comparisons with climatic variations of the last millennium. Quaternary Research 4:128–135.

Sauer, Carl O. 1944 A geographic sketch of early man in America. Geographical Review 34:529–573.

Schobinger, Juan 1972 Nuevos hallazgos de puntas "colas de pescado," y consideraciones en torno al origen y dispensión de la cultura de cazadores superiores toldense (Fell I) en Sudamérica. Proceedings of the 40th International Congress of Americanists, Rome-Genoa.

Simpson-Vuilleumier, Beryl 1971 Pleistocene changes in the fauna and flora of South America. Science 173:771–780.

Simpson, Beryl B. 1975 Glacial climates in the eastern tropical South Pacific. Nature 253:34–36.

van der Hammen, T. 1972 Changes in vegetation and climate in the Amazon Basin and surrounding areas during the Pleistocene. Geologie en Mijnbouw 51:641–643.

———. 1974 The Pleistocene changes of vegetation and climate in tropical South America. Journal of Biogeography 1:3–26.

Weeks, Sam E. 1973 The behavior of the red-winged Tinamou, *Rhynchotus rufescens*. Zoologica-1973 (New York Zoological Society):13–40.

Willey, Gordon R. 1971 An Introduction to American Archaeology, Vol. 2: South America. Englewood Cliffs, N.J.: Prentice-Hall.

Wing, Elizabeth S. 1975 Hunting and herding in the Peruvian Andes. *In* Archaeozoological Studies, ed. A. T. Clason. Amsterdam: North Holland Press.

A stone figure from Chan Chan.

CHAPTER ELEVEN

The Evolution of Andean Civilization

Michael E. Moseley

Dr. Moseley objects to the "horizon framework" traditionally used to structure Peruvian archeology because it "requires the pigeonholing of complex phenomena in one or another epoch of unity or disunity" and gives a distorted picture of human history in this area as having consisted of "static epochs suddenly replaced by other epochs of similar nature," with no mechanism for change except "radical diffusion." Instead, Moseley envisions the evolution of civilization in the Andes as a continuous process, where cultural interaction and ecological pressures are stronger forces for change than the "radical" forces of "invasion and conquest or proselytism and conversion."

In 1532 the largest native empire ever to arise in the New World toppled from the impact of European technology and disease as Pizarro's conquistadores spread like a fungus into the political veins of Tawantinsuyu. Tawantinsuyu—"Land of the Four Quarters," as the Inca called their sprawling realm—stretched more than 4300 kilometers along the mountainous Andean backbone of South America. Cuzco, the imperial capital, exercised political hegemony over northern Chile, the uplands of Argentina, Bolivia, Peru, and Ecuador, as well as the southern frontier of Colombia. There is today no Andean nation of comparable magnitude.

The masters of Tawantinsuyu ruled, by virtue of armed conquest, every major state and polity comprising South American civilization. Inca armies—like their earlier Roman counterparts—marched beyond the frontiers of native civilization to dominate a heterogeneous population and diverse congeries of societies. The Inca attempted to reduce ethnic diversity by combining different tribal and political groups into larger territorial units for administrative purposes. However, this still left Tawantinsuyu with more than 80 governmental provinces reflecting earlier ethnic differences. Linguistic variance was equally pronounced and cumbersome, requiring the Inca to impose their own tongue, Quechua, as the medium of government communication and the lingua franca of the realm.

ANDEAN ARCHEOLOGY

One aim of Andean archeology is to elucidate the origin and development of the societies and institutions that were the components of Tawantinsuyu, in order to understand the evolutionary processes affecting the dynamics of civilization in general.

The dynamics of Andean civilization assumed various configurations in different places at different times. The traditional methodology for dealing with variation in space and time has been to divide Tawantinsuyu into geographical areas, outline man's occupational history in each, and then correlate events in the different areas. Figure 11.1 shows the conventional area divisions of Andean civilization that formed the core region of Tawantinsuyu.

Defining geographical units is an easy, if arbitrary, matter; documenting man's development in each region is not. Nowhere is the archeological record fully preserved; neither has the preserved sector been studied with adequate sampling for the solution of more than simple problems. An inadequate data base encourages the projection of generalizations, drawn from evidence in one setting, to other settings in space or time where comparable documentation does not exist. This situation makes the correlation of different past events in different areas difficult. In principle, correlations are established by associating objects produced or designed in one region, at a known time and in a known social context, with those of another region in a similar controlled context. In practice, less exacting procedures and less complete data are employed.

The Inca state provides the most pervasive archeological model for both covert assumptions and overt, formal criteria employed in assessing interregional unity and correlations. More than 90 percent of Tawantinsuyu was conquered by the Inca within a span of four generations. Because consolidation lasted only a century or less before the Spanish Conquest, Inca dominance is conceptualized as a widespread but short-lived political "horizon."

The horizon analog was first used in Andean archeology at the turn of the century by the German scholar Max Uhle. In Europe he studied cultural materials from the two important sites of Cuzco and Tiahuanaco. The latter settlement, located in Bolivia, was reported by the Inca to have been abandoned before the spread of Tawantinsuyu. While excavating ancient graves in widely scattered areas along the coast of Peru, Uhle later found artifacts which he believed to have been produced at the two sites or to have been copies of such products. The Cuzco and Tiahuanaco materials were generally separate and underlain by graves or other remains whose design and expression varied from region to region. Uhle treated past art styles as being tightly

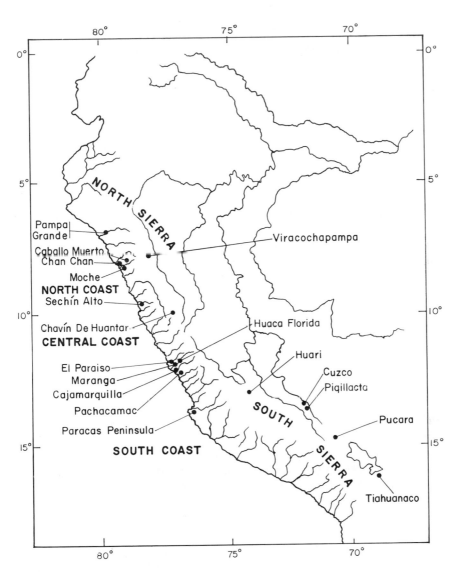

FIGURE 11.1
Archeological sites and areas of Peru.

linked with past societies, and interpreted his finds as patterns of cultural heterogeneity followed by unity. Because Inca unity was a product of political conquest, the earlier manifestation of areal correlation expressed in Tiahuanaco-affiliated grave goods was assumed to be an analogous militaristic horizon, but of smaller scope. This carried the implication that the evolution of Andean civilization was characterized by times of cultural heterogeneity followed by consolidation in progressively larger political horizons.

This model was expanded and modified by the Peruvian archeologists Julio C. Tello and Rafael Larco Hoyle, who, in the 1930s, argued for an even earlier expression of the horizon phenomenon. The highland site of Chavin de Huantar was seen as the center and archetype of a widely diffused art style interpreted as religious in nature and as having been spread by a proselytizing cult. The implication was that native horizons evolved from sacred to secular in nature.

The horizon framework and its implicit evolutionary connotations have dominated Andean archeology for the last half-century. The strength and usefulness of the scheme lay in its ability to organize diverse data from widely separated regions. There are two approaches to the integrative function of the framework. The first employs horizons to define relative periods of time. In theory, archeological remains are then dated by independent means and placed in the appropriate chronological period. The second approach is evolutionary in inspiration and sees native civilization as having developed through a series of progressively more complex stages, three of which correspond to the recognized horizons. In theory, archeological remains can be assigned to one or another stage on the basis of their complexity, form, and degree of elaboration. Stages are sometimes treated as time periods, thus overlapping with the first approach. Figure 11.2 combines two currently popular examples of the horizon space-time framework.

The weakness of the horizon framework is its classificatory nature, which requires the pigeonholing of complex phenomena in one or another epoch of unity or disunity. The resulting historical perspective is one of static epochs suddenly replaced by other epochs of similar nature, and the only means of accounting for cultural change is radical diffusion: invasion and conquest or proselytism and conversion. Classification is, of course, not explanation, nor is radical diffusion the mechanism of cultural adaptation and evolution.

An understanding of certain aspects of Andean civilization can be developed by means of the direct historical approach that uses Tawantinsuyu as a model for interpreting earlier societies. Arguing by analogy from Inca to pre-Inca peoples is most successful when one is dealing with social and political institutions and least successful when one is dealing with specific historical events. For example, the horizon concept inspired by Tawantinsuyu suffers from the uniqueness of the Incas' political fortunes. The empire expanded rapidly and then collapsed even more quickly as a result of foreign influence. There is little reason to suppose earlier states had similar unusual

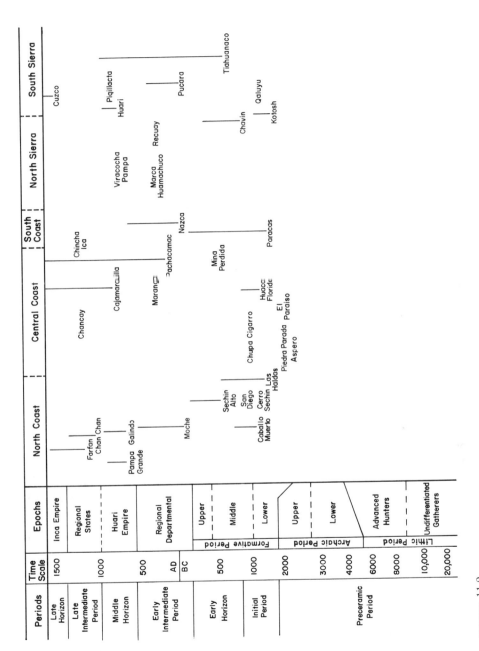

FIGURE 11.2
Stages and periods in Peruvian archeology.

histories. On the other hand, at the institutional level neither the Inca nor their predecessors utilized currency or a monetary system. Here it is reasonable to suppose that the taxation system and other economic principles that underwrote Tawantinsuyu had earlier Andean precedents and that arguments by analogy are legitimate.

GEOGRAPHY OF THE FOUR QUARTERS

The land of the four quarters stretched over one of the most rugged mountain chains on the face of the earth. Consequently, geography had a profound influence upon peoples' lives and the development of civilization. The Andes can be conceptualized as a vast rock wedge driven longitudinally up the continent's western edge to form the spine of South America. The wedge is both wider and generally higher in southern than in northern Tawantinsuyu. The lithic bit is narrow and low in Ecuador before splaying out northward like the fractured cutting edge of a chisel.

Viewed literally, the rocky shim produces a threefold split in the geography. West of the highland massif lies a low and narrow coastal plain abutting the Pacific Ocean, while east of the mountain wall sprawl the immense tropical flatlands of Amazonia. Where the Andes are wide and high in the south, the tripartite split is most pronounced. In the north, as the lithic bit narrows and drops, distinctions between eastern and western lowlands begin to diminish and greater similarities in physical and cultural environments prevail.

Climatic conditions range from dry and cool in the south to moist and warm in the north. This, however, is not a simple gradient. It is crosscut by altitudinal variation introduced via contrasting topographic relief. In general, conditions vary from warm and very dry on the western coastal plain, through cool and moderately moist in the central mountains (called the sierra), to hot and wet in the eastern tropical lowlands (the selva).

Tawantinsuyu embraced great variation in landforms. The edges of the sierra wedge are demarcated by two towering mountain chains called the Eastern and Western Cordilleras. In the south they are connected by a high, flat plain of great width known as the *altiplano*. In the north the river headwaters of the Amazon have cut deep gorges through the Eastern Cordillera and the progressively narrower altiplano. Given this topographic pattern, the sierra has more flat land in the south than in the north, and a more developed eastward than westward drainage system.

The administrative dividing lines of Tawantinsuyu's four great quarters ran approximately north-south and east-west, meeting and crossing at the imperial hub of Cuzco. This was not simply a bureaucratic carving up of western South America but a general expression of Inca cognizance of the physical and cultural geography of the state (Figure 11.3). Taken loosely,

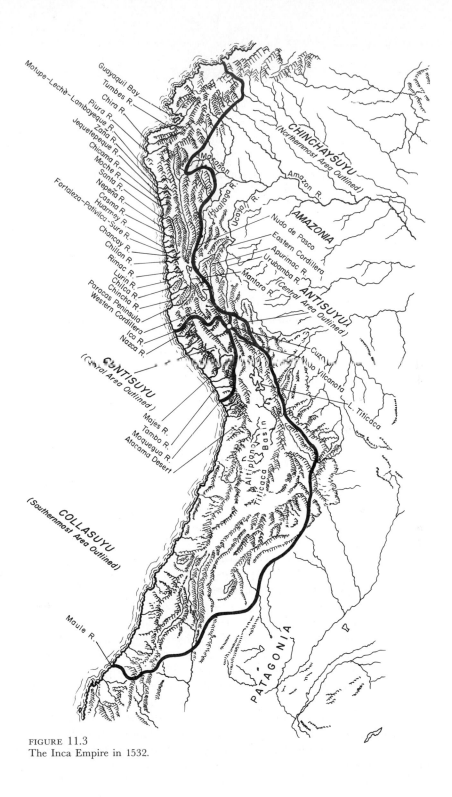

FIGURE 11.3
The Inca Empire in 1532.

the individual quarters of Tawantinsuyu serve as a useful device for summarizing man's adaptation to the diverse physical environments of the Andes.

Collasuyu

Collasuyu was the largest and most southerly of the four quarters. It included the key Titicaca Basin as well as the rest of upland Bolivia, northern Argentina, and Chile.

The Andes are a simple, single chain of mountains in southern Collasuyu. Further north a high, flat plateau stretches between the Eastern and Western Cordilleras and extends northward about 1600 kilometers to near latitude 14° south. This great central mountain plain, or altiplano, is the largest expanse of uninterrupted flatland in Tawantinsuyu. The potential utility of the favorable topography is, however, limited by aridity and altitude.

In Collasuyu's central plain, man found his most amenable environment in the region of Lake Titicaca, which lies on the Bolivian-Peruvian border. The lake is situated at the north end of an extensive landlocked basin some 800 kilometers long, at an altitude of 3800 meters. The north end of the Titicaca Basin is sheltered by a mountain rim, and the area is warmer, with a more constant temperature (about 7°C), than the southern altiplano. More important, however, is the fact that the northern basin receives between 50 and 75 centimeters of annual precipitation. Here rainfall promoted agriculture and animal husbandry which in turn supported the human population density requisite for the development of complex social and political institutions.

High altitude exerted stringent selection factors, and economic adaptation to the altiplano assumed unique forms. Man built his subsistence pattern around specialized domesticates adjusted to a narrow life zone lying between about 3700 meters and the upper alpine limit of plant growth. Plant staples included tubers, principally potatoes (*Solanum tuberosum*), and grains, primarily quinoa (*Chenopodium quinoa*).

Highland animal domesticates included the muscovy duck and the cavy, or guinea pig, as well as the llama and alpaca. Much of the altiplano is either too dry or too high to be exploited by the tuber-quinoa complex and supports only low grassy plants, such as *ichu*. These grasslands, called *puna*, are of no direct utility to man without cameloid intermediaries. In effect, the llama and alpaca allowed man to move above the altitudinal limits of agriculture and extract a livelihood from an enormous but otherwise useless region.

The altiplano subsistence pattern is, then, altitudinally stratified, with puna herding lying above and penetrating into a lower tuber-quinoa economic stratum. This in turn overlies other agricultural strata that developed to meet conditions at various lower elevations.

Antisuyu

Antisuyu was the eastward-facing quarter of Tawantinsuyu, overlooking the vast Amazonian forest. The region included highland areas west and north of Cuzco, but the most striking geographical feature is the eastern slopes of the Andes, where the Cordillera falls rapidly from puna to lowland jungle floor. A very high degree of biotic diversity is compressed into narrow, stratified ecological zones that follow the contours of the mountain faces. These are of two sorts: unforested regions and heavily vegetated regions, called *montaña*, which start at 900 to 1500 meters.

The slopes of Antisuyu hold a great range of resources, the exploitation of which has fostered different degrees of economic specialization. Much of the subsistence technology and most of the domesticates used in exploiting the mountainsides either are more developed in or are principal adaptations in other higher or lower areas of Tawantinsuyu. In general, the region does not, and did not, support the density of population found in other quarters.

Cuntisuyu

Cuntisuyu is the southwesternmost and smallest coastal quarter of Tawantinsuyu, with boundaries stretching out of Cuzco and cutting the Pacific coast near the Ica Valley and the more southerly Moquegua Valley. The territory includes puna, sierra basins, and coastal desert. The Western Cordillera is the dominant structural feature. The mountains combine with prevailing wind currents to promote showers east of the continental divide, but they inhibit precipitation to the west. Most years the coast is completely dry, while 120 to 160 kilometers away, more than 50 centimeters of rain falls seasonally in the uplands and drains into the Amazon. The highlands are broken by mountain basins and are often dissected by narrow valleys. This rough topography distinguishes Cuntisuyu from the flat but elevated plains to the south.

Reflecting dramatic differences in rainfall, the barren Pacific slopes of Cuntisuyu stand in marked contrast to the montaña flanking Antisuyu. Generally, no rain falls below about 1800 meters, and south of Ecuador the coastal lands of Tawantinsuyu constitute one of the driest, bleakest habitats on the globe. Nonetheless, two resource complexes—one marine and the other riparian—support large, stable human populations.

A narrow band of ocean currents, paralleling the coast from latitude 9° south through Cuntisuyu and into northern Collasuyu, supports the richest marine biomass of the Western Hemisphere, if not in all the world's oceans. For millennia, these resources have supported great numbers of people, and their present economic importance is no less than 'it was in the past.

Streams and small rivers were the other resource complex utilized by man in western Cuntisuyu, and in western Tawantinsuyu in general. With head-waters at or near the continental divide, these channels collect a minority of highland runoff and then cascade down the arid side of the Cordillera in steep-sided valleys before discharging their water westward into the Pacific. Fifteen short water courses, 16 to 32 kilometers apart, cross the desert of Cuntisuyu and derive economic importance from irrigation agriculture based on large canals that divert water onto arable desert lands.

The availability of relatively flat land influences coastal irrigation just as it does highland agriculture. Within Tawantinsuyu the configuration of the coastal plain varies not only in width but also in altitude. Mountains push out into the Pacific along the coast of central Peru, and there is no flat coastal shelf. But near the northern border of Cuntisuyu the Cordillera and the sea pull apart, creating a shoreline plain that reaches widths of some 80 kilometers, offering considerable topographic potential for irrigation agri-culture. In the case of the Ica Valley there is more potentially arable land than there is water to irrigate it, and water availability determines the level of agricultural output. This situation is typical of most, but not all, other valleys. The reverse occurs farther south with the Rios Majes and Tambo. These are large rivers, unlike the Ica, but they lie in channels incised far below the high coastal plain. Great quantities of water flow into the sea be-cause man does not have the technology to raise the runoff from the sunken channels onto the desert.

Collasuyu has broadly similar though less frequent streams along its mountain flanks, but less rain falls in the southern Cordillera and the coastal drainages do not exhibit great potential. North of Cuntisuyu the situation changes and hydrographic or topographic conditions are often particularly favorable to coastal irrigation.

Chinchaysuyu

Embracing all of Ecuador and more than two-thirds of Peru, Chinchaysuyu was the second largest quarter of Tawantinsuyu. The territory, reaching from Pacific coast to Amazonian montaña and stretching from Cuzco past Quito, encompassed a greater range of geographical and topographical diversity than any other section of Tawantinsuyu. Likewise, the available resources were the most diverse and abundant of the Inca realm. The most sophisticated Andean societies, as well as the largest states to battle Inca political hegemony, had homelands in Chinchaysuyu.

The northern quarter of the Inca Empire is warmer and wetter than the southern quarter and is warmest and wettest in the north. There is also a marked difference in the topography of the highlands. Just below Cuzco a transverse mountain range, called the Nudo Vilcanota, links the Eastern and Western Cordilleras, and the vast upland prairies of Collasuyu end here. To

the north, other nudos cut Chinchaysuyu, and other parallel ranges lie between the Eastern and Western Cordilleras. This rocky grid of mountain
chains with transecting nudos is, in turn, incised by torrential rivers feeding
Andean runoff to the Amazon.

The effects of the splintered topography are pronounced. The puna grades
into the lower, better-watered *páramo* but occurs as isolated towering islands
or long, meandering, flat-topped ridges. Although these upland meadows
become progressively more lush to the north, their total surface area dwindles,
and the economic role of cameloid herding drops accordingly.

Man's occupation of highland Chinchaysuyu has been most intense in
the eastward-draining river valleys, more in the upper elevations nearer the
puna than the montaña. This is because the valleys are wider and more basin
shaped and water courses less incised at higher altitudes. With decreasing
elevation, rivers collect more water and gain greater velocity, thereby cutting
troughlike gorges with limited arable land.

Settlement in the higher, wider basins was pronounced in the headwaters
of the Rios Marañon, Huallaga, Santa, Mantaro, Apurimac, and Urubamba.
Here man drew upon many of the same domesticates found in upland Collasuyu. None of the Chinchaysuyu basins match the Titicaca plain in size,
and all are several thousand feet lower and receive more moisture. A greater
variety of plant foods, including maize, can therefore be grown. Other important crops are beans, habas, and squashes. These cultivars opened a far-
reaching agricultural stratum underlying the quinoa-tuber stratum and the
higher herding adaptation. While corn and beans cannot penetrate the higher
ecological zones, plant and animal domesticates from these zones can be
tended and in fact prosper at lower elevations. This allows the highland inhabitants of Chinchaysuyu mountain basins to utilize a relatively wide variety of locally adapted plants and animals.

In the far north of coastal Chinchaysuyu, mangrove swamps and tropical
forests grow around Guayaquil Bay, and rainfall is sufficient to support agriculture. Conditions change near the Peruvian-Ecuadorian border as aridity
increases. Most of Chinchaysuyu's western margin is the rainless Pacific desert
that stretches southward into Collasuyu. The bleak landscape of the northern
quarter is broken by some 38 streams, and large-scale irrigation has transformed stream-side strips of desert into the most productive terrain in Tawantinsuyu. The average agricultural output per unit of cultivated land is the
greatest of any area of the Inca's former realm.

The presence of a coastal plain, along with its configuration and elevation,
are the primary determinants of land availability in this area. From the
Ecuadorian border southward for about 550 kilometers there is a well-
developed, flat coastal plain. It reaches a width of more than 100 kilometers
above the Lambayeque drainage before gradually narrowing and disappearing beneath the sea at the south side of the Moche Valley. This is the largest
expanse of potentially arable flat terrain in western Chinchaysuyu and on the

coast as a whole. Ten of the 12 largest rivers crossing Tawantinsuyu's western desert lie in Chinchaysuyu. However, the economic potential of large rivers is dependent upon the configuration of the surrounding topography. The Rio Santa has the greatest discharge; it is the only river to cut through the Western Cordillera and collect abundant water from the heart of the sierra. The river mouth, however, is in a hilly region where there is no coastal plain, and the total amount of irrigated land is small. Likewise, rivers such as the Tumbes and Chira have relatively little potential, since the plain where they cross is elevated and the water courses are incised.

At four points along Chinchaysuyu, sets of rivers enter the sea relatively close together, without rugged intervening topography. These are the most auspicious areas for coastal agriculture. Here man has linked canals and whole irrigation systems, allowing water to be fed to the desert from two or more rivers. These megasystems evolved long ago; the Rios Chillon-Rimac complex and the Fortaleza-Pativilca-Supe complex are still in use on the mountainous coast. The largest megasystems were on the northern coastal plain and collapsed with the Spanish Conquest. They comprised the Chicama-Moche complex and the vast Motupe-Leche-Lambayeque-Zana-Jequetepeque complex.

The ocean waters of Chinchaysuyu hold rich resources, although the northern waters are not nearly as rich as the southern, and man has long exploited the available fish and invertebrates. Along the entire coast of Tawantinsuyu marine produce is the principal source of available protein.

SUBSISTENCE

Geography dictated that the economics of Andean civilization be based upon intensive exploitation of multiple, diverse habitats. The principal resource of these habitats is arable land that man makes productive through an agricultural technology. Secondary subsistence resources are wild plants that man uses either directly or through animal intermediaries. Inorganics—the minerals and metals for which Europeans plundered native societies—were of tertiary importance.

Animal Protein

Anthropologists assume that, as subsistence patterns evolved away from hunting-gathering toward dependence upon domesticates, intake of starch and carbohydrates increased as protein consumption decreased. Protein is, however, a dietary necessity requiring a well-defined minimal intake, and these needs were met by animal foods, but in different forms and quantities in the separate quarters of Tawantinsuyu.

Animals that sustained early hunter-gatherers in Antisuyu and western Tawantinsuyu retained their importance through the advent of Inca sovereignty. Man's adaptation to lowland Antisuyu, and to Amazonia in general, is riparian in nature. River flood plains provide agriculturally favorable soils. At the same time, water courses support a far richer and more abundant vertebrate fauna, principally fish, per unit area than exists in the interfluvial jungle. Consequently, fishing assumed greater dietary importance than hunting and tied the evolution of complex society to river settings and piscine resources (Lathrap 1970). Presumably the use of riparian fauna developed prior to the advent of tuber cultivation and was subsequently perpetuated to satisfy protein demands.

Populations along Tawantinsuyu's western desert have relied upon aquatic fauna for millennia. The extinction of Pleistocene megafauna left the coast lands with a highly impoverished vertebrate biomass. Only in the far north (where increased rainfall supports vegetation and more animals) and in the far south (where guanaco extend their range coastward) could hunting remain a viable subsistence activity.

Rich coastal currents flowing between latitude 9° and 31° south contain bountiful animal life that compensates for the low subsistence potential of the desert. Marine foods found along Andean shores have four characteristics important to man. First, the aquatic biomass is the richest in the Western world, making food abundant. Second, many invertebrates and vertebrates can be exploited with few technological prerequisites. Third, most mollusks and small fish are available year-round. And fourth, much of the animal life is concentrated along the littoral zone and in near-shore waters, thus forming a relatively localized but lenticular resource base. The consequences of these characteristics are twofold: potential support for large exploiting populations and the promotion of sedentism and residential stability.

In highland Tawantinsuyu, native societies extracted protein principally from cameloids, cervids, rodents, and fowl. At first animals were simply hunted, but through time predation gave way to limited pastoralism and ultimately to the domestication of four species.

South American cameloids are indigenous to the upland steppes of Chile and Patagonia and have radiated northward along the Andes in Pleistocene and recent times. The origins and forebears of the domesticated alpaca are obscure. It is a very specialized breed, best adapted to high altitudes. The modern range is principally northern Collasuyu, and the alpaca is most important economically in the region of Lake Titicaca, primarily as a source of wool and only secondarily as a protein source. The Inca state maintained herds in sierra basins and puna areas somewhat farther north and no doubt artificially widened the animals' range. However, the distribution of the alpaca remains the most restricted of all native domesticates, and thus it does not have wide geographical importance.

Adapted to medium as well as to high altitudes, llamas are a less specialized breed than alpacas, and they range throughout sierran Tawantinsuyu. The animals were widely used long prior to Inca consolidation. Llamas were of fundamental importance to the Inca Empire and the state economy, in many ways filling roles analogous to cattle and horse herds in Old World kingdoms. Adult animals, capable of packing up to 60 kilograms of cargo, convoyed marching armies. Great llama trains moved over Inca highway networks transporting tribute and tax produce. The animals were themselves basic forms of wealth and chattel, and the state owned and maintained vast flocks throughout the empire. Religious observances called for sacrificing numerous cameloids, and at some ceremonies more than a thousand beasts were ritually slaughtered. Finally, the llama was a source of wool and ultimately of protein, either cooked or as sun-dried *charqui* rations. In overview, the llama was Tawantinsuyu's most important animal domesticate, not because it was simply a food and wool source, but rather because it could fill many roles integral to an imperial economy.

Today's sierra Indians look to the cavy, or guinea pig, and the muscovy duck for their regular meat supplies. Both domesticates are widely distributed beyond the borders of the Inca Empire, and they have even broader-ranging wild relatives. Both animals are informally but regularly tended household stock, eaten most often on special occasions rather than daily. In folk medicine the cavy is killed and used to divine illness, and it was earlier used in Inca divination and religious sacrifices (Rowe 1946).

Finally, Andean peoples kept dogs, including hairless breeds, but they were pets and had no broad subsistence or economic significance.

In summary, two of Tawantinsuyu's animal domesticates were barnyard stock capable of adjusting to any location suitable for man's agricultural economy. This was not the case with cameloid domesticates. Specialization of the alpaca dictated that man accommodate himself to the animals' high-altitude foraging predilections and restricted range. The llama was less specialized and wider ranging, but maintaining viable breeding stock again drew man into heights where farming was not practical. Nonetheless, the llama and alpaca were fundamental in opening the vast puna and páramo to intensive exploitation. Without these animals, a quarter or more of Tawantinsuyu's extensive land mass would have had little economic utility.

Logistics

Food and other products important to man are not uniformly available in space or time. Because their distribution is irregular, every society must contend with the logistical problem of bringing people and products together to satisfy subsistence wants. Solving this problem depends upon many factors, including the distribution of resources, the nature of peoples' technology, and their systems of allocations and alliances.

Environmental diversity, uneven resource distributions, and a multifaceted agricultural technology combined to ensure that everyone in Tawantinsuyu did not have equal access to all food products, or to the same products. This generated the logistical problem of how people in one setting were to obtain foods from other settings. In many parts of the world the problem is dealt with by formal trade and exchange networks. These existed to some extent in the Andes, but they seem never to have been elaborated to a degree comparable with prehispanic Mesoamerica, where numerous merchants and traders constituted distinct social and economic classes. Other options were pursued in Tawantinsuyu, both at the state and community levels of organization.

The Inca state had what is called a redistributive economy. Currency or money was not used. Instead there was a labor tax known as the *mita*, and people worked a certain amount of time each year doing state-designated tasks. These included such things as military service, construction projects, and the cultivation of government-held lands. The results or products of an individual's mita labor belonged to the state, and this allowed the centralized bureaucracy access to or control over many items produced in different areas of the empire. While all states are predicated upon taking more from their subjects than is given in return, the mita was not a one-way siphon. Laborers were provided food and shelter, and government service was often rewarded with goods that were not locally available. To a degree, this reciprocity facilitated the redistribution of products from distinct areas and settings. This distinctive economic system is probably as old as Andean civilization itself. On the coast a well-defined labor-tax organization can be traced back in time for at least two millennia (Moseley 1975a). It was very likely more pervasive and of greater antiquity than the partially studied archeological record suggests.

At the folk level ethnohistorical sources point to a widespread pattern of "vertical control" as a means by which local communities obtained products from distant settings (Murra 1972). The term *vertical* refers to elevationally stratified habitats or environmental zones, while *control* refers to the fact that members of a community in one zone had use rights to resources in higher or lower zones outside the community's home territory. Utilizing these rights often meant that community members lived in the foreign zone and worked its resources on a permanent basis. In modern arrangements of this type, satellite settlements can be 10 days or more of travel time away from the community, and they may be in open or closed territory. An open territory is one where several communities maintain use rights but no single group claims proprietorship over the entire area. Stretches of puna often constitute open territory. A closed territory is one in which proprietorship is exercised by one community or group, and it most often involves arable land.

The pattern of vertical control has been, as yet, little explored by archeologists. A geographic perspective, nonetheless, supports certain speculations about the pattern's operations. First, the intensity or elaboration of vertical control no doubt increased with elevation. People at lower elevations grow a wider variety of crops than their counterparts at higher elevations who rely on a small number of specialized staples (see Table 11.1). High-elevation crops can more often be grown at low elevations than can low-elevation crops be grown at high elevations. This results in vertical control that has a marked downward thrust; sierra people have a greater need for access to downslope habitats and products than lowlanders have need of the mountain products and environments. A mitigating trend is cameloid herding, which requires puna pasturage. This, however, is offset by fishing, which provides abundant protein supplies both east and west of the Andes.

A second perspective on the vertical control pattern is that it was probably more elaborated on the eastern than the western slopes of the Andes, at least at higher altitudes and on the community level. Stratified ecological zones exist on both flanks. In the west, however, the steeper slope and extreme aridity reduce the agricultural potential of these strata. This produces something of an environmental barrier and economic gap between the coast and sierra. The eastern mountain slopes are entirely different. Here, although the neighboring lowlands offer less incentive for downward movement than the arable lands of the western lowlands, at the middle altitudes one productive zone overlies another, forming an economic continuum like rungs on a ladder. Since man's agricultural pursuits and communication channels often follow water courses, the fact that over three-quarters of the Andean runoff drains to the Atlantic most likely reinforces—at least for short ranges at moderate altitudes—an eastward emphasis for vertical control. This pattern contrasts with the longer, more massive and sophisticated character of the westward pattern, which entailed passing the barrier of the Andes' western slope to profit from the extensive resources of the coast.

Third and finally, the pattern raises questions of how use rights to foreign terrain are obtained and maintained. This speculative matter no doubt involves many factors. One hypothesis holds that relative size and population density in different zones and areas is an important factor. The argument runs that large demographic centers have greater potential for exercising foreign control than small centers. Similarly, large centers are better able to extract use rights in the territory of small populations, while small centers are less likely to secure rights in the territory of large populations. For example, puna herding does not support either large nucleated settlements or dense populations, and this relative demographic void may have been influential in the tendency for upland meadows to be open territory exploited by several large communities from lower elevations.

Perhaps the best example of demographic imbalance combined with the general downward drive of vertical control can be seen in the relationship

TABLE 11.1
Distribution of Peruvian Cultivated Plants by Altitude

	Ann. Mean Temp. Range, °C	Ann. Rainfall (dm)	Altitude Range (m)
Lagenaria siceraria (gourd)	15–27	7–28	850–956
Gossypium barbadense (cotton)	9–26	5–40	320–1006
Erythroxylon coca (coca)	17–27	7–40	450–1200
Nicotiana tabacum (tobacco)	7–27	3–40	57–1000
Solanum tuberosum (potato)	4–27	3–26	2–3830
Oxalis tuberosa (oca)	12–25	5–25	850–1700
Tropaelum tuberosum (mashwa)	8–25	7–14	850–3700
Ullucus tuberosus (olluco)	11–12	14	3700–3830
Ipomoea batatas (sweet potato)	9–27	3–42	28–1000
Manihot esculenta (manioc)	15–29	5–40	46–1006
Aracacia xanthorrhiza (arracacha)	15–23	7–15	850–956
Phaseolus vulgaris (common bean)	5–27	3–42	2–3700
Phaseolus lunatus (lima bean)	9–27	3–42	28–1000
Arachis hypogaea (peanut)	11–27	3–40	46–1000
Cucurbita ficifolia (squash)	11–23	3–17	850–956
Cucurbita maxima (squash)	7–27	3–27	385–1000
Cucurbita moschata (squash)	7–27	3–28	28–1000
Psidium guajava (guava)	15–29	2–42	28–1000
Persea americana (avocado)	13–27	3–40	320–1750
Capsicum annuum (chili pepper)	9–27	3–40	2–1000
Capsicum frutescens (chili pepper)	8–27	30–40	385–1000
Zea mays (maize)	5–29	3–40	2–3350
Chenopodium quinoa (quinoa)	5–27	6–26	28–3878

between the high plains of northern Collasuyu and the coast of Cuntisuyu and Collasuyu. The coastal valleys are small and do not support large populations, while the largest uninterrupted population in Tawantinsuyu lies immediately to the east in the Titicaca region, with ancillary populations along the nearby Apurimac and Urubamba headwaters. By the Early Intermediate period there is strong archeological evidence of connections between the small coastal valleys and the far larger highland populations. Influence moved both ways, but it is evident that the coast received far more input from the mountains than the mountains from the coast. In other words, the record is quite clear about the force of downward flow. A pattern of long-range vertical control issuing from the highlands is implicated as one significant mechanism by which native kingdoms in the Titicaca area maintained Pacific satellite settlements and held coastal use rights on the eve of the Inca conquest (Murra 1968; 1972).

It would be wrong to assign demography and vertical control deterministic qualities in the shaping of Andean civilization, but it would be equally erroneous to dismiss their underlying influences. Demography and vertical control do relate to a number of general prehistoric phenomena. First, coastal Tawantinsuyu as a whole is conceded to have received more influence from the sierra than the sierra from the coast. This presumably is related to the downward thrust of vertical control and the maintenance of more lowland satellite settlements by highlanders. Second, when scholars read the archeological record as indicating military conquest, they generally see highland centers as expanding over both the sierra and the coast and coastal centers as expanding only along the desert and not into the highlands. The first case presumably reflects the economics of vertical control. The second case reflects the economic self-sufficiency of the coast and the fact that the coastal lands are the most productive in Tawantinsuyu. If the object of Andean conquests was to obtain access to rich land, then sierra people would move down, while coastal people would move laterally. Third and finally, the amount of highland influence is generally conceded to be greater on the south coast than on the north. This is probably due to an inverse north-south relationship in highland-lowland demography. The largest concentrations of coastal people are in the north, while the largest concentrations of highlanders are in the south. This situation of the north coast versus the south sierra has long been the major political factor in Andean civilization.

ANDEAN CIVILIZATION

Andean civilization is a density-dependent phenomenon. It developed in demographic settings where substantial numbers of people resided adjacent to one another in contexts promoting intense social interaction. These settings were widespread in Tawantinsuyu by the second millennium BC, and their emergence was underwritten by several types of economic adaptations.

Along the Pacific desert coast, man was engaged in fishing and the exploitation of marine resources some 6000 years ago in both Chile (Bird 1943) and Peru (Engel 1966; Donnan 1964). In central Peru the maritime economy supported a dramatic population explosion, and within several millennia people were residing in very large coastal communities (Moseley 1972; Patterson 1973). Climatic amelioration in northern Chinchaysuyu was associated with increased forestation as well as with coastal mangrove stands. Here man's maritime adaptation entailed adjustment to different types of aquatic resources as well as increased potentials for inland hunting (Richardson 1973; Porras 1973; Meggers, Evans, and Estrada 1965).

In the western lowlands of Ecuador rainfall is frequently sufficient to support farming. There is evidence of an early agricultural way of life at sites producing pottery of the so-called Valdivia type. Valdivia pottery is associated with radiocarbon-14 assays falling shortly before and after 2500 BC. Several sherds have maize kernel impressions, and some decorative motifs can be construed as depicting cobs (Zevallos 1966–1971). A few Valdivia sites are in valley-bottom settings up to 30 kilometers inland. The location of these sites is compatible with hunting and gathering, but the settlements are sometimes of moderate size, implying sedentary life and the high probability of farming. Root crops of the Amazonian tropical forest adaptation are thought by some investigators to have been the principal basis of Valdivia agriculture (Lathrap, Collier, and Chandra 1975). However, both the microliths and the ceramic griddles typical of manihot (manioc) preparation are notably absent. The questions surrounding Valdivia subsistence patterns are the same as those for other early settlements in the nondesert areas of Tawantinsuyu where archeological preservation is wanting.

In the highlands, dry caves are the main source of information on early agriculture. Rockshelter deposits in the upper Santa River drainage point to cultivation of lima and common beans between 8500 and 5500 BC (Kaplan, Lynch, and Smith 1973). Thus highland agriculture had an early inception. By the second millennium BC, cave deposits in the Apurimac drainage reflect both cameloid herding and cultivation of corn, squash, beans, fruit, and possibly quinoa and tubers (MacNeish, Patterson, and Browman 1975). This presumably mirrors a fairly widespread adaptation to upland agriculture in Tawantinsuyu. The inception of tropical forest farming in Antisuyu has left no direct physical evidence of the plants or processes involved. But indirect evidence for manihot and other lowland plants is argued to be present along the Rio Ucayali at sites producing early Tutishcainyo ceramics that are estimated to date as early as 2000 BC (Lathrap 1970).

Early Corporate Undertakings

Andean civilization is density dependent because its character and definition are predicated upon the organized investment of group labor in undertakings not directly concerned with food production. Yet large populations and labor investments are but building blocks, and the structure of civilization is ultimately based upon organizational principles in which the will and work of a majority of individuals are subservient to the directions and dictates of a central body of authority. Simply stated, Tawantinsuyu was a product of populations that behaved like corporate bodies, each subscribing to common norms and rules that facilitated centralized direction of group undertakings. The nature and types of these undertakings were variable. Likewise, the source of allegiance to corporate authority ranged from voluntary at the village or community level to forced by dint of arms at the level of conquest states. The nature of corporate authority also varied. The emperor of Tawantinsuyu was head of state, paramount military commander, supreme religious pontiff, and a divine or semidivine being. Thus, attempts to categorize the evolution of Andean society and sociopolitical organization in terms of European concepts such as theocratic states versus mundane or militaristic states are not rewarding. It is more fruitful to examine different corporate undertakings on their own terms.

In Tawantinsuyu, corporate activity, as expressed in construction projects, assumes archeological definition by the second millennium BC. On the eastern Andean slopes, excavation at the Rio Huallaga site of Kotosh exposed several moderate-sized courts built by group labor (Izumi and Sono 1963). Dating before the local introduction of pottery, the enclosures were built and used successively. Niches ornamented the interiors of the plastered, masonry walls, and friezes depicting crossed human forearms decorated one wall. The structures were not domestic or residential in nature. The specific types of behavior that went on in the courts are not clear, nor is the nature of the authority that commissioned their construction. It is evident, however, that building activity did not confer the same benefits on individual workmen that equivalent labor invested in subsistence activity would have produced. The Kotosh courts both denote corporate organization and imply an economy productive enough to free labor from subsistence concerns. Presumably these are not isolated phenomena, and continued highland exploration will reveal other early group undertakings.

Artificial mound building is present in a Valdivia context at the Santa Elena Peninsula site of Real Alto. Recent excavations at the settlement are largely unreported, and the nature of construction activity is still to be delineated (Lathrap, Collier, and Chandra 1975). People apparently worked together to build low earthen mounds. Erected in several stages, the eminences supported perishable summit structures. The site is thought to date between 2500 and 3000 BC, and this gives considerable antiquity to corporate activity in northern Chinchaysuyu.

The largest known concentration of early settlements with corporate construction projects is along the Peruvian coast between the Rimac and Chicama valleys. These sites belong to the Cotton Preceramic time period, which dates between about 2500 and 1800 BC (Figure 11.4). Building activity included masonry terracing and walling for residential purposes. At least three settlements have artificial platform mounds 2 meters or more in height. At the mouth of the Rio Supe the Aspero site spreads over more than 13 hectares and houses at least six platforms (Moseley and Willey 1973). The largest mound stands over 10 meters high. It was built in multiple stages, each interspersed with periods of use. Use centered upon summit rooms and courts occasionally ornamented with wall niches or geometric adobe friezes (Feldman 1974). Another form of construction appears at the nearby site of Piedra Parada, where three complexes of terrace platforms are built against hill slopes. Each complex consists of two stone-faced platforms, one terraced immediately behind the other. In the largest example the basal terrace is

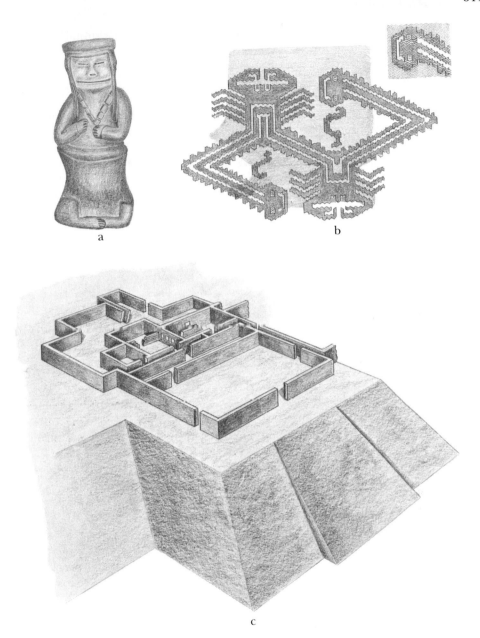

FIGURE 11.4
Artifacts and architecture of the Cotton Preceramic: *a,* unfired clay figurine from Aspero; *b,* reconstructed cotton textile design of double-headed figure with attached rock crabs from the Chicama Valley, with a detail of the twining shown at upper right; *c,* idealized reconstruction of corporate architecture at Aspero. (*a, c,* after Robert A. Feldman, Peabody Museum, Harvard University; *b,* Bird 1963 and Willey 1971.)

over 80 meters long and stands at least 4 meters high. The summit, which divides into symmetrically arranged courts, is about 50 meters wide. The higher, succeeding platform has a similar configuration but is about 20 percent smaller. Immediately in front of this complex is a rectangular court that houses a circular subterranean court about 20 meters in diameter (Moseley 1975a). There is little midden deposit at the settlement and no evidence of a large residential population. This implies that labor for the Piedra Parada corporate constructions was being mobilized on a multisettlement basis.

The largest corporate undertaking for its time period is the architectural complex of El Paraiso, situated about 2 kilometers inland from the mouth of the Rio Chillon. Covering more than 50 hectares, the site is composed of at least six mounds of collapsed masonry buildings. These stand 3 to 6 meters high, and the largest is more than 250 meters long and 50 meters wide. Engel (1967), who excavated at the site, estimates that building activities required no less than 100,000 tons of rock quarried from the nearby hills. Built in multiple stages interspersed with periods of use, the architecture consists of courts and rooms interconnected by corridors. There is little refuse in the buildings, and midden deposits are rare at the site. The lack of refuse and midden deposits implies both a relatively small residential population for a complex of this magnitude and the mobilization of labor for construction purposes on a broad regional basis.

The nature of the corporate authorities that commissioned and directed building activities at Aspero, Piedra Parada, and El Paraiso is as yet undefined. It is fully evident, however, that sociopolitical organization based on a maritime economy was highly evolved along the central coast of Peru. A parallel evolution of corporate organization was underway in the highlands as reflected at Kotosh, where people most likely pursued an agricultural way of life. Analogous developments may have transpired in a Valdivia context somewhat earlier. Yet, by the beginning of the second millennium BC, no known corporate undertaking in Tawantinsuyu or all of South America approached the scope of labor investment or the organizational level expressed in the monumental construction at El Paraiso.

Beginning with the Cotton Preceramic, Andean prehistory is characterized by very big settlements with monumental architecture that increase in numbers and scope through time. In terms of size, and particularly in the required labor investment, the massive sites of any particular period tend to cluster around a common mean and fall into a bell-shaped curve. Yet in every period there is at least one site of disproportional scope that was the product of far greater labor expenditures than those underlying contemporary settlements. This pattern emerges with El Paraiso, which is not only more than three times the size of its largest contemporaries but is also composed entirely of monumental masonry, while the bulk of most preceramic sites is refuse and midden.

Lying well outside the size range of other settlements, the sites of dispro-portional scope were truly the great centers of Andean civilization. It can be argued that these monuments represent products of corporate labor mobilized on broad regional bases and then focused upon a specific locale. Thus, their distribution in space and time reflects upon the evolution of the principal centers of corporate organization.

Although Tawantinsuyu encompassed a vast area, the distribution of the principal corporate centers remained relatively restricted. The coastal spread is about 700 kilometers, running from the Lurin Valley, a short distance below El Paraiso, northward into the Lambayeque irrigation complex. The sierra spread is about twice that of the coast—it starts much farther south with Tiahuanaco in the Titicaca Basin—and most highland centers lie south of their coastal counterparts.

These two expanses of coast and sierra formed the nuclear area of Andean civilization. Beginning with El Paraiso, this region was the seat of the largest, most advanced corporate bodies to evolve in native South America, and it remained the fountainhead of sociopolitical development until the beginning of the Spanish Conquest.

The following archeological summary focuses upon the nuclear Andean area. It documents the early rise of important cultural developments in many widely scattered areas. These areas are then gradually submerged by the evolution of two principal spheres of influence—one southern, comprising the sierra heartland, and the other northern, encompassing the coastal corelands. Finally, these spheres compete on an imperial scale to produce the entity and unity of Tawantinsuyu.

Initial Period

Farming began to supplant fishing as the principal way of making a living along the desert coast of Cuntisuyu and Chinchaysuyu about 1800 BC. The shift in subsistence patterns triggered changes in many aspects of life, and people started producing and using many new commodities. Among the crafts to be adopted was pottery, which probably spread in response to harvest storage demands and new cooking techniques occasioned by the ascendency of cultivated plant foods.

Pottery is the traditional means by which archeologists have studied the prehistory of Tawantinsuyu, and the beginning of the craft in the nuclear area of Andean civilization is used to demarcate the start of the Formative stage as well as the Initial period. Ceramic studies emphasize analysis of the physical properties, shape, and decoration of vessels. This is done for the purpose of recognizing ceramic styles, distinguishing one from another, and graphing their distribution in space and time. Hundreds of styles have been identified, but they are not equally useful in terms of what they reflect about past society. This is because pottery was produced by many people for many different purposes. In the Inca Empire there existed various types of styles. These ranged along a continuum whose base was composed of numerous folk styles. Such forms were made by the common people of different tribes and societies within Tawantinsuyu for their use according to their own canons. Overlying this cluster of folk forms were corporate styles that adhered to the canons of the organization, be it social, religious, or political, which commissioned craft production for formal purposes. The Chincha and the Imperial Chimu styles are examples of corporate forms associated with polities conquered and incorporated by the Inca. At the apex of the Tawantinsuyu style continuum lay the Imperial Inca style. Through the mita, as well as by direct commissions, the state promoted craft production according to specific Inca artistic and technological canons throughout the four quarters (cf. Murra 1962).

Corporate styles are useful to archeological interpretation. While corporate construction reflects upon the scale and focus of labor investments, corporate styles reflect upon the areal size and scope of prehispanic organizations. Interpretation, however, must take into account the fact that not every corporate organization produced a distinctive style and that not every distinctive style was the product of an integrated corporate body.

Figurines and other small objects of clay were made by the preceramic inhabitants of the coast, who sun-dried their crafts and occasionally baked or fired them. This background may have led to an independent invention of the ceramic arts. If not, it undoubtedly facilitated the adoption of pottery making, which could have spread out from earlier beginnings in Ecuador or elsewhere. In ceramic assemblages from the early part of the Initial period, ornamentation is generally based upon a limited repertoire of incised geometric and curvilinear motifs, and vessel-shape categories are not numerous. Styles are therefore relatively unelaborated and often share superficial resemblances because of their simplicity. Early pottery from Kotosh in the northeastern sierra is said to share more attributes with Tutishcainyo sherds and materials from sites of the forested lowlands than with the desert coast (Lathrap 1970). On the other hand, the earliest ceramics from the Andahuaylas region of the Rio Apurimac headwaters share many properties with coastal Initial period ceramics of the Rio Chillon and Rio Rimac region. What such stylistic overlap means in terms of the spread of folkways or corporate organization is not understood. This is a multifaceted problem deriving from the relatively simple nature of the earliest styles and from the poor exploration and limited definition of these styles by archeologists.

A great deal of corporate construction transpired during the Initial period. Huaca Florida, situated near the Rio Rimac, is the largest monument in Tawantinsuyu known to have been built about 1700 BC. The site is of disproportional scope in comparison with other contemporary undertakings.

The principal structure is a platform of cobbles, adobe, and earth fill. In plan, the flat-topped mound is an elongated rectangle more than 250 meters in length by 50 to 60 meters in width, with a summit elevation of some 30 meters. A rectangular court abuts the north side of the platform. Other ancillary structures and the attendant settlement are now covered by a suburb of modern Lima. The size of Huaca Florida implies a very large labor pool, which was probably drawn from the Rimac area as well as the adjacent Chillon and Lurin valleys. It is not clear if the corporate organization responsible for the huaca extended over an even broader area, because the distribution of Florida-style pottery is poorly known.

The huaca is about 14 kilometers from the coast and approximately the same distance south of El Paraiso, the great maritime center that was abandoned at the close of the preceramic stage. Although the two sites reflect an inland shift in the focus of monument building, it is assumed that Huaca Florida represents a continuation of the corporate principles and organizational capabilities developed at El Paraiso. Thus, there is geographical continuity in the location of the largest early sites in Tawantinsuyu.

The inland setting of Huaca Florida results from the shift to farming and the reclamation of desert lands by means of large scale irrigation agriculture. The first construction of canals is thought to have occurred inland along the steeper areas of the coastal valleys. Here inclined gradients make river diversion and water-flow management relatively easy. Three factors allowed reclamation of the desert to proceed rapidly. First, industrial plants, such as cotton and gourd, as well as fruits and dietary supplements, had been cultivated by means of floodwater farming during the Cotton Preceramic period. Thus, there was prior knowledge of plant tending. Second, the maritime adaptation supported population growth, and the labor required for canal building was on hand. Third, the principles of corporate organization needed to mobilize and direct labor forces for building activity evolved in a maritime context. Thus, the administrative abilities necessary for planning and executing large-scale reclamation projects preexisted. Coastal societies were, therefore, preadapted to the demands of irrigation agriculture.

One hypothesis holds that from its onset the development of large-scale irrigation was not in the hands of private farmers or independent agrarian villages but under the direction of preestablished bodies of corporate authority. Such bodies had a monopoly over both water and the land it irrigated. Corporate authority could consequently control the means by which coastal farming populations made a living. This made farmers sharecroppers whose usufruct of arable land was paid for by labor surrendered to corporate authority (Moseley 1975a). Such a scenario could lie at the root of the mita taxation system, as well as the general lack of private landownership among the peasantry of Tawantinsuyu.

Contemporary events in the sierra region of nuclear Andean civilization are not well understood. Ceramic styles are known from a number of areas, and pottery production could well have started somewhat earlier than on the coast. The oldest evidence for metallurgy and gold working in the New World comes from Initial period deposits in the Andahuaylas region (Grossman 1974). In other aspects of technology, the sierra was also more advanced than the coast. Many plants that served as agricultural staples in the desert valleys were either first cultivated in the highlands or diffused via the uplands to the coast. Domesticated cameloids and guinea pigs likewise had origins at the higher elevations.

Group construction of rooms and courts apparently continued at Kotosh. Building may also have started at the site of Pacopampa in the upper Marañon drainage. This is a complex of large stone-faced terraces and megalithic walls that was probably completed after the close of the Initial period (Lumbreras 1974). Other monuments will no doubt prove to have had early beginnings. However, it is evident that neither the number nor the scale of early corporate construction projects in the sierra matched those on the coast. This reflects the different economic origins of complex society in the two regions.

Cultural evolution in the highlands was tied to the gradual buildup and refinement of a broad repertoire of domesticated plants capable of adjusting to very diverse environmental conditions as well as to high altitudes. Man began relying upon beans and perhaps other cultigens by 5000 BC. Yet it required more than three millennia for sierra agriculture and herding to evolve to the point where they could support the numbers of people and organizational institutions needed to match or surpass corporate undertakings on the coast.

As with El Paraiso, Aspero and Piedra Parada were abandoned prior to the introduction of pottery. The two preceramic sites were replaced by a number of sizable inland monuments within the three-valley irrigation complex of the Rios Supe, Pativilca, and Fortaleza. Although this region is of fundamental archeological importance, the early ceramic styles are largely unknown and their associated settlements can only be loosely bracketed within the Initial period and the Early Horizon. Chupa Cigarro is the largest early corporate undertaking and no doubt represents labor input from all three valleys. This unmapped site is more than 20 kilometers inland and consists of at least six platform mounds. The principal structure is an elongated rectangle in plan, measuring more than 175 meters in length and standing over 20 meters high (Kosok 1965:222). In front of it is a circular sunken court, and similar courts are attached to two of the smaller, ancillary platforms.

The building of circular subterranean courts, which began in a preceramic context, witnessed its greatest elaboration in the three-valley irrigation complex where Chupa Cigarro is located. More than 25 such structures are associated with local platform mounds. Other examples occur in different coastal valleys (Williams 1972) and occasionally in the sierra.

One of the few shoreline sites to witness large-scale construction during the Initial period was Las Haldas, situated in the desert about 20 kilometers south of the Casma Valley. The settlement began in preceramic times, but radiocarbon assays date the initiation of corporate construction at 1400 to 1600 BC. The main structure is a multistepped terraced platform, roughly 50 meters wide, built against a hill slope. Stretching out from the terraces for several hundred meters is a series of four aligned, rectangular courts, one of which houses a large, circular subterranean court. A smaller circular sunken court about 12 meters in diameter lies to one side of the rectangular courts. The larger circular court has a stone enclosing wall 6 meters wide, an interior diameter of 17 meters, and a depth of about 3 meters. This is one of the few such structures to be partially excavated, but the specific nature of the activities that went on in the court is not clear (Fung 1969). It probably took more people to build the structure than it could hold upon completion; whatever its use, the activities involved were probably restricted to a relatively small group of people.

The Casma Valley very likely supplied labor for the building of Las Haldas, and the valley contains numerous other important sites. Near the river mouth there is a masonry complex of courts, corridors, and rooms, known as San Diego, that may date to the Initial period (Collier 1962; Thompson n.d.). The inland site of Cerro Sechin is a moderate-sized monument with multiple construction stages, some of which were probably initiated about the same time as the building of Las Haldas. Cerro Sechin is noteworthy for an enclosing wall of megaliths and boulders, each ornamented with a figure of an intact or dismembered human (Figure 11.5). The dating of this garish mosaic is somewhat equivocal, but it belongs to one of the later building phases. North of the Casma a variety of early coastal ceramic styles have been isolated, but monumental construction has received little systematic exploration. In the Moche Valley, one platform in the group of eight mounds comprising the Caballo Muerto complex produced radiocarbon assays falling within the Initial period. However, adobe friezes ornamenting the structure were initially considered to be somewhat later in date (Moseley and Watanabe 1974).

Early Horizon

The great highland site of Chavin de Huantar is the archetype of the Formative stage, and the appearance of Chavin stylistic influence on the coast marks the onset of the Early Horizon (Figure 11.6). The monument is situated at 3000 meters in a small tributary valley of the Rio Marañon. The principal feature is the Castillo, which was built in multiple phases. These phases are grouped into two major stages, called the Old Temple and the New Temple. The former was a U-shaped structure with a circular sunken court in the open space between the arms of the U. The building was subsequently enlarged, principally by expanding one side laterally and then by adding projecting platforms. This created a new U-shaped configuration, the center of

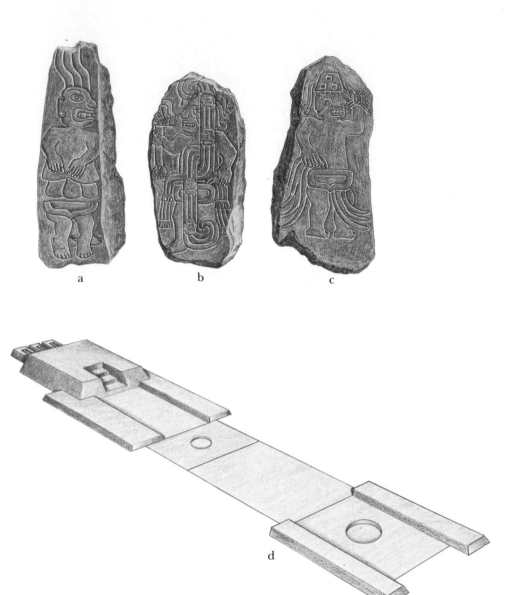

FIGURE 11.5
Coastal art and architecture of the Early Horizon from the Casma Valley: *a–c,* figures incised in stone, from the encircling wall at Cerro Sechin; *d,* reconstruction of the platforms and forecourts of Sechin Alto. The main platform is about 35 m. high. (*a–c,* after Tello 1956; *d,* after Williams Leon 1972.)

b

c

a

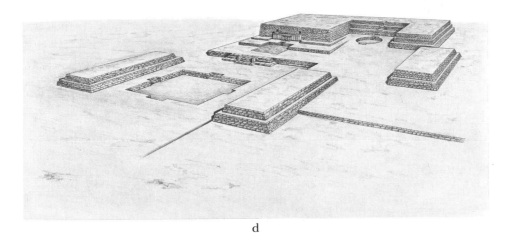

d

FIGURE 11.6

Art and architecture of the Early Horizon: *a,* the *lanzon* or "Great Image," the central upright figure of the middle inner gallery of the old temple at Chavin de Huantar (height, 4.55 meters); *b,* cornice stone from the new temple at Chavin de Huantar, with a feline figure in low relief (height, about 50 centimeters); *c,* the Raimondi stela, a low-relief stone sculpture from Chavin de Huantar (height, 1.95 meters); *d,* the temple complex at Chavin de Huantar—at upper center, the new temple; at lower left, the plaza complex of the new temple; at upper right, the old temple and its circular court. (Temple complex after Kauffman Doig 1973.)

which was occupied by a second sunken court, rectangular in form and measuring about 90 meters on a side. The Castillo, which forms the base of the U and includes both temples, is about 160 meters long, half again as wide, and stands 15 meters high.

Three things are particularly outstanding about Chavin: the masonry, the engineering, and the artwork. The Castillo, its courts, and its flanking platforms were faced with blocks of cut stone. Some blocks weigh over a ton and had to be transported great distances. The engineering is remarkable because the Castillo is about one-third hollow. The interior is occupied by a labyrinth of narrow, stone-lined galleries that often had separate entrances but were interconnected by ventilator and drain shafts. The central gallery in the Old Temple was built around a sculpted megalith 4.5 meters high. The stone depicts a large anthropomorphic being with feline attributes, and it was likely a major cult object. Other galleries have produced sculpture, caches of hundreds of fancy vessels, and the remains of llama, guinea pig, fish, and coastal shellfish. A variety of well-executed stone artwork ornamented the exterior of the Castillo and its ancillary structures. Anthropomorphic beings, felines, birds of prey, serpents, and bats figure in the depictions (Lumbreras 1971; 1974; Tello 1960).

The artwork and engineering at Chavin is distinctive, if not sui generis. However, this site is not unique in terms of size and labor investment, nor in the reflection of sophisticated corporate organization; these features had been extant in the nuclear area of Andean civilization for more than a millennium. Construction and use of the Castillo went on for at least five centuries. Yet the small valley in which it is located does not support a large population, and Chavin must have drawn upon labor from far afield. The nearest large demographic center is the upper Santa basin, about 50 kilometers away, and this must have served as the principal support base for the construction and maintenance of the Castillo. How far beyond this highland basin labor was mobilized depends upon the interpretation of corporate authority at Chavin and upon how the spatial distribution of Chavin-related artistic motifs is read.

The site is traditionally interpreted as being religious in character because of its esoteric art and the "idol" in the Old Temple. The architecture lends support to this interpretation, since the interior galleries could accommodate activities of only a limited number of people and not the bureaucracy of a conquest state. The ornamental stonework has no exact copies at contemporary sites, nor is the architecture or engineering duplicated elsewhere. Thus, Chavin was not a model for the founding of satellite monuments, as Cuzco was for state-built administrative centers in the Inca Empire. On the other hand, close rendering of Chavin style is found in fabrics from as far away as coastal Cuntisuyu, and motif copies in ceramics are found at a number of sierran as well as coastal sites. These considerations suggest that corporate authority at Chavin found its rationalization in transcendental matters and that the spread of Chavin influence was principally on the ideological level. As such, the site has its closest ethnohistorical analogy with Pachacamac in the Lurin Valley, which, in Inca times, was the location of a venerated oracle that mobilized devotees on pilgrimages from many parts of Tawantinsuyu.

Chavin is often thought of as the Formative stage archetype, but it is not the largest corporate undertaking of its day. Julio C. Tello (1956:82) pointed out that the vast platform of Sechin Alto is the biggest structure of its class in the Andes. This Casma Valley mound (see Figure 11.5) is faced with granite boulders, and its rectangular plan measures 300 by 250 meters and has a height of 35 meters—15 times the volume of the Chavin Castillo. There are five ancillary platforms of great size, and stretching out from the main mound for about one kilometer is a complex of aligned rectangular patios and plazas. Two of these contain large, circular sunken courts (Williams 1972; Fung and Williams 1970). Unfortunately, there has been but one small test excavation at Sechin Alto. This was in a lateral mound and suggested a possible onset of construction during the Initial period (Collier 1962; Thompson n.d.) but nothing about the use of the structure.

Casma is a very small valley, and building Sechin Alto obviously demanded a vast labor pool. This must have extended north to at least the lower Santa Valley and south to, or beyond, the Rio Fortaleza. The full areal scope of the corporate body building Sechin Alto and the nature of corporate authority at the site are not known because the architecture and associated styles are unexplored. Yet in its day this was the greatest center in the Andes and, clearly, it was of very different scope and character from Chavin.

During the Early Horizon the coast continued to lead the sierra in corporate construction. Large architectural complexes exist in most valleys from the Caballo Muerto complex in the Moche drainage to the Mina Perdida platform in the Lurin. None of these, however, have either the great artwork of Chavin or the labor investment of Sechin Alto.

Early Intermediate Period

The Early Intermediate period is defined by the emergence of the Nazca ceramic style out of the earlier Paracas style in coastal Cuntisuyu (Figure 11.7). Paracas, which finds expression in both ornate pottery and textiles of exceptional quality, is the most tightly integrated and consistent Early Horizon art tradition on the coast. There is, however, little associated information on subsistence, settlement, or sociopolitical organization, and the art floats in a cultural vacuum.

Nazca is a continuation of the Paracas tradition, both as a distinctive, integrated corporate style and as one that floats in a vacuum. This is not to say that there are no settlements other than cemeteries. Dos Palmas in the Pisco Valley is a planned complex of large rooms, corridors, and courts, while

FIGURE 11.7
Pottery of the Paracas-Nazca tradition. Note increasing stylization of the feline face: *a, b,* early
Paracas; *c,* middle Paracas; *d,* late Paracas; *e, f,* Nazca. (*a,* after Ubbelohde-Doering 1952; *b, e,*
after Willey 1974; *c, d,* after Menzel et al. 1964; *f,* after Sawyer 1968.)

Cahuachi in the Nazca Valley is a conglomerate of platforms, courts, and ancillary buildings covering about three-quarters of a square kilometer (Rowe 1963). Such sites, as well as the Nazca style, are expressions of corporate activity, but the nature and implications of the activities remain unexplored.

To the north, the Rimac region witnessed a fractionation of centralized corporate activity with the abandonment of Huaca Florida. Hereafter, construction often went on simultaneously at several sites. During the Early Horizon, Florida was replaced by a number of somewhat smaller monuments, including Mina Perdida in the Lurin Valley and the U-shaped platform complex at Garagay in the lower Rimac Valley. The appearance of more numerous, but smaller, monuments could reflect either the rise of multiple, autonomous sociopolitical units or the tapping of local labor and resources by a large foreign center such as Sechin Alto.

The oracular center of Pachacamac was established during the Early Intermediate period and gradually developed into a very large complex over a millennium or more of use. The early occupation is associated with Lima-style ceramics that contain both folk and corporate elements (Patterson 1966). The style is distributed north into the Chancay Valley and appears at the large Rimac site of Maranga. Composed of three big platforms and ancillary buildings, Maranga was an important regional center in its day. It did not, however, sustain its position or occupation for the length of time that Pachacamac did. This very likely reflects differences in the basic nature of corporate organization and authority at the two centers.

Early Intermediate period events in the Supe and Casma regions of the coast are not clear, but there is better definition farther north. The Moche Valley site of Huacas Sol and Luna is the largest monumental construction project for its time in Tawantinsuyu. Huaca del Sol, the principal platform, measured at least 340 by 160 meters and stood at a maximum height of about 40 meters. Huaca de la Luna is an interconnected group of three smaller brick mounds. Building was done in multiple stages interspersed with periods of use, and a mitalike labor system was used to mobilize workmen from communities scattered over a broad area (Hastings and Moseley 1975). Courts, corridors, and room complexes occupied the flat-topped platforms. The huacas were used in different manners. Activities on top of Sol were associated with the buildup of refuse and garbage, while Luna was kept clean and its summit structures were ornamented with multicolor murals.

The huacas are associated with a distinct, well-defined corporate art style called Moche or Mochica that finds expression in ornate ceramics, textiles, murals, and other media (Figure 11.8). The ceramic artwork divides into five phases, the first of which was borrowed or imported from an outside source. This is evident in the lack of local antecedents and origins for the corporate style. By contrast, domestic and culinary pottery comprising the folk style is an uninterrupted outgrowth of the preceding Gallinazo phase occupation of the area, as are most elements of Moche subsistence, settlement, and architectural patterns.

FIGURE 11.8

Architecture and pottery of the Moche Empire: *a–c*, fancy ware of the middle phase of the pottery sequence; *d*, plan of Pañamarca, the southernmost major architectural complex of the empire, in the Nepeña Valley. (*a*, after Schaedel 1951; *b–d*, after Sawyer 1968.)

During the third and fourth phases of the ceramic sequence, each valley from Chicama to Nepeña contained at least one sizable monument built in the architectural canons expressed at Sol and Luna. Although the monuments do not approach Sol in scope, each is generally the largest construction in its valley for the period, and each is associated with expressions of Moche corporate style in ceramics and occasionally murals and other media. The two southernmost sites, Pañamarca in Nepeña (Proulx 1968; 1973) and Tembladera in Santa (Donnan 1973), can be interpreted as intrusive phenomena that were spread by means of conquest and served as satellite administrative centers to a polity based at Sol and Luna. As such, Pañamarca and Tembladera foreshadow the Inca practice of establishing state-built administrative centers based upon Cuzco canons in newly conquered territory. Moche cultural hegemony clearly stops in the Nepeña Valley, but its political frontiers probably extended further south. The cultural break predictably coincides with the Casma Valley and the great former center of Sechin Alto, which certainly must have imbued the area with a strong ongoing social tradition even if its political fortunes waned.

Valleys north of the Rio Chicama have received little study, and the local ceramic styles as well as their associated sites and monuments have still to be sorted out. Phase three pottery of the Moche sequence is not in evidence; phase four may be present in the Lambayeque area, but in very minor amounts and apparently not in association with a major settlement. This leaves the northern frontiers of the Moche polity in question.

The sierra occupation of Chinchaysuyu is known from a number of ceramic styles. People from the Cajamarca Basin south to the upper Rio Santa Basin

d

often produced pottery from white clay, sherds and vessels of which appear in coastal contexts on an occasional but repetitive basis. This reflects upon the considerable patterned interchange between the highlands and coast.

Situated in the sierra behind the headwaters of the Rio Moche, the site of Marca Huamachuco was a regional center, and, as with most highland monuments, construction was not focused upon platform building. Rather, the site is a complex of circular and rectangular multistory buildings of·cut stone masonry with walls still standing to heights of 10 meters. This impressive architecture is strung along a narrow ridge and enclosed by a stone wall about 1 kilometer long and standing 4 meters high.

Recuay ceramics are expressions of a distinct, well-integrated corporate style that is very ornate and finds its highest elaboration in the Rio Santa headwaters. Yet there is no single major site or central place to which Recuay style can be tied, and the nature of corporate activity in the region was certainly different from that at Marca Huamachuco. South to Cuzco the sierra occupation is manifested in local ceramic styles, but none have the elaboration of Recuay, nor does corporate construction approximate Marca Huamachuco.

The Titicaca Basin assumes archeological focus as the major Andean demographic center during the Early Intermediate period. The site of Qaluyu and other contemporary settlements of moderate size imply that high-altitude tuber and quinoa farming was a perfected subsistence pattern by 1000 BC in the basin. At the close of the Early Horizon, corporate style and construction are manifest at Pucara, in the northern end of the basin. This unmapped settlement was also occupied in the succeeding period, and remains of domestic habitation cover a considerable area. At least three large buildings composed of courts and rooms were built on an artificial terrace. Associated corporate art includes stonework and statue carving as well as ceramics decorated with realistic and stylized motifs taken from nature. The nearby site of Qaluyu had two occupations, the later of which is associated with Pucara ceramics, as well as an artificial mound built in the shape of a catfish (Rowe 1963:7).

At the opposite end of Lake Titicaca there is evidence of parallel developments in corporate organization, and it is probable that northernmost Collasuyu had become the largest population reservoir in Tawantinsuyu during the Early Intermediate period. This population was initially not unified within a single corporate organization; rather, it was divided between multiple, competing foci of corporate art and architecture. In this respect the south sierra differed from the north coast, where the Moche polity consolidated separate valley populations by dint of conquest, administered its policies from regional state-built centers (as the Inca were to do later), and employed a mitalike labor tax to make Huacas Sol and Luna the largest corporate undertakings in the Andes for their day.

Middle Horizon

The Middle Horizon was a period of broad change throughout greater Tawantinsuyu that is related, among other things, to the ascendancy of centralized organization in the Titicaca Basin. Two sizable sites developed near the south end of the lake at about the same time as Pucara. Chiripa is the smaller, earlier, but less securely dated settlement. It has a ceramic style with corporate elements as well as an arrangement of large, rectangular rooms around a rectangular plaza that may represent a public complex. The great altiplano site of Tiahuanaco is situated somewhat further south, and its long occupation is divided into five phases (Ponce Sangines 1961; 1964). The two earliest phases fall in the latter part of the Early Horizon and are defined on ceramics that share some motifs and attributes with Pucara pottery. The Peruvian archeologist Luis Lumbreras (1974:90) sees these styles, as well as Chiripa ceramics, as an interrelated artistic tradition with close affiliations to the coastal Paracas style. This may reflect upon a pattern of vertical control and the maintenance of satellite communities on the coast.

Large-scale construction becomes evident at Tiahuanaco during its third phase, which falls within the Early Intermediate period. Megalithic stonework was undertaken, including the building of a sunken court measuring about 27 meters on a side. The masonry walls include stone blocks carved in the form of human heads. An anthropomorphic stela 2.5 meters high occupied the court center, and in a subsequent phase a much larger stone being, 7 meters high, was erected in the court. West of this structure was a large rectangular platform known as the Qalasasaya. This earthwork is 2 to 3 meters high, its vertical sides are faced with upright megaliths and stone blocks, and the platform summit has a rectangular patio with an anthropomorphic stela.

Corporate construction and settlement size apparently increased during the fourth and fifth phases of occupation, which fall within the Middle Horizon. Pucara was abandoned by this time, and Tiahuanaco became the paramount center of the Titicaca Basin. The exact dimensions of the settlement remain unestablished. It was vast, however, and stands as the principal candidate for the largest focus of corporate activity in the southern Andes.

Tiahuanaco is of particular note, not only for its large-scale construction and megalithic masonry, but also for an elaborate, highly integrated corporate style expressed in stonework and statuary as well as in ceramics. Elements of the style diffused widely throughout much of Tawantinsuyu during the Middle Horizon. Archeologists originally thought the spread reflected political conquest issuing from Tiahuanaco. This is a logical conclusion, given the size of the site, the demographic resources of the Titicaca Basin, and the survival of satellite communities on the coast up to Inca times.

Recently it has been argued that the sierra site of Huari, rather than Tiahuanaco, was the seat from which most Middle Horizon conquest issued (Menzel 1964; Lumbreras 1974). Based on ceramic analysis, this argument holds that the Tiahuanaco corporate style was spread by a proselytizing movement to Huari, where it was reinterpreted and then diffused by force of arms (Figure 11.9). Huari is located in an upper basin of the Apurimac drainage; the area is something of a population center, but in no way comparable to the Titicaca Basin. Only a sketch map of the site exists, and this suggests that the ruins cover an area about 1.2 by 1.5 kilometers (Bennett

a

b

FIGURE 11.9
Pottery and architecture of the Middle
Horizon: *a, b,* Huari polychrome pottery
from the south coast; *c,* Piqillacta.
(*a,* after Lumbreras 1974; *b,* after
Willey 1974; *c,* after Kauffman Doig
1973.)

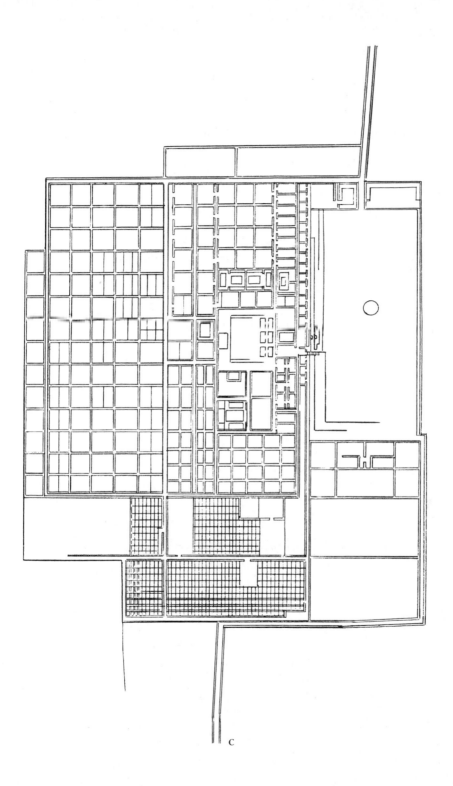

C

1954), which is less than Tiahuanaco. Huari lacks the artistic stonework of the altiplano site, and, while some megalithic masonry is present, it is comparatively rare. There is, however, a substantial amount of multistory masonry. Made of cobbles and unfinished stone, the walls form rectilinear enclosures with internal courts and rooms.

Huari is apparently the largest Middle Horizon sierra center in Chinchaysuyu. Contemporary settlements of substantial size exist in other areas. Two sites are of particular interest, Piqillacta in the Cuzco Basin and Viracocha Pampa, built near the abandoned ruins of Marca Huamachuco. Both are regimented, rectangular architectural complexes laid out according to a preconceived plan. Made of rough stone set in mud, the straight exterior enclosing walls are more than 500 meters long and attain heights of about 5 meters. Inside there are rows of regularly aligned rooms adjoining corridors and large, open courts. The two sites are distinctive because of their strict formal planning. There are no local antecedents for the complexes, and they are interpreted as intrusive, state-built administrative centers. Unfortunately, the architectural prototype for the sites—and by inference the capital of their associated polity—is not as clear as in the earlier Moche and later Inca regimes. The layout and planning at Piqillacta and Viracocha Pampa presuppose building on flat, level land, and no adjustment is made for topographic irregularities such as deep gullies or small hills. Huari, by contrast, is composed of "contour" architecture with building shape and layout adjusted to topographic irregularities. Huari also lacks the formalized plan of Piqillacta and Viracocha Pampa. Unfortunately, Tiahuanaco, which is "level surface" architecture, is insufficiently explored to be offered as an archetype.

On the north coast the polity at Huacas Sol and Luna partially broke down at the end of the fourth phase of the Moche sequence. This coincides with the very beginning of the Middle Horizon, just before the spread of the Tiahuanaco-Huari corporate style. In part the spread of this southern style seems to reflect a filling of the political vacuum created by the Moche collapse.

The political breakdown entailed two things: relocation of the capital and a contraction of the southern frontier. The Moche corporate style continued to be used; however, with the opening of the fifth phase, the southern state-built administrative centers were abandoned, as were the Huacas Sol and Luna. The Moche Valley occupation focused upon the site of Galindo. Domestic architecture there is scattered over more than 4 square kilometers, but there is relatively little corporate construction. The site reflects a sharp break with the previous tradition of building vast platforms. The principal monument is a large, rectangular enclosure measuring about 240 by 130 meters. Floor space is divided into courts, and in the rear of the complex there is a rectangular mound that served as a mausoleum for elite burials (Conrad n.d.).

The capital of the Moche polity shifted north to the immense site of Pampa Grande in the Lambayeque Valley, where architecture is scattered over an area larger than Galindo, and the tradition of building large mounds is retained. The principal huaca measures about 250 by 180 meters and stands about 50 meters high and is thus within the class of Sol and Sechin Alto.

It was once thought that the Moche polity was exterminated by expansion of the Middle Horizon polity in the southern highlands. It now seems, however, that Galindo and Pampa Grande lasted well into the Middle Horizon, while Huari was abandoned by the latter half of this time period. It appears that the nature of Middle Horizon events was rather more complex than originally supposed.

Farther south on the coast, significant changes also occurred as old settlements were abandoned and new centers emerged. Some new sites, such as Cajamarquilla in the Rimac drainage, were of substantial size and exhibit varying degrees of urban planning. Pachacamac continued in use, but the occupation is known from graves and associated offerings rather than from construction. Predictably, the ceramic styles of coastal Cuntisuyu share numerous attributes with the adjacent sierra and altiplano.

One of the more interesting changes to transpire on the coast was in burial practices. Positioning corpses in an extended position on their backs was replaced by burial in an upright, seated position. The latter was practiced in Paracas times but remained localized until the Middle Horizon. By the end of the fifth phase of the Moche sequence, it had spread to the north coast. This imparts a strong ideological overtone to the Middle Horizon.

In summary, the Middle Horizon saw the ascendancy of the southern sierra and northern Collasuyu as dominant foci of corporate activity. Tiahuanaco was the paramount center of both construction and a style that diffused widely, but the smaller center of Huari may have provided a conquest mechanism for this diffusion. While intrusive administrative sites can be identified in the sierra of Chinchaysuyu, they have yet to be found on the coast. There was basic change in coastal settlement and architectural patterns, but in part this could have resulted from the breakdown of the old Moche polity. Yet events over broad areas were tied together by changing burial practices; by inference, the spread of the new ideology was concerned less with life and politics than with death and the hereafter.

Late Intermediate Period

The Middle Horizon is often viewed as a time of unification in the nuclear Andean area, but this is not true of the latter half of the period. Huari was abandoned, the Moche polity at Pampa Grande completely disintegrated, and by the end of the horizon corporate organization at Tiahuanaco fragmented. Thus, if there is an initial impression of unity, the latter part of the Middle Horizon has a far more profound undertone of pervasive collapse, the source and significance of which remains unexplained. Out of the fractured ruins of the old order emerged a series of new corporate bodies that would make up the Late Intermediate period.

The nature of organization in the Titicaca Basin can be inferred from ethnohistorical sources (Murra 1968). Aymara was the common language of the region, but the altiplano population was divided into competing polities. Some, such as the Colla and Lupaqa, were relatively large and are referred to as the Aymara kingdoms. Internecine hostilities prevailed among the kingdoms; yet they shared a number of institutions and practices. Class stratification was pronounced, and a powerful nobility exercised political power. Some polities were associated with loosely defined corporate styles, and a moderate amount of corporate construction went on at some political centers. However, none approached Tiahuanaco in either style or scope. Altiplano people maintained satellite communities on the eastern flanks of the mountains and on the Pacific coast. This was probably a tradition going back to Paracas times and reinforced with the ascendancy of Tiahuanaco.

To the north, the Cuzco Basin was occupied by minor polities. These were often in competition with one another and with people known as the Chanka who inhabited the general area around the ruins of Huari. The Chanka were apparently a loose amalgam of small polities that lacked both distinctive art and architecture (Lumbreras 1974). Thus, the political breakdown following the demise of Huari seems to have been more profound than the fractionation following the collapse of Tiahuanaco. The pattern of small, competing polities characterizes other sierra areas during the Late Intermediate period, and the Aymara kingdoms appear to have been about as large as any highland states became at the time.

The Late Intermediate period occupation of the coast is known from a series of regional corporate styles. These include the Ica, Chincha, and Chancay styles from desert valleys of the same names. The Chincha style is associated with a small, centralized state (Menzel and Rowe 1966), while other styles were apparently shared by minor independent polities. Large settlements and corporate constructions of substantial size were common, but remain generally unmapped and unstudied.

The largest state to develop was, predictably, on the north coast. This was the Chimu Empire (Figure 11.10), which arose phoenixlike out of its Moche predecessor to spread wings of political hegemony over more than 1000 kilometers from the frontiers of Ecuador to the Rimac-Chillon irrigation complex. The imperial capital is the vast site of Chan Chan, located in the Moche Valley, where nucleated monumental architecture covers 6 square kilometers and outlying buildings are loosely scattered over an area three times as large. Dominating the site are 10 large rectangular or rectilinear enclosures with exterior walls 200 to 600 meters long that stand up to 10 meters high. Inside there are formally arranged courts, corridors, and rooms. A dynasty of monarchs ruled Chan Chan and its empire; the large enclosures, built sequentially, served as their palaces and then as their mausoleums. A similar practice later prevailed at Inca Cuzco.

The first enclosure built at Chan Chan closely resembles the rectangular compound at the Moche site of Galindo in layout and construction materials. The continuity in architecture suggests general continuity in function. Thus, the principles by which power was organized and structured at Chan Chan appear to have developed out of local antecedents (Conrad n.d.; Moseley 1975b).

Many institutions underlying the Inca Empire first assumed archeological definition in the Chimu state. Some may have originated with the desert polity; others are undoubtedly older. As with the Inca, political power in the Chimu dynasty was passed to succeeding generations by the principle of "split inheritance." When a potentate died, his successor inherited the office of emperor and the reins of government, but not the dead ruler's material possessions, coffers, lands, or revenues. These went to junior heirs, who formed a lineage or corporation charged with maintaining the dead emperor's veneration. Thus, each new emperor had to build his own palace and raise the revenues to finance his rule (Conrad n.d.). This could be accomplished by levying additional taxes, reclaiming land, or conquering new territory. Because of the nature of the agricultural economy, split inheritance undoubtedly motivated both the Chimu and the Inca royalty to make their polities conquest states as well as to engage in massive irrigation projects on the coast or extensive agricultural terracing in the sierra. Both conquest and reclamation were compatible with the mita taxation systems and labor-intensive economies that new emperors inherited.

In conquest situations the Chimu propagated their policies from state-built administrative centers designed according to the architectural canons of the imperial capital. The large site of Farfan in the Jequetepeque Valley is an example of an intrusive Chimu center. In reclamation situations smaller state-built centers provided direction for canal construction and agrarian administration (Andrews 1974; Keatinge 1974). The state also relocated populations and founded domestic settlements to suit its purposes. The Moche Valley site of Cerro Virgen was a large community of agriculturalists who worked imperial lands and who were forcibly settled beside one of the highways leading to Chan Chan (Keatinge 1975). The Inca later employed population resettlement on a far larger scale, but this institution is quite evident among the Chimu.

In overview, the Chimu Empire was the coastal culmination of progressively larger corporate bodies that grew out of maritime foundations. These foundations lay farther south, where marine resources were richest. The

a

b

FIGURE 11.10
Pottery and architecture of the Chimu Empire: *a*, *b*, fancy blackware; *c*, plan of one of the
major compounds at Chan Chan. (*a*, *b*, after Willey 1974; *c*, after M. E. Moseley and
C. J. Mackey, Chan Chan-Moche Valley Project.)

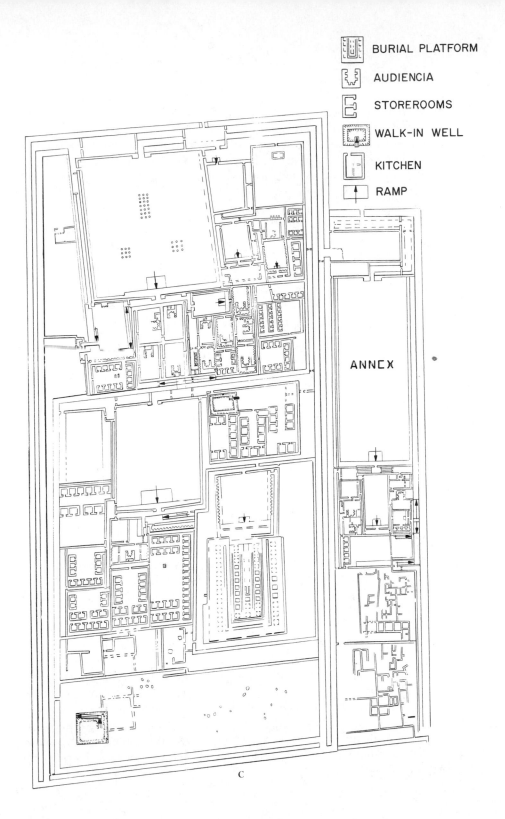

BURIAL PLATFORM

AUDIENCIA

STOREROOMS

WALK-IN WELL

KITCHEN

RAMP

ANNEX

C

advent of irrigation agriculture shifted the seats of corporate authority inland, and El Paraiso was replaced by Huaca Florida. Agriculture also promoted the economic ascendancy of multivalley irrigation complexes and triggered a gradual northward movement of the foci of corporate power. This movement was a response to the greater availability of arable land in the north, and it proceeded in a steplike manner. Southern sites such as Huaca Florida and Chupa Cigarro were surpassed as corporate foci by Sechin Alto. This center in turn yielded to the Huacas Sol and Luna, which were later replaced by Pampa Grande as the Lambayeque complex assumed economic dominance. Emerging out of previous strong political traditions, Chan Chan recaptured power and brought the focus of corporate organization back to the Moche Valley.

In terms of Tawantinsuyu's broader political balance of north coast versus south highlands, the Chimu tipped the balance of power to the desert for the last time. Subsequently the rise of Inca predominance reweighted the political scale, and the south sierra asserted definitive dominance over the land of the four quarters.

Late Horizon

The Inca were a minor polity engaged in raiding their neighbors until about 1438 AD, when a battle at Cuzco defeated the Chanka and a policy of consolidating conquered lands was adopted. The factional populations around the capital were quickly united and campaigns were launched into the Titicaca Basin, first against the Colla and then against the Lupaqa and other groups. Within 20 years the Inca developed into the largest state in the southern highlands. About 1463 a rapid expansion north through the sierra to Quito outflanked the coastal Chimu. Inca armies descended to the Pacific in Ecuador and then marched south to conquer and sack the desert empire of their largest political rivals (Rowe 1946) (Figures 11.11 and 11.12).

By seizing control over both the north coast and the Titicaca Basin, the Inca attained hegemony over the economic and demographic foci of Andean civilization. Suddenly the emerging highland polity was without serious rivals or comparable states in all of native America, and frontiers were quickly expanded to make Tawantinsuyu one of the largest empires ever to arise in the preindustrial world.

In 1532 the quintessence of native civilization toppled with the impact of a single European state. The basic impact came from neither advanced technology nor sophisticated corporate organization. The most effective weapons arming the conquistadores were smallpox, measles, and other Old World diseases. These first undermined and later virtually destroyed the demographic foundations of New World society, making the Late Horizon the last horizon.

a

b

FIGURE 11.11
Pottery and architecture of the Late Horizon; *a*, Inca pottery from Machu Picchu; *b*, a
salient of the fortress of Sacsahuaman. (*a*, after Kauffman Doig 1973; *b*, after Willey 1974.)

538

FIGURE 11.12
Urban planning of the Late Horizon: plan of Spanish Cuzco with the fortress and walls of the Inca City outlined and redrawn as the silhouette of a stylized Puma. (After Rowe 1967.)

References Cited and Recommended Sources

Andrews, A. P. 1974 The U-shaped structures at Chan Chan, Peru. Journal of Field Archaeology 1:241–264.

Bennett, W. C. 1954 Excavaciones en Wari, Ayacucho, Peru. Revista del Museo Nacional (Lima) 23:198–211.

Bird, J. B. 1943 Excavations in Northern Chile. New York: American Museum of Natural History.

———. 1963 "Preceramic art from Huaca Prieta, Chicama Valley." Ñawpa Pacha 1:29–34 (Figure 4).

Collier, Donald 1962 Archaeological investigations in the Casma Valley, Peru. Thirty-fourth International Congress of Americanists, Wien, 1960, pp. 411–417.

Conrad, G. W. n.d. Burial platforms and related structures on the north coast of Peru; some social and political implications. Unpublished Ph.D. dissertation, Harvard University.

Donnan, C. B. 1964 An early house from Chilca, Peru. American Antiquity 30:137–144.

———. 1973 The Moche Occupation of the Santa Valley, Peru. Berkeley: University of California Press.

Engel, F. A. 1966 Geografia humana prehistorica y agricultura precolumbina de la quebrada de Chilca 1. Lima: Universidad Agraria.

———. 1967 Le complexe précéramique d'El Paraiso (Pérou). Journal de la Société des Américanistes de Paris 55:43–95.

Feldman, R. A. 1974 Informe preliminar sobre las excavaciones en Aspero, Peru, y sus implicaciones teoricas. Paper presented at the II Congreso Peruano del Hombre y la Cultura Andina, Trujillo, Peru.

Fung Pineda, Rosa 1969 Las Aldas: su ubicacion dentro del proceso historico del Peru antiguo. Dedalo (São Paulo) 5:(9–10).

Fung Pineda, Rosa, and Carlos Williams Leon 1970 Exploraciones y excavaciones en el valle de Casma. Trabajo presentado al XXXIX Congreso Internacional de Americanistas, Lima, Peru.

Grossman, J. W. 1974 Early Intermediate period settlements and the impact of Huari in the south central highland region of Andahuaylas, Apurimac, Peru. Paper presented to the Thirty-eighth Annual Meeting of the Society for American Archaeology, Washington, D.C.

Hastings, C. M., and M. Edward Mosely 1975 The adobes of Huaca del Sol and Huaca de la Luna. American Antiquity 40:196–203.

Izumi, Seiichi, and Toshihiko Sono 1963 Andes 2: Excavations at Kotosh, Peru, 1960. Tokyo: Kadokawa.

Kaplan, Lawrence, T. F. Lynch, and C. E. Smith, Jr. 1973 Early cultivated beans (Phaseolus vulgaris) from an intermontane Peruvian valley. Science 179:76–77.

Kauffman Doig, Federico 1973 Manual de arqueologia Peruana. Lima: Ediciones Peisa.

Keatinge, R. W. 1974 Chimu rural administrative centres in the Moche Valley, Peru. World Archaeology 6:66–82.

———. 1975 Urban settlement systems and rural sustaining communities: an example from Chan Chan's hinterland. Journal of Field Archaeology 2:215–227.

Kosok, Paul 1965 Life, Land, and Water in Ancient Peru. New York: Long Island University Press.

Lathrap, D. W. 1970 The Upper Amazon. New York: Praeger Publishers.

Lathrap, D. W., Donald Collier, and Helen Chandra 1975 Ancient Ecuador: Culture, Clay, and Creativity 3000–300 BC. Chicago: Field Museum of Natural History.

Lumbreras, L. G. 1971 Towards a re-evaluation of Chavin. In Dumbarton Oaks Conference on Chavin. ed. E. P. Benson, pp. 1–28. Washington, D.C.: Dumbarton Oaks Research Library and Collection.

———. 1974 The Peoples and Cultures of Ancient Peru. Washington, D.C.: Smithsonian Institution Press.

MacNeish, R. S., T. C. Patterson, and D. L. Browman 1975 The Central Peruvian Prehistoric Interaction Sphere. Andover, Mass.: Phillips Academy.

Meggers, B. J., Clifford Evans, and Emilio Estrada 1965 Early Formative Period of Coastal Ecuador. Washington, D.C.: Smithsonian Institution Press.

Menzel, Dorothy 1964 Style and time in the Middle Horizon. Ñawpa Pacha 2:1–105.

Menzel, Dorothy, and J. H. Rowe 1966 The role of Chincha in late pre-Spanish Peru. Ñawpa Pacha 4:63–76.

Menzel, Dorothy, John H. Rowe, and Lawrence E. Dawson 1964 The Paracas Pottery of Ica. Berkeley: University of California Press.

Moseley, M. E. 1972 Subsistence and demography: an example of interaction from prehistoric Peru. Southwestern Journal of Anthropology 28:25–49.

———. 1975a The Maritime Foundations of Andean Civilization. Menlo Park, Calif.: Cummings Publishing Company.

———. 1975b Chan Chan: Andean alternative to the preindustrial city. Science 187:219–225.

Moseley, M. E., and Luis Watanabe 1974 The adobe sculptures of Huaca de los Reyes. Archaeology 27:154–161.

Moseley, M. E., and G. R. Willey 1973 Aspero, Peru: a reexamination of the site and its implications. American Antiquity 38:452–468.

Murra, J. V. 1962 Cloth and its functions in the Inca state. American Anthropologist 64:710–728.

———. 1968 An Aymara kingdom in 1567. Ethnohistory 15:115–151.

———. 1972 El "control vertical" de un maximo de pisos ecologicos en la economia de las sociedades andinas. In Visita de la Provincia de Leon de Huanuco (1562), Vol. 2., ed. Inigo Ortiz de Zuniga, pp. 427–476. Huanuco, Peru: Universidad Nacional Hermilio Valdizan.

Patterson, T. C. 1966 Pattern and Process in the Early Intermediate Period Pottery of the Central Coast of Peru. Berkeley: University of California Press.

———. 1973 America's Past: A New World Archaeology. Glenview, Ill.: Scott, Foresman and Company.

Ponce Sangines, Carlos 1961 Informe de labores 1. La Paz: Centro de Investigaciones Arqueologicas en Tiwanaku.

———. 1964 Informe de labores 2. La Paz: Centro de Investigaciones Arqueologicas en Tiwanaku.

Porras Garces, P. Pedro 1973 El Encanto—La Puna. Un sitio insular de la Fase Valdivia asociado a un conchero anular. Serie La Puna #1. Museo Francisco Piana. Quito: Guayaquil Ediciones Huancauilca.

Proulx, D. A. 1968 Archaeological Investigations in the Nepeña Valley, Peru 1. Amherst: University of Massachusetts Press.

———. 1973 Archaeological Investigations in the Nepeña Valley, Peru 2. Amherst: University of Massachusetts Press.

Richardson, J. B. 1973 The preceramic sequence and the Pleistocene and post-Pleistocene climate of northwest Peru. In Variation in Anthropology: Essays in Honor of John C. McGregor, ed. D. W. Lathrap and Jody Douglas, pp. 199–211. Urbana: Illinois Archaeological Survey.

Rowe, J. H. 1946 Inca culture at the time of the Spanish Conquest. In Handbook of South American Indians, Vol. 2, ed. J. H. Steward, pp. 183–330. Washington, D.C.: Bureau of American Ethnology.

———. 1963 Urban settlements in ancient Peru. Ñawpa Pacha 1:1–27.

———. 1967 What kind of a settlement was Inca Cuzco? Ñawpa Pacha 5:59–76.

Sawyer, Alan R. 1968 Mastercraftsmen of Ancient Peru. New York: Solomon R. Guggenheim Foundation.

Schaedel, Richard P. 1951 Mochica murals at Pañamarca. Archaeology 4:3:145–154.

Tello, J. C. 1956 Arqueologia del valle de Casma. Lima: Imprenta de la Universidad de San Marcos.

———. 1960 Chavin, cultura matriz de la civilizacion andina. Lima: Imprenta de la Universidad de San Marcos.

Thompson, D. E. n.d. Architecture and settlement patterns in the Casma Valley, Peru. Ph.D. dissertation, Harvard University.

Ubbelohde-Doering, Heinrich 1952 The Art of Ancient Peru. New York: Frederick A. Praeger.

Willey, Gordon R. 1971 An Introduction to American Archaeology, Vol. 2: South America. Englewood Cliffs, N.J.: Prentice-Hall.

———. 1974 Das Alte Amerika. Berlin: Propyläen Verlag.

Williams Leon, Carlos 1972 La difusion de los pozos ceremoniales en la costa peruana. Apuntes arqueologicos (Lima) 2:1–9.

Zevallos Menendez, Carlos 1966–1971 La agricultura en el formativo temprano del Ecuador (cultura Valdivia). Guayaquil: Casa de la Cultura Ecuatoriana.

Slash-and-burn agriculture. A Waiwai man with a digging stick plants manioc in a newly cleared field.

CHAPTER TWELVE

Lowland South America and the Antilles

Betty J. Meggers and Clifford Evans

In archeological terms, the New World has its own "dark continent." Although the Andean high civilizations have been intensively studied and extensively reported, the vast, inhospitable, nearly inaccessible interior of South America has been, and remains, nearly unknown. The poor preservation of archeological materials, the difficulties of survey and excavation, and the sheer size of the area involved have combined to limit systematic, thorough research. Drs. Meggers and Evans provide a definitive survey of the research that *has* been done in this little-known area, often drawing on as yet unpublished data, and offer an outline of the many questions still awaiting an answer.

INTRODUCTION

The region discussed in the following pages extends from western Cuba to Tierra del Fuego and from the Atlantic Ocean to the base of the Andes (for a chronological chart of the region, see Figure 12.1). Within these boundaries are large islands, vast swamps, the most extensive forest on the planet, and parts of ancient Gondwanaland. Differences in climate, soil, and elevation create countless kinds of arboreal, terrestrial, and aquatic habitats. Nevertheless, several general topographical and environmental patterns can be discerned.

There are three principal river networks: the Orinoco, the Amazon, and the Plata (Figure 12.2). All have tributaries originating in the Andes as well as the lowlands. The Orinoco flows north and east, the Plata south, and the Amazon northeastward to an exit on the equator. Because of the combination of low relief and high precipitation, there are permanent or temporary links between these river systems. The Casiquiare provides a year-around con-

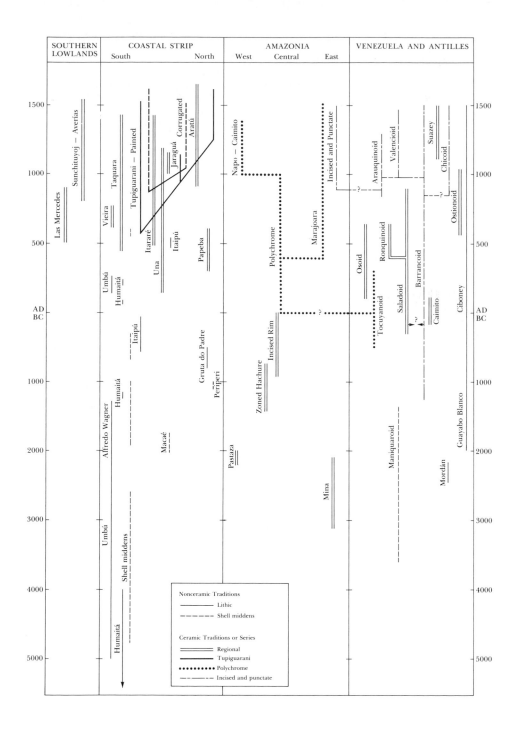

nection between the Orinoco and the Amazon, while southern tributaries of the latter blend with the headwaters of the Plata during the rainy season. On the northern and southern borders of Amazonia, the forest becomes increasingly restricted to the margins of watercourses and the summits of hills, leaving grassy expanses that become the llanos of central Venezuela and the pampas of Argentina and Uruguay.

The Antilles resemble an arc of stepping stones extending between eastern Venezuela and Yucatán; Patagonia, at the opposite extreme, is a triangle of gradually diminishing width and increasingly inhospitable climate that fades out in a jumble of small islands. The strip of coast east of Amazonia is temperate and wet in the south, tropical and arid in the north, but the transition is gradual and movement is facilitated by two large rivers running parallel to its length. The physiographic characteristics permit the recognition of four subregions: (1) Venezuela and the Antilles, (2) Amazonia, (3) the Coastal Strip, and (4) the Southern Lowlands. As we will see, they had different histories during most of the pre-Columbian period, in spite of the seeming ease of communication among them.

The magnitude of the area with which we are concerned is no more impressive than the magnitude of our ignorance of its prehistory. Most of the information available a decade ago consisted of incomplete descriptions of isolated sites and poorly documented artifacts. The principal exceptions were coastal Venezuela and the Antilles, where a time-space framework was developed mainly from the comparison of ceramic complexes. Although a tremendous amount of data has been obtained from the other three areas in recent years, most of the heart of the continent remains unknown. Furthermore, there are no carbon-14 dates from the Southern Lowlands, so that correlation of the numerous lithic complexes recognized there with those from other parts of the continent rests on typological grounds. This lack of knowledge allows conflicting interpretations of the role of the lowlands in the domestication of plants and the development and dispersal of cultural traits. Since a choice among these reconstructions must await information

---

FIGURE 12.1 (*Opposite*)
Chronological positions and postulated relationships of dated archeological traditions in lowland South America and the Antilles. This chart summarizes the information on the maps, but a careful observer will note slight differences in the positions or durations of some of the complexes. For example, the Pastaza phase begins prior to 2000 BC here, but is shown on the map representing the millennium between 2000 and 1000 BC (Figure 12.8). This discrepancy reflects the difference between uncorrected carbon-14 dates and the ages resulting from adjustments for the true half-life and the fluctuations in production of carbon-14 in the atmosphere. These corrections are necessary to compare very recent dates with historical ones. In prehistoric times, the ranges of the plus-or-minus values and the fact that even a large series of dates may not encompass the total duration of an archeological culture make it necessary to consider all carbon-14 ages as approximations. Differences in the durations of complexes on this chart and the periods to which they are allocated on the maps are not significant at the present state of knowledge of the development of culture in lowland South America and the Antilles.

FIGURE 12.2
Lowland South America and the Antilles, showing natural features, political and geographical locations, and the boundaries of the four subregions.

yet to be gathered, there is nothing to be gained by repeating the arguments. The interested reader should consult the literature and form his or her own opinion (e.g., Cruxent and Rouse 1958; Lathrap 1970; Meggers and Evans 1961; 1973). Instead, we will employ a biogeographical approach, making use of data still mainly unpublished, to examine the distribution of general cultural complexes through space and time, to see what kind of picture seems to be emerging, and to see what kinds of interpretative problems its explanation presents.

Because other chapters in this volume discuss subsistence strategies, social systems, and processes of cultural change, it may be well to mention that our approach does not imply lack of interest in these aspects of archeological research. In the tropical lowlands of South America, however, we are still attempting to construct the time-space framework prerequisite to such types of analysis. The geographical distributions of most complexes are unknown, and, although several hundred carbon-14 dates are available, we cannot be sure that they accurately define the inception or termination of any phase or tradition. Moreover, where there are no dates, correlations must be based on typological resemblances, which imply cultural relationships but do not ensure contemporaneity. Diffusion proceeds at varying rates and traditions may persist for millennia; it is risky to assign undated remains to a particular period. To achieve maximum reliability, we will deal only with dated remains. All the complexes and traditions include numerous additional sites and phases, however, which would undoubtedly fill some of the gaps in the time and space distributions if their ages were known.

Two major lacunae in the record deserve comment. The absence of archeological information from Amazonia prior to the Christian era is only partly attributable to lack of search. Surviving groups employ numerous types of perishable materials for tools, weapons, and containers. This situation must have existed in earlier times as well, making it unlikely that much will ever be known of the preceramic inhabitants. Hunter-gatherers subsisted on wild foods in the surrounding areas for at least ten millennia, however, and it seems safe to assume that they also exploited the varied resources of the lowland streams and forests. Poor preservation may also account for failure to encounter projectile points in many nonceramic sites in the other subregions, particularly since bone points have occasionally been reported.

Another effect of the humid climate is destruction of vegetal remains indicative of domestication. Palynology, a potential source of information, has not been applied. Since pottery was adopted in most parts of the lowlands long after cultivated plants became the basis of subsistence in the nuclear areas, it seems likely that its presence signifies the practice of shifting cultivation. The beginning of agriculture may have preceded the use of pottery here, however, as it did in many other parts of the New World.

Our review will advance through space and time with the aid of a series of maps. Except for the first, those before the Christian era represent a millennium; those within it, half a millennium. Because carbon-14 results are approximations, we have emphasized relative rather than absolute ages and clusters or patterns rather than isolated dates. Where a date (a group of dates) departs radically from others for a style or complex, we have considered it invalid. The two principal criteria for rejection are: (1) an excessively long gap (about 1000 years) between the initial occurrence and the other dates and (2) an ambiguous or inconsistent stratigraphic context.

Cultural comparison is facilitated by the widespread use of similar classificatory approaches in different regions. Most investigators in Venezuela and the Antilles have adopted the "series" concept developed by Rouse, which is sufficiently comparable to the "tradition" as defined in Brazil to provide a common denominator for discussing ceramic distributions. Lithic remains have been classified into "complexes" throughout the lowlands, and these also represent similar levels of typological generalization. Our story begins, arbitrarily, about 5000 BC and ends at AD 1500.

CHRONOLOGICAL REVIEW

5000–3000 BC

By the beginning of the fifth millennium BC, populations employing several kinds of subsistence strategies were distributed along the Coastal Strip (Figure 12.3). Two general lithic traditions have been recognized in southern Brazil, one with stone projectile points and the other lacking them. The latter, designated the Humaitá tradition, is represented by numerous sites in forested locations along rivers, lagoons, or swamps. Four subtraditions are distinguishable by their artifact complexes and settlement patterns. The earliest dates are associated with the Tamanduá subtradition, which also possesses the most distinctive tool: a boomerang-shaped biface. Elongated unifacial or bifacial choppers with circular or triangular cross-sections, plano-convex scrapers, and flake knives are also typical (Figure 12.4). This subtradition, known in Argentina as "Altoparanaense," centers on the Rio Uruguay. The related Ivaí subtradition in northern and western Paraná emphasizes a variety of scrapers, unifacial choppers, and chopping tools. Most sites are about 20 meters in diameter, but some reach 200 meters. A third subtradition, Antas, has been reported from several parts of southern Rio Grande do Sul. Sites occupy a broader range of habitats and tend to occur at higher elevations. Refuse is less than 40 centimeters in depth and covers areas ranging from 25 meters in diameter and to 75 by 150 meters. Unifacial choppers, chopping tools, and flake knives are diagnostic; bifaces are absent.

Similar kinds of tools have been encountered more sporadically north of Paraná. Dates have been obtained mainly from rockshelters, but open sites also occur. These data indicate that populations with cultures generally

549

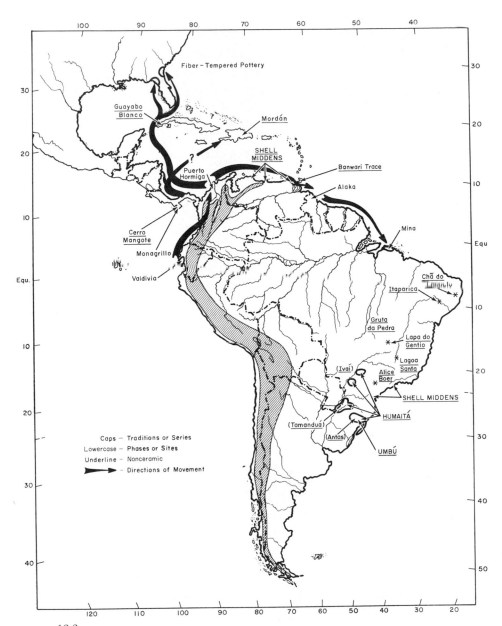

FIGURE 12.3
Location of archeological sites and complexes dated between 5000 and 3000 BC. Arrows show postulated routes of migration.

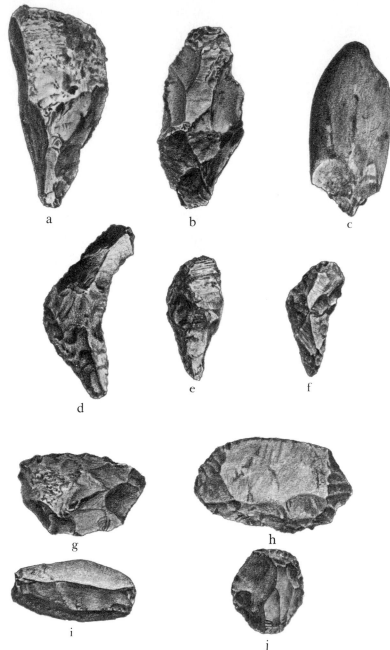

FIGURE 12.4
Characteristic artifacts of the Humaitá tradition, southern Brazil: *a–f,* choppers, some bifacially chipped, others shaped only at one end, boomerang form (*d*) is diagnostic; *g,* "turtle-back" scraper; *h, j,* scrapers; *i,* flake tool. (After Programa Nacional de Pesquisas Arqueológicas 1969a.)

comparable to the North American Archaic prevailed throughout the Coastal Strip during the same time period. Lithic complexes have also been defined in lowland Argentina, but their antiquity has not been established (e.g., Bórmida 1962).

Stone projectile points are ancient in South America and persist in southern Brazil after 5000 BC in the Umbú tradition. Four subtraditions have been recognized, as well as numerous sites of uncertain affiliation. The earliest remains are contemporary with sites of the Humaitá tradition and occur in rockshelters or open locations near the coast, adjacent to streams, lagoons, or swamps. Where not limited by the dimensions of a rockshelter, refuse is distributed over areas ranging from 30 by 40 to 80 by 150 meters. Among the variety of unstemmed and stemmed points are some with serrated margins and others with unifacial chipping. Most common is an elongated triangular form with a parallel-sided or expanding stem and a straight, concave, or convex base. Pounders and small anvil-stones with a central concavity are typical, as are choppers, end scrapers, and chips and flakes showing use. Bolas, semipolished and polished axes, and grinding stones are often associated (Figure 12.5). The Umbú tradition has been reported only from the southern Brazilian states of Rio Grande do Sul, Santa Catarina, and Paraná; whether or not it will prove to be as common in the north as the Humaitá tradition remains to be established.

Several carbon-14 dates from Banwari Trace, a shell midden on southwestern Trinidad, place its occupation between about 5000 and 3000 BC. Some artifacts, notably edge grinders, are shared with Venezuelan shell middens; pounders, pestles, mortars, and grooved axes occur along with flaked implements for cutting and scraping. Projectile points and pins were fashioned from bone. Shell was not used for tools. Rising water during occupation of the site is implied by a change from fresh to brackish water mollusks.

About 4000 BC, shell middens become increasingly numerous on the coasts of Venezuela and southern Brazil (Figure 12.6). They also exist in the intervening region, but only those in eastern Pará are known to be equivalent in age. Excavations in many sites in Paraná and Santa Catarina have provided a considerable number of dates between 4000 and 3000 BC, indicating that exploitation of mollusks was particularly intense. During this millennium, sea level was some 2.5 meters higher than today, inundating the lowlying shore and enlarging the potential habitat for mangrove oysters and other shellfish. Perhaps the same phenomenon explains the existence of shell middens on Cuba and Hispaniola by 3000 BC. The artifact inventories of the Guayabo Blanco and Mordán complexes differ from one another and from mainland assemblages, making their relationships problematical.

Toward the end of this period, pottery appears in the shell middens on the coast of Pará. The shell-tempered ware, simple vessel shapes, and lack of decoration affiliate this Mina phase with the Alaka phase, which occurs in the mangrove swamps along the northwestern coast of Guyana. Mina phase

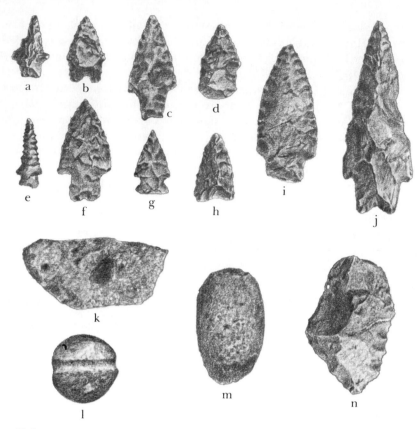

FIGURE 12.5

Characteristic artifacts of the Umbú tradition, southern Brazil: *a–j,* projectile points; *k,* pitted anvil-stone; *l,* grooved bola; *m,* pebble hammerstone; *n,* scraper. (After Programa Nacional de Pesquisas Arqueológicas 1974.)

sites are larger than the known Alaka phase accumulations but have the same compactness, resulting from cementlike layers of calcium carbonates. The dates are unexpectedly early, but are consistent with their relative stratigraphic positions.

Acceptance of this antiquity offers a choice between two explanations: (1) independent invention of pottery making or (2) introduction from elsewhere in the Americas. The second alternative seems more logical because it is compatible with the Colonial Formative dispersal suggested by Ford (1969) to explain the early appearance of pottery in shell middens on the Florida and Georgia coasts. The fiber temper, incised and punctate techniques of decoration, and design motifs of the North American ceramics have counterparts in earlier South American complexes, notably, Puerto Hormiga

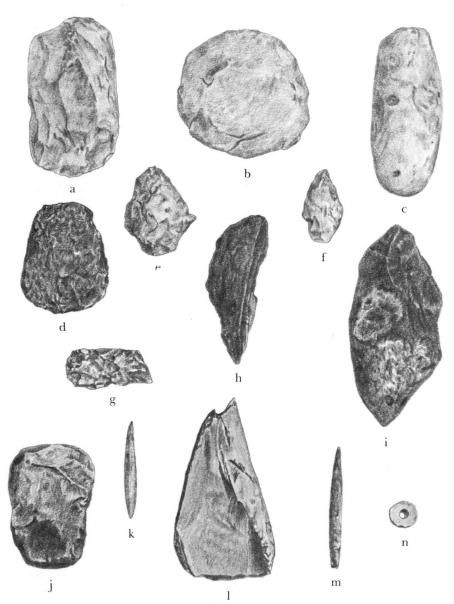

FIGURE 12.6
Characteristic artifacts of the early shell middens of southern Brazil (*a–i*) and the Manicuare complex of Venezuela (*j–n*). *a*, bifacial ax; *b*, bifacial chopper; *c*, semipolished ax; *d*, scraper; *e, f*, projectile points; *g*, flake knife; *h, i*, picks; *j*, hammerstone; *k, m*, bone points; *l*, shell gouge; *n*, shell bead. (*a–i*, after Programa Nacional de Pesquisas Arqueológicas 1971; *j–n*, after Cruxent and Rouse 1958.)

on the Caribbean coast of Colombia and the Valdivia and Machalilla phases of coastal Ecuador, where shellfish were also an important component of subsistence. Mina phase pottery does not share equally specific features with that from Puerto Hormiga, but the presence of the same type of ware on the Guyana coast provides a stepping stone halfway between the Brazilian and Colombian complexes. Although the shell middens that abound along the shore of Venezuela have been considered nonceramic, few have been investigated thoroughly enough to rule out the possibility that similar ceramics may occur.

The hypothesis that the early shell-tempered pottery of northeastern South America and the fiber-tempered pottery of southern North America represent migrations by related coastal-adapted populations receives additional support from the failure of the colonists in both areas to expand beyond this environmental niche or to exert significant influence on neighboring inland groups (Crusoe 1974). The suggestion that the closest affiliations of the Tumucua language of Florida are with Warau, spoken in the Orinocan delta, also fits the Colonial Formative hypothesis. Preliminary calculations placing the linguistic separation around 3000–2000 BC agree remarkably well with the archeological carbon-14 dates (Granberry 1970; see also Noble 1965).

3000–2000 BC

Few dated complexes fall within this millennium, and the majority of these are confined to the earlier half. Persistence of the Umbú and Humaitá lithic traditions is implied by their occurrences during the following period, and the Camurí subtradition, as yet undated, may fill the gap. Four phases have been recognized in Rio Grande do Sul (Figure 12.7). Sites are generally along rivers or swamps but occasionally occupy rockshelters. Scrapers, bifaces, choppers, chopping tools, and stemmed projectile points are diagnostic; polished axes and pitted anvil-stones are rare; grinding stones are absent. Choppers, chopping tools, scrapers, and knives also have been encountered in the Lagoa Santa region, but stone projectile points are not associated. Many shell middens in southern Brazil and the greater Antilles were apparently abandoned by 2500 BC; others, among them the Macaé phase of Rio de Janeiro and the Cubagua complex of eastern Venezuela, date from the latter part of the period. East of the mouth of the Amazon, the pottery-making Mina tradition also disappeared after the first few centuries.

This time-space patterning may be attributable to accidents of sampling, but another explanation deserves investigation. Between about 2700 and 2000 BC, the sea level fell, and this must have reduced lacustrine subsistence resources. If shellfish gathering became less productive, one might expect a compensating increase in the frequency of inland sites, but these too seem to become less common. Although the evidence is mainly circumstantial, this

FIGURE 12.7
Location of archeological sites and complexes dated between 3000 and 2000 BC.

paradox may reflect adaptation to changes also underway in the terrestrial environment. About 3000 BC the lowlands began to experience increasing aridity, which reduced the extent of the coastal and Amazonian forests. The expanding scrub and savanna would have provided fewer and less concentrated food resources for hunter-gatherers; survival would have been enhanced by reducing group size and/or increasing mobility. The archeological result would be smaller sites, less likely to be encountered without intensive search and less likely to provide organic materials suitable for dating.

Pottery continued to be made on the coast of Colombia, where a sequence of several cultural phases has been reconstructed. The Tesca phase is of particular interest because it possesses shell temper and zoned-hachure decoration, both of which turn up in distant parts of the lowlands during the following period (Bischof 1966).

2000–1000 BC

The map for this millennium (Figure 12.8) shows a pattern similar to that between 5000 and 3000 BC. Both the Humaitá and Umbú traditions continue in southern Brazil. The former is represented by the Jacuí subtradition, which has chipped bifaces, semipolished axes, grooved bola stones, and discoidal objects. The Umbú tradition has been encountered in western Paraná and Santa Catarina, as well as Rio Grande do Sul. There is a marked decline in the variety of projectile point forms, although both unstemmed and stemmed types persist. Scrapers are the most common artifact. Other kinds of nonceramic remains have been described from isolated locations. The Alfredo Wagner site in northeastern Santa Catarina has produced unusual amounts of basketry and braided cord. Rockshelters in the Lagoa Santa region of Minas Gerais have pictographs and rare stone implements indicating sporadic occupation. The absence of sites farther north seems more likely to reflect the small amount of investigation and paucity of dates than a decline in population size.

A resurgence of shellfish exploitation is implied by several series of dates from southern Brazil. The majority correlate with a rise in sea level, between 2000 and 1500 BC, to some 3 meters above that at present, which recreated the conditions favoring the earlier florescence of this adaptation. A number of middens date to the latter part of the period, however, when the sea level dropped. Differences in elevation of the shoreline and other local topographical and geographical factors probably account for such variations, as well as for the appearance of shell middens on the coast of Bahia at this time. A comparable situation seems to exist in the north; most sites in western Venezuela (see Figure 12.6, j–n), the Manicuare complex of eastern Venezuela, the Mayaro site on Trinidad, and shell middens of Hispaniola and Cuba also cluster in the early part of this period.

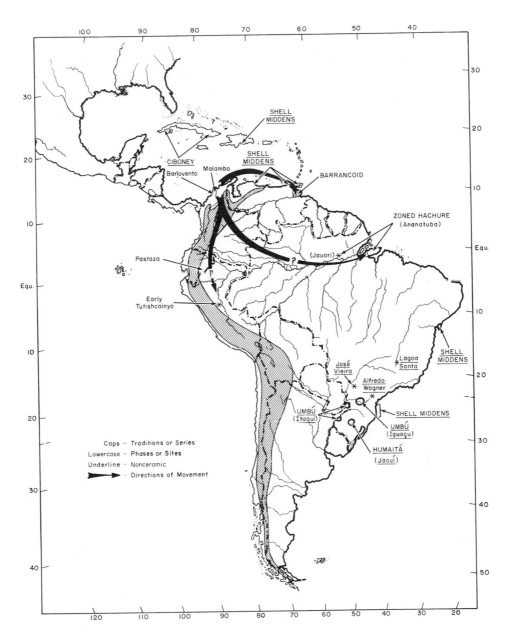

FIGURE 12.8
Location of archeological sites and complexes dated between 2000 and 1000 BC.

As the millennium was drawing to a close, pottery-making groups became established at the mouths of the Amazon and the Orinoco. Although the initial dates are approximately contemporaneous, the ceramic traditions are different. The Ananatuba phase on the eastern half of Marajó Island is characterized by relatively small but comparatively deep refuse accumulations, suggesting that residence was more stable than was usual in Amazonia. The absence of local stone and the unfavorable conditions for preservation of wood, bone, and other organic materials make pottery the principal surviving type of evidence. It was tempered with crushed sherd and decorated by three techniques: exterior brushing, red slipping, and incision. The last was executed with a broad tool to produce scallops along the rim, rectilinear patterns on the exterior wall, or areas filled with hachure (Figure 12.9, a–c). Rounded bowls and jars, sometimes with exteriorly thickened rims, are typical. There are no griddles or other indications of the use of bitter manioc. Whether domesticated plants are associated with the Ananatuba phase remains to be established; some dependence on maize or root crops seems likely in view of the apparent length of village occupancy, but wild terrestrial and aquatic food may have been sufficiently varied and abundant to permit a small population to maintain a sedentary way of life. There is no evidence of ceremonialism, social stratification, or warfare until the end of the phase, when Ananatuba villages appear to have been conquered by a group associated with a different kind of pottery.

The only other place in eastern Amazonia where the Zoned Hachure tradition has been reported is Jauarí, on the northern margin of the flood plain about halfway between Marajó and the mouth of the Rio Negro (Figure 12.8). The pottery possesses several features not represented in the Ananatuba phase. Some vessels were tempered with crushed shell; others were embellished with stylized, anthropomorphic adornos. Pottery was also used to make tubular pipes decorated with stylized faces and zoned hachure (Figure 12.9, d, g, h). Zoned hachure and shell temper also occur in the Early Tutishcainyo phase on the Rio Ucayali in eastern Peru; this phase has not been dated but the ceramics resemble types being made in the adjacent highlands during the second millennium BC (Figure 12.9, e, f). Differences in vessel shapes and other details suggest that the Tutishcainyo and eastern Amazonian Zoned Hachure complexes are not directly related. Zoned hachure is also characteristic of the Pastaza phase in the lowlands of southeastern Ecuador, which shares some motifs and techniques with Formative pottery from the coast of Colombia and the highlands of Peru; carbon-14 dates place the Pastaza phase early in the second millennium BC. This temporal and spatial distribution suggests diffusion of the Zoned Hachure tradition from northwestern South America.

In the delta of the Orinoco, the Barrancoid tradition was established by 1000 BC. Although elegantly sculptured adornos and beautifully incised patterns are its best-known features, the analysis of pottery from stratigraphic

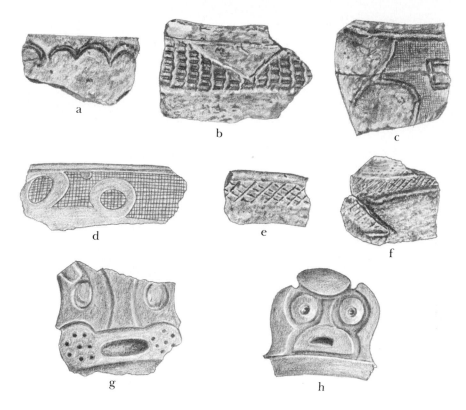

FIGURE 12.9
Pottery of the Zoned Hachure tradition of Amazonia: *a–c,* Ananatuba phase, Marajó Island; *d, g, h,* Jauarí phase, lower Amazon; *e, f,* Early Tutiscainyo phase, eastern Peru. (*a–c,* after Meggers and Evans 1957; *d–f,* after Meggers and Evans 1961; *g, h,* after Hilbert 1968.)

contexts shows that this "classic" style evolved from less elaborate antecedents. The ware is sand tempered, and vessels tend to have thick walls and polished surfaces. Broad-line incision emphasizes scrolls and often separates polished from unpolished zones. Small biomorphic adornos and circular nubbins with a central punctation or slash are also typical (Figure 12.10). The closest similarities are with the Malambo phase from the lower Rio Magdalena in Colombia (Figure 12.8), which is a few centuries earlier. Sites with Barrancoid affinities have been encountered on the intervening coast and along the middle Orinoco, but those dated are too recent to shed light on the initial route of diffusion.

The Barrancoid population had access to productive wild-food resources from the waters and lands of the Orinoco delta. The presence of griddles indicates that bitter manioc was cultivated. This artifact also occurs in the

FIGURE 12.10
Decorated pottery of the Barrancoid tradition of the Orinoco delta: *a,* zoned polishing; *b,* incisions ending in punctation; *c,* low relief bounded by incision; *d, e,* biomorphic adornos. (Courtesy of Mario Sanoja.)

Malambo phase refuse, along with bones of fish, turtle, cayman, rodent, deer, capybara, and birds. The alluvial soil and freshwater ponds, lakes, and river channels provide similar potentials for human adaptation in the two regions, and the small amount of data about the Malambo phase suggests that settlement location and stability were similar to those of the Barrancoid tradition. This, added to the ceramic resemblances, makes a strong case for intrusion of the latter into the Orinoco delta from the west.

1000–0 BC

During the millennium preceding the Christian era, the tropical lowlands gradually assumed their present condition. Patches of forest expanded across intervening savanna until they joined, creating the impressive arboreal vegetation that blankets Amazonia today. Along the coasts, the sea attained its present level. Unfortunately, there is little archeological evidence by which to assess the effects of these environmental changes on human adaptation because nearly all the dated sites are in Venezuela or the Antilles (Figure 12.11).

As is true for earlier times, the vast interior of the continent remains unknown, although the complexity of linguistic distributions at the time of

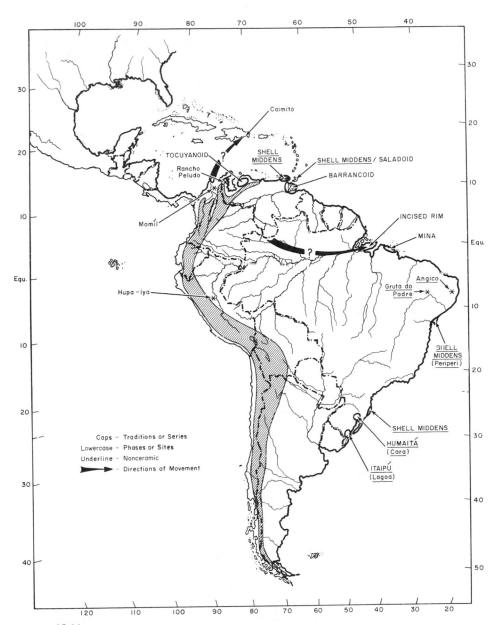

FIGURE 12.11
Location of archeological sites and complexes dated between 1000 and 0 BC.

first reporting and the antiquity of the estimates for differentiation of stocks and families provide indirect evidence of human groups. Few of the shell middens along the southern Brazilian coast that have been dated fall within this period, many having been abandoned during the preceding one. Lithic complexes have been reported from northeastern Brazil, as well as in the south, but these sites too seem less abundant.

The inception of the Itaipú tradition, with a new settlement pattern and artifact inventory, may reflect adaptation to the change in sea level. Sites have been identified along the coast from Rio de Janeiro to Rio Grande do Sul, but only the Lagoa phase in the latter state has been dated. Refuse accumulations vary greatly both in area and depth; whether the larger and deeper ones are the result of reoccupation or longer duration of occupation has not been established. Favored locations were the summits of dunes, natural rises, and small artificial mounds in swampy terrain. Fish and crustaceans were intensively exploited, in addition to birds, mammals, mollusks, and wild fruits. Grooved and ungrooved axes, grinding stones, pitted anvil-stones, and scrapers are characteristic stone implements. Bola stones and store projectile points occur in the southern phases. Beads, pendants, and bone points and awls are more typical in the north (Figure 12.12).

A similar change in adaptation appears to have occurred in the Antilles. Sites from the Dominican Republic and the Virgin Islands contain remains of sea turtle and manatee, as well as terrestrial fauna and flora. Tools made from stone or shell emphasize celts and gouges, which may have been used in woodworking. Although the shell middens of the Ortoire complex on Trinidad and the Punta Gorda complex of eastern Venezuela are associated with different artifact inventories, they probably reflect similar ways of life.

Pottery-making complexes persisted at the mouths of the Orinoco and Amazon. The Barrancoid tradition flourished, to judge from the increasing elaboration of the pottery. Toward the end of the period, modeled and incised decoration, highly polished surfaces, and a variety of vessel shapes were being combined to create impressive works of art. Bats, felines, fish, other animals, and human faces were popular motifs. A decline in wild-food remains in the refuse suggests an increase in dependence on agriculture, with bitter manioc important, if not the principal staple.

On Marajó Island, the Ananatuba phase was assimilated by invaders with a different ceramic tradition featuring open "plates" with rims interiorly thickened to create a horizontal or insloping surface that was often decorated by incision. The derivation of this Incised Rim tradition is uncertain. It has been reported from sites along the lower Amazon and upper Orinoco, but dates are too few as yet to identify the region of greatest antiquity.

Much cruder pottery with no obvious affiliation to any of the traditions thusfar described has been encountered in shell middens on the coast of Bahia. The carbon-14 dates for this Periperi tradition are inconsistent with

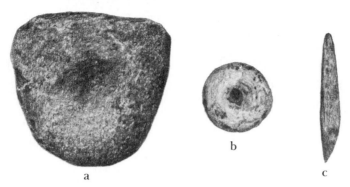

FIGURE 12.12
Characteristic artifacts of the Itaipú tradition of the southern coast of Brazil: *a*, pitted hammerstone; *b*, worked vertebra; *c*, bone projectile point. (After Programa Nacional de Pesquisas Arqueológicas 1971.)

their stratigraphic position and are widely separated in time, making their reliability uncertain. The pottery is thick, undecorated, and sand tempered. If the earliest Periperi dates prove to be associated with pottery, the shell midden context would be consistent with an origin by stimulus diffusion from the Mina tradition to the north. Another enigmatic occurrence is at Rancho Peludo in northwestern Venezuela. The site has a long preceramic occupation, and this may be the source of the early dates attributed to the pottery. The absence of resemblances to Formative ceramic complexes from the adjacent coast of Colombia, together with the occurrence of perforated pedestal bases and other traits found in later western Venezuelan traditions, argues for a more recent chronological position.

By ca. 500 BC, several well-defined polychrome traditions were established in northern Colombia and western Venezuela. The Momíl site on the Colombian coast has a number of traits suggesting influence from Central America, including not only techniques of pottery decoration but also a new subsistence pattern based on maize rather than manioc. The region east of Lake Maracaibo was dominated by the Tocuyanoid series, which features patterns skillfully executed in black and red on a white slip. Application of the colors to the background creates the effect of negative painting without employing a resist technique (Figure 12.13). The occurrence of tripod bowls points to relationships with the west, where both this vessel form and polychrome painting were highly developed at an earlier date.

So far, we have not mentioned the Saladoid series, which constitutes the initial ceramic horizon in the Lesser Antilles. Based on carbon-14 results obtained in the 1950s from the site of Saladero in the mouth of the Orinoco, this tradition has been assigned an origin early in the first millennium BC. Now that additional dates are available from the Lesser Antilles and the

FIGURE 12.13
Decorated pottery of the Tocuyanoid series, western Venezuela: *a*, anthropomorphic jar with low-relief ornament; *b*, *c*, black and red painting applied to a white-slipped surface (*a*, *b*, after Rouse and Cruzent 1963; *c*, from National Museum of Natural History, Department of Anthropology.)

Venezuelan coast, this placement seems less probable. A gap of nearly a thousand years intervenes between Saladero and sites of the white-on-red tradition on Trinidad, where this technique was in use a century or so before the Christian era. The spread of this tradition was a major event of the following period and discussion will therefore be deferred.

The recent discovery on eastern Hispaniola (Dominican Republic) of a ceramic complex that is distinct from the Saladoid tradition and possibly a few centuries older makes it necessary to reexamine the assumptions about the origins of pottery-making groups in the Greater Antilles. The Caimito site is a rockshelter 3 kilometers from the shore in a region with abundant wild-food resources. Preliminary palynological analysis reveals no evidence of cultivated plants. Celts, manos and metates, scrapers, hammerstones, and other artifacts of stone, coral, or shell resemble those from earlier nonceramic sites. The pottery is sparse but possesses several characteristics diagnostic of the initial ceramics from the mainland of South America. Among these are sherd and shell temper and incised decoration in broad lines, occasionally terminating in a punctation. The only other kind of embellishment is application of low ribs to form curves. The vessel surfaces were sometimes well polished. Rounded bowls and jars are the predominate forms, and rim treatment is extremely variable. The similarities between this pottery and earlier coastal Colombian complexes suggest the possibility of a trans-Caribbean route of dispersal.

AD 0–500

Early in the Christian era, pottery began to be made at several places on the Brazilian coast, in the Lesser Antilles, and along the middle Amazon (Figure 12.14). Although it can be assumed that hunter-gatherers continued to occupy much of the lowlands, only three dates are available for nonceramic complexes—one each for the Humaitá and Umbú traditions in Rio Grande do Sul and one for the Potiri phase of the Itaipú tradition in Espírito Santo. Shell middens, largely abandoned during the previous period, continue to be insignificant.

The best-documented event is the spread of the Saladoid tradition, which appeared on Trinidad at the end of the preceding period. The near simultaneity of the initial carbon-14 dates from Puerto Rico and eastern Venezuela implies a very rapid dispersal; whether the immigrants assimilated, replaced, or coexisted with the earlier nonceramic populations remains to be established. Continuing expansion along the Venezuelan coast and into the Orinoco basin is indicated by the appearance of Saladoid pottery in these areas a century or two later. (Although other definitions have been employed by specialists, we have adopted a simple criterion for this discussion. Complexes incorporating white-on-red decoration are considered Saladoid; those lacking this technique are classified as Barrancoid.) Saladoid pottery employs several techniques of decoration in addition to white-on-red painting. Incision defining zones filled with crosshatch, low nubbins with a central punctation or slash, and broad-line incision are typical; small adornos, frequently rising from the rim and concave on the interior, are also characteristic, along with vertical strap handles. The broad incision and style of modeling resemble Barrancoid decoration and may represent influence from that source (Figure 12.15).

Three distinct ceramic traditions appear on widely separated parts of the Brazilian coast during this period. Taquara tradition in eastern Rio Grande do Sul has the most abundant and varied decoration (Figure 12.16). Cylindrical, round-bottomed containers have well-finished surfaces ornamented with pinching, incision, numerous varieties of fingernail marking, or punctations (both single and drag-and-jab). Rocker stamping, cord impressing, and red

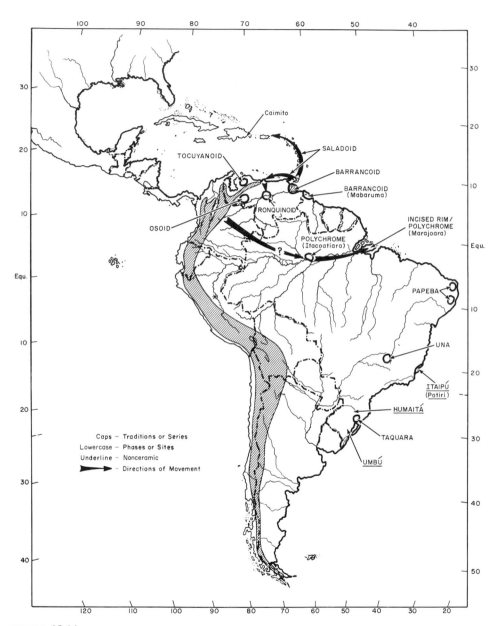

FIGURE 12.14
Location of archeological sites and complexes dated between AD 0 and 500.

FIGURE 12.15
Characteristic decorative techniques of the Saladoid tradition, eastern coast of Venezuela:
a, white painting on red slip; b, red zones bordered by white painting on an unslipped
surface; c, red painting on a white slip; d, e, fine incision; f, low nubbins with central
punctation; g, adorno on vertical strap handle. (Courtesy of Iraida Vargas.)

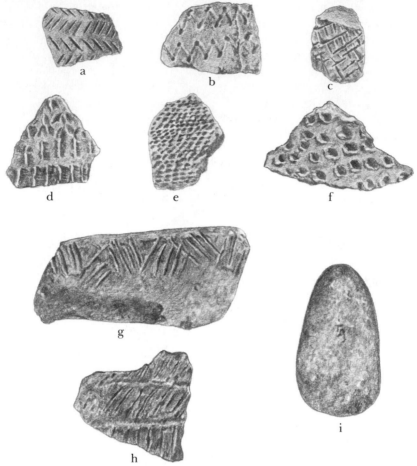

FIGURE 12.16
Characteristic decorated pottery and stone artifact of the Taquara (*a–f*) and Una (*g–i*) traditions of the southern coast of Brazil: *a,* zigzag incision; *b,* rocker stamping; *c,* cross-hatch; *d,* pinching (*top*) and drag-and-jab (*bottom*); *e,* dentate stamping; *f,* deep punctation; *g,* incision; *h,* zoned incision; *i,* pecked stone ax. (After Programa Nacional de Pesquisas Arqueológicas 1971 [*a–f*]; 1969 and 1974 [*g–i*].)

slipping also occur. Only 10 percent of the vessels are plain. Most of the pottery comes from shallow sites in the forest, but some has been found associated with pithouses on the neighboring planalto. These structures often form clusters of three or more, either randomly distributed or encircling a larger pit. They were probably occupied seasonally, during harvest of Araucaria pine nuts. Celts and pestles are extremely common, the latter perhaps used to crush the nuts. There is no evidence of domesticated plants. Rare bone projectile points are the only artifacts indicative of hunting.

The earliest available date for the Uná tradition places its arrival in Minas Gerais a few centuries before the inception of the Taquara tradition. Habitation sites are small and sometimes located in rockshelters. The pottery is much less ornate, the principal technique of decoration being striated polishing; red slipping, punctation, and corrugation occur rarely. Common vessel shapes are deep jars with expanding walls and rounded bases, globular jars, and jars with short, constricted necks. Griddles imply use of bitter manioc. Other clues to food processing are stone pestles. Stone axes and pottery spindle whorls also occur.

The Papeba tradition makes an approximately contemporaneous appearance in Rio Grande do Norte and Pernambuco. This pottery is sometimes red slipped. Circular or elongated nubbins applied to the upper wall or extending above the rim have been perforated vertically, perhaps for insertion of a cord. Simple rounded jars and bowls with outsloping walls are the principal vessel shapes; griddles have not been reported. Polished celts, quartz perforators, hammerstones, and flakes with evidence of use characterize the lithic industry. Fragments of *Strombus* were employed for scraping or punching.

The earliest known pottery from the middle Amazon also dates near the beginning of this period. It comes from Itacoatiara, on the left bank just below the Rio Negro (Figure 12.17). Several other sites have produced similar ceramics decorated by polychrome painting (red and black on white), fine incision, broad incision, double-line incision, punctation, excision, and modeling combined with incision. The paste is tempered with sponge spicules (cauixí). Although Hilbert (1968:207) assigned the Itacoatiara phase to the Incised and Punctate tradition, decoration and vessel shape are more characteristic of the Polychrome tradition. Especially noteworthy are carinated and hollow-rimmed bowls. Pottery figurines and spindle whorls are also widespread (Figure 12.17).

Several dates suggest that the Marajoara phase was established on Marajó by AD 500. It is the best-known representative of the Polychrome tradition, having been reported by travelers and naturalists during the nineteenth century and having received attention from anthropologists in the early decades of the twentieth century. Unlike other Amazonian archeological complexes, Marajoara phase sites incorporate artificial mounds, most of which served as cemeteries for interment of burial urns. This culture was more advanced in every respect than its predecessors on Marajó. Differential treatment of the dead, complicated decoration and standardized vessel forms, articles produced for ritual or mortuary use, and construction of large earthworks are among the features implying social stratification and occupational specialization.

At the mouth of the Orinoco, the Barrancoid series continued to flourish, and Barrancoid elements were incorporated into the Ronquín style, which appeared on the middle Orinoco toward the end of this period. The

FIGURE 12.17

Ceramics of the Polychrome tradition of Amazonia—*a, b, d, g,* are Marajoara phase, Marajó Island; *c, e, f,* are Napo phase, eastern Ecuador: *a,* spindle whorl with excised decoration (enlarged to show detail); *b,* ladle; *c,* corner of a square basin with incised and painted designs featuring double-headed snakes; *d,* anthropomorphic jar with incision on a white slip; *e,* sherd with incised and excised decoration; *f, g,* red and black painting on a white slip in a pseudonegative pattern. (*a, b, d,* after Meggers and Evans 1957; *c, e, f,* after Evans and Meggers 1968; *g,* after Palmatary 1950.)

Mabaruma phase of northwestern Guyana, as yet undated, may reflect Barrancoid expansion to the east about AD 500.

Artificial mounds and causeways were being constructed on the western llanos of Venezuela around the beginning of the Christian era (Zucchi 1973). The subsistence pattern of this Caño de Oso complex combined maize cultivation with hunting and fishing. Metates, manos, pestles, bolas, and celts occur, along with pendants, beads, figurines, and spindle whorls. Although the construction of earthworks and use of certain types of artifacts are shared with the Marajoara phase, the ceramic complexes from these two areas have little in common except the use of painting. The variety of incised and excised techniques, the anthropomorphic urns, and other Marajoara phase ceramic characteristics are absent; popular Caño de Oso vessels are shallow bowls with tall pedestals and narrow-necked jars with angular bodies. Ring and conical supports are also confined to western Venezuela. The "pseudo-negative" style of painting, hollow rims, snake motifs, and anthropomorphic jars of the earlier Tocuyanoid series resemble more closely attributes of the Amazonian Polychrome tradition than do the "positive" painting and footed vessels of the Caño de Oso style. Whether the construction of earthworks in these widely separated regions represents similar adaptations to periodically inundated terrain or diffusion of the concept of mound building and associated sociopolitical organization remains to be ascertained.

Numerous localized ceramic complexes have been reported along the Amazon, and pottery ornamented by drag-and-jab punctation has been encountered in northeastern Argentina. In the absence of relative sequences or absolute dates, it is impossible to assign them a chronological position. Some may belong to this period, but the majority are probably more recent.

AD 500–1000

By AD 500, pottery-making groups were established along the Amazon and Orinoco rivers, throughout most of the Coastal Strip and the Guianas, and on the Caribbean islands. Before AD 1000, they had spread to eastern Cuba and the northern lowlands of Argentina. A few dates document the persistence of nonceramic populations and attest to continuing exploitation of shellfish on a limited scale, particularly in southern Brazil. Sites and artifacts are similar to those of earlier periods, so attention will be restricted henceforth to ceramic complexes.

On the Brazilian coast, the Taquara and Una traditions expanded their distributions. Taquara phases dominated most of northeastern Rio Grande do Sul until the last decades, when they were replaced along the shore by Tupiguaraní immigrants. The Una tradition spread from Minas Gerais to the coast, where incision was added to the repertoire of decorative techniques (Figure 12.18). In the swampy environment of southeastern Rio Grande

FIGURE 12.18
Location of archeological sites and complexes dated between AD 500 and 1000.

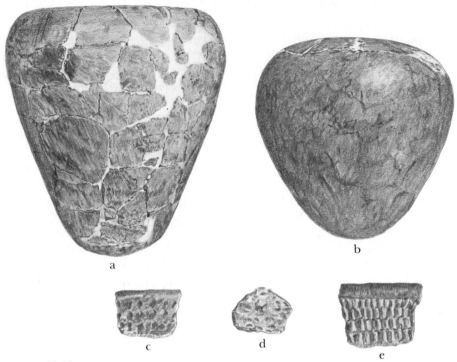

FIGURE 12.19
Characteristic pottery of the Aratú (*a, b*) and Itararé (*c–e*) traditions of coastal Brazil:
a, b, periform burial urns; *c, d,* overall punctation; *e,* dentate stamping. (After Programa
Nacional de Pesquisas Arqueológicas 1971.)

do Sul, the appearance of simple pottery in the upper levels of nonceramic
sites marks the beginning of the Vieira tradition. Rare decoration consists
of one or two rows of dentate stamping adjacent to the rim; typically, vessels
have large, flattened bases and incurving walls. The former locations of small
villages of the Itararé tradition in eastern Paraná are marked by shallow
deposits of sherds mixed with unretouched cores and flakes. Ninety-two
percent of the pottery has well-smoothed, undecorated surfaces; the rest is
red slipped, punctated, or dentate stamped (Figure 12.19, c–e). Deep, rounded
bowls and wide-mouthed jars with slightly everted or exteriorly thickened
rims and flattened bases are typical.

By the end of the millennium, the Aratú tradition was widely distributed
in the state of Bahia on the north-central coast of Brazil. Again, the pottery
is predominantly plain; rare decoration consists of incision, fingernail marking, punctation, red slipping, unobliterated coils, or corrugation. Vessels are
much larger than those of any other regional tradition and include periform
burial urns up to 75 centimeters tall and 60 centimeters in diameter (Figure
12.19, a, b). Cemeteries containing more than 100 urns have been encountered

in many parts of Bahia, as well as in the adjacent states of Goiás, Sergipe, and Alagoas. Spindle whorls and pipes are typical ceramic artifacts.

An event that was to have a major impact over the entire Coastal Strip was the arrival of the Tupiguaraní tradition. Present dates suggest that the earliest immigrants settled in western Paraná around AD 500. This tradition has been identified with speakers of Tupí-Guaraní on the basis of ethnohistoric evidence and the coincidence between the distribution of sites and the area occupied by groups with this linguistic affiliation at the time of first reporting. Close to a hundred regional and chronological phases have been defined, and numerous relative sequences showing a transition from painting to corrugation to brushing as the most common surface treatment provide a basis for recognizing three successive subtraditions. Unfortunately, carbon-14 dates are available for less than a quarter of the phases. Painting in red and black on a white slip, corrugation, red slipping, fingernail marking, incision, punctation, grooving, brushing, fingernail ridging, and rim nicking are characteristic, with plastic treatments most common in the south. By AD 1000, bearers of the Painted subtradition had spread over northern and western Paraná, penetrated southward to Rio Grande do Sul, and advanced northward to the coast of Espírito Santo. In the south, corrugation became more popular than painting, giving rise to the Corrugated subtradition. Survival of the earlier regional traditions is indicated by failure of the intruders to occupy their territories, by ceramic evidence of acculturation and trade, and by contemporaneous carbon-14 dates. The correlation between Tupiguaraní sites and forested habitats suggests that persistence of the populations associated with regional traditions was facilitated by their adaptation to other kinds of environments.

Habitation sites of the Tupiguaraní tradition have all the characteristics diagnostic of ethnographic Tropical Forest cultures. The refuse is shallow (rarely exceeding 10 centimeters in thickness), indicating low village permanency. In many instances, darker patches of soil mark the locations of circular or oval houses, which were often arranged around a plaza. The presence of griddles and the association of the sites with forest are circumstantial evidence of slash-and-burn agriculture with emphasis on bitter manioc. Urn burial was practiced and interments were sometimes isolated, sometimes within or adjacent to a house, sometimes in the center of the plaza. Vessels are extremely variable in form and size, with ovoid or rectanguloid outlines popular in the north. Large polished celts, choppers, and cylindrical lip plugs (tembetás) are common stone artifacts (Figure 12.20).

Pottery making was also introduced into the northern lowlands of Argentina during this period. Sites of Las Mercedes phase consist of scatterings of sherds, along with occasional bola stones, three-quarter grooved axes, and possibly stone projectile points. The incised and painted decoration is reminiscent of the Aguada style of the adjacent highlands. There is no direct evidence of agriculture, but plant and animal remains indicate that hunting, fishing, and gathering were important activities.

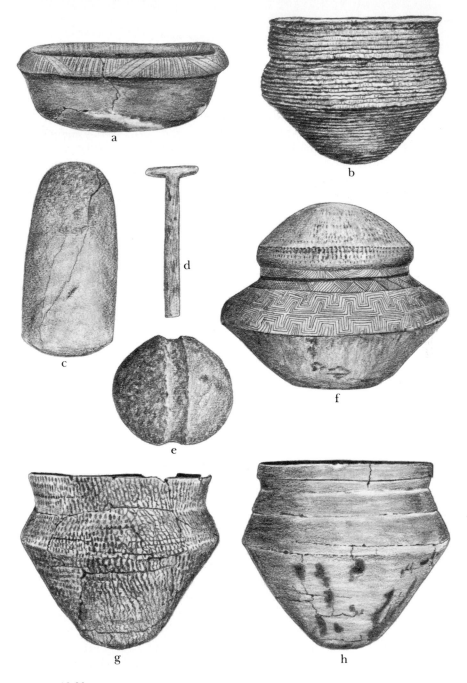

FIGURE 12.20
Pottery and stone artifacts of the Tupiguaraní tradition of coastal Brazil: *a*, square bowl
with the interior painted in red and black on a white slip; *b*, burial urn decorated with
simple corrugation; *c*, polished ax; *d*, quartz lip plug; *e*, bola stone; *f*, burial urn with
red painting on a white slip, lid decorated with complicated corrugation; *g*, corrugated
burial urn; *h*, painted burial urn. (After Programa Nacional de Pesquisas Arqueológicas
1971 [*a, c, e*]; 1969a [*b, d, g, h*]; 1974 [*f*].)

In Amazonia, the Polychrome tradition expanded westward along the flood plain (see Figure 12.18). Dates from several sites between the Madeira and Japurá indicate a dispersal upriver from the vicinity of the Rio Negro. At the mouth of the Amazon, the Marajoara phase was undergoing a decline in general complexity. This tradition displays considerable regional variation, some of which may reflect an unrecognized mixture produced by the reoccupation of shallow sites. Amalgamation with earlier complexes, local evolution, and other kinds of processes also potentially involved cannot be evaluated until local relative sequences and phase distributions are better known.

The principal unifying characteristic of the Polychrome tradition is pottery decorated by painting in red or black or both on a white slip, with "pseudonegative" motifs typical. Associated techniques include excision, red slipping, incision with a single- or double-pointed tool, grooving, and appliqué. Higher relief and modeling were used for the hands and legs of anthropomorphic urns and for small adornos. Square-mouthed vessels and large, shallow bowls with ornately contoured rims are also common. Ceramic artifacts include figurines, stools, flat or roller stamps, and spindle whorls. Stone tools are very rare, as in all Amazonian traditions, their place being taken by objects of wood, bone, or other perishable materials. Anthropomorphic urns were widely used for burial.

The only Amazonian ceramic complex known to belong to this period that is not affiliated with the Polychrome tradition is the Japurá phase. Although painting occurs, the pottery is distinguished by vessels with broad rims ornamented by modeling and incision reminiscent of the Barrancoid style. The proximity of this region to the middle Orinoco, the existence of a water connection between the Orinoco and Amazon drainages, and the differences in antiquity all make derivation from the north seem probable.

Along the middle Orinoco, the Ronquinoid style gave way to the Arauquinoid series, which emphasized modeling and closely spaced, parallel, straight, incised lines, sometimes accompanied by excision or punctation (Figure 12.21, c, d). Increased interaction between the Orinoco and Amazon basins is implied by the mixture of traits exhibited by pottery of the Nericagua phase from southern Venezuela. It shares with Amazonian and Orinocan complexes the use of sponge spicules for tempering and combines vessel shapes characteristic of the Amazonian Incised Rim tradition with modeling reminiscent of Caribbean styles. On the lower Orinoco, Barrancoid pottery began to simplify about AD 750, and there was a decline in village permanency, although the general way of life seems to have continued much the same. Decoration emphasized incision and punctation more than high relief. Western Venezuela continued to be dominated by groups with elaborately painted pottery. Increased complexity in sociopolitical and ritual features probably indicates the emergence of chiefdoms in the highland valleys.

In Puerto Rico, the Saladoid series was replaced about AD 650 by a different style known as Ostionoid. White painting was abandoned, but polished

FIGURE 12.21
Pottery of the Incised and Punctate tradition of the northern lowlands. *a, g,* Santarem style, lower Amazon; *b–d, f,* Arauquinoid series, middle Orinoco; *e,* Mabaruma phase, northwestern Guyana. (*a,* after Palmatary 1939; *b–d, f,* after Cruxent and Rouse 1958; *e,* after Meggers and Evans 1961; *g,* after Willey 1971.)

red slipping remained popular. Geometric or bat-headed rim adornos, curved appliqué ribs, and incision on the rim interior are typical. Bowls are often ovoid or boat shaped, and griddles are common. Since Ostionoid pottery appears at the same time on Jamaica, it should be of equal age on intervening Hispaniola, although the earliest carbon-14 date there is a few centuries more recent. Some authorities consider this change to be a local development, but the addition of petalloid celts, pottery stamps, zemis ("three-pointers"), stone idols, and other new types of artifacts makes outside influence a possibility (Figure 12.22). Ball courts and stone belts are tentatively associated; if the association proves to be true, their widespread occurrence on the mainland would make the case for diffusion even stronger. Many of these traits had spread southward as far as Trinidad by the end of the period, implying more intensive interaction throughout the Antilles than existed during earlier or later times.

AD 1000–1500

During the final centuries preceding European contact, sedentary pottery-making (and presumably agricultural) groups were distributed over most of the tropical lowlands, with Patagonia in the south and western Cuba in the north being the best-documented exceptions. Although hunter-gatherers persisted in the intervening area, many of the gaps on the map are probably filled by complexes that have already been described but not dated.

In the Southern Lowlands, sedentary pottery-making groups continued to occupy the annually inundated portions of Santiago del Estero. Habitations were on river banks, natural elevations, or artificial mounds. The last occur in groups of 5 to 100, some arranged haphazardly and others (particularly the larger clusters) in irregular rows along "streets." Settlements of the Sunchituyoj phase are 3 to 10 kilometers apart, and the circular or oval mounds that compose them are from 20 to 60 meters long. Elevation ranges from less than a meter to 4 meters, the upper 40 to 60 centimeters being composed of habitation refuse. Plain pottery predominates, but some vessels were decorated by appliqué, incision, or black paint. During the succeeding Averias phase, black and red painted designs on a white slip became popular. Bolas and bone or stone projectile points attest to continued dependence on hunting, but maize was grown. Secondary burial in urns was characteristic, and the head was often placed in a different vessel than the rest of the skeleton. Among artifacts indicative of ritual are figurines and tubular pipes. Bone awls and needles, pottery spindle whorls, and metal objects reflect various domestic activities. Where affiliations can be discerned, they are with the West.

Although the Taquara, Itararé, Una, and Aratú traditions persisted in enclaves along the Coastal Strip, most of the region was dominated by the Tupiguaraní. Representatives of the Painted subtradition had reached Bahia

FIGURE 12.22
Artifacts of the Chicoid series of the Greater Antilles: *a*, stone idol or zemi; *b*, stone celt with anthropomorphic carving; *c*, stone head; *d*, pottery figurine. (*a*, *c*, after Fewkes 1907; *b*, after Rouse 1964; *c*, after Willey 1971.)

by AD 1200, southern Goiás by AD 1300, and Rio Grande do Norte before AD 1500. Numerous phases belonging to the Corrugated subtradition have been identified in the south and corrugation had replaced painting as the most popular surface treatment in the Rio de Janeiro area by ca. AD 1300. Whether this change reflects a second wave of migration or a widespread evolutionary trend remains to be established. Although the majority of the later villages fall within the size range typical of the Painted subtradition, large ones (extending over more than 100 meters) are more common. Pitted anvil-stones, pounders, pestles, and small polished celts are characteristic lithic artifacts.

Along the lower Amazon, the Polychrome tradition gave way to pottery emphasizing decoration by incision combined with punctation. The most flamboyant member of this Incised and Punctate horizon is the Santarém culture, which flourished at the mouth of the Rio Tapajós (Figure 12.23). The evenly spaced, parallel incisions terminating in punctates or alternating with areas containing rings or punctates, which are diagnostic of this horizon, have a wide distribution during the final centuries prior to the discovery of the New World. Complexes incorporating these features include the Mazagão phase at the mouth of the Amazon, the Arauquinoid series on the middle Orinoco, the Postclassic Barrancoid and late Mabaruma ceramics of the lower Orinoco and northwestern Guyana, and the Chicoid series of the Greater Antilles (see Figures 12.22 and 12.24). Glass beads or other objects of European origin may be associated. Pottery affiliated with this horizon has not been reported from Amazonia above the Rio Negro.

The Amazonian Incised and Punctate tradition appears to have intruded from the north and broken the continuity of the Polychrome tradition. The upriver diffusion of the latter, underway during the preceding period, continued, and it had penetrated to the middle Ucayali in eastern Peru by about AD 1300. At the opposite side of the continent, the Aristé phase of coastal Brazilian Guiana survived until European contact. Here, rockshelters were used as cemeteries, where small burial urns were set on the surface of the ground.

The Marajoara phase was replaced on Marajó and other islands in the mouth of the Amazon by the Aruã phase. Villages were small and frequently moved, leaving only a scattering of potsherds to mark their former locations along streams near the shore. Rare decoration on the pottery consisted of impressed rings, appliqué ribs, and painting. The dead were placed in large jars, which were not interred. The quantity of urns in some cemeteries implies that they were used by several villages or for a considerable period of time or both. Occasionally, pottery figurines, small pots, polished stone axes or celts, pottery or stone beads, and nephrite pendants were placed in the urn. The immediate origin of this culture was the adjacent Guiana mainland, where stone alignments are an additional feature. Similar monuments have

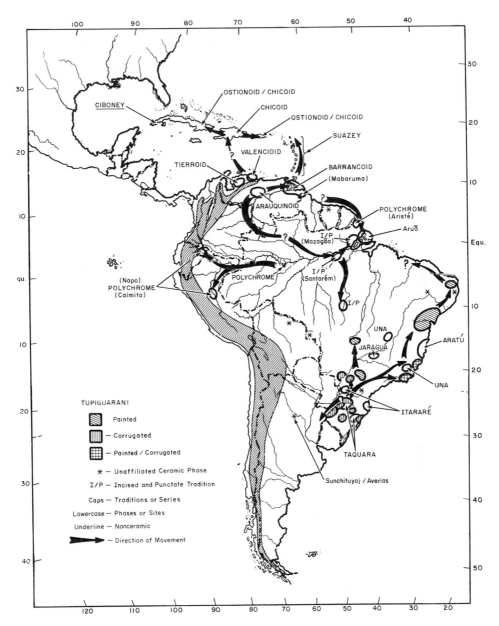

FIGURE 12.23
Location of archeological sites and complexes dated between AD 1000 and 1500.

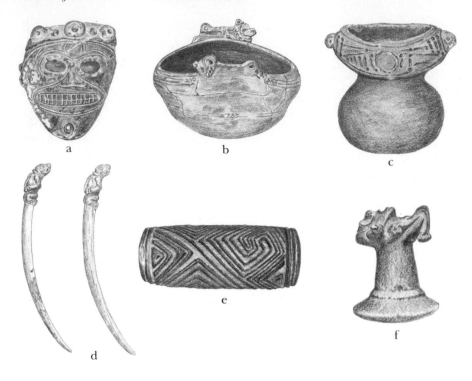

FIGURE 12.24

Artifacts of the Chicoid series of the Greater Antilles. *a*, shell amulet; *b*, *c*, pottery vessels; *d*, spatulae to induce vomiting; *e*, cylindrical stamp; *f*, stone pestle. (From National Museum of Natural History, Department of Anthropology.)

been reported from Guyana, and a number of aspects of the pottery and stone artifacts suggest affiliations with the Caribbean.

In the Greater Antilles, cultural development reached its climax. The increased number of ball courts and the artistic quality of the associated paraphernalia suggest greater ceremonial activity and perhaps sociopolitical complexity. Among the ritual objects beautifully carved from wood, bone, or shell are idols, snuff tubes, spatulae to induce vomiting, large zemis, stools, and a variety of amulets. The pottery was decorated with broad incisions, frequently terminating in punctations, and with modeled and incised lugs (see Figures 12.22 and 12.24). Heart-shaped bottles, often ornamented with anthropomorphic features on the neck, are also diagnostic. The occurrence of some of the same ceramic motifs of the Incised and Punctate horizon on the mainland suggests communication across the Caribbean, as do the numerous similarities between ceremonial objects.

That this communication did not involve the Lesser Antilles seems to be implied by the presence of a different ceramic complex in this region. Suazey pottery has coarse temper, poorly smoothed surfaces, and crude decoration. The coincidence between the distribution of this style and the historic range of the Island Caribs makes it possible to correlate the archeological and ethnographic data. The occurrence of occasional vessels of earlier styles verifies ethnohistorical accounts that the Island Carib invaders married local women, who retained some of their pottery-making traditions. No similar ceramic complex has been encountered in Venezuela or the Guianas that might identify the source of these migrants. The apparently simultaneous movement down the coast to the mouth of the Amazon, represented by the intrusion there of the Aruã phase, may be traceable to a common impetus. The ceramic complexes differ, however, and the Guianas are too poorly known as yet for this to be verified or explained.

"Floating" Complexes

Pottery with characteristics unlike those of traditions and styles for which chronological information is available has been reported from various parts of the lowlands. One such complex on the lower Paraná features decoration by drag-and-jab punctation in lines and zones, along with massive zoo-morphic adornos. It bears no resemblance to any material from adjacent parts of Brazil and is undated. It could be as early as the Vieira or Taquara regional traditions, or it could fall just prior to the migration of the Tupi-guaraní down the Rio Uruguay in the early historic period.

Another "mystery" complex is the painted pottery associated with earth-works in the Mojos region of lowland Bolivia. These remains are also un-assignable to any period with confidence, but we guess that they are no earlier than similar constructions in western Venezuela, which date sub-sequent to AD 1000. The numerous distinctive ceramic complexes along the lower Amazon indicate considerable cultural heterogeneity, but whether this is spatial or chronological or both remains to be established. Other regional traditions have been defined in central Brazil (Minas Gerais and Goiás), but these too are of uncertain age.

Within the Tupiguaraní tradition, dates have been obtained for only a few of the approximately 100 phases that have been recognized. Although the local relative chronological positions of most of the others have been estab-lished either by seriation or by identification of their subtradition affiliation, the south-north slope exhibited by the existing dates for the tradition makes the time of its arrival in Goiás, Maranhão, and Pará speculative without carbon-14 determinations. The fact that groups of Tupí-Guaraní speakers fled inland to escape enslavement by European colonists is another complication, since it implies that some of the archeological phases in the interior may represent such postcontact movements rather than precontact settlement. In northern Venezuela, numerous sites and complexes have been assigned to periods based on typological similarities. Here too, more dates are needed to differentiate contemporary communities from dispersals from various centers over several centuries. Relative sequences are also available from several areas along the base of the Peruvian Andes and from eastern Ecuador, and a number of the component phases have been dated. Those few with clear affiliations to the lowlands have been included in the preceding review; the majority appear to be local developments or related to cultures in the adjacent highlands.

SOME PATTERNS AND THEIR POSSIBLE SIGNIFICANCE

Even if the undated sites and phases were added to the maps, most of Amazonia would remain blank. In spite of this hiatus and numerous smaller gaps, a number of coincidences in the appearances or disappearances of styles or traditions can be discerned. These suggest that widespread factors affected human adaptation several times during the past seven millennia and offer a basis for formulating hypotheses to guide future research.

Examination of the patterning of the nonceramic complexes reveals that the vast majority fall into two periods: 5000–3000 BC (Figure 12.23) and 2000–1000 BC (Figure 12.8); the maps corresponding to the third and first millennia BC (Figures 12.7, 12.11) are comparatively blank. This chronological clustering applies both to inland sites and to shell middens. Although the possibility that accidents of sampling are responsible cannot be eliminated, there are indications that environmental changes may be involved. Shell middens were most abundant when the sea was 2.5 to 3.0 meters above its present level, inundating larger areas of the low-lying shore and expanding the habitat suitable for shellfish. Between about 2700 and 2000 BC, and again between about 1500 and 600 BC, sea level was lower than it is today, and the rarity of shell middens dating within these intervals suggests that this caused a significant decline in the mollusk population.

Whether exploitation of shellfish and other marine resources was a seasonal or year-around specialization, one might expect the reduction of this staple to be reflected in an increased number of inland sites. Actually, however, the density of inland sites declines simultaneously with the decrease in shell midden occupancy. Again, sampling error may be responsible, but another possibility must also be considered. Loss of a dependable marine food supply would have forced more intensive exploitation of terrestrial resources and hastened their depletion unless local groups become smaller or more mobile.

Another response might have been a decline in general population size. In either case, the archeological consequence would be more dispersed, sparser, and shallower refuse accumulations, which would be difficult to discover or to recognize as human in origin. Subsistence resources must have been further reduced by changes in the vegetation resulting from more arid climate. Between about 3500 and 500 BC, the forest was replaced by savanna and drought-tolerant types of flora in parts of Amazonia and along the Coastal Strip. Although evidence from all disciplines is meager, there is enough to suggest that not only man but all plant and animal populations were being subjected to strong environmental stresses during the final millennia preceding the Christian era.

Whether these general fluctuations in climate and sea level set the stage for the dissemination of pottery making during the fourth millennium BC remains to be established. It seems unlikely, however, that the nearly contemporaneous appearance of this new trait in shell middens of southeastern North America and northeastern South America was coincidental. Shell-tempered pottery was made on the Colombian coast, and although the earliest dated occurrence is too recent to be ancestral, additional investigation may reveal complexes with greater antiquity. Whether the large gaps between the known "colonies" and the presumed donor area reflect rapid diffusion or inadequate archeological survey is another problem awaiting future research.

The shell midden ceramic tradition died out in South America early in the second millennium BC, and several centuries elapsed before new kinds of pottery were introduced at the mouths of the Amazon and Orinoco. The Barrancoid series shares enough features with Andean Formative ceramics to suggest its derivation from the west. The Ananatuba phase on Marajó Island has also been interpreted as an intrusion from the northwestern portion of the continent. Support for this inference is provided by the related Jauarí phase on the lower Amazon, which has pottery tempered with shell and decorated by modeling, incision, and zoned hachure—all traits present earlier in the Tesca phase on the coast of Colombia. Consideration of this distribution in the context of the changing environment reveals that the Zoned Hachure tradition appeared on the lower Amazon during the final period of aridity and forest fragmentation. Although the extent to which the vegetation was modified is still open to speculation, a corridor probably extended across the Guianas that would have facilitated the penetration of groups adapted to parkland or savanna.

Just prior to the Christian era, new ceramic complexes "sprouted up" in a number of other regions. The Saladoid or White-on-Red series appeared on Trinidad. Pottery tempered with shell and decorated with broad-line incision was being made on eastern Hispaniola. The Mangueiras phase, which replaced the Ananatuba phase at the mouth of the Amazon, is characterized by shallow bowls with a broad, flat-topped rim. East of Lake Maracaibo, the

Tocuyanoid series initiated an emphasis on polychrome painting that dominated western Venezuela thereafter. These developments are concentrated north of the equator and near the coast. Why? Changed adaptive pressures resulting from coalescence of the forest may be involved, but information is too vague to indicate where and how populations might have been affected.

During the first five centuries of the Christian era, pottery-making groups appeared on the Brazilian coast, the middle Amazon, and the Lesser Antilles. The Saladoid series diffused rapidly over the islands as far as Puerto Rico and onto the Venezuelan mainland. Dates are progressively more recent moving up the Orinoco and westward along the coast, contrary to what would be expected of a tradition with roots in the nuclear areas. Nevertheless, Saladoid pottery from eastern Venezuela shares enough features with late Chorrera ceramics from coastal Ecuador to imply a common derivation. Again, separation in time and space is great, and no similar material has been reported from the intervening area.

The earliest dates from the middle Amazon come from Itacoatiara, just below Manaus, and belong to the Polychrome tradition. This area may provide a link between the earlier Tocuyanoid series of western Venezuela and the Marajoara phase, which flourished a few centuries later at the mouth of the Amazon. The differences in associated traits and the absence of polychrome pottery on the upper Orinoco must be considered in assessing the possibility of direct or indirect affiliations. Three other distinct regional ceramic traditions appear almost simultaneously on widely separated parts of the Brazilian coast: the Papeba tradition in Rio Grande do Norte and Pernambuco, the Una tradition in southern Minas Gerais, and the Taquara tradition in eastern Rio Grande do Sul. The huge hiatus in information between these regions and the western margin of the continent, where cultural development had attained the level of statehood, makes speculations about origins premature. It seems unlikely to us, however, that pottery making was invented independently.

Between AD 500 and 1000, pottery-making groups became dominant in the lowlands. Most of the earlier traditions persisted, some remaining within their original territories and others expanding their distributions. On the Coastal Strip, the Vieira, Itararé, and Aratú traditions were added to the roster of regional ceramic complexes for which no antecedents are evident. About AD 500, an event occurred that was to affect the entire Coastal Strip during the succeeding millennium—the appearance of the Tupiguaraní tradition in the vicinity of western Paraná. Expansion southward was hampered by the Taquara tradition, which appears to have survived in part because its habitat was not sought by the forest-dwelling invaders. Incorporation of Taquara decorative techniques into the Tupiguaraní ceramic repertoire is one indication of communication; another is the occasional occurrence of painted sherds in Taquara habitation sites. Migration northward proceeded faster, and before AD 1000 the tradition was established in Espírito Santo. The Una tradition may have been displaced to the coast by the newcomers, or this movement may have begun earlier.

In Amazonia, the Polychrome tradition expanded up the Amazon and some of its tributaries from the vicinity of the Rio Negro and also continued to dominate the island of Marajó. The ancient Barrancoid style of the Orinoco delta reached a climax and spread to adjacent Guyana. Pottery from the Rio Japurá, a western tributary of the Amazon, exhibits Barrancoid features, but their origin is uncertain because the Nericagua phase, which occupied the intervening upper Orinoco at this time, shows no similar influence. The Arauquinoid series of the middle Orinoco also emphasizes incision rather than modeling.

The Ostionoid series emerged on Hispaniola and Puerto Rico and soon spread to Jamaica. Rather crude adornos are typical, and the pottery has been considered a local development from degenerate Saladoid antecedents. By ca. AD 800, Ostionoid pottery was being manufactured throughout the Lesser Antilles, along with a variety of stone and shell artifacts characteristic of the larger islands. Although the widespread distribution of these traits suggests that the Antilles were more closely integrated culturally than at any earlier or later time, they probably were not unified socially or politically.

This interaction was disrupted around AD 1000 by the appearance in the Greater Antilles of Chicoid pottery, associated with the historic Arawak. Among its diagnostic features are anthropomorphic modeling; broad-line incision, frequently associated with or terminating in punctation; and decorative motifs with a long history on the mainland. Ball courts, stools, stone carvings, amulets, and other ritual elements also have mainland counterparts. Although communication via the Lesser Antilles has not been ruled out, the known distributions of these traits make direct contact across the Caribbean a plausible alternative. By AD 1200, most of the Lesser Antilles were overrun by the Island Carib, whose conquest was interrupted by the arrival of Europeans. The invaders are identifiable archeologically by a ceramic style known as Suazey, and the presence of occasional sherds with Ostionoid features supports historic accounts of their adoption of Arawak women who, being the potters, retained some of their traditional ways.

By AD 1000, the Polychrome tradition was restricted to the upper Amazon, leaving the lower course dominated by representatives of the Incised and Punctate tradition. A band composed of incised lines slanting in alternate directions and defining triangular spaces occupied by rings or punctates is the hallmark of this tradition. The Chicoid series of the Greater Antilles, late Barrancoid phases from the lower Orinoco and Guyana, the Arauquinoid series of the middle Orinoco, the Santarém complex of the lower Amazon, and the Mazagão phase on the Brazilian Guiana coast are among the best-known expressions. Initial dates are closely contemporaneous throughout this distribution, implying rapid dispersal. Whether this reflects a population movement and, if so, what provoked it are questions for which no answer can be offered as yet.

Along the Coastal Strip, the Taquara, Itararé, Una, and Aratú traditions survived, but most suffered reductions in their territories as a result of continuing Tupiguaraní expansion. By AD 1200, the latter were established on the coast of Bahia and two centuries later were in Rio Grande do Norte. They may also have reached Ceará by this time, but dates are needed for confirmation. The chroniclers tell us that these people were migrating in search of an earthly paradise, a quest that was terminated by the arrival of Europeans. Rapid extermination was the fate of most of the lowland population. Jesuit missions were established in southern Brazil by 1557; disease, slavery, and warfare left the coasts, the islands, and the principal rivers free of their aboriginal inhabitants within a short time. Some of those who escaped to the interior have preserved their culture to the present, but now they too are increasingly threatened with extinction.

This review of the state of archeological knowledge of lowland South America and the Antilles shows we have the beginning of a time-space framework, full of gaps but sufficient to reveal a number of major problems. What caused the widespread dispersals during several periods? What accounts for the similarities between complexes widely separated in space and time? Where did the regional ceramic traditions originate? What happened during the millennia when archeological sites appear to decline drastically in abundance? Was there as little significant exchange among the four principal lowland subregions as the existing evidence suggests? There are hints of environmental stress, but data from geology and biology are as tantalizingly incomplete as those from archeology.

In all the natural sciences, we are peering through a clouded glass (Meggers 1975). To see more clearly, we need much more basic research. One thing is certain, however; we cannot dismiss the tropical lowlands as unworthy of attention. A better understanding of the adaptive role of culture will be a significant byproduct of the reconstruction of the prehistory of this fascinating part of our planet.

ACKNOWLEDGMENTS

We are greatly indebted to many Latin American colleagues for permission to use unpublished results of their fieldwork during the past decade. The following Brazilians have provided data on the areas named: Mário F. Simões (Pará, Amazonas), Nássaro A. de Souza Nasser (Rio Grande do

Norte), Valentin Calderon (Bahia), Celso Perota (Espírito Santo, Piauí), Ondemar F. Dias (Rio de Janeiro, Minas Gerais), Silvia Maranca (São Paulo, Piauí), Igor Chmyz (Paraná, Mato Grosso), José Wilson Rauth (Paraná), Walter F. Piazza (Santa Catarina), Eurico Th. Miller (Rio Grande do Sul, Mato Grosso), José Proenza Brochado (Rio Grande do Sul), Pedro Ignacio Schmitz (Rio Grande do Sul, Goiás). Mario Sanoja and Iraida Vargas have made available information on Venezuela and Marcio Veloz Maggiolo on the Dominican Republic.

References Cited and Recommended Sources

Angulo Valdés, Carlos 1962 Evidence of the Barrancoid series in north Colombia. *In* The Caribbean: Contemporary Colombia, ed. A. C. Wilgus, pp. 35–46. Gainesville: University of Florida Press.

Bischof, Henning 1966 Canapote—an early ceramic site in northern Colombia: preliminary report. Thirty-sixth International Congress of Americanists, Actas y Memorias 1:483–491.

Bórmida, Marcelo 1962 El Jabaliense, una industria de guijarros de la Península de San Blas, Prov. de Buenos Aires, República Argentina. Trabajos de Prehistoria del Hombre de la Universidad de Madrid 6:7–54.

Bullen, Ripley P., and Adelaide K. 1976 Cultural areas and climaxes in Antillean prehistory. Proceedings of the Sixth International Congress for the Study of Pre-Columbian Cultures of the Lesser Antilles, pp. 1–10.

Crusoe, Donald L. 1974 The Shell Mound Formative: some interpretative hypotheses. Archaeological News 3:71–77.

Cruxent, José M., and Irving Rouse 1958 An archeological chronology of Venezuela. Social Science Monographs, VI. Washington, D.C.: Pan American Union.

Evans, Clifford, and Betty J. Meggers 1960 Archeological investigations in British Guiana. Bureau of American Ethnology Bul. 177. Smithsonian Institution.

———. 1968 Archeological investigations on the Rio Napo, eastern Ecuador. Smithsonian Contributions to Anthropology, Vol. 6.

Fairbridge, Rhodes W. 1976 Shellfish-eating preceramic Indians in coastal Brazil. Science 191:353–359.

Fewkes, Jesse W. 1907 The aborigines of Porto Rico and neighboring islands. Twenty-fifth Annual Report of the Bureau of American Ethnology, 1903–1904. Smithsonian Institution.

Ford, James A. 1969 A comparison of formative cultures in the Americas. Smithsonian Contributions to Anthropology, Vol. 11.

González, Alberto Rex, and Humberto A. Lagiglia 1973 Registro nacional de fechados radiocarbónicos: necesidad de su creación. Relaciones 7:291–312. Buenos Aires: Sociedad Argentina de Antropología.

Granberry, Julian 1970 Final collation of texts, vocabulary lists, grammar, of Timucua for publication. Year Book of the American Philosophical Society, pp. 606–607.

Harris, Peter O'B. 1973 Preliminary report on Banwari Trace, a preceramic site in Trinidad. Proceedings of the Fourth International Congress for the Study of Pre-Columbian Cultures of the Lesser Antilles, pp. 115–125. St Lucia Archaeological and Historical Society.

Hilbert, Peter Paul 1968 Archäologische untersuchungen am mittleren Amazonas. Marburger Studien zue Völkerkunde 1. Berlin: Dietrich Reimer Verlag.

Hurt, Wesley R. 1974 The interrelationships between the natural environment and four Sambaquis, coast of Santa Catarina, Brazil. Occasional Papers and Monographs No. 1, Indiana University Museum.

Laming-Emperaire, A., A. Prous, A. Vilhena de Moras, and M. Beltrão 1975 Grottes et abris de la région de Lagoa Santa, Minas Gerais, Brésil. Cahiers d'Archéologie d'Amérique du Sud 1. Paris: École Pratique des Hautes Études.

Lathrap, Donald W. 1970 The Upper Amazon. New York: Praeger Publishers.

Lorandi, Ana María 1969 Las culturas prehispánicas en Santiago del Estero. Etnía 10:18–22. Olavarría, Argentina: Museo Ethnográfico "Dámaso Arce."

Lorandi de Gieco, Ana María, and Delia Magda Lovera 1972 Economía y patrón de asentamiento en la provincia de Santiago del Estero. Relaciones 6:173–191. Buenos Aires: Sociedad Argentina de Antropología.

Madrazo, Guillermo B. 1973 Síntesis de arqueología pampeana. Etnía 17:13–25. Olavarría, Argentina: Museo Etnográfico "Dámaso Arce."

Meggers, Betty J. 1975 Application of the biological model of diversification to cultural distributions in tropical lowland South America. Biotropica 7:141–161.

Meggers, Betty J., and Clifford Evans 1957 Archeological investigations at the mouth of the Amazon. Bureau of American Ethnology Bul. 167. Smithsonian Institution.

———. 1961 An experimental formulation of horizon styles in the tropical forest area of South America. In Essays in Pre-Columbian Art and Archaeology, ed. Samuel K. Lothrop et al., pp. 372–388. Cambridge: Harvard University Press.

———. 1973 A reconstituição da pré-história amazônica; algumas considerações teóricas. Pubs. Avulsas 20:51–69. Belém: O Museu Goeldi no Ano do Sesquicentenário.

Noble, G. Kingsley 1965 On the genetic affiliations of Timucua, an indigenous language of Florida. Journal de la Société des Américanistes 54:359–376.

Palmatery, Helen C. 1939 Tapajó pottery. Ethnological Studies 8:1–136. Göteborg: Göteborg Ethnographical Museum.

———. 1950 The pottery of Marajó Island, Brazil. Transactions of the American Philosophical Society (New Series) 39:3:(1949).

Porras Garcés, Pedro I 1975 El Formativo en el valle amazónico del Ecuador: Fase Pastaza. Revista de la Universidad Católica, Año III:10:74–134.

Programa Nacional de Pesquisas Arqueológicas (Belém) 1967 Resultados preliminares do primeiro ano, 1965–66. Museu Paraense Emílio Goeldi, Pubs. Avulsas 6.

———. 1969a Resultados preliminares do segundo ano, 1966–1967. Museu Paraense Emílio Goeldi, Pubs. Avulsas 10.

———. 1969b Resultados preliminares do terceiro ano, 1967–1968. Museu Paraense Emílio Goeldo, Pubs. Avulsas 13.

———. 1970 Brazilian archaeology in 1968: an interim report on the National Program of Archaeological Research. American Antiquity 35:1–23.

———. 1971 Resultados preliminares do quarto ano, 1968–1969. Museu Paraense Emílio Goeldi, Pubs. Avulsas 15.

———. 1974 Resultados preliminares do quinto ano, 1969–1970. Museu Paraense Emílio Goeldi, Pubs. Avulsas 26.

Reichel-Dolmatoff, Gerardo 1965 Colombia. New York: Praeger Publishers.

Rohr, João Alfredo 1967 O sítio arqueológico de Alfredo Wagner. Pesquisas, Antropologia, Nr. 17. Instituto Anchietano de Pesquisas (São Leopoldo).

Rouse, Irving 1964 Prehistory of the Western Indies. Science 144:499–513.

Rouse, Irving, and José M. Cruxent 1963 Venezuelan Archaeology. New Haven: Yale University Press.

Rouse, Irving, José M. Cruxent, Fred Olsen, and Anna C. Roosevelt 1976 Ronquin revisited. Proceedings of the Sixth International Congress for the Study of Pre-Columbian Cultures of the Lesser Antilles, pp. 117–122.

Sanoja, Mario 1977 Las culturas Formativas del oriente de Venezuela: la Tradición Barrancas del Bajo Orinoco. Instituto de Investigaciones Económicas y Sociales, Universidad Central de Venezuela. Caracas.

Sanoja, Mario, and Iraida Vargas 1974 Antiguas formaciones y modos de producción venezolanos. Caracas: Monte Avila Editores.

Schmitz, Pedro I., Irmhild Wüst, Altair Sales Barbosa, and Itala I. B. Becker 1974 Projeto Alto-Tocantins, Goiás (Comunicação prévia). Universidade do Vale do Rio dos Sinos (São Leopoldo).

Simões, Mário F. 1972 Indice das fases arqueológicas brasileiras. Museu Paraense Emílio Goeldi (Belém), Pubs. Avulsas 18.

————. n.d. Situação do ensino e da pesquisa arqueológica na Amazônia Legal Brasileira. Mesa Redonda sôbre Ensino e Pesquisa Arqueológica no Brasil (São Paulo). Dédalo, in press.

Vargas, Iraida 1976 La tradicion saladoide del oriente de Venezuela: la Fase Cuartel. Ph.D. dissertation, Departmento de Antropología y Ethología de América, Facultad de Filosofía y Letras, Madrid.

Veloz Maggiolo, Marcio 1972 Arqueología prehistórica de Santo Domingo. Singapore: McGraw-Hill Far Eastern Publishers.

————. 1976 Medioambiente y adaptación humana en la prehistoria de Santo Domingo. Colección Historia y Sociedad 1:24. Editora de la Universidad Autónoma de Santo Domingo.

Veloz Maggiolo, Marcio, Elpidio Ortega, and Plinio Pina P. 1974 El Caimito: un antiguo complejo ceramista de las Antillas Mayores. Fundación García Arévalo (Santo Domingo), Serie Monográfica No. 3.

Willey, Gordon R. 1971 An Introduction to American Archaeology, Vol. 2: South America. Englewood Cliffs, N.J.: Prentice-Hall.

Zucchi, Alberta 1972 New data on the antiquity of polychrome painting from Venezuela. American Antiquity 37:439–446.

————. 1973 Prehistoric human occupations of the western Venezuelan Llanos. American Antiquity 38:182–190.

Hokule'a, a modern replica of the Polynesian ocean-going vessels, seen here on the return leg of its historic Hawaii-Tahiti voyage.

CHAPTER THIRTEEN

Pre-Columbian Transoceanic Contacts

Stephen C. Jett

Perhaps the largest disparity of beliefs in all of archeology is that between the diffusionists, who believe that "important, even fundamental outside influences" shaped or were directly responsible for many cultural features of the New World civilizations, and the independent inventionists, who emphasize local or regional evolution of New World cultures. Dr. Jett presents a compendium of diffusionist hypotheses, from the diffusionist point of view; no attempt is made to present the alternatives of these hypotheses. What emerges is a collage of possibilities and some tantalizing, inexplicable, but undeniable facts.

INTRODUCTION

Archeologists and other students of culture history are concerned with description of the individual events and gradual cultural changes experienced by particular societies. To this chronological picture the culture-historical geographer adds more of the spatial dimension—the dispersal in space, through time, of cultures and culture traits. All of these scholars also aim to determine how those events, changes, and dispersals came to occur, and an ultimate though elusive goal is the formulation of generalizations about the nature of culture change and culture dispersal (Trigger 1970).

Cultural elaboration takes place both by local innovation and by the selective introduction, adoption, and adaptation of foreign ideas. The relative importance of these two sources of culture-change has long been debated among culture historians and theorists. This debate has often been heated, even acrimonious, particularly concerning the question of possible ancient interhemispheric influences. The reasons for supposedly dispassionate scholars' frequent lapses into partisan polemics over this issue are complex, but emotionalism on both sides has often impeded calm consideration of the evidence.

The majority of Americanists have emphasized local or regional development of New World cultures and have either unequivocally rejected the idea of significant transoceanic impacts or have avoided discussing such possibilities. However, a minority of scholars, which has grown considerably since the Second World War, feels that important, even fundamental outside influences may have helped shape ancient America. These "diffusionists" tend to make certain assumptions about cultural processes, including the following:

1. Each culture's form, at any given moment in time, is the result of the unique sequence of its past experience, which has been shared in toto by no other culture. Cultures' different histories account for the almost infinite variety of cultural forms that have developed.

2. Mankind's conservative tendencies normally outweigh creative ones. Premodern innovation was deviant and rare, and usually resulted from a gradual accumulation of almost imperceptible changes.

3. A complex innovation can occur only when a particular and improbable set of circumstances—cultural, historical, and perhaps environmental—come into conjunction. These concatenations of circumstances, being improbable to begin with, are even more unlikely to have been repeated at other times or places.

4. Therefore, when complex similarities are found to have existed between cultures, these similarities were most likely a result of innovation in one area and subsequent spread to the other(s), rather than being the fruit of multiple, independent innovations. Since it is easier to copy an idea or technique than it is to invent it spontaneously, diffusion is the more economical explanation for such similarities, at least if opportunity for diffusion can be demonstrated.

5. In those rare instances when cultural conservatism *was* overcome and rapid innovation *did* take place, it was usually a consequence of cultural contact, which led to introduction of new ideas, hybridization of these with old ones, and the forced realization that multiple possibilities exist, not just those that were once taken for granted. Such contact was normally a necessary, but not always sufficient, condition for rapid elaboration.

Diffusionists are skeptical of psychological, environmental, economic, or "ecological" determinist theories of culture change, although they acknowledge that each of these factors has played its role in culture history.

The opposing view, briefly stated, is that mankind everywhere is possessed of the same basic psychological and physical makeup and degree of potential inventiveness, and that if an innovation could occur in one society it could just as easily occur in any other comparable society. There were undeniable and often enormous differences between premodern cultures, but there were also many similarities. The latter are attributable to the limited possibilities of natural materials, mechanics, and man himself; to the universal nature of the problems that societies must solve; to the similar challenges of similar physical environments; and to the similar nature of many societies' basic technico-economic and social systems. In this view, mankind is at least moderately inventive and has tended to respond rather readily, via adaptive innovation, to the exigencies of survival. Further, a change in one part of the socio-environmental system generates a sequence of responses throughout the system, and changes initiated in one subsystem may eventually result in changes in other ones. Thus, similar environmental, social, economic, or other alterations in two historically unrelated societies may have generated similar innovations in various areas of those societies, and even complex similarities need not be attributed to diffusion.

Each of the preceding views has its merits and defects, and each requires much more testing before any even moderately reliable "general theory" can be accepted with confidence. Rather than elaborating further on these issues, exceedingly important though they may be, we will turn to the more concrete questions as to whether pre-Columbian transoceanic contacts *could* have occurred; whether in fact they *did* occur; and, if so, what impacts they may have had on New World cultures, particularly on the "high cultures" of Mesoamerica and the Andean region. (I have elaborated on these theoretical themes elsewhere [Jett 1971].)

Means and Motives for Contacts

Since there is nothing to suggest significant diffusion between the high cultures of the two hemispheres by way of the Bering Strait, the question of interhemispheric contacts among these cultures is essentially one of transoceanic voyaging. A major barrier to consideration of possible diffusion by sea routes has been skepticism as to the existence of seaworthy watercraft and adequate navigational techniques in pre-Columbian times. In part, this skepticism has stemmed from the dearth of direct archeological evidence of watercraft (outside of the Mediterranean area). However, it has also been a consequence of lack of appreciation by modern workers of the comparative difficulties of land versus water travel in early times, and of the ethnocentric assumption of historical superiority of Western watercraft, navigational ability, and geographical knowledge.

In recent decades, continuing archeological, historical, ethnographic, and experimental research has tended to alter scholars' perceptions of the abilities of early watercraft and their navigators. Several significant points that have emerged follow. Southeast Asia appears to have been the hearth of early watercraft development; it remained ahead of the West until modern times in the seaworthiness of its craft and the efficiency of sailing rigs and techniques, especially in sailing against winds and currents (Bowen 1953; 1959; Needham 1970; Borden 1967:219–222). Relatively small, flexible watercraft, such as sailing rafts and lashed-plank outrigger and double canoes, are more seaworthy than large, rigid-hulled ships, and these small craft have considerable antiquity (Doran 1973). Navigational techniques were highly advanced in ancient southern and eastern Asia; in China, for instance, celestial navigation, the magnetic "south-pointer," the spherical-earth concept, and the latitude and longitude system of coordinates were all known before AD 200 (Needham 1959:171, 498, 537; 1962:271, 281). In any event, navigating to a target of continental size presents no great difficulties. When good watercraft were available, travel by sea was far easier and swifter than overland travel until modern times.

The earliest great sailing tradition that seems to have emerged, and the one usually pointed to as the probable vehicle for the earliest transpacific voyages, is that of the Southeast Asian and derivative(?) northwest South American sailing raft (Doran 1971). The deep-water sailing abilities of this craft have been demonstrated empirically by Heyerdahl (1950a; 1950b) and others (Edwards 1965:101; 1969). A second major sailing tradition is that of the Indonesian and Oceanian sailing canoe, or vaka. The junk is the third of the great oceanic sailing craft of eastern Asiatic origin. All of these watercraft date to before—in some cases, long before—the Christian era. In the West, the frame-hulled "nao" was the sole great seagoing type of watercraft to evolve, apparently during the Bronze Age (Doran 1973).

That each of these sailing traditions—particularly the eastern ones—early developed watercraft and navigators able to make intentional transoceanic crossings in relative safety now seems beyond serious doubt. In light of these capabilities, we then must ask: Were such voyages actually made? If so, how was initial discovery accomplished? What may have motivated any subsequent crossings? We have little firm data on these points. Suggestions as to early discovery include accidental drift voyages, of which a number of historical Japan-to-America instances have been recorded (Brooks 1875); gradual exploration up the coasts of northeast Asia and along the Aleutians to Alaska and beyond; and direct, intentional easterly sailing to see what lay beyond the sea (flotsom and the paths of migrating birds may have suggested the existence of lands beyond known waters). Similar possibilities exist for the Atlantic.

Heyerdahl (1963) and others (e.g., Ferdon 1963) have discussed the most probable routes of drift-voyage discovery, stressing prevailing winds, currents, and storm tracks (Figure 13.1); it should be kept in mind, however, that at least Asiatic and Oceanian vessels were, under most conditions, quite capable of sailing against these "conveyor belt" systems, and that prevailing winds sometimes shifted direction seasonally and during storms.

Once knowledge of distant shores was gained, what might have motivated return voyages and maintenance of contacts sufficient to account for the massive similarities between the New World and the Old World that diffusionists have attributed to transoceanic contacts? A simple sense of adventure and attendant prestige must not be overlooked as a motive in some instances, particularly in the postulated early phases of exploration. The desire to escape from restraints or invaders at home or the search for more fertile, less populated lands may also have precipitated some crossings. Desire to make

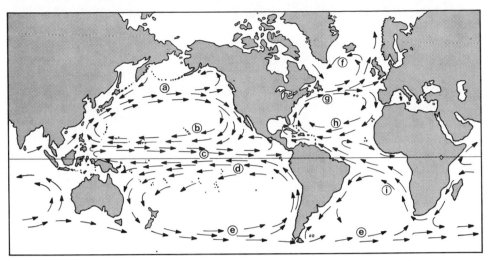

FIGURE 13.1
Generalized map of the principal surface ocean currents: *a*, Japan-North Pacific Current;
b, California-North Equatorial Current; *c*, Equatorial Countercurrent; *d*, Peru-South Equatorial
Current; *e*, Antarctic Drift; *f*, Irminger Current; *g*, Gulf Stream-North Atlantic Current; *h*, Canary-
North Equatorial Current; *i*, Benguela-South Equatorial Current.

astronomical observations may have played a role. Trade in highly valued
luxury or indulgent or sacred products has been suggested as having motivated later transpacific intercourse (e.g., Heine-Geldern 1956:95); possible
materials of these types include precious metals, jade, tropical bird feathers,
and hallucinogenic plants. Religious searches and proselytizing—particularly
Hindu-Buddhist—have also been proposed as potentially effective factors
in stimulating voyaging and even colonization (e.g., Jairazbhoy 1974b;
Ekholm 1953:88).

Kinds of Evidence for Cultural Diffusion

The best kind of evidence for pre-Columbian contacts would be discovery of
easily identifiable objects of Old World origin in unquestionably pre-
Columbian archeological context. Few if any such objects have been discovered, although a few artifacts have been claimed as conforming to these
criteria.

Spectrographic and other chemical and physical analyses of jade, turquoise,
metals, and so on found in Old and New World sites may prove useful for
identification of exotic source areas for these materials, but such techniques

have practically never been applied to the transoceanic diffusion issue (see following discussion).

During the last several years, reevaluation of supposedly forged New World inscriptions in Old World languages and the discovery of additional inscriptions have led to renewed interest in this type of evidence. It has been asserted that the occurrence, in a number of these inscriptions, of usages and constructions, including cryptograms, which were unknown to scholarship at the time of initial discovery, proves their genuineness. Nevertheless, all of these finds have been questioned.

Cultivated plants have long been looked to as excellent evidence of transoceanic contacts—particularly those plants which could not have been carried by way of Bering Strait or by any plausible natural means. The best plants in this respect are tropical cultigens, which survive only with the aid of man. Cultigens can be "invented" only when the appropriate wild ancestors are available, and these are usually confined to only one hemisphere. Transoceanic natural dispersal even of wild plants (other than littoral ones) is minimal.

It is not possible to review the evidence for specific pre-Columbian plant and animal transfers here (see Carter 1950; 1953; 1963; 1974; Heyerdahl 1952; Merrill 1954; Heine-Geldern 1958; Jett 1968). There is historical, archeological, or distributional evidence, of quite variable quality, for the following: plantain (C. Sauer 1950:527; Towle 1961:97; Heyerdahl 1952: 482), sweet potato (Brand 1971), maize (Stonor and Anderson 1949; Jeffries 1971; Mangelsdorf 1974:201–206), peanut (Chang 1973:527), pineapple (Casella 1950; Pohl 1973), coconut (J. Sauer 1971), amaranths (J. Sauer 1967), bottlegourd (Whittaker 1971), cotton (Hutchinson, Silow, and Stephens 1947; Stephens 1971), the chicken (Carter 1971), and a number of others.

Even if all of the Old World artifacts, inscriptions, and cultivated plants that are claimed to be pre-Columbian in the New World were proved to be absolutely genuine and of preconquest date, they would not, in themselves, demonstrate anything more than casual contacts and occasional plant transfers. They would (and, I think, *do*) show *opportunity* for further influences, but to assess the chronologies, extent, and impact of such influences, we must turn to the content and chronology of the cultures themselves.

Because of their lack of specificity, the more general and basic characteristics of cultures—such as food-getting methods, settlement patterns, social stratification, religious and political institutions, and the like—are not very useful *indicators* of diffusion, even though they may in some cases have been profoundly influenced from the outside. To demonstrate likelihood of diffusion, and to achieve some impression of the times and places of its occurrence, we must look for certain cultural "trace elements."

Ideally, these trace elements should possess certain characteristics, although in practice they seldom demonstrate them all. The traits should be arbitrary— that is, not called for or notably favored by man's basic physical and psychological makeup, nor channeled by the nature of the materials he has at his disposal, nor elicited by the characteristics of the physical environment and the culture's technico-economic relationship with that environment. Intrinsically improbable traits—for example, specific lexemes, particular animals associated with particular months or days of the week, divination from entrails, and rump masks in art—though often themselves trivial, provide both evidence of contact and "index fossils" pointing to particular cultural and temporal sources to which, then, more general aspects of culture may at least tentatively be tied.

Suspicion of diffusion is very much strengthened if spatial and temporal clustering of such traits occurs in the postulated donor and recipient areas, because the overall statistical probability of their twice occurring together declines as the product of the individual probabilities of their independent occurrence.

Proof, in one area, of an evolutionary sequence leading up to the traits in question, and their sudden appearance without developmental stages in the other area, are very suggestive of introduction from the first area to the second. However, the incompleteness of the archeological record and the possibility of sequential importation of the developmental stages reduce the usefulness of this criterion.

Finally, temporal overlap of the traits in question should occur between the two areas involved.

Aims of This Chapter

Beyond the preceding synopsis, I will not elaborate on criteria for assessing evidence of transoceanic contacts; these criteria are implicit in the following pages, particularly in that the more "arbitrary" culture traits are emphasized. The principal aim is to survey, in their geographical and chronological contexts, the major hypotheses of transoceanic influences on pre-Columbian America.

Naturally, no one person can be familiar with current findings relevant to all of the many cultures and time periods under consideration or be free of error when dealing with them. I no doubt have, in some cases, followed obsolete chronologies or have been unaware of new data and interpretations. The data themselves, of course, are often far from complete; many gaps and question marks characterize the discussions below. No one need fear a shortage of potential research projects for the future, nor a lack of opportunity for critical reconsiderations of theories presented.

The survey below is written, without apology, from a diffusionist point of view. The aim is *not* to give a detailed assessment of each hypothesis but rather to display these diffusionist theses to the reader. Some critical comments will be made, and some new information given, but on the whole I am presenting the theories as they have been promulgated by their authors, without much reference to alternative explanations for the same data. The reader need not assume that all of the hypotheses described below have gained universal, or even wide, acceptance, nor that the present author unreservedly accepts all of them.

ARCHAIC AND COLONIAL FORMATIVE CULTURES AND OVERSEAS CONTACTS

Australia and the Antarctic

Brief mention may be made of Paul Rivet's (1957) attempt to account for certain lexical and physical anthropological similarities observed between Australian aborigines and the Fuegids of southernmost South America. Rivet proposes that Australoids early reached Antarctica by boat, followed its shorelines to the Antarctic Peninsula, and then paddled to Tierra del Fuego. The rudimentary nature of Australian watercraft and the storminess of the southern seas would, however, seem to preclude any such migration. Presumably, similarities found between the two peoples are either fortuitous or are vestiges of an extremely ancient common Asiatic origin.

Europe and Africa

Transatlantic influence on North America has been suggested for as early as the Late Pleistocene, that is, before 10,000 BC. Greenman (1963) postulates that Upper Paleolithic hunters of the Biscayan region of Europe crossed to northeastern North America in skin boats, utilizing ice floes and bergs, some of which carried glacial gravels suitable for toolmaking. Greenman saw particularly strong similarities to Magdalenian boats, house types, and art among eastern Canadian tribes and, to a lesser extent, among the Eskimo and other groups. Some physical anthropological evidence has been presented that supports this idea (Comas 1973). If correct, this hypothesis could have very important implications for New World prehistory.

Schwerin (1970) has explored the idea that preceramic African farmer-fishermen were blown to the New World and there established cultivation of cotton, bottlegourds, and jackbeans, between 8000 and 5700 BC, and Carter (1977) presents a stimulus-diffusion hypothesis for the further development of American cultivation complexes. Most present workers, however, believe in the independent development of Old and New World agriculture (e.g., Phillips 1966:298–300).

A northern transatlantic impact has been postulated for the late fourth or third millennium BC. Alice Kehoe (1971:285–287) suggests the possibility that fishermen from coastal Norway introduced some of the diagnostic artifacts of Laurentian culture to eastern Canada and the northeastern states. Traits shared at this period include gouges, adzes, plummets, ground-slate points and knives, barbed bone points, and chipped stone projectile points. Ground-slate weapons have priority in America and, if contact is assumed, would represent a reciprocal introduction to Europe. Covarrubias (1957:26–27, 123, 246, 269–272) has also pointed out that the metal weapon types of the contemporary or somewhat earlier Old Copper culture of Michigan and Wisconsin bear strong resemblance to Old World forms.

Extracontinental origins have been posited for New World pottery. The earliest known Woodland pottery of northeastern North America is often said to have been diffused from Siberia, although it does not occur west of the Great Lakes region. Neither does it appear to derive from Formative wares of the Southeast. Kehoe (1971:287–289) pointed out that Vinette 1 pottery appeared without antecedents prior to 1000 BC in New York State and adjacent Canada, and in most respects is very similar to contemporary pottery of Norway, which has a long evolutionary history. Vinette 2 pottery is reminiscent of wares of the contemporaneous western European maritime Bell Beaker cultures and is absent in western North America. Kehoe further suggests that European funerary practices, including barrow building, may be reflected in use of burial mounds during the Early and Middle Woodland of about 1100–500 BC. The latter period includes the Hopewell culture of the Midwest, in which a number of ceramic traits have European parallels. Evidence now indicates, however, that burial mounds may occur as early as Laurentian times (Dragoo 1976:16). Huscher (1972; 1974) has argued for North American linguistic borrowing from the Baltic region. The sweat bath could also represent a transatlantic transfer (Lopatin 1960; Jett 1969:20).

Barry Fell (1976) has attributed megalithic and other stone structures of New England, including astronomical temples, dolmens, and menhirs, to Iberian Celts who colonized there during the first millennium BC. He has described many inscriptions on these monuments as being in Celtic ogam and Iberian Punic. His proposed decipherments are so recent that they have not yet had adequate assessment.

In regard to the New World pottery types usually lumped under the heading "Formative," James Ford (1969) has summarized the basic data. This pottery first appeared, as far as is known, in northwestern South America prior to 3600 BC, and it was distributed from Peru to Georgia by 2100 BC or before, primarily, apparently, by shell-fishing folk. The question of Old World origins has naturally arisen. The American Formative is in many ways reminiscent of the Old World Neolithic, but attempts to identify explicit Old World antecedents for the Formative have so far been unsuccessful. Alcina (1969) and Kennedy (1971) have suggested a possible Mediterranean source for many of the ceramic traits, but much more development of the evidence is needed.

Japan

A possible East Asian origin for Formative pottery and other traits has received far more attention. Meggers, Evans, and Estrada (1965:157–172; Meggers 1971:242–246) have argued in detail for a Japanese origin of what they believed to be America's oldest pottery, unearthed at Valdivia, Ecuador, and dating from about 3600 BC. There are many striking similarities in decorative designs and techniques, as well as in rim and base forms, between Early Middle Jomon pottery of western Kyushu and Valdivia phase pottery. The Kyushu-Valdivia similarities are greater than those between Kyushu and Honshu Jomon or between Valdivia and other Formative wares. Although a number of archeologists (e.g., Ford 1969; Kidder 1964:474) accept the Meggers, Evans, and Estrada hypothesis—perhaps because it relies on potsherds—others (e.g., Patterson 1967; Pearson 1968; Muller 1971:70–71) perceive weaknesses in it. These include selection of traits from various Jomon sites and from various Jomon and Valdivia time periods, the lack of comparisons of overall decoration and vessel forms, and the existence of similar pottery at other, distant places and times. Furthermore, pre-Valdivia pottery, without Jomon parallels, has recently been discovered at Valdivia (Bischof 1973).

Some workers now view Valdivia and Jomon not as being directly related but rather as variants of an early, more or less circumpacific ceramic style associated with fishing cultures. In any event, no matter how striking the Jomon-Valdivia similarities may be—and I believe that they are very striking—Jomon apparently cannot now be considered the source to which, by way of Valdivia, all Formative pottery may be traced. Jomon Japan could, nevertheless, represent a contributing element.

Southeastern China

In regard to other possible Asiatic sources of influence on the American Formative, Covarrubias (1954:60) illustrates some interesting comparisons between certain Neolithic and Bronze Age western Chinese vessel forms and those of the Mesoamerican Preclassic (Formative). However, Southeastern China is probably a more promising area for investigation. Its Neolithic horizons are poorly known, but there are several Lungshanoid vessel forms— particularly of the lower Yangtze River area—which also occur in the Formative. I have not investigated this matter at all thoroughly, but some forms of early Preclassic pottery are like the Chinese *hsien* (tripod bowls with mammiform legs), *ting* (carinated bowls), *tou* (round-bottomed shallow dishes on tall, concave-profile, flaring pedestals, seemingly used as incense burners), *chüeh* (lipped, tripod pitchers), annular-based shallow dishes, and other shapes (Chang 1968:139; Caso and Bernal 1973; Chadwick 1971; Ford 1969:101– 117, Charts 13–15; Piña Chan 1971:160–161, 177). Some of these forms also

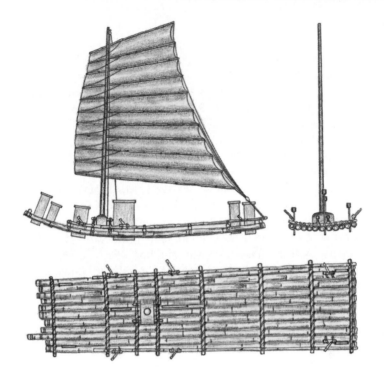

FIGURE 13.2
Taiwanese bamboo sailing raft with daggerboards to control leeway. (After Ling 1956.)

occur in early Southwest Asia and the Mediterranean (as do small terra-cotta figurines, a Preclassic hallmark).

The peanut, a South American domesticate with an uncertain date of arrival in Mesoamerica, has been reported from two sites near the coasts of Kiangsu and Chekiang provinces, with dates of about 3300–2800 BC (Chang 1973:527). If dating and identification are correct, human transpacific carriage seems almost certain, although there are no clues as to possible motives for the implied round-trip voyaging. It is notable, however, that "The [ancient] Southeastern Culture [of China] is essentially maritime oriented and is historically known as the Pai-Yueh, the navigators" (Chang 1959:97).

Firm evidence of use of seaworthy sailing rafts (Figure 13.2) off the coasts of China exists for the fifth century BC, with traditions indicating their use as many as 2000 years earlier (Ling 1956:47, 49, 51). Pre-Columbian sailing rafts also occurred in Ecuador (Doran 1971; Edwards 1965). The possibility that a third culture area—Malaysia—was involved in such transfers is discussed in the next section, but the idea of early Southeastern Chinese contacts fits well with suggestions of later Chinese influences in the Americas (also discussed later).

The Neolithic of Southeastern China seems a likely source for the Meso-american bark-cloth-manufacturing complex. The date of stone bark-cloth beaters in Southeast Asia is earlier than 2400 BC (Taiwan), and nearly identical beaters dating to about 1500 BC are known from southern Mesoamerica (Ford 1969:85–86, Chart 3). Although the Mesoamerican bark-cloth complex most closely—and very strikingly—resembles that of Celebes in Indonesia (Figure 13.3), Tolstoy (1963) finds certain Mesoamerican traits that suggest a relationship to the southern Chinese industry which gave rise to true paper making about the time of Christ and which was probably preceded by Celebes-type bark-cloth making. Tolstoy (1966:72, 77–79) recognizes 121 individual traits characterizing bark-cloth and paper making, 92 of which are shared by Southeast Asia and Mesoamerica. Forty-four of these shared traits are "not required by any of the other steps in the procedure of which they are part or by the goal itself of making bark-cloth. . . . Even when essential, many of these traits are still but one of several known alternatives. . . . [37 of the traits] are redundant, i.e. they co-occur with their alternatives, thus casting doubt on their competitive advantage or determination by function" (Tolstoy 1972:835).

Malaysia

Indonesia and the nearby mainland coasts are the hearth for what is probably the oldest, most diverse, and most efficient of premodern watercraft complexes. The origin of sailing rafts is seemingly attributable to this region, as is the emergence of double and outrigger sailing canoes. The area also apparently gave birth to a tradition of navigation and seamanship unequaled elsewhere until recent times. By 1500 BC or earlier this maritime complex had reached the Southwest Pacific, and over the centuries it spread to the most isolated habitable islands of the South Seas, presumably carried by Austronesian-speaking peoples. Coastal South China and perhaps early Japan also participated to a large degree in this tradition (Doran 1971; 1973; Bellwood 1975).

In view of the seagoing proclivities of these peoples, it would be surprising if they did not reach the shores of the Americas. In fact, as I have proposed elsewhere (Jett 1968), Malaysians may well have had an extremely important impact on the tropical rain forest regions of the New World. There is virtually no archeological evidence bearing on this question, so that attempting any dating is difficult; ethnographic information must be heavily relied upon in making comparisons. Nevertheless, physical anthropological data and the evidence of cultivated plants lend weight to a hypothesis of trans-pacific voyaging.

In brief, data on tribes of interior Borneo and on Caribs and Arawaks of equatorial South America demonstrate greater physical similarity between

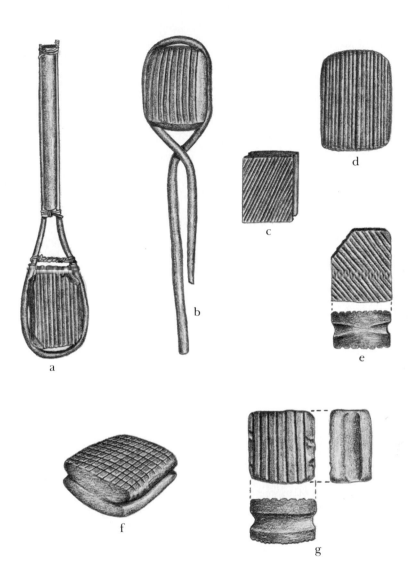

FIGURE 13.3
Southeast Asian and Mesoamerican bark beaters: *a*, central Celebes; *b*, Puebla, Mexico; *c*, El Salvador; *d*, Costa Rica; *e*, Guerrero, Mexico; *f*, central Celebes; *g*, Oaxaca, Mexico. (After Tolstoy 1963.)

these two groups than between either group and its neighbors. This greater similarity suggests actual migrations rather than simply contacts. However, the populations involved need not have been large if settlement by Malaysians began prior to the development of rain forest farming in the New World, so that the farmer newcomers could gradually have expanded at the expense of sparse indigenous populations of gatherers, without being drastically changed through genetic mixture.

It is possible that the entire system of vegetative-reproduction-shifting cultivation in the New World owes its origin to Malaysian or other Southeast Asian immigrants. If so, local plants—such as sweet potato, yautía, and manioc—were largely substituted for similar Asian ones, such as yams and taro. However, there is evidence (of variable quality) that certain Southeast Asian food plants, such as the plantain, were brought to pre-Columbian tropical America (see the introduction).

The old cultural pattern of Indonesia and that of equatorial America are strikingly similar. Points in common range from long houses to headhunting, and include a host of specific traits. Of these, the blowgun complex has been studied in detail and was found to share a very large number of common points in the two areas concerned (Jett 1971). It may also be relevant that the Tucano of southern Colombia, though an inland tribe, have a tradition of having come from across the Pacific (Fulop 1954:105).

The aforementioned similarities have been attributed by some to similar physical environments. Many of the shared traits, however, have no specific adaptive value in such environments. Further, the distribution pattern of the relevant traits—decreasing in frequency as one moves away from north-westernmost South America—is suggestive of transpacific introduction over a long period and sequential diffusion into the Amazon Basin, the Guianas, and Central America. As to those traits which clearly *are* adaptive, Malaysians' earlier adaptation to equatorial environments in Asia is exactly what would have enabled them to occupy such environments successfully in the New World while at the same time excluding them from other environments.

As to dating the postulated period of Malaysian migrations, it is not possible at present to be at all exact. I have, however, suggested a probable time range from 3600 to 300 BC and a possible principal Malaysian source area on the shores of the Celebes Sea. Suggestions of possible transatlantic influences from Indonesia (via India, Madagascar, and Africa) have also been made, especially with respect to domesticated plants and birds (Whitley 1974; Carter n.d.).

Some evidence for Melanesian and Polynesian contacts with western South America has also been adduced (e.g., Hornell 1945; Rivet 1957). However, any such contacts seem likely to have had minimal impact on that continent and will not be elaborated upon here.

What the combined evidence of cultivated plants, pottery types, bark-cloth making, the blowgun, and other traits seems to suggest is that during the Colonial Formative significant transoceanic influences on both New

World continents took place in the realm of mundane affairs. This is in contrast to the apparent usual emphasis in later periods on religion, religious architecture, luxury goods, and sophisticated art and their association with elite classes of society.

DYNASTIC CHINA AND THE AMERICAS

Shang China and the Olmec

The Shang, the first Bronze Age civilization in the Yellow River valley area of northern China, developed upon a Lungshan Neolithic base during the sixteenth century BC or earlier. It was a hierarchical civilization, with a capital and administrative and religious centers often built on earth platforms with north-south orientation. The Shang possessed ideographic writing, produced richly decorated ritual bronze vessels, knew gold and silver, valued jade, and buried their elite with retainers and grave furniture in subterranean tombs. They practiced water control, had long-distance trade networks, made war with chariots, and controlled a large area.

On the Gulf of Mexico, in Veracruz and Tabasco, lay the heartland of what has been called America's first civilization, the Olmec. It possessed a hierarchy of leaders, constructed complex north-south-oriented ceremonial centers on artificial earth platforms, erected large earthen mounds, produced monumental stone sculptures and superb lapidary work in jade and other stones, practiced water control, had long-distance trade and widespread influence, and apparently used systems of enumeration and ideographic writing. It was, however, nonurban, without metals, draft animals, or the wheel. Its recalibrated radiocarbon dates are about 1450–650 BC. Nearly every commentator has remarked on its sudden flowering in the environmentally unlikely swampy rain forest of the Gulf coast, many miles from the sources of stone used in its huge carvings and lined drains.

Some scholars believe that the evolutionary steps leading to the Olmec florescence will be found in Veracruz's volcanic Tuxtla Mountains (e.g., Heizer 1968:24), perhaps under lava flows. Others look to Guerrero in western Mexico (e.g., Griffin 1972:302) or Izapa in southeastern Chiapas (Malmstrom 1976) as the early Olmec homeland and place of development. Still others seek overseas sources for the dramatic inception of Olmec culture (Jairazbhoy 1974b; Meggers 1975).

The Olmec origins question is particularly important because it relates to general theories of the emergence of civilization, and because from Olmec culture there developed a significant part of the content of later Mesoamerican cultures and perhaps Andean and southeastern North American ones as well.

Much has been made of a "feline cult" in comparing archaic China (tiger) with Olmec and later Mesoamerica (jaguar). Emphasis on animals of such power and hunting prowess is not surprising, but certain specific shared aspects of feline representation, such as frequent absence of a lower jaw, are more arbitrary. Meggers (1975:14, 17) points out that felines appear to have been earth gods in both regions. Additional themes common to the Shang and the Olmec are felines protecting (devouring?) children (Chêng 1960: Plate 50; Bernal 1969:172–173), which is a variant of the alter-ego motif, and monster-mask headgear (Fraser 1967:31, 37, 43, 45–46). Birds or bird monsters are iconographically significant in both areas. The plumed(?) or winged serpent (Quetzalcoatl) and the four-legged fire serpent are said by Coe (1968a:100–101, 114) to have been two of the principal Olmec deities, and serpents and dragons are abundantly depicted in Shang China (Figure 13.4). Other similarities have been pointed out, but perhaps the ones most deserving of detailed examination here are those relating to the use of green stones, particularly jade.

Various green through blue stones, to which special powers were attributed, were highly valued in early times in Eurasia, the Americas, and the Pacific. Particularly in China and Mesoamerica the most cherished of these stones, jade, was sought after, skillfully worked, and venerated. In both areas, the very word *jade* also meant "precious" and "verdant," and an esteemed person had a "heart of jade" (Stirling 1961:43; 1968:24–25; Ruff 1960).

The jade of ancient China was nephrite ("true jade"), imported from the Khotan area of Turkestan. Jadeite, from upper Burma and adjacent Yünan, is usually said not to have been used before the eighteenth century AD, although Kinle (1962:234; see also Yü 1967:175) contends that it is known archeologically from Han times (206 BC–AD 220). Nephrite was used for making celts in Neolithic times in China and became a true art medium during the Shang Dynasty (Hansford 1968:27–29).

In Mesoamerica, a few pre-Olmec jadeite beads are known (Ford 1969:58), and a nonjade greenstone celt and pendant date from 1450–1300 BC at Olmec San Lorenzo de Tenochtitlán, Veracruz. However, about or before 1100 BC, the Olmec site of La Venta, Tabasco, seems suddenly to exhibit mastery of unprecedented jadeite-working skills, which were never equaled in later periods.

Because of the lack of known Mesoamerican jade deposits, the question of possible importation from Asia was raised as early as 1880 (Beck 1966). It now seems clear, however, that at least the bulk of Chinese and Mesoamerican jade came from Asia and America, respectively. The provenience of much Olmec jade was certainly the middle Río Balsas drainage of Guerrero (Coe 1968a:94; Feldman 1973:88, 91). The emerald-green jadeite "of Oriental [Burmese] quality" found in important La Venta graves (Stirling and Steward 1943:323) now seems attributable either to the recently rediscovered Guatemalan deposits that supplied the later Maya with jadeite (Foshag and Leslie 1955) or to Costa Rica (Easby 1968:15, 86–87). Nevertheless, some transoceanic carriage—most likely from Middle America to China—is not ruled out.

a

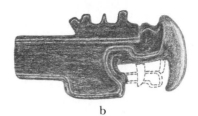
b

FIGURE 13.4

a, Shang Chinese *k'uei* dragon motif from bronze vessel; *b*, Olmecoid jade "dragon spoon" from Costa Rica. (*a*, after Willetts 1958; *b*, after Balser 1968.)

Spectroscopic analysis of 25 impure Mesoamerican jades, 5 from Asia, and 1 from New Zealand showed that "the resemblance . . . is striking" between 1 Chinese "nephrite" piece on the one hand and a Chichén Itzá object and the late Olmecoid Tuxtla Statuette on the other (Norman and Johnson 1941); however, the mineralogical validity of these tests in dubious (see Foshag 1955; 1957). Analyses of "suspicious" archaic Chinese jades would be desirable, to determine if they might be of American origin. In view of the fact that China's nephrite supply was in foreign hands and that there were Shang conflicts with the intervening Western Chou, voyaging to Mexico to obtain jadeite does not seem inconceivable (although jadeite also occurs in Japan).

On the whole, Shang and Olmec jade objects are quite distinct. Common to both areas, however, are rounded jade celts, often interred with corpses. Celts sometimes carried faces engraved or painted in red. In China, ritual objects such as the slender *yüan kuei* seem to have evolved from celts; artifacts of similar form and size occur in buried offerings at La Venta. Meggers (1975:11–14) interprets objects carried by dignitaries on Stela 3 at La Venta as *yüan kuei,* but in the original relief it is by no means clear what the figures are holding. Other classes of jade objects common to Shang and Olmec include beads, bird and animal plaques, pendants, and figurines (Willetts 1958:61–62, 67–74; Chêng 1960:Plates 15–17; Drucker, Heizer, and Squier 1959; Smith 1963:122, 126–127, 216–217).

Covarrubias (1954:103–109) and others (Ruff 1960: Needham 1971:544–555; Towle 1973) have stressed the similarities between Chinese and Mesoamerican jade prospecting, working, and use. Although not documented for early times, ethnographic Asians and Americans believed that "exhalations" helped prospectors locate jade. Little of an explicit nature is known about early techniques of working these extraordinarily hard stones, which also lack cleavage planes; but sawing, drilling, and polishing with abrasives were held in common. In Shang China and later (Chêng 1960:69–70), shell, turquoise, or jade was put in corpses' mouths, and at some point in history rice was.

At least in Classic Maya times, jade and maize were put in corpses' mouths; funerary jades in both areas were sometimes coated with or associated with cinnabar. Jade seems to have been used medicinally in both areas.

Far less attention has been paid, in the transoceanic context, to turquoise than to jade. Turquoise mosaic work, as on dagger handles, was common in Shang through Han China (Willetts 1958:87, Plate 4; Chêng 1960:99). It is not reported for the Olmec, but there is evidence of turquoise mosaic work in the Preclassic of Central Mexico. It was rarely used in Classic times but was abundantly employed in later periods (Noguera 1971:258–259), including use on dagger handles (Carmichael 1970:16). Perhaps its late ascendancy was as a partial substitute for jade as that material became increasingly rare.

Green birds gave to jadeite one of its names in China (kingfisher) and in Mesoamerica (quetzal) (Ruff 1969; Balser 1968:61). Feathers of these birds were used for ceremonial occasions in both regions, although how early is not known: at least by AD 1000 in China (Hansford 1968:28–29) and by Classic times in Mesoamerica (Dillon 1975:106). Heine-Geldern (1956:95) has suggested that jade, feathers, and precious metals were motivating factors in Asian-Nuclear American contacts. Perhaps such wealth seeking began as early as Shang times. If so, transport or a middleman function may have been performed by coastal peoples of Kiangsu and Chekiang, outside of the Shang state, where a reservoir of transpacific knowledge may have existed (see previous discussion); the Shang themselves are not known to have been seafarers.

A more dramatic hypothesis has also been proposed, involving an exodus of Shang elite and craftsmen to the New World when the dynasty was overthrown by the Western Chou, apparently in 1122 BC (but possibly in 1027). Jairazbhoy (1974b:102) summarized traditions relating to this event (here condensed): "[Before attacking the Shang ruler] the Chou leader accused him of thinking only 'of palaces, buildings, terraces, groves, dikes, pools, and extravagant clothes' and 'spreading pain and poison over the four seas.' He distinguished the families of the clever men among the enemy who had gone away." Jairazbhoy cites a historical parallel: the eighth-century-AD Omayyad Dynasty of Syria fleeing civil war and establishing a new kingdom in Spain. He connects the dikes and pools of the Shang emperor (drains have been found at the Shang capital [Meggers 1975:13]) with those in the Olmec "heartland" of ca. 1300–1000 BC (Coe 1970:26).

Any Chinese landings would have been on the Pacific coast. The primary Olmec jade source and the area of most frequent finds of Olmec jade objects is the archeologically almost unknown middle Río Balsas area of the Pacific coast state of Guerrero. The nearest port city today is Acapulco, which the Spaniards found to be the most convenient location for their transpacific trade.

Meggers (1975) has suggested that the impact of putative Shang contacts on Mesoamerica was fundamental, introducing the Shang system of "centralized control and social stratification in the context of a dispersed settlement pattern," extensive long-distance trade in luxury items for major ceremonial centers, organized religion centering on felines, calendrics, and the idea of writing. The sudden appearance of Olmec "civilization," the chronological framework, and the sharing of certain arbitrary traits all support the basic idea of Shang influence on the Olmec. However, such influence, if it occurred, was not thoroughgoing enough to have introduced metallurgy and associated decorative styles or wheeled vehicles, nor does it account for the monumental sculpture so characteristic of the Olmec heartland (to be discussed later).

Of possible interest in reference to Shang-Olmec comparisons is the finding of what may be a hematite magnetic compass of Olmec manufacture dating to before 1000 BC. The earliest evidence for Chinese use of the lodestone pointer does not predate 300 BC (Carlson 1975). Nevertheless, the possibility of an ultimate Olmec origin of what has been thought of as a Chinese invention must now be considered.

China and Chavín

Many workers have noted similarities between the Olmec of Mesoamerica and the Chavín-Cupisnique culture in Peru, the earliest "high culture" of that region. Influence of the Olmec on the latter culture has often been postulated. Radiocarbon dating has now shown Chavín to be similar in age to the Olmec (Signorini 1969), and, although the question of interinfluence remains, the possibility of direct Chinese impact on Peru has also been raised, particularly by Heine-Geldern (1959; 1972:787–791). Among the similarities are feline motifs, including sculptured felines with mortars on their backs, conventionalized "tiger" stripes, felines with rump mask, horned and jawless feline faces, eyebrows kenned as snakes, and representational ambiguity, as well as the scale band on tails of dragons and feline monsters in China and Peru, respectively. Heine-Geldern also suggests that use of gold was introduced to Peru from China during the Chavín period (although gold working is now known to be pre-Chavín). He thought in terms of Chou influences, in light of the supposed age of Chavín, but the new dates take the latter's beginnings back to late Shang times. Heine-Geldern expresses the opinion that Chinese influences may have stimulated the emergence of Chavín.

Some significant features of the highland site of Chavín de Huántar are north-south orientation, stone-lined drains, and a stepped-platform building with stone-faced walls and subterranean rooms. On the coast, fairly elaborate adobe brick and stone buildings with platforms, stairways, and clay columns occur, as do platforms and terraces. Whatever the possible Chinese impact on Chavín culture, that influence does not account for such features as stone-faced walls, subterranean rooms, adobe brick, and large, sculpted stone heads, which will be discussed in reference to possible Mediterranean connections.

Among additional possible Chinese importations into both Mexico and Peru are practices relating to domestic dogs. In these three areas "toy" dogs were bred, special breeds were kept as temple and sacrificial animals, and dogs were raised for eating (Fiennes and Fiennes 1968:26, 53–55, 103–110; Loayza 1948:191–196). Dog sacrifice and eating are known from Shang times (Simoons 1961:95), and Coe (1968b:59) found that dogs, especially juveniles, were eaten at Olmec San Lorenzo.

Chou and Ch'in China and the Americas

Despite a change of dynasty occasioned by the Western Chou conquest of the Shang, the basic Shang styles and ways of life persisted for centuries. There is currently no evidence that the Western Chou voyaged to nuclear America. However, the subsequent Eastern Chou period (770–222 BC) was a time of rapid expansion, during which Chou hegemony extended increasingly southward in coastal Kiangsu and Chekiang and foreign intercourse increased. Transpacific contacts have been suggested for this period.

The principal indicator of such contacts is the distinctive Tajín decorative style of Classic and early Postclassic Mesoamerican art (Proskouriokoff 1954; Kampen 1972), which exhibits some remarkable similarities to decorative styles of Chinese bronze and jade work of middle Chou through Ch'in times (770–207 BC). Typical motifs (Figure 13.5) are fields of low-relief commas, single and double interlaced ribbons usually representing serpents or dragons, scale bands, the double-contour design element border, and the double-headed dragon and *sisiutl* motifs (Covarrubias 1947:110–111; 1957:176–180; Heine-Geldern 1959a; 1966:277–283). These are quite specific, arbitrary traits, associated with two recognized stylistic complexes. The similarities are such that, as Heine-Geldern (1966:278) has written of the Ulúa Valley marble vases of Honduras: "The Chinese character of the designs . . . is so conspicuous that, had these been found, not in America, but somewhere in Asia, no one would doubt that they represent a colonial version of Chinese art."

MIRRORS □ One class of artifacts in the two hemispheres of particular interest for comparison is that of mirrors (Ekholm 1973).

The Shang had a few metal mirrors, although none are yet known from the Western Chou period. Small flat or concave pyrite, magnetite, or ilmenite "mirrors," the latter apparently for ceremonial solar fire making, occurred among the Olmec after about 1100 BC. They were pierced and suspended from the neck. Ekholm sees a possible connection with Chinese concave bronze mirrors used for the same purpose and notes that Garcilasso de la Vega referred to concave metallic mirrors with this function in Peru (see also Nordenskiöld 1926).

a

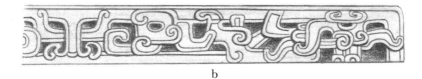

b

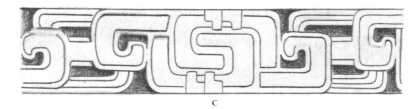

c

FIGURE 13.5
Chou Chinese and Mexican interlaced, double-outlined band designs: *a,* from Chou bronze vessel; *b,* from stone frieze, El Tajín, Vera Cruz; *c,* from wall painting, Temple of Agriculture, Teotihuacán, Mexico. (After Covarrubias 1954; 1957.)

In Eastern Chou times, bronze mirrors became common in China. They were usually round (sometimes lobed in Han and later times) but occasionally were square. Diameters ranged from 5.5 to 20 centimeters; thicknesses ranged from 0.35 to 0.4 centimeters. The reflecting surface was usually flat and occasionally convex or concave. The back had a central loop for a suspension cord and was usually decorated. A few mirror backs had painted or inlaid decoration; other mirrors had a separate back in open work or relief soldered or bolted to the face; still others consisted of a single cast piece. The color of the bronze ranged from black to chocolate or an acquired green patina. Mirror-back designs of the Eastern Chou (770–222 BC) and Ch'in (221–207 BC) periods included teeming, interlocking groups of animals, snakes, dragons, or geometric elements. Often the zoomorphic elements degenerated to nearly or solely decorative designs. Sometimes whole mirror backs or background areas were made up of small commas, "bean sprouts," or "wing" curves, giving the impression of chains or networks. There were usually separate rim, main-design, and center areas; a blossom or a stemmed flower occasionally occupied the central area. Inlaid mirror backs (in glass, turquoise, shell, jade, gold, or silver) frequently featured animal or human motifs. Mirrors were ubiquitous in Eastern Chou China and were traded beyond the frontiers. They were used cosmetically and as grave offerings, but later dynasties, at least, accredited them with magical powers, including divinatory usefulness (Chêng 1963:249–254; Anon. 1934:92–93, 122–123, Plates 39–41).

Mesoamerican pyrite-mosaic mirrors are known from the Formative of El Arbolillo, Cholula (Ford 1969:74). Mirrors of the Mesoamerican Classic period were very widely made and traded. Many from Kaminaljuyú, Guatemala, have been described, although preservation of these artifacts is poor. They were usually round (7.5 to 25 centimeters in diameter and 0.5 centimeters thick), but occasionally they were square. Their faces were of polished, closely set pyrite plates; a few small examples probably had only one piece of pyrite. Some larger specimens had adorned bands encircling the pyrite-encrusted area. Mirror-face inlays of hematite, jade, shell, and other materials are known. Although at least one solid stone mirror with a pyrite-vein face is reported, mirror backs were normally of slate or sandstone. They were pierced near the edges, or, later, near the center, for suspension. Usually the backs had beveled edges but were not sculpted; they were painted red or, in one instance, in blue-gray with a marginal green band. Sometimes backs consisted of more than one edge-joined piece. In one case of this kind, a supplemental slate backing was added; smaller supplemental, encrusted slate disks on mirror faces have been noted. Some mirror backs were elaborately carved or stuccoed in relief and painted. Usually these had a central anthropomorphic-design area and a surrounding tracery decorative zone or a decorative band (Kidder, Jennings, and Shook 1946:126–133, 237, Figs. 155–156; Woodbury 1965:172–175; Proskouriakoff 1965:569). Aztec period obsidian mirrors were used for divination (Ekholm 1973:135).

The similarity between the basic forms, probable functions, and decorative styles of Chinese and Mesoamerican mirrors is most suggestive of historical relationship. Typical Tajín-style interlocking meanders and scrollwork and the scale-band motif on mirrors, palma stones, and buildings have been emphasized by Covarrubias (1947:110–111) and Heine-Geldern (1959a; 1966:227–282), as have those on the Ulúa marble vases. Figure 13.6 illustrates some similarities.

THE CHRONOLOGICAL PROBLEM □ The scale-band motif is not known on Chou bronzes after 400 BC. The other Chou-Ch'in bronze work motifs of which the Tajín style is reminiscent lasted until about 200 BC in China proper (Lefebvre d'Argencé 1966:82–83, 88–89, 122–123; Anon. 1934: 90–93, 122–123, Plates 32, 35, 39–41). Tajín-style stone carving has not been dated before about AD 300–700. Heine-Geldern (1958:204–205; 1966:280–283) has tried to show that a mural at Teotihuacán in Tajín-like style *might* date to the second century BC, but a third-century-AD date would better fit

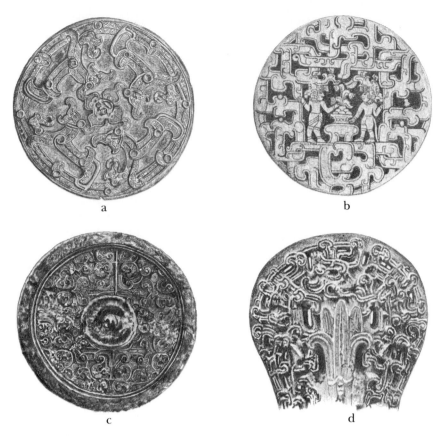

a

b

c

d

FIGURE 13.6
Chinese and Mexican decorative motifs: *a*, Late Chou bronze mirror back; *b*, Tajín-style
slate mirror back, Kaminaljuyú, Guatemala; *c*, Late Chou or Ch'in bronze mirror back,
"Huai Valley style"; *d*, detail of Tajín-style palmate stone, Vera Cruz. (*a*, after Willetts
1965; *b*, *d*, after Covarrubias 1957; *c*, after Anon. 1934.)

the chronological evidence. Thus, an important time gap still remains between the Chou-Ch'in and Tajín styles. Nevertheless, Heine-Geldern's hypothesis that the Tajín style might long have been applied in ephemeral
painting and woodcarving prior to its common translation into durable stone
has considerable appeal. Palmas actually used in ballgames must have been
of a relatively light material such as wood, and carved wood could well have
served for early mosaic mirror backs. A wooden backing was probably used
to reinforce the thin slate of a compound mirror from Kaminaljuyú, and
a wood-backed turquoise and pyrite plaque was found at Chichén Itzá.
Wooden frames for later Mexican obsidian mirrors are also known (Kidder,

Jennings, and Shook 1946:127, 133). It has been supposed that perishable carved wooden objects were important in pre-Buddhist China; the impression of a wooden object carved in late Shang decorative style was found on the clay of a tomb at Anyang (Chêng 1960:Plate 6). Since Chou-Ch'in style is known primarily in bronze (but to some extent in jade), and since metal working was not introduced to Mesoamerica until later, it is plausible that the Chinese decorative style was introduced primarily in woodcarving. It may be noted, too, that a few late Olmec or post-Olmec stone relief sculptures have spiral motifs that may reflect this style (Monument C, Tres Zapotes; relief, Chalcatzingo [Bernal 1969:61, 139]).

The ancient Chinese coastal state of Wu (which included modern Kiangsu Province) was nominally within the Chou Empire, although it was a peripheral area and came under Chou influence rather late. Wu briefly dominated the Chou Empire in the late sixth century BC but was soon conquered and destroyed by Yueh, in present Chekiang Province. By the early fifth century BC Yueh, in turn, had been conquered by the inland state of Ch'u. The entire period from then until 222 BC is known as that of the "Warring States," and after a brief period of unification, warfare and rebellion reasserted themselves toward the end of the Ch'in Dynasty (221–207 BC) (Chêng 1963:xxvii–xxxii). We may speculate that some middle Chou motifs (e.g., the scale band) lasted longer in the coastal areas than in the inland core area and that some coastal peoples responded to the prolonged strife of the times by emigrating to Mesoamerica, but as yet we have no direct evidence for these speculations.

Traditions recorded by 90 BC do tell, however, of Taoist belief in three mountain islands in the Yellow Sea, on which were found the drugs of longevity. From the early fourth century BC, sailors are said to have been sent in search of these isles, without success. In 219 BC the Ch'in emperor sent Hsü Fu of Ch'i (Shantung) to search for the islands. Hsü reported that the king of one of these lands in the Eastern Sea required virgins and workmen of all trades in exchange for the drugs. Three thousand young men and women were then sent out with Hsü Fu in 210 BC, but he is said to have become a king in a land of plains and great lakes and never to have returned to China (Needham 1971:551–553; Yü 1967:182–183). There has been speculation that this expedition ended in America. The emphasis on drugs does bring to mind Middle and South American hallucinogenic plants. However, there is good reason to believe that Hsü colonized Honshu, Japan (Hsieh 1967: 87–90). Nevertheless, this bit of history does confirm maritime exploration by China proper in pre-Han times.

Drug plants could have represented a high-value, easily transported commodity that might have provided a motive for early Chinese voyaging— voyaging perhaps interrupted during the period of strife of late Chou times. As noted above, jade is also possibly relevant in this context. It is interesting to compare known and probable jade sources near Pacific shores with the areas thought by some scholars to exhibit archaic Chinese influences. Jade: Japan, Indonesia (Celebes), New Guinea, New Zealand, Costa Rica, Guerrero, British Columbia (Fraser and Turnagain rivers [Hansford 1968:27]). Putative Shang-Chou-Ch'in artistic or other influence: Japan, Indonesia (especially Sumatra, Borneo, Flores), New Guinea (Sepik River, Trobriand Islands), New Zealand, Peru, Costa Rica, Guerrero-Veracruz, British Columbia-southern Alaska (Heine-Geldern 1959a:205; Fraser 1962:144). For Peru, Sumatra, and Borneo, gold and tropical bird feathers could have been the relevant precious materials.

CHINA AND THE NORTHWEST COAST □ A number of scholars have pointed out similarities between aspects of Northwest Coast art and that of Shang and Chou China. The similarities seem particularly close between surface decoration of bronze vessels and Middle Chou jade carvings on the one hand, and northern Northwest Coast (Haida and Tlingit) wooden boxes and bone and ivory shamans' charms (e.g., the "spirit-catcher") on the other.

Although Northwest Coast art has some clear Eskimo affinities, as well as its own unique aspects, a large number of motifs are shared with Middle Chou China (Fraser 1962:301–304; 1967). Inverarity (1972) has made what is so far the most thorough analysis of these similarities. They include curving, swelling lines, utilization of all available space, small animal figures attached to larger ones, "x-ray" designs, representational ambiguity, C-shaped, oval, and S-shaped areas, "scale" shapes, split images, dragons, the alter ego, the *sisuitl* motif, and others.

Northwest Coast culture is clearly anomalous in comparison with surrounding cultures. It was a hierarchical society with an elaborate material culture and complex art style in the midst of far simpler, egalitarian hunting cultures. It was coastal, washed by the Japan current, and maritime oriented, and it shared many traits with ancient Asia. Japanese slaves were found there in early contact times, and the people of the coast were of a different physical type from those of the interior. Despite a lack of proven time depth for this society, there is a strong presumption of implantation of many of its characteristics, by sea, from Asia. Whether the similarities between archaic China and the Northwest Coast derive from a common third culture, or whether China influenced the Northwest Coast directly, is an item for debate. Fraser (1972:652) discusses the possibility that archaic Chinese motifs spread to various points around the Pacific in the form of a popular but archeologically perishable woodcarving style rather than in the form of stylistically more sophisticated items of nonperishable materials used by the aristocracy. Certain traits, such as trophy head taking, long houses, boat-building techniques, and animal heads on boat prows, suggest a South Chinese connection rather than the northern Chinese or Siberian ones sometimes suggested.

Dong-son Culture and American Metallurgy

By Late Chou times there existed beyond the southern borders of the Chinese state, in present-day Yünnan and Tonkin, a culture referred to today as Dong-son. It persisted into the early Christian era. The kingdom of Nan Yüeh, set up by a Chinese general in Ch'in times, included much of this area; it was annexed by the Han emperor in 112 BC.

The still poorly known Dong-son people were workers in copper and bronze. Some objects—drums and urns with lids supporting sculpted figures and buildings—are very distinctive. Others, including types of belt buckles and socketed tools, suggested to Heine-Geldern (1954; 1972) derivation from earlier cultures around the Black Sea (or in Latin, *Pontus*). He postulated a "Pontic Migration" to Indochina to account for the observed similarities. Heine-Geldern takes note of earlier workers' recognition of the similarity of metal objects from the Black Sea region to those of northwestern South America and proposes that this could be accounted for by transpacific carriage of these styles by Dong-son voyagers, artifacts of whose culture have been discovered widely in Southeast Asia and New Guinea.

Heine-Geldern distinguished two putative impact areas: the central Andean region and the region from northern Ecuador to Costa Rica. In the northern area, there are some metal artifacts and metallurgical techniques strikingly like those of Dong-son. Objects include: small, globular bells; open-work scenes framed with simple or plaited rope designs with spiral appendages; frogs decorated with the plait motif; and others. Chronologies, unfortunately, are not well established for these objects. Earliest present dates for metal working are from Bahía, Ecuador, at ca. 500 BC–AD 500. However, the relevant style is not attested to before ca. AD 100–200 (Mountjoy 1969:27).

The Andean area presents more problems than does the northern area. Here are found socketed tools, trunnion axes with broadened necks, star-shaped mace heads, tweezers, double protomes of animals, and a large variety of metal pins that so closely resemble Pontic types that either some historic relationship exists or most criteria for use of stylistic resemblances to identify diffusion must be discarded (Figure 13.7). Unfortunately for the Heine-Geldern hypothesis, none of these objects is yet known in Dong-son archeology. Heine-Geldern suggests that these classes of objects may not have been included with burials in Southeast Asia and may have been melted down when their usefulness or vogue ended. At present, a major chronological gap exists between most of the few approximately dated Andean finds of the object types in question and the end of Dong-son culture. A far greater gap occurs when the Pontic material is considered, and the Pontic peoples were not maritime. One may point out that some of these pin types *are* known from early times in maritime areas—the Aegean (Piggott 1965:74–75) and

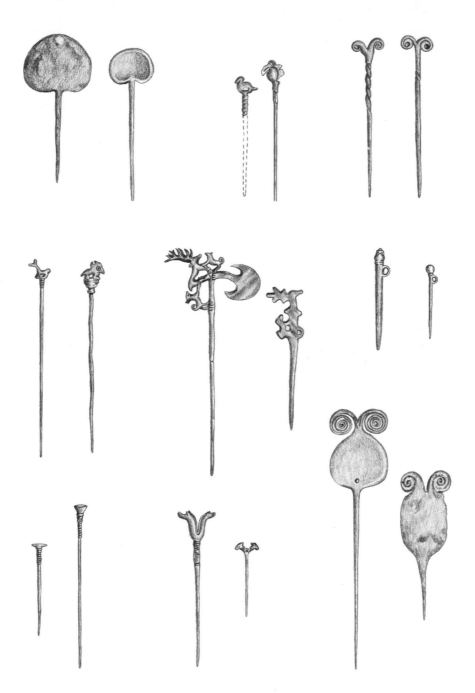

FIGURE 13.7
Bronze and copper pins from the Caucasus region (left-hand specimens of each pair) and from the Andean region (right-hand specimen). (After Heine-Geldern 1972.)

the Indus Valley (Wheeler 1966:51). The question of an extracontinental origin for these metal objects in the Andean region seems possibly tied to that of the origin of other traits with seeming Mediterranean-Southwest Asian affinities. These will be discussed in a subsequent section.

Similarities between Dong-son sculptured bronze drums and urn lids and the unique terra-cotta house models and "village scenes" on round or rectangular bases from southern Nayarit, Mexico, have been noted (von Winning 1969; Bell 1971:715–716). The chronology of the latter is not yet established, but they are estimated to date between the first and seventh centuries AD. From early in the shaft tomb period of southwestern Nayarit (ca. AD 100–200) also come the vaguely Oriental-faced "chinesca" figurines (von Winning 1974:69, 172–176). It is to be noted as well that the Han Chinese, who conquered the Dong-son area (see the following section), made ceramic house models as grave offerings and utilized shaft tombs.

In South America, the Bahía culture of Ecuador also produced ceramic house models, many of which exhibit overhanging eaves or saddle roofs or both (Estrada and Meggers 1961; Meggers 1971:244–248). The latter roof type is otherwise unknown in the Americas but exists or existed at scattered localities in South India, Southeast Asia (including Tonkin), South China, Japan, and western Oceania (Noble 1969:266–267). The Bahía culture also exhibits other traits rare or otherwise absent in America but found in southern and eastern Asia. Among these are neck rests, symmetrically graduated panpipes (see also Marschall 1965; Tekiner 1974), a type of ceramic net weight, "golf-tee" ear plugs, and the coolie yoke. The dates of this complex lie somewhere between 200 BC and 1 BC, a time compatible with either Dongson or Han, or a fusion of the two. The contemporaneous occurrence in the Bahía area of the earliest American Dong-son-like metal work is also of note. Bahía culture was highly developed and had maritime trade relations with areas from Mexico to southern Peru (Kidder 1964:476–477).

Han China and the New World

The Han Dynasty in China (206 BC–220 AD) was, on the whole, a time of political reunification, expansion of frontiers, and development of long-distance foreign contacts. Voyaging to India was common during the Western Han (206 BC–AD 8). A third-century-AD writer wrote that the Han had "won through across the Western Seas to reach Ta-Chhin (the Roman Empire) . . . but the Eastern Ocean is yet more vast, and we know of no one who has crossed it" (Needham 1971:550). Nevertheless, trade was carried on with Korea and Japan (Yü 1967:183–186), and some have suggested contacts with the Americas.

Heine-Geldern (1959b; 1966:283–284) and Ekholm (1964a) have pointed out the similarity of Teotihuacán II–III cylindrical tripod pottery (beginning

a   b   c   d

FIGURE 13.8

Chinese and Mesoamerican cylindrical tripod pottery vessels: *a,* Han Dynasty, North Viet Nam; *b,* Teotihuacán III style, Kaminaljuyú, Guatemala; *c,* Han Dynasty, model granary; *d,* "stuccoed" (lacquered) Teotihuacanoid vessel, Uaxactún, Guatemala. (*a, c,* after Heine-Geldern 1959b; *b,* after Kidder et al. 1946; *d,* after Kelemen 1956.)

in the third century AD[?]) to ceramic, metal, and lacquer cylindrical tripod vessels of Han China (Figure 13.8). Besides general form, points in common include conical lids (sometimes with aviform or ring-form apical knobs); decorative zones encircling the vessel's body, separated by ridges or incisions; thickened tops and/or bottoms of vessel walls; and mold-made applied decoration. The cylindrical tripod vase is an unprecedented form in Mesoamerican archeology when it appears at Teotihuacán, and it is associated with the earliest known Mesoamerican use of ceramic molds and appliqué mold decorations. Ekholm suggests that the Mesoamerican ceramic forms imitated Chinese metal ones, which had mold-made parts.

Heine-Geldern also sees Han or pre-Han influence in Middle American bowls on high, flaring stands pierced by triangular perforations.

LACQUER □ Although developed by Shang times, lacquer work came into preeminence in China in Han times. The sap of the lac tree (ch'i<ts'iet) was used as the vehicle for pigments and then dried to a bright, usually glossy finish. This technique was used on wood, cloth, metal, pottery, and other materials. Usually a gessolike primer layer of bone ash or white earth (huan) was first applied to the wood, but sometimes a technique called chia chu ("lined with hemp cloth") was used. Successive layers of lacquer, sometimes of different colors, were painted on. Decoration techniques included simple painting, inlaying with precious materials (sometimes imitated in painted lacquer), carving (including exposure of different-colored lower layers and filling of incisions with white or red pigment), and reliefs of built-up lacquer putty. The most common colors were black and red (Willets 1958:188–205).

In India, Ceylon, and Burma, resin (or in Sanskrit, laksha) secreted by a Coccus insect, parastic on gummy-sapped trees, is used. A scale insect, pela, is also used in China to produce a white wax.

Mesoamerican lacquer work apparently dates to at least the first century BC, although most of what is known of processes used comes from post-contact observations. Salvia-seed oil (chia or chian) was one major lacquer medium used, particularly in western Mexico; the other was aje (axin, nij, ni-in, nün), the fat rendered from a tree-sap-sucking coccid insect (for example, kurrón) native to the hotter parts of Middle America. Lacquers were used on gourds, wood, stone mirror backs, pottery, and probably metal, over a gessolike white-earth primer. Successive layers, sometimes of different colors, were applied. Red and black were common colors. Decoration techniques involved painting, painted inlay, carving (Jenkins 1967; B. Gordon 1957), exposure of different-colored undercoats, and incision filling. Covarrubias (1957:96–97, 139) believed lacquer work to have originated in Mesoamerica in late Preclassic times on the Pacific coast of western Mexico, and to have reached its acme on Teotihuacán pottery, whence it spread. One technique used early in western Mexico but not at Teotihuacán until the Late Classic was pseudo-cloisonné, in which a dark lacquer coat was cut away, leaving only design outlines, which were then filled in with contrasting-colored laquer (Holien 1975:158–161). This is reminiscent of Chinese true cloisonné of enamel and metal.

ADDITIONAL EVIDENCE OF CHINESE CONTACTS □ A number of Chinese objects and inscriptions have been reported from Mexico and Peru, sometimes in archeological contexts but not excavated under controlled conditions. Some of the written characters are said to be of forms attributable to Han times, others of about the sixth century AD. The principal archeological zones involved are those of Teotihuacán, Mexico, and Chan Chan, Peru (Loayza 1948:44–94; Lou 1968; Carter 1976). These objects are suggestive but, because of the uncertainties surrounding their discoveries and the complexities of Chinese epigraphy, no great weight can be assigned to them at present.

It may be noted that the layout of Teotihuacán is reminiscent of that of the Chinese city in emphasizing an interrupted north-south axial street and a rough gridiron layout and in being composed largely of walled household compounds with courtyards. Unlike the Chinese city, Teotihuacán lacked an encompassing wall (Millon 1974; Willetts 1958:655–677). Further, in Middle America it was believed that lunar eclipses occurred in certain proportion to the number of lunar months. This same proportion was believed in by the Han Chinese, but in reality this supposed rate is almost one and one-third times the actual frequency of occurrence (Campbell 1974:146–147).

Relevant to the finds of the Chan Chan area, Loayza (1948:101–154) listed 95 Peruvian place names that have meaning in Chinese but not in local languages, plus 130 Peruvian place names corresponding to Chinese place names. These are concentrated particularly from Lima northward. Among additional traits shared by China and Peru, the following are of especial interest: metal disks or coins put into cadavers' mouths, tally strings (*quipus*), suspension bridges, great walls (Needham 1971: 544–546; Loayza 1948:161–173, 213–222), and elaborate agricultural terraces (Spencer and Hale 1961).

Heine-Geldern (1966:284) states that there is no evidence of post-Han Chinese contacts with the New World. Others, however, have disagreed. Since the eighteenth century, some workers have postulated that Fu-Sang, a land said to lie thousands of miles east of China, was in America. The land was referred to as early as Late Chou times and was reportedly visited by Afgani Buddhist monks in AD 485 and by a monk named Hui-Shen a few years later. Rock crystal was said to have been brought to China from Fu-Sang about AD 520 (Needham 1971:540–541; Mertz 1975). Although some aspects of the descriptions of Fu-Sang are compatible with a Mesoamerican identification, others—such as the presence of oxen, horses, and deer milking—seemingly are not. In any event, the Chinese did believe in a land far to the east, and the much condensed records that have survived may point to the conclusion that some voyages were made.

THE MEDITERRANEAN AND MEXICO

Almost from the moment of Cortez's landing in Mexico, Europeans began speculating on possible links between New World civilizations and those of the ancient and classical Near East and Mediterranean. So many unfounded surmises, religious theories, and even fraudulent "finds" had occurred by the early twentieth century (Wauchope 1962) that serious study of possible early

Mediterranean-American relations became, through "guilt by association," even more of an anathema to scholarship than did consideration of possible transpacific ties. This is still true to a large degree, which perhaps helps explain why most works on the subject have been written either by amateurs or by scholars from fields other than anthropology, history, or geography. Not surprisingly, many of these works are flawed or are at least held suspect by specialists. I believe, nevertheless, that some of the proposals of these writers merit serious scrutiny.

Ancient Egyptians

During the early decades of this century, surgeon G. Elliot Smith (1924; 1927; 1933), founder of the "British School" of diffusionism, promoted the idea that Egypt was the fountainhead of much of the world's civilization. Though this was rejected by the scholars of the 1930s and 1940s, there has been a recent revival of interest in some of his ideas by publishers of a journal known as *The New Diffusionist*. In a resultant book, R. A. Jairazbhoy (1974b) argues that Egyptians of the time of Rameses III were among the founders of the Olmec culture.

Olmec specialists have frequently noted analogies between that culture and ancient Egypt, without suggesting any actual historical link. The apparent seasonal use of corvée laborers, expending incredible amounts of effort to transport, sculpt, and emplace colossal, excellently executed stone statues, reliefs, drainways, and the like and to build earth platforms and mounds has been compared to Egyptian practice, as has dependence upon the annual inundation of river flood plains for farming. The sudden, unprecedented appearance of these works and other evidence of advanced knowledge and organization in the unlikely environment of the swampy Gulf coast of Veracruz and Tabasco has often been remarked upon.

Jairazbhoy proposes to explain these similarities not simply as analogues but as the result of a purposeful expedition, in the early twelfth century BC, of Egyptians dispatched by the Pharaoh to discover the underworld paradise to which the setting sun repairs at night. Jairazbhoy believes that the Maya *Popol Vuh* and Mexican traditions recorded by Sahagún and others, which tell of ancestors coming across the sea from the east, seeking the sun and searching for a terrestrial paradise, referred to this expedition.

Briefly summarized, these Mesoamerican traditions relate that mankind was created in the East and lived there in darkness. The ancestors left the East, crossing the sea in a fleet of seven vessels carrying "many companies," and sailed along the Gulf of Mexico coast to its furthest westward point, at Panuco, where the people debarked. They were led to "Tula" by priests, "bookmen" who carried their symbols of rank and their gods. When the sun did not appear, the leaders, disappointed, left, either for home or to continue their quest. Those voyagers who remained then settled near the highest mountains they could find, and for them the sun rose. They married into the local population, to whom they taught the arts of civilization. When their leaders returned, the settlers would not accompany them homeward. Sons of the priest-kings returned to the East, where they received from the king of the East the insignia and symbols of royalty, including the canopy and throne. They then returned to rule the tribes.

In most versions, these culture-bearer ancestors came to Tula; the Aztec and the Maya both seem to have inherited the legend from the Toltecs (who, in turn, apparently adopted it from Teotihuacanos). One version, however, places the arrival of these ancestors in the Olmec period (Goetz and Morley 1951:63, 165–189, 204–210; Heyerdahl 1950b:277–280; Sorenson 1955; Irwin 1963:11–12, 35–38; Jairazbhoy 1947b:8–11). Jairazbhoy views the seeking of the highest mountains as a search for the two peaks flanking the entrance to the Egyptian underworld and feels that the crater of San Martín de Tuxtla, in the Olmec heartland, was accepted by some of the pilgrims as the entry itself. The fluted earthen mound at La Venta is considered a surrogate for this volcano.

Jairazbhoy (1974a; 1974b; 1975) points to a number of traits and institutions that he believes were introduced at this time, including cylinder seals, terra-cotta animals with moving parts, colossal stone sculpture, the calendar, divine kingship, military and funerary customs, and the idea of writing, among others. His emphasis is on religious concepts, however, and he describes more than a score of Mesoamerican "deities"—about half of which are depicted in Olmec period carvings—that he believes to be of Egyptian derivation. Although some of the comparisons seem flimsy, others include some striking similarities: for example, the Mexican goddess Tlazoteotl, who ate people's sins upon confession, and the Egyptian Amemil, "the devouress," who would eat the hearts of condemned sinners after they had confessed to her.

Jairazbhoy also compares Egyptian and Mexican beliefs about passage through various stages on the journey through the western underworld, and finds a serpent guard at stage 2 in each area, deserts in stage 4, and a stage 8 (Aztec *Tlalocán*) in which inhabitants dwell in an enjoyable watery underworld. He also believes he has identified aspects of the Babylonian Gilgamesh legend in Mexican and Mayan texts and sees the earliest Mesoamerican stepped temple mounds (of which there is a small one at La Venta) as reflections of the Babylonian ziggurat.

Jairazbhoy gives far more material than can be summarized here, and much of what he does present would benefit from additional elaboration. Adjusted dates for the Olmec now put that culture's origins well before the reign of Rameses III. Nevertheless, Jairazbhoy's suggestions are most pro-

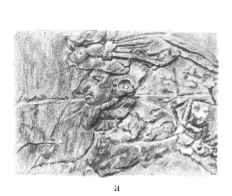

a

b

FIGURE 13.9
Olmec stone sculptures depicting faces with Old World racial traits: *a*, detail, Stela 3, La Venta—note exaggeratedly large, convex, "Levantine" nose and false (?) beard; *b*, Monument 1, San Lorenzo—note Negroid features: broad, flat, low-rooted nose with forward-directed nostrils; thick, everted membranous lips with ridged seams; slight prognathism. (*a*, after Heyerdahl 1971c; *b*, after Clewlow et al. 1967.)

vocative and deserve further analysis. If modified and accepted, his theories could go far toward explaining the enigma of Olmec origins—as a grafting of Egyptian and Chinese branches onto a preexisting Formative American root, to yield a distinctive new "high culture."

One aspect of the "Olmec problem" has been the ostensible presence, in Olmec (and later) art, of depictions of exotic racial types, including Negroids and "Semites" or Armenoids (Heyerdahl 1952:286–295, Plates 17–22, 29–32; 1971c:229–236; Irwin 1963:121–138; von Wuthenau 1970; C. Gordon 1971: 21–35). In most cases, it appears to me, depictions are either too stylized or too generalized for any racial attribution. However, a small number of apparent portraits seem to be sufficiently explicit (Figure 13.9) to justify calling some of them Caucasoid (especially in an Olmec bas-relief and among late Preclassic and Classic Veracruz and Oaxaca terra cottas) and others at least partially Negroid (Olmec colossal stone heads from San Lorenzo and some Veracruz terra cottas). The fact that a number of "portraits" cannot be racially classified, though they are quite realistic, suggests that genetically mixed individuals may be portrayed. Wiercinski (1969) has concluded that there is skeletal evidence for a Negroid component at Tlatilco, Mexico, and elsewhere, although Comas (1973) does not accept this conclusion. For those who do feel that foreign racial types are indicated, a hypothesis of Egyptian or Phoenician voyagers bringing Negro troops or slaves is usually invoked. The wearing of beards is often pointed to as an indication of Caucasoid affiliations of certain individuals depicted in Olmec and later art. Some of these beards seem to be quite genuine, but many appear to be false. It is of note that false beards were worn both in ancient Egypt and in China.

Canaanites and Carthaginians

The Bronze Age Minoans and other "sea peoples" of the ancient Aegean and eastern Mediterranean seem to be prime candidates for early transatlantic transmissions, but as yet only the most dubious, ambiguous, or circumstantial evidence suggests actual impacts (e.g., Hapgood 1966; Cohane 1969; C. Gordon 1971:68–105; Bailey 1973). However, for the Iron Age Phoenicians—Canaanites and their Carthaginian descendants—we have more substantial grounds for hypothesizing influences upon the New World.

Although they had long occupied the Levantine littoral, the northwest-Semitic-speaking Canaanites become prominent in history—as "Phoenicians"—beginning about 1200 BC. They were merchant mariners located at a cultural crossroads, and they developed trade and established colonies along the Mediterranean and on the European and African shores of the Atlantic. They were skilled manufacturers, ambitious traders, and the navigators par excellence of the day, and they were not infrequently employed in the service of the land-based empires of the times.

Several classical sources beginning in the fourth century BC speak of an immense land beyond the Atlantic, many days west of Africa. This land was said to have mountains, plains, and navigable rivers and to be inhabited by strange people who had substantial houses, wealth, and cultivated land through which ran streams. The land was, according to Diodorus Siculus (first century BC), discovered by a storm-blown Phoenician ship sometime after the 1104 BC founding of Gadeira (Cádiz, Spain). Some Carthaginians went to settle this land (Carthage's traditional founding date is 814 BC but may have been as early as the twelfth century). Etruscans also wished to establish a colony there, according to a fourth-century-BC Aristotelian source, but the Carthaginians prevented them from doing this. Then, worried that other nations would establish a foothold there, as well as about an exodus of its own people, and wishing to reserve a secret refuge in case of calamity, Carthage forbade further emigration and killed all of the settlers already there. Tradition places one voyage to this land at about 370 BC (Pohl 1961:17–35; Irwin 1963:119, 220–224; C. Gordon 1971:38–42, 193; Bailey 1973:36–41).

Constance Irwin (1963) has raised the question as to whether Carthaginians ever resorted to this refuge and whether any Canaanite-Carthaginian influence can be detected in the Americas. She believes that likely times for flight might have included the siege of Tyre by Babylonians about 600 BC and the Punic Wars, which began in 264 BC and ended with the destruction of Carthage in 146 BC. Of these dates, she favors the first because of what she believes to be indications of Phoenician influence on the Olmec and because she feels that the Phoenicians introduced the first calendar to Mesoamerica, for which internal evidence is said to suggest a beginning date of about 600 BC.

The great Olmec earthworks and colossal stone sculptures-in-the-round are now clearly too early to have been a result of such a Phoenician immigration. However, certain traits—such as relief carvings showing "Levantine" physical types wearing pointed, curling-toed shoes; ritual self-laceration; possible infant sacrifice; wheeled animal models; and Jairazbhoy's (1974b:20–27, 114–115) "Babylonian complex"—could be attributable to a Phoenician source. These people could conceivably also have inspired the ancestors-from-the-east legends and the beards that crop up in Mesoamerican archeology, not to mention more generalized traits. What some believe to be a terra cotta head of a Phoenician god—either Melqart or Bes—was found under uncontrolled conditions in the Río Balsas drainage (Vaillant 1931).

One of the Phoenicians' hallmarks was the making of a coveted and costly purple dye from the shellfish *Murex* and *Pupura*. *Pupura* dye was also extracted and used in pre-Columbian Middle America and Peru and long ago was pointed to as an indication of Phoenician contacts (Nuttall 1909; Jackson 1916; Gerhard 1964).

In support of the probability of Phoenician transatlantic voyaging is the famous "Paraíba Inscription." Reported in 1872 and long dismissed as a forgery, the authenticity of this now lost inscription from Brazil has recently been championed by Semitic linguist Cyrus H. Gordon (1971:115, 120–127; 1974:22–29, 71–92). Although his position has not gone unchallenged (Cross 1968), his argument—that the text contains several organizational and linguistic usages unknown to scholarship at the time of the supposed forgery, as well as cryptograms—seems convincing to a nonspecialist. The inscription tells of the landing of a Sidonian ship in 531 BC, after a voyage around Africa from the Red Sea port of Ezion-geber. Gordon notes Herodotus's report of an Egypto-Canaanite circumnavigation of Africa about 600 BC and proposes that the Sidonians intentionally sought Brazil via the Red Sea rather than via the Straits of Gibraltar because subsequent to the Persian conquest of Canaan in 539 BC the Carthaginians barred Sidonian voyaging through the straits. The motivation, Gordon proposes, was provided by Brazil's iron deposits.

Further, Barry Fell (1976:157–173) has recently identified purported Iberian Punic (Canaanite) inscriptions from New England, Iowa, and Oklahoma and has given evidence that the language of the Arizona Pima's creation chant is Semitic. These matters are still under investigation.

The Classical World and Mexico

As Sorenson (1971) and others have shown, a very large number of basic ideas, beliefs, and technologies are shared by the Mediterranean and Near East on the one hand and Mesoamerica on the other—even though the styles of these regions are quite distinct. The sharings could represent parallel or convergent evolution, or a legacy of the proposed Egyptian and Phoenician impacts of the Theocratic Formative period, or they could be importations from one or more other sources.

In many instances, it would be impossible to choose between the Mediterranean, India, Southeast Asia, and China as the potential source area for traits that are shared by some or all of those regions. In recent decades, consideration of the Mediterranean and Near East has been neglected by diffusionists in favor of studies involving eastern Asia, but Southwest Asia and the Mediterranean deserve, I believe, close examination in this connection.

The classical world—Greece and Rome—certainly represents one possible source for certain of the aforementioned similarities. However, others date from well before the classical civilizations, and the evidence regarding other traits has, as of yet, been very little studied. Teotihuacán seems to be the most promising Mesoamerican area for investigations relating to possible classical ties.

Despite the lack of comparative studies between Mexico and the classical Mediterranean, a few clues point to actual round-trip Roman voyages. These include a terra cotta head, said to be Roman, of about AD 220, found *in situ* by José García Payon with a twelfth-century-AD burial in the Valley of Toluca, Mexico, and a small torso of Venus collected by Seler in the Huaxteca on the Gulf of Mexico (Heine-Geldern 1967). Scattered finds of Roman period coins have been reported from the eastern United States (C. Gordon 1971: 175–179). Further, the pineapple, a South American domesticate, is depicted in murals and a mosaic at Pompeii (Casella 1950; Pohl 1973), which was destroyed in AD 79. The identification was accepted by plant taxonomist E. D. Merrill (1954), a staunch foe of diffusionism.

What influences, if any, classical civilizations may have had on Mesoamerica is still an open question. Sorenson's list should provide grist for many years of research in reference to classical and earlier times.

Medieval Voyages

Little will be said here regarding putative medieval voyages to America, since they seem unlikely to have had very important impacts on indigenous cultures (although this judgment may require reassessment in the future).

Among proposed voyagers are the Welsh (Deacon 1966), the Irish, the English, the Portuguese (C. Sauer 1968), and, of course, the Norse (Pohl 1961;

Ingestad 1971; C. Gordon 1974), about whom there is a vast literature. Arab voyages have also been postulated, particularly by M. D. W. Jeffreys (1971), as having resulted in pre-Columbian introduction of maize into the Old World. Possible late West African crossings have also received some slight attention (Davidson 1969; Clegg 1969).

SOUTHWEST ASIA AND THE MEDITERRANEAN, AND PERU

Egypt and the Andean Region

Jairazbhoy (1974b: 83–99) theorizes that the "Egypto-Olmecs" continued their search for the underworld paradise and were an element in the formation of the early Andean high cultures, their legacy persisting to the time of the conquest. This migration, as Jairazbhoy perceives it, required several generations.

Similarities between Olmec and Chavín have often been discussed; the two cultures were approximately contemporaneous and had much in common. Although not adequately dated, San Augustín in Colombia certainly has some relationship to Chavín as well. Chavín and its coastal variant Cupisnique together exhibit monumental stone construction, use of adobe brick, large stone sculptures, tenoned stone heads in walls, and other distinctive attributes. Other, poorly dated traits peculiar to Peru in the New World but also found in Egypt include solar religion, the royal title Son of the Sun, the marriage of the ruler to his sister, hunchback dwarfs as court attendants, the equal-arm balance, the horizontal loom staked onto the ground, and mummification with layered wrappings, false heads, and jars for viscera (Rowe 1966; Jairazbhoy 1974b:85–88, 98–99). In addition, T-shaped and epsilon-shaped axes, virtually identical in form, are essentially restricted to the Egyptian region, parts of Mexico, and the Central Andes (Bierne 1971:153, 157).

Jairazbhoy (1974b:92–99) believes that the Egyptians' descendants finally decided that the plains of Lake Titicaca were the equivalent of Iaru, the fields of the city of Re, the sun god whose dwelling is in an underworld lake. The Peruvian paradise Yaro and the fields of Yarocaca in the place of the dead are cited as equivalences (c.f., as well, the Uru Indians now inhabiting the lake's shore). Of course the importance, in Andean religion, of Titicaca's Island of the Sun is well known. Jairazbhoy finds a few architectural parallels between the lakeshore site of Tiahuanaco and Egypt, but his case is far from proved. Tiahuanaco has probably generated more speculation than any other South American site, particularly in view of the uncertainties of its dating, and much about its origins and history remains a mystery.

Heyerdahl (1952:228–238, 247–274, 282–284) has emphasized the occurrence in South America, particularly in Peru and Bolivia, of traditions of white, long-bearded, long-robed culture-bearers who came from somewhere to the East in early times. These people were priests and proselytizers, who—in the Central Andean version of the legend—settled the Island of the Sun in Lake Titicaca and built the great edifices of Tiahuanaco. Some of the party married native women, and the Inca royal family claimed descent from this line.

Heyerdahl (1952:295–328, Plates 23–27, 34–36) points to depictions of bearded individuals and to portraits of non-Indian-appearing persons in Andean art, and discusses the occurrence of pre-Incan Peruvian mummies whose hair is silky, wavy, and of auburn color like that of Caucasoids rather than coarse and black, as is typical of the local Indian populations. Although he does not elaborate on the specifics of the ultimate origins of these physically anomalous individuals, Heyerdahl (1971a; 1971b) makes clear his belief that the Mediterranean—particularly North Africa—is the most likely source area. This idea is, of course, completely compatible with Jairazbhoy's theory of a seminal Egypto-Olmec presence in Peru, focused on Tiahuanaco, and completely at variance with conventional thinking about Andean cultural evolution.

Relevant to the Egyptian question is the recent work of H. B. Fell, published in his *Occasional Papers of the Epigraphic Society* (Summarized in Carter 1975). Fell claims to have deciphered a Chilean inscription that records, in Libyan script, an Egyptian "annexation" of the South American coast in 231 BC. Among Fell's (1976:174–191; 253–276) other startling proposals are that the Zuni language of New Mexico is Libyan (related to Ancient Egyptian), that the Micmac script of maritime Canada is modified Egyptian hieroglyphics, and that the Davenport Stele from Iowa contains inscriptions in Egyptian, Libyan, and Iberian Punic.

"Greco-Roman" Traits in the Andean Area

Although he was attempting to discredit diffusionist theories, John H. Rowe (1966; see also Jett and Carter 1966; Birrell 1964) has compiled a trait list that is of much potential interest to diffusionists. It includes a substantial number of Andean traits that are also present in the Mediterranean and Southwest Asia. The following are known from Archaic or Classical Greece (and, in a number of cases, from other Old World areas) and, in the New World, *exclusively* from the Andean region: pack animals, divination from entrails (Obayashi 1959), sacrifice of domestic animals, oracles, a deity implied to be superior to heavenly bodies because of their regular movements, divine kingship, the sling (weapon), military tents, cubical dice, the whipping top, the abacus, the equal-arm balance, the bismar (Nordenskiöld 1921), the pointed plumb bob, the *peplos* dress, bronze mirrors with handles, metal tweezers, metal nails, the cylindrical drum with two skin heads, the bell-mouthpiece trumpet, the corbeled-dome roof, metal cramps in masonry, handling-protruberences left on building stones, rustication and entasis (techniques for worked stone), the building of stories directly over one another, the siphon, and the sickle. Other shared traits are also notable, including the arch (Larco Hoyle 1945:164), bronze metallurgy and artifact types, staffs with bells for town leaders, wheel-thrown pottery (Lynch 1974: 383), and some striking resemblances in subject matter and in decorative style and technique between Greek Attic and Corinthian pottery and Peruvian Mochica wares.

In addition to the preceding are the following traits known from Roman culture: convents, rectangular land survey, taxation census, standard-number military units, animal-manure fertilizer, and press-mold-made pottery.

Finally, there is in Peru, the *qanat,* or horizontal well—a Mediterranean-Southwest Asian device associated particularly with Persia (English 1968)—and the *badgir,* or wind scoop, found from Egypt to Pakistan as well as in Mochica ceramic house models (von Hagen 1965:56, Plates 35, 36).

Foci in the Andean region for these traits seem to be the Mochica area of the North Coast and the Titicaca Basin. Rowe is correct in considering his list an important test of diffusionist theory. If the archeologically recoverable traits in question should prove to be chronologically irreconcilable—and some are not yet attested to in Peru early enough to be attributable to the classical world—the whole process of comparison would be brought into question. Still, dating of Andean cultures is far from complete.

Although H. S. Gladwin's (1947) transpacific Alexandrian fleet must be viewed more as allegory than history, one *could* hypothesize a Greco-Roman Persian Gulf or Arabian Sea trading colony in which certain Hellenic styles (of pottery decoration, for example) persisted in provincial form and from which voyagers reached Peru. The Romans *were* in contact with Han China and Indochina, where transpacific knowledge may well have been present. No such trading colony is known to me, and it represents, at present, pure speculation; but I believe the question of a classical Greco-Roman–Andean connection to be one of the most critical for future research relevant to the transoceanic diffusion controversy.

INDIA, INDIANIZED SOUTHEAST ASIA, AND MESOAMERICA

India appears to have had seaborne trade relations with areas around the Indian Ocean since quite ancient times. But beginning in the first century AD the search for wealth—particularly gold—resulted in increasingly massive influences by India, especially southern India, on both mainland and island Southeast Asia. Hindu-Buddhist kingdoms were established in Burma, Malaya, Sumatra, Java, Cambodia, Vietnam, and elsewhere (Sarkar 1970:1–4, 18–25). Probably the earliest of these kingdoms was the maritime realm of Funan, in the Mekong delta; this area was later to develop into the Khmer Empire (Briggs 1951).

Many comparisons have been made and contacts postulated between Indianized Southeast Asia and Mesoamerica. It has been suggested that Indian expansion led to acquisition of knowledge of the Americas from Chinese or Southeast Asian merchants and sailors and ultimately resulted in Indian and Indianized Southeast Asian voyages to the New World; large, oceangoing ships were unquestionably in use at the time. The earliest suggested concrete evidence of Hindu influence in Mesoamerica is at Teotihuacán, where the chank shell appears in art, sometimes with a deity emerging from it. This imagery, in which the deity was Tlaloc, the rain god, continued to the conquest, along with the association of the chank with the moon and fertility and its use as a ceremonial trumpet. In India, the sacred chank was blown as a trumpet and otherwise used ceremonially; had associations with the moon, waters, and fertility; and the world creator is sometimes shown rising from it (Jackson 1916a; 1916b; Rouget 1948; Vokes 1963).

The principal proponents of Southeast Asian influences in Mesoamerica have been archeologist Gordon Ekholm (1950; 1953; 1955; 1964b) and Robert Heine-Geldern, an art historian influenced by the early twentieth-century Kulturkreis school of diffusionism (Heine-Geldern 1964a; 1964b; 1966:286–293; Heine-Geldern and Ekholm 1951). The emphasis has been on Cambodian impact upon the Maya and the Toltec, although comparisons with Java and India itself are also made. These scholars' contentions (here much condensed), plus a few additional observations, follow.

During the Amarāvatī period (second to fourth centuries AD), merchants, adventurers, and Buddhist priests from southeastern India colonized Funan and other areas, introducing their religion and art styles; the latter may have persisted there longer than in India, although, the medium having been almost exclusively wood, practically no art has survived. Elements of Amarāvatī style, particularly the lotus (water lily) motif, were introduced directly or indirectly into the Maya country. The most Amarāvatī-like expressions of this motif were not translated into imperishable stone in Mesoamerica until centuries later (particularly at Palenque in Chiapas and at Chichén Itzá in Yucatán); they are not attested to before the sixth century AD, at Uxmal, Yucatán. (The Goodman-Martínez-Thompson calendrical correlation for Maya dates is used herein.) However, the large number of detailed and arbitrary points of similarity (see also Rands 1953) suggests a historic relationship (Figure 13.10). Another possible link with Amarāvatī is the Mesoamerican sun disk-calendar disk and thrones, which recall the Indian symbolism of the wheel and which sometimes carry motifs reminiscent of Indian lotus-petal-rimmed disks and the three-pronged *triratna* (e.g., Hürlimann 1967:138, Plate 161).

a

b

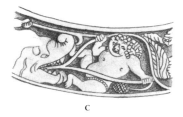

c   d

FIGURE 13.10
Lotus-water lily friezes, India and the Maya country: *a, c,* Amaravati, southern India; *b, d,* Chichén Itzá, Yucatán. (After Heine-Geldern and Ekholm 1951.)

Hindu-Buddhist stylistic and iconographic developments in India continued to be transferred to Southeast Asia and, directly or indirectly, to Mesoamerica. During the Pallava period of maritime activity by South Indians (AD 550–750), corresponding approximately to the Chenla period in Cambodia (AD 550–802), the following Hindu-Buddhist devices may have reached Mayaland: a monster mask from whose lower-jawless mouth emerge plant stems; the *makara,* a crocodile- or fish-bodied, elephant-trunked monster (see also Naudou 1962); and, possibly, Ganesha, the elephant-headed god (Elliot Smith 1924).

By the Indian Nalanda-Pala period (AD 750–900), Cambodia (and possibly Java) seems to have been the focus for Asian-American relations. It may be relevant that the later eighth century was the great period of expansion of the seafaring Malays—from Sumatra to Malaya, to Java, and along the coasts of all Indochina. Chenla, Funan's successor state, was conquered by maritime Malays from Java in the late eighth century. This event may in some way have triggered the massive Cambodian-American interinfluences suggested for the eighth and early ninth centuries. In the Mesoamerican Late Classic period, many of the shared traits are centered at Palenque. Putative Asiatic traits appearing here at this time include roof profiles, trefoil corbeled arches, the building-within-a-building sanctuary, the image of a deity standing on a reclining or crouching human, the feline throne, the seated figure with one leg bent and a lotus in one hand, possibly the lotus throne, and the conch shell or chank with a plant growing from it. Fired brick was a common structural material in Southeast Asia and also appears at Palenque-influenced sites of Tabasco (Pollack 1965:396, 427). Relief "court scenes" from Borobudur, Java (eighth to ninth centuries), and Piedras Negras, Guatemala, have also been compared, as have high-relief figures from Copán, Honduras, and from India and Java (Meggers 1971:250–255, 258–259). Asian-style symbols of rank, such as parasols, fan standards, and litters, are in evidence at this period.

In Cambodia, round stone colonnettes and half and three-quarter columns imitating turned wooden ones were used to fill windows and blind windows and to mark door jambs and exterior building corners. Except for not being used in real windows, stone columnar detail was used in the same contexts, as well as for molding decoration, at ninth-century Puuc-style sites of the Late Classic phase of the Yucatán Peninsula, such as Uxmal, Labná, and Sayil. These features have no precedents in Mesoamerica but show an evolutionary sequence in Cambodia, where round ones were particularly characteristic of the pre AD 802 Chenla period but also continued into the subsequent Angkor period. Atlantean figures, phallic iconography, and monster-mouth doorways in Campeche and Quintana Roo may also represent Southeast Asian imports. Possible America-to-Asia reciprocal influences of this era are the temple pyramid, which appeared in Java and Cambodia toward the end of the eighth century, and stucco-relief decoration. It may also be worth noting that at Belūr (AD 1117), in India's Mysore state, semidetached round columns and colonnettes are used as building-corner and molding decorations. In a high-relief scene on a temple facade at the nearby site of Helebīd (AD 1141) there is a deity holding in his left hand what appears clearly to be an ear of maize (Hürlimann 1967:84, 91–92, Plates 82, 84, 88). Thus, a Yucatán-Cambodia-Mysore diffusion seems to be a possibility (Figure 13.11).

Iconographic features manifested at Tula in Central Mexico (ca. eighth to eleventh centuries[?]) and at "Toltec"-influenced Chichén Itzá in Yucatán (ca. AD 900–1200) have also been attributed to Cambodian or Javan influences of slightly later date. Among the common traits are colonnaded corbel-vaulted galleries with realistic relief scenes on the walls, seated guardian feline statues, head-downward serpent (Hindu *naga* or *makara*) columns and stairway balustrades, and possibly the reclining god (Vishnu-Chac Mool) and aspects of the Quetzalcoatl cult. In support of the purported Southeast Asia-Tula-Mayaland journeys led by priests is a Guatemalan tradition: "From the west we came to Tulán, from across the sea . . ." (Sorenson 1955:426, 435).

The preceding discussion has dealt primarily with quite specific, datable archeological evidence. More general comparisons between such things as the similar cosmological considerations in the layout of ceremonial centers and

FIGURE 13.11

Reciprocal influences on Indic Asia(?): *a*, Temple pyramid 2, Tikal, Guatemala, ca. AD 699; *b*, temple pyramid Baksei Chankrong, Angkor, Cambodia, ca. AD 947; *c*, detail of relief, Halebid, Mysore, India, twelfth century AD—note ear of maize in figure's hand. (*b*, after Stierlin 1964; *c*, after Hurlimann 1967.)

similar settlement patterns have been made for Cambodia and Mayaland (Coe 1956; Shimkin 1973:291–295). Further, conquest period Mesoamerican traits of unknown age have been tentatively attributed to South and/or Southeast Asian contacts. Among these are details of administrative hierarchy, belief in a series of worlds destroyed by natural catastrophes and recreated, concepts of heaven and hell, the idea of the rabbit in the moon, and so forth. Also mentioned are the games *pachisi* in India and Southeast Asia and *patolli* in Mexico (Tylor 1896) and the hook-swinging rite of India and the volador ritual of Mexico (MacLeod 1931). The specialized *chinampa* agricultural system of Mexico has also been compared to almost identical Burmese and Kashmiri systems (Sturtevant 1968). Putative pre-Columbian maize pollen has been reported for Kashmir (Vishnu-Mittre and Gupta 1966), and Stonor and Anderson (1949) have argued for early maize in northeastern India. The list could be lengthened.

The closely related Mexican and Mayan lunar calendars have been compared with Asiatic ones (Kelley 1960; Kirchhoff 1964a; 1964b; Moran and Kelley 1969), in a search for relationships. Mesoamerican calendrics date to before 200 BC, which is too early for them to have been introduced by the above-postulated South and Southeast Asian contacts, nor does the Mesoamerican calendar appear to derive from the Chinese, at least according to Kelley's comparisons. Nevertheless, there is evidence favoring Indian-Southeast Asian *influence* on a Mexican calendar already in use, and to a lesser extent on the Mayan calendar. Without going into the complexities of the various comparisons, we may note that Kelley has found *in-order* primary correspondences of seven and four, respectively, between the 28 Hindu lunar mansions and their gods on the one hand, and the 20 Mexican and 20 Mayan day names and day gods on the other. Further, significant correlations exist between South and Southeast Asian lunar animals and Mesoamerican animal day names. The probability that these correspondences are the result of chance is very low.

The question of an Old World origin for the original Mesoamerican calendar system is far more problematic. A possible clue is the finding, in Maya day names, of four in-order similarities with letters of the Hebrew and Greek alphabets that have been postulated as having derived from now unknown lunar calendric signs. If this Northwest Semitic calendar system still existed in the twelfth century BC, it could have been one of the postulated Levantine contributions to the Olmec, from whose calendar the Mayan and Mexican ones seem to have been derived (see subsequent discussion).

The association of a color with each of the cardinal directions is a widespread and probably very ancient phenomenon, one found primarily in southern, central, and eastern Asia and in Middle and North America. Particular color-directional associations vary tremendously, and the spread of this idea and associated ones (such as directional gods, animals, times of day, seasons, jewels, elements, winds, and sky bearers) was undoubtedly quite complex. However, relevant to possible Hindu-Buddhist influences in Meso-america is the fact that exact correspondences in the four-directional color assignments exist between certain of the several Hindu-Buddhist systems and certain of the Mexican and Mayan ones, and that the Javan system is the same in order of colors but not in their positions (although the Javan and the New Mexico Tewa Puebloan systems correspond exactly). An ascending series of sequentially destroyed world ages—the first, 4800 divine years long—each with a symbolic color, occurs, in the same order, in India and Mesoamerica (Singhal 1969:65). The essentially identical games *pachisi* and *patolli* are symbolic of this cosmic scheme (Tylor 1896). In relation to suggested South Chinese-Mexican contacts, it is notable that the color-direction orders of Burma and of the Nakhi of South China are duplicated only in Mexico (Damais 1969:114; Riley 1963:Table 1; Bogue 1966–1967; Nowotny 1969).

Essentially all of the postulated Hindu-Buddhist influences in Mesoamerica are in the realm of religion and religious art and architecture, and few if any are in the area of technology unrelated to religion. This suggests that any such contacts were restricted to missionary and perhaps trading relations but did not involve conquest and colonization in the later European manner, in which foreign technology and organizational principles were used in combination with native labor for purposes of economic exploitation.

It has been pointed out that the gruesome practices of Mexican and Mayan human sacrifice are totally at odds with the Hindu-Buddhist tradition of *ahimsā*, nonviolence. Thus, it is perhaps noteworthy that the historic Quetzalcoatl (Kukulkan), the priest-king who seems successively to have ruled in Tula, Cholula, and Chichén Itzá in the late ninth and tenth centuries, initiated and preached "a new religion that combated excesses and human sacrifices," and which may have included autosacrifice, penitence, and mystic unity through meditation (Hedrick 1971; Singhal 1969:64). This Quetzalcoatl appears to have been native born, but his teachings sound quite compatible with Hindu-Buddhist doctrine. Perhaps he had studied with Asian priests. The version of the Quetzalcoatl tradition in which he departs for the East on a raft of serpents (Heyerdahl 1952:276) compares with Vishnu's floating on the cosmic waters on a *naga* (serpent-monster) raft (Ions 1967).

It is not amiss to consider the possible relationship of Southeast Asian-Mayan contact and the collapse of Classic Maya civilization. Widespread depopulation occurred immediately following the period for which there is maximum evidence for such contacts, that is, about AD 900. Many causes have been suggested for this decimation, but as Shimkin (1973:279–284) and others have observed, disease has been underestimated as a possible cause. Aboriginal Americans' general lack of immunity to Old World diseases is well known, and this, more than warfare, accounted for their early postcontact decline and, often, extinction. If ninth-century Southeast Asians inadvertently introduced Old World infections to Mayaland, precisely the effects observed would have been the result. The Toltec influx, which seems to have concentrated surviving lowland Mayan priests and artisans at Chichén Itzá, probably occurred in a near vacuum rather than substantially contributing to the collapse.

Perhaps the fall of the Classic Maya and the abandonment of Tula caused the termination of Cambodian relations with Mesoamerica. Certainly none continued after dissolution of the Khmer Empire in the thirteenth century. One important remaining question is: If imported disease led to the demise of Classic Maya civilization, why did a substantial Mexican population survive? Possibly a series of earlier contacts, as previously discussed, had resulted in development of a degree of disease immunity among Mexicans. In this connection, it is notable that the areas of high cultures with whom massive early Old World relations have been suggested, namely, Mexico and the central Andes, had native populations that best survived the post-Columbian pestilences brought by Europeans (although environmental factors no doubt also played a role in this connection).

CONCLUSIONS

Without attempting to present detailed arguments for and against various theories of transoceanic influences, this chapter has surveyed the most important diffusionist theses and has summarized—and occasionally augmented or questioned—the evidence supporting these theses. Further, I have endeavored to arrange diffusionist schemes into a framework that gives a broad chronological and geographical view of how the ancient Americas *may* fit into the larger picture of world history.

For Americanists, the principal interest of this survey will be in its implications for the reconstruction of the course of New World culture growth, particularly in reference to the high cultures of nuclear America. Most scholars admit to the likelihood of sporadic, accidental transoceanic contacts but tend to discount the possibility of significant extracontinental influences. However, with the demonstration of means and potential motives for intentional transoceanic traffic (Jett 1971), the question of important foreign contributions to New World cultures becomes critical.

If one were to present a contemporary, capsule, "diffusionist's-eye view" of the role of foreign contacts in the development of nuclear America, it might look something like the following:

1. Significant contacts may have occurred in preceramic times and may have resulted in the introduction of a few cultivated plants and even the idea of cultivation, but this, as yet, can be considered little more than speculation.

2. The appearance and spread of Colonial Formative pottery, beginning before 3600 BC, justifies a tentative presumption of introduction from the Old World. Although possible Mediterranean sources have been cited, at present eastern Asia seems to exhibit better evidence of having been a source area. By the end of the

Colonial Formative (ca. 1450 BC), village farming life, well-developed ceramics, bark-cloth making, color-directional symbolism, religious emphasis on felines and serpents, nagualism, and a number of other trait complexes had been introduced to southern Mesoamerica, probably largely from the Yangtse River area of Neolithic coastal China, via the North Pacific current. Return voyages were made, introducing the peanut to China.

3. In the meantime, Malaysians, probably from the shores of the Celebes Sea, had reached the Gulf of Panama, aided perhaps by the Equatorial Countercurrent. For many centuries these settlers continued to maintain contacts with island Southeast Asia, perhaps in the fashion that the migratory Polynesians later preserved ties with relatives on their home islands. Vegetative-reproduction-shifting cultivation, long houses, houses on piles, headhunting, the blowgun complex, signal gongs, and other traits were introduced over a long period of time, and American food plants were carried back to Asia. In lower Central America, the Southeast Chinese and Malaysian influences met and merged.

The nature of these early contacts differed from later ones in that, at least in some areas, migrations had significant genetic impact because of the technological superiority of the intruders, the small populations of the indigenes, and the toll taken by Old World diseases. Cultural impacts were even greater; they encompassed the whole gamut of life, both secular and religious, and formed the basis for the subsequent distinctive development of nuclear American cultures and the foundations onto which later imports were added. The motives for these early voyages are obscure, but simple adventuring and the search for new, relatively empty lands may have played important roles.

4. Beginning about 1450 BC, quantum changes, including hierarchical social organization, construction of large-scale religious monuments and ceremonial centers, extraordinary lapidary work (Middle America) and metal working (Peru), and water control, appeared suddenly at San Lorenzo, Veracruz, and at Chavín de Huántar, Peru. A theocratic system involving a pantheon, a priesthood, craft specialists devoted to creating religious art in so-called great styles, rigid social stratification, corvée labor, and perhaps calendrics and writing all seem to have been introduced and grafted on to the well-established Colonial Formative base. Many traits of this earlier cultural manifestation were retained, adapted, and elaborated, while others were eliminated over wide areas. Possible outside sources for the theocratic stimuli include Shang China (with the search for jade and gold providing a motive), Egypt (via religiously inspired explorations), and (somewhat later) Phoenicia (for purposes of raw-material acquisition, perhaps including *pupura* dye). Despite the religious and organizational emphases of these impacts, important technological additions to nuclear America also occurred, including advanced techniques of weaving, metal working, stoneworking, and, probably, more intensive agricultural methods.

Based on a strong economic base—including an expanding long-distance trade network—new technologies, and highly structured religious and sociopolitical organization, regional nuclear American cultures, benefiting from inputs from several cultural sources, consolidated and developed their own distinctive styles during the later Formative.

5. The great Olmec emphasis on jade seems first to have manifested itself at La Venta, perhaps about 1100 BC. For several centuries thereafter, there is little

or no evidence of East Asian influences in Middle America. Yet it is for about this time period that Northwest Coast stylistic similarities to Middle Chou art seem to suggest contacts. Perhaps local takeover of the Middle American jade deposits led to a development, by southeast Chinese, of Fraser River jade as a substitute.

6. Apparently no earlier than 500 BC, and perhaps a century or two later, Chinese influences on Mesoamerica seem to have resumed. This may be related to Taoist voyages seeking the "drugs of longevity," perhaps vaguely remembered from earlier contacts; but the Guerrero jade mines were never reopened, possibly because the Burmese jadeites had been discovered by this time. The introduction of Late Chou-Ch'in art styles, mainly in woodcarving, occurred during this period. These, in modified form, were later translated into stone carving in Veracruz (Tajín) and elsewhere.

7. Dong-son people of northern Vietnam, falling increasingly under Chinese influence, also established relations with the Americas, focusing, apparently, on the Bahía area of Ecuador, and introducing certain metal-working techniques and object types. Dong-son was conquered by the Han Chinese, and by the first century AD influence from this area was being felt in Nayarit—the probable debarkation area—as well as in the Valley of Mexico. The Chinese presence, though probably not demographically large, may have contributed to the planning and layout of a growing Teotihuacán, and may have introduced certain pottery forms and lacquering techniques. The Chinese may also have been active in coastal Peru about the same time.

8. Classical Mediterranean influences are strongly suggested in nuclear America, especially Peru. Exact source areas remain to be pinpointed, but some indications exist that a trading colony on the Persian Gulf or the Arabian Sea may have been involved.

9. Important transatlantic contacts all but ceased during the European Dark Ages, not to be resumed until the Renaissance. Chinese Pacific voyaging seems also to have dwindled away after Han times. Simultaneously, however, there occurred a waxing of voyaging from South India and its Southeast Asian colonies, particularly Cambodia. Resulting influences, from about AD 400 to 1000, were manifested largely in religion and religious art and architecture and were concentrated almost exclusively in the Maya Lowlands and at Tula in Central Mexico. Ultimately, introduced diseases led to the Maya collapse and, shortly thereafter, to the end of significant pre-Columbian transpacific voyaging.

Phillips (1966) has presented a more conventional view than the somewhat startling scenario outlined above. He has argued against the idea of transoceanic contacts as a source of "decisive" impacts on nuclear American culture growth, defining "decisive" developments as (1) the initiation of food production, (2) the emergence of pottery making, (3) the commencement of village farming life, (4) the addition of minor ceremonial centers to the village pattern, and (5) the inception of major ceremonial centers.

These "events" probably are, with the possible exception of pottery making, too general to be amenable to direct proof for internal or external origin, and Phillips ultimately concludes that pottery is not, in itself, of any great cultural significance anyway. He also goes on to question the existence of village ceremonial centers. He does not discuss urbanization as a "decisive" development.

In any event, a few workers *have* speculated on a possible stimulus-diffusion origin of New World crop raising as well as on human introduction of certain early cultivated plants of foreign origin, such as the bottlegourd. Practically nothing is known about the emergence of village farming (Flannery 1972), and we can hardly yet come to any firm conclusions as to how it originated. Certain of the hypotheses outlined in this chapter have suggested transoceanic contacts at time periods compatible with their having contributed to the formation of a village farming society and to the introduction of some associated traits; Phillips mentions jade carving, turquoise mosaics, tripod vessels, and figurines, all of which have been discussed in a transoceanic context.

Phillips concedes that, with the appearance of early temple centers, the question of diffusion becomes acute. Among "critical elements," he mentions (1) monumental architecture, (2) planned arrangement of structures, (3) sculpture, (4) metallurgy (Peru), (5) hieroglyphic writing (Mesoamerica), and (6) great art styles. He also lists nonarcheological items, such as widespread religious movements, complex sociopolitical institutions, craft specialization, and trade. Most of these have been dealt with in some detail here, in reference to the transoceanic question. This is not to say that the derivation of these phenomena from abroad has been proved, nor that Phillips has not raised some legitimate questions about the validity of certain areas of the evidence. Nevertheless, this chapter *has* demonstrated, I believe, that transoceanic influences must be seriously reckoned with in any consideration of these fundamental cultural developments. In addition, myriad minor cultural phenomena may be "trace elements" indicating contacts that provided *opportunity* for more "decisive"—but less demonstrable—impacts. None of this is intended to suggest that any New World culture "*is*" Egyptian, Chinese, Cambodian, or what have you. The intent has been to show how Old World cultures may have contributed important threads to the fabric of the distinctive civilizations that we call nuclear American and perhaps have provided significant stimuli for the evolution of those civilizations.

References Cited and Recommended Sources

Alcina Franch, José 1969 Origen transatlántico de la cultura indígena de América. Revista Española de Antropología 4:9–64.

Anon. 1934 The exhibition of early Chinese bronzes. The Museum of Far Eastern Antiquities, Bulletin 6:81–136.

Bailey, James 1973 The god-kings and the titans: the New World ascendancy in ancient times. London: Hodder and Stoughton.

Balser, Carlos 1968 Metal and jade in lower Central America. Congreso Internacional de Americanistas, Actas y Memorias, 37:4:57–63.

Beck, Louis 1966 Jade. Anthropological Journal of Canada 4:1:12–22.

Bell, Betty 1971 Archaeology of Nayarit, Jalisco, and Colima. *In* Handbook of Middle American Indians 11:2:694–753.

Bellwood, Peter 1975 The prehistory of Oceania. Current Anthropology 16:1:9–28.

Bernal, Ignacio 1969 The Olmec World. Berkeley and Los Angeles: University of California Press.

Bierne, Daniel Randall 1971 Cultural patterning as revealed by a study of pre-Columbian ax and adz hafting in the Old and New Worlds. *In* Man Across the Sea: Problems of Pre-Columbian Contacts, ed. Carroll L. Riley et al. Austin: University of Texas Press.

Birrell, Verla 1964 Transpacific contacts and Peru. Congreso Internacional de Americanistas, Actas y Memorias 35:1:31–38.

Bischof, Henning 1973 The origins of pottery in South America—recent radiocarbon dates from southwest Ecuador. Congresso Internazionale degli Americanisti, Atti 40:1:269–281.

Bogue, Patricia 1966–67 The world directions in Greece, India, and Meso-America. The Wisconsin Sociologist 5:1–2:1–10.

Borden, Charles A. 1967 Sea Quest: Global Blue-Water Adventuring in Small Craft. Philadelphia: Macrae Smith Company.

Bowen, Richard Le Barron, Jr. 1953 Eastern sail affinities. The American Neptune 13:2, 3: 81–117, 185–211.

———. 1959 The origins of fore-and-aft rigs. The American Neptune 19:3, 4:155–199, 274–306.

Brand, Donald D. 1971 The sweet potato: an exercise in methodology. *In* Man Across the Sea: Problems of Pre-Columbian contacts, ed. Carroll L. Riley et al. Austin: University of Texas Press

Briggs, Lawrence P. 1951 The ancient Khmer Empire. Transactions of the American Philosophical Society, 41:(1).

Brooks, Charles Wolcott 1875 Reports of Japanese vessels wrecked in the north Pacific from the earliest records to the present time. Proceedings, California Academy of Sciences 6:50–66.

Campbell, Joseph 1974 The Mythic Image. Princeton: Princeton University Press.

Carlson, John B. 1975 Lodestone compass: Chinese or Olmec primacy? Science 189:4205: 753–760.

Carmichael, Elizabeth 1970 Turquoise Mosaics from Mexico. London: Trustees of the British Museum.

Carter, George F. 1950 Plant evidence for early contacts with America. Southwestern Journal of Anthropology 6:2:161–182.

———. 1953 Plants across the Pacific. Memoirs, Society for American Archaeology 9:62–71.

———. 1963 Movement of people and ideas across the Pacific. *In* Plants and the Migration of Pacific Peoples, ed. Jacques Barrau, pp. 7–22. Honolulu: Bernice P. Bishop Museum.

———. 1971 Pre-Columbian chickens in America. *In* Man Across the Sea: Problems of Pre-Columbian Contacts, ed. Carroll L. Riley et al. Austin: University of Texas Press.

———. 1974 Domesticates as artifacts. *In* The Human Mirror: Material and Spatial Images of Man, ed. Miles Richardson. Baton Rouge: Louisiana State University Press.

———. 1975 Some comments on the Egyptians in the Indo-Pacific region. Anthropological Journal of Canada 13:2:6–11.

———. 1976 Chinese contacts with America: Fu-Sang again. Anthropological Journal of Canada 14:1:10–24.

———. 1977 A hypothesis suggesting the possibility of a single origin of agriculture. *In* Charles A. Reed, ed., Origins of Agriculture. Chicago: Aldine Publishing Company.

Casella, Domenico 1950 La frutta nelle pitture pompeiana. *In* Pompeiana 11–13.

Caso, Alfonso, and Ignacio Bernal 1973 Ceramics of Oaxaca. *In* Handbook of Middle American Indians 3:2:871–895. Austin: University of Texas Press.

Chadwick, Robert 1971 Archaeological synthesis of Michoacan and adjacent regions. *In* Handbook of Middle American Indians 11:2:657–693.

Chang, Kuang-chih 1959 A working hypothesis for the early cultural history of South China. Bulletin of the Institute of Ethnology, Academia Sinica 7:43–103.

———. 1968 The Archaeology of Ancient China. Rev. ed. New Haven: Yale University Press.

————. 1973 Radiocarbon dates from China: some initial interpretations. Current Anthropology 14:5:525–528.

Chêng, Tê-kun 1960, 1963 Archaeology in China, 2, 3. Cambridge: W. Heffer & Sons.

Clegg, Legrand H., III 1969 The beginning of the African diaspora: black men in ancient and Medieval America? Current Bibliography in African Affairs 2:2:13–34.

Clewlow, C. William, Richard A. Cowan, James F. O'Connell, and Carlos Benemann 1967 Colossal heads of the Olmec culture. Contributions of the University of California Archaeological Research Facility, 4.

Coe, Michael D. 1956 The Khmer settlement pattern: a possible analogy with that of the Maya. American Antiquity, 22:4:409–410.

————. 1968a America's First Civilization. New York: American Heritage Publishing Company.

————. 1968b San Lorenzo and the Olmec Civilization. In Dumbarton Oaks Conference on the Olmec, ed. Elizabeth P. Benson, pp. 42–71. Washington, D.C.: Dumbarton Oaks Research Library and Collection.

————. 1970 The archaeological sequence at San Lorenzo Tenochtitlán, Veracruz, Mexico. Contributions of the University of California Archaeological Research Facility 8:21–34.

Cohane, John Philip 1969 The Key. New York: Crown Publishers.

Comas, Juan 1973 Transatlantic hypothesis on the peopling of America: Caucasoids and Negroids. Journal of Human Evolution 2:2:75–92.

Covarrubias, Miguel 1947 Mexico South: The Isthmus of Tehuantepec. New York: Alfred A. Knopf.

————. 1954 The Eagle, the Jaguar, and the Serpent: Indian Art of the Americas. New York: Alfred A. Knopf.

————. 1957 Indian Art of Mexico and Central America. New York: Alfred A. Knopf.

Cross, Frank Moore, Jr. 1968 The Phoenician inscription from Brazil: a nineteenth-century forgery. Orientalia 37:4:437–460.

Damais, Louis-Charles 1969 Etudes javanaises III: à propos des couleurs symboliques des points cardinaux. Bulletin de l'Ecole d'Extrême-Orient 56:75–118.

Damon, P. E., C. W. Ferguson, A. Long, and E. I. Wallick 1974 Dendrochronological calibration of the radiocarbon time scale. American Antiquity 39:2:350–366.

Davidson, Basil 1969 Africans before Columbus? West Africa 2714:649.

Deacon, Richard 1966 Madoc and the Discovery of America. New York: George Braziller.

Dillon, Brian D. 1975 Notes on trade in ancient Mesoamerica. Contributions of the University of California Archaeological Research Facility 24:79–135.

Doran, Edwin, Jr. 1971 The sailing raft as a great tradition. In Man Across the Sea: Problems of Pre-Columbian Contacts, ed. Carroll L. Riley et al., pp. 115–138. Austin: University of Texas Press.

————. 1973 Nao, junk, and vaka: boats and culture history. Texas A & M University Lecture Series.

————. 1974 Outrigger ages. The Journal of the Polynesian Society 83:2:130–140.

Dragoo, Don W. 1976 Some aspects of eastern North American prehistory: a review. American Antiquity 41:1:3–27.

Drucker, Philip, Robert F. Heizer, and Robert J. Squier 1959 Excavations at La Venta, Tabasco. Bureau of American Ethnology Bulletin 170.

Easby, Elizabeth Kennedy 1968 Pre-Columbian jade from Costa Rica. New York: André Emmerich.

Edwards, Clinton R. 1965 Aboriginal watercraft on the Pacific coast of South America. University of California, Ibero-Americana 47.

————. 1969 Possibilities of pre-Columbian maritime contacts among New World civilizations. Mesoamerican Studies 4:3–10.

Ekholm, Gordon F. 1950 Is American Indian culture Asiatic? Natural History 59:8:344–351, 382.

————. 1953 A possible focus of Asiatic influence in the Late Classic cultures of Mesoamerica. Memoirs, Society for American Archaeology 9:72–89.

————. 1955 The new orientation toward problems of Asiatic-American relationships. In New interpretations of aboriginal American culture history, pp. 95–109. Anthropological Society of Washington.

————. 1964a The possible Chinese origin of Teotihuacán cylindrical tripod pottery and certain related traits. Congreso International de Americanistas, Actas y Memorias 35:1:39–45.

————. 1964b Transpacific contacts. *In* Prehistoric Man in the New World, ed. Jesse D. Jennings and Edward Norbeck, pp. 489–510. Chicago: University of Chicago Press.

————. 1973 The archaeological significance of mirrors in the New World. Congresso Internazionale degli Americanisti, Atti 40:1:133 135.

Elliot Smith, G. 1924 Elephants and Ethnologists. London: Kegan Paul, Trench, Trubner & Company.

————. 1927 Culture: The Diffusion Controversy. London: Norton.

————. 1933 The Diffusion of Culture. London: Watts & Company.

English, Paul Ward 1968 The origin and spread of qanats in the Old World. Proceedings, American Philosophical Society 112:3:170–181.

Estrada, Emilio, and Betty J. Meggers 1961 A complex of traits of probable transpacific origin on the coast of Ecuador. American Anthropologist 63:5:913–939.

Fell, Barry 1976 America B.C.: Ancient Settlers in the New World. New York: Quadrangle/ The New York Times Book Company.

Feldman, Lawrence H. 1973 Stones for the archaeologist. Contributions of the University of California Archaeological Research Facility 18:87–104.

Ferdon, Edwin N., Jr. 1963 Polynesian origins. Science 141:3580:499–505.

Fiennes, Richard and Alice Fiennes 1968 The Natural History of Dogs. London: Weidenfeld and Nicholson.

Flannery, Kent V. 1972 The origins of the village as a settlement type in Mesoamerica and the Near East: A comparative study. *In* Man, Settlement and Urbanism, ed. Peter J. Ucko, Ruth Tringham, and G. W. Dimbleby, pp. 23–53. London: Gerald Duckworth & Company.

Ford, James A. 1969 A comparison of Formative cultures in the Americas: diffusion or the psychic unity of man? Smithsonian Contributions to Anthropology 11.

Foshag, William F. 1955 Chalchihuitl—a study in jade. American Mineralogist 40:11, 12: 1062–1070.

————. 1957 Mineralogical studies on Guatemalan jade. Smithsonian Miscellaneous Collections 135:(5).

Foshag, William F., and Robert Leslie 1955 Jadeite from Manzanal, Guatemala. American Antiquity 21:1:81–83.

Fraser, Douglas 1962 Primitive Art. Garden City, N.Y.: Doubleday & Company.

————. 1967 Early Chinese Art and the Pacific Basin: A Photographic Exhibition. New York: Columbia University.

————. 1972 Early Chinese artistic influence in Melanesia? *In* Early Chinese Art and Its Possible Influence in the Pacific Basin, 3, ed. Noel Barnard. New York: Intercultural Arts Press.

Fulop, Marcos 1954 Aspectos de la cultura Tukana: cosmología. Revista Colombiana de Antropología 3:97–137.

Gerhard, Peter 1964 Shellfish dye in America. Congreso International de Americanistas, Actas y Memorias 35:3:177–191.

Gladwin, Harold Sterling 1947 Men Out of Asia. New York: McGraw-Hill Book Company.

Goetz, Delia, and Sylvanus G. Morley 1951 Popol Vuh: The Sacred Book of the Ancient Quiché Maya. The Translation of Adrian Recinos. Norman: University of Oklahoma Press.

Gordon, B. L. 1957 A domesticated, wax-producing, scale insect kept by the Guaymí Indians of Panama. Ethnos 22:1–2:36–49.

Gordon, Cyrus H. 1971 Before Columbus: Links Between the Old World and Ancient America. New York: Crown Publishers.

————. 1974 Riddles in History. New York: Crown Publishers.

Greenman, Emerson F. 1963 The Upper Palaeolithic and the New World. Current Anthropology 4:1:41–91.

Griffin, Gillett G. 1972 Xochipala, the earliest great art style in Mexico. Proceedings, American Philosophical Society 116:4:301–309.

Hansford, S. Howard 1968 Chinese Carved Jades. New York: New York Graphic Society.

Hapgood, Charles H. 1966 Maps of the Ancient Sea Kings: Evidence of Advanced Civilization in the Ice Age. Philadelphia: Chilton Book Company.

Hedrick, B. C. 1971 Quetzalcoatl: European or indigene? *In* Man Across the Sea: Problems of Pre-Columbian Contacts, ed. Carroll L. Riley et al. Austin: University of Texas Press.

Heine-Geldern, Robert 1954 Die asiatische Herkunft der südamerikanischen Metalltechnik. Paideuma 5:7/8:347–423.

———. 1956 The origin of ancient civilizations and Toynbee's theories. Diogenes 13:81–99.

———. 1958 Kulturpflanzengeographie und das Problem vorkolumbischer Kulturbeziehungen zwischen Alter und Neuer Welt. Anthropos 53:361–402.

———. 1959a Chinese influences in Mexico and Central America: The Tajín style of Mexico and the marble vases from Honduras. Congreso Internacional de Americanistas, Actas 33:1:195–206.

———. 1959b Chinese influence in the pottery of Mexico, Central America, and Colombia. Congreso Internacional de Americanistas, Actas 33:1:207–210.

———. 1959c Representation of the Asiatic tiger in the art of the Chavin Culture: a proof of early contacts between China and Peru. Congreso Internacional de Americanistas, Actas 33:1:321–326.

———. 1964a One hundred years of ethnological theory in the German-speaking countries: some milestones. Current Anthropology 5:5:407–418.

———. 1964b Traces of Indian and Southeast Asiatic Hindu-Buddhist influences in Mesoamerica. Congreso Internacional de Americanistas, Actas y Memorias 35:1:47–54.

———. 1966 Problem of transpacific influences in Mesoamerica. In Handbook of Middle American Indians 4:277–295.

———. 1967 A Roman find from pre-Columbian Mexico. Anthropological Journal of Canada 5:4:20–22.

———. 1972 American metallurgy and the Old World. In Early Chinese Art and Its Possible Influence in the Pacific Basin, 3, ed. Noel Barnard, pp. 787–822. New York: Intercultural Arts Press.

Heine-Geldern, Robert, and Gordon F. Ekholm 1951 Significant parallels in the symbolic arts of southern Asia and Middle America. International Congress of Americanists, Proceedings 29:1:299–309.

Heizer, Robert F. 1968 New observations on La Venta. In Dumbarton Oaks Conference on the Olmec, ed. Elizabeth P. Benson, pp. 9–36. Washington, D.C.: Dumbarton Oaks Research Library and Collection.

Heyerdahl, Thor 1950a The voyage of the raft Kon Tiki. Geographical Journal 115:1:20–41.

———. 1950b The Kon-Tiki Expedition. London: George Allen & Unwin.

———. 1952 American Indians in the Pacific. London: George Allen & Unwin.

———. 1963 Feasible ocean routes to and from the Americas in pre-Columbian times. American Antiquity 28:4:482–488.

———. 1971a The Ra Expeditions. Garden City, N.Y.: Doubleday & Company.

———. 1971b Isolationist or diffusionist? In The Quest for America, ed. Geoffrey Ashe, pp. 114–154. London: Pall Mall Press.

———. 1971c The bearded gods speak. In The Quest for America, ed. Geoffrey Ashe et al., pp. 198–238. London: Pall Mall Press.

Holien, Thomas 1975 Pseudo-cloisonné in the Southwest and Mesoamerica. In Collected Papers in Honor of Florence Hawley Ellis, ed. Theodore R. Frisbie, Papers of the Archaeological Society of New Mexico 2:157–177. Norman, Okla.: Hooper Publishing Company.

Hornell, James 1945 Was there pre-Columbian contact between the peoples of Oceania and South America? Journal of the Polynesian Society 54:167–191.

Hsieh, Chiao-min 1967 Geographical exploration by the Chinese. In The Pacific Basin: A History of Its Geographical Exploration, ed. Herman R. Friis. New York: American Geographical Society.

Hürlimann, Martin 1967 India. New York: Viking Press.

Huscher, Harold A. 1972 The keeper of the game: a demonstration of Old World-New World acculturation. Anthropological Journal of Canada 10:2:13–21.

———. 1974 Pre-Columbian trans-Atlantic contacts recorded in material culture vocabularies. Congresso Internazionale degli Americanisti, Atti 40:2:25–30.

Hutchinson, J. B., R. A. Silow, and S. G. Stephens 1947 The Evolution of Gossypium and the Differentiation of the Cultivated Cottons. Oxford: Oxford University Press.

Ingestad, Helge 1971 Norse sites at L'Anse au Meadows. In The Quest for America, ed. Geoffrey Ashe, pp. 175–197. London: Pall Mall Press.

Inverarity, Robert Bruce 1972 Observations on Northwest Coast Indian art and similarities between a few art elements distant in time and space. In Early Chinese Art and Its Possible Influence in the Pacific Basin, 3, ed. Noel Barnard, pp. 743–785. New York: Intercultural Arts Press.

Ions, Veronica 1967 Indian Mythology. London: Paul Hamlyn.

Irwin, Constance 1963 Fair Gods and Stone Faces. New York: St. Martin's Press.

Jackson, J. Wilfrid 1916a The Aztec moon-cult and its relation to the chank cult of India. Manchester Literary and Philosophical Society, Memoirs 60:(6).

———. 1916b The geographical distribution of the shell-purple industry. Manchester Literary and Philosophical Society, Memoirs 60:(7).

———. 1916c Shell trumpets and their distribution in the Old and New World. Manchester Literary and Philosophical Society, Memoirs 60:(8).

Jairazbhoy, Rafique A. 1974a Egyptian gods in Mexico. Congresso Internazionale degli Americanisti, Atti 40:2:203–212.

———. 1974b Ancient Egyptians and Chinese in America. London: George Prior Associated Publishers.

———. 1975 Further evidence of Egyptian intrusion in pre-Columbian Mexico. The New Diffusionist 5:18:5–11.

Jeffries, M. D. W. 1971 Pre-Columbian maize in Asia. In Man Across the Sea: Problems of Pre-Columbian contacts, ed. Carroll L. Riley et al., pp. 376–400. Austin: University of Texas Press.

Jenkins, Katharine D. 1967 Lacquer. In Handbook of Middle American Indians 6:125–137. Austin: University of Texas Press.

Jett, Stephen C. 1968 Malaysia and tropical America: some racial, cultural, and ethnobotanical comparisons. Congreso Internacional de Americanistas, Actas y Memorias, 37:4:133–177.

———. 1969 A French origin for the "beehive" structures of Ungava? Anthropological Journal of Canada 7:2:16–21.

———. 1970 The development and distribution of the blowgun. Annals, Association of American Geographers 60:1:662–688.

———. 1971 Diffusion versus independent invention: the bases of controversy. In Man Across the Sea: Problems of Pre-Columbian Contacts, ed. Carroll L. Riley et al., pp. 5–53. Austin: University of Texas Press.

Jett, Stephen C., and George F. Carter 1966 A comment on Rowe's "Diffusionism in Archaeology." American Antiquity 31:6:867–870.

Kampen, Michael Edwin 1972 The Sculptures of El Tajín, Veracruz, Mexico. Gainesville: University of Florida Press.

Kehoe, Alice B. 1971 Small boats upon the North Atlantic. In Man Across the Sea: Problems of Pre-Columbian Contacts, ed. Carroll L. Riley et al., pp. 275–292. Austin: University of Texas Press.

Keleman, Pál 1956 Medieval American Art: Masterpieces of the New World Before Columbus. 1 vol. New York: Macmillan Company.

Kelley, David 1960 Calendar animals and deities. Southwestern Journal of Anthropology 16:3:317–337.

Kennedy, Robert A. 1971 A trans-Atlantic stimulus hypothesis for Mesoamerica and the Caribbean, circa 3500 to 2000 BC. In Man Across the Sea: Problems of Pre-Columbian Contacts, ed. Carroll L. Riley et al., pp. 266–274. Austin: University of Texas Press.

Kidder, Alfred Vincent, Jesse D. Jennings, and Edwin M. Shook 1946 Excavations at Kaminaljuyú, Guatemala. Carnegie Institute of Washington, Publication 561.

Kidder, Alfred, II 1964 South American high cultures. In Prehistoric Man in the New World, ed. Jesse D. Jennings and Edward Norbeck, pp. 451–486. Chicago: University of Chicago Press.

Kinle, Jan 1962 Jadeite—its importance for the problems of Asia-America pre-Columbian relationships. Folia Orientalia 4:231–242.

Kirchhoff, Paul 1964a The diffusion of a great religious system from India to Mexico. Congreso Internacional de Americanistas, Actas y Memorias 35:1:73–100.

———. 1964b The adaptation of foreign religious influences in pre-Spanish Mexico. Diogenes 47:13–28.

Larco Hoyle, Rafael 1945 A culture sequence for the North Coast of Peru. Handbook of South American Indians 2:149–175, Bureau of American Ethnology, Bulletin 143.

Lefebvre d'Argencé, René-Yvon 1966 Ancient Chinese Bronzes in the Avery Brundage Collection. Berkeley: De Young Museum Society.

Ling, Shun-sheng 1956 Formosan sea-going raft and its origin in ancient China. Academia Sinica, Bulletin of the Institute of Ethnology 1:1–54.

Loayza, Francisco A. 1948 Los Chinos llegaron antes de Colón. Lima: Los Pequeños Grandes Libros de Historia Americana, Ser. 1:14.

Lopatin, Ivan A. 1960 Origin of the Native American steam bath. American Anthropologist 62:6:977-993.

Lou, Dennis 1968 Chinese inscriptions found in pre-Columbian objects. Congreso Internacional de Americanistas, Actas y Memorias 37:4:179-182.

Lynch, Thomas F. 1974 Andean South America. American Antiquity 39:2:383-386.

MacLeod, William C. 1931 Hook Swinging in the Old World and in America: a problem in cultural integration and disintegration. Anthropos 26:551-561.

Malmstrom, Vincent H. 1976 Izapa: Cultural Hearth of the Olmecs? Proceedings, Association of American Geographers 8:32-35.

Mangelsdorf, Paul C. 1974 Corn: Its Origin, Evolution, and Improvement. Cambridge: Harvard University Press.

Marschall, Wolfgang 1965 Die Panpfeife im circumpazifischen Raum. Abhandlungen, Berliner Statliche Museum Völkerkunde 25:127-151.

Meggers, Betty J. 1971 Contacts from Asia. In The Quest for America, ed. Geoffrey Ashe, pp. 239-259. London: Pall Mall Press.

———. 1975 The transpacific origin of Mesoamerican civilization: a preliminary review of the evidence and its theoretical implications. American Anthropologist 77:1:1-27.

Meggers, Betty J., Clifford Evans, and Emilio Estrada 1965 Early Formative Period of coastal Ecuador: the Valdivia and Machalilla Phases. Smithsonian Contributions to Anthropology, 1.

Merrill, Elmer Drew 1954 The botany of Cook's voyages. Chronica Botanica 14:(5/6).

Mertz, Henriette 1975 Gods from the Far East. New York: Ballantine Books. (Formerly: Pale Ink. 2d ed. Chicago: Swallow Press.)

Millon, René 1974 The study of urbanism at Teotihuacán, Mexico. In Mesoamerican Archaeology: New Approaches, ed. Norman Hammond. London: Gerald Duckworth & Company.

Moran, Hugh A., and David H. Kelley 1969 The Alphabet and the Ancient Calendar Signs. 2d ed. Palo Alto, Calif.: Daily Press.

Mountjoy, Joseph B. 1969 On the origins of West Mexican metallurgy. Mesoamerican Studies 4:26-42.

Muller, Jon D. 1971 Style and culture contact. In Man Across the Sea: Problems of Pre-Columbian Contacts, ed. Carroll L. Riley et al., pp. 66-78. Austin: University of Texas Press.

Naudou, Jean 1962 A propos d'un éventuel emprunt de l'art Maya aux arts de l'Inde extérieure. Internationalen Amerikanistenkongresses, Akten 34:340-347.

Needham, Joseph 1959-1971 Science and Civilization in China, 3, 4(1, 3). Cambridge: Cambridge University Press.

Noble, William A. 1969 Approaches toward an understanding of traditional South Asian peasant dwellings. The Professional Geographer 21:4:264-271.

Noguera, Eduardo 1971 Minor arts in the Central Valleys. In Handbook of Middle American Indians 10:1:258-269.

Nordenskiöld, Erland 1921 Emploi de la balance romaine en Amérique du Sud avant la conquête. Journal de la Societé des Americanistes de Paris (New Series) 13:169-171.

———. 1926 Miroirs convexes et concaves en Amérique. Journal de la Societé des Americanistes de Paris 18:103-110.

Norman, Daniel, and W. W. A. Johnson 1941 Note on a spectroscopic study of Central American and Asiatic jades. Journal of the Optical Society of America 31:1:85-86.

Nowotny, Karl A. 1969 Beiträge zur Geschichte des Weltbildes; Farben und Weltrichtungen. Wiener Beiträge zur Kulturgeschicte und Linguistik, 17.

Nuttall, Zelia 1909 A curious survival in Mexico of the use of the pupura shell-fish for dyeing. In Putnam Anniversary Volume, pp. 368-384. New York: G. E. Stechert & Company.

Obayashi, Taryo 1959 Divination from entrails among the ancient Inca and its relation to practices in Southeast Asia. Congreso Internacional de Americanistas, Actas 33:1:327-332.

Patterson, Thomas C. 1967 Review of Meggers, Evans, and Estrada 1965. Archaeology 20:3:236.

Pearson, Richard J. 1968 Migration from Japan to Ecuador: the Japanese evidence. American Anthropologist 70:1:85-86.

Phillips, Philip 1966 The role of transpacific contacts in the development of New World pre-Columbian civilizations. In Handbook of Middle American Indians 4:296-315.

Piggott, Stuart 1965 Ancient Europe from the Beginnings of Agriculture to Classical Antiquity. Chicago: Aldine Publishing Company.

Piña Chan, Román 1971 Preclassic or Formative pottery and minor arts of the Valley of Mexico. *In* Handbook of Middle American Indians 10:157–178.

Pohl, Frederick J. 1961 Atlantic Crossings Before Columbus. New York: W. W. Norton & Company.

———. 1973 Did ancient Romans reach America? The New Diffusionist 3:10:23–37.

Pollack, Harry E. D. 1965 Architecture of the Maya Lowlands. *In* Handbook of Middle American Indians 2:1:378–440.

Proskouriakoff, Tatiana 1954 Varieties of Classic Central Veracruz sculpture. Carnegie Institute of Washington, Contributions to American Anthropology and History 12:58:61–94.

———. 1965 Classic art of Central Veracruz. *In* Handbook of Middle American Indians 11:2:558–72.

Rands, Robert L. 1953 The water lily in Maya art: a complex of alleged Asiatic origin. Bureau of American Ethnology, Bulletin 151:75–153.

Riley, Carroll L. 1963 Color-direction symbolism: an example of Mexican-Southwestern contacts. América Indígena 23:1:49–58.

Rivet, Paul 1957 Les origines de l'homme américain. Paris: Galimard.

Rouget, Gilbert 1948 La conque comme signe des migrations océaniennes en Amérique. Congrès International des Américanistes, Actes 28:297–305.

Rowe, John Howland 1966 Diffusionism and archaeology. American Antiquity 31:3:334–337.

Ruff, Elsie 1960 The jade story: part one—jade in America. Lapidary Journal 14:4:296–309.

Sarkar, Himansu Bhusan 1970 Some Contribution[s] of India to the Ancient Civilization of Indonesia and Malaysia. Calcutta: Punthi Pustak.

Sauer, Carl O. 1950 Cultivated plants of South and Central America. *In* Handbook of South American Indians. Bureau of American Ethnology, Bulletin 143:6:487–543.

———. 1968 Northern Mists. Berkeley: University of California Press.

Sauer, Jonathan D. 1967 The grain amaranths and their relatives: a revised taxonomic and geographical survey. Annals, the Missouri Botanical Garden 54:2:103–137.

———. 1971 A reevaluation of the coconut as an indicator of human dispersal. *In* Man Across the Sea: Problems of Pre-Columbian Contacts, ed. Carroll L. Riley et al., pp. 309–319. Austin: University of Texas Press.

Schwerin, Karl H. 1970 Winds across the Atlantic. Mesoamerican Studies, 6.

Shimkin, Demitri B. 1973 Models for the downfall: some ecological and culture-historical considerations. *In* The Classic Maya Collapse, ed. Patrick T. Culbert. Albuquerque: University of New Mexico Press.

Signorini, Italo 1969 The Heine-Geldern theory in the light of recent radiocarbon dating. Internationalen Amerikanistenkongresses, Verhandlungen 38:1:467–469.

Simoons, Frederick J. 1961 Eat Not This Flesh: Food Avoidances in the Old World. Madison: University of Wisconsin Press.

Singhal, D. P. 1969 India and World Civilization, 2. East Lansing: Michigan State University Press.

Smith, Tillie 1963 The main themes of the "Olmec" art tradition. The Kroeber Anthropological Society Papers 28:121–213.

Sorenson, John L. 1955 Some Mesoamerican traditions of immigration by sea. El México Antiguo, 8:425–439.

———. 1971 The significance of an apparent relationship between the ancient Near East and Mesoamerica. *In* Man Across the Sea: Problems of Pre-Columbian Contacts, ed. Carroll L. Riley et al., pp. 219–241. Austin: University of Texas Press.

Spencer, J. E., and G. A. Hale 1961 The origin, nature, and distribution of agricultural terracing. Pacific Viewpoint 2:1:1–40.

Stephens, S. G. 1971 Some problems of interpreting transoceanic dispersal of the New World cottons. *In* Man Across the Sea: Problems of Pre-Columbian Contacts, ed. Carroll L. Riley et al., pp. 401–415. Austin: University of Texas Press.

Stierlin, Henri 1964 Living Architecture: Mayan. New York: Grosset and Dunlap.

Stirling, Matthew W. 1961 The Olmecs: artists in jade. *In* Essays in Pre-Columbian Art and Architecture, ed. Samuel Lothrop, pp. 43–59. Cambridge: Harvard University Press.

———. 1968 Aboriginal jade use in the New World. Congreso Internacional de Americanistas, Actas y Memorias 37:4:19–28.

Stirling, Matthew, and Richard H. Steward 1943 La Venta's green stone tigers. National Geographic Magazine 84:3:321–332.

Stonor, C. R., and Edgar Anderson 1949 Maize among the hill peoples of Assam. Annals, Missouri Botanical Garden 36:3:355–404.

Sturtevant, William C. 1968 Agriculture on artificial islands in Burma and elsewhere. International Congress of Anthropological and Ethnological Sciences 8:11–13.

Tekiner, Roselle 1974 Trans-Pacific contact: the evidence of the panpipe. Congresso Internazionale degli Americanisti, Atti 40:2:31–38.

Tolstoy, Paul 1963 Cultural parallels between Southeast Asia and Mesoamerica in the manufacture of bark cloth. Transactions, New York Academy of Sciences, Ser. 2, 25:6:646–662.

———. 1966 Method in long range comparison. Congreso Internacional de Americanistas 36:1:69–89.

———. 1972 Diffusion: as explanation and as event. *In* Early Chinese Art and Its Possible Influence in the Pacific Basin, 3, ed. Noel Barnard, pp. 823–841. New York: Intercultural Arts Press.

Towle, Jerry 1973 Jade: an indicator of trans-Pacific contact? Yearbook of the Association of Pacific Coast Geographers 35:165–172.

Towle, Margaret A. 1961 The ethnobotany of pre-Columbian Peru. Viking Fund Publications in Anthropology, 30.

Trigger, Bruce G. 1970 Aims in prehistoric archaeology. Antiquity 44:173:26–37.

Tylor, E. 1896 On American lot-games as evidence of Asiatic intercourse before the time of Columbus. Internationales Archiv für Ethnographie 9 (Supplement).

Vaillant, George C. 1931 A bearded mystery. Natural History 31:3:243–252.

Vishnu-Mittre and H. P. Gupta 1966 Pollen morphological studies of some primitive varieties of maize (*Zea mays* L.) with remarks on the history of maize in India. The Paleobotanist (Lucknow) 15:176–185.

Vokes, Emily H. 1963 A possible Hindu influence at Teotihuacán. American Antiquity 24:1:94–95.

von Hagen, Victor W. 1965 The Desert Kingdoms of Peru. New York: New York Graphic Society.

von Winning, Hasso 1969 Ceramic house models and figurine groups from Nayarit. Internationalen Amerikanistenkongresses, Verhandlungen 38:1:129–132.

———. 1974 The shaft tomb figures of West Mexico. Southwest Museum Papers, 24.

von Wuthenau, Alexander 1970 The Art of Terracotta Pottery in Pre-Columbian Central and South America. New York: Crown Publishers.

Wauchope, Robert 1962 Lost Tribes and Sunken Continents. Chicago: University of Chicago Press.

Wheeler, Mortimer 1966 Civilizations of the Indus Valley and Beyond. London: Thames and Hudson.

Whitley, Glenn R. 1974 The Fulvous Tree Duck as a cultural tracer. Anthropological Journal of Canada 12:1:10–17.

Whittaker, Thomas W. 1971 Endemism and pre-Columbian migration of the bottle gourd, *Lagenaria siceraria* (Mol.) Standl. *In* Man Across the Sea: Problems of Pre-Columbian Contacts, ed. Carroll L. Riley et al., pp. 320–327. Austin: University of Texas Press.

Wiercinski, Andrzej 1969 Ricerca antropologica sugli Olmechi. Terra Ameriga, 18–19.

Willetts, William 1958 Chinese Art. 2 vols. Harmondsworth: Penguin Books.

———. 1965 Foundations of Chinese Art. New York: McGraw-Hill Book Company.

Woodbury, Richard B. 1965 Artifacts of the Guatemalan Highlands. *In* Handbook of Middle American Indians 2:163–179. Austin: University of Texas Press.

Yü, Ying-shih 1967 Trade and Expansion in Han China. Berkeley: University of California Press.

Epilogue

Jesse D. Jennings

In this short concluding section, it is appropriate to make a few general remarks about the nature of prehistoric research in the Americas, including concepts or principles used (if not always made explicit) by the authors of this book.

The whole of American culture history is a network of continuous interaction and interinfluence between the major culture areas over the millennia. This network is so striking that I was once impelled to speak lyrically of North American prehistory "as a series of patterns . . . details [that] fade into one another to create an overall design or pattern." Part of the pattern is distinctive areal adaptation, the use made of innovations from other localities. For example, the Plains peoples (Chapter 5), even while they borrowed from cultures to the east, abandoned little of their previous utilization of the bison; the schedule for harvesting bison was merely rearranged. The eastern Plains and the Mississippi valley (Chapter 6) shared a knowledge of horticulture, architecture, ceramics, and even some ceremonies, but they were adjusted to very different environments, exploiting a different overall spectrum of resources. In no way could the two regional cultures be confused with each other, even though the eastern Plains boundary has always been difficult to identify because of transitional cultures—for example, are Iowa, Quapaw, and Santee really *Plains* cultures? In the same vein, the contrast between the gardening techniques used in the rich river valleys of the well-watered Southeast (Chapter 7) and those of the Southwest (Chapter 8), where water is always scant, are extreme. But both are food-producing lifeways, utilizing the same cultigens. It should also be noted that maize is found under cultivation in the Southwest before it is securely documented as a staple food east of the Mississippi River. But on the earliest levels the eastern corn is the Basketmaker variety. The later varieties of maize known east of the Rockies seem to be different from those of the Southwest. Therefore, the transmittal of cultigens to the Southeast at different times must have taken several routes, no doubt from different points of origin in Central America.

Another interesting point to be made is an inescapable fact of scholarship—"new" trends often are not truly new. For example, archeologists have long done ecology at a crude level in studying what has been labeled a man-land-culture relationship—such as anthropogeography or historical geography or human ecology of the better geographers of the 1920s and 1930s. A recent awareness of environment among the public, as well as among scholars, has led to a much more frequent use of the modish word *ecology* by archeologists. Thus, while often using the word *ecology*, every author here has documented, as he or she has done before with varying explicitness, primarily the adaptation of human groups to quite local environments and to regional resources, be they floral, faunal, or mineral. One should even, perhaps, call this volume a history of American Indian adaptation to a virgin world. As such, its stance is implicitly ecological. In connection with adaptation, the extent to which continental and local environments have changed has been often emphasized herein. The most dramatic change was the first—the final retreat of the ice, followed by the expansion of floral zones and the ensuing pattern of wider human exploitation that came to be called the Archaic stage. Subsequent, more complex cultures developed on both continents from the hunter-gatherer cultures of the Archaic.

The development from the Archaic cultures into the later horticultural systems is regarded by many of us as an evolutionary process. What the causes were, what the mechanisms were, or why adoptions of innovations varied could be endlessly debated. But few prehistorians feel any great urge to discuss the matter; the evolutionary model is usually implicit in the culture historian's thinking.

Another point of interest is that the intensity of research varies so greatly from one geographical or topical area to another. Careful readers will have noticed that some of the bibliographies are studded with very recent—post-1970—publication dates. The activity is heavy in such subjects as the Paleo-Indian remains on the east slopes of the Appalachians, the reconstruction of paleoclimates and the accompanying changes in associated natural resources (Chapter 11), the matter of transoceanic contact over the past 6000 years (Chapter 13), and a revamping or complete overhaul of the cumbersome and vague classification of subareal variants of Southeastern culture. Much insightful attention is also being paid currently to the archeological resources of the High Plains hunting peoples from Texas to Canada, and to the Arctic, particularly Alaska (Chapters 2 and 3). Particularly noticeable is the accumulation of new knowledge of, as well as debate about, the vast lowlands of South America.

But possibly more important, at this stage, is the concern with theory and culture process revealed by some of the authors. For example, the chapter on Andean cultures (Chapter 11) is organized entirely around the hypothesis that the pattern of Inca civilization was an ancient one, one that has influenced the evolution of Andean cultures for about 3500 years. And the Southeast section devoted space to an entirely theoretical problem, that of states versus chiefdoms. The concern is a "borrowed" one, drawn from important hypotheses developed by cultural anthropologists, but it is proving to be useful to a limited degree to archeologists, who are beginning to attempt to deal with social organization and other intangibles of culture. Yet another trend, closely allied to the use of ecological principles, is the effort to involve systems theory in archeological interpretation. However, little evidence of this trend shows up among the authors, largely because few examples of successful use of systems theory, except of the most general kind, are reported in the literature.

There is another aspect of adaptation that must be touched on. It is live and becoming terribly important to everyone; this is the destruction of resources and intangible values resulting from the deleterious impact that land and other development programs have on the natural environment. The fragile archeological remains are identified as a segment of the resource base; thus, archeological sites are part of the environment. The impact of roads, dams and reservoirs, airports, urban sprawl, and development of new energy sources on archeological sites is fully and finally destructive. But archeologists had emerged as conservationists decades before the disastrous deterioration of resources was widely recognized. At first, the only recourse was the excavation of jeopardized prehistoric locations. But today a new breed of archeological conservationist has emerged. He does what is called "resource management." The term implies much more than mere emergency or salvage excavation. In fact, the resource manager prefers to protect and preserve the finite and dwindling reservoir of archeological sites rather than to excavate them. Excavation is a final act; while it may preserve the data, it also destroys one more location. The role that resource managers have to play in government agencies in connection with the Environmental Protection Agency is of great importance; it makes archeologists active, key participants in conserving the national heritage of North Americans.

It seems necessary to comment upon the extremely uneven availability of the data upon which the reconstructions of past events are based. The paucity or plentitude of information derives from a multitude of factors. Personnel available for archeological research is a prime consideration. Archeology is a slow and costly pursuit. Without trained people who are interested in specific geographical areas or particular scientific problems concerning prehistoric users of the land, no study is undertaken. And, without significant funding, no amount of interest on the part of scholars will result in the gathering of new archeological information; meanwhile costs continue to rise. Salaries, transportation, equipment, supplies, and laboratory overhead costs are soaring.

In addition to money and personnel, many types of ancillary scientific advice are required by the archeologist who wishes to extract all he can from his data and to represent accurately the lifeway his archeological findings sample or represent. Modern archeological interpretations therefore require the assistance of climatologists, geomorphologists, biologists of several kinds (such as mammalogists or botanists), palynologists, physicists, geologists, statisticians, and computer specialists, to name a few. Unless such specialists are available, the archeologist is doomed to produce substandard analyses and interpretations, because no one person can be expert in so many fields.

But there is much more to the matter than mere money and people. Discoveries are made for reasons remote from scholarship. For example, data from the American Southwest have become available because the prehistoric (as well as historic) minor crafts—ceramics, fibers, and jewelry—are aesthetically pleasing and have long been sought by museums and art dealers. The Plains are now better known because of massive emergency archeological programs organized to save information from destruction by the enormous lakes created by dams built since 1945 along the many waterways, notably, the mighty Missouri. Mandatory salvage programs with vastly increased federal subsidies are continuing and accelerating this trend over the whole country. Similar mitigation of the despoliation effected by the Alaskan pipeline has produced new information that might not have been gained in decades of "normal," problem-oriented research in a region where there are few scholars. And, again, the majesty of Mayan and Mexican monuments and the beauty of their artifacts has led to intense study since the ruined cities were discovered and described over a century ago by the explorer John L. Stephens. Peru came to early antiquarian, and then to scientific, notice for identical reasons. Other examples could be adduced showing how random or irrational or even serendipitous factors sometimes influence the local abundance of data.

Suffice it to say that *only* since 1950 has there been enough information to allow even a partial culture history to be written about the Plains (Chapter 5), Great Basin (Chapter 4), Pacific Northwest, Alaska (Chapter 2), the Arctic and Sub-Arctic (Chapter 3), or lowland South American (Chapter 12) regions. The increased numbers of archeologists, the tenfold increase in departments of anthropology and institutional interest in prehistoric research, a research concern for treating problems rather than collecting objects of art, and, recently, the national concern with conservation of resources other than natural have made possible the North American chapters.

As a closing note, perhaps a word on the social values of archeology is not amiss. Everyone who chooses archeology as a profession must sooner or later answer the question, often asked by his friends and relatives and occasionally by his own social conscience, "What good does it do?" This is somewhat reminiscent of the nineteenth-century gentlemen of the utilitarian persuasion who demanded to be told in what way the reading of poetry was conducive to the spinning of cotton. A more germane and answerable question is, "Does archeology contribute to or enrich the life of modern man? And, if so, how?"

An interest in the origins of one's species and society seems to be a universal human trait; even the simplest cultures have myths of origin. But in modern man this interest has expanded to include the rise and fall of cultures and the lifeways of distant and ancient people. Archeology has a unique capacity to satisfy this curiosity about origins.

Another nearly universal human interest is that in things antique. Old buildings, clothes, tintypes, and newspaper advertisements fascinate us; how much more fascinating is the vicarious experience of ancient and prehistoric cultures that archeology provides. Those banes of the archeologist, the arrowhead collector and the pot hunter, although we tend to picture tham as malicious vandals, are often honest, ordinary people who are attracted to these tangible evidences of the past.

A third human interest that archeology satisfies is that curiosity about exotic places and other cultures which has made *National Geographic* more of a tradition than a periodical. The phenomenal and long-lasting popularity of works by world explorers results from a combination of the exotic and the antique.

But archeology, in addition to satisfying our curiosity, enriches our lives as well—by unearthing objects of great aesthetic beauty, for example. Indeed, the beauty of many artifacts has, archeologically, been a curse rather than a blessing. Figurines and pots, even frescoes and obelisks, have become the objects of an enormous, lucrative, and illicit international trafficking in antiquities; tragically, removing these articles from their context for their aesthetic (and monetary) value destroys their one-time, irreplaceable archeological value.

Not only are objects of such obvious beauty as jades and porcelains sought; even everyday tools and utensils of past cultures are of intense interest to modern man. In part this may be an expression of urbanite frustration with assembly line products and their eternal sameness, in part an awareness that artisan and artist were once one and the same rather than the discrete, self-conscious classes they are today. And, too, these "mundane" objects fascinate us as tactile, physical remnants of cultures long lost and otherwise unknowable.

Finally, archeology offers several historical and sociological lessons. By tracing the emergence of what we call civilization, it invites the humbling discovery of how little we have progressed, in some ways, beyond the achievements of "primitive" cultures—indeed, how we have retrogressed from their achievements. An increased understanding of the mechanisms by which cultures have risen, influenced one another, and fallen gives food for thought, if not object lessons, for today. But perhaps most important, archeology preserves a sense of heritage and cultural continuity in our fragmented and sometimes seemingly rootless world. As Lipe has written in another context:

Peoples came and went, and man's relationship to the land changed in some major ways. But throughout, these past cultures had some basic things in common, differing from our modern industrial-based culture of today. The prehistoric local groups were small, ranging from a few tens to a few hundred persons. Tools were simple, and work depended entirely on human muscle-power. With few exceptions, food and materials for home and livelihood came from local sources rather than through elaborate trade and distribution networks. Most local groups were not only economically but politically independent. They knew nothing of such institutions as kings, nations, armies, judges. Life was hard. Babies often died in their first year. But the basic, universal components of human society and culture were there: family and kinship; language as rich and infinitely expandable as any spoken today; means of education and social control; a sense of community and history; techniques for getting food, shelter, and clothing; music and art; conceptions of how things came to be and of the supernatural; and ceremonies for coming to terms with that world beyond nature and tangible reality.*

---

*From *Plateau,* vol. 49, no. 1, Summer 1976.

Glossary

adornos Appliqués applied to pottery vessels as decoration.

altiplano The high-altitude plain between the Western and Eastern Cordilleras of Peru.

anadromous Referring to saltwater fish that swim upstream into freshwater areas to spawn.

apatite radiocarbon dating A technique for dating bones or bone artifacts by extracting carbon from the mineral apatite.

aspartic acid racemization A technique for dating archeological finds that tests a crystalline amino acid found especially in plants.

atlatl A stick or board with a handle at one end and a peg or groove at the other, used in throwing a dart or lance.

baleen A horny substance, found in the mouths of some species of whale, used as a strainer to collect food from the water.

bannerstone A polished stone artifact that has a variety of forms and is usually perforated. Probably used as an atlatl (q.v.) weight; possibly has ceremonial functions as well.

barrio A delimited area of a city whose inhabitants are related by kin and/or craft.

Beringia The land area exposed between Siberia and Alaska when sea level fell drastically during the Ice Age.

biome A unit of associated plant and animal life.

blade A long, narrow flake of stone with parallel sides, usually struck from a prepared core (q.v.). Has a thin, sharp, acutely angled working edge (cf. scraper).

blowout An area of variable size in which the surface soils or sediments have been removed by wind, leaving a resistant lower level. Associated with dune fields.

bolas A hunting weapon comprised of two or more grooved stone balls tied by thongs to a longer line.

burial *Bundle* burial is reburial of defleshed and disarticulated bones tied or wrapped together; *extended* burial has body in supine or prone position with legs extended and arms at sides; *flexed* burial has arms and/or legs bent up against body. Also referred to as fetal position.

657

burin   A flake or blade stone tool with a small, angled chisel edge or a sharp, beaked point.

check stamped   A pottery decoration design of small, impressed squares produced by a paddle or stamp.

chinampas   Artifically created islands used for intensive agriculture.

conchology   The study of shells.

core   A stone from which flakes have been removed to make tools. A prepared core is worked to a conical or domed shape before the flakes are struck so that the shape of the pieces removed can be controlled.

econiche   Generally describes a zone of narrow or limited resources to which one or more species have made a complete adaptation.

flensing tool   Used for stripping blubber or skin from a whale.

fleshing tool   Used to scrape fat and flesh from the inner surface of a hide.

gorget   A flat ornament, usually worn over the chest. Often perforated for suspending on a cord or otherwise attaching to clothing.

gracile   Slender or slight in build.

Holocene   The most recent geological epoch, that is, the last 10,000 years.

interstadial   The period between glacial advances.

Inuit   The word those whom we call Eskimos use when referring to themselves— means "the people."

jacal   A construction technique similar to wattle-and-daub (q.v.).

kayak   An arctic canoe. It has an enclosed cockpit and is covered and decked with sealskin.

kazigi   The Eskimo combination ceremonial house and men's house.

labret   An ornament worn in a perforation of the lip.

lanceolate   In archeological usage, refers to a long, slender chipped stone point or knife, pointed at one or both ends.

leister   A barbed, three-pronged fish spear.

linear stamping   A pottery decoration technique. The wet surface is pressed with a grooved paddle, producing narrow, impressed corrugations.

lomas   Fog-supported vegetation in an otherwise arid environment.

mano   The upper half of a hand-worked milling stone assembly.

metate   The lower half of a hand-worked milling stone assembly.

midden   The accumulation of refuse near a dwelling or habitation site.

mita   A tax paid in labor.

montaña   The heavily vegetated slopes of the Amazonian Andes.

nagualism   Belief in a fetish or personal magic spirit.

ocher   Red ocher is an oxide of iron very often used for ceremonial purposes.

ossuary   A depository for the bones of the dead; usually refers to a multiple burial.

paleo-   Prefix meaning "dealing with ancient forms or conditions."

paleontology   Study of life in past geological periods by means of fossil remains.

palette   A flat surface for mixing paint pigments.

palynology   Study of past environments through analyses of pollen samples.

páramo   The lower, better-watered areas of the puna (q.v.).

percussion flaking   A toolmaking technique (usually with stone as the raw material) using sharp blows to remove large flakes.

playa   A shallow basin or dry lake bed in which rain or runoff collects.

Pleistocene   The geological period immediately preceding the present period.

pochteca   A class of professional traders in Postclassic Mexico.

potlatch   A ceremonial feast, usually given to announce an event of social significance for the kin group, at which gifts were given to the guests according to their rank.

pressure flaking   A toolmaking technique utilizing pressure from an implement of antler or bone to remove flakes. Permits greater control over size and direction of removal of the flake than does percussion flaking (q.v.).

provenience   The location of objects and features in an excavation. Described in terms of map grids, stratified levels, and/or depth from ground surface. Provides for the study of associations of artifacts once they are removed from context.

puna   High Peruvian grasslands.

Quechua   The language of the Inca.

raclette   A term used mostly in Europe to describe a flint knife or saw with serrated edges.

retouch   Secondary flaking of a stone implement to remove surface irregularities and refine or modify the cutting edge. Always done by pressure flaking (q.v.).

rocker stamped   A pottery decoration design of connecting zigzag lines produced by rocking a sharp-edged implement back and forth on the wet clay.

savanna   Usually a tropical or subtropical grassland with scattered trees and drought-resistant undergrowth.

scraper   A stone tool with a blunt, steeply angled working edge.

shaman   An individual possessing supernatural powers to cure ailments or interpret strange phenomena.

slash-and-burn   A technique of clearing ground for agricultural use by cutting and burning the vegetation on the spot.

spokeshave An artifact with a rounded notch in an edge, used to scrape arrow shafts or other slender cylindrical objects.

steatite A variety of talc used for pots and other utilitarian items. Also called soapstone.

steppe Level, treeless land with vegetation adapted to dry conditions, often subject to extremes of temperature.

taiga Swampy area of coniferous forest south of the tundra (q.v.) zone.

tembetas Cylindrical lip plugs.

tree ring dating A dating method, also known as dendrochronology, based on the variation of annual growth ring thickness in some trees in comparison with variation in rainfall. Regional master charts of variation patterns over time permit absolute dating of samples.

tundra Treeless plain within the Arctic Circle, marshy in summer, frozen in winter. Subsoil is permanently frozen; surface soil supports small, cold-adapted vegetation.

ulu A knife with a semicircular blade, usually fitted with a slotted wooden handle.

umiak A flat-bottomed open arctic boat, made of a wooden frame covered with walrus hide.

wattle-and-daub A construction technique in which a frame of poles and interwoven twigs is plastered with mud or a similar substance.

Index